SETTING NATIONAL PRIORITIES

Agenda for the 1980s

JOSEPH A. PECHMAN *Editor*

SETTING NATIONAL PRIORITIES

Agenda for the 1980s

Essays by   Barry P. Bosworth
Ralph C. Bryant and Lawrence B. Krause
Hans H. Landsberg
Lester B. Lave
Louise B. Russell
David W. Breneman and Susan C. Nelson
George F. Break
William W. Kaufmann
William B. Quandt
Helmut Sonnenfeldt
Kenneth G. Lieberthal
Philip H. Trezise
Christopher J. Makins
John W. Sewell and John A. Mathieson
James L. Sundquist

THE BROOKINGS INSTITUTION
Washington, D.C.

353.007
Se7
117819
apr. 1981

THE BROOKINGS INSTITUTION is an independent organization devoted to nonpartisan research, education, and publication in economics, government, foreign policy, and the social sciences generally. Its principal purposes are to aid in the development of sound public policies and to promote public understanding of issues of national importance.

The Institution was founded on December 8, 1927, to merge the activities of the Institute for Government Research, founded in 1916, the Institute of Economics, founded in 1922, and the Robert Brookings Graduate School of Economics and Government, founded in 1924.

The Board of Trustees is responsible for the general administration of the Institution, while the immediate direction of the policies, program, and staff is vested in the President, assisted by an advisory committee of the officers and staff. The by-laws of the Institution state: "It is the function of the Trustees to make possible the conduct of scientific research, and publication, under the most favorable conditions, and to safeguard the independence of the research staff in the pursuit of their studies and in the publication of the results of such studies. It is not a part of their function to determine, control, or influence the conduct of particular investigations or the conclusions reached."

The President bears final responsibility for the decision to publish a manuscript as a Brookings book. In reaching his judgment on the competence, accuracy, and objectivity of each study, the President is advised by the director of the appropriate research program and weighs the views of a panel of expert outside readers who report to him in confidence on the quality of the work. Publication of a work signifies that it is deemed a competent treatment worthy of public consideration but does not imply endorsement of conclusions or recommendations.

The Institution maintains its position of neutrality on issues of public policy in order to safeguard the intellectual freedom of the staff. Hence interpretations or conclusions in Brookings publications should be understood to be solely those of the authors and should not be attributed to the Institution, to its trustees, officers, or other staff members, or to the organizations that support its research.

Foreword

THIS is the eleventh volume in an annual series published by the
Brookings Institution since 1970. It presents analyses of federal policy issues that emphasize the problems of choice and seek to identify
the alternatives available. Most of the books in this series have examined presidential budget decisions and evaluated their implications for economic and social policy. This one departs somewhat
from the usual format, as did its 1976 predecessor: it examines
longer run problems that confront the nation as it prepares for both
presidential and congressional elections.

Both domestic and foreign issues receive detailed attention here.
The contributors address the problems of inflation, slow productivity
growth, and energy. They explain how the world's economic interdependence affects the United States and discuss fresh approaches
for improving federal policy toward the regulation of economic activity, medical care, education and training, and intergovernmental
fiscal relations. They argue for changes in the nation's defenses in
response to the volatile world situation, and they define the positions
they believe the United States should take in its dealings with the
Soviet Union, China, Japan, the countries of the Middle East, Western Europe, and the developing world. They conclude with an analysis of the reasons for the decline of confidence in the competence of
government and how that confidence might be restored.

The contributors, writing during December 1979 and January
1980, took the rapid and unusual developments of the recent past

into account to the extent they could, but the reader should be aware that the book does not reflect events after February 15, when it went to press.

All three Brookings research programs collaborated in the preparation of this volume. Joseph A. Pechman is director and Barry P. Bosworth, Ralph C. Bryant, David W. Breneman, Lawrence B. Krause, Lester B. Lave, Susan C. Nelson, and Louise B. Russell are members of the staff of the Economic Studies program; William B. Quandt and Philip H. Trezise, of the Foreign Policy Studies program; and James L. Sundquist, of the Governmental Studies program. George F. Break is professor of economics at the University of California, Berkeley; Hans H. Landsberg is at Resources for the Future, Inc.; William W. Kaufmann, a consultant to the Foreign Policy Studies program and to the secretary of defense, is a member of the faculty of the Massachusetts Institute of Technology; Kenneth G. Lieberthal is professor of political science at Swarthmore College; Helmut Sonnenfeldt is a former counselor of the U.S. Department of State and currently a Brookings guest scholar; Christopher J. Makins is a member of the staff of Science Applications, Inc.; and John W. Sewell and John A. Mathieson are president and fellow, respectively, of the Overseas Development Council.

The risk of factual error in this volume was minimized by the work of Penelope Harpold and her associates, Judith Lynn Cameron, Ellen W. Smith, and Clifford W. Wright. Karen J. Wirt, Alice M. Carroll, Elizabeth H. Cross, Diane Hammond, and Caroline Lalire edited the manuscript.

The Brookings Institution is grateful to the Ford Foundation for financial support of this project. The views expressed here are those of the authors and should not be ascribed to the trustees, officers, or other staff members of the Brookings Institution, to the Ford Foundation, or to the other organizations with which the authors are affiliated.

BRUCE K. MACLAURY
President

February 1980
Washington, D.C.

Contents

Tables

Contents xiii

Figures

SETTING NATIONAL PRIORITIES
Agenda for the 1980s

CHAPTER ONE

Introduction and Summary

JOSEPH A. PECHMAN

THE United States enters the 1980s beset by enormous difficulties at home and abroad. The domestic economy is plagued by double-digit inflation, slow productivity growth, and excessive oil imports. Confidence in the ability of government to provide needed services has eroded. U.S. interests are threatened in many parts of the world, most acutely in the Middle East and Southwest Asia, while the nation's military power and foreign policies are widely regarded as inadequate to cope with such threats. U.S. relations with the Soviet Union—never harmonious—have deteriorated as a result of the impasse over the second strategic arms limitation agreement and the Soviet invasion of Afghanistan. In short, the prospects for achieving a healthy economy and maintaining peace are not good.

The problems confronting the nation today are not new. Inflation has been festering for over a decade; the 1973 oil boycott and the 1979 interruption of Iranian oil production merely dramatized the consequences of greater U.S. dependence on imported oil; domestic economic policies have been increasingly constrained by the growing interdependence of the world economy; and world peace remains uneasy as a result of the instability of governments in the Middle East and the expansionism of the Soviet Union.

I thank the authors of this volume, John C. Baker, and Robert P. Berman for their assistance in the preparation of this chapter; Henry J. Aaron, A. Doak Barnett, Raymond Garthoff, Robert W. Hartman, and John D. Steinbruner for their comments; and Evelyn M. E. Taylor and Val J. Harris for their efficient secretarial assistance.

These problems will not disappear, and the consequences of inaction will become ever more serious. Continued inflation distorts economic activity, undermines the values of the dollar, and increases social tensions. Vacillation on energy conservation exposes the United States to the danger of economic paralysis at home and to blackmail from abroad. Foreign policy cannot be conducted effectively when the economy is heavily dependent on foreign oil, and domestic economic policy options are greatly restricted by economic and political developments overseas.

This book deals with these and other crucial domestic and foreign policy issues. While the individual chapters were prepared by different authors, a common theme running through them all is that many of the nation's problems are interrelated and cannot be resolved piecemeal. The problems of inflation, slow productivity growth, international competitiveness, and energy supply must be addressed simultaneously. To achieve its foreign policy objectives, the United States must have a coordinated defense policy and a consistent strategy governing its relations with its friends and adversaries. And attaining any set of national goals, whether those suggested in this book or in others, depends on public confidence in the competence of the government to make policy and to execute it.

Domestic Policy

The decade of the 1970s was a period of growing disenchantment and conflict over the conduct of domestic policy. Much of the controversy has been a direct outgrowth of the failure to contain inflation. More recently, the problems have expanded beyond inflation to include sharply reduced productivity growth, falling real earnings, a declining value of the dollar, and an inadequate energy policy. Regulatory and social policies, particularly those regarding medical care and education, and the mechanisms used by the federal government to funnel money to the state and local governments have also been subject to increasing criticism.

Economic Policy

Traditionally, emphasis has been placed on fiscal and monetary restraints to combat inflation, but in the 1980s the cost of exclusive reliance on these measures in terms of unemployment and lost output will be high. If the experience of recent recessions is a guide, an increase of the unemployed by one million persons, maintained over a two-year period, would reduce inflation by less than one percentage point. Yet there are no simple alternatives: voluntary programs for wage and price restraint seem weak, and mandatory controls raise the risks of serious economic disruptions. Thus there is no consensus on the appropriate means of reducing inflation.

The momentum of the inflation is only loosely related to current cyclical demand conditions. It reflects to a considerable extent the efforts of labor and business to catch up with past price and wage increases and the expectations that the process will continue in the future. An effective program to break this momentum will require a combination of policies. Despite the severe difficulties, some direct government intervention in price and wage decisions will probably be needed. Whatever form this intervention may take—whether a modification of the voluntary guidelines or more formal controls—it will require the cooperation of government, business, and labor groups to agree on a policy and then to cooperate in its implementation. No price-wage policy will be successful, however, unless aggregate demand is kept in check by responsible fiscal and monetary policies. In periods of high employment, the federal budget should be balanced and growth in money supply should be consistent with bringing down the inflation.

Sharply rising energy, food, and housing prices have not been caused by general conditions of excess demand in the economy as a whole. But price increases in specific sectors are important because they raise the general price level and stimulate new rounds of wage increases. They have been important also in initiating episodes of inflation. Nevertheless, attempts to hold down relative prices of such key commodities as energy and food interfere with necessary structural adjustments by business firms and consumers to changing circumstances.

The sharp expansion of the federal government's regulatory activities in recent years has contributed to inflation. The government is attempting to meet various goals by means that are neither reflected in its budget nor paid for through higher taxes. Rather, efforts to improve the environment and meet other health and safety problems have been undertaken through regulation—by ordering changes in the private sector that lead to higher prices. Similarly, many administrative and legislative actions such as foreign trade restrictions, minimum wage requirements, and price supports raise business costs and prices. The government should establish a capability to assess the effect of these actions on the economy and to provide some form of accountability and should develop a means of improved coordination. Wherever possible, economic activities should be deregulated in order to capture the advantages of competition to set prices and allocate resources.

The worsening inflation since the mid-1960s has been paralleled by a sharp slowing of productivity growth. While the causes of growth in productivity are many and complex, attention has focused on the role of capital formation and on the potential benefits of increased tax incentives for investment and saving. The issue of tax incentives is important because inflation has increased the effective tax rate on income from capital. How best to offset this effect is highly controversial because the effects of taxes on saving and investment and of increased capital formation on productivity are disputed by experts.

An optimistic interpretation of the evidence suggests that an investment tax credit generates investment spending equal to the revenue loss. An additional credit costing $25 billion of revenues annually (about one percent of gross national product) would initially raise annual productivity growth by about 0.2 percentage point annually. More typical empirical studies put the investment response at only half of this optimistic estimate. Moreover, although higher investment raises the *level* of productivity, its effect on productivity *growth* is temporary; a sustained increase in productivity growth would require increasingly higher rates of investment. Thus, while more investment is needed and tax incentives can help, the direct contribution of more investment to reducing inflation will be small, and other approaches (such as increased research and development expenditures and improved incentives for innovation and risk-taking) will be required to increase national productivity growth on a sustained basis.

The evidence of the effect of taxes on private saving is even more tenuous, and there is the additional complication that higher private saving may not translate into a higher level of total saving or increased business investment. If there is a problem of inadequate capital formation in the United States, it is more the result of a weakness of investment incentives and uncertainties about the payoff from investment than a shortage of saving. This is particularly true during a period of economic slack, when demand for investment is low. When the economy is operating at high levels, reducing the budget deficit or running a surplus offer more certain means of increasing funds for investment than do tax preferences for saving. The reduced deficit or the surplus would also help to fight inflation.

Thus it is possible to improve the performance of the economy, but the measures needed are not easy for the public and politicians to accept. Restraints on wage-price behavior, higher prices for energy, more efficient government regulation, more business investment, federal budget surpluses in high employment years, and moderation of money supply growth are minimum elements of a coordinated economic program. The United States must undergo painful economic readjustments, and the transition cannot be made without significant near-term costs and sacrifices.

Impact of World Interdependence

The United States is now subject to the discipline of the international economic system much like any other country. Evidence of interdependence is apparent in the impact of international trade on the volume and price of domestic output. The average of exports and imports as a percentage of total output almost doubled in the 1970s. As much as one-third of the inflation in the prices of consumer goods and services in 1979 can be attributed to the devaluation of the dollar in 1978 and the rise of world oil prices in 1979. Increasingly, the balance of payments is recognized as an important barometer of what is happening in the domestic economy. Furthermore, rapid growth in the international creditor-debtor relationships of the United States is augmenting the financial interdependence of the U.S. economy, as illustrated by the 24 percent of the federal debt held outside the government that is owned by foreigners, up from less than 5 percent at the end of 1969.

Increasing interdependence means that, to a considerable degree, U.S. economic policy must conform to the policy stances in the rest of the world. The monetary policies of other countries, for example, spill over in part to the United States, thereby complicating Federal Reserve efforts to control inflation or influence output. Similarly, policy actions taken by the United States spill over into other countries. Because the domestic economy is influenced by the monetary decisions of other nations, U.S. efforts, say, to raise or lower interest rates are more difficult to make and more uncertain in their consequences. The complications for U.S. policy stemming from interdependence are not eliminated by flexible exchange rates (although in some instances they are mitigated). Further complications come from the use of the dollar as a world currency and the conflicting regulatory environment in which American financial institutions operate.

There is simply no escaping the fact that the United States is both constrained by and constrains the rest of the world. The lesson to be drawn from this is that cooperation among countries is increasingly important. The need for international cooperation was seen most dramatically when cooperation did not exist. In the 1930s individual countries adopted protectionist policies to try to export their unemployment. Each failed because other countries retaliated, and the situation was made worse for all countries. This disaster must not be repeated in the 1980s.

International cooperation is impeded by a lack of analytical understanding of how the international economy works, by a clash of national interests, and by a universal unwillingness to surrender national sovereignty. The problem is compounded for the oil-importing countries by their dependence on a cartel of nations that supplies a vital natural resource, oil.

World attempts to recover from the expected global slowdown in 1980–81 will strain international cooperation. Oil-importing countries should agree on an allocation of petroleum products from the Organization of Petroleum Exporting Countries (OPEC) because excess demand would drive up prices. A macroeconomic strategy for expansion that avoids excessively rapid rates of recovery should be developed. Countries that have low inflation rates, balance-of-payments surpluses, and sizable external assets (or smaller debts) should expand sooner and more vigorously; other countries should postpone actions until the spillover effects from the rest of the world become evident. A coordinated effort should also be made to replace monetary tightness by fiscal restraint in order to make investment more attractive and thus to increase the share of investment in output in all countries.

The implications of this analysis are especially important for the United States. If the rest of the world has a more contractionary policy than is desirable, the United States will then also have to be more restrained because of its lack of independence. The United

States must take independent action to solve its energy problems (see below). It should adopt other supply-management policies that improve its productivity and its international competitiveness. While avoiding protectionism, it must endeavor to improve its balance of payments, eventually moving toward a surplus on its current account in order to transfer real resources to the developing countries. The United States can afford expansionary policy only when it is clear that its inflation is decelerating and its balance-of-payments position is improving relative to the payments positions of the other oil-importing countries.

Energy

Six years after the upheaval by OPEC, neither the United States nor the rest of the world has adjusted energy consumption to high and rising energy costs. The supply of alternative sources of energy has increased only slightly relative to the supply of oil. Improvement of efficiency in the use of energy is modest. And plans to deal with future supply shocks and surprises are primitive.

One of the principal tasks for the 1980s is to improve the efficiency of energy use. Among the tools are dissemination of technical information on energy use, improved standards and regulations, and subsidies to encourage businesses and households to reduce energy consumption. These means cannot be successful unless controls are removed from energy prices and higher prices are allowed to influence purchasing and operating decisions of energy users. Rising prices aggravate inflation and hurt some consumers more than others, the poor above all. But in the long run, making energy artificially cheap for all users will help neither the fight against inflation nor the poor. Subsidies or tax credits should be devised to avoid imposing hardships on the poor.

Current legislation to improve the fuel efficiency of automobiles terminates with the 1985 models; for that year the new-fleet average is set at 27.5 miles per gallon, 8.5 miles per gallon above the 1980 standard. This schedule should be observed. In addition, the price of gasoline should be raised by taxation to encourage conservation. At a minimum, the average federal and state gasoline tax of 12 cents a gallon should be increased to offset the eroding effect of inflation. Few realize that the federal 4 cent tax has not changed in more than twenty years, and that the average state tax has risen only from 6.5 to

8 cents since 1960. In France the tax doubled between late 1973 and 1979 and stood at $1.59 in the latter year. In Italy it rose by 150 percent to about the same level as that in France, and in the United Kingdom, it rose from 38 to 88 cents.

On the supply side, the 1970s have been a decade of ambitious programs and small accomplishments. The energy balance sheets of major energy-consuming countries reveal no significant move to coal, a continuing slowdown in nuclear growth and, except for a few countries where domestic oil production increased because of important discoveries, no substantial decline in the dependence on imported oil. Thus the world is entering the decade of the 1980s with the obvious imperative of finding new sources of liquid fuel.

The United States is just beginning a synthetic fuel program to build a small number of demonstration plants that will provide cost, environmental, and other information to serve as a base for deciding on a more ambitious step. The phased program, with ample but not excessive funding, is a step in the right direction and a welcome modification of the initial massive, forced-draft approach suggested by President Carter in July 1979. But fascination with the synthetics technology should not reduce efforts to develop other energy resources and to promote greater efficiency in energy use.

Coal is the nation's most abundant energy source, and actions should be taken by both government and business to increase its use. Pollution policy is a major impediment; it should be modified—as the Environmental Protection Agency recently has begun to do—by moving to market-like regulatory devices that will make compliance easier and remove many of the uncertainties and burdens now discouraging potential coal consumers. In addition, coal-burning technologies suitable for industrial and utility users should be developed.

The 1980s will be the critical decade for nuclear energy. For the first time, there is a real risk that the United States will abandon nuclear power as a source of energy. Because each of the major contemporary energy sources involves health, environmental, or political problems, the need is not to abandon nuclear energy, but to strengthen its public acceptance through institutional reforms such as those recommended by the Kemeny Commission in late 1979, and through technological improvements, international cooperation, and credible timetables. This is doubly important because eroding support for nuclear power would also jeopardize breeder research. That technology should not be abandoned at so early a stage of development. Alternative breeder designs need to be investigated, but a decision to deploy the breeder can be deferred.

Contingency plans for energy shocks are sorely needed. An adequate national petroleum reserve is a first line of defense, but the Carter administration's effort to build a reserve of one billion barrels is far behind schedule. Rationing in the event of an emergency has been neglected for too long. To minimize the surprises when a plan is put into action, it should be developed now and given wide publicity.

In the next ten years solar energy will not make a significant contribution to energy supplies; but policies should be implemented to remove institutional obstacles against its adoption and to provide financial aid to match open and hidden subsidies to other energy resources. Thus far the obvious technologies have received most attention (for example, roof collector panels). Research may reveal that these are not the most attractive or the least costly. Particularly if one believes that solar energy will eventually be the world's principal energy source, the years ahead should be spent on widening and deepening the understanding of its potential.

Health, Safety, and Environmental Regulations

Beginning in 1965, a large body of legislation was enacted by Congress to regulate health, safety, and the environment. Congress declared that the environment should be clean, highways and consumer products safe, workers protected, and automobiles efficient in gasoline consumption. It set stringent standards and tight timetables and required that standards be "practicable." While progress has been made, the goals have not been met. Still, surveys show that the public endorses the goals and is concerned about risks to health. Some sort of regulatory reform seems inevitable, but proposals range from one extreme of making it easier for the regulatory agencies to promulgate and enforce regulations to the other extreme of abandoning the regulations and relying on the marketplace.

Better health, safety, and environmental quality are legitimate goals, but they often conflict. Resources used to clean the environment are not available to protect workers. Resources expended on making automobiles safer cannot be used to curtail their emissions; making them more fuel-efficient requires trimming weight and size, which tends to make them less safe. Attaining the goals requires simultaneous consideration of such interactions.

A series of recent controversies illustrate the complexity of the process of setting standards and enforcing them. In some instances, such as vinyl chloride (the basic ingredient in the second most commonly used plastic in the United States), both the regulatory agency and the firms vastly overestimated the cost of complying with the regulation. In other cases, such as benzene (a basic chemical used in industry and products such as gasoline), the agency failed to muster evidence that further tightening of the standard would produce a measurable reduction in occupational illness. In still other cases, exemplified by sulfur dioxide (an air pollutant that is expensive to abate), the agency is regulating a compound, which is easy to measure and straightforward to control but not much of a health hazard, rather than the chemical derivatives (acid sulfates), which are difficult to control but are a health hazard. Administration is an inherent problem because it is impossible to enforce the entire set of social regulations in detail. Finally, there is a desperate need for better data and analysis in setting and enforcing regulations.

After fifteen years, it seems evident that the legal mechanisms of regulation do not work satisfactorily. As an alternative, economic mechanisms, such as effluent fees or transferable pollution rights, should be encouraged. These mechanisms have their own difficulties, but they are worth pursuing.

Even without any change in legislation or in enforcement procedures, one step should be taken immediately. Each agency must do more to set and articulate the reasons for priorities. The objective should be to communicate to Congress, the public, and those regulated the goals and plans of the agency and to encourage a reasoned dialogue about whether the activities of the agency are consistent with the legislation and with the public interest generally. The agency should also provide a basis for judging its success. The resulting information could enhance coordination among agencies, help Congress evaluate the regulations, and involve the public in planning.

The creative phase of social regulation has passed. The public desire for a clean, safe environment will prevent any general retreat from current goals. The next phase must improve the legislation and the regulatory frameworks for setting standards and for enforcing them. The problem is to strike the right balance between the desirable social goals of environmental improvement, enhanced safety, and better health on the one hand and the economic goals of growth, price stability, and preservation of market forces on the other.

Medical Care

The decade of the 1970s was marked by a series of battles over national health insurance and cost control, but neither cause made much headway. At the end of 1979, Congress had yet to pass any of the major cost-control proposals of the Ford or Carter administrations. The national health insurance bills of the early 1970s faded away and a new set was introduced, but no action was taken in 1979.

The current stalemate is an inevitable consequence of the history of medical care financing, which has been dominated during most of this century by the development and expansion of third-party payment. During the 1940s and 1950s private insurance became a major financing mechanism. In the 1960s medicare and medicaid gave the federal government a major role in paying for medical care. By the late 1970s over 90 percent of the population had some sort of coverage under private insurance, public programs, or both. Over 90 percent of hospital costs and about 60 percent of physicians' and nursing home costs were paid through third parties.

The philosophy behind third-party payment, whether private or public, is that medical care should be provided whenever it will help the patient, without regard to cost. In pursuit of this goal, the new forms of financing were reinforced by programs to provide funds for constructing hospitals and for training doctors and other health workers and by large increases in the research budget of the National Institutes of Health.

The result has been an enormous influx of resources into medical care. Private and public costs rose rapidly, from $13 billion in 1950 to $192 billion in 1978, or from 4.5 to 9.1 percent of the gross national product. The strain was so great, particularly on the federal budget because of medicare and medicaid—both of which cost far more than anticipated—that costs became the central concern in medical care, and cost-control proposals a major issue in Congress.

The issues of unlimited needs and limited resources have been joined in the new round of national health insurance bills. The major plans would all cover more people than are now covered and cover some of them more completely. Both the plan proposed by Senator

Russell Long and the Carter administration's National Health Plan would provide catastrophic coverage for the employed population and their dependents and for people enrolled in medicare. For most people, financial protection against catastrophic illness is the most important kind of coverage they now lack. The administration's plan also includes more comprehensive coverage for the poor; the plan envisages further expansion of coverage, but at a gradual pace in the hope of gaining greater leverage on costs. The Health Care for All Americans Act proposed by Senator Edward Kennedy would cover all U.S. residents and would provide all services included in the plan without charge.

Neither the administration's plan nor the Kennedy plan give an open-ended commitment to provide services. The administration's plan includes the cost-containment bill that failed to pass Congress in 1979. It would set limits on the rate of growth in hospital budgets and on investment spending. The Kennedy plan stipulates that spending for the services included would not be allowed to grow faster than the gross national product. This limit would stop the steady increase in the share of gross national product spent on these services and would constitute a sharp break with the past.

Both plans implicitly abandon the principle that services should be provided without regard to cost. Rationing would become necessary, and because both plans use budget limits on providers as their method of controlling costs, rationing would be the responsibility of the providers. Realistically, cost control—with or without national health insurance—requires acceptance of the principle that some medical services produce benefits that are worth less than their costs; otherwise, the opportunities for spending are unlimited. But the proponents of these plans have not admitted the need to ration, or that their plans will make it necessary. As a result, the debate over national health insurance and cost control has not yet dealt with the crucial issues—how much the nation is willing to spend on medical care and how to accomplish the rationing that must take place. The choice between limited services at moderate costs and generous services at high costs is not an easy one. But that is the choice before the nation, and the issues should be debated openly and honestly.

Education and Training

For the past two decades, outlays on education and training have increased rapidly. State and local governments scrambled during these years to keep pace with growing enrollment; and the federal government launched many new programs to increase the educational and employment opportunities of disadvantaged young people.

Falling enrollments at the elementary-secondary school level will force state and local governments to choose between maintaining current real spending (a "quality enhancement" option) or reducing real spending as enrollments decline (a "constant quality" option). The decision is likely to turn, in part, on the receptivity of teachers and administrators to proposals—such as the use of teacher proficiency exams—that hold the promise of genuine quality improvement.

Although the National Education Association has called for a sharp increase in the federal share of education support, such a shift is unnecessary. The federal agenda for education developed in the 1960s is essentially complete, and the federal government will continue to face greater claims compared to its resources than will state and local governments. The 1983 legislative reauthorization of the Elementary and Secondary Education Act will witness a push for unrestricted aid to schools, but this pressure should be resisted.

Growing interest of many parents in alternatives to public schools will keep the pressure on for tuition tax credits or voucher initiatives. Tax credits fail to measure up as either sound educational or tax policy because they mainly help the families with higher incomes. Those who are convinced that large public school systems are beyond reform see vouchers as the answer. But there is no assurance that a voucher system would improve educational quality, and there is a danger that it would seriously damage the public school system.

Policymakers concerned with the transition from school to work will confront old problems left unresolved from the 1970s as well as new challenges in the decade ahead. Youth unemployment, a persistent problem, has worsened dramatically for minorities. Programs to combat youth unemployment have accomplished little in the past and have provided few leads on how to do better in the future. Should the programs be aimed at those most in need of assistance, or should they be spread more broadly across a larger number of less disadvantaged youth? Should the training be work experience or vocational or general education, and which institutions should provide it? How can the private sector be productively involved in training hard-to-employ youth? The Carter administration's youth initiative, which would add about $2 billion a year to federal spending on youth, is an improvement over past programs. Focused on youth in depressed areas, the proposals would expand remedial education for teenagers lacking basic skills as well as increase training programs for hard-to-employ youth. Planning, standards of progress, and coordination among schools, industry, and training programs would be emphasized.

Colleges and universities will face a severe challenge in the coming years as the population aged eighteen to twenty-four drops by 21 percent between 1981 and 1995. The major research universities will have great difficulty maintaining excellence in research and graduate education because they will be unable to hire many junior faculty, a group that is highly active in research. Former state teachers' colleges, many of which are stranded in a state of semi-development and with unclear missions, will suffer much of the enrollment loss in the public sector. The less selective, heavily tuition-dependent private colleges will struggle for existence, and many will not survive the decade. Community colleges face an equally uncertain future, their fate depending in large measure on the demand for community-based, nondegree education from older part-time students.

The most important decisions affecting higher education in the 1980s will be made at the state, institutional, and private levels. The federal government will face pressure to become involved in the fate of individual institutions, but it should avoid that temptation. Unlike the previous decade when federal spending for higher education increased rapidly, the education agenda for the 1980s should emphasize consolidation and improvement of existing programs. In particular, the college student loan program should be overhauled; this program provides subsidies to many students who do not need it and has recently been abused by the state and local governments through the issuance of tax-exempt securities backed by federal loan guarantees.

Federal Grants-in-Aid

Federal financial assistance to state and local governments has grown rapidly during the past thirty-five years. From a mere 0.5 percent of the gross national product in the mid-1940s, federal grants-in-aid to the states and their political subdivisions increased to more than 3.5 percent by the mid-1970s. Current estimates indicate the percentage will decline in 1980 for the first time, and projections as far ahead as 1982 show that decline continuing.

As more federal revenues have been channeled to lower levels of government, the mechanism for transferring the funds became a major issue. Agreement about the relative merits of different methods of handling this transfer is needed as general revenue sharing comes up for renewal in 1980.

Three broad types of intergovernmental grants have been developed and are in current use. Categorical grants are directed specifically toward designated goals, with policy guidelines laid down by the federal government and recipient jurisdictions held answerable for expending the money according to the terms of the agreement. This approach gives Washington some assurance that its money will meet specific needs, but it imposes significant administrative and compliance costs and produces a fragmented grants system often criticized for its lack of flexibility and failure to deal efficiently with the interrelated problems of a large and complex society.

Block grants are funds provided by the federal government for broad functional areas, such as education, law enforcement, transportation, community development, and manpower training. They constitute a heterogeneous group of broadly aimed programs that give state and local governments greater flexibility in meeting their needs than do the more closely controlled categorical grants. Two factors, however, make it difficult to evaluate the real effectiveness of block grants. One is the fungibility of grant funds, which makes it virtually impossible to determine precisely how the money is spent. The other is the rapidly increasing number of procedural requirements attached to the expenditure of all federal funds. These have to do with civil rights and nondiscrimination, environmental protection, planning and project coordination, and wage and procurement standards. Such requirements complicate goal achievement, a problem that is compounded when programs have multiple, sometimes conflicting, goals. Hiring unskilled people to perform public services may not be the most efficient way of delivering adequate services in poor communities. Direct transfer payments would better serve needy persons, while fewer restrictions on the use of grant funds might aid the communities.

The most controversial type of federal assistance is general revenue sharing, which provides funds that can be used for whatever purposes the recipient governments choose. The current appropriation of $6.85 billion a year is distributed to each state and the District of Columbia on the basis of population, tax effort, per capita income, urbanization, and state income tax collections. One-third of each state's allocation goes to the state government; the remaining two-thirds is divided among all the general-purpose local governing jurisdictions. The division of money among localities is complicated and satisfies few critics, but it is politically acceptable.

Revenue sharing is opposed by those who believe that the federal government should control the use of its funds at the state and local levels. It is supported on the ground that the state and local governments can allocate the proceeds among regional or local programs better than can the federal government. The wide differences among states and localities with respect to both needs and tastes for services are strong arguments for allowing them the flexibility that unrestricted aid offers. In addition, revenue sharing can be an effective device for improving the financial ability of the poorer states and localities to provide public services. If for these reasons revenue sharing is made a permanent part of the federal grant system, the program should continue to allocate funds to the states because they have been playing an increasingly significant role in providing essential public services and in helping to finance local government activities.

Defense Policy

The United States is now in the midst of a public debate about its defense priorities and spending levels that results from the widespread perception that Soviet military strength has grown faster in recent years than that of the West. Much of this debate is reminiscent of the debates that occurred over twenty years ago. The central questions are: how much emphasis should be placed on nuclear and conventional forces and what contingencies should be prepared for by future nonnuclear force improvements.

There is now a nuclear stalemate between the United States and the Soviet Union. The stalemate exists because the two countries have sufficiently diverse and survivable forces that preclude either side from acquiring a meaningful and exploitable nuclear advantage. Even though some believe that the Soviet Union could obtain strategic superiority, the situation is unlikely to change as long as both sides continue to be reasonably cautious and conservative in planning their future nuclear forces.

To prolong the stalemate, the United States must maintain long-range second-strike nuclear forces that are flexible and reliable enough to cover a variety of targets. Toward this end, the United States is already planning to add a mobile land-based ballistic missile (the MX) to its intercontinental ballistic missile force and is considering a larger and more accurate missile (Trident II) for its submarine-based missile force. Additional investment may be required to improve the American command, control, communications system and to reduce the vulnerability of its nuclear forces based overseas.

Even though the stalemate will continue, there is a preoccupation in the United States with nuclear forces that diverts attention from the pressing issues concerning the adequacy of the nation's conventional forces; these latter forces are more directly relevant to prospective Western security problems in the 1980s. U.S. nuclear forces overseas are already being modernized and improved, but this should not be regarded as an alternative to an urgently needed nonnuclear force program. The Western alliance seems to be on the verge of making this mistake.

Despite a tradition of doubts to the contrary, nonnuclear defense of Western Europe is feasible given the resources available to the West and the constraints on the Warsaw Pact forces. Indeed, the Carter administration has continued to strengthen the conventional forces in Europe and the Far East, although the problems of old equipment and low operating rates continue to exist. The North Atlantic Treaty Organization (NATO) defense capability has been upgraded by the deployment of additional air and ground units to Europe, and steps have been taken to develop a system of rapid deployment of forces based in the continental United States in the event of conflict.

However, the threats to American security interests in the 1980s are more likely to arise from circumstances outside Europe and the Far East. Particularly around the Persian Gulf and the Indian Ocean, turbulent political events, intense Western economic interest, and the close proximity of the Soviet Union combine to produce potential security problems for which U.S. forces are poorly positioned. Although historically U.S. defense planning has attempted to provide forces with sufficient flexibility to respond to threats in any part of the world, in actuality American nonnuclear forces have become so rigidly committed to Europe and Korea that they are not readily available for serious military operations elsewhere, and lack sufficient airlift for two simultaneous contingencies.

One solution to this problem would be to seek a division of labor with European allies whereby they would augment their own defense efforts in order to release more American nonnuclear forces for service in other areas, including the forward deployment of forces in the Arabian Sea. Even in the absence of an explicit arrangement of this sort, security problems during the 1980s might require a reduction in the U.S. conventional forces permanently committed to Europe and Asia. Alternatively, the United States should consider increasing the readiness of selected ground and tactical air force reserves.

Redeployment and more flexible commitment will not by themselves meet the needs of the 1980s, however. The threat to U.S. and allied interests has not merely shifted—it has increased. The United States will need more capability for moving forces by air and by sea to distant parts of the world and the combat capabilities of the nonnuclear navy will have to be increased. Consequently, protecting U.S. interests in the 1980s will require a significant real increase in defense spending over the next several years, most of which should be dedicated to improving U.S. nonnuclear force capability.

Foreign Policy

U.S. foreign policy will remain heavily preoccupied with the Middle East and the Soviet Union. It will also be concerned with improving U.S. relations with China, Japan, Western Europe, and the developing countries.

The Middle East

In the 1980s, American Middle East policy is likely to shift from its long-standing concern with the Arab-Israeli conflict to the region surrounding the oil-rich Persian Gulf. Three developments in 1979 served to accelerate this trend.

First, the shah of Iran, once viewed as a pillar of stability and moderation in the volatile Middle East, was forced from his throne by Islamic revolutionaries under the stern leadership of Ayatollah Ruhollah Khomeini. With the departure of the shah, Iran entered a period of domestic turmoil, reduced oil production, and intense anti-Americanism.

Second, the signing of a formal peace treaty between Egypt and Israel greatly reduced the dangers of another Arab-Israeli war. While accomplishing far less than the comprehensive settlement that the Carter administration sought, the treaty was nonetheless seen by most Americans as a major achievement. Inevitably, less priority has been given to the second stage of the Camp David process, settlement of the Palestinian issue, than to the first.

Third, oil prices doubled in 1979, from less than $13 a barrel to more than $26, in large measure because Iranian production fell and because consumers, anxious to build oil stocks to hedge against uncertainty, engaged in panic buying. Although OPEC could not agree on a uniform pricing schedule or on a prorationing scheme, the actions of its individual members drove prices to unprecedented levels. OPEC's disarray does not appear to spell its demise, nor would its demise necessarily lead to lower oil prices.

The 1970s closed on two notes that had a profound impact on American public opinion. In November 1979 Iranian militants seized the American embassy in Tehran and held its occupants hostage. As the crisis dragged on for weeks, then months, American frustration at the impotence of the United States mounted. Adding to this angry mood was the massive Soviet invasion of Afghanistan the following month. This display of Soviet power and ruthlessness in a country beyond the established Soviet orbit has seriously upset the balance of power in the region and is already having wide international repercussions.

Taken together, these events have created a new strategic setting in the Middle East and in the world. The central feature of this environment is competition between the superpowers for influence in the Persian Gulf region. Iran's future orientation will be the prize, with U.S.-Saudi relations also in the balance. In these circumstances, the United States will commit more military resources to the region—by substantial arms transfers to Israel, Egypt, and Saudi Arabia, and probably by increasing military assistance to Jordan, Pakistan, Oman, Somalia, and other countries. It is also important for the United States to develop a capability for direct local intervention, complete with access to air and naval facilities, if not full-fledged bases.

Although the Egyptian-Israeli peace treaty is likely to endure, tensions between Israel and its other Arab neighbors will continue. Failure to find a political solution to the Palestinian question will be a major impediment to close U.S. relations with a number of Arab countries, and may be a factor for instability in Lebanon, Syria, Jordan, and the Gulf states. Furthermore, divisions will continue within the Arab world, as Arab nationalism gives way to the realities of state interests. Iraq will carry more weight as a regional power; Egypt will pursue an independent course; and sectarian differences will cause internal problems in many Arab countries. Islam will remain a strong factor in the political life of the area, but it will not prove to be a unifying bond transcending national borders and interests.

Thus U.S. policymakers will confront difficult choices in the Middle East. Efforts will have to be made to resolve, or at least contain, the Palestinian dimension of the Arab-Israeli conflict. Beyond that lies the challenge posed by an assertive Soviet drive for influence in the region, with Iran as the most important target. A combined American diplomatic, economic, and military strategy is needed to convince the Soviets of the need to exercise restraint. A vital part of such a strategy is an energy policy that will reduce U.S. vulnerability to disruptions of oil supply from the Middle East.

The Soviet Union

The 1980s, which began ominously with the Soviet invasion of Afghanistan, will see the United States and the USSR confront each other in many places; yet they will also continue to grope for a measure of safety and predictability in their relations. For the Soviet Union, the preoccupation with the United States will remain complicated by fears about China and the possibility that the United States and China (along with Europe and Japan) may form a hostile coalition. The United States must cope with the expanded Soviet military power and with their increasing involvement in international affairs.

The United States must identify its interests more clearly than it has in recent years and pursue a conscious policy of defending them against Soviet encroachments. It should work with others who have similar or compatible interests and concerns. More broadly, the United States should make clearer how the various elements of its policy toward the Soviet Union are related to one another. The USSR should not expect a flow of benefits, particularly economic ones, while conducting expansionist policies.

The 1980s will see conflict and instability in many parts of the world. The Soviet Union's capacity to exploit such situations continues to grow. Footholds and positions of influence obtained by supporting some faction or government in a conflict are increasingly used for Soviet military purposes. This has been the case recently in Angola, Mozambique, Ethiopia, South Yemen, and Vietnam; it has long been true in Cuba. In the case of Afghanistan, the intervention was climaxed by a sudden takeover by Soviet forces with overwhelming military power. The reasons were probably a combination of fear and opportunism, and the outcome remains uncertain. Inevitably, however, the United States and other countries must be concerned about such thrusts.

Potential areas of Soviet political or military intervention in the 1980s are to be found in virtually all parts of the world. The Middle East, where the Soviet Union already has numerous military advisors in the Arabian peninsula and nearby Ethiopia as well as armed forces in Afghanistan, is the most worrisome because of its petroleum resources and strategic location. In Europe, still the area where the largest Eastern and Western military forces are arrayed against each other, the Soviet Union is likely to remain cautious in the use of force, but will seek to advance its objectives through enticements and threats. The Tito succession in Yugoslavia might be an occasion for renewed Soviet pressure, including, in some circumstances, military intervention. Any significant shift in Yugoslavia's alignment toward the USSR would be a serious setback for the United States and Western Europe.

Arms control negotiations and agreements were more numerous in the 1970s than ever before. As a means of reducing hostility and the risks of conflict, however, they did not prove particularly successful. The strategic arms limitation talks (SALT) process produced some modest limits on existing strategic forces and inhibited some future programs. But it failed to cope with the most serious problems posed for the United States by the momentum of Soviet programs or with parallel threats that the USSR sees from the U.S. programs. Neither side has thus been willing to rely on SALT to solve its strategic arms problems, and this situation will probably not change significantly in the 1980s. Talk of possible deep cuts in strategic forces is almost certainly misleading, but specific measures may still be sought. The Soviet Union will probably opt for mobility to protect its land-based forces as the United States plans to do with the MX missile, but whether the USSR will constrain itself by the verifiability criteria of SALT and whether the United States will continue to do so is open to question. It may also prove necessary for the United States to consider hardening the defenses for its land-based missiles, if necessary by seeking modification of the Treaty on the Limitation of Anti-Ballistic Missile Systems of 1972.

Arms control in Europe does not appear to hold any more promise than SALT for coping with U.S. military problems. The mutual and balanced force reductions negotiations, even if invigorated, are unlikely to relieve the disparities that exist in the East's favor. Negotiations on nuclear forces in the European theater, if they were to proceed, would not obviate the need of NATO to modernize these forces. Such negotiations also run the risk of being confined to longer range forces, thus leaving the USSR with the advantages of its cumulative modernization of shorter range nuclear delivery systems. These problems are serious for the West, because NATO—in addition to improving its conventional defenses—will undoubtedly continue to rely on possible use of nuclear weapons by the United States to supplement deterrence of massive conventional attack.

Given Soviet economic needs, economic relations could play a significant role in shaping U.S.-Soviet relations as a whole and Soviet international conduct generally. Although there is long-standing resistance in the United States to political intervention in economic relations, the United States curtailed almost all its contacts with the USSR as a result of the Afghanistan crisis early in 1980. However, restrictive legislation has not allowed U.S. policy to develop a coherent economic strategy in dealing with Soviet power. The erratic approaches that have marked U.S. policies to date also hamper efforts to achieve some degree of coordination in the policies of the industrial democracies. If U.S. legislation is to be modified in the 1980s, the overriding purpose should be to integrate economic policies toward the USSR into overall policy. Failing this, the United States would deny itself an important instrument for influencing Soviet conduct in a period when Soviet interest in expanded economic relations is likely to grow.

Human rights concerns have always played a role in American attitudes and policies toward the USSR. As a result of action by the Carter administration as well as by Congress in the 1970s, this issue became one of direct confrontation between the United States and the USSR. Clearly, the United States must seek to alleviate the condition of people under Soviet rule, but U.S. influence in this respect is limited. Over the longer run, the policies aimed at moderating Soviet international conduct will also be the most beneficial ones in the area of human rights.

China

The immense strides in relations during the 1970s between the United States and the People's Republic of China have created a full agenda of issues for the 1980s on four overlapping levels: bilateral, strategic, regional Asian, and global.

Bilaterally, rapid progress is being made toward clearing away the legal debris of thirty years of hostility, but potential problems remain. While the Agreement on Trade Relations between the United States and the People's Republic of China is crucial to the entire economic edifice that is being constructed, Congress now requires that the president declare explicitly that China has met the free emigration test of the Jackson-Vanik amendment to the Trade Act of 1974 *each year* in order to keep the trade agreement in force. Additionally, China hopes to increase exports of light manufactures, including such items as textiles and footwear, to help rectify its sharply negative trade balance with the United States. But protectionist sentiment— expressed largely through Congress—runs strong in America. However, the key economic issues should be resolved soon, including arranging projects by U.S. government agencies on a compensatory basis and providing loans and guarantees.

Politically, the fate of Taiwan—an issue that normalization of diplomatic relations finessed but did not resolve—remains a dangerous problem. Taiwan itself could upset the status quo and provoke counterpressure by China, such as a blockade, which would in turn require a U.S. response. Or people in China who oppose current policies toward modernization might seek to weaken Deng Xiaoping (Teng Hsiao-ping) and his colleagues by accusing them of accepting a de facto U.S. two-Chinas policy and demanding that they adopt a more aggressive policy toward Taiwan. In either case, if Taiwan is brought to the front burner, U.S.-China relations could be badly singed.

In the strategic arena, China values the connection with the United States as a counterweight to the Soviets in Asia and elsewhere, and it has therefore tried to secure U.S. support for a consistently hard-line stance against Soviet initiatives. Until recently, Washington viewed its relationship with China in triangular terms and was in principle evenhanded in its dealings with the Soviet Union and China. The Soviet invasion of Afghanistan has outmoded this policy in non-military activities and suggests that this approach should be modified even in the security area. However, the United States should carefully restrict any future change in its security ties with China to activities —such as military consultations, intelligence sharing, and agreements to transfer particular technologies that may have military as well as peaceful applications—that do not create rigid, potentially irreversible commitments. The United States should also initiate a dialogue on strategic weaponry with Chinese leaders; conceivably that might eventually contribute to the broader arms control discussions with the Soviet Union. But Washington should resist the temptation to alarm Moscow through rhetoric about U.S.-China security relations.

Shared concerns about Soviet aggression, and the recognition that in some respects Chinese and U.S. military capabilities complement each other in Asia, may make a more far-reaching Sino-American security relationship attractive to some. But many considerations— such as the opposition of America's allies elsewhere in Asia, the possibility that the Soviet Union would be provoked into more rather than less aggressive behavior, and the recognition that Washington cannot control China's actions—make any such effort unwise. The United States, in brief, should not commit itself to providing China with military hardware or to defending it against attack.

Some key Asian regional problems cannot be resolved without U.S.-Chinese cooperation. For example, any effort to neutralize Kampuchea (Cambodia) will almost certainly fail unless the United States and China cooperate to bring about a solution (and unless Hanoi decides that neutralization is preferable to the costs of continuing the level of military effort necessary to pacify Kampuchea on its own terms). The Korean peninsula remains volatile; parallel political efforts of the major powers to encourage reconciliation between North and South Korea hold the best hope for peaceful evolution of the situation there. Since the start of their rapprochement, the United States and China have talked about their parallel interests and the importance of cooperation. The relationship has now developed to the stage at which efforts to change this rhetoric into reality in Asia should be high on the agenda.

The United States and China confront common global issues from the perspectives of the first and the third worlds, respectively. These issues cover a wide range—including not only developmental funding and the issues raised by the advocates of the New International Economic Order, but also the need for common efforts to stabilize world food prices, control international pollution, and cooperate in international scientific and technical research. Active cooperation in all these fields is still to be achieved, but one test of the maturity of the U.S.-China relationship in the 1980s will be the degree to which the two countries can help promote progress on this agenda of global concerns.

Japan

Japan is a military ally and a key element in the American strategic position in Asia and in the world. The U.S.-Japan mutual security treaty in many ways parallels the better-known North Atlantic treaty. It links the United States closely to a major industrial power and to a strong democracy on a continent otherwise antipathetic to representative government and political freedom. It also provides access to facilities and bases that are indispensable to U.S. strategy in the western Pacific.

The similarity between Japanese and American interests has if anything been reinforced by the U.S. rapprochement with China. If China looks to the United States as a potential military counterweight to the Soviet Union, it looks to Japan as a principal market and supplier of capital; and it has accepted the U.S.-Japan military alliance as a factor contributing to Chinese security. Among Western countries, Japan's influence will be second to that of the United States in affecting events and policies in China.

While the China connection has altered the strategic scene in Northeast Asia, it has also reemphasized the value of the many U.S. ties with a stable Japan. Japanese-American security relations, once a matter of domestic political controversy in Japan, have improved steadily in recent years. After more than two decades of arm's-length coexistence, the self-defense forces and the American military command in Japan have agreed to begin joint planning and to coordinate their operations. The American forces stationed in Japan are now officially described by the Japanese as being "indispensable to the security of this nation." Japanese spending in support of the American bases is now about $1 billion a year. Even in the politically sensitive matter of the role of Japan in regional defense, it has now become possible to study jointly the assistance that Japan can extend to the United States "in situations in the Far East outside of Japan."

These developments, which give or promise to give the alliance a mutuality of purpose and procedure heretofore absent, reflect remarkable gains in popular support or tolerance for the security treaty and for the continued presence of about 46,000 American military personnel in Japan. They do not presage Japanese "rearmament," if that term means a large increase in the defense budget from the current level of less than 1 percent of the gross national product (or about 1.5 percent if military pensions are counted, as they are in the NATO figures). The domestic constituencies supporting a large increase in defense spending—say, to 2 or 3 percent of the gross national product—are too weak to give this idea much promise.

American-Japanese economic relations are extensive, as befits the world's leading market economies, and they have been subject to periodic strains, such as those of the 1976–78 period. Strains and tensions aside, the two economies are heavily interdependent at both the macroeconomic and microeconomic levels, so that policies decided in either country affect the other.

Recent difficulties in the relationship have been primarily in the area of trade. During the past decade, Japan has typically had a global and a bilateral surplus in merchandise trade; these surpluses reached new highs in 1977–78. Their existence, together with allegations of unfair import restrictions and export incentives in Japan, led to a well-publicized series of bilateral negotiations, intertwined with the multilateral negotiations of the General Agreement on Tariffs and Trade. Some issues were resolved but, most important, the negotiations produced a number of agreements designed to reduce or to end resort to so-called nontariff measures that restrict imports or foster exports. The manner in which these understandings are carried out will help to shape bilateral (and multilateral) trade relations in the 1980s. If the parties entering contracts take their commitments seriously, market forces will have a larger role in world trade and fewer controversies will spill over into the political spheres.

Japan and the United States have overlapping or common interests in, among other things, fostering agricultural trade, coping with the energy problem, and seeking to adjust to each other's macroeconomic policy choices in ways that will contribute to satisfactory economic performance. Flows of direct investment in both directions, if not arbitrarily impeded, would smooth the structural adjustments that will have to be made in major industries in the United States and Japan. The yen promises to become a significant reserve currency during the decade, with substantial implications for the management of national monetary policies in all major countries.

A long-standing characteristic of U.S. relations with Japan has been their essentially bilateral character. This has been inescapable in the defense realm because Japanese legal and political constraints prevent any extension of mutual security beyond the home islands. In economic affairs, bilateralism has been more nearly a matter of custom and convenience; its limitations for the decade ahead need to be given more attention. Few economic issues are in fact bilateral. Most involve the interests of all the industrial states and the developing countries as well; and putting American-Japanese differences into a narrowly bilateral mold has often seemed to have connotations of discriminatory treatment. The United States should take the lead in changing the pattern.

Western Europe

Despite predictions of the early 1970s, the U.S.-West European relationship has remained of central importance to the United States and Western Europe alike. Both have interests in maintaining and in changing the balance of the relationship, but there are conflicting objectives. Whether it will be possible to continue managing the relationship successfully depends both on the internal political evolution of the United States and Europe and on broader international developments. The elections in the United States, Germany, and France in 1980–81 create uncertainties, as does the possibility of a serious international economic downturn. Political fragmentation and polarization in the United States and a more inward-looking European Community, beset by internal financial problems and slow economic growth, could make the outlook for transatlantic relations bleaker.

In the security field, the U.S.-European relationship has been complicated by the arrested development of East-West détente. The dimmed prospects for détente have increased U.S. fears of the "finlandization" of Western Europe, while the consecration through the SALT process of U.S.-Soviet strategic nuclear "parity" has crystallized European anxiety about the U.S. security guarantee of Europe. In nuclear force policy, the alliance will have to define more precisely the role of theater nuclear forces in deterrence and defense. Conventional force improvements have become even more important in the age of strategic parity. Efforts to promote human rights, contacts, and cultural improvement through the follow-up mechanism of the Conference on Security and Cooperation in Europe will also remain important to most European countries. Alliance cohesion in this situation will depend on truly multilateral handling of both defense policy and East-West negotiations. The continuing hope of the alliance for a bilateral U.S.-Soviet negotiation on long-range theater nuclear forces is fraught with risks for allied solidarity.

Political changes outside the Atlantic area will challenge Atlantic solidarity. Europeans typically see changes as the unavoidable product of national and regional causes and emphasize political and diplomatic ways of dealing with them; the United States stresses the geopolitical dimension and contemplates the use of military means. The Iranian crisis of 1978–79 exemplified these differences. Africa and the Middle East will be the two critical areas for the future. Possible Soviet involvement in the Persian Gulf, following the intervention in Afghanistan, will further complicate problems in that area.

Economic issues will be the keystone of the transatlantic relationship. Earlier fears that an increasing divergence between a socialist Europe and a capitalist United States would strain transatlantic relations have not materialized. European countries and the European Community have increasingly accepted the need for liberal, open economic arrangements, though this is still a fragile trend. Despite continuing protectionist tendencies in both Europe and the United States, trade and industrial policy disputes will probably be resolved pragmatically in the 1980s. Disagreements over macroeconomic management and monetary policy have also diminished in severity, but they could grow again if present policies fail. Energy policy, especially that for oil, will be crucial. Inasmuch as a consumer-producer agreement on oil supply and pricing seems unlikely, the Atlantic countries will have to concentrate on conservation and the development of alternative energy sources. A more effective international policy for conservation can be achieved. Nuclear safety, the international regime for nuclear fuel services, and environmental problems associated with increased coal use all require the cooperation of the Atlantic countries.

The common thread running through future transatlantic problems is the interaction between the rigidities of domestic politics and the requirements of international policy. This problem is more acute than it has been in the past, but the allies adjusted to new realities in the 1970s with less difficulty and greater political stability than many feared. This fact and the broad common interests of the United States and Western Europe provide the foundation for a sound Atlantic relationship in the future. Common interests do not, however, translate automatically into common policies, and in some areas competition and divergence are inevitable. But the North Atlantic countries can avoid fundamental damage to the relationship and enhance their mutual understanding of the domestic constraints on one another's policies. With modest adaptations to the institutional structure, which has already been improved during the 1970s, a stronger, less acrimonious and more mature relationship should be within reach in the 1980s.

Developing Countries

U.S. relations with developing countries have changed significantly in recent years. Until the late 1960s the United States was considered the predominant economic and political power. The view held then was that the United States would sustain its allies in nearly any part of the world and take the lead in assisting developing countries to achieve their economic aims. This view was shattered by the U.S. failure in Vietnam, the decline in U.S. economic and military hegemony, and the perception that the United States was taking a much more introverted, even isolationist, approach toward economic relations with the South in such areas as trade and aid. Developing countries began to question the depth of U.S. resolve to provide its allies with generous economic assistance and military protection.

Despite these adverse political and economic trends, there has been a significant growth of U.S. interests in and dependence on the third world. Developing countries supply about 40 percent of the oil consumed in the United States and significant amounts of other essential commodities. The advanced developing countries are rapidly penetrating the markets of industrial countries with such low-cost, labor-intensive consumer goods as textiles, apparel, footwear, and consumer electronics. Approximately two-fifths of total U.S. exports are sold to developing countries, more than to East and West Europe, the Soviet Union, and China combined. The developing countries are the most rapidly growing markets for U.S. machinery, transportation equipment, high-technology goods and services, and agricultural products. U.S. banks and corporations have large stakes in the developing countries. The third world is also important to the United States strategically for access to raw materials and supplies and for maintenance of lines of communications.

Drained by the Vietnam debacle and by adverse economic conditions, the United States has attempted to limit military and economic commitments to developing countries, except in the Middle East. The Nixon doctrine, designed to reduce the need for direct military involvement abroad, minimized the level of direct U.S. intervention in numerous third world conflicts, but greatly expanded U.S. arms transfers. Even though it has tried to take a more neutral stance, the United States continues to be viewed by the developing countries as controlling the regimes it supports. Yet the assistance actually extended has declined as a percentage of U.S. gross national product and is often insufficient or unsuited to meet internal political, economic, and security requirements. U.S. attempts to influence policies in individual countries on such significant matters as human rights and nuclear nonproliferation have been both supported and criticized by third world leaders.

After totally rejecting the developing countries' initial demands for a New International Economic Order, the United States since the mid-1970s has taken a slightly more open, step-by-step approach toward reforms in the areas of trade, aid, debt, investment, and technology transfer. Some modest progress has been made in several aspects of North-South economic relations (for example, commodity agreements, debt relief for some of the poorer countries, multilateral trade negotiations, and better access to international financing), but these steps have been considered insufficient by the developing countries. The Carter administration has continued to emphasize that the scarce resources available for economic assistance should be directed at meeting basic human needs. While acknowledging this goal to be the ultimate objective of economic development, third world leaders point out that the basic needs strategy is not backed by an expanded flow of resources; they claim that it is designed to block the reforms envisaged in the new economic order and permit interference in the domestic affairs of developing countries. The result of these differences has been stalemate in negotiations and general acrimony in North-South relations.

The Carter administration has acknowledged the importance of North-South relations, but to date has yet to assign them the operational priority they warrant. Overloaded by domestic concerns and relegated to the defensive in the international arena, the administration has been unable to design an overarching strategy that is acceptable to developing countries and is consistent with the long-run economic and political needs of the United States. In the current environment, even positive steps taken by the United States—in Panama, Zimbabwe, and the Middle East—are regarded as minimal.

The United States and the other democratic industrial countries should reopen the North-South dialogue in good faith. The new policy should recognize the needs of developing countries, the areas in which mutual gains can be achieved, and the capabilities of the industrial countries to contribute. A clear financial commitment should be made to assist countries planning concerted efforts to meet the basic needs of their poor majorities. The policy should recognize the diversity of developing countries, but accept their need for unity.

The United States should now give relations with developing countries the same priority it gives relations with its industrial partners or to the Soviet Union and China. It will have a number of opportunities to demonstrate its commitment to the third world in the months and years ahead. The Presidential Commission on World Hunger and the Brandt Commission have suggested priorities and specific measures to be taken. Global negotiations will resume in the United Nations this year, and preparation for an international development strategy for Development Decade III is under way.

Third world reaction against the Soviet invasion of Afghanistan and a general softening of criticism of the United States may have provided an opportunity for the development of a more constructive set of North-South relations. The challenge will be to use this opportunity wisely and decisively.

Competence in Government

In his national "malaise" speech of July 1979, President Carter concluded that the country was suffering from a crisis of confidence. Polling data support the president clearly enough: confidence in the people in charge of American institutions, particularly the presidency and Congress, had fallen precipitously by 1979 from a high point reached in the mid-1960s, when the bold measures of Lyndon Johnson's Great Society were being passed.

The alarming decline of confidence in government is rooted clearly in a series of traumatic events that are perceived to reflect a failure of national leadership. The lost war in Vietnam, the riots in the ghettoes and on the campuses, the Watergate scandal, the forced resignation of a president, the worst economic downturn since the Great Depression, double-digit inflation, the energy crisis and the gasoline lines—all have turned a nation that was confident and optimistic in the mid-1960s to one that is gloomy about the future and distrustful of the White House and Congress. But it is faith in the present generation of politicians that has been lost, not belief in the system itself; Americans still believe that the government *can* work. If whoever is elected president in 1980 has a program reasonably well calculated to cope with the problems that now confront the country—above all, inflation, energy, and foreign policy—and if after election the president is able to deliver on his campaign promises, confidence in government could be restored. A record of governmental success, in short, can overcome the effects of fifteen years of failure and mistakes. The crisis of confidence, then, becomes a crisis of competence in government.

Competence in government—never easy to achieve under the American constitution and political tradition—will be more difficult than ever to attain in the coming decades because of certain fundamental trends within the political and government system and because of the complexity of the problems that the nation faces.

For policy to be made effectively, three centers of power—the president, the Senate, and the House—have to achieve a reasonable degree of harmony and collaboration. In the past, the bridge between the branches of government was the political party. In periods when party organizations and party attachments were strong, the president as leader of his party was normally accepted by the majorities in Congress as leader of the legislature. But in the absence of strong party organizations and attachments—as is the case now—anything more than minor, incremental changes in policy is exceedingly difficult to implement.

With the deterioration in party organization since 1968 has come the proliferation of state presidential primary elections, to the point where they are the rule rather than the exception. Primaries put a premium on popular appeal, as distinct from party standing. When the voters at large make the choice, without the intermediation of a party elite, a candidate who is a complete outsider to the party establishment can reach the White House. The country's leader may take office, then, without acceptance as the natural leader of the party, and hence without followership in Congress, and perhaps also without experience in dealing with world affairs or the national economy.

The fourteen years of divided government during the Eisenhower, Nixon, and Ford administrations were years of struggle and discord between president and Congress, which reached their climax at the end of the first term of Richard Nixon. Congress, angered and aroused to assert itself against the president, moved decisively to reverse its long decline and recapture lost authority. It regained control of the power to make war and the power of the purse, in particular, and it took steps to tighten control and supervision over the executive branch, and to enlarge its role in policy formation, considerably augmenting its staff resources for those purposes. But a trend toward assertiveness in Congress has been accompanied by another trend— toward fragmentation of authority in the legislature. If Congress is to reject presidential leadership, it needs the capacity to develop comprehensive, integrated policies of its own. But power in Congress has been diffused from a few leaders and key committee chairmen to a large number of members only weakly bound by party allegiance. If Congress is to continue to reject presidential leadership, it is in no position to serve as a substitute source of policy coordination and integration.

The ability of the government to execute policies and programs is also in question. For more than a quarter of a century there has been a sharp trend toward politicization of the bureaucracy, with the result that governmental administration is increasingly in the hands of transient people—chosen for qualities besides skill or experience in management, unfamiliar with the organizations they head, and likely to leave government service before they learn how to use effectively the resources at their disposal.

It will not be easy to modify these adverse trends; they are rooted in powerful historical events and fundamental forces operating within the political system. Parties will be revived only as new issues may arise to dominate politics and polarize the country. The tide of direct primaries may, at some point, spontaneously begin to recede in reaction to the ordeal that presidential campaigning has become. If, for that reason or because of happy accident, the voters elect a succession of presidents whom the congressional majorities are willing to accept as their leaders, collaboration between the branches will improve. As for governmental management, if a consensus were to be reached that the federal government should move toward development of a professional managerial corps on the pattern of other democratic countries, the Senior Executive Service established in 1979 provides the appropriate institutional base on which to build. But the major step toward restoring competence in government—and, with it, public confidence —is to stop blaming the particular leaders who happen to be in office for what is wrong and to look hard at the system in which they work.

CHAPTER TWO

Economic Policy

BARRY P. BOSWORTH

THE DECADE of the 1970s was a most traumatic period for American economic policy. As the dominant concern of the policymakers vacillated between the problems of inflation and unemployment, there were repeated sharp shifts of direction in both fiscal and monetary policy. By the end of the decade, both inflation and unemployment had worsened, and the economy was on the verge of its third recession in ten years. At the same time, the nation was beset by increasingly severe problems of declining productivity growth and exploding energy prices. All these problems were reflected during the decade in a 20 percent decline in the value of the dollar on foreign exchange markets.

In the optimistic world of the mid-1960s the Keynesian "new economics" achieved a considerable degree of consensus. Under this view, fiscal and monetary policy could be used to prevent major deviations of demand from a smooth growth of aggregate supply. By avoiding the extremes of excess demand and recession, economic policy could provide a reasonable and acceptable compromise on inflation and unemployment. But within a few years the optimism of the mid-1960s had given way to intense debates about the relative efficacy of fiscal and monetary policies and calls for replacing discretionary policy with formal rules.

I thank Robert W. Hartman, Arthur M. Okun, and George L. Perry for their many suggestions. Kathleen Elliott Yinug assisted in preparing the manuscript.

Much of the disenchantment is a direct outgrowth of the deteriorating economic performance of the 1970s in comparison to the previous decade. Real output growth slowed from an annual average of 4.1 percent to 2.8 percent, and the unemployment rate averaged about 1.5 percentage points higher.[1] Most dramatically, inflation averaged more than 7 percent in the 1970s, compared to 2.3 percent during the 1960s. In the early years of the 1960s the United States had essentially no inflation; yet by the end of the 1970s consumer prices were rising at an annual rate in excess of 13 percent.

A simple review of the deteriorating performance of the U.S. economy, however, is not an adequate basis for condemning the policies of the last decade. The essence of policy decisions is frequently the choice between unattractive alternatives. And in many areas economic events during the last ten years did not present the government with attractive choices. The inflation problem originated with the excessive fiscal stimulus of the Vietnam War years. And certainly the world economy was not subjected during the 1960s to economic disruptions of the magnitude of the 1970s—in particular, the world grain crisis of 1972–74 and the abrupt rise of energy prices in late 1973 and again in 1979. In addition, the role of the United States in the world economy has changed significantly. The spread of technology, increased mobility of capital, and industrialization in other countries have sharply reduced the dominating position of the United States in many of its traditional markets, and the growth of financial centers abroad has reduced foreign dependency on the dollar. Today there is a more open competitive world economy with a high degree of interdependency among countries. As a result, foreign economic events are of far greater importance to the domestic economy of this country.

The public perception of economic policy, on the other hand, is not that it has made the best of a bad situation. Government policies are perceived as a major contributor to that poor performance. The effectiveness of fiscal and monetary policies as means of regulating aggregate demand, however, should not be the issue of major debate.[2]

---

1. The overall unemployment rate may exaggerate the amount of labor market slack because of demographic shifts during the 1970s toward a less experienced work force.
2. The economic forecasts of gross national product that underlie the economic policies of the government had smaller errors in the 1970s (0.75 percent) than in the 1962–69 period (1.30 percent). Far larger errors were made in projecting the split of that income growth between real output and inflation.

Instead, the problem has been that the ability to control aggregate demand has not translated into control of inflation. It is the issue of inflation and the apparent failure of past anti-inflation policies that destroyed the policy consensus of the 1960s; and it is the question of whether there are more effective alternative means of combating inflation that is at the center of the current conflict over economic policy.

Today the United States is faced with three major economic difficulties: inflation, slow productivity growth, and an uncertain energy supply. Yet the interrelated nature of these problems and the policy conflicts that arise among them frustrate efforts to develop solutions. In addition, the current inflation differs in several important ways from the traditional situation of an inflation fueled by excess demand pressures. If fiscal and monetary restraint are to be the primary means for reducing that inflation, the costs to unemployment will be extremely high. A focus on the supply side of the economy and the role of government policy as it affects supply decisions does offer some insights into the causes of the problems, but it does not offer any simple solutions. The United States is faced with the need to make some painful readjustments of its economic policies, and the problems cannot be solved without imposing some significant near-term costs and sacrifices.

Demand-Management Policy

Economic policy as it evolved during the 1960s emphasized the management of the demand side of the economy. The growth of aggregate supply was viewed as an autonomous process reflecting longer term, structural factors such as growth in productivity and in the labor force. These determinants of supply were viewed as relatively immune to short-run changes in economic policy. In fact, elaborate efforts were made to estimate their trends and to project the growth of supply—"potential gross national product"—that would be associated with maintaining a specific rate of overall resource utilization. The unemployment rate of labor was also stressed as a measure of overall resource utilization. Although it was recognized that variations in the rate of capital formation would affect the growth of labor productivity and capacity, these effects were viewed as small; and the impact of policy on investment was emphasized more from the perspective of investment as a component of demand than from its role in expanding supply.

Fiscal and monetary policy could be used to control the level of aggregate demand relative to supply. This would determine the level of production, employment, and unemployment. Most important, an unemployment rate target for policy was based on the assumption of a stable inverse relationship between unemployment and inflation. Thus desires for a lower rate of unemployment had to be evaluated against the costs of increased inflation. Inflation was the antithesis of unemployment as high levels of aggregate demand implied shortages in a large proportion of individual markets and consequent upward pressures on wages and prices.[3]

Within this framework, economic policy during most of the 1960s was viewed as successful. The combination of an expansionary fiscal policy and an accommodative monetary policy succeeded in maintaining a strong economic expansion that stretched over nine years and reduced unemployment to 3.5 percent of the labor force. The mistake of policy was seen as the failure to moderate the growth in demand as the unemployment rate dropped below the target rate of 4 percent—the failure to dampen pressures of excess demand on the inflation in the latter half of the decade. This was widely interpreted as a political rather than an economic mistake because the administration feared the implications for public support of increasing taxes to pay for the war in Southeast Asia.

Events in the late 1960s and the 1970s, however, made clear that the fundamental problem for economic policy was that control of demand did not translate in a simple and direct way into control of inflation. Moreover, once the inflation became imbedded in the economy, efforts to remove it with demand restraint required unacceptable high levels of unemployment. The adoption of restrictive demand policies in late 1968 and the recession of 1969–70 did not undo the mistakes of earlier years. Despite a substantial increase in unemployment (to 6 percent in 1970), inflation continued at a high rate and spawned a new economic term: "stagflation," or the joint occurrence of high rates of unemployment and inflation. There has not been a

3. This notion of a trade-off between inflation and unemployment was summarized empirically in the Phillips curve, which charted, on the basis of historical experience, feasible combinations of the two goals. This empirical model is illustrated in Robert J. Gordon, "Inflation in Recession and Recovery, *Brookings Papers on Economic Activity, 1:1971,* pp. 105–58. (Hereafter *BPEA.*)

stable inverse relationship between unemployment and inflation, and during the 1970s any given level of unemployment came to be associated with increasingly high rates of inflation.

The continued attempt throughout the 1970s to view the inflation problem within the confines of an excess demand framework—as a conflict between unemployment and inflation goals—led to repeated changes of direction in fiscal and monetary policies. During periods of economic expansion, as unemployment declines, public concern about inflation intensifies and the government responds by adopting more restrictive demand policies. In the subsequent period, inflation recedes; but sharp rises in unemployment result in a reversal of policy, demand expansion, increased employment, and worsening inflation. In each of these cycles the average levels of both unemployment and inflation is higher than in the previous cycle.

The sharply expanded role of external factors during the 1970s, such as the world food and energy crises, also created a dilemma for demand-management policies. In concept, higher food and energy prices could be treated as a simple change in relative prices as the increased expenditure on these items reduced demand for other items. The stickiness of industrial wages and prices, however, implies that a concurrent, offsetting reduction in those prices would require severe restraints on domestic demand. In effect, U.S. policy seems called on to respond to a sharp rise in the price of oil set by the Organization of Petroleum Exporting Countries (OPEC) by raising the number of unemployed workers in this nation. The undesirability of these consequences has put great pressure on fiscal and monetary policies to accommodate the food and energy price shocks by a rise in the average price level; this, too, has proven unsatisfactory, but there is no clear guidance as to what the optimal policy should be.

Cost and Supply Issues

The growing problem of inflation and the evident frustrations with the existing policy framework have been important motivating factors behind a resurgence of interest in the supply side of the economy and the linkages between supply and demand. This development of a supply-side economics over the last decade has had several different themes.

First, the obvious inadequacies of the unemployment-inflation trade-off as an explanation of the inflation process have stimulated efforts to develop a better understanding of wage and price dynamics. In particular, why are wage rates and industrial prices so insensitive to large increases in unemployment and idle capacity?

Second, the disproportionate impact on the overall economy of supply-demand disruptions in individual commodity markets during the 1970s and the rapid growth of government policies—particularly regulation—directed at individual industries have generated interest in the development of a microeconomic policy framework that would complement macroeconomic fiscal and monetary policies. In one sense, it is a call for more government planning with an analogy to the role of government in the Japanese economy. On another level, it reflects the recognition that government, through its regulatory and administrative decisions, does have substantial impacts on the economy; and that, because they are carried out by a vast array of single-purpose agencies, these policies are frequently inconsistent and uncoordinated. In any given year, policy decisions at the micro level can do as much or more than fiscal and monetary policies to determine the course of inflation, yet their economic effects are seldom subjected to the same evaluation.

Finally, there has been a growing concern about the process of supply creation and, in particular, the effects of relative prices and taxes on incentives to supply capital, work effort, and savings. This is an old theme in economics and a major element of the resurgence of neoclassical economics; it contrasts with the emphasis in earlier years on demand-management policies and income rather than price effects.

Wage-Price Dynamics

Today the United States is experiencing an inflation that is not being driven primarily by pressures of excess aggregate demand. Instead, it can be characterized as an inflation that has built up a momentum of its own, while shocks or disturbances to the economy exacerbate the ongoing inflation or initiate a new one. The momentum process is reflected in a self-perpetuating underlying rate of inflation in the industrial sector as all individuals view themselves as responding defensively to the inflationary excesses of others. Wage increases are fueled by a desire to match past price increases and the wages of others, and by expectations that the process will continue.

On the price side, business firms also see their own actions as reflecting a pass-through of past cost increases. This continual cycle of wage and price increases is only loosely related to overall demand conditions and is more the result of a long history of past inflation and expectations that it will continue. While most participants recognize that they do not gain from the process, no one dares to restrain their own actions because of fears that others will not.

The shocks or disturbances that exacerbate this inflation momentum come from a variety of sources. At times, such as the mid-1960s, excess aggregate demand has been an important factor. In 1972–73 a sharp worldwide economic expansion created strong demand pressures in many basic materials markets. In addition, the increased exposure of the United States to a more integrated world economy leaves it vulnerable to events such as world crop failures or a disruption of petroleum supplies. Finally, there has been a great growth in the involvement of government in individual markets, and its actions often initiate upward pressures on prices or wages.

These disruptions in major individual markets can have a dramatic direct effect on the average inflation rate. But a secondary and longer-lasting impact results because a surge of inflation that originates with sharp price increases in a few markets rapidly spreads throughout the economy as other participants accelerate their own wage and price increases in an effort to catch up. The result is an upward ratcheting of the underlying inflation rate in the industrial sector and a carry-over of inflation into future periods.

The distinction between the underlying rate or momentum of inflation in the industrial sector and the overall inflation rate is illustrated in figure 2-1. As shown in the top panel, most of the volatility of the inflation rate reflects changing conditions in a few markets dominated by special factors: food, energy, and housing. The underlying rate of increase in wage rates and other prices is much more stable and persistent from one period to the next. The bottom panel shows that these volatile components account for nearly all the acceleration of inflation in recent years. The distinction between the underlying rate and the role of specific shocks is important because each calls for quite different policy actions. If the causes of inflation extend beyond excess demand, effective policy responses will require more than fiscal-monetary restraint. Policy must deal with the difficulties of breaking the momentum of a wage-price inflation that has

Figure 2-1. Consumer Price Inflation, by Source, 1968–79

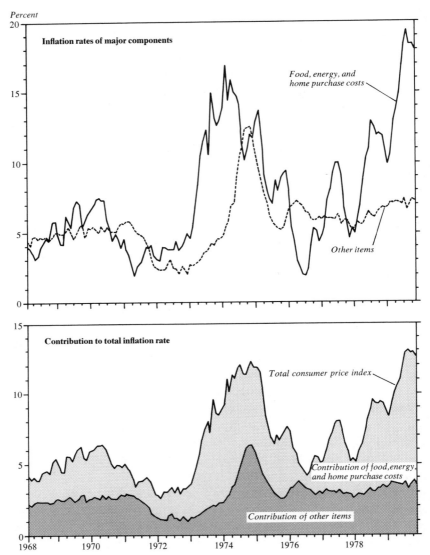

Source: U.S. Department of Labor, Bureau of Labor Statistics. The "other items" category excludes the following components of the consumer price index: food, energy, home purchases, used cars, and home financing, insurance, and taxes. The contribution of each component to the total increase is equal to its rate of increase multiplied by its share in the total index. Changes are measured over six-month intervals at annual rates.

become deeply ingrained in the institutional structure of the industrial sector. At the same time, policy must develop effective means to avoid new shocks to the system or, at a minimum, dampen their influence on the rest of the economy.

The major change in the inflation process during the 1970s was the increased frequency and magnitude of the shocks. But there was also too little appreciation of the role of catch-up efforts by others and the strength of the momentum process. Thus, unless governments were prepared to accept large increases in unemployment, a relative price increase in one market translated into a higher overall price level and a continuing impact on inflation in future periods.

The process is well represented by the events of 1973–74. Food and energy items combined represent about one-fourth of consumer expenditures. The explosive increases in these prices during that two-year period had a direct but temporary impact on the overall inflation of consumer prices of about 4 to 5 percentage points annually. This shift of real income to farmers and energy producers represented a large drop in the real incomes of those in the industrial sector. But, in addition, the resultant conflict over who would bear that burden— the effort to maintain one's own real income and to pass the costs of the shortages to others—together with the end of controls led to an escalation of wage increases from 7 percent in 1972 to 11 percent in 1974 and a near fourfold increase in the overall inflation rate from 3 to 12 percent. The subsequent recession was a direct result of that worsening of inflation, and the cost in terms of unemployment and forgone income were ultimately far larger than the initial costs of higher food and energy prices. Yet the rate of inflation, exclusive of farm prices, never declined below 6 percent annually.

Given the magnitude of the disruptions in world commodity markets during the 1970s, a worsening of inflation was not a surprise; but the persistence of high inflation rates long after the reversal of the initiating factors and in the face of recession and high unemployment was. The experience of recent recessions, for example, suggests that, at best, an increase of 1 percent in the unemployment rate—about 1 million persons—if maintained over a two-year period would reduce inflation by only about 1 percentage point. This persistence of inflation is the predictable result of structural differences between markets in a complex modern economy and the idealized model of the textbooks. While competitive factors exert strong long-term pressures on wage rates and prices, there is substantial discretion in the adjustment to short-run fluctuations in market conditions. The factors that contribute to the momentum of the inflation process and its insensitivity to variations in demand are not new to the 1970s. However, they have been made more evident by the shocks and disruptions that escalated the process to a sharply higher plateau.

WAGE RATES. The role of structural factors in modifying the response of wage rates to variations in unemployment is most evident in the case of collective bargaining. Although the individual in an idealized competitive economy is pictured as choosing between the offered wage and other available alternatives, collective bargaining is similar to the dealings of a bilateral monopoly because the result is a group decision and the decision to reject the wage offer can also include the denial of the job to others. As a result, individuals lose perception of a linkage between their own wage demands and the risk of losing their jobs. At the empirical level, it is reflected in the fact that wage agreements in the large union establishments show little or no sensitivity to cyclical changes in labor market conditions.[4] These tendencies are reinforced by the practice of multiyear bargaining under which the current year's wage increase reflects economic conditions of previous years or is indexed to current rates of price inflation. In a typical year, less than half of union pay increases are the result of contracts negotiated during that year.

Collective bargaining agreements cover about 30 percent of total employment in the private nonfarm sector; and, because of higher-than-average wage rates in unionized industries, they represent about 40 percent of the total nonfarm wage bill. In addition, about 20 percent of the American work force is employed in the public sector where the effect of competitive pressures or cost minimization are reduced. Nonunion pay practices are also influenced by union wage rates—employers with a mixed labor force need to maintain historical wage differentials, while others wish to avoid the potential for unionization of their own work force.

Even in the absence of collective bargaining, wage rates cannot be expected to adjust quickly to cyclical fluctuations. The heterogeneous nature of the work force, when combined with costly and imper-

4. See, for example, Daniel J. B. Mitchell, "Union Wage Determination: Policy Implications and Outlook," *BPEA, 3:1978*, pp. 537–82.

fect means of evaluating workers before employment, leads firms with strong concerns about quality to adopt practices that minimize long-run employment costs rather than to adjust wage rates fully to cyclical changes in the labor market. Employment practices in such situations have many aspects of an implicit contract between the employer and the employees as the employer seeks to adopt policies that achieve long attachments and low quit rates. During periods of temporary or cyclical declines in demand, these firms will maintain some on-the-job underemployment and temporarily lay off workers rather than reduce wage rates. Such policies substitute for additional new-hire costs in the future expansion and are viewed as less damaging to the firm's reputation as a "good" employer—thus minimizing the impact on future quit rates.

In reality there are enormous variations in the characteristics of labor markets, ranging from close approximations to an auction market to highly tenured types of arrangements. Arthur Okun has labeled the two extremes "casual" and "career" jobs.[5] In casual jobs, employees can be used as though they were homogeneous and the job requirements can be tailored to the lowest common denominator. Without job attachments, wage-rate changes will be an active part of the adjustment of supply and demand because the employer does not value experience and expects considerable job turnover: few alternatives are available to wage-rate increases in strong markets and few inhibitions to cutting wage rates in slack markets. In career job markets, however, the focus of employment practices shifts away from maximization of short-run advantage to a concern for longer term stability of the employer-employee relationship.

PRICES. A limited response to cyclical variations in demand is also evident in the behavior of industrial prices. Many empirical studies, in fact, fail to find any cyclical sensitivity in the average level of industrial prices—they identify only a pass-through of input-cost changes. Again, this stability is in many respects the logical result of important institutional distinctions between industrial markets and

5. An extensive discussion of the cyclical insensitivity of wage rates is provided in Arthur M. Okun, *Prices and Quantities: A Macroeconomic Analysis* (Brookings Institution, forthcoming). That book also includes an annotated bibliography of research on implicit contracting and other characteristics of these markets. A summary of recent research work is provided by Robert J. Gordon, "Recent Developments in the Theory of Inflation and Unemployment," *Journal of Monetary Economics,* vol. 2 (April 1976), pp. 185–219.

the auction market of the competitive model. In auction markets the individual firm cannot influence the price and focuses its attention on the quantity to offer for sale. Auction markets dominate in situations in which many buyers and sellers produce a homogeneous product—typified by the markets for agricultural products and financial assets.

In most markets, however, the firm sells a differentiated product for which it sets a price and stands ready to supply the quantity demanded by the market. The firm establishes a price as a markup over standard unit costs. In many industrial processes, standard unit costs are relatively constant over wide variations in capacity utilization and are therefore not significantly altered by small variations in demand. Similarly, competitive conditions, which determine the magnitude of the optimal markup, are not necessarily changed by cyclical shifts in the level of demand. The potential entry or exit of firms from the market does represent a change in competitive conditions, but because of the importance of fixed costs, these are long-term decisions that are not drastically altered by cyclical factors. Thus prices tend to be sticky and responsive only to changes in the costs of input.

In addition, as with labor markets, there are significant search costs associated with gathering information on prices that create advantages to both buyers and sellers of establishing a continuing relationship. The buyers economize on the cost of search; and the sellers gain a higher level of sales through repeat business if they can discourage their customers from shopping elsewhere. In effect, the costs of shopping introduce a bilateral monopoly surplus that can be shared between buyers and sellers.[6]

The concern with maintaining a continuing relationship introduces an intertemporal relationship between today's prices and tomorrow's sales. Today's customers have a value beyond their current purchases because of the potential for repeat business in the future. Therefore, a firm will not fully adjust prices to transitory changes in today's market conditions as it looks forward to the impact on future sales. The absorption of some temporary cost increases will provide the firm with a cushion of repeat business if market conditions weaken in the future. The result will be a dampening of variations in pricing markups over the business cycle.

6. The rationale for customer relationships and their implications is discussed by Arthur M. Okun in "Inflation: Its Mechanics and Welfare Costs," *BPEA, 2:1975*, pp. 360–65; and Okun, *Prices and Quantities*, chap. 4.

Microeconomic Policy

The previous section highlights some of the characteristics of the private sector that reduce the effectiveness of demand restraint as a tool for reducing inflation. But there have also been considerable changes in the role of government. Public discussions of government economic policy normally revolve around the budget as a summary of the government's economic policies. Significant efforts have been made to improve the budgeting process and to ensure that Congress considers the competing claims and priorities of alternative national objectives and allocates the resources available to it in a more rational way. Today, however, important aspects of the government's economic policy lie outside the budget process. These nonbudget actions cause difficulties because they are not subject to the usual budgetary review, their economic effects are often not considered, and there is a lack of coordination among the numerous agencies with overlapping authority.

The worsening inflation in recent years, for example, cannot be ascribed primarily to government fiscal policies that overstimulated the economy. Unemployment remains well above levels of the 1960s, and wage-rate increases have not been a leading element in the acceleration of inflation. But it is clear that the government did contribute to the inflation in a direct way through its regulatory activities, direct administrative actions, and a shift in the tax structure toward a greater emphasis on taxes that were reflected in higher prices. The government has increased the minimum wage; sharply boosted social security and unemployment taxes; removed agricultural land from production, raised price supports for sugar, dairy, and other agricultural interests; and extended trade protection to several domestic industries. At the same time, the expansion of social regulations has added approximately one-half of a percentage point to the annual inflation rate by reducing productivity growth. In many areas complex licensing requirements and delays sharply lengthen the lag of the economy's adjustment to changing market conditions. These actions were often desirable and provided important benefits to some, but a thorough evaluation of the costs and benefits was often absent.

ECONOMIC REGULATION. There is a long tradition of government oversight of individual industries where a "natural monopoly" or related aspects of unrestricted competition were thought to pose a threat to consumers. In most cases, the regulatory authority resides in a single agency that is familiar with the industry and is capable of evaluating the consequences of its decisions. The major problem with this type of regulation results from changes in the competitive environment after the regulatory authority is established. Restriction of entry and determination of joint rates keep prices at high levels when reform or deregulation offers an opportunity to lower prices by strengthening competition and improving efficiency. The decline in airline fares after deregulation is an example of the potential benefits. That a problem exists is most evident in the major opposition to reform that usually comes from the groups being regulated: the regulatory agency has been captured by those it regulates and has become a means of sheltering them from competition.

SOCIAL REGULATION. The government has also entered into a new area of regulation with the passage of a series of laws aimed at protecting the environment, increasing worker health and safety, setting safety standards for consumer products, limiting energy use, and so on. This represents a sharp shift in government policy from the period when it sought to achieve most national goals through the direct expenditure of tax revenues. Ordering the private sector to spend its resources in certain ways, however, has the same impact on the use of the nation's resources as an increase in taxes. The only difference is that the costs emerge in the form of higher prices rather than higher taxes.

The problems that the regulations address are important and generally require some form of regulation, but major issues arise about the *means* of intervention. To date, the regulators have emphasized design standards that specify in detail the means of compliance. There are few incentives for firms to find more efficient methods of achieving the goals because they will only be compelled to do more. In some cases, the concept of maximum feasible effort has been perverse— the standards are tightened for efficient firms while inefficient firms are allowed to delay implementation where the alternative is bankruptcy. The imposed costs to achieve an increment of benefits vary widely among industries and among firms in the same industry.

The alternative is to develop approaches to regulation that create incentives for firms to meet the goals at minimal costs. In some instances, effluent taxes can be an effective means of encouraging innovation since reducing pollution implies reducing costs. In other cases, greater reliance on performance standards that set goals would leave firms with the incentive to develop efficient means of compliance. But much of the problem lies with the regulatory agencies, and efficiency or a concern for economic consequences is not part of their mandate.

The determination of specific goals or standards requires a balancing of costs and benefits. These benefits frequently are more difficult to quantify than the costs. Uncertainty and conflict over the benefits, however, are not unique to these regulations. Estimates of program benefits and costs within the budget are often subject to error, and groups within society differ sharply in their perception of the value of the benefits that are achieved; but the process of considering competing programs within the confines of the basic scarcity of resources is of considerable value. There is a need to develop the equivalent of a budgetary process for regulations, and to apply the same basic principle that resources are scarce. The beginnings of such a process are evident in recent requirements that the agencies undertake an economic analysis of their new regulations.[7]

INCOME DISTRIBUTION. Other actions by the government having a direct impact on the price level are undertaken for the purpose of improving the relative economic position of specific groups. They include agricultural price supports, foreign trade restrictions, minimum wage legislation, and measures such as the Davis-Bacon Act. In the past, government intervened in the distribution of income, but the major focus of the public debate has been on the use of taxes and budgetary transfers. The effort to do this outside the budget often reflects a desire to avoid political accountability for situations in which direct budgetary payments to the affected population might not survive public scrutiny. These indirect methods, however, impose higher costs on consumers than would result from a direct budgetary outlay.

In agriculture, for example, government can choose between several systems to support farm incomes at socially desirable levels. Direct payments, which would be included in the budget, can be aimed at the small-farm population by setting payment limits to the individual producer. This approach would leave the price charged to consumers free to vary in response to changing market conditions.

7. The economic issues surrounding these regulations are discussed in more detail in chapter 5.

Alternatively, the government can specify a minimal market support price and intervene to restrict production or to withdraw supplies whenever market prices decline to the support level. This approach shifts the cost of supporting farm income from budget outlays to higher market prices. But maintaining prices above market-clearing levels weakens the competitive position of the United States in world markets and focuses the effort to raise incomes on reducing production. In addition, the benefits are not limited to the small farmer. Political and budgetary pressures, however, traditionally tilt policy toward reliance on support prices and production restrictions; consequently, the costs are hidden within the general inflation.

Similarly, in the area of foreign trade policy, direct budgetary payments to domestic producers who are hurt by imports would involve significantly less cost to the public than trade restraint actions that push up market prices and distort consumer decisions. When the United States limits the importation of color television sets, for example, consumers pay more. At the same time, the costs are not fully reflected in gains to domestic producers because the higher market price also reduces total sales. In addition, other countries can be expected to respond through restrictions on U.S. exports.

Many of the microeconomic actions of government are dismissed on the grounds that their individual costs and effects on the price level are small. The cumulative impact of these actions, however, has become substantial; and because there is a continual procession of such actions, they are a major element in the inflation. In addition, when the costs are reflected in higher prices, they become subsumed within the overall inflation and initiate the catch-up of wages and other prices to such cost increases that compounds the inflation effect.

The proliferation of these microeconomic policy decisions among a large number of individual agencies also creates severe problems of coordination and integration with other national priorities. The government has neither the capability to evaluate the cumulative effects of the myriad agency actions that affect individual industries nor the means of sorting out the conflicting claims of jurisdiction. At the same time, the focus of business concern is shifting away from minimizing the costs of production to an effort to establish a favorable regulatory environment relative to competitors. If this process is to be brought under control, the government will need to establish its own capability to assess the economic effects of these regulations within and among industries. This implies an extension of the concept of budgeting beyond its present focus. The development of a micro-economic policy framework is also important to establishing some form of accountability for the actions that lie outside the budgetary process. At present, they are difficult to control in a political framework because the benefits to the specific group are large and evident. Yet the general costs to consumers in the form of rising prices are diffuse, and there is no organized constituency to oppose them.

SUPPLY SHOCKS. Nearly all the acceleration of inflation since 1975 can be attributed to the worsening of price increases in the three areas of food, energy, and home purchases (see figure 2-1). Yet, as discussed earlier, in such circumstances no good options are available for macroeconomic policy: the choice is between accommodating a worsening of inflation, or monetary restraint with its consequences for unemployment. Thus there is an interest in the development of microeconomic policies of supply management that would prevent the basic disturbances themselves or provide offsetting actions that would dampen their impact on the overall price level.

There are parallels in past policies. During the early 1950s the government provided special tax incentives to expand capacity in several basic materials industries that were judged important to national defense. The United States has also maintained a large stockpile of critical materials against the risks of war, and the sale of surplus holdings from this stockpile has been a major stabilizing force in some of these markets in past years. Although the government was criticized for accumulating large reserves of agricultural products in the 1950s and 1960s as part of its effort to boost farm income, the reduction of those stocks in the early 1970s demonstrated that the holding of reserves in the face of uncertain supply can be a prudent policy. Perhaps the rationale for grain reserves—supporting farm prices above market-clearing levels—was faulty, but this does not mean that holding grain reserves, as a price-stabilizing action, is without benefit.

The maintenance of government reserves is the most obvious example of supply-management policies to ameliorate price shocks. Private speculators will not hold reserves adequate to meet the small probabilities of a large supply disruption because they believe that export restrictions or similar government interferences will prevent their reaping the full benefits of such shortages. Furthermore, private evaluations of the benefits and costs will not take account of the secondary inflation implications of wide commodity-price fluctuations—namely, that changes in these prices will initiate catch-up efforts of others and exacerbate the general inflation. It is difficult, however, to achieve sufficient agreement between producers and consumers on the operating rules required to guarantee that the reserve will act as a stabilizer of cyclical fluctuations and not delay the adjustment to basic secular trends or simply substitute for normal private reserves. The financing also is frequently inadequate to cover the extremes of shortage situations that have the greatest inflation consequences.

Some countries have provided a buffer between world market price fluctuations and their domestic economy by erecting barriers to imports that are varied inversely with domestic market conditions. Such policies are particularly common for agricultural products. Although they dampen domestic price fluctuations, they amount to a substitution of high average prices for reduced variability. European food prices are controlled in this way, and the policy has proved to be very expensive for the consumer.

It is also possible to develop industrial policies to coordinate the various government programs that have an impact on specific industries and evaluate them relative to future national requirements. Such programs have been suggested for the steel and automobile industries and a few other basic material producers. They, too, can easily become perverse if government subsidies are used to promote production in areas where the United States does not have a comparative advantage; or they may simply delay the date at which the industry must face its own competitive difficulties.

Supply-side shocks could be offset by reducing indirect taxes or other government fees that add directly to prices. In the case of the United States, such actions would be limited to a federal buy-out of state sales taxes or a reduction in employment taxes. In effect, higher income taxes would substitute for lower indirect taxes. Such a shift in the mix from indirect to direct income taxation would leave a net gain in the form of a lower price level.

On the other hand, it is extremely difficult to obtain a prompt adjustment of sales taxes. In effect, state governments would be asked to surrender their authority to impose future sales taxes. The federal government would also be committed to making a permanent annual payment to the states in return for the one-time benefits of a tax rate reduction. In the case of social insurance taxes, only the employer portion of the tax is anticipated to result in lower prices. If political factors dictate that any reduction in employer rates must be matched by an equal reduction in the employee rate, only half of the revenue loss is reflected in prices.

Thus there are major barriers to the development of a comprehensive supply-management policy. However, it is important to remember that the potential for major supply shocks is limited principally to grains and petroleum. Few other markets are of sufficient size with the potential for instability of supply to create serious problems. In the 1972–74 period excess demand pressures in other basic commodity markets were important elements in the inflation. But, in part, they were symptomatic of more general excess-demand problems that resulted from an unusual synchronized expansion of the world economy.

Supply Creation

The worsening inflation of the 1970s has been intertwined with several other disappointing economic trends. There has been a sharp falloff in productivity growth; many basic material industries have experienced significant capacity shortages; and the rapid expansion of the labor force has not been matched by a similar acceleration of capital formation. This combination of events has suggested to some observers that a major part of the country's economic problems results from the supply side and, in particular, that U.S. investment rates are too low. The argument is strengthened by concerns that the declining international competitiveness of the United States can be attributed to the larger share of national output that other countries devote to capital formation. An argument that the inflation problems can be solved by expanding supply rather than restraining demand also has political appeal.

A decline in private-sector productivity growth is evident in the period since 1965 (see table 2-1). After averaging 3.3 percent annually in the 1948–65 period, the growth rate for labor productivity declined to 2.3 percent in 1965–73, and only 1.2 percent in 1973–78. The growth of industrial capacity also slowed between 1948 and 1978. Even when adjusted for different stages of the business cycle, studies by the Council of Economic Advisers indicate that there has

Table 2-1. Rates of Growth of Labor Productivity, Capacity, Capital, and Labor, Private Domestic Sector, Selected Periods, 1948–78

Annual average (percent)

Item	1948–65	1965–73	1973–78
Labor productivity	3.3	2.3	1.2
Manufacturing capacity	4.2	5.0	3.2
Net capital stock	2.6	3.7	2.0
Labor force	1.2	2.2	2.5
Hours worked	0.4	1.4	1.4
Ratio of capital to labor	2.2	2.2	0.6

Source: J. R. Norsworthy, Michael J. Harper, and Kent Kunze, "The Slowdown in Productivity Growth: Analysis of Some Contributing Factors," *Brookings Papers on Economic Activity*, 2:1979, pp. 387–422; and Board of Governors of the Federal Reserve System, *Capacity Utilization: Manufacturing and Materials*, series G.3, various issues.

been some deterioration in the balance between industrial capacity and labor supply since the mid-1960s and that it is most pronounced in the basic materials industry.[8]

The rate of business capital formation also slowed significantly. The treatment of the post-1965 period as a single phenomenon, however, ignores the sharply different patterns before and after 1973: 1965–73 was a period of exceptionally strong capital formation, and all the shortfalls from trend occurred in the period since 1973. Thus the decline in productivity growth predates the decline in capital formation.[9]

Two recent studies of the productivity slowdown reach the unsatisfying conclusion that much of the slowdown is inexplicable.[10] The basic problem is to provide a consistent explanation for the two subperiods of 1965–73 and 1973 to the present. If capital is assumed to play a dominant role in the productivity process, the latter period is not a puzzle, but the earlier period is. If other factors are allocated a larger role and that of capital reduced, the situation is reversed. Both studies are valuable, however, for emphasizing the complexity of the

8. The council report also showed a similar shortage of capacity in the early 1960s that was overcome by a subsequent rapid rise of capital formation. However, if shifts in the mix of the labor force toward more inexperienced workers have increased the full-employment unemployment rate, the evidence of a capacity-labor imbalance is weak. See the *Economic Report of the President, January 1978*, pp. 157–61.

9. This conclusion is unaffected by adjustments in order to exclude investments to meet the more stringent regulatory goals of the 1970s.

10. Edward F. Denison, *Accounting for Slower Economic Growth: The United States in the 1970s* (Brookings Institution, 1979); and J. R. Norsworthy, Michael J. Harper, and Kent Kunze, "The Slowdown in Productivity Growth: Analysis of Some Contributing Factors," *BPEA, 2:1979*, pp. 387–421.

process of productivity growth and the diversity of factors that affect it.

The slowdown is concentrated in a few industries such as mining, construction, public utilities, and retail trade, but a pervasive component is evident in nearly all sectors. The frequently discussed role of a shift to a services economy is largely a statement about the shrinking role of agriculture and the growth of government; sectoral shifts do not explain the slowdown in the private nonfarm economy.[11] The costs of increased social regulation, a less experienced work force, and the decline of research and development are contributing factors, but much remains unexplained.

Similar questions can be raised about the decline of capital formation. As shown in figure 2-2, the decline in the proportion of gross national product that went into investment was largely a result of the 1974–75 recession. In addition, investment in equipment is not abnormally low, and most of the post–1973 difficulties are the result of the failure of investment in nonresidential structures to recover from the recession. Some decline in structures investment dates back to the late 1960s. The slowdown in structures investment is also not distributed across industries in a pattern that is in accord with the distribution of the productivity slowdown.

Another possible contributor to the productivity slowdown is the direct influence of a weaker growth in demand. Although demand growth exerts an influence on capital formation, research and development, and thus on productivity growth, the effects on productivity are not limited to these. Instead, much of the improvement in productivity is seen as the results of the pressures and opportunities for innovation that a rapid expansion of the economy creates. This interpretation places less stress on capital formation and attributes a much larger proportion of the productivity growth slowdown to the failure to maintain a strong economic expansion during the 1970s. Such an explanation, however, cannot account for the poor performance of productivity growth during the 1976–79 expansion.

Despite the uncertainty concerning the causes of the productivity slowdown, several important points should be emphasized. First, unlike other inputs, the capital stock is an accumulation of past efforts. Even if investment does not decline as a share of output, a recession like that of 1975 and the subsequent recovery still leave the economy

11. Denison, *Accounting for Slower Economic Growth*, pp. 142–43.

Percent

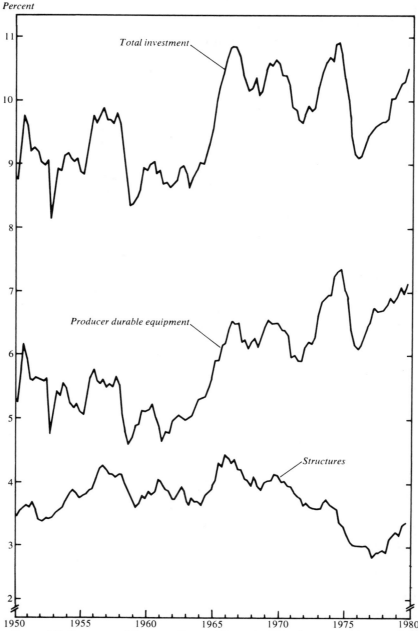

Source: U.S. Department of Commerce, Bureau of Economic Affairs. Investment and gross national product are measured in 1972 dollars.

with a smaller capital stock. That is, a recession can quickly wipe out the gains of other efforts to stimulate capital formation. Second, the role of capital formation in the productivity growth and inflation processes must be kept in perspective. If the business investment share of gross national product could be raised by 1 percentage point (approximately $25 billion in today's prices, or about a 10 percent increase in investment) and maintained in future years, an optimistic interpretation of its impact would imply a rise in labor productivity initially of about 0.2 percentage point annually. This effect on productivity growth would progressively decline because the expansion of the capital stock implies that the additional 1 percentage point of investment has a shrinking impact on the net capital-stock growth rate—an increasing allocation to replacement of the existing stock. This is a significant effect on a productivity growth rate currently averaging only about 1 percent, but it cannot be interpreted as an important means of reducing an inflation that is currently in the range of 10 to 15 percent.

Assuming that agreement would be achieved on the desirability of a higher rate of capital formation, there are still substantive issues concerning the means. First, given the level of total production, can government tax and monetary policies significantly affect investment? Would a higher rate of private savings translate into increased investment, and can government policies affect this decision? The heightened concern about the effects of tax policy in a world of high inflation has led to renewed interest in these issues.

Inflation interacts with the existing tax system to alter tax burdens in two distinctly different ways. First, there is a tax-rate effect as inflation pushes individuals at a given level of real income into progressively higher tax brackets. This is because most exemptions, credits, and the tax brackets themselves are defined in nominal terms. Although this is of considerable political interest, it is of limited economic concern because Congress has acted to offset, by periodic discretionary actions, much of this tendency toward a higher tax rate, and the potential allocative effects on the economy seem small.

A more serious issue is raised by the effects of taxation on the tax base. With a tax system based on nominal income, inflation implies an increasing tax on the income from wealth because the tax applies to that part of receipts required to maintain real capital. It is an important issue for business income where depreciation is limited to historical costs and for income from capital gains and interest. Again, the inflation effects could be offset by the discretionary actions of Congress; but the offsetting adjustments are more complex and the potential burden varies among different types of income, so that there is a greater potential for distorting savings and investment incentives.[12] For this reason, many economists have suggested that the tax base should be adjusted for inflation in its entirety, but this would be extremely complex and is often opposed on administrative grounds. Thus most of the current proposals focus on more partial measures.

INVESTMENT STIMULUS. Taxes and interest rates affect investment demand primarily through their impact on the cost of capital and on the profitability of adopting more capital-intensive production processes. The magnitude of this effect has been an issue of long-standing controversy. While nearly all the studies agree that some substitution between capital and labor is possible in response to changes in their relative prices, there is considerable disagreement over its empirical importance. The complexities and long lags in the investment process and the inability to conduct controlled laboratory experiments continue to frustrate efforts to resolve this empirical question. It is possible, however, to illustrate the range of potential effects of tax measures. If the objective is to maximize the impact on investment per dollar of lost revenue, an investment tax credit would have the largest "bang for the buck." The optimistic studies suggest that one dollar of annual tax cuts would generate about one dollar in additional annual investment demand in the first five years.[13] Thus, if this estimate of the role of taxes is combined with the earlier estimate of the effect of investment on productivity, a tax cut of about $25 billion annually would be needed to increase the rate of productivity growth by 0.2 percentage point. A more common estimate produced by many econometric models is that the payoff in investment of a dollar of investment tax stimulus is only 50 cents, so that the tax cut required to produce the same result would be double, or about $50 billion.[14]

12. These issues are discussed in detail in Henry J. Aaron, ed., *Inflation and the Income Tax* (Brookings Institution, 1976).

13. This assumes that interest rates are not increased by the higher demand; and the estimate does not take account of the feedback effects of investment on total demand—increasing U.S. Treasury receipts and generating a second round of investment growth. The feedback effects would exist for any demand stimulus policy and are not relevant to the choice between investment incentives and other tax cuts.

14. Studies by Dale W. Jorgenson restrict the analysis to a specific form of the production function in which capital-labor substitution is important and combine it

Comparable effects on investment and productivity can be derived for changes in the depreciation treatment of future investment. Depreciation changes, limited to new investment, are equivalent to a loan from government to business because a faster write-off of depreciation lowers today's taxes but increases taxes in the future. In this analogy, a tax credit is an outright grant. Both actions will have equivalent effects on investment when the present discounted value of the loan and the tax credit are equal. Thus, for an equal investment impact, a depreciation change requires a larger immediate revenue loss to the Treasury with some recovery in future years.[15]

SAVINGS INCENTIVES. If the share of national output devoted to investment is to be raised, increased incentives for investment alone will not be enough. It is equally important that the saving rate rise by a matching amount. This can be achieved by increased incentives for private saving or by reduced government dissaving (a smaller budget deficit).

It is important to remember that, while total economy-wide saving and total investment must be equal, the components of private saving and business investment can change in quite dissimilar directions. An intention by households to increase their savings in the absence of a willingness of other sectors to utilize it can translate into reduced consumer demand, production, and total income—and ultimately to reduced investment. An increase in private saving may also be offset by an increase in the deficit (dissaving) of federal or state and local governments. It can add to home purchases, or it can be reflected in a change in the foreign account balance. In fact, it is difficult to con-

---

with an assumption that firms perceive and fully utilize all opportunities to minimize costs; a study by Charles W. Bischoff imposes less restrictive assumptions but still concludes that there is a major role for capital-labor substitution. The work of Robert Eisner is most representative of the alternative view that tax effects are relatively small. Examples of these approaches and an extensive discussion of the issues are found in Gary Fromm, ed., *Tax Incentives and Capital Spending* (Brookings Institution, 1971). A wider range of models than those discussed above has been explored. They include models that allow for cash-flow restrictions on investment and the market-valuation approach that focuses on the ratio of market to replacement values for the existing capital stock. In addition, because energy inputs may be complementary with capital, the price of energy may be a major element of the investment decision. The diversity of views on tax effects, however, remains.

15. Any future congressional debate of these issues will not be limited to a comparison of their impact on total investment. Such a focus ignores the concern about the impact of inflation on the tax base and the distortions that various depreciation proposals may have for the choice between short- and long-lived capital assets and the distribution of tax benefits among industries.

clude that reduced private saving has imposed serious limits on business investment in recent years. The federal government has run large deficits for the purpose of absorbing private saving and maintaining aggregate demand in the face of what it interpreted as weak business demand for those funds. In addition, in a world of highly mobile capital in international markets, it is difficult to argue that high-return capital projects are not being exploited in the United States because of reduced domestic private saving. The lack of strong incentives for investment itself would seem to be the more immediate problem.

Components of private saving within the United States display substantial cyclical fluctuations. The household saving rate increased throughout the 1960s and most of the 1970s and declined within the last two years back to the levels of the early 1960s. Total private saving, including business retained earnings, however, has continued throughout at a stable 15 to 16 percent of gross national product.

Recently several empirical studies have challenged the conventional wisdom that household saving was insensitive to interest rates or to government programs such as social security. While theoretical considerations imply that a higher cost of capital will lower investment, in theory the effects of an increased rate of return on saving are ambiguous.[16] Thus the question must be resolved empirically. But the range of estimates is extremely wide, with little evidence of any convergence toward agreement.[17] In the present circumstances a more certain stimulus to capital formation can be obtained by concentrating tax incentives on the investment side of the capital-formation process. At the same time, reductions in the federal budget deficit provide a more obvious and certain means of supplying the increased saving. The issue of incentives for private saving becomes

16. A higher return makes saving more attractive, but it reduces the need to save currently to meet a given wealth objective.

17. See, for example, Michael J. Boskin, "Taxation, Saving and the Rate of Interest," *Journal of Political Economy,* vol. 86, pt. 2 (April 1978), pp. S3–S27 for some results on the role of interest rates; and Martin Feldstein, "Social Security, Induced Retirement, and Aggregate Capital Accumulation," *Journal of Political Economy,* vol. 82 (September–October 1974), pp. 905–26, for a discussion of the impact of social security. A result contrary to that of Boskin is reported by E. Philip Howrey and Saul H. Hymans, "The Measurement and Determination of Loanable-Funds Saving," *BPEA, 3:1978,* pp. 655–85. An evaluation of the social security studies is provided by Louis Esposito, "Effects of Social Security on Saving," *Social Security Bulletin,* vol. 41 (May 1978), pp. 9–19; and "Comments," *Social Security Bulletin,* vol. 42 (May 1979), pp. 33–40.

more relevant in an economy of strong demand and a balanced government budget.

In summary, developments over the last decade do support the notion that the U.S. economy is increasingly short of capital. This is reflected in the contribution of capital to the productivity slowdown, some evidence of capacity restrictions, and the rising proportion of investment needed to meet the goals of social regulation. Inflation has also had the effect of increasing the effective tax rate on income from capital. But there is a need to keep in perspective the potential contribution that capital formation can make to reversing the decline of productivity growth. The latter is the product of many factors, not all of which can be influenced by government policy. A greater concern with supply creation is clearly justified as a means of reviving productivity growth. It also may be a means of minimizing longer-term inflation problems; but it cannot be expected to be an important element of a near-term effort to break the momentum of inflation that has built up over the last decade.

Policy Constraints

For the next several years economic policy will be dominated by three major concerns: inflation, energy prices, and productivity growth. It will be difficult to develop a consistent policy that addresses these problems with the tools available to government. Inflation has worsened to the point that the underlying momentum of the process is approaching double-digit rates. The vulnerability of the United States to foreign oil developments and uncertainties about the agricultural outlook raise the prospect of continued external shocks that will maintain the inflation rate above 10 percent. One of the most surprising aspects of the current inflation is that there has not been an explosive catch-up effort of wages and prices in the industrial sector such as that which occurred in 1974. On the other hand, how long this can last is a great cause for concern.

The bill for imported oil has escalated from $4.3 billion in 1972 to $39.1 billion in 1978, and is currently running at an annual rate in excess of $60 billion. World spot market prices of $30 to $40 a barrel are well above OPEC contract prices and raise the prospect for large increases in future prices. The United States cannot earn sufficient income on the remainder of its current account to pay this bill, and the inevitable prospect is for continued downward pressure on the dollar. The higher costs of imported goods, in turn, add to the inflationary pressures.

For the next several years the pressures on world energy markets and the increasing burden of imported oil can be met only by reducing petroleum consumption. The government is urging conservation, but it also attempts to operate a system of controls that holds gasoline prices down. In the face of shortages, the controls are ineffective because suppliers find ways to avoid them. It also is difficult to urge restraint on OPEC when spot market prices for crude oil are above the official cartel prices. Yet, active efforts to raise domestic prices to reduce demand are opposed because they add to the inflation and alter the distribution of income.

The implications of reduced productivity growth are evident in the average hourly earnings of American factory workers, which are no higher now in real terms than a decade earlier. This effect of slower productivity growth on the income of industrial workers is being compounded by sharp price increases for the nonindustrial products they buy, such as energy, food, and housing. The growth of per capita disposable income was maintained only because a rising proportion of families have two earners; foreign borrowing increased; and the growth of personal income and employee payroll taxes slowed sharply during the 1970s, while the rate of growth of transfers accelerated. This buffering influence of the government, however, was financed by increasing the budget deficit and reducing nontransferable expenditures in areas such as defense.

These trends cannot be sustained in the 1980s. For example, a large rise in employment taxes is scheduled for 1981, and the pressures for expanding the defense share of the budget are strong.

A slower rate of productivity growth adds directly to the inflation problem by adding to the rate of growth of unit labor costs. Its most important impact, however, probably is to slow real-income growth, increasing militancy and dissatisfaction of workers and reducing the public desire to cooperate with any anti-inflation program that calls for restraint on income gains.

Policy Conflicts

In late 1978 the administration adopted an anti-inflation program that focused on a tightening of fiscal policy to induce a pause in the economic expansion, a set of voluntary wage-price standards, and an effort to develop a microeconomic framework to evaluate and reduce the inflationary effect contributed by government actions. During the following year that program gradually fell apart. The slowdown in demand growth was delayed and some pressures from shortages pushed up raw material prices. Housing prices continued to rise at a rapid pace, and there were no contingency plans to deal with the unanticipated sharp increases first in farm and later in petroleum prices. In these areas, which were dominated by shortages, the voluntary standards could not be effective. In addition, support for the standards was further eroded by the perception that the standards were "bent" in a few large union settlements and by the growing problem of wage rate inequities that arose because of the indexing of some wage rates to the price inflation. Without the provision for real-wage insurance, the program lost much of its equity for workers who complied with the wage standard. Moreover, little progress was made on the individual microeconomic actions that government could take on its own to reduce inflation because in isolation the inflationary effects seemed small and the political costs of conflict with individual interest groups seemed large. On the other side, those government actions that raised prices were easy to ignore in a world of double-digit inflation. The government did not convince the public that it regarded inflation as serious or that it was taking the lead in exercising the restraint necessary to solve the problem.

Currently anti-inflation policy has shifted to a greater emphasis on demand restraint, but it is still a policy of gradualism, in which the goals are moved progressively further into the future. Judging from the past and the current high rate of inflation, to reduce inflation to a tolerable level, fiscal and monetary policies of demand restraint must induce a recession far more severe than that of 1975 or lasting for a considerably longer period of time. All the historical experience suggests that a mild recession will have little effect on inflation. The government must also anticipate that many interest groups will try to avoid the costs of recession and that the political pressures to restrain imports, increase price supports, and further restrict competition are likely to exacerbate the long-run problem.

In addition, a successful policy will face the need to manage the subsequent expansion to restore employment to more normal levels despite the fact that the recession will have reduced investment and worsened the problem of capacity shortages. At the same time, it would be futile to embark on a program of stimulating capital formation in the face of the depressing influences of severe demand restraint. Clearly, the losses to the capital stock from reduced investment during the recession will be larger than any possible increase that might be generated by new tax incentives.

Monetary policy is currently the leading element of the restraint program, and high interest rates are justified as necessary to reduce domestic spending and to attract foreign capital inflows as a means of financing the trade deficit. But the shift toward higher interest rates has been met by increasing rates in other countries and a consequent dilution of the effect on the relative rates and capital flows.[18] In the meantime, the immediate domestic effect of higher interest rates is to worsen the overall rate of price increase; the long-term effect is to reduce capital formation. A tight money policy is being pursued for the explicit purpose of reducing demand and employment and thus slowing inflation. But at the same time the government acts to offset its impact in the major area where its effect is most pronounced and where there is the greatest evidence of excess demand—housing.

Policy Alternatives

In view of an economic situation that is steadily deteriorating and the difficulties of maintaining support for a policy of gradualism, a program that attempts to address all the major problems in a more comprehensive way should be discussed. The following is a brief outline of some of the dimensions of policy action that are available if the numerous political restrictions are ignored.

DEMAND POLICY. A general policy of some demand restraint must be one element of the program. Alternative policies might serve as a complement, but no anti-inflation policy can be effective in the face of general market pressures that are forcing up either prices or wage rates. Demand restraint can, however, be made more consistent with other goals by shifting the fiscal-monetary policy mix. A shift

18. In addition to its influence through reduced demand, monetary policy can affect inflation through the foreign-exchange market. If the dollar strengthens as a result of capital inflows, there is an inflation benefit of lower increases in import prices. In a world of flexible rates, there can be significant benefits to those countries who give the appearance of acting strongly against inflation because that leads to currency inflows, exchange rate appreciation, lower import prices, and a self-fulfilling reduction in inflation. Such policies cannot be pursued by all countries, however, and do represent an effort to pass inflation problems to others. See chapter 3.

toward a more restrictive fiscal policy offset by an easing of monetary policy would put a larger portion of the burden on consumption and a smaller burden on investment—thus improving the climate for capital formation.

A less restrictive monetary policy can be criticized, at present, for its potential effects on the foreign exchange rate and the inflationary effect of increased demand in an already tight housing market. High interest rates, however, have had a weak impact on exchange rates because other countries have simply raised their own interest rates in a competitive upward spiral. As discussed below, a more direct attack on the fundamental sources of weakness in the dollar—a rising oil import bill, high domestic inflation, and low productivity growth— would seem to be a more effective means of addressing concerns about the competitive position of the United States. Similarly, alternative means will be required to remove the excess demand pressures on the housing market.

ENERGY POLICY. From the perspective of energy policy and foreign pressures on exchange rates, petroleum imports need to be cut by a significant amount from current levels. That can best be accomplished by a direct limitation on imports. Such an action will, however, create a shortage within the domestic market, and the United States will have to choose between direct rationing or price increases to reduce demand.

The choice is most explicit in the comparison between a gasoline excise tax or the so-called white coupon system of rationing in which the ration coupons may be bought or sold. Both methods raise extremely emotional issues about who is going to bear the burden: in the case of coupons, it surfaces in the issue of who receives them initially; in the case of an excise tax, in the question of who gets a rebate. An excise tax is administratively simpler—particularly if one ignores any complex equity considerations and simply rebates the tax by lowering other taxes. Alternatively, given the uncertainty about the response of consumer demand to higher gasoline prices, a rationing system produces a known quantity effect, and the resale value of the coupon would not be included in official indexes that are used to escalate other wages and prices. Thus rationing focuses the consumer's attention directly on the need to reduce the quantity purchased and seems less inflationary. An explicit discrete increase in the excise tax, however, identified as a specific element of a comprehensive economic policy, may not have the same effect on inflationary expectations as continually rising prices, and thus the feedback on the overall inflation might be reduced. In addition, it would be possible to use some of the increase in excise taxes as a substitute for the scheduled increases in social insurance taxes—thus neutralizing part of the inflationary impact.

To be significant in its effect on world market prices, the reduction in imports would need to be initially of the order of 10 percent. If the demand reduction were concentrated exclusively in gasoline usage, the percentage decline would be of similar magnitude.[19] The best available evidence on the price sensitivity of demand suggests that a tax well in excess of 50 cents a gallon would be needed to reach this objective in the first year, but the impact on demand would rise substantially in future years as people adjust their new car purchases to higher gasoline prices.

In any case, the inflationary effect of these energy policy actions is reduced when they are compared to the alternative of doing nothing. Continued high demand will lead ultimately to a further escalation of the OPEC price. In addition, the heightened pressures of the deficit on the exchange rate will add to inflation through the mechanism of higher prices for other imported goods. Only by reducing demand can the oil-consuming nations develop a credible countervailing force to future OPEC price increases. In some respects, higher energy prices are certain. The policy issue is whether the higher prices will all be paid to OPEC or will they be accomplished in part by taxes that can be rebated.

WAGE-PRICE POLICY. The above actions will still leave the United States with the problem of inflation. There is no policy that can break the current momentum of the wage-price spiral without high costs; yet a continuation of recent trends is also costly. A mild recession is too weak and voluntary incomes programs have lost their credibility. Given a desire to slow the inflation, the choice is rapidly being reduced to one of severe recession versus wage-price controls.

Past experience indicates the major problems and risks of controls. But the lessons learned in those periods can also be used to avoid some of the problems. No incomes policy can succeed in the face of shortages, and the previous effort to use controls as a substitute for

19. Oil imports are approximately 8 million barrels a day; gasoline consumption is about 7 million barrels a day.

fiscal-monetary restraint was a mistake that led to distortions and exacerbated the supply problem. The possibility still exists that a combination of controls and demand restraint can reduce the magnitudes of unemployment and idle capacity substantially below those required by a policy of relying on demand restraint alone.[20]

When the government, however, adopts a voluntary or mandatory wage-price program, it becomes responsible in the public's view for all prices—even those in relatively competitive markets or those that are externally determined. Thus government efforts to stabilize prices in the areas of food, energy, and housing take on added importance. In both 1973 and 1979 the government's anti-inflation program was severely damaged by developments in these markets for which the government had no response.

SPECIAL SECTOR PROBLEMS. It is important that anti-inflation policy distinguish between the momentum aspect of the inflation and the special problems of food, energy, and home purchase prices that have done so much to exacerbate the process in recent years. A stabilization of grain prices is the key element to avoiding sharp increases in food prices. The current beef shortage is primarily a continuing reflection of the previous grain crisis when high feeding costs led to sharp reductions in beef herds. If the government focuses on stabilizing the grain market, there is a very limited potential for inflation shocks in other areas that cannot be quickly reversed by normal market responses. Under present policies, reserves in 1980 will be approximately equivalent to those that existed before 1972, but substantially below the peak levels of the early 1960s. A policy of reducing support prices for dairy products and removing many of the marketing restrictions on fruits and vegetables could also provide some direct benefits in the form of lower prices.

The recent pattern of soaring housing prices is a classic case of excess demand. Demand is fueled by a speculative element that reflects strong expectations of continuing future inflation and some increase in the population of homeowning age. More importantly,

20. The distinction between voluntary and mandatory incomes programs is largely a matter of degree. But within a voluntary program it is extremely difficult to convince individual groups that others will go along. On the other hand, a mandatory program can only be maintained for a few years. It is being used only to break the momentum that has built up over the last decade and is not an element of a permanent solution. The choice between rationing and a gasoline tax is also affected by controls because they can prevent the feedback onto those wage rates that are escalated in step with the consumer price index.

those pressures have been augmented by government actions that sharply expanded the volume of funds available for mortgage lending. The federally sponsored agencies that supported the mortgage market during the 1974 credit squeeze did not withdraw from the market during the subsequent recovery; and modification of government regulations allowed the mortgage-lending institutions to attract funds with high-yield money-market certificates. These changes have reduced the importance of credit rationing as a restraining influence during periods of tight money. Yet it is not possible to expand supply in the short run by an amount sufficient to meet these pressures. The excess demand has spilled over into large price increases. The current high interest rates in the market will reduce the demand for housing; but they will also reduce supply by restricting the funds for construction loans to builders. High interest rates have a weak influence on demand in part because they are deductible from income taxes. Alternative measures could relieve some of the demand pressures, while maintaining a higher level of construction. These would include reducing the lending of the federally sponsored agencies and invoking selective credit controls to raise down-payment requirements as a means of limiting speculation.

GOVERNMENT ACTIONS. An incomes policy is dependent upon a public perception of a strong government commitment to its objectives. The government cannot expect restraint from the private sector unless it can demonstrate a willingness to overcome the pressures of individual interest groups and develop a more effective microeconomic policy that addresses the inflationary effect of its own actions. One initial step that would serve to highlight the inflationary impact of government actions would be to maintain a regularly published scorecard that estimates the inflationary impact of actions and proposals of Congress and the administration. Because so many of these actions seem inconsequential in isolation, a cumulative record may be the most effective means of highlighting their implications for inflation.

PRODUCTIVITY GROWTH. There are severe limits on the short-term effectiveness of government policies to promote productivity growth, but the avoidance of another episode of severe demand restraint, additional tax incentives to promote investment, and expansion of research and development are measures that operate in the right direction. The arguments for a significant expansion of tax incentives for capital formation seem particularly strong because the interaction of inflation and the existing tax structure has increased the effective tax burden. Although the precise magnitude of the effect on investment is subject to dispute, the general conclusion of past studies is that it is significant. The arguments for focusing on tax incentives to expand saving over the next few years are significantly weaker.

Conclusion

For the longer term, the arguments that government must pay more attention to the supply-side implications of its actions seem compelling. The wide swings of demand-management policies in past years and the continuing uncertainty of the regulatory environment seem to have had a serious destabilizing influence: investment is misdirected and expansion of capacity among related industries has gotten out of balance. The cumulative effect of programs to increase productivity can be substantial, and alternatives to petroleum will take on a greater role in energy supply. But the benefits from these efforts will not be immediately obvious, and they do not provide a means of breaking the momentum of the inflation that has been inherited from the past.

A program of general wage and price controls, restrictions on housing and energy demand, and a continuation of slow demand growth are not easy measures to sell even on a temporary basis. Yet it may be that government today can address its problems only within such a crisis framework. The one constant element in the inflation, for example, has been that each successive round of government policy has consistently underestimated the magnitude of the problem. Each failure contributes to a loss of public confidence that the government can solve the problems, thereby reducing the probability that future policies will succeed.

In many respects the problems are as political as they are economic. The country remains deeply divided over the merits of alternative means of reducing inflation. Fiscal and monetary restraint sufficient to stop inflation will require extremely high levels of unemployment. On the other hand, wage and price controls will also impose costs and inequities that are different but no less important. The opinions of most people regarding the options are formed on the basis of whether they expect to be among the unemployed in the next recession. Yet regardless of the direction that U.S. economic policy takes, there is no fast or simple solution, and each option raises risks of failure and imposes significant costs. Conservation must be a dominant element of near-term energy policy; the continued slow growth of productivity will severely limit real-income gains and intensify the conflicts among social groups, and there is no cheap means of breaking an inflation that has become deeply imbedded in the economic structure. The political problem is to shift the focus of public discussion away from the fruitless search for painless solutions to the question of how the costs of the adjustments can be allocated in the most equitable way. The alternative of a continued drift in policy is becoming increasingly unpalatable and makes the ultimate solution more difficult.

CHAPTER THREE

World Economic Interdependence

RALPH C. BRYANT *and* LAWRENCE B. KRAUSE

DURING the past two decades Americans have become increasingly dependent on economic relationships with the rest of the world for their well-being. American economic policy has been forced to pay correspondingly greater attention to international developments.

Several occasions have recently provided dramatic evidence of those facts. For example, the decisions of the Federal Reserve to restrict the growth of the U.S. money supply have been critically influenced by the behavior of the dollar in foreign exchange markets. After a gradual but persistent depreciation of the dollar during the year from September 1977 to September 1978, unsettled market conditions began to emerge in October 1978. By the last week of October, both foreigners and Americans were frantically selling dollars for foreign currencies, and the chaotic trading conditions were spreading to the stock and bond markets. Left with no choice but to alter policy to respond to the crisis, the administration and the Federal Reserve on November 1 announced a sharp tightening of domestic monetary policy and a resolve, backed by expanded financial resources, to intervene vigorously in defense of the dollar in exchange markets. The cause and effect relationship between the exchange-market crisis and the tightening of domestic monetary policy could not be mistaken. Both at home and abroad, the Novem-

The authors acknowledge the comments they received from Robert Z. Lawrence. Research assistance was provided by Stephen L. Smith, and the manuscript was typed by Kirk W. Kimmell and Charlotte Kaiser.

ber 1 policy package was interpreted as a "sea change" in policy, indicating that the American government would henceforth give significantly greater weight in its domestic policy decisions to the external value of the dollar. That judgment was confirmed in the late summer and early fall of 1979. The reappearance of exchange-market pressure on the dollar played a significant role in Federal Reserve decisions to tighten monetary policy in August and September; international concerns continued to be a contributing factor in the additional restrictive actions by the Federal Reserve announced on October 6, 1979.

The economic dependence of the United States on the rest of the world was illustrated even more dramatically after the Iranian revolution in early 1979 led to a cutback in the global supply of crude petroleum. The links between domestic energy consumption and the availability of petroleum imports became easier for American motorists to comprehend when they were forced to wait in long lines to buy gasoline at $1 or more a gallon. No doubt the further oil price increases announced by the Organization of Petroleum Exporting Countries (OPEC) in December 1979 will drive home that lesson still more clearly.

Even in the 1950s the United States depended significantly on the world economy. But for the majority of Americans that dependence was hidden from view and seemed of little direct consequence. That perception contrasted with the experience of citizens in other nations, where the problems of dependence on the rest of the world have been commonplace and highly visible. With the increasing openness of the U.S. economy in the 1970s, a new view is becoming widespread among American citizens: despite the size and power of the United States, it is only one of many nations in an international system and is subject to the same disciplines of that system.

Being dependent on other countries makes Americans uncomfortable. Having domestic policy options constrained by international forces makes them unhappy. Having domestic prosperity undermined by foreign events makes them angry. One natural response to these situations is to consider ways of reversing the dependence of the United States on the world economy. That response makes sense in the case of oil because of the global energy problem and the political instability in oil-exporting countries. In general, however, a more thoughtful and constructive response is to ask how to live with the dependence and to turn it to U.S. advantage. Other nations, after all, are dependent on the United States. Indeed, that aspect of American foreign economic relations has been stressed for the past thirty-five years.

Before Americans had fully experienced dependence themselves, they had difficulty in understanding its implications for others. Perhaps the true nature of interdependence can be comprehended only when all major nations are subject to the tensions of mutual dependence. The decade of the 1980s may prove to be a time for new forward steps in managing economic policy in an interdependent global economy.

Types of Interdependence

Among the types of transactions linking the United States to other countries, those involving international trade in goods and services are the most visible. Exports in response to the demands of foreigners directly affect the outputs and prices of a wide range of goods and services produced in the United States. Imports into the United States also have powerful if indirect impacts on outputs and prices in the United States.

In the early 1950s only a small fraction of the output produced in the United States was exported, and imports represented a correspondingly small fraction of total expenditures by American residents; the value of trade in goods and services, measured as the average of exports and imports, was less than 5 percent of the value of output. The proportion of trade to output began to grow steadily, however, and by the early 1970s was more than 6 percent; by 1979 it was more than 11 percent (see table 3-1).

The proportion of trade to output measured in current prices can change solely because of price effects. In the early postwar years the prices of traded goods rose more slowly than the average of all prices. In recent years, however, and especially because of the huge increases in international oil prices since 1973, the reverse has occurred. Thus some part of the slow rise of the ratio of the value of trade to the value of output in the early postwar years and some part of the rapid increase in recent years is attributable to these price effects. When expressed in constant rather than current prices, the ratio of trade to output shows substantial and fairly steady increases.

Table 3-1. U.S. Trade in Goods and Services and Ratio of Trade to Output, Selected Years and Periods, 1950–52 to 1979

Billions of dollars, except as noted

Unit of measurement and year or period	Trade in goods and services		Gross domestic product	Ratio of trade to output (percent)[a]
	Exports	*Imports*		
Current prices				
1950–52[b]	17.0	14.3	319.8	4.9
1960–62[b]	29.0	23.9	528.0	5.0
1970–72[b]	66.9	66.2	1,066.2	6.2
1975	147.3	126.9	1,518.3	9.0
1978	207.2	217.5	2,107.0	10.1
1979[c]	257.4	260.9	2,343.3	11.1
Constant 1972 prices				
1950–52[b]	24.2	18.7	567.6	3.8
1960–62[b]	37.2	31.5	759.7	4.5
1970–72[b]	69.2	70.0	1,111.5	6.3
1975	90.0	67.5	1,197.5	6.6
1978	108.9	97.9	1,391.1	7.4
1979[c]	119.8	102.1	1,423.2	7.8

Source: National income and product accounts of the United States, *Survey of Current Business*, various issues.
a. The ratio is calculated as half the sum of exports and imports divided by the gross domestic product.
b. Average for the period.
c. Preliminary.

The aggregates shown in table 3-1 are broad indicators for the U.S. economy as a whole. The extent of trade interdependence is considerably greater in the production of goods alone (output excluding services). For the first three quarters of 1979, the average value of merchandise exported and imported was 19 percent of the value of the output of American goods (the comparable figure for 1960–62 was about 6 percent). For some sectors of the economy, international transactions have still greater importance. More than 20 percent of the agricultural output of the United States is now exported. Exports account for more than half the total output of such agricultural products as rice, sunflower seeds, wheat, soybeans, and cattle hides and such manufactured goods as track-laying tractors, oil and gas drilling equipment, and civilian aircraft. Roughly one-half of American petroleum consumed comes from imports.

International trade flows are accounted for in the balance of payments. The U.S. balance on current account is the difference between what the United States pays for the goods and services it receives from other countries (and gifts it makes to them) and what it earns through exports of its own goods and services. In most years since the end of World War II, the United States has had a comfortable surplus on its current account and has thus added to its net international assets. In 1977 and 1978, however, the current account showed a large deficit, and the United States had to borrow from others to cover its current expenditures. Part of this change can be attributed to cyclical factors in the U.S. and foreign economies. But some analysts attribute another part to a persistent deterioration in the competitive position of the United States in international markets.[1] If present, such a trend will add to the difficulties of managing the U.S. economy in the future.

The international debtor-creditor relationships of the U.S. economy are less well documented and understood than international trade in goods and services. But increases in financial interdependence in the last decade have been at least as rapid as for trade. This interdependence may now be more important than trade in transmitting external influences to the American economy and American influences to the global economy.

Table 3-2 gives an indication of the increasing financial interdependence of the U.S. economy. For selected years beginning in 1952, data are shown for the outstanding claims of American residents on foreigners and their liabilities to foreigners. Data for the financial assets held by broad sectors of the U.S. economy, taken from the flow-of-funds accounts, are shown for comparison. As the table suggests, the international financial links of the American economy to the rest of the world are still small in relation to domestic financial magnitudes, but are growing rapidly.

Like trade, the interdependence in some financial markets and for some types of financial assets is much greater than the averages for the economy as a whole. The federal government debt is an important example. Of the debt held by investors (besides that owned by the Federal Reserve and agencies and trusts of the government itself), about 24 percent was owned by foreign investors (private and official combined) in September 1979. The ratio was as high as 27 percent

---

1. Robert Z. Lawrence, "Toward a Better Understanding of Trade Balance Trends: The Cost-Price Puzzle," *Brookings Papers on Economic Activity, 1:1979,* pp. 191–210; and Lawrence, "The United States Current Account: Trends and Prospects," prepared for the Joint Economic Committee, Special Study on Economic Change (U.S. Government Printing Office, forthcoming).

Table 3-2. International Assets and Liabilities of the U.S. Economy and Financial Assets of the U.S. Private Sector, Selected Years, 1952–78

Billions of dollars, end of year, except as noted

Type of asset	1952	1962	1972	1975	1978
Total U.S. assets abroad	59	97	199	295	450
U.S. private assets abroad	23	60	150	237	377
Direct investments	15	37	90	124	168
Assets except direct investments	8	23	60	113	209
Total liabilities of the United States to foreigners	21	46	162	220	373
Liabilities to foreign private sector	n.a.	n.a.	99	134	198
Direct investments	4	8	15	28	41
Assets except direct investments	n.a.	n.a.	84	106	157
Total financial assets of the U.S. private sector	1,003	2,040	4,603	5,269	7,219
Households	522	1,094	2,387	2,551	3,422
Nonfinancial business	140	236	499	610	826
Commercial banking	169	270	638	826	1,130
Private nonbank financial institutions	172	440	1,079	1,282	1,841
U.S. private assets abroad divided by total financial assets of U.S. private sector (percent)	2.3	3.0	3.3	4.5	5.2
Total U.S. liabilities to foreigners divided by total financial assets of the U.S. private sector (percent)	2.1	2.3	3.5	4.2	5.2

Source: U.S. Department of Commerce, Bureau of Economic Analysis, tables on international investment position of the United States; and Board of Governors of the Federal Reserve System, flow-of-funds accounts.

n.a. Not available.

at the end of 1978. As recently as December 1969 it was less than 5 percent and in 1952 a mere 2 percent.

The financial interdependence of the U.S. economy has also been promoted by the widespread use of the dollar outside the United States. Significant proportions of trade transactions and movements of capital among foreign nations are denominated in dollars. Those uses in turn give rise to demands by non-Americans to hold assets and incur liabilities denominated in dollars.

Because trade and financial interdependence are so quantitatively important, all parts of the American economy are affected. Firms, financial intermediaries, and households that do not directly engage in international transactions feel the influence indirectly. As an example, consider the rate of inflation of the overall U.S. price level (measured by, say, the consumer price index). The overall inflation rate is self-evidently an important economic variable for every wage-earner, consumer, and investor. And the inflation rate can be significantly affected, directly and indirectly, by international influences.

The dependence of the U.S. price level on foreign developments is most dramatically evident when the OPEC nations raise the price of oil by a large amount; the higher price of oil imports adds directly to the cost of gasoline and heating oil, which in turn gives an upward push to other prices and to wages. The Organization for Economic Cooperation and Development has estimated that 1.5 percentage points of the 9.0 percent rise of the U.S. personal consumption deflator (similar to the consumer price index) in 1979 was due to higher oil prices. Failures in food grain crops abroad are another highly visible instance; U.S. food prices may rise sharply in response to increased demands for food grain exports from the United States. But international influences on the U.S. price level are pervasive and are not restricted to these readily visible cases.

When the dollar declined relative to other currencies during 1978, the dollar prices of U.S. imports were pushed up. Consequently, the prices of American goods that compete with imports (for example, small automobiles) also tended to rise. In addition, the prices of American goods exported to other countries rose. Finally, the prices of nontradable goods in the United States also rose as consumers shifted to them because traded goods became more expensive and because wage costs in the whole economy were pushed up in response to increases in the price level caused by the dollar depreciation itself. It is difficult to quantify these direct and indirect effects, which can differ depending on whether the cause of the dollar's decline is external (events occurring in foreign nations) or internal (for example, expansive Federal Reserve monetary policy or an unexpected surge in domestic spending). When the cause is external, a reasonable estimate is that a 10 percent depreciation of the dollar will lead to a 1.5 to 2.5 percent increase in the U.S. price level over a period of two to three years.

In practice, inflation of the U.S. price level is the result of a complex combination of domestic and foreign causes. In quantitative terms, domestic economic policies and disturbances are normally more important than the foreign factors. Moreover, a correct analysis of inflation must acknowledge the many institutional and behavioral characteristics—largely domestic—that generate inertia in the wage-price process. Those characteristics explain why inflation is a slow-starting phenomenon, and why it is slow in stopping once it begins.[2] Nevertheless, the externally generated causes of American inflation—and not only the increases in the world price of oil—have become increasingly important in the 1970s.

Constraints on U.S. Economic Policy from Interdependence

In an interdependent world economic system, each nation cannot be assured of effective control over its own national economy. The United States may have seemed an exception to this generalization in earlier decades, although in fact it was not. In any case, for the reasons already given, the constraints resulting from interdependence will be a major factor determining the evolution of the American economy in the 1980s. Increasing interdependence has made macroeconomic policy in the United States more difficult to formulate and more uncertain in its consequences. Therefore, for better or for worse, it has become less possible than it once was for economic and financial conditions in the United States to differ greatly from those in the rest of the global economy.

International involvement can bring benefits as well as costs, and the United States enjoys substantial benefits as a result of its economic transactions with the rest of the world. These include the more efficient allocation of productive resources brought about by international trade and capital movements, an expanded range of consumption possibilities, and a dampening of inflationary pressures generated internally within the American economy. The result is a higher standard of living for Americans than would otherwise be possible.[3]

2. See chapter 2 in this volume and Arthur M. Okun, "The Invisible Handshake and the Inflationary Process," the Seidman Prize Lecture, *Challenge,* vol. 22 (January–February 1980), pp. 5–12 (Brookings Reprint 356).

3. In real terms, the share of gross domestic product produced for export at the end of the 1970s was 8.4 percent, compared to 6.2 percent at the start of the decade; the figures for the share of imports in total expenditures were 7.2 percent and 6.3 percent, respectively. U.S. national income rose at an average annual rate of 3.2 percent over the decade, after correction for inflation. Calculations based on a method pioneered by Edward F. Denison suggest that 0.02 percentage point of that annual improvement in national income can be attributed to the augmented role of international trade.

Demand-Management Policies

The reduction of policy autonomy brought about by increasing interdependence is an important problem for all decisions about U.S. macroeconomic policies. The complications are especially troublesome for demand-management policies—that is, the decisions of the Federal Reserve about monetary policy and those of the administration and Congress about general fiscal policy.

The complications can be appreciated by considering what happens when the Federal Reserve tightens monetary policy in an effort to control U.S. inflation. Not only do interest rates rise in the United States, but they rise for dollar lending everywhere. Because foreigners also borrow dollars and invest in dollar assets, their borrowing of dollars is discouraged and their desire to invest in dollar assets is encouraged just as it is for domestic residents. As a consequence, money from other countries is attracted to the United States. Hence, financial conditions are not as tight in the United States as they would have been in the absence of international capital flows and are tighter in the countries from which the money came. The capital flows also raise the value of the dollar in foreign exchange markets, with further consequences such as discouraging U.S. exports and encouraging imports.

In short, because of the financial and real-sector links of the U.S. economy to the rest of the world, a part of the contractionary effects of Federal Reserve action leaks abroad. If market forces are permitted to strengthen the dollar against foreign currencies, the amount of the leakage is smaller than in the case in which foreign central banks or the Federal Reserve intervene in the exchange markets to prevent the dollar from appreciating. But some part of the Federal Reserve action does spill over, regardless of the presence or absence of variability in dollar exchange rates.

In general, the growing financial openness of the American economy makes it increasingly difficult for the Federal Reserve to pursue a monetary policy greatly out of step with financial conditions in the rest of the world. Rapid inflation in the global economy is more likely to be transmitted to the United States—despite anti-inflationary actions of the Federal Reserve. International capital flows have an increasing tendency, if not to hold Federal Reserve policy hostage, at least to render an anti-inflationary policy less effective than it otherwise would be.

Similar complications arise if U.S. monetary policy attempts to induce less restrictive financial conditions in the United States than exist elsewhere in the world—a situation that could occur in 1980–81. Stimulative U.S. policies would be partially dissipated through international linkages. The leakage would be greatest if the Federal Reserve or foreign central banks intervened to prevent depreciation of the dollar, but some leakage would occur even if the dollar did decline. Furthermore, a falling dollar could cause private investors to panic and sell dollars, forcing a large and rapid depreciation of the dollar and precipitating a foreign-exchange crisis. In such an event, U.S. inflation could be exacerbated before much of an expansion of real output took place. The expansionary policy would likely have to be abandoned in the face of that crisis.

Until recently, it was believed that the United States and other nations could pursue independent monetary policies if exchange rates were permitted to be perfectly flexible. That generalization is now understood to be analytically incorrect and a misleading guideline for policy. Flexibility of dollar exchange rates cannot insulate the U.S. economy. The effects of foreign policy actions and disturbances tend to have *less* effect in the United States when dollar exchange rates are flexible than when exchange rates are kept from adjusting. If American policymakers want to buffer the U.S. economy against most types of foreign policy actions and against many types of disturbances originating in the real sector of foreign economies, they should let the dollar appreciate in response to external stimuli that are expansionary and depreciate in response to those that are contractionary. But the buffering tendencies associated with exchange rate variability do not apply to every type of disturbance originating abroad. Nor is it always desirable to have the U.S. economy buffered against the rest of the world. During periods when the United States is predominantly influenced by real-sector disturbances originating *in the United States,* for example, it is in its interest to share, to the greatest extent possible, the adverse consequences of those disturbances with the rest of the world.[4]

Financial interdependence would cause difficulties for U.S. economic policy even if the dollar were not widely used by foreigners as

---

4. The analysis summarized in this and the preceding paragraphs is presented in detail in Ralph C. Bryant, *Money and Monetary Policy in Interdependent Nations* (Brookings Institution, forthcoming), pts. 3, 5.

a currency for international transactions and a store of value. Those uses of the dollar, however, exacerbate the difficulties by increasing the opportunities and incentives for capital flows into and out of dollar assets, thereby magnifying the cross-national transmission of policy actions and disturbances.

Federal Reserve decisions are constrained in a subtle way by still another set of international considerations. The regulatory and supervisory environment within which banks and other financial intermediaries operate in the United States differs in important ways from the corresponding environments in other nations. The United States relies heavily on the use of minimum reserve requirements; many other nations with highly developed financial sectors (for example, Switzerland, France, the United Kingdom, Belgium, and Luxembourg) do not. Taxes on the profits of intermediaries are considerably lower in some foreign locations (for example, the Bahamas and Cayman Islands) than in the United States. Bank examination procedures are more highly developed and intensive in the United States than in many foreign countries. Disparities of this sort give strong incentives to the intermediaries to conduct their business in the countries with least stringent regulations.

Many nations are affected by these disparities in national regulatory environments. Indeed, most major nations contribute to and in turn are confronted by an *international* problem: national regulations discriminate in favor of banking activities conducted in nonnational currencies, especially vis-à-vis nonresidents (so-called Eurocurrency banking).[5] The United States encounters more severe problems with these disparities than other nations because of its reserve requirements, tax rates, and supervisory procedures.

The existence of the competitive differences in national regulatory environments and the unusually rapid growth of Eurocurrency banking that is associated with those differences do not mean that the Federal Reserve has lost control over domestic monetary policy. In principle, the Federal Reserve can adjust its policy actions to allow

5. For example, external-currency banking in some locations is free of any reserve requirements and any quantitative restrictions on lending activities; in most other nations this banking is subject to fewer and less restrictive regulations than those applicable to domestic-currency banking. The United States is one of the few nations that has not discriminated in favor of external-currency banking. The proposal presently before the Federal Reserve to permit banks in New York to establish an international banking facility would be a departure from this past policy.

for shifts in the location of banking activity. In practice, however, the shifts are an additional source of uncertainty about the consequences of monetary policy and yet another international factor complicating the efforts of the Federal Reserve to influence the U.S. economy.[6]

For illustrative purposes, our discussion here has concentrated on monetary policy. Had we chosen to focus on the implications of the increasing openness of the U.S. economy for fiscal policy, analogous points and conclusions would have been stressed. The impacts of changes in tax rates and changes in discretionary government expenditures do not fall entirely on the domestic economy but instead partly spill over into the global economy. And limitations exist on the degree to which American policymakers can use fiscal-policy actions to promote macroeconomic conditions in the United States widely at variance with macroeconomic conditions in the rest of the world. There is thus no easy way to escape the international constraints on U.S. economic policy simply by placing the burden of demand management on fiscal policy rather than on monetary policy.

Supply-Management Policies

Even if there were no international constraints on the use of monetary and fiscal instruments, the experience of the last three decades strongly suggests that demand-management policies by themselves are insufficient to guarantee noninflationary economic growth. Demand management needs to be supplemented by supply-management policies. Supply management can help to achieve domestic goals— such as increasing growth without worsening and possibly even improving the inflation experience—while at the same time easing constraints from the interdependence of the world economy.

Supply-promotion policies can be general, as in the case of investment tax credits to promote investment, or they can be specific, such as special deductions for conversion of energy use in industrial plants from oil to coal. The rationale of such policies rests on the belief that

6. Interdependence also drastically changes the economic rationale for American antitrust policy. Effective competition must be considered in global rather than national terms. Thus a rule that establishes presumption of a violation of American law simply because a domestic firm controls a dominant share of the domestic market is inappropriate. For example, it may be poor public policy to weaken a large U.S. corporation such as International Business Machines in an effort to strengthen other domestic firms because of the severe international competition with Japan and Europe.

private firms cannot react sufficiently to rising real market prices and that the supply response can be improved by public policy, particularly if existing policies that interfere with market adjustments are modified.

Obviously the most important supply-promotion policy in the United States concerns energy: the private market, acting alone, is unlikely to satisfy national needs. The principal goal of U.S. energy policy should be to increase domestic sources of energy. Various methods for doing this are discussed in chapter 4, along with measures to reduce demand through conservation.

A successful energy policy would mitigate some of the current international constraints on U.S. economic policy. With increased domestic sources of energy, U.S. imports of petroleum would be scaled down to relieve some of the pressure on dollar exchange rates coming from current-account deficits in the balance of payments. A reduction of petroleum purchases from OPEC countries relative to real economic activity in the United States would reduce OPEC's balance-of-payments surplus, which in turn could have stabilizing consequences for the international monetary system. A reduction in U.S. oil imports would also add some moderation to the rise of petroleum prices worldwide. Finally, if foreigners could be convinced that the United States is able to respond effectively to the economic challenges that lie ahead, confidence in the dollar would be bolstered and world events would not lead to destabilizing asset shifts away from the dollar that are as large or occur as rapidly as those of the past.

Another goal of U.S. supply-promotion policies should be to improve productivity performance by increasing research and development expenditures and domestic real investment as a share of total output. An increase in capital formation relative to output may not be a sufficient condition for reversing the lackluster performance of productivity in recent years. But in the judgment of many economists it is a necessary condition.[7]

---

7. Edward F. Denison, *Accounting for Slower Economic Growth: The United States in the 1970s* (Brookings Institution, 1979); Peter K. Clark, "Issues in the Analysis of Capital Formation and Productivity Growth," *Brookings Papers on Economic Activity, 2:1979*, pp. 423–31; and J. R. Norsworthy, Michael J. Harper, and Kent Kunze, "The Slowdown in Productivity Growth: Analysis of Some Contributing Factors," in ibid., pp. 387–421.

Changing the mix of U.S. national income to include more investment and less consumption—in addition to the desirable domestic
effects—could ease the constraints on U.S. economic policy stemming from weakness in the current account of the balance of payments. It could facilitate an improvement in the international competitiveness of U.S. goods for a given level and rate of growth of U.S.
national income. The improved competitiveness could in turn lead
to larger exports, smaller imports, a higher valued dollar and lower
domestic inflation. Thus the international involvement of the United
States could be instrumental in stimulating increased domestic growth
with less inflation because the U.S. gains from competitiveness would
be reflected in the world market rather than just in the smaller
domestic market. Improvements in U.S. productivity performance
that come from regulatory reform would have a similar effect through
enhanced U.S. competitiveness in world markets.

Choice of Macroeconomic Goals

Policymakers in the United States are increasingly limited in their
choice of macroeconomic goals by the growing openness of the
American economy—in particular, goals for U.S. output, employment, and inflation are constrained so they cannot differ sharply from
corresponding objectives in the rest of the world.

If U.S. macroeconomic policy is formulated without realistic perceptions of international constraints and hence with exaggerated
perceptions of the ability to achieve American goals, policy decisions
may have consequences quite different from those intended, and
serious policy mistakes may result. It is thus essential for American
policymakers to concentrate on a *feasible* set of policy goals, and to
understand how they are limited by international economic relationships.

We do not want to overstate the case. The international constraints
on American economic policies, while important, are not so dominant as to render the policies hostages to global economic conditions.
The trade and financial channels of interdependence are not so wide
and deep that there is no significant scope for divergences between
conditions here and abroad. What we do want to stress is that the
scope for such divergences has been perceptibly narrowing. American
policymakers in the 1980s will thus have to be more and more concerned with the international aspects of their policy decisions.

The Need for International Economic Cooperation

If national governments adopt policy actions with only their domestic economies in mind (ignoring the consequences of the actions for other nations), the global outcome may be adverse for all nations.

The industrial countries learned that lesson in international trade policy in the 1930s, but only after suffering immense pain. The Great Depression was significantly worsened because individual nations took protectionist measures to support domestic employment; those measures called forth protectionist retaliation. The result, intended by none, was a serious undermining of the world economy. Four decades later, even during the sharp recession that occurred in 1974–75, industrial nations did not try to export their unemployment by restricting imports. Indeed, the major nations explicitly pledged not to do so in the series of international economic meetings held at that time.

Conceivably the lesson of the 1930s about protectionist trade policies could be forgotten in the future. Significant domestic pressures for additional trade protection exist in all nations and are likely to intensify in the troubled economic environment that lies ahead. But the experience of the 1970s, including the largely successful completion of the Tokyo Round of multilateral tariff negotiations, suggests that cooperative trade policies will continue. The major challenge in the years ahead is to generalize the lesson of the 1930s for other areas such as energy and general macroeconomic policies.

In virtually all areas of policy, national governments may be able to improve the performance of their own economies—and hence, indirectly, the global economy—by adjusting national policies to take better account of the interactions among their economies. Because the cross-national impacts of policy actions and disturbances are increasing relative to own-country impacts, moreover, the potential benefits from more collaborative decisionmaking are augmented. If each nation made an effort to assess the impacts of its actions on others and was willing to commit itself to a mutually consistent set of actions, it would become possible to enter into a bargain whereby each nation achieved a better performance for its economy than would otherwise have been possible under noncooperative decisionmaking.

The potential benefits from collective decisionmaking are especially great when noncooperative national decisions threaten to produce—inadvertently—an excessive boom or bust for the global economy as a whole. For example, the global outcomes in the 1972–73 period of synchronized excess demand in the industrial countries and the 1974–75 coordinated contraction of output were both situations that could have been mitigated by improved cooperation in macroeconomic decisionmaking among the major countries.

It will, nevertheless, be difficult for the United States and other nations to make much progress in collaborative decisionmaking. One basic problem is the lack of sufficient analytical understanding of how the global economy functions. National governments cannot effectively identify alternative outcomes and bargain about which outcomes to aim for unless they can use a common model of the interaction among their economies. Such an analytical framework currently does not exist.

Even with improved knowledge of the functioning of the global economy, other basic obstacles will have to be overcome. For example, international cooperation in setting economic policies requires the explicit surrender of some national sovereignty. Domestic political acceptance of this surrender is difficult to obtain because of the continuing dominance in domestic politics of ideas and institutions that are exclusively national in orientation.[8]

Moreover, there is a natural reluctance for a single nation or group of nations to take the initiative in cooperative decisionmaking. International cooperation is in essence what economists label a "public good," that is, a good that benefits everybody rather than any particular consumer.[9] Like other public goods, the supply of interna-

---

8. The extent of the surrender of sovereignty is commonly exaggerated in domestic politics. Richard N. Cooper observed: "Widespread reluctance to make the required political commitments [to greater cooperation] reflects in part a confusion between formal sovereignty and real freedom of action. Autonomy may have been lost long before the public recognizes it and is prepared to yield the sovereignty which can actually restore a certain freedom of action." See Cooper, *The Economics of Interdependence: Economic Policy in the Atlantic Community* (McGraw-Hill, 1968), p. 264.

9. If a public good is supplied, all who value the good tend to benefit whether or not they contribute to the cost of supplying it. See, for example, Mancur Olson, *The Logic of Collective Action: Public Goods and the Theory of Groups* (Harvard University Press, 1971).

tional cooperation is likely to fall short of what would be mutually beneficial because each nation—acting rationally on an individual basis—ignores the potential benefits of the greater cooperation for others. Collective decisionmaking about macroeconomic policies is also likely to be plagued by the "free rider" problem; because the world economy is composed of many nations and because most of those nations have a tendency to perceive themselves as "small," the probability is high that a disproportionately large share of the costs of cooperation will fall on a few countries willing to take an initiative for the benefit of the world economy as a whole.

Despite the undoubted difficulties in encouraging greater cooperation, national governments cannot sustain the status quo by simply remaining passive. As the evolution of political institutions lags behind the increases in economic interdependence, tensions build that either catalyze a more rapid political evolution or restrain (possibly even reverse) the pace of economic advance.

In principle, national governments could decide to inhibit the growth in economic interdependence by creating additional impediments to the movements of goods, assets, and people across national boundaries. Conceivably, international cooperation could even be harnessed to such an objective: nations could try to find mutually acceptable ways to restore a greater measure of autonomy for national policies.

Suggestions for cooperative action to reduce interdependence deserve further study. In the case of the dependence of oil-importing nations on the production and pricing decisions of the OPEC cartel, proposals for reducing interdependence should receive priority. In our opinion, however, there are no low-cost ways to achieve a general reduction in interdependence, and the economic costs would greatly outweigh the economic benefits. Moreover, the political costs incurred from a noncooperative retreat into protectionism and financial controls could be high indeed.

All things considered, there is a strong case for the United States and other nations to move forward rather than backward. The trend toward increasing economic interdependence should be accepted, but stronger collective efforts should also be made to manage that trend, and a corresponding evolution of national and intergovernmental institutions should be actively promoted.

Trend toward Economic Pluralism in the World Economy

The 1980s will be a challenging decade for industrial countries. The worldwide energy shortage, by forcing up the real price of petroleum, will limit real growth and exacerbate inflation. These twin problems are extremely difficult for industrial democracies to solve. Political power is diffused among many groups, each with a capability of shifting burdens to others. Hence, even small income losses are magnified severalfold before adjustment is finally accomplished. Industrial democracies are good at parceling out gains, but are bad at distributing losses.

Many developing countries that are importers of oil do not seem to have this problem, at least to the same extent that industrial countries do. As a result, they adjusted to the oil price rise of 1973–74 and then rapidly returned to or near their earlier paths of rapid growth. Brazil, Colombia, Korea, the Philippines, and Thailand (and many others) are examples. Moreover, a number of the more advanced developing countries are likely to continue to outperform industrial countries significantly in the 1980s.[10] Economic growth, economic wealth, and economic power are thus likely to be more widely diffused by the end of the decade than at its start. If one adds the oil-producing countries themselves, a much larger number of important players will participate in the policy decisions affecting the world economy.

The further diffusion of world economic power will have many implications that cannot now be easily perceived. For example, the methods, procedures, and negotiations that have been used by developed countries to sustain and advance the postwar liberal international trading regime will have to be altered to accommodate the new powers; but the actual changes that will occur cannot yet be predicted in detail.[11] Similarly, changes seem likely in the participation of the advanced developing countries in decisionmaking about international monetary arrangements, especially pertaining to the role of the dollar. Indeed, every dimension of international economic relations is likely to be affected in some manner that will strain the

10. For more complete description and analysis, see Lawrence B. Krause and Sueo Sekiguchi, *Economic Interaction in the Pacific Basin* (Brookings Institution, 1980).

11. See the discussion in chapter 15 of this volume.

ability of intergovernmental institutions responsible for overseeing and guiding such changes.

Fostering Greater International Cooperation

If a strong case exists in principle for more international cooperation, how might efforts to encourage such cooperation proceed?

The most critical area is energy supplies and uses. The experience of the last few years suggests that the world petroleum market can work perversely: the more oil demanded from OPEC by oil-importing nations, the less they may receive. This is so because higher demand can lead to higher prices, which in turn can yield much larger incomes to OPEC than are needed for current expenditures. In the face of world inflation (in part caused by increases in oil prices themselves), oil producers may decide that oil in the ground is the best investment they can make and accordingly react by cutting output. Therefore, consumers may be able to obtain more oil—and perhaps on more favorable terms—by collectively limiting their demand.

Cooperative efforts to limit the demand for OPEC oil could involve policies to allocate available world supplies to consuming countries, including guidelines for the accumulation and use of oil inventories; to stimulate domestic (non-OPEC) production of traditional sources of energy; to induce conservation; and to hasten the innovation process whereby alternative energy technologies become commercially feasible. Allocation policies will become urgent if there is a deliberate OPEC decision to cut output or a political crisis in the Middle East that results in a fall in that output. At a minimum, workable allocation policies need to be available on a contingency basis.

International collaboration on energy policy cannot be easily achieved, as suggested by the modest success thus far attained in the International Energy Agency and at the Tokyo economic summit in 1979. There are few incentives for a nation acting individually to participate in a cooperative energy policy. Each nation has a basic interest in securing for itself a sufficiently large share of scarce world energy supplies to avoid adjustment in its own policies. But what a single nation may be able to do by itself cannot be done by the entire community of oil-importing nations. And the global consequences of such a scramble among individual nations could be highly adverse for all. Hence, effective cooperation to manage the energy crisis can have a large payoff for all oil-importing nations.

Another fertile area for cooperation, as suggested above, is greater coordination of domestic macroeconomic policies. The best way to make incremental progress in this difficult area is to encourage more intensive and candid exchanges of information, analysis, and projections among national macroeconomic policymakers and their staffs.

Important institutions already exist for promoting cooperation among industrial countries by means of economic summits and certain organs of the Organization for Economic Cooperation and Development.[12] Some degree of broad-based consultation also occurs within the Executive Board and the Interim Committee of the International Monetary Fund.

Not much actual coordination of national policies has yet been achieved in these forums. This is not surprising because, as noted above, modest progress at best can be expected when there is such an imperfect understanding of the functioning of the world economy. Indeed, some analysts argue that the state of knowledge is so poor that little confidence can be placed in efforts to determine national policies jointly; they fear that mistaken joint policies may lead to worse outcomes than those resulting from noncooperative decisions.

Nevertheless, in our judgment a possibility already exists to foster modest but significant improvements in macroeconomic cooperation through mutually discussed but differentiated policy actions. Efforts to achieve those improvements are worthwhile. Equally important, national governments and intergovernmental institutions should be giving greater support to analytical research that promotes understanding of the cross-national impacts of policy actions and economic disturbances. Such research cannot bear fruit in the immediate future. Yet if a practical global macroeconomics is ever to be available as a guide to international coordination of national policies, the analytical foundations of that framework first must be laid.

Another way to improve macroeconomic cooperation is to increase the number of countries participating in information exchange and economic consultations. As noted above, the advanced developing countries are already having a significant impact on the world econ-

---

12. The work of the Economic Policy Committee and that of its Working Party Three are the most significant activities, but useful exchanges also occur in the other working parties and at the ministerial level.

omy; their inclusion in enhanced consultative arrangements would be mutually beneficial. Intensified consultations at the global level in institutions such as the International Monetary Fund can contribute to this goal; but for many purposes the International Monetary Fund is a forum that is too inclusive. Another possibility would be to have some of the advanced developing countries join the Organization for Economic Cooperation and Development; but expanding the membership of that organization could impair its functioning by preventing it from doing what it now does well. Many advanced developing countries are located in the Pacific basin; a case exists for forming a new regional institution within that area to promote economic consultation among its developed and developing countries.[13] Coordination between the Organization for Economic Cooperation and Development and the new institution could easily be accomplished through dual membership for some members.

One of the benefits to the advanced developing countries from a fuller participation in economic consultations among national governments would be better information about world economic developments and the policies of other governments, including other advanced developing countries. Furthermore, participation in a forum in which the policies of developed countries are explained would give advanced developing countries an opportunity to express their concerns and thereby have some influence on policy formation. An appropriate channel must be provided for the advanced developing countries because their real impact on the world economy is increasing. As part of participation in this process, the advanced developing countries would recognize that they are no longer "small" and that they should not behave as irresponsible outsiders. With size comes responsibility; it is time that the rights and responsibilities of the advanced developing countries be adjusted to the realities of the world economy.[14]

Yet another necessary condition for success of greater international coordination of national macroeconomic policies is a more intensive effort, within national governments, to incorporate international con-

13. This issue is discussed in Krause and Sekiguchi, *Economic Interaction in the Pacific Basin,* and by Peter A. Drysdale and Hugh Patrick, *An Asian-Pacific Regional Economic Organization: An Exploratory Concept Paper,* prepared by the U.S. Library of Congress, Congressional Research Service, for the Senate Committee on Foreign Relations, 96 Cong. 1 sess. (GPO, 1979).

14. See chapter 15.

siderations in domestic policymaking. Governments have a strong tendency to compartmentalize domestic and international decision-making. The fact that domestic economic policy cannot be separated from foreign economic policy, which in turn cannot be separated from foreign relations in general, causes an understandable dilemma for governments; a few officials cannot possibly make all decisions. No perfect organizational chart for intragovernmental decisionmaking can be developed to resolve this dilemma. In any case, the purely organizational issue is secondary. The solution lies in the careful screening of priorities so that only the most important ones are considered by the senior officials as a group.[15]

World Recession, Recovery, and Constrained World Energy Supply

The guidelines for cooperation outlined in the preceding section provide an appropriate frame of reference for assessing the outlook for the U.S. economy and the world economy over the next several years.

The U.S. government and the majority of private forecasters of the outlook for the U.S. economy foresee a recession during 1980. All forecasters, however, emphasize the great uncertainty about defense spending; the faster and larger the rise in military expenditures, the less protracted and milder the projected economic slowdown. The rate of inflation is projected to remain high. Even in forecasts predicting a sizable recession, the inflation rate falls only modestly from the high rates observed in the second half of 1979. If only a mild slowdown occurs, the inflation problem may be even worse.

Other developed countries are also likely to have economic slowdowns in 1980–81. Just as the first oil crisis caused a synchronized recession in 1974–75 when all countries simultaneously responded to the same external disturbance, so the escalation of oil prices in 1979–80 will tend to reduce real output, increase inflation, and worsen the balance of payments of all oil-importing countries. Growth of international trade among oil importers is likely to suffer

15. A similar problem exists in the U.S. Congress, which by necessity is organized into committees and subcommittees. Because of the large role that Congress plays in both domestic and foreign economic policy, better information must be available to individual members than is now provided by the hearings process.

and provide an unwelcome surprise for policymakers. Some countries in 1974–75 tried to avoid the world slump through domestic stimulation; they achieved some short-term success, but the temporary gain proved costly as their rates of inflation and balance-of-payments deficits worsened considerably. Because few countries will want to repeat or emulate that experience, a 1980–81 slowdown could be even more synchronized and more general than it was previously.

If world commodity markets behave as they have in the past, the synchronized slowdown will cause prices of internationally traded commodities (besides oil) to stabilize or even decline, with negative impacts on developing countries that export them. In 1974–75 many developing countries sustained their growth despite weak export prices, but accumulated large external debts in the process. Given the recent large increases in oil prices, the developing countries will have to increase external borrowing further. In the face of a world slowdown, developing countries may not want or be able to increase their current borrowing to the extent that would be needed to sustain output growth. Thus a world slowdown could be reflected in the developing countries faster and more completely in the next few years than in 1974–75.

Such a macroeconomic outlook poses a dilemma for almost all industrial countries and many of the advanced developing countries. What growth of nominal aggregate demand should be the aim of demand-management policy? With inflation rates so high, few governments want to take substantial risks of worsening inflation by aiming at too high a rate. A policy of vigorous expansion that could prevent a rise of unemployment would seriously undermine the long-run prospects for controlling inflation. But with output weak, stagnating, or possibly even declining, most governments will also feel political pressure to promote a recovery in real activity. Moreover, there are sizable risks with a sharply restrictive demand-management policy; if the aim of that policy is to reduce the rate of increase of nominal aggregate demand too rapidly (from the experience of 1978–79, when there was high inflation and positive real growth), the rapid slowdown in nominal demand will produce mainly a decline in output rather than a reduction in inflation. Given a nation's labor market practices, tax system, and regulatory environment, it also faces the difficult problem of deciding what supply-management policies, if any, can be used to supplement its demand-management strategy. The international aspects in many cases may prove to be decisive in selecting macroeconomic policy. If any individual nation chooses a strategy that ignores what is happening in the rest of the world, its objectives will not be achieved.

Natural economic forces—for example, cessation of cutbacks in inventory accumulation—will help to bring the slowdown to an end. And the recovery in developed countries will be aided by the moderation or decline in world prices of raw materials. Nevertheless, the recovery is likely to be quite modest if private-sector forces alone are relied upon without any policy measures for expansion.[16] Yet a sharp recovery, fueled by rapidly rising military expenditures in the United States and possibly elsewhere, would run unacceptable risks of exacerbating inflation. What is needed, for the world as a whole and for most individual nations, is a middle-of-the-road demand-management policy that avoids the extremes of vigorous restimulation and aggressive restriction.

The global outlook is significantly darkened by the medium-term prospects for energy supplies and energy prices, and the crux of the macroeconomic problem will be to determine how much expansion in the world is possible without causing a worldwide energy shortage. The large increases in oil prices in 1979–80 are the most important factor contributing to the 1980 outlook for adverse inflation rates and sluggish growth in output. The surplus of oil-producing countries in the current account of the balance of payments will rise substantially in 1980 from the high rates already reached in the second half of 1979. Apart from the global macroeconomic effects of the rise of oil prices (weakening activity and pushing up price levels), the OPEC surplus will create added strains for many countries in the external financing of the counterpart current-account deficits. Other things being equal, the lower the rate of OPEC oil production in the future, the worse will be the inflation and the weaker the real activity in oil-importing countries.

The *least* pessimistic energy scenario for the first half of the 1980s that seems plausible requires successful conservation efforts in oil-

16. In contrast with the 1973–74 period, the recent expansion of output in the United States and most other industrial countries has proceeded with a better balance between inventory accumulation and final sales, and there has been less speculative building of inventories. The prospective slowdown in 1980–81 is thus likely to have fewer characteristics of the classic inventory cycle.

consuming countries and the availability of significant additional sources of energy supply from non-OPEC sources. Under such circumstances, demand for oil imports from OPEC would not rise greatly, even if activity began to recover vigorously in industrial countries. Hence, the world oil price and other energy prices would not rise much further, if at all, in real terms even with little or no increase in OPEC output.

But it is not difficult to imagine a less-comfortable outcome in which increased demand for OPEC oil puts substantial upward pressure on (real) oil prices. Rises in price would then bring forth no increase—and possibly a decrease—in OPEC production. In scenarios of this more pessimistic type, the global economic environment becomes much more fragile, and world political tensions would worsen.

The situation for each individual nation in this scenario would be less problematic if a consensus existed among the major nations about the broad outlines of a global demand-management strategy. Such a consensus, if it could be obtained, would constrain total world activity within available energy supplies; it would presumably have to be a middle course that eschewed the extremes of vigorous restimulation and aggressively restrictive policies. One merit of this effort to achieve a mutually acceptable *global* strategy for demand management (albeit in a rough and tentative way) would be the avoidance of the imbalances and strains that result when the economies of individual countries diverge markedly from the average experience of all of them.

Countries will inevitably have different levels of inflation, unemployment, balance-of-payments deficits, and external indebtedness. In principle, middle-of-the-road expansionary policies to counter the downturn should be undertaken first by countries with the lowest inflation rates, the strongest balances of payments, and the least burdensome accumulation of external debts. Later, other countries could add further stimulus if the spillover effect from the first group of countries was inadequate and if there were still sufficient supplies of world energy. Thus there could be a coordinated yet differentiated world economic expansion. The effort to agree on a global strategy could create a global environment more conducive to the attainment of each nation's individual objectives (as constrained by the process of shaping the international consensus). The national governments, by more directly confronting the interactions of their economies and their policies than they had in the past, could collectively reduce the uncertainty about the evolution of the global economy, and hence about the performance of their own economies.

The case for trying to achieve a broad international consensus extends even to the mix of fiscal and monetary policies. Many, if not all, major nations that participate in such a consensus—like the United States—would probably want to provide greater incentives to investment than to consumption expenditures (in the belief that productivity would thereby be enhanced). If a single country acting in isolation attempted a radical change in the policy mix, tightening fiscal policy while easing monetary policy, that country could find its currency depreciating in exchange markets and thereby would be under pressure to abandon its change in the mix. If countries could agree to move together in the direction of changing the mix, what is difficult or impossible for a single country acting in isolation would become feasible for all of them acting collectively.

Implications for U.S. Economic Policies

Because of the large relative size of the U.S. economy and the prominence of the dollar as an international currency, the challenges posed by the increasing interdependence of national economies are especially important for the United States. American policies for the early 1980s should be consistent with the framework for international cooperation outlined above. If implemented, these policies would go far toward making the United States a responsible leader and participant in world economic affairs.

When formulating fiscal and monetary policies, the administration and the Federal Reserve should be especially sensitive to the desirability of developing an international consensus on demand management. They can set a good example for the rest of the world by advocating and implementing in the United States the middle-of-the-road course that should characterize the global consensus. In particular, the United States must be careful not to repeat the fiscal mistakes of the Vietnam period. Any projected increase in military strength must be financed on a pay-as-you-go basis.

At present, even more than during the Vietnam War, the United States cannot have a macroeconomic outcome that diverges greatly from the rest of the world without sharply confronting the constraints imposed by the openness of the economy. If other industrial nations should choose to follow aggressively restrictive demand-management policies throughout a 1980–81 world slowdown, it would be especially dangerous for the United States to unilaterally implement a vigorous expansionary strategy. Although such a strategy might yield faster growth in real output in the short run, the financial-market and exchange-market consequences would soon force a retrenchment of that U.S. expansion and leave an even more difficult problem in its wake.

Even a middle-of-the-road expansionary policy in the United States could fail in the face of aggressively restrictive demand-management policies abroad. In the absence of an international consensus on middle-of-the-road policies, the United States will inevitably be driven to more restrictive macroeconomic policies than would otherwise be desirable.

In the area of energy policy, the United States must implement policy adjustments to correct existing distortions of the U.S. economy. Those adjustments will in turn have beneficial effects on (though of course they cannot solve) the global energy problem. In particular, U.S. policies need to bring about a higher price for energy promptly that reflects its current scarcity value (including the political and security aspects of that scarcity value). Decontrol of domestic energy prices is thus essential. Adjustments are called for in government tax revenues and transfer payments to try to offset the macroeconomic and distributional consequences. But difficulties in making those adjustments must not be allowed to prevent the implementation of decontrol. For the United States and for the rest of the world the establishment of a realistic relative price for energy is an overriding priority. Other adjustments in U.S. energy policies can help. These include more intensive efforts to promote research and development of alternative energy technologies; more effective implementation of the U.S. strategic petroleum reserve; design of a flexible, long-run strategy for increasing domestic sources of energy supplies; and better surveillance of government regulations to ensure that regulations do not have unintended and undesirable side effects on energy demands and supplies.[17]

Other supply-management policies, although less urgent than those

17. For further details, see chapter 4.

in the energy area, are needed to encourage capital formation and productivity. Such policies are desirable on domestic grounds alone, but are needed a fortiori to improve the international competitiveness of the U.S. economy. Changes in the tax incentives applicable to investment and to expenditures on research and development are examples. Protectionist actions to shield U.S. companies from world competition would be especially inconsistent with the need to improve U.S. productivity and competitiveness.

Sensible energy and supply-management policies can be expected to strengthen the U.S. balance-of-payments position over time, helping to avoid continuing and excessive deficits on current account. The current-account position that is reasonable for the United States in any given year depends on the current-account surplus of the oil-exporting countries and on the relative cyclical situation in the United States and the world economy. So long as the surplus of the oil-exporting countries remains large (the likely prospect for 1980–82), the oil-importing nations will inevitably experience counterpart deficits. If all oil-importing nations, acting individually, tried to eliminate their deficits in the short run, their efforts would be self-defeating and ensure a deep worldwide recession. The existence of a large OPEC surplus, however, does not relieve the United States of the need for caution in adopting domestic policies that could weaken its balance-of-payments position. Over the longer run, the U.S. economy should achieve a current-account surplus, thereby aiding in the transfer of resources to developing countries to promote their more rapid growth.

Finally, the United States should take a leadership role in demonstrating an awareness of and a sensitivity to the issues of interdependence. Decisionmaking procedures within the U.S. government need to be strengthened to achieve a better integration of the international and domestic aspects of problems. Improvement of those procedures would indicate to the rest of the world that there is an altered awareness in the United States. Another important manifestation of U.S. leadership would be an enhanced commitment to support and strengthen the international economic organizations. As one looks toward the latter part of the 1980s and even further into the future, a gradual strengthening of international institutions and decisionmaking procedures will be essential for a peaceful and prosperous evolution of the world economy.

CHAPTER FOUR

Energy

HANS H. LANDSBERG

THE UNITED STATES and the rest of the world are facing an energy problem long in the making and certain to persist. The era of abundant, reliable, low-cost energy is past, and the normal condition henceforth will be scarcity—and a continuing need to manage the complex and difficult issues associated with the use, supply, pricing, and trading of energy to prevent economic, political, environmental, and military crises.

The broad, long-run aims of energy policy are not hard to define: to help users adjust to high and rising energy costs; to encourage transition to a different mix of energy sources, away from crude oil (a process that, as shown in table 4-1, has not yet begun in the United States); to provide incentives for greater efficiency in the use of energy; to avoid irreversible damage to the environment; and to establish contingency plans for major interruptions in energy supply, whatever their cause. The agenda for the 1980s is to marshall the political wisdom and the consensus necessary to move toward these objectives.

Reducing Energy Demand

Imported oil is at the heart of the energy problem: it is produced mainly in politically unstable areas, making massive supply interrup-

The author gratefully acknowledges the help of his colleagues Douglas Bohi, Joel Darmstadter, and Milton Russell, who read a draft of this chapter and made valuable suggestions for improving substance and exposition; and the help of Lee Carlson, who untiringly typed draft after draft.

99

Table 4-1. U.S. Energy Consumption, by Source, 1973 and 1978

Source	Consumption (quadrillions of BTUs)		Share of total (percent)	
	1973	1978	1973	1978
Petroleum	34.9	38.0	46.8	48.4
Natural gas (dry)	22.5	20.0	30.2	25.5
Coal	13.3	14.1	17.8	18.0
Hydroelectric	3.0	3.1	4.0	4.0
Nuclear	0.9	3.0	1.2	3.8
Other	*	0.2	*	0.3
Total	74.6	78.4	100.0	100.0

Source: U.S. Department of Energy, *Monthly Energy Review* (December 1979), p. 6.
*Less than 0.1.

tions possible; it is difficult to replace in the short run and thus encourages political accommodations to avoid supply problems; its use
is pervasive in most industrialized economies; and its high price and
volume creates large international trade and payment disequilibria.
It is important, however, to distinguish between short-term and long-
term dependencies on large oil imports. Both create problems, but
there is good reason to believe that in the long run dependency can
be alleviated. In the short run, on the other hand, there are no good
escape routes, only ways of containing the damage. Reducing consumption appears to have the greatest quantitative potential.

The Role of Prices

It is an elementary economic principle that the prices consumers
pay for any commodity or service should reflect their true value or
replacement cost. This principle takes on particular importance in the
case of energy. Replacement-cost prices for energy would give proper
signals to guide consumers in the allocation of their expenditures, including their choice of amounts and kinds of energy and of energy-
using equipment and facilities. Similarly, producers would be given
proper signals regarding both the appropriate energy sources to use
in production and the appropriate investment in exploration and
development of other energy sources and technologies. In short, demand and supply efficiencies would be enhanced.

To achieve these objectives it is necessary to eliminate the controls
on the prices of domestic oil and natural gas that keep them below

replacement cost.[1] Aside from the improvements in the allocation of resources, decontrol would eliminate the heavy administrative and compliance costs of the regulations. In addition, in the case of oil, it would end the allocation and entitlement system that levies a tax on domestically produced oil to subsidize the high cost of imported oil and thus perversely increases imports of oil at a time when national policy calls for reducing them.

Under present legislation, oil and gas prices are scheduled to be decontrolled. However, decontrol of gas prices will not be completed until 1985 and oil prices not until September 1981. Even then a legacy of price control will remain in the arrangements for a windfall profits tax, which defines the base price as the May 1979 world price plus an inflation allowance. Advocates of controlled prices could use this fictitious price to gain support for reimposing controls, especially with gas and oil prices rising rapidly. In addition, decontrol has undesirable economic effects: high fuel prices are inflationary; and they fall most heavily on the poor (the differential effect). These problems should not be allowed to dominate the price issue. They should be resolved through other policies.

INFLATION. Estimates of the inflationary impact of higher energy prices differ; but history offers some guidance. The U.S. retail price of regular gasoline doubled between mid-1973 and the end of 1978 and the price of other energy sources also rose sharply. Nevertheless, had energy prices paid by consumers risen only in step with inflation, the consumer price index would have been only about 1 percent lower at the end of 1978 than it actually was.[2] Although it ignores secondary effects, this exercise strongly suggests that factors other than energy prices have had a dominant role in fueling inflation—at least until the surge in oil prices in 1979.[3]

1. Replacement cost may be either the cost of production or the scarcity cost— both costs are real. The often-heard argument that the oil price of the Organization of Petroleum Exporting Countries (OPEC) is not a "real" price because it is not based on the cost of producing oil and thus should be disregarded in domestic price policy ignores the nature of scarcity cost. Who captures the rent that forms part of that cost is an important matter, but the existence of that rent hardly makes the resulting price a phantom. Further, it does not matter whether that rent arises from true scarcity or from monopoly behavior. In either case the value of goods that importing countries must give up to import an additional barrel of oil is the same.

2. Sam H. Schurr and others, *Energy in America's Future: The Choices Before Us* (Johns Hopkins University Press for Resources for the Future, 1979), p. 447.

3. An examination of all the dynamics of the situation would have to include the cost of shifting to new technologies and the cost of new, more energy-efficient capital, which also generate higher labor productivity. These effects, partly triggered by higher energy prices, are here neglected.

In 1978 total raw energy expenditures in the United States were just over 6 percent of the gross national product. That percentage undoubtedly rose in 1979. Nonetheless, if real energy cost doubles in the next two decades the consequent direct effect on the general price level will not exceed 0.5 percent a year. There will also be indirect effects from the increase in nonenergy prices resulting from rising energy costs and from the probably higher wage settlements. But a reasonable guess is that energy costs will cause a rise in prices no greater than 1 percentage point annually.[4]

Thus while it is true that letting oil and gas prices catch up with world market prices will have a significant inflationary effect it is equally true that energy is merely one of the many forces that cause inflation. Given the advantages of restoring market prices for energy, the inflationary effect must be accepted. Since legislation now has set us on this course, it would be unwise to backslide. Offsetting policies should be sought elsewhere.

EQUITY. Assisting those hardest hit by energy prices is preferable to controlling prices and thus making energy cheap for everybody, poor or not. What little research has been done on the subject suggests that the share of energy purchases in total spending falls somewhat as income rises. This relation is pronounced for direct purchases of energy (gasoline, heat, electricity) but quite moderate when indirect purchases of energy (that is, energy incorporated in goods) are included.

The inclination of Congress has been to provide income supplements for easily identified needy consumers (supplemental social security and welfare recipients, low-income taxpayers, and so on), who are made needier by energy price increases. Income supplements are preferable to energy stamps or other measures that make energy available directly at low cost, for they preserve the right of recipients to choose where to save: on energy or on, say, food or medical

4. The price of oil nearly doubled between the beginning and the end of 1979. Thus the 0.5 to 1.0 percent increment a year may not look as "reasonable" as it did in 1978. Note that the assumption of doubling rather than the impact calculation is in question. For example, the Council of Economic Advisers in late 1979 estimated the inflationary impact of the near-doubling in oil prices to be 2.4 percentage points in 1979 and 3.1 percentage points in 1980, when the entire year will be affected. At a November 1979 conference sponsored by the Massachusetts Institute of Technology the inflationary effect of only the mid-1979 OPEC price boost was estimated at 1.1 and 2.8 percentage points for these years. If this price doubling (of oil only, to be sure) were spread over twenty years the annual effect would be small.

services. Negotiable energy stamps would also meet the choice criterion but would be more complex to administer.

Another distributional aspect of decontrol that stirs up controversy is the transfer of income from consumers to producers. The amounts involved, especially aggregated over ten years, are huge, but so is the gross national product. The potential transfers at their peak will be about $15 billion to $20 billion a year, depending on the price of OPEC oil and other factors. However, the net gain to oil companies will be substantially smaller once income taxes, state severance taxes, and royalties are deducted from gross accruals to oil companies. Additionally, one-third to one-half of the gain from controls on the prices producers pay never reached consumers but accrued to oil refiners. To that extent decontrol will cause smaller losses to consumers than those shown by calculations based on the assumption that the entire difference between controlled and decontrolled prices represents a transfer from consumers to producers. Nonetheless, several billion dollars annually will be transferred from users to producers of crude oil.

Congress has decided that some producer revenues resulting from decontrol should be taxed away by a special ad valorem excise levy, misnamed a windfall profits tax (which conveys the idea that this money is some kind of costless bonanza, thus making it more difficult for consumers to realize that the money taxed away comes from the higher prices they pay for decontrolled oil). Whether or not one endorses the underlying philosophy, there is much to be said for reassigning the income arising from lifting price controls from oil discovered and in production before 1973. Higher prices for this oil would not significantly increase supplies, and oil producers cannot claim to be treated unfairly because their investments were made in anticipation of much lower prices. The same arguments cannot be made with equal force for post-1973 oil, however, and certainly not for oil discovered and produced in the future. Indeed, taxing the revenues from newly discovered oil is bound to discourage investment in exploration not only for oil but also for gas, as potential investors will rightly wonder whether decontrol in 1985 will in fact be allowed to take place and, if so, will not be coupled with some kind of windfall profits tax. Also, as the entire system takes its cue from the OPEC price—and the difference between that price and the base price—the odds are high that the oil industry will continue to be semiregulated.

A task for the 1980s, then, is to decide what kind of oil industry the country wants: one approaching the status of a utility or one essentially free of government regulations other than those protecting safety, health, and the environment. Given the risks involved in oil exploration and development, with oftentimes large rewards for gamblers, the industry does not seem suited for becoming a utility, with a set profit rate and penalties for successful gambling. The alternative is a regime with a minimum of government regulation but with cost, price, and profit characteristics that remove it from the role of the villain in the energy story. A tax applicable principally to old oil and phased out with the depletion of such oil would serve this purpose, but an open-ended tax regime, embracing all oil, seems the more likely outcome of congressional activity.

To summarize, a move toward market pricing would increase demand and supply efficiencies (less would be demanded, more would be produced), eliminate the entitlement system with its subsidy to imported oil, and minimize the administrative costs and the burdens of regulation (and its evasion), both for government and for industry. There is no consensus on the efficiency gain to the economy from decontrol; for 1978 it has been estimated at between $2 billion and $5 billion a year and thus is smaller than the conjectured size of the income transfers from consumers to producers. But the balance is reversed when one considers nonquantifiable effects of controls: less aggressive exploration, less risk-taking, a preference for foreign investment, a slower pace of development, the use of costly technology (for example, tertiary oil recovery) and, most important, the diminished attractiveness to consumers of alternative, higher-priced sources of energy.

The Conservation Potential

Most alternatives to imported oil are supply substitutions requiring a long time to develop. The outstanding exception is increased efficiency or conservation, not as a solution in a crisis but as a continuing undertaking. Past success on that score has been poorly publicized. Energy consumption in 1972, the last full pre-embargo year, reached 62,063 British thermal units for each dollar of gross domestic product; by 1978 this measure was 56,613 BTUs, about 10 percent improvement in aggregate energy efficiency in six years (see table 4-2). Indeed, the 1978 level was the lowest ever in U.S. history, and pre-

Table 4-2. U.S. Energy Consumption and Gross Domestic Product, Selected Years, 1960–78

Year	Consumption (quadrillions of BTUs)	Gross domestic product (billions of 1972 dollars)	Consumption of BTUs per dollar of gross domestic product
1960	45.2	733.6	61,574
1965	53.8	919.9	58,481
1970	67.4	1,069.8	63,038
1971	69.0	1,100.3	62,705
1972	72.2	1,164.1	62,063
1973	75.1	1,227.4	61,192
1974	73.4	1,211.0	60,585
1975	71.3	1,197.5	59,530
1976	75.1	1,266.2	57,308
1977	77.2	1,332.9	57,913
1978	78.8	1,391.1	56,613

Source: Information provided by Jack Alterman, Resources for the Future.

liminary 1979 statistics show a continued decline, with economic growth up 2.3 percent and energy consumption up only 0.3 percent. To be sure, the ratio is a crude measuring instrument. A decline in the coefficient can reflect deliberate efforts at using less energy as well as the consequence of a great many other factors that shape the two aggregates. Moreover, the decline in energy use began in 1971. Nonetheless, the trend suggests what effect conservation can have: the equivalent of about 4 million barrels more oil a day would have been used in 1978 had the 1978 coefficient remained at the 1972 level.[5]

Without exaggeration, then, conservation was a "source" of energy during the 1970s. Analysts expect conservation to be a significant source in the future, also. Projections for U.S. energy demand in the year 2000, which ranged between 150 quadrillion and 175 quadrillion British thermal units a decade ago, now cluster around 110 quadrillion to 120 quadrillion. The two critical factors in the projections are the rate of economic growth and the level of energy intensity; a reduction in the level of intensity is believed possible, and capable of making an increasing contribution to saving.

5. This does not suggest that this saving was all or even mostly oil, though the obstacles to increased coal and nuclear production imply that the energy saved was mostly reflected in keeping oil imports below the level they would otherwise have reached.

A few years ago, it was generally believed that conservation is a one-time affair. Some obvious adjustments are made (the equivalent of tightening a few nuts and bolts) and then the upward trend of energy demand, based on population and income growth, resumes. By late 1979, few held that belief and they held it less firmly. A case in point is gasoline consumption. Automobile manufacturers met government-imposed fleet mileage standards on schedule, and at times exceeded them. Few now doubt that continued advances will enable producers to reach the 1985 standard of 27.5 miles a gallon average for new cars (as measured by the Environmental Protection Agency), about twice the average efficiency of all vehicles in 1973. Roughly speaking, by 1995 the 1985 *new-fleet* average will be the *total-fleet* average. This lends credence to a recent calculation that by the year 2000 a stock of automobiles about 40 percent larger than the present one, with each automobile driven about the same number of miles a year as now, will burn 30–50 percent less gasoline.[6] Similarly, making old homes and, more importantly, newly built ones more energy-efficient holds out the promise of less residential energy use by the end of the century.[7]

Efforts by industry to become more energy-efficient are driven by continuous cost calculations that take account of higher energy prices, whereas private users—individuals and families—lack the information and motivation for engaging in such calculations. They do not as a rule draw up profit and loss statements that help them guide their energy expenditures. Indeed, the diversity of decision-makers in the private, nonindustry, noncommercial, segment of the economy (that accounts for 40 percent of the nation's energy consumption) is the biggest single obstacle to greater conservation. The gap between potential and reasonably expectable energy savings is large. Thus, the most urgent task is to assist consumers in reaching that potential, first by having sellers provide more efficient equipment and buildings and second by motivating purchasers to acquire and use them efficiently.

Entrepreneurial inertia in providing energy-efficient buildings and equipment rests on the lack of incentive to do otherwise, at times

6. Schurr and others, *Energy in America's Future*, pp. 143–59.
7. This would occur despite a sizable increment in the housing stock. The slow turnover of the housing stock, however, sets a slower pace for savings than is true of motor vehicles.

reinforced by the disincentive of higher costs. And failure in this aspect of the task not only impairs the second aspect, consumer behavior, but downgrades the effectiveness of conservation. Thus, the fact that the choice of energy-efficient automobiles was once quite limited and that, therefore, the growth rate of gasoline consumption during 1973–78 slowed only a little has been incorrectly interpreted as proof of low gasoline-demand elasticity and has been used to deride the hope of reductions in consumption following higher prices.

Landowners, developers, individual builders, architects, lenders, landlords, tenants, utilities, and public agencies determine the form and efficiency of energy use in the home. Each has a specific, narrow objective, while none has the responsibility for building a truly energy-efficient structure. Multifamily dwellings lack individual metering and, as in overgrazing of common grasslands in medieval England, restraint is not matched by perceived benefit—and the result is excess use. Removing or at least weakening these obstacles calls for institutional pioneering in the coming decade.

Another important impediment is consumer ignorance of technical matters. It is necessary, for example, that consumers know that continuous operation of a heating or cooling system is under most conditions less energy-efficient than cycling and that gasoline can be saved by cutting off the engine if idling time will exceed half a minute or so. The real and perceived difficulties in the maintenance and costs of energy-efficient facilities can be alleviated through consumer education.

Thinking "energy efficiency" is new to this country. Energy conservation is in its infancy and needs an initial impetus, somewhat akin to the situation many decades ago when infant industries were believed to need tariff protection. (In both instances, of course, the principle can be abused.) The following are ways in which the potential for conservation in the years ahead can best be exploited:

1. Information should be provided to illuminate the murky areas described above: product information, technical knowledge, and cost data, among others. Consumer behavior in the face of high and rising energy prices must be understood so that policy takes it into account. Institutional impediments need to be defined and ways found to overcome them at least cost. (Is the cost of individual metering in multifamily dwellings worth the resulting savings? If not, are there other ways of motivating apartment dwellers?)

Table 4-3. U.S. Automobile Efficiency, Selected Years, 1967–78

Year	Average fuel consumed per car (gallons)	Average miles traveled per car	Average miles per gallon
1967	684	9,531	13.93
1970	735	9,978	13.57
1973	763	9,992	13.10
1974	704	9,448	13.43
1975	712	9,634	13.53
1976	711	9,763	13.72
1977	706	9,839	13.94
1978	715	10,046	14.06

Source: U.S. Department of Energy, *Monthly Energy Review* (December 1979), p. 19.

2. The role of legal standards needs to be assessed so that hostility to regulation does not kill useful initiatives. In that respect, the implications of government-imposed automobile mileage standards should be carefully considered. Pending acquisition of more knowledge about demand elasticities, this particular regulation is probably a good second-best, moving us in the right direction. Its essential merits are that it reversed a trend to progressively fewer miles per gallon (see table 4-3) and fostered reconsideration of the value to consumers of such energy-using accessories as air conditioning.[8]

3. Building regulations deserve greater attention. Reforms to save on fuel have been introduced in a number of states and in late 1979 were the subject of a major federal initiative.[9] Caution is, however, indicated, lest we get entangled in another bureaucratic net. Above all, regulations should stress the end result, that is, performance, not the technical specifications for getting there. For example, taxes levied on energy consumption above a set standard—adjusted for location and perhaps certain other factors—are better than detailed prescriptions for thickness of foundation, number and size of windows, and kind of attic insulation.

4. There is a place for subsidies in support of home-fuel conservation. (The first session of the Ninety-sixth Congress enacted several.) They are hard to justify on strict economic grounds since over a number of years the energy savings pay for the initial investment.

8. Between 1960 and 1972, for example, the number of automobiles leaving U.S. assembly lines with built-in air conditioners rose from 6.9 percent to 68.6 percent.
9. The federal proposals, known as Building Energy Performance Standards, are designed to achieve this objective, but the crucial ingredient will be acceptable ways of enforcing them.

But there are counterconsiderations. First, there are social benefits, such as lessening the adverse effects on the environment and reducing the hazards and insecurity of importing oil. Second, while most conservation investments are self-liquidating, they typically require substantial initial outlays and if the payoff period is long and a resale market does not develop to reflect them adequately, the homeowner may refrain from making these improvements. This is especially important in light of the fact that Americans change residence about every five years, on the average. Finally, as long as fuel costs are subsidized directly and indirectly, there is something to be said for subsidizing conservation, too. Subsidies should, however, be cost-effective and favor long-run, durable installations.

5. A higher tax on gasoline has reappeared in the public debate as a method of reducing consumption, largely as a consequence of rising political instability in the Middle East. As the debate develops, two striking facts are worth keeping in mind. First, gasoline taxes in this country have risen only slightly in the past two decades and thus have been cut by more than half in real terms. The federal tax has been at 4 cents a gallon since 1960, while the average state tax has risen only 1.5 cents, from 6.5 to 8 cents. Second, gasoline taxes abroad have always been much higher than U.S. taxes, and they have been increasing steadily. In 1979, the tax on a gallon of gasoline was $1.59 in France, $0.88 in the United Kingdom, $1.14 in Germany, and $1.58 in Italy. A minimum objective for the United States is to raise the tax enough to offset inflation since 1960. That by itself would add about 15 cents to the current tax; an increase later would then be less formidable.

6. Decontrolled prices will encourage efficient energy practices. It is remarkable that the moderate increase in real costs to the final consumer since 1973 has already slowed the increase in energy consumption. Rising energy prices in the future should give added momentum to conservation.

7. Rationing is a short-term, crisis-oriented palliative. Particularly focused on quick imposition, it is badly needed for coping with sudden, drastic interruptions anticipated to be of short duration; but for reducing demand for an indefinite period it is either too blunt or too complex. Rationing of gasoline—the most likely candidate— by any rigidly structured system is no less unfair than gasoline rationing by price, although it affects a different group of users; and if,

as is desirable, ration coupons can be sold, ability to purchase will again be a major determinant of who gets the gasoline. Divisiveness, bickering, lobbying, cheating, and enforcement problems can all be tolerated in short-term emergencies but not for the long run. All this is apart from the important fact that the price incentive to efficiency in both consumption and production would be lost.

Utility Rate Reform

There is a growing consensus among analysts on the merits of marginal cost pricing for utilities, but there is uncertainty regarding the disposition of the large amounts of revenue that would thus accrue to the utilities.[10] One attraction of marginal cost pricing is that it would encourage consumers to install and use energy-efficient equipment. Another is that, if at the price required to cover the cost of a high-cost source people will not buy it, then the demand is not there and it should not be produced. If a high-cost source cannot have its cost averaged (rolled in) with a lower-cost source, high-cost sources will not emerge prematurely.[11]

Various rebating systems that do not vitiate the energy-saving effect have been suggested to redistribute excess utility revenues. These schemes tend to be complicated, but it is becoming hard to argue that the energy-saving is not more important than the difficulties of redistributing revenue. Studies now under way should be vigorously pursued so that additional pilot systems can be tried before a massive modification of the rate structure is attempted.[12]

Rate reform is only one of the changes that face the public utilities. Another is capturing the potential electricity outside the utility grid and introducing it into the general supply stream.[13] The opportunities

---

10. For a more extensive discussion of utility pricing see *Energy: The Next Twenty Years,* Report by a study group sponsored by the Ford Foundation and administered by Resources for the Future; Hans H. Landsberg, chairman (Ballinger, 1979), chap. 3; and Philip Mause, "Price Regulation and Energy Policy," *Selected Studies on Energy: Background Papers for Energy the Next Twenty Years* (Ballinger, forthcoming).

11. By the same token, by subsidizing high-cost sources, rolling in is an obstacle to the introduction outside the utility system of perhaps cheaper technologies such as solar energy.

12. Moreover, these problems need to be viewed in the context of the utility issues discussed under "Coal" below.

13. The catchphrase for this is "cogeneration." The term itself is neutral; it denotes merely the simultaneous production of both heat and electricity, with each being commercially utilized, thus spreading costs over more services. Cogeneration

for increasing energy supply in this way are substantial and should be vigorously exploited.

Summary

The demand-side agenda is pretty clear. Its rationale is the urgent need to reduce energy consumption and especially oil imports. Its objective is to move rapidly toward greater efficiency in energy use, potentially the largest "source" of energy in the eighties. Its elements are market prices for fuel; marginal cost pricing in regulated uses; consumer information and education; modification of established practices so as to provide incentives (for example, in housing); regulation where ingrained habits are especially slow to yield to market incentives or where conditions are not conducive to close cost calculations; cogeneration to utilize energy sources more fully and reduce their cost to the user. The principal obstacles are the vast numbers and variety of decisionmakers; the inflationary effect of decontrolled rising prices; social and political conflict over allocation of economic rent from rising prices; and the unequal impact of higher prices, especially but not solely on low-income groups. On the last point, it is no exaggeration to argue that any redress of income inequalities would remove a major obstacle to managing the energy problem, much superior to many highly touted technical solutions to the energy problem.

Supply Outlook and Strategies

In the short run, demand reduction is probably the most promising method of balancing demand for energy with prospective supplies, but conservation can only "supply" so much energy. Over the long run, supply must be enhanced, not only to replace energy from present sources but to provide additional energy to support a growing economy and a growing population. Perhaps the most important question Americans must decide soon is whether, to what extent, and on what terms to use conventional sources of energy—nuclear, oil and gas, and coal—until more acceptable and benign permanent sources become available. The problem has different dimensions for the different sources.

---

may use waste heat from power generation for space heating, or generate electricity from the waste heat in industrial operations, or merely feed into utility grids non-utility electricity in excess of industrial requirements.

Nuclear Energy

Decision time is closest in nuclear energy. With increased erosion of public support since the Three Mile Island accident in March 1979, the demise of the U.S. nuclear power industry has become a distinct possibility, not by shutting down existing reactors but by stopping all further construction. Whether implementation of reforms such as those suggested by the presidential commission investigating the accident (the Kemeny Commission) could reverse the increased hostility to nuclear power is largely up to the electric utility industry. If it judges the demanding regulations as too burdensome, the added public involvement as too unattractive, and the financial risk in case of accidents as too high, it will simply stop ordering reactors. No referendum and no congressional vote would be needed to shut the industry down. Indeed, it would take positive action by Congress to keep the industry alive. Such a move is probably feasible only by shifting to the public a large part of the financial and other risks—an unlikely possibility barring a radical change in public opinion.

Public acceptance of nuclear energy—and, therefore, the willingness of utility companies to continue to invest in nuclear power—can be influenced by education on the feasibility of living with the atom. For that reason the early 1980s is the time for decision. At least five areas call for action: operating practice, waste management, breeder development, international cooperation and safeguards, and resource management.

OPERATING PRACTICE. The Kemeny Commission in late 1979 presented a large agenda. It will take time to discuss, digest, and institute the suggested reforms. Rather than adding to them one can suggest priorities: (1) improved training and higher levels of skill for those monitoring operations; (2) greatly increased government supervision of personnel competence; (3) specific roles for utility companies and local, state, and federal government authorities in emergency procedures; and (4) rapid and effective communication with all interested parties about experiences with any one reactor.

Reactor operating practices will no doubt greatly improve. But no matter how assiduously improved safety is pursued, the public may not be reassured and, as mentioned above, the industry may abandon what it considers a troublesome technology. To be sure, for some companies nuclear facilities are so large a part of their capacity that they will find it no cheaper to extricate themselves than to continue, but others are even now considering abandonment. Orders for plants are at a standstill, raising the question of the viability of nuclear equipment manufacturers once their backlog of orders is worked off. The Three Mile Island incident demonstrated the poor state of preparation and coordination for protecting the public in the event of a serious accident. Remedies must be practical and put into effect rapidly.

While deviations from routine functioning of reactors are regularly reported to the Nuclear Regulatory Commission there is doubt whether (a) questions raised outside this network receive adequate recognition and (b) the information collected by the federal government percolates to the government layers below, to industrial operators, to utility companies, and to equipment manufacturers. Means must be devised to remedy these omissions.

As mentioned before, the nuclear industry can be killed off by overattention to small irregularities as much as by a serious accident. Fear of accidents, of being accused of neglect, and of the financial burden could lead to the shutdown of reactors at the slightest hint of trouble. In fashioning better safeguards and especially in determining the federal role, this should be kept in mind.

The Three Mile Island accident also drew renewed attention to the siting of nuclear reactors. Reevaluation of the location of a number of early nuclear power plants close to large, densely populated centers will be difficult to avoid. Debate on future location of nuclear plants must also consider the possibility of limiting the number of sites and utilizing them for clusters of plants. Despite drawbacks, the use of "power parks" would decrease the number of battles over sites.

WASTE MANAGEMENT. Until the Three Mile Island accident, waste management was the biggest bone of contention in the nuclear area. Plagued by a history of neglect, promises of easy management, false starts, postponements, and the prospect of inadequate temporary storage space, the nuclear waste management program continues to flounder. Yet, it need not be so, for there is broad agreement, even among some critics of nuclear energy, that there are no insurmountable technological problems.

At the probable future size of nuclear energy in the United States —perhaps no more than 150,000 megawatts by the end of the century—the accumulation of waste material is slow enough that for some time to come a modest expansion of temporary holding facilities, at nuclear sites first and away from reactors later, will do. Thus, there is time to determine (1) whether geologic environments other than salt are suitable sites for waste, and what they will cost; (2) the advantages and drawbacks of disposing of entire fuel elements instead of reprocessed, separated components; (3) ways to retrieve waste material; (4) the length of time it takes for radioactive material to escape from deep burial sites, the paths it takes, and the possible barriers to escape; and (5) the effect of escape under various assumptions.

The federal role in waste disposal urgently needs to be determined to cope with state prohibitions against waste disposal sites. Monetary incentives may be the answer. State moratorium referenda frequently specify that safe disposal must be "demonstrated." How is this to be done? When half-lives of some fission products are in the tens of thousands if not hundreds of thousands of years, state governments and public opinion must accept computer or laboratory calculations and stipulated permanent solutions that are widely perceived as tolerably safe. Any demand beyond this stamps the requirement of demonstrated safe disposal as a disguised call for terminating the nuclear energy program; absolute safety is an illusion and produces an unproductive stalemate.

THE BREEDER. Nuclear energy is attractive over the long run because of the nuclear breeder. For all practical purposes the breeder will be free of resource limitations, raising the efficiency of a unit of uranium fifty or more times over its efficiency in a nonbreeder (or burner). Indeed, if it were not for the breeder, the conventional nuclear reactor would be only a brief transition to other energy sources, significantly affecting the energy industry only half a century or so.

Given coal's adverse effects on human health and the natural environment and the political risks of large oil imports, the nuclear breeder is the best supply alternative unless more attractive energy sources materialize in the next ten or fifteen years. Yet, opposition to the breeder is even stronger than to conventional reactors. It focuses on the breeder's use of plutonium or highly enriched uranium.

There is no denying that the production, transportation, trade, and use of plutonium carry the danger of abuse, that is, the building of weapons or other nuclear explosive devices by national governments or terrorist groups. On the other hand, numerous technical and institutional proposals have been made to reduce the hazard to a tolerably low level. The most urgent task therefore is to allow breeder *research* to continue until either acceptable ways of handling the risks are found or it is clear that efforts must be abandoned. That judgment will be rendered in the coming decade.

To fight the battle over breeder *deployment* now simply worsens the outlook for nuclear energy generally. The federal government must make it clear that a sharp line separates research and development from deployment—that is, a commitment to research carries no prior or implied commitment to deploy a technologically proven breeder. A statement to that effect will probably assure support for needed research as well as for the examination of foreign breeders for eventual licensing in the United States. Indeed, U.S. research could benefit from foreign research and development, which continues undisturbed by misgivings in this country, and could in turn influence such research. The U.S. research and development program should embrace broad technological alternatives, should be specific in the objectives that a breeder must meet, and should be clear in what is to be demonstrated in any hardware short of a commercial-sized facility. Moreover, all nuclear research and development in the next few years must emphasize technical, locational, and institutional-political resistance to the proliferation of radioactive materials that can be used in weapons or other explosive devices.

INTERNATIONAL COOPERATION AND SAFEGUARDS. Nuclear development is an international issue. A reactor that goes wrong anywhere affects nuclear operations and development everywhere. A serious accident can jeopardize all life. However, different countries evaluate nuclear energy differently. Those poor in fossil fuels tend to look at nuclear energy, and specifically at reprocessing, recycling, and above all the breeder, as their means of liberation from imports and resource dependence, though they too recognize the possibility of abuse through weapons production.

The U.S. policy of denying resources and technology to other countries was designed to dissuade these nations from reprocessing, recycling, and enriching nuclear materials. That strategy, while producing a useful pause, has been sufficiently unsuccessful in changing other countries' minds to suggest that policy be directed toward positive incentives. One possibility is to open U.S. nuclear waste sites to other nations or to construct internationally managed sites. Another is to establish nuclear fuel banks—uranium inventories with specified terms of access in case of supply interruption—thus deemphasizing uranium supply as a policy tool.

For such a policy to be taken seriously, the handling of domestic waste must be realistic. Foreign nations observing the snail's pace of progress in this country are bound to look skeptically at any U.S. offer to play host to their waste. Even if this specific issue is resolved, friction between the United States and some of its allies will persist until the United States ceases to make decisions unilaterally and to act unpredictably. An early opportunity for changing course is the completion of the International Nuclear Fuel Cycle Evaluation program, scheduled for February 1980. This is a review of the technical and institutional alternatives in nuclear power, with special attention to nonproliferation. About fifty countries are participating. A second opportunity is the July 1980 review of the 1968 Treaty on the Nonproliferation of Nuclear Weapons.

URANIUM RESOURCES. While the nuclear outlook is bearish, other energy sources are so uncertain that a reversal in the fortunes of nuclear energy cannot be categorically excluded. In that event, the nation would be well-served by answers to fairly elementary resource and supply questions. With the declining possibility of strong nuclear growth and the real price of uranium falling, some uranium producers are finding it difficult to sell their ore at a price at which in the spring of 1977 it was eagerly bought. Nonetheless, the government's effort to improve knowledge of the country's uranium resource should be encouraged. Particularly important are firmer estimates of potential resources whose cost and other characteristics make them likely to become producible soon. Related questions concern manpower availability, lead time for new facilities, and environmental constraints.

PUBLIC CONFIDENCE. Whatever the specifics—and they are bound to change during the decade—it is useful to keep in mind when setting priorities that the attitude toward nuclear energy of much of the American public is uneasy or hostile. Attempts to gain public acceptance must be (a) credible, largely by being wholly frank, and (b) realistic about specific goals and the time it will take to achieve them. Downplaying the risks ("nuclear energy is safer than any other energy source"), setting unrealistic goals only to have to postpone them, and being reluctant to admit mishaps, will only further erode public confidence. At the same time, those informing the public must present nuclear hazards in the context of the adverse effects of competing energy sources, so that the question, "If not nuclear, then what?" is never far from the core of the energy debate. When quantification is feasible and convincingly demonstrable, it should be undertaken. When it is not, qualitative judgments are less compromising than poorly supportable quantifications that are miles apart; these merely produce cynicism about quantification generally.

Crude Oil and Natural Gas

Two questions dominate the discussion of supply of oil and gas: (1) How much conventional crude oil and natural gas is in the ground? (2) What are the magnitudes and the characteristics of liquid and gaseous energy that are now marginal but that might be feasible resources as costs of conventional fuels continue to climb?

CONVENTIONAL SOURCES. More and more, informed opinion holds that domestic crude oil and natural gas are irreversibly depleting. Domestic output began to fall in 1970 for oil and in 1974 for gas. Higher prices can temporarily slow the decline by making risky exploration, tertiary recovery, and the drilling of small fields worthwhile; by shifting some exploration from foreign areas (like the North Sea) to domestic areas; and by bringing known and operating deposits into production sooner. These moves are likely to slow the decline but not to reverse it. Despite the large amount of money that major oil companies have invested in new offshore areas, their experience has on the whole been disappointing.

Abroad, the situation is less clear. How many more North Seas or Mexicos will there be? How serious are the resource and supply limitations in the Soviet Union and how soon will their effect be felt? Happy surprises cannot be categorically excluded. However, what would have been a very large discovery fifteen years ago when world crude production was about 30 million barrels a day would not be so viewed today, with production about twice that amount. Annual world production is now 22 billion barrels; even a giant new field capable of producing 10 billion barrels, or one-third of U.S. reserves, would be only a modest addition. Alaska, hailed in the mid-sixties as ushering in a new era in U.S. petroleum history, now contributes less than 10 percent of U.S. oil supplies. Moreover, one recent study makes a convincing case that the odds are against discovering giant fields.[14] Realistically, the most that can be expected is that new discoveries will be large enough for a while to offset depletion.[15]

MARGINAL SOURCES. Of the nonconventional naturally occurring oil and gas resources, some have long been known and routinely utilized on a small scale while others have attracted attention only recently. Liquid fuel is derived from oil shale, tar sands, and bituminous sands, and occurs as heavy crude. Gaseous fuels are natural gas in tight sand formations, in coal seams, in geopressured brines, and in Devonian shale. The quantities of these fuels are many times the estimated reserves of crude oil and conventional natural gas.

The location, dimensions, and characteristics of tar sands, heavy crude oil, and oil shale are well-known. Oil has been extracted for a number of years from tar sands, mostly in Canada, and thus the technologies, costs of production, and characteristics of the end product are known. The same is true of heavy crude oil, though there is less experience in environmental impact, such as results of steam injection, and in production technology, which is still costly for some very viscous types, such as those from the region of the Orinoco River in Venezuela. As for oil shale, there is need for considerable experimentation to learn how to dispose of nonoil residual material and how to preserve clean water. Experience suggests that development of oil shale facilities could easily become a battleground, unless environmental issues are resolved soon.

Data are in shorter supply regarding gaseous hydrocarbons. The extent of occurrence, the methods of production, and the magnitude of likely supplies are all uncertain. There has been sporadic, com-

14. Richard Nehring, *Giant Oil Fields and World Oil Resources* (Rand Corp., June 1978).

15. For the world as a whole, there are several questions for which the 1980s must find the answers. First, are we seeing the final, irreversible downward slope of the production curve? Can supplies therefore be increased only by producing them faster? If so, is a raise in prices the best method? And what are the costs? Second, industry has not recovered a significant amount of fuel from the oil left in the ground after production by conventional means of recovery. Is the payoff insufficient or are the reasons technological and institutional? In the United States alone the remaining oil is about 300 billion barrels. In light of the past record, this figure is a very misleading indicator of what we can realistically expect to recover; at the same time it is a spur to increased application of known technologies and to research on new technologies. Third, what areas have been inadequately explored and why—lack of prospects of discovering oil or lack of capital and attractive institutional arrangements? Special efforts to test theories of large oil-bearing formations in these areas should shed light on the matter.

mercially sponsored activity in drilling, but cost estimates are only approximate and are subject to rapid obsolescence. Yet estimated resources in this country alone are massive.

The obvious alternative to supplies from these marginal hydrocarbon resources is conversion of coal to both gas and liquid form. However, as described below, coal conversion will not be quick, cheap, and easy, and thus rapid acquisition of information on marginal sources is urgent. Given the stakes, government will have to play a major role and act without delay. The Carter program of July 1979 included a funding proposal for nonconventional hydrocarbons, but coal conversion has so far greatly overshadowed them.[16] A more balanced effort is needed, assigning greater urgency to the advancement of knowledge and the exploitation of these marginal resources.

Coal

The clouded outlook for alternative energy sources highlights the role of coal, an abundant resource in this country and in many other parts of the world. Coal could provide energy far into the next century and beyond, until energy from the sun, the nuclear breeder, nuclear fusion, biomass, or other sources is technologically satisfactory and can be made available at affordable costs.

A flourishing coal industry in the United States, producing perhaps twice the present tonnage by late in this century, will not come about simply because prices are rising. Government policy and behavior deeply affect both coal supply and coal demand. However, supply issues either do not involve especially high costs (for example, strip mine regulations) or do not pose especially novel problems (for example, transportation and community development). A variety of means are available to reduce these problems, including fiscal incentives, grants, loans, and training programs. This is much less true on the demand side. Improvements in technology are needed to encourage users, especially small firms, to use coal, and new ways to regulate air pollution are required to provide incentives for coal users to reduce emissions which pollute the air without discouraging their use of coal.

LAGGING DEMAND. For many reasons the use of coal worldwide in the 1970s lagged (table 4-4). Energy growth as a whole was much

16. Shale oil is included in the federal government's synthetic fuel program and thus shares the limelight with coal conversion ventures.

Table 4-4. Energy Consumption, by Source, Selected Countries, 1960, 1973, and 1977

Country and source	Consumption (millions of tons of oil equivalent)			Share of total (percent)		
	1960	1973	1977	1960	1973	1977
United States						
Petroleum	453	788	866	45	45	48
Natural gas	294	543	459	29	31	25
Solid fuels	230	326	353	23	19	20
Nuclear	. . .	21	64	. . .	1	4
Hydroelectric and other	37	66	56	3	4	3
Japan						
Petroleum	30	255	257	31	75	74
Natural gas	1	5	12	1	2	3
Solid fuels	50	57	55	53	17	16
Nuclear	. . .	2	7	. . .	1	2
Hydroelectric and other	14	18	19	15	5	5
France						
Petroleum	27	125	106	30	68	60
Natural gas	2	14	18	2	7	10
Solid fuels	47	31	32	52	17	18
Nuclear	. . .	3	4	. . .	2	2
Hydroelectric and other	14	11	18	16	6	10
West Germany						
Petroleum	31	148	139	21	56	53
Natural gas	1	28	39	1	10	15
Solid fuels	110	84	71	75	32	27
Nuclear	. . .	3	9	. . .	1	3
Hydroelectric and other	4	3	4	3	1	2
United Kingdom						
Petroleum	44	111	93	25	50	44
Natural gas	. . .	26	36	. . .	12	17
Solid fuels	124	79	72	73	35	34
Nuclear	1	7	10	1	3	5
Hydroelectric and other	1	1	1	1	*	*

Sources: Calculated from data in International Energy Agency, *Energy Balances of OECD Countries, 1975–1977* (Paris: OECD, 1979); ibid., *1973–1975* (Paris: OECD, 1977); and ibid., *1960–1974* (Paris: OECD, 1976).
*Less than 1 percent.

slower than anticipated, and the growth of coal's principal customer —the electric utilities—also slowed (in the United States the 7 percent annual growth in electricity use that prevailed for so long dropped to 5.4 percent from 1970 to 1979 and was only 3.5 percent in 1973–79). Utilities resist government programs designed to make them switch from oil and gas to coal, largely to avoid the cost and inconvenience of meeting clean air standards and the uncertainty regarding requirements, standards, timing, and implementation. Moreover, the fuel adjustment clause allowing utilities to pass on increased fuel costs to the customers reduces the incentive to move to a less expensive fuel. Not surprisingly, the electric power industry has attempted to make air standards less stringent and to postpone the dates when they must be met.

Sudden changes in federal policies have not helped to boost demand for coal. For example, the use of natural gas was discouraged following the natural gas shortages of 1976 and 1977, but in 1979 Washington exhorted the industry to switch back to gas. Finally, the utilities have been plagued by excess generating capacity and have not found it easy to raise capital in the face of continuing uncertainties. Nor have coal strikes helped the image of the coal industry as a reliable supplier.

Other industrial countries have had similar experiences. Most members of the Organization for Economic Cooperation and Development had planned to rely more heavily on coal, supplied partly by West Germany and the United Kingdom and partly by Eastern Europe, the United States, South Africa, and Australia. But like the United States, most countries continued to rely on oil and gas (see table 4-4). In the densely populated countries, hostility to coal on environmental grounds is pronounced; in Japan, the installations required for greater use of coal—ports, storage, and transportation— are inadequate and will be hard to acquire. Coal conversion involves high costs everywhere, and, for whatever purpose coal is used, few wish to exchange dependence on a few oil exporters for dependence on a few coal exporters, with the United States frequently singled out as an unreliable source whose domestic needs and policies are apt to override export commitments.

If utilities have been slow to switch to coal, manufacturing industries have been even slower. The major impediments are location, process requirements, costs of changeover, nonavailability of equipment for small-scale operations, and lack of sites for coal storage and ash and sludge disposal. Such problems were given little attention in the early stages of the post-1973 planning for energy use. Their neglect helps explain the great gap between potential and reality and underlies the urgent need to catch up, technologically, institutionally, and economically.

AIR POLLUTION: A MAJOR CONSTRAINT. Coal-caused air pollution and the regulatory regime associated with its reduction remains a severe obstacle to greater use of coal. It has been a highly controversial subject ever since the revision of the Clean Air Act in 1970. Ambient air quality standards were established listing maximum amounts of the major pollutants (sulfur oxide, nitrogen oxide, particulates, carbon monoxide) and dates were set for achieving these standards everywhere. Subsequent modifications in the law tightened the standards, setting different goals for different regions depending on the degree to which they fall short of or exceed the standard. In addition, a ruling requires all emitters to adopt the best available controls.

Most economists argue for replacing air standards with monetary charges for emissions, giving the coal users an incentive to introduce the most effective antipollution techniques. The usual argument against this proposal is that charges are no more easily set than standards. This may well be true; but the great advantage of charges is that the emitters are given the flexibility to meet the standards by any legal method—using new technology, modifying their processes, or changing their product, the raw material, or the location of their plant.[17]

Federal policy recently began to move in this direction. For example, experiments are being conducted in the use of offset provisions, under which emitters identify existing pollution sources and buy offsetting emission reductions; and the "bubble" concept, which allows some emissions from closely associated sources to exceed the limit as long as aggregate emissions meet the standards. These experiments could lead to major revisions in the philosophy and techniques of air pollution regulation and to significant savings throughout the economy.

17. A recent study puts the advantages of market devices clearly and tersely: "In applying market devices to air pollution control, their fundamental advantage should be kept in mind, so that it is not lost in the details of implementation. Market devices allow the processes of government to concentrate on 'external' matters that only they can handle—such as determining where emissions come from, where they go, what harm they do, and how much it is worth to society to reduce them. Individual emitters are given the incentive and the opportunity to evaluate and respond to the 'internal' technological and economic details that each can best deal with individually. This is a natural and efficient division of responsibility of the type that is essential for successful management of any complex and dynamic system, whether a modern corporation or an economy. To the extent that market devices of various kinds can effect this kind of division, they can help solve difficult environmental management problems." *Energy: The Next Twenty Years*, p. 390.

At least three priorities emerge from these considerations. First, effort must be redoubled to understand the relation between emissions and health and the environment, not to buttress legislated standards but to improve policy through better information. Second, Congress has in the past legislated as though environmental goals were absolutes, capable of being cast into targets and standards set by the executive branch on a scientific basis: at a certain number we were presumed "safe," at another we were in peril. In the light of the new information and the rising uncertainty about the sequences and agents of pollution and the relation of costs to results, it is time for Congress to examine the philosophy and strategy behind air pollution control. Congress should be forthright in stating the cost that is justified to avoid or remedy pollution effects. In the past this judgment was considered a technical one made implicitly by the administration in setting standards. Far from being only technical and administrative, this judgment is most importantly political and social. Third, the invention of market devices, including marketable emission rights, charges, and so on, should be forcefully pursued. Both energy and environmental objectives are likely to benefit. The argument that such approaches are tantamount to a "right to pollute" equally applies to any regulatory system with standards above zero pollution. The difference is that in the latter instance, the right to pollute is accorded free; in the former it is paid for and goes to those willing and able to pay.

A special issue within the air pollution area is the easing of coal into industrial facilities not using it now, and especially into smaller-sized plants. Coal-burning technology that reduces noxious emissions and can be profitably operated on a small scale exists in the form of small gasifiers and fluidized-bed combustion. Because oil would be replaced, the introduction of such equipment into industry is a high priority for the 1980s and justifies government assistance not only in research and development but also in facilitating acquisition and installation of the equipment. High cost of acquisition and waiting until day-to-day reliability has been established are major retarding factors. Loan guarantees and perhaps tax rebates are no less justified here than for energy conservation investment. It is estimated that by the end of the century up to 400 million tons of coal could be substituted for industrially burned oil and gas. In assessing this figure it is useful to remember that this much coal is equal to about 4.5 million barrels a day of oil, or only about one-fourth of current U.S. oil consumption. Thus a quick and substantial dent in the oil market through coal substitution in industry is not in the cards.

OBSTACLES TO SUPPLY. The list of obstacles to increasing the supply of coal is long, but their characteristics are not novel. Most predate the events of 1973–74, and while failure to make progress on any one of them will retard the increase in coal use, none is as critical as are those discussed above.

Environmentally motivated regulations on strip mining and water quality are complex. There is concern about the problems arising from sudden, substantial population growth in heretofore sparsely settled locations, often with no expectation of permanence (the boomtown). Transportation poses problems: some eastern railroads are run-down; some western railroads need more trackage and rolling stock; some major hauling roads that would have to carry greatly increased coal tonnage are in poor condition; and coal slurry pipelines have failed to develop because of opposition by the railroads and by some western state and environmental interests that do not favor coal mining west of the Mississippi or that oppose the use of water as the carrier in such lines.

There is considerable opposition based on environmental grounds to leasing federally owned coal land, most of it west of the Mississippi. Whether the prospect of much greater government involvement in the plans and operations of mines on newly leased federal land will retard their development remains to be seen.

Finally, workers in the eastern coal mines are mostly very old and very young; few are in their middle years. This unusual age pattern, which has resulted in lack of good supervisory personnel, further aggravates sagging productivity.

Two aspects of coal remain to be discussed. Coal conversion is taken up in the next section. The other is increased carbon dioxide in the atmosphere, which could drastically change the global climate. A ten-year perspective need not focus on the event itself but on improving our understanding of the problem. The carbon dioxide syndrome is a potentially powerful impediment to the use of fossil fuels, especially coal, worldwide. It thus deserves continuing and methodical attention. Responsibility for research must be firmly lodged in a government unit with links to policymaking bodies so that the problem is not shrugged off as a scientific curiosity. Publication of the periodic Status Report, issued by the Department of Energy's Carbon Dioxide and Climate Research Program, is a step in the right direction.

Selected New Technologies and Sources

Many are looking to new energy sources and technologies to help supply the nation's future energy needs. Most of these new sources and technologies are reasonably well-known. The great unknowns are how quickly they can be expected to provide significant amounts of energy and at what cost. Discussion here is confined to a few that figure prominently in the public debate but not always with adequate information or perspective.

Coal Conversion

High on the list of possible substitutes for oil—at least in the United States because of its rich resource endowment—is coal conversion. Germany converted coal to liquid fuel during the Second World War and South Africa is producing liquid fuel this way now, but on a small scale in each case.[18] In July 1979 President Carter recommended a program widely considered overambitious; though the program is still under discussion, the chances are that Congress will substantially reduce it.

The dimensions of coal conversion are awesome. A plant producing 50,000 barrels of oil a day—about the size one would wish to establish—would require a daily coal supply of 15,000 to 25,000 tons, the total output of a coal mine with an annual capacity of 5 million to 8 million tons. It would occupy about a square mile of land, employ 4,000 people, and its equipment would operate at high temperatures and pressure. An industry that would supply, say, 10 percent of current U.S. liquid fuel consumption, that is, roughly 1.8 million barrels a day, would call for thirty-six plants of such size. These would consume 270 million tons of coal annually from some forty new, very large surface mines or sixty to eighty very large underground coal mines. Total resources of the coal land supporting this output would be in the neighborhood of 8 billion tons. To put such numbers in context, a 50,000-barrel-a-day plant would consume about two to three times as much coal as the largest U.S. coal-burning electric power plant now in operation. Cost estimates for a single plant range from $1.5 billion to $3 billion, but such estimates must be regarded with caution because plants of this size have never been

18. The entire German wartime capacity hardly exceeded 100,000 barrels a day. In late 1979, South Africa's capacity was less than 20,000 barrels a day, but additional capacity is under construction.

built. A capacity of 1.8 million barrels a day would thus cost between $50 billion and $100 billion, not counting investment in associated facilities in coal mining, transportation, and engineering.

This is a very large, capital-intensive undertaking. Consequently, capacity should be built up in steps, with the intent to learn from experience so that the technologies will not be locked in prematurely. As of late 1979, Congress appeared to be favoring this route, with a moderate but still ambitious first five-year plan limited to a few plants using various technologies. Barring contrary legislation in 1980, new decisions are not due until the middle of the decade, by which time the first plants should have provided the information to permit policy decisions on the second phase, building a large synthetic fuel industry. Information is needed on costs, costs of competitive fuels, environmental impact, and difficulties in site selection (until early 1980, when all federal permits had been secured for a new oil refinery on the Chesapeake Bay, no new site had been agreed to in this country for ten years even for such a conventional enterprise). Of course, radically higher oil prices may have changed the market enough by then that industry will act without significant government initiative. As the program unfolds, the elements that merit assessment are (1) the relative importance of this enterprise versus other means of relieving the supply-demand pinch;[19] (2) the environmental problems and the means of resolving them, especially the handling of solid waste; and (3) the comparative advantage of western and eastern coal.

Shale Oil

The major problem in extracting oil from shale in significant quantities is environmental. The technology of mining the shale and then retorting ("cooking") it above ground is well-established—it has been commercially used on a small scale in other parts of the world. Tearing up the land and disposing of the huge quantities of residual material is the principal problem; the material itself is a nuisance and its potential for polluting water adds to its unattractiveness. Production in place is being tried experimentally; by breaking up the rock, heating it, and thus coaxing the oil out without mining, residual material is not generated.

The second objection to the creation of a sizable industry is that it

19. This feature argues strongly against attempts to isolate the synthetic fuel program through special institutions or dedicated tax revenues.

would disturb community life in sparsely settled areas, creating boom-towns. Modest payments by the industry or government for attractive and efficient community services should meet this concern.

Water availability is a third problem and is largely institutional. There is little doubt that the shale oil industry could successfully bid for water, but water rights are tenaciously held. These rights are being tested in the courts and no quick solution is in sight. Water-conserving technologies thus are of great interest.

As with nuclear energy, the fate of the shale oil industry will be known in the 1980s. Having been looked at longingly by Americans since the beginning of the century, this potentially abundant source of energy will make it in the next ten years or not at all.

Solar Energy

Relatively few believe that solar energy will capture a significant share of energy use in the 1980s.[20] Hardware cost is high. Operating and maintenance costs are uncertain. Buildings partially supplied by solar energy will need a supplementary energy source, and this is likely to be expensive. Moreover, location imposes a substantial constraint, both in the macrodimension (geographical) and the microdimension (each building's access to sunlight).

A significant amount of switching from conventional to solar energy is thus not likely in the 1980s. Subsidy plans, some already on the statute books, are certain to affect new construction rather than help retrofit existing buildings. Since new housing units are added at a rate of no more than 2 million a year to an inventory of about 70 million, the growth rate of housing itself sets a modest pace. The rising cost of fuel-dependent residential energy may predispose people towards solar energy, which will not cost anything outside of equipment cost and maintenance. However, the high initial cost is likely to be a significant deterrent, especially in an era of high interest rates. The next two or three years should shed some light on how these two tendencies will balance out.

In the long run solar energy is likely to be a major energy source

20. The narrow definition of solar energy is the most useful and is used here: solar radiation intercepted for sun-heated water and sun-heated space (passively heated—or without special equipment, and actively heated—or with special equipment); and for generating electricity by photovoltaic cells, focused mirrors, and so on. In its broad sense, solar energy also includes hydroelectricity, biomass, wind, and ocean.

for buildings. Consequently, experimentation with different ways of capturing solar energy merits high priority. Current methods such as heating with roof panels may not be the most desirable and least costly. Attention should be devoted to developing low-cost materials, since materials and their treatment is what makes solar energy expensive. Research in heat transfer and storage is also needed. And the door should be left open for new technologies.

Considerable progress has been made in the development of solar cells for generating electric power. The cost of cells has been lowered from about $50 per peak watt to $10, and some experts expect it can reach $1 to $2 before long. However, not until the cost is reduced to something like 50 cents, will solar cells be competitive. Past accomplishments are impressive, but the final step will be arduous because there are few materials that permit the needed cost reduction not only of the cell but also of the array and supporting structure.

These considerations suggest that research and development is the top priority in the photovoltaic field. Government's primary role should be to supply a moderate-sized market for small modules (for use in navigational aids, satellites, emergency equipment, and defense). At the same time, a research effort is called for to assess the institutional implications if solar cells become commercially feasible: compatibility with existing utility grids, optimum size of installations, and the role of installations for individual customers. There is no law that says we need always be taken by surprise when research bears fruit.

A task awaiting resolution in the eighties is the use of solar energy as a regular source of residential and commercial heat. Technology has so far focused on individual water and space heating installations, typically with public utilities providing backup electric service. The large initial outlay needed for equipment is an obstacle to its adoption, and though special loans have been advocated and may soon be available, they may not be sufficient to overcome the resistance of potential users who have the lower-cost option of tying into existing gas or electric systems. Bringing the utilities into the picture—for example, by having them lease the equipment to customers—is one alternative, though this arrangement might cost the user more to achieve a utility-prescribed level of maintenance. Also, as solar enthusiasts frequently have a strong bias against utilities and large corporations, this alternative might create problems. Yet, financing by the utilities probably is the most effective approach, and practical schemes for making such financing acceptable to all concerned need to be developed.

Conclusion

Energy is now firmly established as one of modern society's major problems. It takes its place alongside the urban problem, the health problem, the national security problem, and others. Moreover, its many facets touch on most other social issues and national objectives —from environmental quality to income distribution. Unfortunately, there is no policy or set of policies that will once again give us abundant, reliable, cheap energy. Even the idea of a comprehensive national energy policy may be an illusion; the best one might hope for is a reasonable degree of consistency in policies that deal directly or indirectly with energy. Achievement of greater efficiency in the use of energy requires both a turnover of energy-using facilities, like motor vehicles and buildings, and a change in energy-using habits and practices. Both will take time. Lead times for new energy sources and technologies are also long. Moreover, energy is now so intertwined with other objectives that sorting out their effects on each other is likely to continue to be time-consuming but inescapable. Consequently, little can be accomplished in less than half a decade.

Given these characteristics of the energy problem, a few guidelines can be suggested. First, there is ample room for lowering demand without changing life-styles—through realistic fuel prices and programs to offset their effect on low-income users and inflation; through simplified regulations and cost-effective subsidies; and through wide distribution of technical information. Second, a balanced supply program is needed to keep us from becoming dependent on specific resources and technologies that in the long run may be more costly and environmentally less attractive than others. Third, energy being an international problem, an exclusively U.S.-oriented policy is neither desirable nor practical. International understandings, some already on the books, are essential; and the effect of high energy costs on developing countries, and ways to alleviate it, needs attention. Fourth, while all conventional energy sources are flawed and carry risks, there is little prospect of significant changes over the next decade. Thus, the major effort must be to reduce risks and to demonstrate that those remaining are the price we must pay for a rising standard of living, both here and abroad. For the same reason, utmost care is called for before any conventional source is permitted to vanish. To reverse an idiom, use well before shaking. Finally, contingency plans are vital for dealing with shocks and surprises to make them less wrenching.

If 1979 presages things to come, we are in for rapid change and unforeseen disturbances; projections and prescriptions are likely to have brief life spans; the ability to respond quickly but without panic will carry a premium. In this context, it is worthwhile to keep two points in mind when thinking about the future of energy. First, the problem did not appear suddenly in October 1973; it resulted from trends in consumption and production long in the making. Just as it did not arise full-fledged so it will not be terminated by the stroke of the legislative pen. Second, as the slow and often zig-zag course of energy policy unfolds, it must be recognized that energy policy is only a mirror reflecting a society fractured into an ever-increasing number of interest groups; the energy debate is simply a convenient arena in which citizens can do battle over their convictions. Unfortunately, even the best institutions can perform no better than willingness to trade and compromise will allow them. Thus the highest priority for the 1980s is the forging of a national consensus on a few objectives, in the recognition that asking energy policy to help resolve all of society's problems is preordaining it to frustration and failure.

CHAPTER FIVE

Health, Safety, and Environmental Regulations

LESTER B. LAVE

THE DECADE beginning in 1965 was a time for statements of purpose and for ringing rhetoric about health, safety, and environmental regulation. Congress passed legislation declaring that automobiles should be made safe, should be virtually emission-free, and should conserve fuel; that workers should be protected from accidents and exposure to hazardous substances; that consumers should be protected from dangerous products, and that steps should be taken for a cleaner environment.

This "social legislation" is qualitatively different from previous regulations. To be sure, clean air and clean water acts, acts to protect workers, and acts to protect consumers had been passed. With the possible exception of the Food, Drug and Cosmetic Act, however, none delegated such broad powers to the newly created regulatory agencies or such broad missions to solve social problems.

Despite recession, the hostility of business, plant closings, losses in productivity, and particular cases of consumer dissatisfaction, the fundamental goals have not changed; but there is growing dissatisfaction with the results and the high costs. Regulatory reform is a powerful slogan, but it is supported by people advocating repeal of all regu-

I thank Henry J. Aaron, Morton Corn, Robert W. Crandall, Michael Gough, Raphael Kasper, Roger G. Noll, Paul R. Portney, Louise B. Russell, Eugene P. Seskin, and Steven M. Swanson for their comments; Lewis S. Alexander for extraordinarily competent research assistance; and Val J. Harris for secretarial assistance.

131

lation at the one extreme and those wanting to increase the speed with which new regulations are enacted and enforced at the other. The dissatisfaction and opposing proposals for reform are the inevitable result of the previous failures to obtain agreement on short-term goals and to face the difficult trade-offs among noble social goals.

Costs of Social Regulation

Estimating the costs of social regulation is extremely complicated. For example, there is evidence that saccharin, a nonnutritive sweetener used principally in soft drinks, is a carcinogen, although the evidence is open to a wide range of interpretation, especially about its potency. What would be the social loss associated with banning saccharin and thus nonnutritive sweeteners? Some argue that the benefits would be zero because people do not *need* sweeteners; others contend that the public would be willing to pay billions of dollars a year to have the current array of sweetened foods. Cost estimates are tenuous. There is much to be learned by displaying the "hard" estimates of costs and then listing separately the most complete estimates.

Table 5-1 shows the 1978 budget allocations for health, safety, and environmental regulatory agencies. The list is incomplete because, for example, the Interstate Commerce Commission is excluded but has a social regulatory role.

More complete, and highly speculative, estimates of total costs were made by the Office of Management and Budget and then submitted for comment to the General Accounting Office and the staff of the Committee on Government Affairs. The estimates for total environmental regulation are $40–$60 billion a year, with a much smaller estimate of $14.4 billion in 1975 by the Council on Environmental Quality. Of this total, about $6 billion a year was the estimated cost of controlling automobile emissions. Safety regulation was made up of $500 million and $3.5 billion annually for automobile safety and occupational safety, respectively. Finally, the quality standards for food and drugs set by the Food and Drug Administration were estimated to cost just less than $500 million a year. Murray Weidenbaum and Robert De Fina estimate that health, safety, and environmental regulations cost about $20 billion in 1976. Although large in absolute terms, these costs represent a small proportion of gross national product—about 1 percent. If they were

Table 5-1. Costs of Social Regulation, 1978
Millions of dollars

Agency	Budget allocation
Consumer Product Safety Commission	$40.6
National Highway Traffic Safety Administration	54.6ᵃ
Federal Railroad Administration	7.3ᵇ
Federal Aviation Administration	203.7ᶜ
National Transportation Safety Board	15.4
Occupational Safety and Health Administration	136.6
Occupational Safety and Health Review Commission	7.2
Mine Safety and Health Administration	99.3
Department of Agriculture	206.5ᵈ
Food and Drug Administration	288.7
Nuclear Regulatory Commission	141.4ᵉ
Environmental Protection Agency	643.5ᶠ

Source: *Study on Federal Regulation*, vol. 6, *Framework for Regulation*, Senate Committee on Governmental Affairs (Committee Print) 95 Cong. 2 sess. (U.S. Government Printing Office, 1978), pp. 36 and 37.
a. Excludes research and state contracts.
b. Railroad safety only.
c. Administration of flight standards program only.
d. Meat and poultry inspection only.
e. Excludes research.
f. Excludes research and grants.

spread evenly across the entire economy, they would represent less than one year's increase in real income (at productivity increases prevailing before 1973); however, they are concentrated in a few industries or consumer products. For example, the costs of occupational health standards for cotton mills and coke ovens are estimated to be $688 million and from $241 million to $1,280 million, respectively. The costs of water pollution control must be borne primarily by industries such as paper; the costs of air pollution control by automobiles and steel.

Social Goals

A central paradox is that Americans are safer now than ever before, but at the same time they are more concerned about health and safety than ever before. There is a general perception that we are exposed to so many risks from toxic materials in the environment and from accidents that we are in the midst of a crisis. Certainly life-threatening risks abound, from new chemicals in the environment to new safety hazards, but no evidence exists that overall risks increased in the recent past or will increase in the foreseeable future. Occupations such as coal mining and lumbering are hazardous, and further steps must be taken to reduce the rates of injury and chronic disease. But most agency attention has gone to regulating exposure to low concentrations of toxic substances. Progress in the biomedical sciences has shown some chemicals to be carcinogens in animals and has raised suspicion about others. Advances in analytical chemistry, which have shown these chemicals to be in minute concentrations in air, water, and food, have created public concern. Once aroused, the fears cannot be calmed because of the paucity of both data and accepted scientific models. This dearth of scientific evidence on the magnitude of risk has intensified the perception of *possible* risk that dominates public thinking.

Perhaps the best indicator of overall health is life expectancy at various ages, particularly at birth. All life-shortening risks from accidents and from disease are incorporated into this measure. Life expectancy rose rapidly during the early part of this century, and has continued to rise steadily, although slowly, during the second half.[1] Certainly there is room for improvement; compared with other nations, significant further enhancement is possible, and part may be attained through social regulation. Indeed, much has been accomplished in the battle to lower the overall risk, control emissions into the air and water, and reduce the exposure of workers.

How can such a wide discrepancy occur between this decreasing risk and the perception that more must be done to abate environmental pollution and prevent accidents? Is it irrational to demand that health, safety, and environmental regulations lower these risks further?

Since the turn of the century, real income per capita has quadrupled, and life expectancy at birth has almost doubled. Although no evidence exists that Americans have become sated with the products of the U.S. industrial economy, it is natural that they should want a

1. The life expectancy at birth in 1900 for a white male was 46.6 years and for a white female, 48.7 years; the figures in 1975 were 70.7 years and 77.7 years, respectively. Life expectancy at age forty for white males and females rose from 27.7 and 29.2 years to 33.4 and 39.8 years. After subtracting respiratory cancer (due principally to cigarette smoking), the data show that the overall cancer mortality rate has fallen steadily; the decline in cardiovascular mortality rates is even more dramatic. See U.S. Department of Health, Education, and Welfare, *Health United States, 1979* (U.S. Government Printing Office, 1980), pp. 144–45, 153, 157; and L. A. Fingerhut, R. W. Wilson, and J. J. Feldman, "Health and Disease in the United States," in Lester Breslow, Jonathan E. Fielding and Lester B. Lave, eds., *Annual Review of Public Health*, vol. 1 (1980).

more pleasant environment, lower risks associated with their products and work places, and general health improvements to accompany their increases in real income.

What appears to be a paradox is resolved by recognizing the rapidly increasing desire for lower risk. Short of economic disaster, the goals for a cleaner, safer environment are unlikely to change. Nothing is to be gained by questioning whether the goals are widely shared or considered important. Americans should proceed with the task of attaining the goals more efficiently.

Conflicts among Goals

But translating deeply felt human desires into worthwhile goals is difficult. In particular, at the most basic level, the goals conflict. To clean the environment, resources must be expended; those resources will not be available for hospitals, education, or private consumption. Implicit in each social goal must be some notion of priorities or balancing.

The automobile offers one of the best illustrations of contradictions among goals. In 1966 Congress declared that the automobile must be made safe; in 1970 it declared that its emissions must be reduced at least 90 percent; in 1975 it declared that automobiles must be fuel-efficient. A catalytic converter designed to reduce emissions also adds weight; furthermore, there is a physical relationship between combustion efficiency and emissions, particularly for nitrogen oxides. Curtailing emissions necessarily leads to a deterioration in fuel economy, other factors held constant.

It is possible to build automobiles that offer better protection to the occupants in a collision, have lower emissions, and achieve better fuel economy, but only at the cost of making an automobile that is less pleasant to drive, ride in, and look at—and is much more expensive. In general, one of the attributes can be enhanced only at the expense of others. These social goals would have been achieved more efficiently by considering all attributes simultaneously and thereby resolving the conflicts.

Public Perceptions

In 1965 few Americans thought that reducing air and water pollution were high-priority tasks. Within five years, however, environmental concerns were rated as the second most important social problem (after reduction of crime).[2] The rapidity of this rise in public concern suggested a frivolous phenomenon that had caught the public attention, but would disappear from view. Opinion surveys, however, have continued to find that the environment is a major concern. People want a clean environment and give it high priority whether they are asked to identify major social problems or answer complicated questions about trade-offs between the environment and either inflation or unemployment.

For example, in a series of polls conducted between 1973 and 1978, people were asked to state which programs were not being supported adequately by the federal government; a little more than 60 percent of the respondents named the environment in 1973, while about 50 percent listed it in 1978, despite the greatly increased expenditures for such purposes during that period. People are in favor of slowing economic growth and of paying higher prices, if necessary, to protect the environment. Furthermore, most people think that progress to date has been too slow and that air and water pollution still will be serious problems in the year 2000.

Some polls indicate that only about one-quarter of Americans would choose a job in which they were exposed to dangerous substances, in contrast with a job that paid one-third less but was not associated with dangerous exposure.[3] Economic studies of jobs with such risks find that workers demand a wage premium of $200–$1,000 for each additional risk of one in one thousand that death will result from exposure.[4] More direct evidence of society's goals for health and safety is seen in the expenditures on health care, health research, and the environment itself. As the first children of the baby boom reach their forties in the mid-1980s, they will see some of their friends suffer from various chronic diseases such as cancer and, especially, cardiovascular disease. If anything, health concerns are likely to

2. Robert Cameron Mitchell, "Silent Spring/Solid Majorities," *Public Opinion*, vol. 2 (August–September 1979), pp. 16–20, 55.
3. Gene Pokorny, "Living Dangerously . . . Sometimes," *Public Opinion*, vol. 2 (June–July 1979), pp. 10–13.
4. Robert Stewart Smith, *The Occupational Safety and Health Act* (American Enterprise Institute for Policy Research, 1976), p. 91; Richard Thaler and Sherwin Rosen, "The Value of Saving a Life: Evidence From the Labor Market," in Nester E. Terleckyj, ed., *Household Production and Consumption* (National Bureau of Economic Research, 1976), pp. 265–98; and W. Kip Viscusi, "Employment Hazards: An Investigation of Market Performance" (Ph.D. dissertation, Harvard University, 1976), chap. 6.

increase as the demographic composition of the population shifts toward a greater proportion of older people.

History of Recent Legislation

The agencies created to administer the social legislation have far broader mandates and powers than previous agencies such as the Interstate Commerce Commission or the Federal Aviation Administration. Indeed, the evolution of this legislation over time has given even greater latitude to the agencies. Congress has reacted to past inadequacies both by setting specific regulations and by delegating even broader power. For example, Congress has retained the authority to set automobile emission standards by writing detailed standards into law; it ordered the Environmental Protection Agency to consider air pollution standards for areas that were currently clean, without ever defining what "currently clean" meant or what constituted "significant deterioration." By both the specificity and generality of legislation, Congress has muddied the role it traditionally gave to regulatory agencies: Congress defines a general goal and set of workable goals and charges the agency with carrying out the day-to-day operations. If the agency fails to behave according to congressional mandate, the mechanisms of oversight, appropriations hearings, the need for senate confirmation of the agency head, and special laws serve to discipline the agency. However, Congress has rarely defined workable goals for social legislation. It alternates between assigning the agencies problems it cannot solve (through legislation that states only the most general goals) and acting itself to set detailed goals.

Air Pollution

Although there have been federal acts regulating air pollution since 1955 and local regulations for more than half a century, a major change took place in the 1967 amendments to the Clean Air Act. Congress ordered the Secretary of Health, Education, and Welfare to define air quality control regions, set general goals for ambient air quality, and then to induce state and local governments to formulate detailed goals for air quality and plans to achieve them in each region. By 1969 it was apparent that not much progress had been made in defining these regions.[5] Even after designating a region, little

5. Of perhaps 300 regions, the Secretary had designated 20 regions, and 37 were in process.

cleanup took place because no government wanted to push out industry.

Congress realized that the 1967 amendments had not been successful and made sweeping changes in the 1970 amendments. It ordered the Environmental Protection Agency to define primary and secondary ambient air quality standards and emissions standards designed to achieve these objectives. Rather than make the effort entirely federal, detailed plans and enforcement policies were to be left to the states. The primary air quality standards were to protect the health of the population, even the most sensitive members with respiratory problems. The basic notion was that there was some threshold level of air pollution below which no one's health would be threatened.

Secondary standards were to protect property, vegetation, visibility, and other nonhealth values. Congress believed that achieving these more stringent standards would be more difficult, expensive, and time-consuming.

Automobiles were singled out for special attention in the 1970 amendments. Congress mandated a 90 percent reduction in emissions levels over 1970 models and a detailed timetable for implementation.[6] Congress, however, has found itself embroiled in this problem, with periodic reviews of the time schedule and standards.

Besides changes in the timing of the automobile standards, another set of major amendments was passed in 1977. These decreed that clean areas could not be allowed to suffer significant deterioration and that coal-fired electricity generator plants would need to have flue gas desulfurization, even if they met emissions standards. Among other changes, the amendments created a National Commission on Air Quality, which, under the aegis of the Congress, was to study air pollution goals and regulations. The creation of this commission was simply one additional step in a continuing review of air pollution regulations.[7]

---

6. Levels of hydrocarbon and carbon monoxide were to be reduced by 90 percent in 1975 models; levels of nitrogen oxides were also to drop by 90 percent, but 1971 levels were used as a base, with implementation in the 1976 models. None of these objectives was achieved on schedule, and the most stringent standard for nitrogen oxides still awaits implementation.

7. See David P. Rall, "Review of the Health Effects of Sulfur Oxides," *Environmental Health Perspectives,* vol. 8 (August 1974), pp. 97–121; and National Academy of Sciences, Commission on Natural Resources, "Perspectives on Technical Information for Environmental Protection," vol. 1, U.S. Environmental Protection

The 1977 amendments represented a major departure from a policy of deciding on desired air quality and then estimating the extent of emission control required. The administrator of the Environmental Protection Agency was ordered to determine a standard for removal of sulfur from coal that would apply, even when abatement was not required to meet ambient air standards and when little sulfur was being emitted—for example, when low-sulfur coal was burned. Requiring abatement equipment, without regard to protecting air quality, has its justification in political, not environmental, considerations. Surely attaining the goal of an enhanced environment is sufficiently difficult that it is folly to append unrelated political barriers.

Extensive hearings and major new amendments on air pollution control policy are likely in 1980–81. For example, the National Commission on Air Quality will make its report, and the automobile emissions regulations will require review. As energy policy emphasizes the role of coal, past compromises will require reexamination. There are also likely to be proposals for modifying the process by which standards are set, for example, using benefit-cost analysis; changing the implementation of abatement policy, for instance, effluent fees or transferable pollution rights (discussed below); and altering the nature of judicial, congressional, or executive branch review of regulations under the semblance of regulatory reform. Progress has been made in lowering emissions of sulfur oxides and particulates, but many cities have increasing photochemical smog resulting largely from automobile emissions. Major changes are likely.

Water Pollution

Important legislation governing water pollution was passed first in 1899, prohibiting the dumping of waste materials into navigable waters. Although the 1899 Rivers and Harbors Act exerted the most stringent controls until the Federal Water Pollution Control Act amendments of 1972, it was little used until 1970. The 1972 amendments provided that discharges were basically to be determined by the best available control technology rather than by goals for water

---

Agency Analytical Studies Series (NAS, 1977), and other volumes in the series. The National Academy of Sciences has also published studies on stationary sources of air pollution, automobile emissions, and specific pollutants such as nitrogen oxides, ozone and other photochemical oxidants, sulfur oxides, and carbon monoxide.

quality. Industry was instructed to use the best practicable technology by mid-1977 and the best available technology by mid-1983. These steps were taken to protect fish, shellfish, and wildlife in waters, to provide for recreation by July 1983, and to eliminate all discharges of pollutants into navigable waterways by 1985. To ensure that these laws were being enforced, any citizen could sue polluters when they did not observe the standards or the government when it did not proceed expeditiously with the setting of standards. Although some industries complied, the deadlines were generally not met, and the Clean Water Act of 1977 delayed many of these deadlines.

The most important political aspect of these acts has been the allocation of major federal funds for sewage control and other projects to control water pollution. Congress used the goal of eliminating discharges by 1985 to justify large expenditures for local control projects—pork barrel. So powerful were the joint attractions of environmentalism and pork barrel that Congress overwhelmingly overrode President Nixon's veto of a bill whose price tag he described as "staggering, budget-wrecking."

Toxic Substances

The Toxic Substances Control Act, passed in 1976, was an attempt to deal comprehensively and on a prospective, rather than reactive, basis with the myriad chemicals to which Americans are exposed. Earlier legislation addressed toxins in foods, food additives, drugs, and cosmetics; air and water pollution; and exposures at the work place. The new act was an attempt to deal with chemical exposures comprehensively. In a radical departure from previous practice, Congress required a manufacturer to demonstrate that a chemical was safe before its introduction. Previously the regulatory agency was responsible for showing that the use of the chemical caused problems. Certainly Congress was facing a difficult problem and was providing more guidance on procedures and priorities than it had in the past. But it did not reckon with the complexity and size of the problem. Three years after passage, the basic procedural steps of the act still have not been taken, in part because Congress did not appropriate a sufficient budget or manpower.

Although there are thousands of toxic chemicals in use, regulation that would prohibit or significantly delay the introduction of new chemicals could slow both economic growth and the increase in real income. Congress required that authority under the act "should be exercised in such a manner as not to impede unduly or create unnecessary economic barriers to technological innovation while fulfilling the primary purpose of this Act to assure that such innovation and commerce in such chemical substances and mixtures do not present unreasonable risk of injury to health or the environment."

To accomplish this balancing, the Environmental Protection Agency is to establish standards and review them at least annually, establish a "most wanted" list of potentially dangerous chemicals and review these annually, and begin testing on the substances with highest priority. To prevent unnecessary risk, companies must give ninety days notice before manufacturing a new chemical or before any significant new use of an existing chemical. Finally, to ensure that the agency is properly administering the Toxic Substances Control Act, private citizens have the right to sue or petition for enforcement, amendments, or repeal of standards.

But no one anticipated the difficulty in formulating and implementing the rules and procedures associated with regulating chemicals. Furthermore, suits by private citizens have disrupted the ability to proceed systematically. To date, enforcement of this statute has hardly begun.[8]

The Resource Conservation and Recovery Act of 1976 ordered the Environmental Protection Agency to set criteria for the disposal of toxic wastes. Like the Toxic Substances Control Act, administration of the Resources Conservation and Recovery Act has hardly gotten started. One might doubt that the task is feasible. Are there any criteria for disposal of toxic wastes that will prove acceptable to local communities? Even if there were, the costs of a system that meets these criteria are likely to be greater than that which can be borne by the plants affected.

Occupational Safety and Health

Congress passed the Occupational Safety and Health Act in 1970 to guarantee that "Each employer—shall furnish to each of his employees employment and a place of employment which are free from recognized hazards that are causing or are likely to cause death or serious physical harm to his employees." Congress emphasized that

8. John Walsh, "EPA and Toxic Substances Law: Dealing with Uncertainty," *Science*, vol. 202 (November 10, 1978), pp. 598–602.

this protection was to extend over the entire period of employment; thus workers were to be protected from exposures whose accumulation over forty or more years might cause harm.

To achieve these goals, Congress established an Occupational Safety and Health Administration within the U.S. Department of Labor. They began by adopting and promulgating about 7,000 voluntary or consensus standards published by industry groups. Many of the voluntary standards were never intended to be mandatory and hundreds had little relationship to health or safety.

The majority of the agency's efforts have been devoted to enforcement, with inspectors visiting places of employment to see that standards are being met and that no hazardous conditions exist. Most violations carry minimal fines, although "willful" violations can result in large fines or prison sentences. Only recently have violations been cited as willful, and a few fines have gone beyond a minimal level.[9]

The agency initially had 400 inspectors to cover almost 5 million places of employment; the chances were nil that a randomly chosen place of employment would be inspected. The largest firms have been the focus of attention because these employ about 50 percent of the work force; work places with ten or fewer employees receive only sporadic inspection. Furthermore, there are so many standards that it is inconceivable that an inspector can do more than look for a few obvious violations.

The standard-setting procedures have proved to be so time-consuming that only a handful of health standards have been set. Large amounts of personnel time are required to collect information, conduct hearings, distill that information, and revise a standard. In addition, virtually all standards are challenged in the courts, and so vast resources are devoted to litigation.

Recently 928 standards and parts of standards not pertaining to health and safety were eliminated. While this is to be commended, many more standards are irrelevant to health and safety (about 1,100 were initially identified for elimination by the agency).

The relationship between this regulatory agency and the National Institute of Occupational Safety and Health has not been a satisfactory one. The agency complains that the latter, a research agency, publishes superficial or untimely studies more rapidly than they can be used, and generally pursues a course unrelated to the requirement

9. Nicholas A. Ashford, *Crisis in the Workplace* (MIT Press, 1976), p. 260.

for regulation—a common complaint of regulatory agencies. More recent efforts at coordination may have alleviated some problems.

Progress in enhancing occupational health and safety to date is generally perceived to be unsatisfactory. The agency has failed to reduce accident rates significantly, even in industries that the agency selected for attention.[10] Only a few toxic substances have been regulated; many cases are still in litigation; and compliance is usually slow. The agency has not developed a comprehensive program or a set of priorities, although internal priority-setting exercises have been conducted. Congress, and probably the agency also, still does not appear to have made a realistic appraisal of the magnitude of the problems. Instead, the agency plods along, setting individual standards and sending inspectors to individual plants.[11] Ten years of experience show that the agency cannot promulgate more than a few standards a year, and its inspectors cannot possibly visit most work places or uncover most violations. Clearly, trying harder is not going to accomplish the goals set by Congress. More radical changes in procedure are necessary.

Highway Safety

In 1966 Congress passed the National Traffic and Motor Vehicle Safety Act to reduce the number of people being injured or killed on highways. The National Highway Transportation Safety Administration issued its first set of standards for 1968 model automobiles, with requirements such as seat belts (lap only). Subsequently, the agency has regulated the design of door handles and other objects that protrude into the interior of the vehicle, the crash-worthiness of bumpers, and so forth. Many of the safety standards would not disappear even if they were no longer required, both because of the increasing safety consciousness of purchasers and the automobile manufacturers' fears of product liability.

In 1975 Congress ordered the agency to regulate the fuel economy of automobiles: model 1978 vehicles were to achieve a fleet-weighted

10. Smith, *The Occupational Safety and Health Act,* pp. 67–70; and Aldona DiPietro, "An Analysis of the OSHA Inspection Program in Manufacturing Industries 1972–73," Draft Technical Analysis Paper (U.S. Department of Labor, August 1976).

11. A generic carcinogen standard was proposed in 1978, but compared with other agency regulations it was so unrealistic and contradictory that it has been delayed. A revised standard has been published, but it will undoubtedly be tied up in court for several years.

average of 18 miles per gallon; model 1985 vehicles, 27.5 miles per gallon. Interim standards for 1981–84 were to be set by the agency. The regulations have brought about large changes in design, virtually all of which would have occurred with some delay after the rise in gasoline prices.

Like other social regulation, highway safety regulation has been immersed in controversy since its inception. Perhaps the most controversial regulation was that requiring an interlock device that rendered vehicles inoperable if occupants were not wearing their seat belts. A combination of public resentment and problems with the technology led Congress to bar the requirement for this device. More recently the decision to require passive devices (ones that do not require action by the passenger to make them effective) has revived the controversy.

Compared with other social regulation, setting auto safety and interim fuel-efficiency standards has been easy; enforcement has been especially simple. The success stems from several factors. First, Congress was subjected to intense lobbying from the auto industry before enacting the legislation. Thus many of the controversies were settled by Congress, rather than delegated to the agency. Second, the public has supported both safety and fuel economy; the agency seemed to be codifying public desires, rather than serving a narrow constituency (for example, many of the 1968 safety requirements were introduced in 1964 to 1967 model automobiles). Third, the agency had only a few firms to deal with in setting and enforcing standards, in contrast to the agencies regulating occupational health and safety, consumer product safety, or environmental quality. A fourth factor is that enforcement consists of reviewing company procedures, rather than making visits to thousands of separate plants or testing thousands of products. Fifth, measuring the magnitude of the problem and progress is easy; the effects of highway accidents are immediately apparent and statistics are available for a long period of time—in contrast, for example, to lung cancer for which there are many causes, long intervals between initial exposure and diagnosis of the disease, and poor statistical records. Finally, the agency has collected data and performed analyses from its inception; it has a comparatively firm foundation for justifying its regulations. It is unfortunate that few of the factors that enabled this agency to be successful apply to other social regulatory agencies.

Consumer Products

The Consumer Product Safety Commission was created in 1972 as a focal agency for regulating products used by consumers. The commission is required to balance costs and benefits, and it bears the burden of proof when it seeks to ban a product. Its efforts to date have been largely ineffectual. For example, it required that children's sleepware meet flammability standards; this led to treating the fabrics with Tris (2,3-dibromopropyl), which was subsequently found to be a carcinogen that could be absorbed through the skin. The efforts of the agency to be open and fair led to charges by one commissioner that the public generally learned about staff activities before commissioners; that private negotiations with manufacturers would have resolved many of the initiatives that subsequently were litigated, delayed inordinately, and sometimes defeated; and that work was paralyzed by giving equal attention to all petitions. Although recent attempts have been made at improvement, the commission is often cited as an example of how good intentions, amorphous objectives, and poor leadership can make social regulation a fiasco.

Recent Controversies

It is difficult to formulate general policies in social regulation because of the unique circumstances associated with each case. In this section I attempt to draw out lessons from a series of recent controversies.

At the center of each controversy is the estimate of risk. Social regulation is designed to lower human risk or environmental damage. But quantifying the expected reduction in injury, illness, or death is inherently controversial; recent history rarely provides data sufficient for a satisfactory estimate. More often, risk is calculated from undertested theory or laboratory experiments with animals. There is general agreement that these estimates are subject to great uncertainty, and some scientists believe that the uncertainty precludes quantitative risk calculations.

But no matter how difficult or uncertain the results may be, there is no reasonable alternative to numerical estimates and their use in regulation. Without some notion of the magnitude of risk, society must rely either on the visceral reactions of a few individuals or must regard all possible fears as being of equal concern. Clearly, I am more likely to be killed by an automobile than a meteorite, by cancer than by botulism. Regulations that cost society billions of dollars each year and result in bankruptcies, unemployment, and dislocation must be backed by more than the hunches of a few regulators. As the following cases illustrate, social regulation is inescapably embroiled in risk quantification and in using the uncertain estimates properly.

Occupational Exposure to Vinyl Chloride

Vinyl chloride, a gas, is the principal ingredient in the second most widely used plastic in the United States.[12] In 1974 the B.F. Goodrich Company reported that three workers died of angiosarcoma, an extremely rare cancer of the liver, and a fourth had died five years before. The workers had been exposed to vinyl chloride in concentrations of several hundred parts per million. Laboratory data showed that rats contracted angiosarcoma when exposed to 250 parts per million of vinyl chloride. Subsequent experiments produced tumors at much lower concentrations. As a result of the Goodrich announcement, and with consideration of the laboratory results, the Occupational Safety and Health Administration used an "emergency temporary" standard to lower the exposure ceiling for humans from 500 to 50 parts per million. In late 1974 a permanent standard of 1 part per million was set.

If the form of cancer (angiosarcoma) had not been extremely rare, it would have been impossible to associate four cancer deaths with exposure to vinyl chloride. Also crucial in this case was the laboratory result, which showed that vinyl chloride produced this same rare cancer in rats at exposures similar to those experienced by workers.

The question was whether to set a standard so low that it would prohibit use of vinyl chloride or one that might still subject workers to risk. The first alternative would have been extremely expensive and disruptive—temporarily costing tens or hundreds of thousands of workers their jobs, disrupting manufacturing processes in many fabrication industries for lack of raw material, and removing many products from the market. It could also have led to discovery of a safer substitute. Clearly, there was pressure to find an exposure level

---

12. David D. Doniger, *The Law and Policy of Toxic Substances Control* (Johns Hopkins University Press for Resources for the Future, 1979), p. 23.

that would protect workers, yet was technically and economically achievable.

Regulation generally proceeds by taking exposure levels found toxic in humans or in animals and then using a "safety factor" to arrive at a permissible exposure level or virtually safe dose. Human exposure data suggested that 250 parts per million of vinyl chloride was sufficient to cause angiosarcoma. Animal data showed this cancer at exposure levels of 50 parts per million, with some evidence of mammary tumors even at 1 part per million. This evidence suggests that the agency was balancing economic costs and jobs against the risks of cancer, and was not terribly conservative—at least if the objective was to prevent all cancer in workers exposed for forty years.

The feasibility of attaining a standard of 1 part per million was disputed by the industry, and the agency contractor agreed. Indeed, in its *Federal Register* notice of October 4, 1974, the agency stated: "There is virtually no dispute that most, if not all, fabricators are currently capable of reaching exposure levels of 1 ppm through engineering controls." But a paragraph below in the same document the agency added: "We agree that the PVC and VC establishments will not be able to attain a 1 ppm TWA level for all job classifications in the near future. We do believe, however, that they will, in time, be able to attain levels of 1 ppm TWA for most job classifications most of the time."

The Occupational Safety and Health Administration did not attempt to estimate the cost of meeting the standard because the feasibility was in doubt. The only cost estimate came from the Firestone Tire and Rubber Company: $450 million to $1 billion, with a best estimate of $750 million, but Firestone did not believe these expenditures would meet the standard. Even assuming the standard was feasible, the cost per incident of cancer avoided by lowering the standard from 50 to 1 parts per million would be in the hundreds of millions of dollars.

The agency regarded such a balancing to be inappropriate; three questions were relevant. Is the substance a carcinogen? Is control at the level of the standard technically feasible? Can these costs be borne by the industry? Affirmative answers were obtained to all three questions (although there was dispute concerning the second and third), and the agency promulgated the standard of one part per million.

When it became clear that the standard would actually have to be met, industry began research on how to do it cheaply. The result was the discovery and introduction of technology that made it possible to meet the standard for much less than the above estimate; indeed, current estimates are that the recovery of vinyl chloride previously wasted offsets much of the cost of control.

The vinyl chloride case is probably unique in two respects. The first is the confidence with which the ill effects of the substance could be identified and related to the amount of exposure. The second is the substantial progress in research and development that allowed the standard to be met at virtually no cost. Although research and development can be expected to result in some reduction in the cost of implementation of other regulatory standards, the extent of the reduction for vinyl chloride is unlikely to be typical, judging from the experience of other social regulation.

Occupational Exposure to Benzene

Occupational studies show that workers exposed to high levels of benzene (a ubiquitous chemical used by industry and an ingredient in products such as gasoline) develop leukemia and other blood abnormalities more frequently than workers not exposed.

In 1977 a proposal was made to lower worker exposure from a maximum of 10 to 1 parts per million of benzene. There is no epidemiological evidence to establish that benzene is a carcinogen at 10 parts per million or even at levels many times higher. However, the Occupational Safety and Health Administration established in its hearings that experts could not ensure that no cases of leukemia were caused at 10 parts per million of benzene, nor that any level of exposure was safe. A level of 1 part per million was shown to be technologically feasible to achieve in most industrial applications. Accordingly, there was a presumption that lowering exposures would lower leukemia rates and that the costs would not serve to bankrupt the industry. Therefore the standard was promulgated.

The American Petroleum Institute headed a group of plaintiffs in bringing suit against the government. The United States Court of Appeals for the Fifth Circuit suspended the regulation on the grounds that the benefits of the regulation did not bear a reasonable relationship to costs and that the agency had failed to quantify the benefits of lowering the concentration of benzene from 10 to 1 parts per million.

The case was heard by the United States Supreme Court in October 1979. The government argued that it was impossible to quantify the benefits with confidence, and that such a requirement would paralyze the agency.

Although the agency has been in existence for almost a decade, there have been no previous Supreme Court rulings on its procedures for setting regulations; and there are no relevant decisions regarding other health, safety, and environmental agencies. Thus the decision of the Court is likely to have wide ramifications for social agencies setting regulations. Benzene is particularly important because more complete evidence exists on the effects on humans than will be found for most other cases concerning toxic substances in the work place or in the environment generally. If this evidence is deemed insufficient for quantifying risk, the regulatory agencies will be directed to give little weight to scientific evidence in assessing the absolute and relative risks of each toxic substance.

To quantify risk, one must estimate the expected ill effects on workers of amounts of exposure much lower than those found to be carcinogenic in previous studies (or, for most substances, from laboratory experiments on animals).[13] Three difficulties arise. The first is extrapolating from the effects on rats to those on humans. The second is extrapolating from high to low amounts of exposure. And the third is extrapolating from one human environment, or a laboratory environment under carefully controlled conditions, to countless human environments and genetically heterogeneous persons having different personal habits and experience and multiple low-level exposures to toxic substances. Benzene exemplifies these difficulties since different biological and statistical models produce differing estimates of the incidence of leukemia at 10 and 1 parts per million.

The fundamental question in the benzene case is whether scientific information can be used to do more than suggest the existence of risk. If not, regulations must proceed on the basis of arbitrary judgments, and all toxic substances must be reduced to levels as low as is feasible

13. Interagency Regulatory Liaison Group, "Work Group on Risk Assessment, Scientific Bases for Identifying Potential Carcinogens and Estimating Their Risks" (Interagency Regulatory Liaison Group, 1979), pp. 33–35, 72; "Identification, Characterization and Control of Potential Human Carcinogens: A Framework for Federal Decision Making," Staff Paper (Executive Office of the President, Office of Science and Technology, 1979), pp. 8–9; and Lester B. Lave, "Interagency Working Group on State II Assessments of Food Additives," Working Paper (Brookings Institution, forthcoming).

or they must be banned altogether. Furthermore, agencies could not set priorities and find levels at which benefits are commensurate with costs.

This is a political, rather than a scientific, question. If the agencies are instructed not to estimate risks (as they were in the Delaney Clause), or choose not to collect data and perform analyses, quantitative risk estimates will not be available to decisionmakers.[14] Congress must instruct the agencies to quantify risks to the extent feasible and weigh benefits against costs, as it did when creating the Toxic Substances Control Act and the Consumer Product Safety Commission, among others.

Sulfur Oxides Emissions

A host of acute air pollution episodes, such as the 1952 London Fog, made it evident that high concentrations of air pollution have grave health effects.[15] A large literature of laboratory and epidemiological studies has helped to narrow the uncertainty about which pollutants cause the problem and the nature of the resulting health effects. Sulfur oxides and suspended particulates, separately and in combination, are the air pollutants responsible for the greatest health effects in the United States. Accordingly, the Environmental Protection Agency has embarked on a program of curtailing emissions of these pollutants to improve air quality.

If pollution abatement were inexpensive, the matter would be closed. There are health effects, and it is prudent to lower emissions and reap these benefits. But pollution control, particularly for sulfur oxides, is expensive. Furthermore, stringent control could result in the prohibition of technologies such as direct burning of coal and reduced use of such fuels as high sulfur coal. Thus there have been repeated reevaluations of the health effects of sulfur oxides. The fundamental issues to decide are: What are the health effects of sulfur

14. The Delaney Clause, part of the Food Additives Amendment of 1958, instructs the Food and Drug Administration that no substance shown to be a carcinogen in laboratory animals can be added to foods, even in minute quantities with a minimal or nonexistent risk.

15. Benjamin G. Ferris, "Sulfur Dioxides and Particulates: Human Exposure-Response Relationships," in Robert W. Crandall and Lester B. Lave, eds., *The Scientific Basis for Environmental and Health Safety Regulation* (Brookings Institution, forthcoming); John R. Goldsmith and Lars T. Friberg, "Effects on Health," in Arthur C. Stern, ed., *Air Pollution,* 3d ed. (Academic Press, 1977), pp. 458–610; and Lester B. Lave and Eugene P. Seskin, *Air Pollution and Human Health* (Johns Hopkins University Press for Resources for the Future, 1977), p. 9.

dioxide and other sulfur oxides? How far are these sulfur oxides transported from the source of emission? What abatement techniques will serve to reduce emissions and the consequent health effects? What other effects, such as reduced visibility and acid rain, are important and how can they be controlled?

Sulfur dioxide is relatively easy to measure, and its control does not pose serious technological problems. The Environmental Protection Agency has set emissions and ambient air standards for sulfur dioxide. But both laboratory and epidemiological work indicates that sulfur dioxide may not be the primary culprit affecting health, at least not at the concentrations occurring in urban areas. In contrast, sulfates, particularly acid sulfates, are harmful to health. However, they are difficult to measure and result from chemical transformation of sulfur dioxide in the atmosphere. Accordingly, it is not easy to determine whether ambient air quality is "satisfactory"; emissions regulations on these pollutants would be irrelevant.

A major difficulty has resulted because sulfur dioxide is regulated, but is not terribly harmful, while acid sulfates are harmful but unregulated. This has led the agency to be unresponsive to the issues raised by its critics, and vice versa.

Although it has not been *proved* that sulfates are harmful in the concentrations that occur in urban areas, analysis of groups exposed to different pollution levels demonstrates a statistical association between sulfates and mortality rates that persists even after adjusting for the principal factors that might vitiate the relationship.[16] However, there are contradictions in the epidemiological evidence.[17] For a number of reasons, laboratory experimentation sheds little light on the issue of harm at these levels.[18]

The underlying uncertainties are the focus of industry's arguments

16. For example, see Lave and Seskin, *Air Pollution and Human Health,* pp. 237–44; and Lester B. Lave and Eugene P. Seskin, "Epidemiology, Causality, and Public Policy," *American Scientist,* vol. 67 (March–April 1979), pp. 178–86.

17. F. W. Lipfert, "The Association of Human Mortality with Air Pollution: Statistical Analyses by Region, by Age and by Cause of Death" (Ph.D. dissertation, Union Graduate School, Yellow Springs, Ohio, 1978); and Thomas D. Crocker and others, *Methods Development for Assessing Air Pollution Control Benefits,* vol. 1, *Experiments in the Economics of Air Pollution Epidemiology* (U.S. Environmental Protection Agency, February 1979).

18. Lave and Seskin, *Air Pollution and Human Health,* pp. 14–15; and Eugene P. Seskin and Lester B. Lave, "Enhancing the Contributions of Science and Technology in Environmental, Health, and Safety Regulations," Working Paper (National Science Foundation, 1979), pp. 26–29.

because they must bear the cost of sulfur dioxide emissions regulations. Industry points to the billions of dollars of annual control costs and asks whether these are worthwhile, given the uncertainties.

Visibility, the concentration of fine particulates in the atmosphere, is also a problem.[19] A large proportion of the particulates are sulfate aerosols.[20] Another consequence of sulfur emissions is acid rain, which has become much more of a concern as measured levels of acidity have worsened.[21] Although neither reduced visibility nor acid rain has the emotional quality of life-endangering air pollution, they are important. Who would visit the Grand Canyon if the other side could not be seen? What would happen if acid rain made many lakes in the northeast biologically dead, as appears to have occurred in Scandanavia?

Thus the costs of abating sulfur dioxide have served to intensify the debate. It is not sufficient to point to vague evidence of health, aesthetic, and environmental effects to justify the expenditure of billions of dollars each year on control and the resulting dislocation of persons, plants, and products. The adverse health consequences of highly polluted air are evident and appear to exist for less polluted air, but proving causality is difficult. Complicating the discussion is agency regulation of sulfur dioxide, which is not as harmful as acid sulfates, but is easier to regulate. There are sufficient uncertainties and questionable policies to preclude consensus on sulfur oxides emissions policy.

Research in a Policy Agency

In 1967 the Community Health and Environmental Surveillance System was inaugurated by the Environmental Protection Agency to study the effects of air pollution on health.[22] In an elaborate program that was conducted over a decade, many millions of dollars were ex-

19. Environmental Protection Agency, Strategies and Air Standards Division, "Protecting Visibility," Report to Congress (Research Triangle Park, North Carolina: EPA, Office of Air Quality Planning and Standards, 1979), pp. 2-12 to 2-44.

20. David P. Rall, "Review of the Health Effects of Sulfur Oxides."

21. *Air Quality and Stationary Source Emission Control*, prepared by the National Academy of Sciences and National Research Council for the Senate Committee on Public Works, 94 Cong. 1 sess. (GPO, 1975), pp. 4–13.

22. *The Environmental Protection Agency's Research Program, with Primary Emphasis on the Community Health and Environmental Surveillance System (CHESS): An Investigative Report*, prepared for the House Committee on Science and Technology, 94 Cong. 2 sess. (GPO, 1976), p. 5.

pended. But the resulting work has been largely discredited and is not used by the scientific community.

In view of the commitment of funds and personnel, it is important to consider what went wrong and how the mistakes can be avoided in the future. The main issue is the conduct of basic research by a regulatory agency; subsidiary issues are the planning, pace, and reporting of research that takes place in this setting.

A major difficulty with previous epidemiological work, which was to be rectified in this work, was improved measurement of the amount of exposure to air pollution that people received. This measurement required better instruments for calculating ambient air quality, beginning with the development of reliable instruments in the laboratory; more problematic was finding methods that worked in the field under extremes of temperature, humidity, sunlight, and wind, which were maintained and observed by semitrained technicians, with delays in analyzing samples. At the inception of the research, proven field instruments neither measured the desired pollutants nor had the required sensitivity. Because time constraints precluded waiting for the development and testing of new instruments, the researchers decided to utilize instruments previously used only in laboratories. The result was aerometric data of deplorable quality, with large errors of observation.

Time constraints also created problems in the analysis and in writing up the conclusions.[23] Usual scientific procedures were not followed in reporting the results; for example, there were allegations that the conclusions were changed to reflect the viewpoint of the agency. Further, the work was not reviewed by peers before it was published by the agency. These problems led epidemiologists to reject the results; parts of the research that did have a firm scientific basis also tended to be rejected. The conduct of this project wasted vast resources and time and damaged the reputation of the Environmental Protection Agency.

These problems are the extremes of those that occur in every agency. Regulatory agencies are under pressure, and it is inevitable that they demand quick results from researchers. Moreover, research results from a regulatory agency are inherently suspect. Employees

23. *Conduct of the EPA's Community Health and Environmental Surveillance Systems (CHESS) Studies,* Hearings before the House Committee on Science and Technology, 94 Cong. 2 sess. (GPO, 1976), and W. B. Rood, "EPA Study—The Findings Got Changed," *Los Angeles Times,* February 29, 1976.

are likely to believe in the mission of their agency. It is natural for them to seek to prove what they believe; the more subtle the analysis and interpretation, the more danger that the research conclusions will reflect the agency's mission, especially if researchers must justify each conclusion when they report to agency administrators.

The alternative to the regulatory agency undertaking its own research is to give that mission to a separate agency and attempt to establish a cooperative arrangement between the two agencies. The Environmental Protection Agency and the National Institute of Environmental Health Sciences have used this method, as have the Occupational Safety and Health Administration and the National Institute of Occupational Health. However, as the histories of these pairs of agencies have shown, each develops its own constituency and agenda; each is responsible to different executives. Cooperation is difficult to achieve under those conditions. Even within one agency, the regulatory officials often charge that the research officials are working on irrelevant matters and not delivering reports on time or in a form that is suitable.

A number of procedures can be adopted to lessen these problems. For example, researchers can be given sole responsibility for a project and the organization structured to protect them from time constraints or pressures to find the desired results. A scientific advisory board with stature could remind researchers and administrators of scientific standards and act as an impartial arbiter in disagreements about timing, research design, and the interpretation of results. However, some of the pressures must inevitably be faced by the researcher.

Steel Industry Emissions

According to the steel industry:[24]

By their very nature, steelmaking processes incidentally generate large volumes of pollutants. The American steel industry has already spent huge sums and implemented far-reaching and effective programs to protect the environment and reduce hazards. Although environmental benefits have been obtained, these expenditures have diverted capital from income-producing and cost-reduction applications. Meeting environmental standards has also had an inflationary impact by significantly increasing operating costs of producing steel.

24. American Iron and Steel Institute, *Steel at the Crossroads: The American Steel Industry in the 1980's* (AISI, 1980), p. 3.

David M. Roderick, chairman of the U.S. Steel Corporation, testified "that the steel industry is being involuntarily liquidated."[25]

As the industry asserts, environmental and health regulations have imposed heavy costs on steel production. The steel industry spends more on air and water pollution abatement than any other industry except electricity generation.[26] The acts governing air, water, and related environmental problems have had major impacts on the processes by which steel is made because air and water are used to carry off much of the effluent.

The steel industry estimates that complying with environmental and occupational safety laws will cost approximately $800 million a year (initial investment plus operating costs).[27] The cost of steel will be increased by an estimated $5 to $8 per ton, or less than 3 percent. However, the investment in abatement technology could represent about 25 percent of the total funds available for investment over the next several years.[28] The steel industry claims that the funds are needed to modernize plant and equipment if the industry is to be viable at a time of fierce international competition.

The investment requirements for the steel industry undoubtedly will be large. Certainly, investing 25 percent of new capital in environmental and safety control is a much heavier than average burden. And there is no doubt about the intensity of foreign competition and the need to modernize plant and reduce costs. However, the increased costs are a tiny proportion of the cost of making steel. If the industry were robust and profitable, sufficient funds could easily be secured to cover mandated investments and the small increases in cost would have little effect on sales. The scarcity of investment funds stems from the unattractiveness of the industry to new investors; low rates of return to investment have resulted from foreign competition, the rapid rise in wages and, to a small extent, social regulations.

Thus the lesson is that the steel industry is in a difficult position because of its low profitability, compounded by its failure in the past

25. Testimony before the Subcommittee on Environmental Pollution of the Senate Committee on Environment and Public Works, 96 Cong. 1 sess. (May 23, 1979).

26. Environmental Protection Agency, *The Cost of Clean Air and Water,* Report to Congress (EPA, 1979), p. vii.

27. American Iron and Steel Institute, *Steel at the Crossroads,* pp. 69–71.

28. Council on Wage and Price Stability, *Report to the President on Prices and Costs in the United States Steel Industry* (GPO, 1977), p. 35; and American Iron and Steel Institute, *Steel at the Crossroads,* pp. 39–41.

to control emissions. If conditions are created that make the industry viable, health and safety regulations will not stand in the way. If conditions do not change, these regulations will not be the cause of the industry's reduction in capacity. The steel industry's dilemma is a social and economic problem, not one of environment and safety.

Automobile Regulation

The automobile has done more to shape American society than any other modern innovation. In addition to transporting most of us to work, school, and other destinations quickly and cheaply, it is a symbol of adulthood and status. The unpleasant consequences of the automobile include 50,000 people killed in highway accidents each year, 2 million people injured, and the emissions that produce photochemical smog and other air pollution. About one-quarter of the petroleum used in the United States is consumed by automobiles.

As noted above, Congress has attempted to regulate safety, emissions, and fuel economy, but the conflicts among regulations and with consumer desires has impeded progress. It was evident that the 1960 model automobile could be improved in design to reduce injuries to pedestrians and occupants and to prevent some accidents. In its initial actions in 1967, the National Highway Transportation Safety Administration required the installation of seat belts on all cars, together with energy-absorbing steering columns, dual braking systems, and other safety features, some of which had been introduced voluntarily by automobile manufacturers. The General Accounting Office estimates that 1966–68 models were safer, resulting in a 15–25 percent reduction in serious injuries and fatalities compared to pre-1966 models (1971–73 models were equivalent to 1969–70 models).[29] If the entire fleet of automobiles were as safe as the 1969–70 models, 12,000 fewer people would have been killed in 1978 than if all cars were as safe as the pre-1966 models. If all people actually buckled their seat belts (only about 10 percent currently do), an additional 7,000 fatalities a year would be averted.[30]

Debates have focused on the role of government in protecting in-

29. U.S. General Accounting Office, *Effectiveness, Benefits, and Costs of Federal Safety Standards for Protection of Passenger Car Occupants,* report to the Senate Committee on Commerce (GAO, 1976), p. 17.
30. Donald F. Huelke and James O'Day, "The National Highway Traffic Safety Administration Passive Restraint Systems—A Scientist's Viewpoint," in Crandall and Lave, eds., *The Scientific Basis for Environmental and Health Safety Regulation.*

dividuals from risks they accept voluntarily. Should the role of the government be limited to providing consumers with information and ensuring that safe vehicles are available to be purchased? Should the government require people to fasten their seat belts? Protect people unwilling to use seat belts by requiring passive protection devices?[31] If passive seat belts or air bags are required on 1982 models, as currently mandated, people who now buckle up will find themselves paying more (seat belts cost about $80, passive belts about $130, and air bags about $300) for passive restraint systems that are less effective than *buckled* lap-shoulder belts. Is this paternalism necessary? Is it desirable?

Automobile safety policy is being made under the assumption that Americans cannot be trusted to look after their own welfare and will not use safety devices that are even slightly inconvenient. Policy based on this assumption boosts the price of automobiles, but allows people to disconnect "inconvenient" safety features. If safety is to have top priority, the agency must enforce the use of mandated safety features.

Automobile emissions is another problem area, as mentioned above. No individual driver can have an appreciable effect on the air pollution in an area; pollution results from the emissions of all automobiles. Consequently, there is a strong case to be made for some sort of governmental intervention. In the Clear Air Act Amendments of 1970, Congress showed its distrust of the executive branch by setting the detailed emissions regulations and timetables noted above, rather than delegating these tasks. Congress refused to believe that it was impossible to invent and install the required technology in the time allowed.[32] There seemed to be a judgment that only when under pressure would the automobile industry try to find new technologies and then install them. The legislation was therefore designed to be "technology forcing."

The result was an increase in research expenditures and many new discoveries, although the original timetable was not met. However,

31. Glenn Blomquist and Sam Peltzman, "Mandatory Passive Restraint Systems and Social Welfare," Huelke and O'Day, "The National Highway Traffic Safety Administration Passive Restraint Systems," and Carl E. Nash, "The Science and Policy of Automatic Crash Protection," in Crandall and Lave, eds., *The Scientific Basis for Environmental and Health Safety Regulations.*

32. Charles O. Jones, *Clean Air: The Policies and Politics of Pollution Control* (Pittsburgh University Press, 1975), pp. 195–201.

hastily conceived technologies were developed in the early years (with automobiles that had poor fuel economy and were difficult to start and drive), and there was a premium on technologies that were certain to work, at the expense of more promising technologies that entailed more risk.[33] Although the catalytic converter solved some problems, it created new ones. The catalyst is poisoned by small amounts of lead in the gasoline. An estimated 10–20 percent of catalysts have been poisoned and are no longer functioning to abate emissions.[34] More energy must be put into refining unleaded gasoline to obtain the required octane. The catalyst also created a problem in retailing because a new grade of gasoline—unleaded—must be sold by each station. Finally, emissions goals would prohibit diesel engines and require new, more complicated technologies, such as three-way catalysts.

As a result of emissions regulations, fuel economy had fallen to 14.2 miles per gallon in the 1974 model. Smaller, fuel-efficient cars sold well in 1974, but lost popularity as the oil embargo crisis receded; gasoline was readily available and not much more expensive than it had been in 1973. By early 1979 the fuel-economy standards were subjected to intense criticism as automobile manufacturers had to reduce the size of vehicles and substitute other materials for steel, thereby increasing the price. But a new oil crisis and higher gasoline prices shifted demand toward fuel-efficient automobiles in mid-1979.

Automobile purchasers responded to both the price and availability of fuel in 1974 and 1979. Certainly higher gasoline prices will be required to sustain the demand for fuel-efficient automobiles. But higher gasoline prices strike a raw nerve. Lobbyists for the poor, teamsters, suburban homeowners, and many other groups seek relief for their clients, even when they recognize the need to conserve gasoline. With the exception of rationing, no other proposal will sustain and enhance the demand for fuel-efficient automobiles.

33. Eugene P. Seskin, "Automobile Air Pollution Policy," in Paul R. Portney, ed., *Current Issues in U.S. Environmental Policy* (Johns Hopkins Press for Resources for the Future, 1978), pp. 68–104.
34. Charles A. Lave and Lester B. Lave, "Curbing 'Lead Poisoning' by Drivers," *New York Times,* February 2, 1979; and Sobotka and Company, Inc., "An Analysis of the Factors Leading to the Use of Leaded Gasoline in Automobiles Requiring Unleaded Gasoline," report prepared for the Environmental Protection Agency (EPA, September 29, 1978), pp. 3–5.

Lessons from the Controversies and Possible Solutions

The above controversies demonstrate that setting standards is both time-consuming and cumbersome, that often the wrong substances are regulated, and that implementation and enforcement are expensive and inadequate. Moreover, there are contradictions among regulations—perhaps because of a general failure to step back to look at the complete picture. Although social regulation has brought society closer to achieving its desired goals, the last decade and a half has revealed major flaws. Regulatory reform is desirable; indeed, it is necessary. But regulatory reform is confronted with diverse proposals that must be sharpened to deal with the underlying problems. It is important to understand the sources of the current difficulties in order to arrive at some notion of what reforms are necessary and likely to work.

Both the praise and blame for social regulation to date rests primarily with Congress. It writes the legislation, oversees it, amends it, sets appeal mechanisms and budgets, and confirms the regulators. To its credit, Congress quickly understood the problems and the public's desire for improvement. The initial legislation drafted to deal with these problems was less praiseworthy because Congress succumbed to rhetoric rather than trying to deal with those problems. Even worse, Congress failed to perceive the inadequacies in the legislation and correct them. Congress has not solved the difficult problems associated with giving the agencies practical goals, resolving conflicts among legislation, and finding workable mechanisms for implementation. Certainly there are no easy or obvious solutions, as demonstrated by the welter of proposals for reform. But there are some problems that only Congress can handle.

Much of the responsibility for the current situation belongs to the regulators themselves. It is not a sufficient qualification for agency administrators to know the law (or the science, the engineering, or even the economics) and have a true desire to protect the environment (or workers or consumers). The achievement of a goal—even one supported by the majority of people and written into law—by means of setting and enforcing standards requires all these disciplines in addition to good sense and political judgment.

The views of the standard-setting and enforcement process that are often expressed by regulators are "it is all politics"; "science speaks for itself"; and "our hands are tied." The first view is that, because the electorate wants a clean environment, any progress toward this goal is desirable—as long as political forces support it. Thus scientific evidence and analysis, the weighing of costs and benefits, or even engineering feasibility are viewed as either irrelevant or as tools for gathering support. But how long will popular and congressional support persist for hasty, ill-conceived regulations and implementation plans? Congressional disciplining of the Federal Trade Commission and the Consumer Product Safety Commission (at least until recently) provides one answer.

The second view is that the scientific facts speak for themselves and determine each decision. Unfortunately, this evidence is rarely clear or unequivocal. The laboratory studies find that animals react to a particular toxic substance at high levels of exposure; an extrapolation is necessary to estimate the effects at low levels (for example, in the case of vinyl chloride). Generally there are no data on human effects. Scientific analysis will, at best, provide a range of estimated effects and help identify a number of possible exposure levels that might be chosen. However, other considerations will be necessary to choose a particular exposure level. If quantitative analysis is not used to identify the proper range and nature of uncertainties, the result is likely to be decisions that waste resources and fail to protect—decisions that can be challenged in court or before Congress.

The third view is expressed by regulators when explaining why they cannot accommodate a reasonable request or why they are spending time on secondary problems when first-order problems are neglected. Their unsatisfactory performance resulted, they say, because of the restrictions of the statutes; there was no reason to muster the best scientific evidence, to sponsor research that would improve the evidence, to perform analysis, or to monitor the successes and failures of past regulations and implementation techniques. Indeed, anything except what they did seems to have been prohibited by Congress or the courts. Yet as solicitors and regulators have changed and as the courts have had a chance to rule, it has become evident that the legislation is sufficiently broad to support diverse interpretations. There is no excuse for being carried away by current crises and failing to engage in systematic thinking.

Improvements in Legislation

The fundamental problems cannot be solved until Congress confronts the task of setting workable goals for each agency and reconciling conflicts among the goals.

Instructing one agency to protect the environment, another to protect workers, and a third to protect consumers invites chaos. Each agency must be instructed on priorities and what to do when conflicts emerge. For example, it is not sufficient to order an agency to make the environment sufficiently clean to protect health. Who is to be protected (for example, cigarette smokers with emphysema, persons who suffer from eye irritation)? What margins for safety are needed? How should conflicts such as that between electricity costs and clean air be resolved? These are questions of values; although they are difficult to resolve, Congress is the body that must do so.

But Congress should not attempt to set detailed regulations, as it did for the automobile. It does not have the time or technical knowledge to write standards and is not organized to negotiate compromises. Instead, it must set workable goals and then oversee the agency to ensure that the emerging implementation is consistent with congressional intent.

Better Data and Analysis

Better collection and analysis of scientific and technical data is fundamental to better social regulation. If the Environmental Protection Agency had undertaken such research in 1970, much better answers could now be given to the issues of which specific pollutants affect health and which risks are associated with alternative levels of air quality. Data collection and analysis are of utmost importance in formulating policy on toxic substances.

Analysis is needed to identify the implications of decisions and contradictions among them and to clarify the trade-offs among various goals. Although the analysis cannot be expected to anticipate all problems, much can be done to foresee and take account of contradictions and trade-offs that arise, such as those discussed above for the automobile. Better data collection and analysis will occur only if the agency and Congress jointly recognize the need and provide the resources.

Reconciling Conflicting Goals

Better analysis cannot resolve the inherent differences in goals among the various participants in the process. Environmentalists have goals that differ from those of industrialists, and no amount of data gathering or analysis will make their views coincide. But, somehow, a set of workable goals and priorities must be developed.

Agencies themselves are incapable of developing goals. Professionals join agencies whose missions they believe to be important; an agency's political constituency believes the mission is important. Thus the agency is not and cannot be a neutral party. The role of setting workable goals and priorities belong to Congress.

Improving Implementation

Even supposing that Congress and the agencies make changes that will result in better regulations, there is still the problem of implementation. It is literally impossible to have detailed checking and supervision of all polluters or work places. Economists assert that improving implementation requires restructuring incentives so that polluters are motivated to abate pollution rather than to circumvent the law. This is best done with monetary incentives rather than legal standards.[35]

Current enforcement procedures begin with identification of a violator. The inevitable response of the violator is that technology does not exist to abate pollution in the particular case. After being shown that technology is available, the response is that it is so costly that the firm will be severely penalized or even bankrupted. Even after resolving all these difficulties, the polluter is motivated financially to delay ordering, installing, and operating the abatement equipment. Perhaps the best evidence of the time and resources re-

35. Edwin S. Mills, *The Economics of Environmental Quality* (Norton and Company, 1978), pp. 91–96; Larry E. Ruff, "Federal Environmental Regulation," in *Study on Federal Regulation,* Senate Committee on Governmental Affairs, vol. 6, appendix, 95 Cong. 2 sess. (GPO, 1978), pp. 251–347; Edwin S. Mills and Lawrence J. White, "Government Policies toward Automatic Emissions Control," in Ann F. Friedlander, ed., *Approaches to Controlling Air Pollution* (MIT Press, 1978), pp. 348–409; Allen V. Kneese and Charles L. Schultze, *Pollution, Prices, and Public Policy* (Brookings Institution, 1975), pp. 98–104; Martin L. Weitzman, "Prices versus Quantities," *Review of Economic Studies,* vol. 41 (October 1974), pp. 477–91; and Marc J. Roberts and Michael Spence, "Effluent Charges and Licenses Under Uncertainty," *Journal of Public Economics,* vol. 5 (April–May 1976), pp. 193–208.

quired to go through these steps is all the missed deadlines in the air and water pollution abatement programs.

One proposed solution to this lack of progress is to expedite the process by removing the appeals mechanisms, by increasing fines, or even by imposing criminal penalties. For example, "willful violation" of occupational safety standards can entail criminal convictions and imprisonment. But it seems a safe prediction that increased fines will rarely be levied or that executives will be sent to jail. Fines are rarely collected now because a company can argue that the money will be better spent on abatement equipment.

The legal mechanisms underlying current implementation procedures are a major part of the problem. Attention has been shifting to economic incentives such as the experiment of the Environmental Protection Agency with a "noncompliance charge," a fine that aims to remove the financial incentive to delay acquiring and installing abatement equipment. Economists argue that the whole procedure could be improved by levying effluent charges and letting each polluter decide how much to emit. Levying a charge based on the general damage to the environment would remove any necessity for the government to ascertain that technology was available at a feasible cost. Instead, each polluter could decide when to order the equipment and to what extent it will be used. Rather than being motivated to circumvent the law, each polluter would be motivated to curtail emissions in order to lower cost.

One major objection to effluent fees is that they are regarded by many as "a license to pollute": more affluent polluters could pour out their emissions with impunity or pass along the costs to their customers. However, although some enterprises have a sufficient profit cushion that they would not be bankrupted by paying effluent fees (in contrast to abating pollution), the fees would nonetheless shrink their profits. Certainly, it is implausible that a profit-making firm would willingly throw away its profits because it was too lazy to abate pollution. Even a public utility could not engage in paying the fee and polluting the environment because its rates are subject to regulation, and it seems unlikely that the rate-setting authority would allow these costs to be passed through quickly and completely to consumers. Furthermore, one of the favorite devices of government is using tax policy to accomplish social goals: providing investment tax credits stimulates investment, while deducting interest payments stimulates ownership of homes. Is it possible that economic incentives can be regarded as powerful stimuli in tax policy but ineffective in health, safety, and environmental regulations?

A second major objection to effluent fees is that they require voluminous data—too much information—to set properly. As Edwin Mills points out, setting effluent fees in a theoretically correct manner requires precisely the same information that is needed to set emissions standards or to use any other abatement mechanism.[36] In practice, this detail is never available. Thus the question is whether partial information allows better attainment of environmental goals through effluent fees or emissions standards. Emissions standards inevitably result in litigation and administrative procedures listing the problems with each facility and the specific technology required for abatement. Effluent fees require estimates of both the cost of abating pollution from each source and the cost of the harm caused to society. The estimates can be erroneous for individual polluters and still lead to an improvement. Furthermore, the regulatory agency need not investigate and certify abatement technologies in detail.[37]

Transferable pollution rights have also been suggested as a way of creating economic incentives to control pollution. Such a right would give its owner authority to emit, say, one pound of sulfur dioxide into the air. Regulators would create the number of rights corresponding to desired air quality and either give them to existing polluters or sell them at auctions. Polluters exceeding their rights would be fined. This proposal has the advantage of fixing total emissions, with the price of a right being determined in the market. In contrast, effluent fees fix the price and let the quantity of emissions be determined in the market.

In addition, economic incentives have been suggested to control occupational injury.[38] The current approach is to set standards that will protect workers from injury or chronic disease. This requires detailed examination of current processes and equipment. An agency is required to regulate at the most detailed level—for example, safety

36. Mills, *The Economics of Environmental Quality*, p. 93.
37. A major series of studies has been carried out by Resources for the Future. See Allen V. Kneese and Blair T. Bower, *Environmental Quality and Residuals Management: Report of a Research Program on Economic, Technological and Institutional Aspects* (Johns Hopkins University Press for Resources for the Future, 1979). They specify existing abatement technologies, estimate the cost of abatement, and calculate some of the benefits.
38. *Economic Report of the President*, 1977, pp. 154–56.

equipment for each machine. There is no realistic possibility that a regulatory agency could ever have the professional personnel to set such standards and enforce them. One proposed alternative is to levy a fine on employers for each injury, for instance, $500 for every work-day lost to an accident and $500,000 for each accidental death. The notion is that these fines would serve to motivate employers to find safety problems in their operations and correct them; the regulator would need accident reports but would not have to know the problem or preventive measures. There is some limited evidence that workers' compensation premiums have led employers to take steps to lower accident rates.

An issue that inevitably arises in discussions of effluent fees is the use to be made of the resulting revenues.[39] Should they be used to abate pollution? To compensate victims? Or should they simply act as a tax to raise revenue? The answer to this question is not crucial; additional tax revenues could hardly be an embarrassment to the government. Economists have learned to be suspicious of clever plans to tailor fee revenues to abating pollution or compensating victims. Such plans are inevitably filled with loopholes. Even worse, as cir-cumstances gradually change, these programs continue after having lost their justification. One would want to be careful about paying the heirs of a worker killed in an accident $500,000 or paying an injured worker $500 per day lost from work. Both sums are large enough to give rise to fraudulent behavior.

The point is not that effluent fees, transferable pollution rights, or economic incentives generally are simple to implement and are free of problems. Certainly they would involve litigation and have faults. Rather, the notion is that they emphasize efficiency of imple-mentation while legal mechanisms stress equity. Experience to date suggests that more emphasis on efficiency of implementation is re-quired and that the economic incentives are worth trying. Indeed, the Environmental Protection Agency employs limited versions of the transferable rights mechanisms in its "bubble" and "offset" concepts; the former allows a firm to trade off one emission source for another, as long as total plant emissions are within permitted levels, while the

39. Frederick R. Anderson and others, *Environmental Improvement Through Economic Incentives* (Johns Hopkins University Press for Resources for the Future, 1977), pp. 45–46.

latter permits new plants to be opened in a polluted area if they reduce emissions by more than they will add (through controlling or shutting down existing polluters).

Enhanced Enforcement

As the preceding discussion shows, enforcement of current regulations is negligent. One possible solution is to increase greatly the resources devoted to enforcing regulations. For example, the number of environmental or occupational inspectors could be increased tenfold and given a daily quota of inspections. Such a change would certainly reveal more violators, raise more revenue from fines, and perhaps even enhance abatement and safety. However, it would first highlight the problems in the current standards. Many, perhaps most, of the major work places in the nation could be shut down by strict enforcement of the health and safety regulations. Such expanded enforcement would certainly lead to resentment of the regulations and demands for reform or even elimination of them.

Changes in Agency Rulemaking

The Administrative Procedure Act, passed in 1946, calls for a sequence of steps from notice of proposed rulemaking to hearings; the final regulation must be based on evidence in the hearing. Following these steps requires thousands of days of professional time and results in long delays in setting standards. One proposal is to change these steps so that new regulations can be issued quickly. However, the Environmental Protection Agency now goes through the entire process, even though it is not a requirement. It believes that there is so much to learn about the costs and benefits of abatement, the difficulties of compliance, and the nature of the uncertainties that the time is well spent. Furthermore, it is difficult to imagine that the nation would tolerate the setting of rules imposing costs of billions of dollars on various groups without an elaborate process in which all viewpoints were heard.

Indeed, a proposal has also been made to enhance the comments process by funding groups that would otherwise not be able to participate. For example, the Food and Drug Administration has embarked on a program to pay the travel and legal fees of consumers who want to testify. Extending the proceeding in this way will cost time and money. However, it is hoped that the extended procedure will result in better regulations and that, after all interested parties have had the opportunity to make their views known, there will be less litigation after the standard is set.

Agency frustration with delays in rulemaking is understandable, and the enormous effort required to gather information, study opposing views, and sort through contrary scientific evidence is both time-consuming and expensive. Yet too many regulations have been promulgated without sufficient exploration of their scientific, economic, and political implications. Hearings are especially important because Congress generally has not resolved value conflicts. If the agency also fails to air and to try to resolve these conflicts, resistance is likely to go far beyond litigation. Social regulation will work better if the quality of regulations is improved and conflicts are anticipated.

Mechanisms for Immediate Improvements

Many of the above proposals would require either changes in legislation or long delays before social regulation is improved. But one step that would require no legislation and could be taken by agencies immediately is listing and publishing their priorities. Although agencies have gone through internal priority-setting exercises—indeed, zero-base budgeting requires such an exercise—rarely have they published criteria for this priority setting and the resulting priorities. (An exception is the Consumer Product Safety Commission, which published criteria in 1977 and has published detailed priorities annually since then.) The public and Congress are unaware of the priorities of each agency and have no basis on which to approve their goals or their allocation of resources among research, standard setting, and implementation, or among various programs. The information contained in an agency's budget is generally aggregated and sketchy; priorities are difficult to discern.

If agencies gave more attention to priority setting and then discussed the priorities with Congress and the public, much would be done to clarify public goals and the conflicts among those goals. Developing and publishing such information would not be a radical change in current procedures. Some of this information is developed in the budget process; publishing it should enhance the care with which the information is developed. The Regulatory Council could set guidelines for publication of the information. Congress could use this information in oversight and budget hearings to obtain more insight into goals and efficiency.

One other step that would help rationalize environmental policy would be to utilize the materials balance framework and estimate in an integrated way the amount of exposure to toxins that people receive.[40] Boundaries drawn for media, locations, and type of emissions are artificial—for example, setting rules for work-related exposure in isolation from other exposures. As more is learned about the toxicity of various chemical compounds and about how the combination of environmental problems affects people, the need for this integration will be even greater.

The creative phase of social regulation has been completed. Public desires for a clean, safe environment will prevent any general retreat for our current ambitious goals. The next phase must improve the legislation and the regulatory frameworks for setting and enforcing standards; Congress must debate and settle some of the crucial conflicts among values. The lessons of the first decade and a half of social regulation have much to contribute in shaping this change. Making social regulation work is difficult, but the rewards are better health and safety, an enhanced environment, and more economic growth.

40. The framework recognizes that matter is neither created nor destroyed in the economy, but merely changed in location and chemical form. For example, the sulfur in coal must be emitted into the air or water, placed in the ground, or used as a raw ingredient in another process.

CHAPTER SIX

Medical Care

LOUISE B. RUSSELL

IN RETROSPECT, the 1970s were a time of stalemate in health policy. Proposals for new programs withered and died in the shadow cast by the high costs of existing programs; efforts to constrain costs were equally unsuccessful because of fears that they threatened what had already been attained. At the beginning of the decade numerous national health insurance bills were under consideration by Congress. But as costs continued to rise, these bills were put aside, unpassed, and were replaced by a series of increasingly broad proposals for cost containment, culminating in the administration's bills to limit the rate of growth in hospital expenditures. After several years of hard fighting by the principals on both sides, the House approved a token cost-containment bill at the end of 1979; the Senate had still not taken final action. In the same session of Congress, a new set of national health insurance bills was put forward. These bills were more cautious in outlook than their predecessors. The administration, for example, proposed only the first phase of its National Health Plan, as part of a strategy to minimize the effect of the plan on costs.

Medical care in the 1970s presented the nation with the classic dilemma between unlimited needs and limited resources to meet those needs. As the national wealth has grown, the goal of providing medical care whenever it is needed has been pursued by means of private and

I am grateful to Richard J. Rosen for research assistance, to Charlotte Kaiser for typing the manuscript, and to Henry J. Aaron, James D. Farrell, Paul B. Ginsburg, Klaus-Dirk Henke, Lester B. Lave, and Susanne A. Stoiber for their comments.

Table 6-1. National Health Expenditures, Selected Years, 1950–78

Millions of dollars

Type of expenditure	1950	1955	1960	1965	1970	1975	1978[a]
Hospital care	3,851	5,900	9,902	13,935	27,799	52,138	76,025
Physicians' services	2,747	3,689	5,684	8,474	14,340	24,932	35,250
Drugs and drug sundries	1,726	2,384	3,657	5,771	8,406	11,812	15,098
Dentists' services	961	1,508	1,977	2,809	4,750	8,237	13,300
Nursing-home care	187	312	526	2,072	4,677	9,886	15,751
All others[b]	3,190	3,952	5,149	9,941	14,770	24,460	37,023
Total[c]	12,662	17,745	26,895	43,003	74,740	131,465	192,448
Percent of gross national product	4.5	4.4	5.3	6.2	7.6	8.6	9.1

Sources: Data for 1955 are from Barbara S. Cooper, Nancy L. Worthington, and Mary F. McGee, *Compendium of National Health Expenditures Data* (U.S. Government Printing Office, 1976), table 6, p. 34. All other data are from Robert M. Gibson, "National Health Expenditures, 1978," *Health Care Financing Review*, vol. 1 (Summer 1979), tables 1 and 3.

a. Preliminary data.

b. Other services, appliances, administration, public health activities, research, and construction.

c. Columns may not add to total due to rounding.

public programs of third-party payment—private health insurance, medicare, medicaid, and the like. These programs pay most of the costs of care and encourage doctors and patients to use medical resources as though their costs were zero, or almost zero, leaving them free to arrange for whatever services the patient needs.

But need does not mean that the benefit is greater than the cost, only that the benefit is greater than zero. When need is the only criterion, the number of worthwhile things that can be done in medical care is limitless—new services such as the CT scanner or kidney dialysis, better services such as improved nursing homes, and more services for groups that have been neglected. Under the present system of third-party payment, the nation is trying to do them all, no matter how small or costly the gain. We have deliberately chosen to spare patients and their doctors the painful task of deciding when a medical benefit is, in some sense, worth the resources it draws from other uses.

The result has been an enormous influx of resources into medical care, and the end is nowhere in sight. The share of gross national product devoted to medical care rose rapidly during the 1960s and 1970s and exceeded 9 percent in 1978, as shown in table 6-1. Even for a nation as rich as the United States, to provide medical care on the basis of need alone is an expensive proposition, possibly more expensive than we are willing to accept much longer. Caught between the unpleasant alternatives of spending still more or rationing care, the nation has chosen—for the past decade at least—to do nothing.

The purpose of this chapter is to describe the history that produced this stalemate, the main features of health policy in the 1970s, and the proposals for what might be done in the future.

History[1]

The history of health policy in this century has been primarily one of expanding access to care through the development of third-party payment mechanisms. The first major landmark in this history was the formation in 1912 of a Committee on Social Insurance by the American Association for Labor Legislation, a group composed of social scientists and others interested in social reform. Fresh from a successful campaign to get workmen's compensation laws enacted by the states, the association turned its attention to the development of model legislation the states could use to introduce health insurance for the general population. The suggested bill included the principles that the scheme should be compulsory, with payments and management shared by employers, employees, and the public; that those not automatically covered by the plan should be permitted to join if they wished; and that preventive care should be emphasized. Bills were introduced in some states, but the movement lacked popular support. No state legislature actually approved a plan.

In 1932 the issue was revived by the report of the Committee on the Cost of Medical Care, a group financed by a consortium of private foundations. After five years of work that produced a benchmark study of medical care in the United States, the majority of the committee recommended group payment for medical care (meaning the insurance principle, or third-party payment) and the organization of the system into prepaid group practices. The dissenting minority endorsed only the concept of insurance. Their endorsement was subject to a number of qualifications—for example, that any plan should be nonprofit and controlled by doctors and hospitals, and that patients should have free choice of physician—intended to avoid the defects they saw in the systems of other countries.

Partly in response to the possibility of a government plan, and partly because of the financial difficulties of hospitals and their cus-

---

1. The initial paragraphs in this section draw heavily on Odin W. Anderson, *The Uneasy Equilibrium: Private and Public Financing of Health Services in the United States 1875–1965* (New Haven: College and University Press, 1968), pp. 1–120.

tomers during the depression, the American Hospital Association began to encourage the development of private insurance plans for hospital care. It helped pass special enabling legislation for these plans in the states, and in 1936 formed a national center to set standards for member plans and act as a clearinghouse. This center became the Blue Cross Association. Somewhat later the American Medical Association played a similar role in promoting and coordinating the development of Blue Shield plans sponsored by state medical societies. Other private insurance companies also gradually began to offer health insurance policies.

Although proposals for government action continued to be put forward, the programs actually undertaken were short term or were designed for groups such as veterans for which the government had a particular responsibility. Private insurance rapidly became the major form of third-party financing, a position it held until the 1960s. In 1940, only 9 percent of the population had some kind of insurance for hospital care, 4 percent had surgical insurance, and a little more than 2 percent had insurance for nonsurgical services provided in the hospital by physicians. By 1950, the figures were 51 percent, 36 percent, and 14 percent, respectively. And by 1960, 72 percent of the population had hospital insurance, 65 percent had surgical insurance, and 48 percent had nonsurgical, or medical, insurance.

The proportion of people aged sixty-five or older with insurance also grew rapidly, but remained well below the national average. In the early 1960s about half the aged population had hospital insurance, up from one-quarter in 1952, but still about 20 points below the percentage for the population as a whole. The insurance policies bought by the aged also tended to provide less comprehensive coverage. These facts caused concern because the medical expenses of the elderly were (and are) high: in 1961 they averaged $315 per person, two and one-half times the average of $128 for younger people. Eight percent of households headed by elderly people incurred medical expenses of more than $1,000 in 1962. As a result, insurance was both more important for the aged and more expensive. But a disproportionate number of the aged were poor—in 1964, 31 percent of the aged, compared to 18 percent of the population as a whole, lived in households with incomes below the poverty line—and thus were less able to purchase either the care or the insurance.

The idea of enacting a program for the aged grew in popularity with the Congress during the 1950s and early 1960s. The Kerr-Mills bill was passed in 1960, increasing the federal matching money available for the medical care of people receiving old age assistance from the states, and authorizing for the first time matching funds to help pay the medical bills of the "medically needy"—elderly people who were not on welfare, but who were nevertheless having trouble paying their medical bills. Also for the first time, matching funds—for the medically needy—were available with no upper limit on what the federal government would pay.

Bills to provide medical benefits through the social security program to all the elderly, regardless of income, continued to be introduced and debated in each session of Congress. In 1965, five years after the Kerr-Mills bill, the medicare program became law. It went into effect on July 1, 1966. The program had two parts: hospital benefits, subject to both a deductible of $40 and limits on long stays and financed by an addition to the payroll tax; and insurance to cover 80 percent of physicians' fees (after a deductible of $50), which was financed in equal parts by premiums collected from enrollees and by general revenues. Everyone aged sixty-five or older was automatically entitled to hospital benefits when the program began. Enrollment for physicians' insurance was and is voluntary.

The potential costs of the program had been a sticking point in the congressional debate. Frequent revisions, even before the bill was passed, underlined how much more difficult it was to project costs for a program to provide services rather than for one, like the retirement program, that paid cash benefits.[2] The estimates published soon after passage of the bill were therefore made according to assumptions about the future that were considered to be quite conservative at the time. The costs of hospital insurance were estimated at slightly less than $3 billion for calendar 1970 and about $4.2 billion for 1975. At the legislated tax rate for employers and employees combined of 1.0 percent in 1970 and 1.1 percent in 1975, the hospital trust fund was expected to have money left over. Costs for the medical insurance part of the program were projected only two years ahead because the law allowed the premiums to be adjusted as neces-

2. Martha Derthick, *Policymaking for Social Security* (Brookings Institution, 1979), p. 330.

sary every year. On the assumption that 95 percent of the elderly would choose to enroll, the high estimate was that costs would be $1.3 billion in 1967.[3]

Almost as an afterthought, Congress also expanded the federal-state grant program to help pay the medical expenses of those on welfare (medicaid). Federal matching funds were authorized without limit, not only for welfare recipients, but if a state chose, for the medically needy as well, regardless of age. Standards were set for the kinds of care, although not the amounts, the states had to offer. Apparently no one thought the states would make much use of the generous matching funds. Estimates were that this expansion would add about $200 million a year to the federal cost of the existing program, which was $550 million in fiscal 1965.

During the 1950s and the 1960s the federal government not only established major programs to pay for care, but added and expanded programs to advance the frontiers of medical care and to increase the resources, especially manpower, available to produce it. The research budget of the National Institutes of Health was increased year after year; new institutes were created; and the responsibilities of old ones enlarged. The Institutes spent $28 million in 1950, and more than $1 billion in 1970. The National Cancer Act of 1971 crowned this period of growth, giving the Cancer Institute new visibility and much larger budgets. The total for all the Institutes reached $2 billion in 1975; of this, the Cancer Institute spent $700 million, compared to less than $200 million in 1970.

The manpower programs were designed to ensure that the supplies of medical professionals were large enough to meet the need for them, and estimates of need were stated in numbers of doctors, dentists, nurses, and so on, relative to the population. Because meeting need was the primary goal, the annual costs of maintaining these workers once they were in the system were seldom considered. When they were, it was generally argued that the added resources would reduce costs, or at least moderate their rise, by reducing the prices of services at the same time that quantities were increased. The argument is valid when applied to areas of the economy where the limited

3. Robert J. Myers and Francisco Bayo, "Hospital Insurance, Supplementary Medical Insurance, and Old-Age, Survivors, and Disability Insurance: Financing Basis Under the 1965 Amendments," *Social Security Bulletin*, vol. 28 (October 1965), pp. 24–28.

income of the customer means that when quantities increase, price per unit must decrease. No one realized that the growth of third-party payment, which backed the unlimited goal of need with an unlimited commitment to pay, was removing this constraint from medical care and making it possible for the industry to absorb large quantities of resources without a decline in their prices. More fundamentally, once again no one realized that need did not add up to a small, tidy number of dollars.

Manpower shortages were announced regularly during the 1950s and 1960s. Virtually all the health professions eventually received federal funds for training, but existing and projected shortages of physicians were given the most attention. The Bane Committee warned in 1959 that medical school classes would have to be enlarged almost 50 percent to ensure that the physician-population ratio did not decline by 1975.[4] Beginning in 1963, a succession of laws made available increasing amounts of money to subsidize the operating and construction costs of medical schools and to provide loans and scholarships for students. The money was linked to requirements that class sizes be increased: for example, the Comprehensive Health Manpower Training Act of 1971 specified a minimum increase in the entering class each year, and offered bonuses for larger increases. Similar programs were legislated for dentists, nurses, and other health professions.

The programs very quickly succeeded in increasing class sizes and, in sequence, numbers of graduates and practitioners also grew. Between 1965 and 1975, the number of medical school graduates increased 70 percent (from 7,800 to 13,300); dental graduates increased more than 50 percent; and registered nurse graduates doubled. The subsidies that produced these results were substantial. In 1975, federal training funds for education—grants to schools, student scholarships, and the direct outlays of student loan programs —averaged $4,966 per medical student, $4,121 per dental student, and $636 per nursing student.

In 1967, not long after these programs began, the report of the National Advisory Commission on Health Manpower agreed that there was no longer any danger that the physician-population ratio

4. U.S. Department of Health, Education, and Welfare, *Physicians for a Growing America: Report of the Surgeon General's Consultant Group on Medical Education* (U.S. Government Printing Office, 1959), p. 12 (Bane Committee Report).

would fall, but cautioned that rising demand for services might nonetheless lead to shortages.[5] The pressure remained to increase supplies. Two other concerns were expressed in the manpower legislation and in the debate surrounding it. The first was that medical workers were not located where they were most needed, and that local shortages were particularly serious in rural and inner-city areas. The second was that, with more and more physicians training for the specialties, the population's need for nonspecialist care would not be met. But these issues were subordinated to the overriding concern with national shortages until later.

The Hill-Burton program to promote the construction of hospitals predated the training programs by many years. After the depression and World War II, when little investing was done, many people argued that the nation did not have the hospital beds it needed, particularly in rural areas. The Hospital Survey and Construction Act of 1946, which created the program, specified that construction subsidies could be provided until a state had 4.5 general hospital beds per 1,000 people; the limit for sparsely populated states was higher. The law was later amended to permit subsidies for renovation and for the construction of facilities besides hospitals. The Hill-Burton program was an important source of funds during the 1950s and 1960s; it provided as much as 15 percent of the money for hospital construction in some years and, through its requirements that some funds be raised from other sources, exerted leverage on considerably more.

Meanwhile, throughout the postwar period, expenditures on medical care claimed a larger and larger share of the gross national product, primarily because of the new resources being drawn in to produce more care, and new kinds of care, for more people.[6] After 1965, when medicare, medicaid, and private insurance coverage combined to loosen the economic constraints on the industry still further, the growth in resources, and thus in costs, accelerated. Expenditures under medicare and medicaid quickly outdistanced the original estimates. As costs continued to grow, Congress and state legislatures began to search for ways to slow them. Holding to the principle that people should be given the care they need, they enacted measures to

5. U.S. National Advisory Commission on Health Manpower, *Report of the National Advisory Commission on Health Manpower*, vol. 1 (GPO, 1967), p. 13.
6. Martin Feldstein and Amy Taylor, "The Rapid Rise of Hospital Costs," A Staff Report of the Executive Office of the President, Council on Wage and Price Stability (January 1977).

reduce unnecessary care, waste, abuse, and fraud. The presumption was that these were important sources of higher costs and that, if they were eliminated, the growth in costs would drop to a comfortable level.

The first major federal initiative was to establish the professional standards review organizations. Congress created these organizations —generally groups of physicians—through the Social Security Amendments of 1972, and asked them to review the care given patients in their respective areas to determine whether it was necessary and of good quality. Their first responsibility was the hospital care given medicare and medicaid patients, and if a review group disapproved hospital admission, or a longer stay, medicare and medicaid would not pay. The plan was to expand the reviews as the groups gained experience to include nursing homes and outpatient care.

Certificate-of-need legislation—laws requiring hospitals to obtain state approval for investment projects or changes in service—began with the states. Three states passed laws before 1970, and many more followed in the early 1970s as costs continued to rise. The purpose of the laws was to reduce costs by preventing the addition of beds or equipment beyond the needs of an area, but not to cut back on investments with real benefits for patients. Certificate of need and health planning were brought together in the National Health Planning and Resources Development Act of 1974. This law replaced the voluntary planning agencies created by the Comprehensive Health Planning and Public Health Services Amendments of 1966 with a new network of more than 200 agencies; their job was to review the medical resources in their areas, recommend long-term plans for development, and advise the states on applications for certificates of need. The 1974 act also required that every state have a certificate-of-need law.

The government nibbled at the edges of costs by other means as well, some administrative, some requiring new legislation. Medicare reduced the degree by which a physician's fee could exceed the average for the area and still be reimbursed, and cut payments to nursing homes by tightening its criteria for approving claims. The Social Security Amendments of 1972 gave medicare the authority to limit hospital payments, but thus far this has been applied only to the routine, or "hotel" costs, of hospitals. States froze the fees paid to physicians under medicaid, and Congress approved money for a more careful screening of medicaid eligibility and of the validity of claims for reimbursement.

Medical Care in the 1970s

By 1978, more than 90 percent of the population was covered by some form of third-party payment for medical expenses—private health insurance, medicare, medicaid, the programs of benefits administered by the Veterans Administration and the U.S. Department of Defense, other smaller programs, or some combination of these. Coverage was most complete for hospital care, with less than 10 percent of hospital costs paid directly by patients and the rest financed by third-party payment. Third-party payment reimbursed 66 percent of the costs of physicians' services, 54 percent of the costs of care in a nursing home, and smaller percentages of the costs of other kinds of medical care.

The poor and the elderly have made substantial gains under medicare and medicaid. Historically, the poor have used less medical care than those who are better off, even though their health is generally not as good. In 1964, for example, visits to physicians averaged 2.7 per year for children in families with incomes below $4,000, compared to 5.1 for those in families with incomes of $10,000 or more. By 1975, poor children averaged as many visits as those who were better off, and poor adults made more visits than better-off adults. The more frequent visits by poor adults were explained by their health problems; when the poor were compared with people of higher incomes who had similar problems, the frequency with which they saw physicians was about the same. Rates of surgery, which were considerably lower for the poor before medicaid, also increased, and by 1970 there was little difference between income classes.[7]

The medicare and medicaid programs both help pay the medical expenses of people aged sixty-five or older. About 95 percent of the elderly are currently entitled to hospital insurance under medicare; nearly as many elect to buy coverage for physicians' services. Medicaid pays the premiums for this coverage for many of the poor elderly and helps them pay the deductibles and coinsurance. Medicaid is also the major source of coverage for care in nursing homes: it supplied 85 percent of the third-party funds paid to nursing homes in 1978.

7. Karen Davis and Cathy Schoen, *Health and the War on Poverty: A Ten-Year Appraisal* (Brookings Institution, 1978), pp. 42, 45, 48.

Together medicare and medicaid paid about 60 percent of the total medical costs of the aged in 1977—44 percent from medicare, and the rest from medicaid. When other sources of third-party payment are added, the aged paid only one-quarter of their medical expenses directly, compared to 53 percent shortly before medicare began. Not all services are covered equally—for the elderly as for the general population, the proportion of expenses paid by third-party payment is very high for hospital care, and lower for physicians' services and nursing homes.

The use of medical services by the elderly has also grown since 1965. Visits to physicians did not change much, but hospital admission rates rose 31 percent between 1966 and 1976, from 277 to 363 per 1,000 people aged 65 or older. At the same time, hospitals took advantage of the new sources of funds to invest in better care and new types of care—intensive care units, open-heart surgery, new forms of radiotherapy, and other services—so that patients received more services once they were admitted to the hospital. The number of elderly in nursing homes rose even more sharply, from 22.8 per 1,000 people aged sixty-five or older in 1963 to 45.1 in 1973.

There is considerable controversy about just how much additional medical care contributes to better health and longer life in countries like the United States, where the use of medical care has been relatively high for years. Many people argue that exercise, good nutrition (and not too much of it), not smoking, and a clean, safe environment are far more important. Whatever the cause, death rates declined somewhat more rapidly after 1965 than they did in the preceding fifteen years, and some of the statistics suggest that the improvements have been concentrated among the elderly and the poor. The life expectancy of men at age sixty-five was 12.8 years in 1950, and was still 12.8 years in 1965; by 1977, it had risen to 13.9 years. For elderly women, life expectancy rose in both periods, but by more after 1965 than before. For white women, life expectancy at 65 rose from 15.0 years in 1950 to 16.3 in 1965 and 18.4 in 1977; for nonwhite women, it was 14.5 in 1950, 15.5 in 1965, and 17.8 in 1977—a gain of 2.3 years between 1965 and 1977. The death rate for infants during their first year fell from 24.7 per 1,000 in 1965 to 14.1 in 1977, compared to a decline of less than 5 per 1,000, from 29.2 to 24.7, between 1950 and 1965. The decline was particularly striking for blacks: their infant mortality rate edged downward between 1950 and 1965, and then plummeted from 41.7 per 1,000 in 1965 to 23.6 in 1977—a great improvement, but still well above the rate of 12.3 for whites in that year.

These accomplishments—the greater use of medical services by the poor and the elderly and the declines in mortality, to the extent that they are the result of those services—have been overshadowed by the high costs accompanying them. The costs of hospital benefits under medicare had been projected at $3 billion for 1970; instead they were almost $5 billion. By 1978, with the disabled and people with kidney failure added to the program (in 1973), hospital benefits cost more than $18 billion; the combined employer-employee tax rate necessary to finance them, which provides a measure of cost largely free of the effects of general inflation, was 2.0 percent—0.8 more than the rate originally estimated, in spite of several increases in the maximum amount of earnings subject to tax. The total costs of the program in 1978 were $25 billion.

The federal share of medicaid had been estimated at about $200 million annually at the time the bill was passed. As it turned out, the federal share was $3 billion by 1970 and more than $10 billion in 1978. The total cost of the program in 1978, including state funds, was $18 billion.

Medicare and medicaid were only part of the picture. Total national expenditures on health rose from $13 billion in 1950 to $43 billion in 1965 and $192 billion in 1978 (see table 6-1). General inflation was an important reason for the increase, but much of the growth reflected the increasing amounts of resources committed to medical care—more physicians and nurses, more hospital and nursing home beds, more equipment and new kinds of equipment—and the greater numbers of services they produced. The proportion of the gross national product committed to medical care, an approximate measure of the growth in resources, rose from 4.5 percent in 1950 to 6.2 percent in 1965, and 9.1 percent in 1978, doubling in less than thirty years.

Hospital expenditures have always been the largest item in the total and their share has increased. In 1978 they amounted to $76 billion, 40 percent of total expenditures. Payments for care in nursing homes, though smaller, have grown even faster, and were $16 billion in 1978. These two expenditures together are almost half of the total spent on medical care nationally. They are far larger shares of the payments made by medicare and medicaid and are at the center of the financial difficulties of the two programs. Spending for care in nursing homes under medicare is minuscule, but hospital care accounts for almost three-quarters of the program's outlays. Hospital and nursing home care are about equally important to medicaid, with nursing homes accounting for 39 percent of program payments in 1978, and hospitals 37 percent.

Despite the new programs and the large expenditures, not everyone is covered, not everyone shares in the abundance, and many people can still draw up long lists of needs that remain to be filled. For example, not all the poor are eligible for medicaid—no more than two-thirds of them by one estimate.[8] Each state sets its own income standards to determine eligibility for welfare, and these may be lower than the federal poverty standard. In many states, welfare is available only to poor families in which one parent is missing or disabled and to the aged, the blind, and the disabled. (Income payments for the last three groups were taken over entirely by the federal government in 1974.) Single people, childless couples, and many families with both parents present do not qualify regardless of how low their income is. And in the twenty-one states that have not extended coverage to the medically needy, those who are close enough to poverty to have trouble paying large medical bills are not protected by the program.

More generally, some people at all income levels do not have protection against catastrophic medical expenses, variously defined as very high expenses—for example, more than $5,000—or expenses that are high in relation to income. If one point about third-party payment commands agreement, it is that such programs should provide protection against these medical catastrophes, which are usually the result of a prolonged stay in a hospital or nursing home. Yet an estimated 5 to 8 percent of the population is not covered by any private or public program. These people are disproportionately young and unemployed. Over half are members of poor families. Interestingly, almost half are in families in which the head of household is covered by insurance or a public program. In addition, some of those who have coverage do not have enough, or do not have the right kind, to protect them against catastrophic expenses, although this number has been declining with the rapid spread of major medical insurance.

8. Ibid., p. 54.

In 1965, 34 percent of the population had private major medical insurance; by the mid-1970s, the figure was over 60 percent. Public programs protect some of the rest.

It is not possible to estimate the number of people who are still vulnerable, either because they lack health insurance or because they lack the right kind, but recent estimates are available of the number who actually incur catastrophic expenses. The Congressional Budget Office estimated that, in 1978, 6.9 million families (9 percent of all families) had out-of-pocket expenses for medical care that exceeded 15 percent of their gross income. The definition of catastrophe here is important. Many of these families were poor—4.1 million had incomes of less than $5,000—so that an expenditure of less than $1,000 was catastrophic for them, although it would not have been for families with higher incomes.

In the wake of rising costs, the debate about health resources was turned on its head in the 1970s. Warnings of shortages were replaced by warnings of surpluses, or impending surpluses. In part, projections of needs expressed relative to the population had to be revised when it became clear that the decline in population growth that began in the mid-1960s was going to last for some time. But more and more frequently, the cost of maintaining current levels of resources, or future additions to resources, was brought into the discussion and lent weight to arguments that additions should be made cautiously, and that, in some cases, current levels should be cut back.

The Comprehensive Health Manpower Training Act of 1971, seen as the culmination of the health manpower policies of the 1960s and the pattern for the future, was scarcely in place before some began to suggest that physicians were no longer in short supply, and would soon be in oversupply.[9] Not only had population growth been less than projected, but the growth in medical school classes in response to the new federal legislation had been greater. One analyst estimated that each new physician cost the medical care system roughly $250,000 in 1972; the estimate includes the physician's income and office expenses and the costs of services ordered, such as hospital care.[10] And

9. Carnegie Council on Policy Studies in Higher Education, *Progress and Problems in Medical and Dental Education: Federal Support versus Federal Control* (Jossey-Bass, 1976), pp. 2, 8.

10. U. E. Reinhardt, "Health Manpower Policy in the United States: Past and Prospective" (Woodrow Wilson School of Public and International Affairs, Princeton University, 1976).

the Carnegie Council on Higher Education warned of the heavy costs of building the new medical schools that were still being planned.

Some observers saw in the large classes of American medical students an opportunity to reduce the country's reliance on graduates of foreign medical schools. Graduates of foreign schools accounted for 20 percent of the physicians practicing in the United States in the 1970s, and it was argued that they were not as well trained as domestic graduates and that, in any event, the United States should not depend on poorer countries to finance the training of its physicians. The Carnegie Council projected that even if the net inflow of foreign medical graduates declined to zero by 1987, there would be between 210 and 218 physicians per 100,000 people by 1985 and between 221 and 232 by 1990, compared to 174 in 1975 and 148 in 1960. The projected ratios are much higher than current levels in most industrialized countries, although they may not be much higher than future levels—several other countries have also encouraged large increases in medical school classes in the 1970s.

In the Health Professions Educational Assistance Act of 1976 Congress declared that there was no longer a shortage of physicians and ended both the preferential treatment given foreign physicians entering the country and the requirement that schools increase class sizes in order to receive federal subsidies. The Carter administration went further. Announcing its hope that class sizes would be cut back in future, it recommended that the subsidies be eliminated; by the end of 1979 Congress had agreed to reduce them, but had not yet decided to eliminate them. The 1976 act shifted the focus of federal policy to the geographic and specialty distributions of health manpower, and the National Health Service Corps, which requires graduates to practice for several years in a "medically underserved" area in return for scholarships and loans, has been the only major manpower program to be recommended for larger appropriations.

Although not everyone agreed that there would soon be too many physicians, a consensus seemed to form in the mid-1970s that there were already too many hospital beds. Again, this conclusion was based less on any precise notion of the correct number of beds, if such a calculation is even possible, than on a concern about costs and a sense that many existing beds were being used for care that was not important or that could be provided more cheaply elsewhere. The irony of the new view was that the national average in 1975 was 4.4

beds in nonfederal short-term hospitals per 1,000 people, slightly less than the maximum originally set for the most populous states by the Hill-Burton law. Further, the national occupancy rate was marginally higher in the mid-1970s than it had been in the late 1940s and early 1950s.

The amount of grant money available under the Hill-Burton program declined from its peak of the late 1960s and the program shifted to offering loans with federal subsidies and guarantees. In 1974 its planning functions were merged with the National Health Planning and Resources Development Act. A committee of the National Academy of Sciences subsequently recommended that, as one of the national guidelines required by the planning act, the U.S. Department of Health, Education, and Welfare should set a goal of reducing beds from 4.4 to 4.0 per 1,000 people within five years, "and well below that in the years to follow."[11] The department took the advice, and in the final guidelines published in March 1978 stated that planning agencies should consider 4.0 beds per 1,000 as a maximum, except in extraordinary circumstances, and that fewer beds were better.

By the mid-1970s hospital administrators and physicians were beginning to think there was a surplus of regulation in addition to the other surpluses. The paperwork necessary to be reimbursed by the new federal programs and the number of regulations to improve the safety and quality of care and to control costs had all increased. Hospitals did not direct their complaints solely at state and federal regulation, but included as well the activities of private groups like the Joint Commission on Accreditation of Hospitals. In view of the growing pressure to keep costs down, hospitals were particularly concerned about the additional costs imposed by regulation itself, and several state hospital associations sponsored studies of those costs.

Studies by researchers outside the industry examined the effect of cost regulation specifically. As mentioned earlier, this regulation was undertaken in the hope that significant cost savings could be achieved through improved efficiency and the elimination of wasteful duplication, without cutting into services of real benefit. The early results cast doubt on this premise. An analysis of state experience with certificate of need before the 1974 planning law concluded that the review process had reduced investment by hospitals in additional beds,

11. Institute of Medicine, "A Policy Statement: Controlling the Supply of Hospital Beds" (National Academy of Sciences, October 1976), p. ix.

but that investment of other kinds increased to make up the difference.[12] The effect on costs was negligible, and thus there were no savings to balance the costs of the review process. Under the 1974 law,
and in light of this experience, planning agencies are looking more
carefully at a broad range of investment projects. It is too early to tell
whether the new emphasis will produce different results.

Similarly, professional standards review organizations have not yet
produced enough savings through their review of admissions and
lengths of stay to make up for the costs of the reviews. The second
annual evaluation of these groups by the Department of Health, Education, and Welfare found that they had succeeded in reducing the
number of days spent in hospitals by medicare beneficiaries and were
saving the program $1.10 for every $1.00 spent on review. But when
medicare denies payment, more of the hospital's fixed costs are shifted
to other payers. The Congressional Budget Office estimated the savings to all parties and concluded that review saved $0.70 for every
$1.00 spent.

Experience in Other Countries

The other major industrialized countries do not have before them
the question of whether to introduce national health insurance. All of
them have it in some form, although the many differences in form
among countries belies the uniformity suggested by the term.[13]

The British National Health Service provides care to patients directly. It owns and operates all but a few of the country's hospitals
and establishes contracts with doctors for outpatient care. Most of
the costs are financed out of general revenues. The National Health
Service is often considered a typical European medical care system,
but in reality it is not. The Swedish system is perhaps closest to it,
but in Sweden hospitals are run by county governments and financed
by local taxes. The program officially titled "national health insurance" covers some outpatient care and provides cash payments during

12. David S. Salkever and Thomas W. Bice, *Hospital Certificate-of-Need Controls: Impact on Investment, Costs, and Use* (American Enterprise Institute for
Public Policy Research, 1979).

13. The major source for the next several paragraphs is Joseph G. Simanis,
"National Health Systems in Eight Countries," SSA 75-11924 (U.S. Department of
Health, Education, and Welfare, January 1975).

illness; it contributes only a small part of the total costs of medical care in Sweden.

The systems in West Germany, France, and the Netherlands depend on "sickness funds" (health insurance funds) that are usually organized along occupational or regional lines. Enrollment in the funds is compulsory for most people. In France almost everyone is required to belong to a sickness fund. The funds enroll beneficiaries and process claims, but the system is directed as a whole and financed through a payroll tax on all workers. Deficits are made up from general revenues. In Germany those with incomes above a certain amount were entirely excluded from membership in the funds at one time; they are now given intermittent opportunities to join and may, of course, buy private insurance. Each fund is supposed to be self-sustaining, with the contributions of its members financing the benefits required by law plus any supplementary benefits the fund chooses to offer. Government revenues, in the form of various subsidies and special programs, supply only about one-quarter of the total expenditures for medical care. In the Netherlands people with high incomes are also excluded from the compulsory insurance system. They may buy private insurance, and since 1968 they, along with the rest of the population, have been covered by a government program that pays catastrophic medical expenses.

Canada offers yet another variation. Under its national health insurance plan, the federal government makes grants to the provinces that cover about half the cost of providing hospital and medical benefits. Each province runs its own program, and the details of administration, reimbursement, and supplementary benefits vary from province to province.

When it comes to results, these different ways of providing national health insurance have much in common. And while there are differences between them and the system of medical care in the United States, even here the similarities are often more striking than the differences.

First, virtually the entire population is covered. All residents are entitled to services in Britain, Canada, and Sweden. Under the systems based on health insurance funds, a few people are not covered. In France more than 98 percent of the population is covered. In Germany 90 percent of the population is covered by the compulsory system; the major omitted group is people with high incomes, most of

Table 6-2. Expenditures for Medical Care as a Percent of Gross National Product, Selected Countries, 1969 and 1975

Country	1969	1975
United States	6.8	8.4
Canada	7.3	7.1
France	5.7	8.1
Netherlands	5.9	8.6
Sweden	6.7	8.7
United Kingdom[a]	4.8	5.6
West Germany	5.7	9.7

Source: 1969 data from Joseph G. Simanis, "Medical Care Expenditures in Seven Countries," *Social Security Bulletin*, vol. 36 (March 1973), p. 39; 1975 data supplied by the Social Security Administration.
a. The United Kingdom includes Great Britain (England, Wales, and Scotland) and Northern Ireland.

whom buy insurance. In the Netherlands everyone is covered for extraordinary expenses, but only about 70 percent of the population is covered under the compulsory system for basic benefits; most of the rest, the high-income group again, usually buy private insurance. In general, the group without coverage—when there is one—is smaller in these countries than in the United States, and tends to be made up of people with high rather than low incomes.

Second, third-party payment covers a high proportion of medical expenses. The exact proportions differ with the country and the type of care, and the data do not permit precise comparisons. Based on descriptions of benefits—which necessarily omit such things as care sought outside the system and extra fees—it appears that the proportion of expenses paid by third parties is generally somewhat higher in these countries than in the United States. Hospital care is, as here, the most completely covered. In France, where the emphasis on retaining direct payments by patients suggests that these may be relatively high, third-party payment still covers slightly more than 90 percent of hospital costs, about the same as in the United States. For other types of care, third-party payments are often lower, either because of patient payments required by the program or because limits on reimbursement leave the patient responsible for any additional amounts physicians choose to charge.

Third, together with the United States, many of these countries have watched costs rise rapidly during the postwar period. Table 6-2 shows the percent of gross national product spent on medical care by each country. Precise comparisons between countries are impossible, and no two sources give exactly the same numbers for the same year.

But two points illustrated in the table appear to be true regardless of which data are chosen: the United States was one of the high spenders in the group in the late 1960s; but the costs of medical care have grown more rapidly in many other countries so that, by the mid-1970s, the United States was one of a growing crowd. An observer of the French medical care system notes that, in some respects, it seems as though the United States and France have been following a common model.[14] The level and distribution of expenditures in France, particularly expenditures for hospital care, have approached those of the United States more and more closely. In every country the reason medical care costs have grown faster than gross national product is, of course, that an increasing share of the economy's resources have been allocated to medical care.

Many of the measures that have been introduced in other countries in response to rising costs resemble the measures being tried or debated in the United States. The French, for example, passed a hospital reform law in 1970 to regulate the purchase of expensive equipment by hospitals. Under the law, applications from hospitals are approved or disapproved in light of the facilities already in the region and the ratio of facilities to population recommended by the Ministry of Health. Such items as dialysis machines, CT scanners, and linear accelerators are explicitly covered and others may be added to the list as the Ministry decides. Also, the French are currently experimenting with different ways of reimbursing hospitals, particularly with setting a hospital's total budget in advance each year.

In West Germany the especially rapid cost increases of the early 1970s led to great pressure on the federal government to take action.[15] After several years of discussion and debate, a cost containment act was passed in 1977. Under the new law, the rates of increase permitted each year in payments to physicians and dentists must be set in advance. The rates are negotiated between the health insurance funds and provider groups, taking into account the rate of growth in gross national product, the rate of inflation, and other indicators of the

14. Simone Sandier, "Comparaison des Dépenses de Santé en France et aux U.S.A., 1950–1978," preliminary report, Centre de Recherche pour l'Étude et l'Observation des Conditions de Vie (Paris: August 1979).

15. Ulrich Geissler, "Health Care Cost Containment in the Federal Republic of Germany" (Bonn: Wissenschaftliches Institut der Ortskrankenkassen, November 1978).

economy's ability to finance medical care. A national advisory group created by the law issues recommendations to guide the negotiations, and should they break down, the law provides for compulsory arbitration.

Hospitals were not included in the law, in large part because the existing power of the states to set hospital reimbursement rates already gave them a mechanism for controlling these costs. The mechanism was not, however, much used for this purpose until the growth in costs became particularly severe. Then the states did apply the brakes, allowing only small increases in the reimbursement rates. Together with the voluntary efforts of the health professions, undertaken in an unsuccessful attempt to prevent legislation, these efforts produced rates of increase in costs for 1977 and 1978 that were smaller than the rates of increase in gross national product, the first time this had happened in thirty years. It is too soon to tell whether the new law will do as well.

As the table indicates, Britain has succeeded in holding its medical care expenditures to a much lower level than other countries, even though it offers universal coverage and requires few direct payments from patients. It has accomplished this by strictly limiting the budget of the National Health Service: the policy for the late 1970s was to permit the budget to grow only 1.8 percent a year in real terms. But medical care expenditures are the outcome of a constant struggle between unlimited needs and limited resources. By solving the problem of cost control, the British have set themselves a different problem: that of trying to decide which needs will be filled. The waiting list for hospital care is long—500,000 in a country of 50 million people; and people with low-priority conditions, such as those waiting for a hip replacement, often turn to the private sector for treatment. Proportionately fewer people receive dialysis in Britain than in other European countries or the United States. In 1979 a trade union broke with tradition and negotiated supplementary insurance coverage for its members that covers care in the private sector, where there are no waiting lists.

Perhaps the most important lesson to draw from the experience of other countries is, once again, that there is no completely satisfactory solution to the dilemma. Trying to do everything worthwhile means escalating costs. Controlling costs means going without.

Where Next?

The United States has gone quite far in the direction of making
medical care widely available without adopting a formal national
health insurance plan. Because it has been left until so late in the development of our medical system, the issue of national health insurance has run head-on into the issue of cost control. In other countries
national health insurance came first and the problem of costs developed afterward. But mechanics aside, the essential question is the
same: what point shall we choose on the continuum between low
costs and stringently limited medical care at one end, and very high
costs and abundant medical care at the other?

Three major plans, representing different choices along that continuum, have been proposed: President Carter's National Health Plan,
which is designed to be the first phase of a more comprehensive plan;
the Health Care for All Americans Act developed by Senator Edward
Kennedy; and several variations of a plan for catastrophic health
insurance submitted by Senator Russell Long. The rest of the chapter
describes and compares these proposals.

Coverage and Benefits

The administration and Senator Long both propose catastrophic
insurance for the general population. The administration's plan adds
to this an expanded program of benefits for the poor, and it is expected that Long's final bill will do the same. Senator Kennedy's plan
would provide comprehensive coverage for the entire population.

NATIONAL HEALTH PLAN. Under the administration's National
Health Plan employers would be required to provide catastrophic
insurance for their employees and the employees' families. This coverage would include the provision that the total amount spent by the
family on coinsurance and deductibles for the required services could
not exceed $2,500 in 1980. After 1980 the limit would be adjusted
upward each year by the rate of growth in per capita medical expenses. If, for example, per capita expenses grew 10 percent between
1980 and 1981, the limit would be raised from $2,500 to $2,750 in
1981. Following medicare, the plan would cover hospital and physicians' services, but most nursing home and dental care would not be
covered, and there would be limits on the amounts of home health

and mental health care. Care related to pregnancy and care for infants less than a year old would be provided without cost-sharing.

The aged, the disabled, people with chronic kidney failure, and those with low incomes would be enrolled in a federal plan called Healthcare, which would cover the same services. For purposes of the plan, the low-income group would be defined as everyone in a family whose income was 55 percent of the poverty level or less, or those whose income after medical expenses fell to that level, and everyone receiving welfare or supplemental security income payments. (Supplemental security income is the federal program that took over welfare payments for the aged and disabled in 1974.) Care given the low-income group would be reimbursed in full by the plan, without cost-sharing or premiums. A residual medicaid program would continue to pay for care in nursing homes and a few other items.

All groups except the poor would pay deductibles, coinsurance, and premiums in much the same fashion as they do now under medicare. There would be a deductible for the first day of hospital care, a deductible, coinsurance, and a monthly premium for physicians' services, and so on. But each individual would be protected by a stipulation that direct payments, including premiums, could not exceed $1,250 in 1980. After 1980 the amounts set in dollars—deductibles, premiums, and the limit of $1,250—would automatically be adjusted upward every year by the rate of growth in per capita medical expenditures.

If they chose, employers could meet their legal obligation by buying Healthcare coverage for their employees, rather than a private plan. Individuals who would not otherwise be covered could also pay to enroll. This coverage would be subject to the $2,500 ceiling, rather than the $1,250 set for enrollees (except the poor) who are the federal government's responsibility.

HEALTH CARE FOR ALL AMERICANS. Senator Kennedy's plan would also require employers to provide insurance for employees and their families. The services included in the plan, again patterned after medicare, would be paid in full—with no deductibles or coinsurance for anyone. Hospital and physicians' services would be covered. Most nursing home and dental care would not be covered, and coverage of home health and mental health services would be limited. The National Health Board, the agency that would oversee the insurance system, could itemize other services that would or would not be covered, or the conditions for coverage, on the basis of information about the cost and effectiveness of the service.

State or federal welfare recipients or people living in state or federal institutions would be enrolled in insurance plans by the government responsible, and would receive the same benefits. The aged, disabled, and those with chronic kidney failure would enroll directly with the National Health Board, which would administer their benefit program, or with a health maintenance organization.[16] Besides the services already listed, these people would receive help paying for drugs prescribed for chronic conditions. If a resident of the United States required care at a participating hospital or doctor's office and was not enrolled in any plan, the bills would be sent to the health board of the state. The state board would arrange to enroll the person in a plan, and premium payments for the year would be due at that point. As under the administration's plan, a residual medicaid program would remain to pay for care in nursing homes and a few other services not covered by the national health insurance plan.

LONG PLAN. Senator Long's plan has been proposed in several different versions, each embodied in a separate bill. The description of the plan can be only approximate because it was, at the close of 1979, being reworked as the Senate Finance Committee prepared final legislation to be proposed to Congress.

As worked out in committee thus far, the Long plan would require employers to provide catastrophic health insurance for their employees and the employees' families. The self-employed would not have to insure themselves. The insurance would pay all expenses for covered services after the first $3,500—or for families with incomes of less than $14,000, after expenses equal to 25 percent of income. After the first full year of the program, this limit would be adjusted every year to reflect increases in the prices and use of services. The same services now covered under medicare would be included in the plan: hospital care and some posthospital nursing home and home health services; and physicians' care, with limits on mental health services. Medicare would remain as it is except for the addition of a provision that no enrollee would have to pay more than $1,000 for deductibles and coinsurance in a year; after that limit was reached, the program

16. Health maintenance organizations are groups of physicians who agree to provide as much of a specified, and usually comprehensive, set of services as a patient needs, in return for a single annual payment.

would pay all reasonable costs of covered services. If the enrollee not only met the $1,000 limit, but spent a specified additional amount on drugs, the program would also help pay any further drug bills.

In addition to a catastrophic health insurance plan, the bill originally introduced by Senator Long and Senator Abraham Ribicoff, the Long-Ribicoff plan, proposed to expand the medicaid program and reduce the differences in its coverage among the states. The new program would cover everyone now eligible for medicaid (those on state or federal welfare) and those not now covered whose incomes fall below a certain level or whose medical expenses reduce their incomes to that level. By and large the same services now provided under medicaid would be paid for, without the limits and cost-sharing imposed by some states. But at the end of 1979 the Senate Finance Committee had not decided what kind of program for the poor should be included in the final legislation.

DISCUSSION. A federal plan can accomplish two results that the unregulated private system would achieve only by chance: universal enrollment and uniform benefit provisions. While government action can achieve universality and uniformity, it will not do either automatically. Each of the plans can be measured against these yardsticks and judged satisfactory or not according to the preferences of the measurer.

All three plans would increase the proportion of the resident population with coverage. The Health Care for All Americans plan would cover everyone, although individuals could choose not to use the plan by dealing only with providers of health care who did not participate in it. Under the National Health Plan, people who did not receive coverage because of their employment, low-income status, or age could choose to buy private health insurance, and might choose not to. But few people would be missed by this plan either—no one with an income less than 55 percent of the poverty level. It is impossible to know who would be omitted under Senator Long's plan because the bill is not yet complete.

The National Health Plan sets minimum benefit provisions for all insured people, but builds in its own variation above that level. No family would have to pay more than $2,500 a year for its own use of insured services. Some families would pay less—the low-income group in particular, which would not be expected to share costs at all. Of course, many people would continue to carry other policies that reimbursed some of the expenses not covered by the national plan.

The Long plan is developing along similar lines. The Kennedy plan aims for complete uniformity, and prescribes exactly the same benefit provisions for everyone. The extent to which people would be tempted to supplement either the catastrophic or the comprehensive benefits through nonparticipating providers would largely depend on what the uniform benefits package amounted to in practice, and this would depend on how, and how strictly, cost-control measures were applied.

None of the plans can claim to provide complete coverage of catastrophic expenses because none offers coverage of care in nursing homes beyond the relatively small amount that qualifies as convalescent care after a hospital stay. Custodial nursing home care is a particularly troublesome item to include in a health plan. The rapidly growing expenditures for nursing homes are not easy to characterize as a matter of unpredictable risks or technological advances. They involve a large element of choice: people choose to admit the elderly to nursing homes rather than care for them at home. The choice may be best for everyone, but it makes the costs of complete coverage under a national plan difficult to predict and unnerving to contemplate. All the plans would leave this area largely untouched—depending on the plan, the current or a residual medicaid program would cover nursing home expenses for some of the poor and the medically needy.

Financing and Costs

A major concern about any national health insurance plan is how it is to be financed and how much it will cost. All the proposed plans combine a number of methods of financing and would not only increase expenditures, but would shift responsibility for meeting them.

NATIONAL HEALTH PLAN. Under the National Health Plan employers could choose any policy offered by a private insurer, as long as it included at least the minimum benefits, and would pay the premium set by the insurer; the employee could be required to pay as much as 25 percent of the cost of the minimum benefit package. Employers who preferred to buy coverage through the federal Healthcare program would pay an amount equal to 5 percent of their payroll. The costs of others enrolled in Healthcare—the aged, the poor, and the disabled—would be paid by the revenues from the medicare premiums and payroll tax, which would be continued, by contributions from the states based on their payments under the medicaid program, and by general federal tax revenues. The state contributions would gradually be redefined to be simply a portion of the Healthcare costs for the low-income population of the state.

HEALTH CARE FOR ALL AMERICANS. The Health Care for All Americans plan is to be financed almost entirely by taxes. Each year the National Health Board would set a payroll tax—called a premium rate—sufficient to cover the costs of care for employees and their families. The tax would apply to the employer's entire payroll; the employee could be required to pay as much as 35 percent of the tax assessed against his or her earnings. For many people—the elderly being the major exception—the tax would also apply to amounts of nonwage income in excess of $2,000 for an individual and $4,000 for a married couple. It is estimated that the premium rate would be between 7 and 8 percent.

Each year the National Health Board would also determine premium amounts for families of different sizes; these premiums, if actually paid, would produce the required revenues. If the taxes paid on nonwage income by a family, plus 35 percent of its wage-related taxes, exceed this premium, the family can apply for a refund. There is no maximum on the amount paid by employers so that the total amount paid on behalf of the family could be several times the premium. The excess for some families would, of course, make up the deficits of others whose earnings did not generate enough taxes to match the premium.

The states and the federal government would use general revenues to pay premiums for people receiving welfare or supplemental security income, and for those living in state or federal institutions. The premium rates would be set each year on the basis of the costs for these populations. The medicare payroll tax would be retained and expanded to cover people who do not pay it now, and medicare premiums would still be assessed. If the revenues from these sources were not sufficient, general federal taxes would make up the difference. The total would then be distributed to five consortia of insurers —Blue Cross and Blue Shield plans, other private insurers, health maintenance organizations, independent practice associations, and self-insurers—and each consortium would be responsible for apportioning the revenues among the individual insurers.[17]

LONG PLAN. Under Senator Long's plan employers would pay the cost of catastrophic coverage with a $3,500 ceiling on direct pay-

17. Independent practice associations are a type of health maintenance organization in which the physicians practice as individuals rather than as a group.

ments for all employees. The employee could be required to contribute as much as 25 percent of the premium. Employees whose incomes qualified them for a lower deductible would note this on their insurance forms, and the insurance company would reimburse them on the basis of the lower deductible. The insurance company would then submit a bill for the extra payments (those between the employee's deductible and $3,500) to the federal government, which would pay the insurer from general tax revenues. The program for people with low incomes proposed in the Long-Ribicoff plan would be financed by contributions from the states based on their current medicaid payments and by general federal revenues; at the end of 1979 no agreement had been reached on whether to include this proposal in the new plan being prepared by the Senate Finance Committee.

DISCUSSION. Table 6-3 provides estimates of the costs that would be incurred in 1980 under the National Health Plan, Senator Kennedy's plan, and two bills sponsored earlier by Senator Long—the Long-Ribicoff plan and a bill that proposes only the catastrophic insurance program from the Long-Ribicoff plan; the latter will be referred to as Long's catastrophic insurance bill in order to distinguish it from the incomplete compromise plan discussed in the text so far. These estimates are purely illustrative because none of the plans will be in effect in 1980. Moreover, they measure the costs that would be incurred if each plan had already been in effect for several years, giving all participants time to adjust fully to its provisions.

Total costs and the shares paid by four sectors—the federal government, employers, individuals, and state and local governments—are presented.[18] The "current law" estimates show the amounts that would be paid in 1980 for the services covered by the plan if the plan

18. Federal costs include medicare payments except for revenues from premiums; federal contributions to medicaid and to various grant programs; payments for care in the Veterans Administration, the Indian Health Service, and other programs that provide care directly; and the federal share of any new plan. Because the medical care system of the U.S. Department of Defense will not be affected by any of the proposed plans, these payments have been excluded from the estimates. Employer costs include the employer share of health insurance coverage provided to employees; payments for workers' compensation and temporary disability insurance; the costs of employer health clinics; and the employer share of any premiums mandated by a proposed plan, less any federal subsidies. Individual costs include direct payments to hospitals, doctors, and other providers; charitable contributions; and all insurance premiums paid by individuals, whether paid to a government plan, as the employee's share of job-related coverage, or for an individual policy. All payments for insurance by the self-employed are counted as payments by individuals. State and local costs include state contributions to medicaid, to grant programs, and to any new plan, and the deficits of state and local medical facilities.

Table 6-3. Estimated Costs of Selected National Health Insurance Proposals, Fiscal 1980

Billions of dollars

Proposal	Federal government	Em-ployers	Individuals	State and local governments	Total
National Health Plan					
Current law[a]	45.9	47.2	50.3	8.1	151.5
Plan	63.2	54.1	41.3	6.9	165.5
Difference between plan and current law	17.3[b]	6.9	−9.0	−1.2	14.0
Health Care for All Americans plan					
Current law[a]	46.5	47.5	53.6	8.4	156.0
Plan	72.0	79.5	33.8	5.7	191.0
Difference between plan and current law	25.5[b]	32.0	−19.8	−2.7	35.0
Long-Ribicoff plan[c]					
Current law[a]	54.0	47.4	57.6	16.0	175.0
Plan	80.0	49.9	45.9	14.7	190.5
Difference between plan and current law	26.0[b]	2.5	−11.7	−1.3	15.5
Long's catastrophic insurance bill[c]					
Current law[a]	45.5	47.3	50.2	9.0	152.0
Bill	51.9	49.8	45.5	7.8	155.0
Difference between bill and current law	6.4[b]	2.5	−4.7	−1.2	3.0

Sources: Estimates for the administration's National Health Plan are from the U.S. Department of Health, Education, and Welfare; these estimates assume that the Child Health Assurance Plan and the Hospital Cost Containment Act are in effect. Estimates for the other plans were made by Gordon R. Trapnell of Actuarial Research Corporation, using assumptions and methodology consistent with those used for the administration's estimates.

a. Costs under the current law are those that would be incurred for services covered by the plan if it were not in effect in 1980 and the services were paid for by the private and public programs now in force. The total for the current law varies because each plan covers a different set of services.

b. The difference between federal outlays under the plan and under current law (net federal outlays) is not the same as the net effect on the federal budget because the latter concept includes changes in tax revenues that would result from the plan. See text for discussion and estimates.

c. Cost estimates are not available for the version of the Long plan discussed in the text because it is not yet complete. The estimates in the table refer to two earlier bills introduced by Senator Long. The Long-Ribicoff plan combines catastrophic insurance for the general population with a new program of benefits for the poor, including complete federal financing of the nursing home care currently reimbursed by medicaid. The second bill proposes only catastrophic insurance for the general population. In both, catastrophic coverage is provided in part through a federal program rather than by simply requiring employers to provide the coverage as the more recent Long plan would.

were not passed. These are not the same for all plans because each covers a different set of services. They are also not the same as total medical care expenditures, which are estimated at $209 billion for personal health services in 1980 and $238 billion when such items as research are included, because no plan covers all care. The costs estimated for each plan can be compared with the corresponding current law estimates to see how much additional spending is likely and how costs will shift among sectors. Estimates are not shown for years after 1980 because the history of forecasting medical program spending suggests they would be too far off track to be useful.

It is important to realize, however, that the costs of any program covering only catastrophic expenses will rise rapidly with time if the deductible is specified in dollars and is not adjusted upward. This is inherent in the fixed deductible and does not depend on any stimulus the plan may give to the development or use of expensive care. As medical costs grow and the deductible remains fixed, a larger and larger share of the total will be above the deductible, and thus the costs of the program will always rise faster than total costs. Only if the deductible rises at the same rate as total costs will the share covered by a catastrophic program remain the same. Both the administration and Senator Long appear to be thoroughly aware of this problem. All dollar amounts specified in the National Health Plan are to be adjusted upward each year by the rate of growth in per capita medical costs. The limit on direct payments in Senator Long's plan would be similarly adjusted.

The careful distinctions drawn in each plan about how much of the premium or payroll tax is to be paid by the employer and how much by the employee also warrant comment. The generally accepted view among economists is that whether the tax is called an employer or employee tax is largely a matter of semantics. The total amount available for compensation—wages plus fringe benefits—is the same in either case, and the amount paid directly to the employee will be reduced by whatever amounts the employer must pay the government or private insurers.

The estimates in the table show that all the plans would result in larger expenditures in 1980 for the services covered. Total spending would increase by $14 billion under the National Health Plan and by $35 billion under the Health Care for All Americans plan. The two other sets of estimates suggest the costs of the possibilities being considered for the current version of the Long plan: the Long-Ribicoff plan, which includes an expansion of the medicaid program, would add between $15 and $16 billion to expenditures for covered services; Long's catastrophic bill would add about $3 billion. Each of the first three plans in the table would add substantially to federal outlays.

Senator Kennedy's plan would also impose considerably higher payments on employers. All four plans would reduce state and local government outlays by a relatively small amount. They would reduce payments by individuals by much larger amounts, an extremely large amount in the case of Senator Kennedy's plan.[19]

Another important characteristic of each plan is its net effect on the federal budget. This is not the same as its net effect on federal outlays, which is shown for each plan in the first column (third row of each set of estimates). The net budget effect adds to the net federal outlays the effects of changes in tax revenues brought about by the plan —proposed changes in the tax laws, new taxes proposed to finance the plan, and changes in tax revenues because income is shifted from one category of taxation to another by the plan. The last change is a major item for all the plans because health insurance provided by employers is not taxable; each plan requires employers to provide more insurance than they do currently, and on the assumption discussed earlier that employee wage payments are reduced by a like amount, this reduces the amount of taxable income and, accordingly, reduces tax revenues. The net budget effect for each plan thus shows the amount that must be financed by borrowing or by taxes beyond those proposed in the plan. (The Long catastrophic insurance bill is the only one of the four that has specified new taxes to cover most of the new federal costs of the program.) Estimates of the net budget effect for the four plans are

National Health Plan	−$17.6 billion
Health Care for All Americans plan	−31.9 billion
Long-Ribicoff plan	−22.0 billion
Long catastrophic insurance bill	−2.9 billion

Cost Control

If one of these plans is passed, its actual costs over the longer run will not be the mechanical outcome of the benefit provisions included in it. More accurately, what the benefit provisions mean in practice will depend on the money committed to back them up. How much of our national resources to allocate to medical care is a matter of our choosing, and choices about this amount are implicit in the cost-

19. Any given set of assumptions will produce an estimate that can be expressed with great arithmetic precision. That does not mean that the estimate is truly precise to the tenths of billions as shown in the table. The estimates are better treated as approximations, or as midpoints of a range.

control measures proposed by each plan. These measures are probably the most important part of each plan because they would fix the point on the continuum between low costs and high costs, restricted benefits and liberal benefits.

LONG PLAN. Senator Long's plan does not currently include cost-control measures. It would be subject only to the controls already in effect. In the absence of further controls, passed separately, it implicitly chooses to continue the rapid growth in costs and resources of the past decades.

NATIONAL HEALTH PLAN. The centerpiece of the cost controls proposed by the National Health Plan is the Hospital Cost Containment Act of 1979, which, as separate legislation introduced in 1979, was rejected in all but name by the House. Under this bill, the Department of Health, Education, and Welfare would announce the maximum permissible growth in hospital costs for the nation for the year. If this maximum was exceeded, more detailed limits would be set on the rate of increase allowed in inpatient revenues per admission the following year. The rate set for each hospital would equal inflation—the inflation index would use the hospital's own purchasing pattern to weight the component price indexes, and its own wage rates for nonsupervisory staff—plus an adjustment based on the hospital's costs relative to similar hospitals. If the routine costs of the hospital were lower than those of similar hospitals, it would be allowed a rate of increase greater than inflation. If its routine costs were higher, the permitted rate of increase would be the same as, or less than, inflation. Small hospitals, new hospitals, hospitals receiving most of their patients from health maintenance organizations, and hospitals in states with approved state cost-control programs would be exempt from the legislation.

The plan also includes a separate bill to limit the dollar amount of major hospital investment projects—projects valued at $150,000 or more—that could be approved by the state agencies dealing with certificates of need. Starting from a base of $3 billion for the nation in 1979, the limit would be increased each year by the rate of growth in construction prices. The Department of Health, Education, and Welfare would assign each state a share of the national total.

The remaining elements of cost control in the National Health Plan have not been developed in as much detail. Payments to nursing homes and home health agencies could be based on either costs or rates set prospectively. Physicians participating in the Healthcare program would have to abide by a fee schedule for their Healthcare patients; they could charge higher fees to other patients if they wished. Health maintenance organizations would be paid 95 percent of the average costs incurred by fee-for-service patients, or less if experience warranted it.

HEALTH CARE FOR ALL AMERICANS. Senator Kennedy's plan proposes broader limits. It would restrict the rate of growth of spending for all the services covered by the plan to no more than the average rate of growth in the gross national product for the preceding three years. Thus the resources committed to these services could only grow as fast as the resources available to the economy and, once the plan was in effect, the share of covered services in the gross national product would remain approximately constant. This policy would be a clear break with the past: as already noted, medical care increased its share of the gross national product from 4.5 percent in 1950 to 6.2 percent in 1965 and 9.1 percent in 1978.

The total budget established by this method would be divided among the states, with states whose per capita expenditures were below the national average receiving a larger share of the total than they do now. The state boards would then be responsible for negotiating budgets with hospitals and fee schedules with physicians and other individual practitioners that were consistent with the state budget. Separate limits would be established for other goods and services. If claims for payment nonetheless exceeded the total budget at the end of the year, reductions would be negotiated in the individual budgets and fees, or insurers would be expected to absorb the losses. If the overrun was due to exceptional circumstances, additional money would be provided.

DISCUSSION. Both the National Health Plan and the Health Care for All Americans plan would also encourage health maintenance organizations as a form of cost control. The interest in health maintenance organizations stems from the observation that they often have considerably lower rates of hospital use than more traditional arrangements. But lower hospital use does not always mean lower costs because the use of other services can be high enough to offset the savings from hospital care.[20] Even when costs are lower, studies are beginning to show that selection bias has something to do with the

20. Peter A. Weil, "Comparative Costs to the Medicare Program of Seven Prepaid Group Practices and Controls," *Health and Society*, vol. 54 (Summer 1976), pp. 339–65.

lower use of hospitals; people who join health maintenance organizations tend to be those who, before they joined, used hospitals less than other people of the same age and sex.[21]

But there is no question that a strictly enforced budget limit can control costs, whether that limit is applied to a health maintenance organization, a hospital, a state, or the entire country. Money that is not available cannot be spent. And when less money is provided than could be spent, choices have to be made about how to spend it—whether to add a pediatrician to the staff, expand the intensive care unit from ten beds to fifteen, or buy a CT scanner. Not everything can be provided, and decisions must be made about which things are most important.

Setting budget limits for the people who provide care while eliminating direct charges for those who receive it places the responsibility for deciding these issues squarely on the providers. The patient has no reason to ask what kinds of care make the best use of the limited medical budget. Providers must decide whether buying a CT scanner is more important than expanding the intensive care unit, or whether the newly admitted patient needs intensive care more than the ten already filling the unit. Both the National Health Plan and the Health Care for All Americans plan would give the provider this responsibility, although only the latter explicitly eliminates direct patient payments for everyone. The current level of basic coverage is already so high, especially for hospital care, that any plan to introduce budget limits on providers would produce much the same result.

Both plans thus abandon the principle that care should be provided whenever it is needed, that cost should not be a consideration when life or health is at stake. Implicitly they accept the principle that some medical benefits are too small, too costly, or both, and that the resources can be put to better use elsewhere. Their proponents do not admit that this choice is implicit in the plans. They would have the public believe, and appear to believe themselves, that it is possible to have everything of benefit, while at the same time setting budgets by rules that do not consider the gains that might be achieved if more were spent. It is a fair choice, but one that should be debated openly.

Both plans represent a choice not only to ration, but to do it in a

21. Harold S. Luft, "HMOs, Competition, Cost Containment, and NHI," paper presented at the American Enterprise Institute for Public Policy Research, Conference on National Health Insurance, October 1979.

collective way—by deciding on budgets at the national level and giving the provider responsibility for operating within those limits. Alternatively, the responsibility could be shifted to patients by charging them directly for a larger percentage of the medical care costs incurred. The percentage could be related to each patient's income, to put everyone on a more nearly equal plane. Direct charges would mean that patients would have to weigh costs and benefits themselves and that they could choose to spend more or less, according to preference. Such a system would give patients a larger part in the final decisions. The choice between systems of rationing depends on whether, as patients, we value that responsibility more than we fear it.

Neither rationing through regulatory means, such as budget limits or the item-by-item approach typified by certificate of need, nor rationing through direct charges to patients avoids the conflict between meeting medical needs and restraining medical costs. The issues raised by the debate over national health insurance and cost control reduce to a choice between two basic alternatives. If we decide to limit the flow of dollars into medical care, then we must decide what the limits will be and choose methods for deciding what to do, and for whom, within those limits. Besides direct charges to the patient, the possibilities include waiting lists, criteria based on the medical condition of the patient or on information about the cost and effects of particular procedures, and so on. If, on the other hand, we reject rationing for now and decide to continue to provide everything that is needed, we must expect further large increases in costs, keeping in mind that a dollar spent on medical care is a dollar that cannot be spent on something else. The choice is as much a choice between problems as between solutions.

CHAPTER SEVEN

Education and Training

DAVID W. BRENEMAN *and* SUSAN C. NELSON

FOR the past two decades, education and training have been premier growth areas in the U.S. economy. Total public expenditures rose from $24.7 billion (5.1 percent of gross national product in 1960) to $163.0 billion (8.6 percent in 1978), an increase of 69 percent in real (inflation-adjusted) terms. Federal spending went from a virtually nonexistent base of $569 million (0.7 percent of federal outlays in 1960), to $23.3 billion (5.2 percent in 1978). At the state and local levels, education consistently claimed between 35 and 40 percent of rapidly growing budgets.

Such remarkable growth in spending in recent decades is the result of the sheer increase in the number of young people during these years—the "coming of age" of the postwar baby boom generation born between 1947 and 1961. The impact on the elementary schools was greatest during the 1950s and early 1960s, with enrollment in kindergarten through grade eight peaking in 1969 at 36.8 million pupils. High school enrollments also soared during the past two decades, rising from 9.7 million in 1960 to a peak of 15.7 million in 1976. College enrollments virtually exploded from 3.6 million in 1960 to 11.4 million by 1978, reflecting the increased numbers of eighteen-year-olds, the growing percentage of high school graduates

A number of persons provided valuable comments on early versions of this chapter; we are especially grateful to Henry J. Aaron, Denis P. Doyle, Robert W. Hartman, Jack W. Peltason, Audrey M. Ryack, and Marvin M. Smith. Research assistance was provided by Carol J. Rapaport; Margo S. Cibener typed the manuscript.

continuing on to college, and increased participation by young women, minority students, and adults. State and local governments scrambled during these years to keep pace with enrollment increases by building new schools and campuses and enlarging teaching and administrative staffs.

The federal government began to support training and education in a major way with the enactment of the Manpower Development and Training Act in 1962, the Vocational Education Act of 1963, the Neighborhood Youth Corps and Job Corps in 1964, and the Elementary and Secondary Education Act and the Higher Education Act, both in 1965. These acts, reflecting the spirit of President Kennedy's New Frontier and President Johnson's Great Society, addressed the issues of poverty, unemployment, civil rights, and equal educational opportunity by concentrating resources on disadvantaged young people. Following the federal lead, many states further increased outlays on education by creating their own categorical programs to aid disadvantaged students. Programs outside the schools that provide employment training for youth have been financed primarily by the federal government rather than by state and local governments. Established by the U.S. Department of Labor in response to rising unemployment rates, falling productivity, and the belief that the schools were failing to prepare a substantial number of young people for productive working life, these programs grew from 77,000 youth participating in 1964 to nearly 650,000 by 1978.

The next decade promises to be different from the two that preceded it, however, as enrollment decline, not growth, becomes the common experience for schools and colleges. Many elementary schools have already faced falling enrollments since the early 1970s because the number of live births dropped from a high of 4.3 million in 1961 to roughly 3.1 million annually from 1973 through 1976. Nationally, enrollments in kindergarten through grade eight dropped from 36.8 million in 1969 to 33.6 million in 1976 (an 8.7 percent decline), and are projected to fall to 31.2 million by 1983. Thus the prospect of school closings, reductions in force, and other features of retrenchment will plague the elementary schools in many parts of the country for another few years. What will be new in the 1980s is that enrollment decline will spread to the high schools and colleges. High school enrollments nationally began to decline in the late 1970s and are projected to fall from 15.7 million in 1976 to 13.2 million by 1986, a drop of 16 percent. College and university enrollments are more difficult to project because attendance is optional and not limited to the population aged eighteen to twenty-two; however, enrollments of full-time, degree-credit students, a group that is dominated by youth aged eighteen to twenty-two, can be expected to decline on many campuses by the early to mid-1980s. What is unknown is the extent to which part-time, adult enrollments may make up for the loss of the younger segment of the college population. For training programs, a central question that changing demography poses is whether the need for these programs will diminish as the number of young people declines.[1]

Elementary and Secondary Education

The nation's public schools enter the 1980s with a legacy from the 1970s characterized by dissent and disappointment, attributable in part to the extraordinary (and, in retrospect, unrealistic) expectations of the 1960s and the failure of the schools to fulfill those hopes. An educational historian could, no doubt, document numerous periods in the history of the schools when public enthusiasm for them surged and then receded, but the experience of the 1960–80 period would loom large in such a chronicle. The drive for academic rigor and excellence prompted by the shock of Sputnik and the fear of falling behind the Soviet Union had barely begun when, under the aegis of President Johnson's Great Society, the schools were turned into a central weapon in the War on Poverty and the struggle for civil rights. School desegregation plans and new federal programs with evocative titles such as Head Start, Follow Through, and Upward Bound sought to use the schools to end racial discrimination and

1. In this chapter we examine policy issues in two areas that influence opportunities for the nation's youth—education and training—but not in the third important area of the military. There currently exists no national youth policy that cuts across these activities, forcing an integrated and holistic view of these youth-dependent institutions; instead, there are separate and largely unrelated policies for education, training, and military recruitment, all drawing on and affecting the members of this age group. Some contend that in the 1980s the military will experience increasing difficulty in attracting volunteers from a shrinking number of youth. If that happens, revisions in public policy may be necessary, leading possibly to a reinstatement of the draft or to some form of national youth service that covers the entire youth population. The impact on education and training of such a change would be pronounced because policies governing these areas would have to be integrated with the requirements of the military or with the more inclusive concerns of a comprehensive youth policy.

eliminate poverty. For a brief period during the 1960s, education was considered by many as the solution for all of society's ills: "The answer for all our national problems," said President Lyndon Johnson, "comes to a single word. That word is education."[2]

If education appeared to be taking on the trappings of a secular religion, however, its hallowed position was shortlived, as disillusionment set in rapidly in the late 1960s and early 1970s. The divisiveness and political turmoil caused by the Vietnam War alone might have been enough to wreck the Great Society, but the findings of social science research and other events also contributed. Press reports of the early evaluations of the new federal programs carried the message that increased resources had little effect on education outcomes, while other studies reported that education was not as effective as some had thought as a means for redistributing income and opportunity within society.[3] Meanwhile, school desegregation, proceeding under court order in several northern cities, erupted in widely publicized episodes of racial violence, particularly where busing was involved. "White flight" to the suburbs or to private schools was widely discussed in the news, only to be followed by reports of "black, middle-class flight" from central city schools. As the 1970s progressed, newspapers were filled with stories of vandalism, drug and alcohol abuse, physical attacks on teachers, the breakdown of discipline, and teacher strikes, not to mention the apparent failure to teach and to learn shown by the steady drop in College Board Scholastic Aptitude Test scores and the periodic reports of poor educational performance issued by the National Assessment of Educational Progress. From a position of being "the solution for all our national problems," education had become one of those problems itself.

Public Attitudes toward Schools

The change in public attitudes toward the schools can be traced in the annual opinion polls conducted since 1969 by the Gallup or-

2. Cited in Diane Divoky, "A Loss of Nerve," *The Wilson Quarterly*, vol. 3 (Autumn 1979), p. 123.

3. For a thorough survey of the evaluation literature and its impact on public thought, see Henry J. Aaron, *Politics and the Professors: The Great Society in Perspective* (Brookings Institution, 1978), especially chap. 3, pp. 65–110. The debunking of education as a means of achieving greater economic equality was given its strongest statement in Christopher Jencks and others, *Inequality: A Reassessment of the Effect of Family and Schooling in America* (Basic Books, 1972).

ganization.[4] Over time, the surveys report a steady drop in public regard for the schools. In 1974, 18 percent of those surveyed gave the schools a rating of A; by 1978, this figure had dropped to 9 percent. At the other end of the scale, 11 percent gave the schools a D or fail rating in 1974, while 19 percent did so in 1978. Elaborating on the 1978 survey, the authors note that: "Attitudes are far more favorable in the smaller cities and towns than in the larger cities. In fact, residents of the central cities give their schools the lowest ratings in the nation. . . . Of all groups, blacks living in the North give their public schools the lowest rating."[5] Even more troubling, in 1978 "A surprisingly large number of persons volunteered the comment that people with children in the schools should pay a special tax and that the elderly and those without children in the schools should not have to pay any tax to support the public schools."[6] In an overview chapter, George Gallup sums up the significance of changing attitudes: "Educators should no longer assume that citizens feel deeply committed to support public school education. . . . heroic efforts must be devoted to restoring this lost confidence and respect."[7]

It is against this background of public perceptions that the educational issues of the 1980s will be decided. But more than attitudes changed during the past decade. The racial composition of many urban school districts shifted dramatically; private school enrollments reversed a long-term decline; bond issues failed at much higher rates than in the 1960s; and teacher strikes became a common occurrence. Any analysis of the prospects and policy issues confronting the public schools in the next decade must take these trends into account.

Recent Trends Affecting Schools

Table 7.1 presents enrollment trends that are disheartening to those who care about central city schools and racial integration. Between 1968 and 1976, twenty-nine urban school systems studied by Diane Ravitch lost a total of 680,000 students (a 12 percent decline), producing a shift in the proportion of white enrollment in

4. Stanley M. Elam, ed., *A Decade of Gallup Polls of Attitudes Toward Education, 1969–1978* (Phi Delta Kappa, 1978).

5. Ibid., pp. 337–38.

6. Ibid., p. 362.

7. Ibid., pp. 5–6.

Table 7-1. Racial Change in Urban Public Schools, 1968 and 1976

Number of students in thousands

		1968			1976		Loss of students (percent)	
		Percent of total				Percent of total		
City	Total students	White students	Minority students[a]	Total students	White students	Minority students[a]	White students	Total
New York City	1,064	43.9	56.1	1,077	30.5	69.5	29.8	...[b]
Los Angeles	654	53.7	46.3	593	37.0	63.0	37.5	9.3
Chicago	582	37.7	62.3	524	25.0	75.0	40.4	10.0
Detroit	296	39.3	60.7	239	18.7	81.3	61.6	19.2
Philadelphia	283	38.7	61.3	258	31.8	68.2	25.1	8.7
Washington, D.C.	149	5.6	94.4	127	3.5	96.5	45.8	14.9
Jacksonville	123	71.8	28.2	111	66.6	33.4	16.2	9.7
Columbus, Ohio	111	73.8	26.2	96	67.1	32.9	20.8	12.9
Atlanta	111	38.2	61.8	82	11.2	88.8	78.3	25.8
San Diego	128	76.1	23.9	121	66.0	34.0	18.3	5.8
Kansas City	74	53.2	46.8	51	34.4	65.6	44.4	31.2
Eighteen additional cities[c]	2,293	53.7	46.3	1,903	39.2	60.8	39.5	17.0
Total: twenty-nine cities	5,868	48.6	51.4	5,183	34.7	65.3	36.9	11.7

Source: Diane Ravitch, "A Bifurcated Vision of Urban Education," in Jane Newitt, ed., *Future Trends in Education Policy* (Lexington Books, 1979), app. 5A, pp. 88–90.

a. Minority students include blacks, Hispanics, Asians, and American Indians.

b. Unlike the other cities, New York City had a gain of 1.3 percent.

c. These cities are Baltimore, Boston, Cleveland, Cincinnati, Dallas, Denver, Houston, Indianapolis, Memphis, Miami, Milwaukee, Nashville, New Orleans, Pittsburgh, San Antonio, San Francisco, St. Louis, and Seattle.

these districts from 49 to 35 percent.[8] (During this same period, total enrollments in kindergarten through grade twelve nationally fell by 1,409,000, a drop of 2.9 percent.) Although disagreement exists regarding the causes of white flight from central city schools, these data leave no doubt about the reality. By 1976, white students were in the minority in twenty-one of these twenty-nine cities, and represented less than 30 percent of enrollments in ten cities (Atlanta, Baltimore, Chicago, Detroit, Memphis, New Orleans, St. Louis, San Antonio, San Francisco, and Washington, D.C.). One hypothesis regarding white flight suggests that there are "tipping points," or levels of black enrollments, at which the outflow of whites accelerates;[9] the sharp and rapid drops in white enrollments in these cities is at least consistent with such an hypothesis. But regardless of

8. Diane Ravitch, "A Bifurcated Vision of Urban Education," in Jane Newitt, ed., *Future Trends in Education Policy* (Lexington Books, 1979), pp. 75–90. Data are computed from app. 5A, pp. 88–90.

9. See, for example, Martin T. Katzman, "The Quality of Municipal Services, Central City Decline, and Middle-Class Flight," Research Report R78-1 (Harvard University, Department of City and Regional Planning, 1978), particularly chapter 3. The original theoretical work on tipping points was done by Thomas Schelling.

the explanation, integration policies for central city schools will have to be reexamined in light of the ability and willingness of whites to abandon large, urban school systems.

Although most students who left the central city schools enrolled in public schools in the suburbs, a substantial number shifted into nonpublic schools. These institutions encompass a wide range of independent and religiously affiliated schools, dominated by Roman Catholic schools that account for roughly 75 percent of nonpublic enrollments.[10] It is unfortunate that the data available on private schools, even such basic information as enrollments, are sparse; only in the last three years has the National Center on Education Statistics begun systematic data collection for these schools. Erickson, Nault, and Cooper indicate that nonpublic enrollments dropped from 6.3 million (12.8 percent of total) in 1965 to 4.5 million (9.0 percent of total) in 1975, but have stabilized or increased slightly since then, while public enrollments have continued to fall. Most of the decline from 1965 to 1975 was registered in Catholic parish schools, which tended to obscure the growth that was occurring elsewhere in the nonpublic sector. Based on interviews with leaders in both public and private schools, Erickson and others tentatively conclude that the resurgence in nonpublic enrollments is a direct response to dissatisfaction with the public schools, and they see profound implications for public education in these recent enrollment shifts. Federal and state policies toward private education promise to be among the most controversial and far-reaching issues of the next decade.

Successful passage of school bond elections is an important index of public willingness to support the schools, and a decided drop has occurred in the percent approved since the late 1960s. During the early and middle years of that decade, more than 70 percent of school bond elections passed; the number dropped to 50 percent in 1969–70, and has remained at about that level ever since.[11] This drop in approvals coincided with a sharp reduction in the number of school

10. Donald A. Erickson, Richard L. Nault, and Bruce S. Cooper, "Recent Enrollment Trends in U.S. Nonpublic Schools," in Susan Abramowitz and Stuart Rosenfeld, eds., *Declining Enrollments: The Challenge of the Coming Decade* (U.S. Government Printing Office, 1978), pp. 81–127. This excellent article is the most comprehensive, current treatment of its subject.

11. U.S. Department of Health, Education, and Welfare, Education Division, National Center for Education Statistics, *Digest of Education Statistics, 1979* (GPO, 1979), p. 72.

bond elections on the ballot, suggesting that some localities may have decided it was pointless to try for passage.

Labor unrest in the schools is another sign of growing problems. From a single teacher strike in 1961–62, the number rose slowly for several years, and then jumped to 114 strikes in 1967–68, involving over 163,000 teachers. Since that time, in only one year (1971–72) have there been fewer than 100 strikes, with the high point reached in 1975–76, when 203 strikes idled over 218,000 teachers. The publicity that surrounds these strikes tends to dominate the news about schools each September. (School desegregation—particularly if disruptive—has been the only other serious contender in recent years for extensive back-to-school news coverage.) While the teachers' grievances may be justified in many instances, these strikes highlight the collapse of the old public school coalition of teachers, parents, and administrators, and surely contributed to the negative public attitudes documented in the Gallup surveys.

Although other educational and social trends not mentioned here will influence policy debates during the 1980s, the examples above should provide a sense of the unstable base on which new policies must be built. Financing issues will crystallize these debates at federal, state, and local levels as priorities for education are set during the next decade.

Policy Issues for Public Schools

Elected officials at the local, state, and national levels will have to decide during the next decade how much to spend on education at a time of enrollment decline. These decisions, coupled with trends in total public spending and competing demands on the public purse, will determine education's share of public outlays. How that share should be financed raises the additional question of whether foreseeable trends may require some redistribution of the burden among the three levels of government. To answer that question, it is necessary to examine the purposes served by existing programs and financing methods and ask whether the conditions of the 1980s are likely to bring about changes in the educational responsibilities of local, state, and federal governments.

QUALITY OF EDUCATION. The certainty of enrollment decline in the high schools, and the continued drop in elementary enrollments for at least the early years of the decade, will present public officials with interesting and distinct opportunities in deciding how much to spend on education. One option would be to increase resources per student in a relatively painless way by maintaining the current level of total expenditures in real terms; another would be to shift resources away from education by reducing real outlays as enrollments decline, keeping educational resources per student constant. The first option, quality enhancement, would mean that no reduction would occur in the teaching force, that pay increases would keep pace with inflation, and that few, if any, school closings would be necessary; under this option, average class size would fall, teacher-student ratios would rise, and real resources per student would increase. The second option, constant quality, would require reductions in the teaching force (or sharp wage cuts per teacher) and a willingness to continue closing schools. Although these extremes bracket the realistic possibilities, numerous intermediate positions entail some increase in real resources per student but a drop in total real outlays on education.

We use the terms quality enhancement and constant quality cautiously because we suspect that the decision on which way to proceed will depend, in part, on the prospects for converting increased resources into genuine gains in educational quality. The need, and the desire, to improve the quality of education are clearly present, but so too is skepticism regarding the ability to do so. For example, there is growing public interest in developing proficiency exams to remove inept teachers and to screen new applicants, but the teacher unions are strongly opposed to such measures. If the promise of increased resources could be used to break down union resistance, public support for such outlays would probably be forthcoming. If the unions remain adamant, however, the public is likely to view increased outlays as simply swelling the paychecks of a work force whose competence is increasingly suspect, and a cut in education spending will be the likely result. The 1980s will provide interesting opportunities to use financial incentives to improve school performance, and the level of spending on education will be determined in part by the receptivity of teachers and administrators to such efforts.

SCHOOL FINANCE. Complicating any attempt to project future levels of support for the schools is the fact that revenues are supplied by three levels of government. In 1976–77, public elementary and secondary schools received total revenues of $75.3 billion, of which

$36.0 billion (48 percent) was provided by local government, $32.7 billion (43 percent) by state government, and $6.6 billion (9 percent) by the federal government. In the wake of California's Proposition 13, which sharply cut local property taxes, concerned educators were predicting that a growing tax revolt would undermine state and local support of the schools. This fear prompted the National Education Association to intensify efforts on behalf of a federal Department of Education, in the hope that a cabinet-level agency would help to increase the federal government's share of education support. (The Association's stated goal is to increase the federal share to 33 percent.) How realistic are these fears of tax revolt, and does it make sense for educators to look to Washington for a dramatic increase in aid?

Despite much publicity, tax reduction measures as extreme as Proposition 13 have not spread; instead, the tax revolt of 1978 has taken the less severe form of setting limitations on future spending increases.[12] Voters seem to be saying that the government's share of the gross national product should not increase over current levels, but with few exceptions, they have not voted to roll back this share or sharply curtail services.[13] Thus the fear that voters nationwide would deprive local and state governments of the revenue necessary to support the schools seems thus far to have been exaggerated.

When one considers the effects that the changing age distribution of the U.S. population will have on the budgets of the various levels of government, the desire of the National Education Association to shift a heavier burden for educational support onto the federal government seems particularly ill-advised. Education is the largest single component of most state and local budgets, while retirement and disability programs are the largest component of the federal budget. Because the school population will decline as a percentage of the population while the retired group will grow both absolutely and proportionately from now until well beyond the year 2000, it seems

---

12. For a summary of the measures passed in 1978, see Richard L. Lucier, "Gauging the Strength and Meaning of the 1978 Tax Revolt," *Public Administration Review,* vol. 39 (July–August 1979), pp. 371–79.

13. In fact, state and local government spending as a percentage of gross national product has been relatively stable over the last ten years, fluctuating around 11 percent. See *Facts and Figures on Government Finance* (Tax Foundation, Inc., Washington, D.C., 1979), p. 33.

likely that the federal government, rather than state and local governments, will face greater claims on its resources.

Furthermore, a significant increase in the federal share of support would require new federal goals for education, goals that would carry the national government far beyond its current emphasis on support for disadvantaged groups within the school population. The original federal agenda, as set forth in the Elementary and Secondary Education Act and in subsequent legislation such as the Education for All Handicapped Children Act, is now largely complete: categorical aid programs have been established for virtually every disadvantaged group in society. In the absence of an expanded legislative agenda, federal policy for education in the 1980s will largely be confined to administrative improvements in existing programs. Although many of these programs have not been fully financed (being subject to annual appropriation rather than statutory entitlement), and thus have room to grow, the federal share of the total education budget is unlikely to increase much beyond its current level in the absence of new initiatives. Are any on the horizon?

The most obvious candidate would be some form of general aid provided directly to public schools for support of basic operating expenses. The major education associations can be expected to make a concerted push for institutional support during the next reauthorization of the Elementary and Secondary Education Act in 1983. Federal officials have steadfastly resisted that type of aid because once started down that path, there is no obvious place to stop; furthermore, direct operating support could hardly be provided without introducing federal control into the curriculum, staffing policies, testing standards, and other matters central to educational policy. The debate surrounding the creation of a federal Department of Education made it clear, however, that little enthusiasm exists in any quarter for increased federal control over education.

A problem arises, though, because few people are satisfied with the way current federal programs are operating and being administered. By creating a separate categorical grant program for each interest group and for every distinct objective, the number of programs has risen to more than seventy—all with separate regulations and reporting requirements. These regulations often conflict with one another and with state requirements, and add up to a staggering administrative burden for district administrators, principals, and teachers. It is virtually certain that the 1980s will witness an attempt by the Department of Education to streamline these numerous programs because improved management was the main argument advanced in favor of the new department. During the next reauthorization of the Elementary and Secondary Education Act, Congress can also be expected to simplify the programs in response to the growing volume of complaints about paperwork and detailed regulation. School administrators will apply pressure to loosen the strings, allowing federal money to become, in effect, general aid; the same forces will also be at work on the state categorical programs. Countervailing pressures will be exerted, however, to demonstrate that, after nearly twenty years of operation, federal programs do make a difference in the educational achievements of disadvantaged students. Because a shift toward general aid would reduce the extra resources that flow to disadvantaged students, and therefore the likelihood of increased achievement, the pressures for simplification and for results will pose a painful dilemma for the Congress. Only if it can be demonstrated that some loosening of the regulations actually aids disadvantaged students is Congress likely to move significantly in that direction.

A more realistic initiative for the 1980s may be to provide federal aid to reduce disparities in per-pupil expenditures among school districts or among states. During the past decade, over twenty-five states have changed their school finance systems in an effort to reduce inequities among districts with differing property tax wealth per pupil. Often instigated in response to legal challenges dating from *Serrano* v. *Priest* (1971) in California, the typical remedy has involved increased state aid for poorer districts. There appears to be growing interest in considering whether the federal government should enter this arena, with policies to reduce differences in spending per pupil, either within or among the states. Although the Supreme Court ruled in *San Antonio* v. *Rodriguez* (1973) that expenditure disparities do not violate the Constitution, the federal government still has a legitimate interest in policies that advance equal educational opportunity. Apart from the inherent inequity of large differences in spending per pupil, such disparities may offset federal efforts to provide supplemental funds for particular groups of students. The pros and cons of a federal initiative to equalize expenditures on education will be thoroughly investigated as part of a congressionally mandated study of school finance, authorized by the Education Amendments of 1978. The prospects for a federal initiative in this area will depend, in part, on the findings of that study.

TAX CREDITS AND VOUCHERS. Another initiative that might develop at the federal or state level—and the most far-reaching in its implications for the schools—would be enactment of a tuition tax credit or some form of voucher system to underwrite the costs of private schooling for parents who choose that option. Although neither idea is new, the political environment may be unusually supportive of such proposals, particularly if disenchantment with the public schools continues to grow. In fact, a federal tuition tax credit, covering both elementary-secondary and higher education, was narrowly defeated in the 1978 session of Congress, and proponents can be expected to continue pressing the case. Similarly, ballot initiatives were recently circulated in California both for a tuition tax credit and for a modified form of voucher system, the "Initiative for Family Choice in Education." Although neither proposal secured the 554,000 valid signatures required for the June 1980 ballot, continued efforts on behalf of such proposals can be expected.

Sponsored by the National Taxpayers Union, the first initiative would have provided a credit of up to $1,200 against the California state income tax for every full-time student of any age, kindergarten through postgraduate, enrolled in any eligible public or private institution. The second, or family-choice initiative, was the brainchild of law professors John Coons and Stephen Sugarman, who developed the philosophical basis for the initiative in a recent book, *Education by Choice*.[14] These initiatives are worth evaluating because it is likely that similar proposals will be advanced with some regularity during the next decade.

The principal obstacle to tax credits has been a series of Supreme Court rulings that such aid, if it flows to parents whose children are enrolled in religiously affiliated schools, violates the first amendment, and is thus unconstitutional. Not deterred by these decisions, proponents of a tax credit argue that the Court is incorrect in its interpretation of that amendment and advocate a strategy of "debate, liti-

14. John E. Coons and Stephen D. Sugarman, *Education by Choice: The Case for Family Control* (Berkeley: University of California Press, 1978).

gate, and legislate" as the way to change the Court's opinion.[15] Even if such obstacles are cleared, however, the fundamental question for public policy remains: is a strategy of increased competition and choice the best way to improve the schooling of young people?

A conceptual approach to questions of this type has been brilliantly developed by Albert O. Hirschman through his analysis of the relative effectiveness of the competitive market ("exit") versus the political process ("voice") for encouraging reform.[16] Those who support tax credits or vouchers advance a number of arguments, including the desirability of supporting educational diversity and greater family involvement in the choice of schools, but a principal claim is that increased competition in the market for schooling is the best, and surest, way to force the schools to improve. Deprived of a near-monopoly position, public schools could no longer rely on an assured source of revenue and would have to attract parents, and their children, by the quality of their offerings. Emphasis would be placed on exit to penalize poorly performing schools, and there would be little need to rely on voice—parents working actively from within the system to improve it for all students. Those who were dissatisfied with the local school would simply take their business elsewhere, rather than spend time and energy to improve it.

Critics of this market approach argue that it would encourage further flight from the public schools by those families that are most needed if reform from within is to have any chance of success. Particularly in the case of tax credits, there is reason to worry about the selective withdrawal from public schools of the more active and concerned families, leaving behind less-advantaged students in a public system that has lost all motive force for change. In this view, the decision that a parent makes in removing a child from the public schools is not simply a private, market transaction, but a social decision with consequences for others that cannot be ignored. Rather than improving the public schools through competition, tuition tax credits would consign many of them, and their students, to a permanent position of inferiority.

Tuition tax credits have other undesirable features that make them

15. Daniel Patrick Moynihan, "What Do You Do When the Supreme Court Is Wrong?" *The Public Interest* (Fall 1979), pp. 3–24.

16. Albert O. Hirschman, *Exit, Voice, and Loyalty: Responses to Decline in Firms, Organizations, and States* (Harvard University Press, 1970).

both inequitable and inefficient policy instruments.[17] The proposed California income tax credit exhibited these deficiencies clearly. The credit of $1,200 per student would have been highly regressive in the sense that a disproportionately large amount of the benefits would have accrued to higher income families; in fact, only families with state income tax liability of at least $1,200 (corresponding to income of over $30,000) could have received the full credit. At the level of elementary and secondary schooling, the proposal was inefficient because much of the benefit would have gone to families that had already made the decision to enroll their youngsters in a private school; those families would receive a windfall gain, without the credit influencing their behavior in any way.

The tuition tax-credit proposal, then, does not appear to be either sound educational or tax policy. Despite its apparent similarity to tax credits, the type of voucher system that Coons and Sugarman have proposed avoids some of these shortcomings. Their plan called for the elimination of local property tax support for the schools to make them fully state-supported by 1981. Unlike laissez-faire versions of the voucher, such as that proposed years ago by Milton Friedman, the Coons-Sugarman proposal had numerous regulations built in—the prevention of discrimination, the requirement of lotteries for over-subscribed schools, and so forth. It would have allowed three types of publicly funded schools: public, independent public, and family choice, with families able to enroll children in any of the three. The state would have supported the public schools directly, based on their enrollments, while state certificates, equal to 90 percent of public school costs, would have been available to parents who enrolled children elsewhere. Limits would also have been placed on allowable increases in education costs and on total administrative costs.

Whereas tax credits at the elementary-secondary level would only be utilized by part of the eligible population (parents who chose a private school), a voucher system would be more likely to engage all families. Competition among the schools would be more active under vouchers than under tax credits, for all schools would have to compete for enrollments in order to receive support. Under tax credits, public elementary and secondary schools would not be chal-

17. For more detailed discussion of these points, see David W. Breneman, "Education," in Joseph A. Pechman, ed., *Setting National Priorities: The 1979 Budget* (Brookings Institution, 1978), pp. 117–25.

lenged so fundamentally and directly; the only change would be that the tax system would cover part of the cost of private schooling for parents who make that choice. While the Coons-Sugarman voucher proposal was more equitable than the proposed California tax credit, a voucher system does represent a radical departure from the philosophy and tradition of the common school. Supporters are convinced that vouchers should be tried because—in their view—the evidence is clear that some public school systems, as currently organized and managed, are impervious to reform. Reform should be possible, however, particularly as more is learned about the components of a successful school; a sharp departure from current policy, such as a voucher system, is likely to have unintended, adverse consequences, and is therefore risky to try. The next decade will not witness a more fundamental debate than this one over educational policy.

Training Programs for Youth

For most young people who do not plan to attend college, the transition from high school to employment proceeds fairly smoothly and predictably. A substantial and growing minority of youth, however, has serious difficulty entering the world of work. For them unemployment occurs more frequently and lasts longer than for the average youth, and some may not try to find a job at all. In 1979 the federal government spent approximately $2.9 billion to ease the transition for these youth, and at least another $6 billion came from federal, state, and local governments for vocational education programs. Despite the magnitude of these undertakings, questions far outnumber answers in this area, even on such basic issues as the nature of the problem, its causes, and the effectiveness of previous efforts to address it. With most of the federal employment and training programs for youth expiring in 1980, policymakers must address these questions left unresolved from the 1970s as well as the issues raised by demographic changes and economic conditions that will prevail in the years ahead.

The Problem

To some observers the problem of youth unemployment is a general affliction of immaturity and inexperience, while to others, only the problems of certain disadvantaged groups merit government at-

Table 7-2. Unemployment Rates, by Race and Age, Selected Years, 1954–79

Race and age	1954	1960	1971	1979
All races				
16–19	12.6	14.7	16.9	16.1
20–24	9.2	8.7	9.9	9.0
25–54	4.7	4.5	4.2	4.1
White				
16–19	12.1	13.4	15.1	13.9
20–24	8.3	7.9	9.0	7.6
25–54	4.2	4.0	3.9	3.6
Nonwhite				
16–19	16.5	24.4	31.7	33.5
20–24	15.1	15.1	16.7	18.8
25–54	9.0	8.6	6.6	7.6

Source: *Employment and Training Report of the President*, 1979, pp. 238–39, 244, 246, 257–59; and U.S. Department of Labor, Bureau of Labor Statistics.

tention. The latter, more limited view of the problem is supported by an examination of the experiences of youth in the labor market, as shown in tables 7-2 and 7-3, and consideration of the implications of youth unemployment.

As the tables show, the unemployment rate—that is, the percentage of the labor force that cannot find a job—is substantially higher for young people than for adults. In 1979, 4.1 percent of the prime-age civilian labor force (aged twenty-five to fifty-four) was unemployed, while 16.1 percent of the teenagers (aged sixteen to nineteen) and 9.0 percent of the young adults (aged twenty to twenty-four) in the labor force experienced unemployment. The differential between youth and adults has generally increased during the postwar years, even at comparable levels of adult unemployment, as the data for 1954, 1960, and 1971 suggest.

Within the youth cohort, the risk of unemployment is much higher for nonwhites (particularly blacks) than for whites. In 1979, nonwhite youth—both men and women aged sixteen to twenty-four— were two and a half times as likely to be unemployed as were whites of the same age. Racial differences are more extreme among black and white youth of the same educational status, as table 7-3 indicates. White high school dropouts also have problems finding jobs, but even their unemployment rate is only slightly worse than for black youth with college degrees. Hispanics generally fare worse than whites but not nearly as poorly as blacks.

Table 7-3. Youth Unemployment Rates, by Educational Status, Age, Race, and Hispanic Origin, 1978

Educational status and age	White	Black	Hispanic[a]
In school			
All, 16–24	10.7	31.3	13.8
Elementary-secondary, 16–19	14.9	37.0	21.5[b]
College, 16–19	9.0	35.9	...
College, 20–24	5.1	18.9	5.7[b]
Not in school			
All, 16–24	8.3	23.0	12.5
16–19	13.4	33.4	n.a.
20–24	6.6	20.0	n.a.
High school dropouts, 16–24	16.5	29.7	16.0
High school graduates, 16–24	6.4	20.4	n.a.
College, one to three years, 16–24	4.5	16.5	n.a.
College graduates, 16–24	5.7	15.1	n.a.

Source: U.S. Department of Labor, Bureau of Labor Statistics, *Students, Graduates and Dropouts in the Labor Market, October 1978*, Special Labor Force Report 223 (Bureau of Labor Statistics, 1979).
a. Hispanic designates ethnic origin, not race. In this table Hispanics are also included as whites or blacks as appropriate; most Hispanics are white.
b. The figures are for youth aged sixteen to twenty-four.
n.a. Not available.

Most important for policy, only nonwhite youth have experienced a severe deterioration in labor market status over time. While the unemployment rate for white teenagers rose slightly between 1954 and 1979 (largely explained by increased labor force participation of young women), the rate for nonwhites soared from 16.5 percent to 33.5 percent.[18] This deterioration was more concentrated among nonwhite men than women.

Measures of labor market experience besides unemployment rates also show that only for nonwhite youth has the job market worsened. Over the last two decades the fraction of the population in the labor force and the fraction employed have risen dramatically for whites, while they have fallen for minorities. These diverging patterns are true for students and nonstudents and for all levels of educational attainment.

In sum, these statistics describe a situation in which all youth experience higher risks of unemployment than do prime-age adults, but with those risks highest and rising only for minorities and high school dropouts. But do these differentials—between young and old,

18. The unemployment rate for nonwhite adults actually improved slightly during this period.

between 1979 and earlier years, and between whites and minorities —constitute a problem that requires a policy response?

A given level of youth unemployment, it can be argued, merits less concern than unemployment among adult heads of households. Some differential between unemployment rates for young and older workers is no doubt inevitable, even desirable. Part of the difference stems from the higher frictional unemployment of youths as they explore the labor market before settling into a career and from the limited opportunities for students looking only for part-time work. Although all unemployment produces economic hardship for the person out of work through loss of income and for society through a lower level of production, these two factors are less compelling for the young than for older workers. Youth are less apt to be the primary breadwinners, and they may still be productively occupied— in school or in the military—even though they are not employed or in the labor force. Indeed, in October 1978 when the official unemployment rate for blacks aged sixteen to seventeen was 39.2 percent, only 6.9 percent of the population of that age was unoccupied, neither in school nor working. At the same time, the unemployment rate for their white counterparts was 16.3 percent, but only 5.7 percent of that population was also out of school and out of work. These differences between unemployment rates and unoccupied rates stem largely from high enrollment rates (approximately 90 percent for both whites and blacks), and indicate that unemployment is not synonymous with idleness for these teenagers of high school age.

On the other hand, there is concern that negative initial experiences in the labor market will have a "scarring" effect on youth and handicap their future. This is an appealing presumption, but it has not yet been demonstrated conclusively.[19] Similarly, high unemployment of youth is correlated with social problems such as crime and teenage pregnancy, but evidence of causality has not yet been found.

These considerations suggest that some differential between unemployment rates for youth and adults is acceptable, although how much remains unresolved. The most serious youth employment problem clearly exists among nonwhites, however, and to a lesser extent

19. In the most thorough investigation to date of the long-run effects of early spells of unemployment, Marvin M. Smith of the Brookings Institution has thus far identified only a weak negative impact of unemployment early in a career. Although his results are still preliminary and are handicapped by problems of small sample size, his work suggests caution in ascribing future harm to current unemployment.

among high-risk whites. These are the youth who will present a challenge to policymakers in the 1980s.

Causes of the Problem

Why do some youth move with ease from high school to a job while others have great difficulty? Does the problem lie with the youth or with the labor market? The answers to these questions crucially affect the strategies for dealing with youth unemployment in the 1980s.

On the supply side, the employability of the youth and the growth in their numbers over recent decades are the most likely explanations for the current problem. Under the label of employability fall many personal attributes—education, attitudes, dependability—that undoubtedly influence a youth's labor market experience, though to what extent and through what processes continue to be debated. What is clear, however, is that the formal educational attainment of blacks cannot be held responsible for their deteriorating job prospects; in that respect their position has been improving compared to that of whites.[20] This relative gain in formal education can be interpreted in two ways. It could indicate that the job market and not the young person is primarily at fault if, even with a high school degree, a black youth has trouble finding a job. Or it could mean that the quality of education has deteriorated so much in the schools these youth attend that a diploma has been devalued—and that employers know it. While the former view is plausible, the malaise and resegregation of urban public schools discussed earlier make the second interpretation more likely.

According to most analysts, the changing age composition of the labor force—from 16.6 percent under twenty-five years of age in 1960 to 24.1 percent in 1979—tended to depress the wages of youth relative to adults and to raise the unemployment rate of the former.[21]

20. Between 1967 and 1977, blacks increased the probability that they would be enrolled in school in the appropriate grade or higher for their age (from 70.5 percent of students to 75.3 percent) and that they would graduate from high school (from 55.9 percent to 67.5 percent). While whites still do better on both counts, the gap has narrowed. And black high school graduates stand as great a chance of going on to college as do their white classmates.

21. On relative wages, see Finis Welch, "Effects of Cohort Size on Earnings: The Baby Boom Babies' Financial Bust," *Journal of Political Economy,* vol. 87, pt. 2 (October 1979), pp. S65–S97; and Richard B. Freeman, "The Effect of Demographic Factors on Age-Earnings Profiles," *Journal of Human Resources,* vol. 14 (Summer 1979), pp. 289–318. On employment rates, see Michael L. Wachter, "The Demographic Impact on Unemployment: Past Experience and the Outlook for the Fu-

It is doubtful, though, that cohort size contributed to the deteriorating employment situation of black youth relative to whites. In fact, the white teenage and young adult labor force grew more rapidly than the nonwhite labor force, even though the nonwhite youth population was growing faster than the white youth population.[22] The more important question concerns the future: will demographic forces solve the current problem of youth unemployment? The most likely answer is no, but demography should help, particularly by the end of the decade. On the supply side, a 16.3 percent drop between 1980 and 1990 in the number of persons aged sixteen to twenty-four should ease the youth unemployment rate to some extent. In addition, maintaining a constant size for the military would require an increasing fraction of the youth cohort, further reducing supply pressures in the civilian labor market. Particularly in the early 1980s, however, these trends will be offset by continued growth in the number of young women in the labor force, suggesting that demography will have more influence on youth unemployment rates at the end than at the beginning of the decade.[23] How many minority and other high-risk youth will benefit from this general downward pressure on youth unemployment rates is more problematic, in part because the nonwhite labor force keeps growing several years after the white labor force has peaked. In addition, the demand for labor must be considered. Employers apparently do not view white and nonwhite youth as pure substitutes in the work place. In the past two decades, the economy was able to provide jobs for nearly all (90 percent) of the additional 11 million young whites who entered the labor force but for only two-thirds of the 1.5 million minorities. To the extent that the past is an indicator of the future, it seems unlikely that the baby bust will solve the problem of high unemployment among minority youth, though it may improve the situation somewhat.

ture," in National Commission for Manpower Policy, *Demographic Trends and Full Employment,* Special Report No. 12 (Washington, D.C., National Commission for Manpower Policy, 1976), pp. 27–99.

22. In 1960, 12.8 percent of both the population aged sixteen to twenty-four and the labor force was nonwhite. By 1979, the nonwhite share of the youth population had risen to 14.9 percent, but their share of the labor force had fallen to 12.0 percent.

23. According to the U.S. Department of Labor's "intermediate growth" projections, between 1977 and 1985 the number of men aged sixteen to twenty-four in the labor force will drop by 424,000, while the number of young women seeking jobs will rise by 1.1 million. Between 1985 and 1990 the youth labor force is projected to decline by 2 million.

On the demand side, a number of explanations have been offered for the insufficient opportunities for youth employment: the state of the aggregate economy, racial discrimination, the minimum wage, and changes in the structure and location of industry. Empirical studies consistently find that the condition of the national economy has a disproportionate influence on the employment prospects of young workers, particularly nonwhites. For example, it has been estimated that a rise in the aggregate unemployment rate from 6.0 to 7.2, representing an overall decline of 1.7 percent in employment, would produce a 3.1 percent drop in the number of white teenagers employed, but a 10.8 percent decline in nonwhite teenage employment.[24] While this estimate reflects the inferior labor market opportunities for minority youth, it does not explain that situation nor the secular deterioration in their unemployment rates. Although a full-employment economy would improve the outlook for both white and black youth, the economic prospects for the coming decade (discussed in chapter 2 of this volume) provide little hope that macroeconomic conditions will reduce the rate of youth unemployment to that of adults.

Although little doubt exists that racial discrimination still affects blacks, the success of the civil rights movement in influencing the conscience and the laws of the nation suggests that the effects of discrimination should be moderating. Quantitative evidence supports this view with respect to earnings differentials.[25] But other hypotheses indicate that discrimination may indeed be contributing to the deteriorating employment prospects of black youths. One view, advanced by Elijah Anderson,[26] describes a widening cultural mistrust between black youth and prospective employers as young blacks have become more assertive in dress, speech, and behavior, while employers feel threatened by these changes and by an increasing association of black youth with violent crime. A second hypothesis suggests that

24. Ralph E. Smith, Jean E. Vanski, and Charles C. Holt, "Recession and the Employment of Demographic Groups," *Brookings Papers on Economic Activity, 3:1974*, calculated from tables 2 and 3, pp. 746, 748–49. (Hereafter *BPEA*.)

25. For example, see James P. Smith and Finis R. Welch, "Black-White Male Wage Ratios: 1960–70," *American Economic Review*, vol. 67 (June 1977), pp. 323–38.

26. Elijah Anderson, "Some Observations of Black Youth Employment," in Bernard E. Anderson and Isabel V. Sawhill, eds., "Youth Employment and Public Policy," a collection of papers emanating from the American Assembly on Youth Employment (Arden House, Harriman, New York, August 9–12, 1979), pp. 3-1 to 3-25.

affirmative action itself may have contributed to the unemployment of black youth by making it more difficult for employers to treat blacks differently from whites on the job, for any reason. Instead, employers have found it easier not to hire the blacks in the first place. The validity of these ideas requires further investigation, but both theories represent plausible explanations for increased discrimination.

The minimum wage, by virtually all accounts, reduces the employment of less productive workers, a high proportion of whom are young, unskilled, and poorly educated.[27] While the size of this disemployment effect continues to be debated, most of the evidence suggests that increases in the level and coverage of the minimum wage did not contribute greatly to the deteriorating labor market for youth.[28] The question for policymakers is the advisability of setting the minimum wage for youth below the level for adults. Although such a measure would increase youth employment, some opponents fear it would adversely affect the distribution of income and displace adult workers. Supporters of a differential argue, however, that the main rationale for a minimum wage—income redistribution—is not as valid for youth as it is for adults. Not only is the income of a teenager of less social concern than the income of a head of household, but Gramlich has shown that teenagers who earn low wages come from more affluent families on average than do teenagers who earn higher wages, suggesting that the minimum wage may have perverse redistributional consequences for this age group. In addition, a youth differential may lead some employers to substitute youth for adult workers, but the existing estimates suggest that this effect would be small, primarily offsetting some of the advantage that the minimum wage now gives adult women relative to youth.

The structure and location of industry also affect youth employment prospects, but they do not appear to have been responsible for current problems. While jobs and white households have been moving to the suburbs in the past two decades, employment prospects for blacks in central cities have been only slightly harmed, apparently because blacks now have a better chance at the jobs still in the

27. For a recent summary of the literature, see Steven P. Zell, "The Growth of Youth Unemployment: Characteristics and Causes" (Federal Reserve Bank of Kansas City, June 1979).

28. Edward M. Gramlich, "Impact of Minimum Wages on Other Wages, Employment, and Family Incomes," *BPEA, 2:1976*, p. 442, note.

central city and because living in the suburbs would lower their unemployment rate no more than a few points. According to one estimate, if black teenagers had the same residential pattern as whites of that age group in 1977, the unemployment rate for black youth would only have fallen from 40.5 percent to 35.1 percent.[29] Changes in the industrial composition of the economy have probably affected youth employment adversely, but it is not clear that nonwhites have suffered more than whites. The decline in agricultural employment disproportionately affected black youth, though the increase in the service sector may have worked to their advantage. Both white and nonwhite youth who are out of school are highly concentrated in manufacturing, which has shrunk as a fraction of total employment. On balance, recent analyses conclude that these compositional effects have contributed to the deteriorating employment situation of young black men.[30] The sensible policy response to this trend, however, would focus on the quality of the supply of youth labor, not the demand for it. Structural changes in industry should not be impeded to increase options for youth. Instead, policy should help young people compete for the jobs available, thereby increasing productivity, not inefficiency.

This brief overview of the causes of youth unemployment has several implications for policymakers:

1. The future holds no automatic solutions. Some relief will come from demographic forces, but not until the end of the decade, and even then the fundamental barriers to the employment of high-risk youth will persist. The prospect of sluggish economic growth suggests that an upsurge in demand for young workers is unlikely.

2. Renewed consideration of a youth differential in the minimum wage seems advisable. It will not work miracles, but the increase in youth employment might more than offset the displacement of older workers, increase productivity in the economy, and reduce inflationary pressures.

3. The deteriorating employment experience of young minorities remains largely unexplained, but a number of factors, on both supply

29. *Employment and Training Report of the President,* 1978; p. 73.
30. "An Assessment of Youth Employment Policies for the 1980s," in *Expanding Employment Opportunities for Disadvantaged Youth,* Fifth Annual Report of the National Commission for Employment and Policy (forthcoming).

and demand sides of the labor market, appear to have contributed to it. Consequently, policy must address both the employability of the youths and the availability of jobs. Some of the demand-side causes, however, imply supply-side remedies, suggesting that policy should tilt toward employability. The form that efforts should take to increase employability and the availability of jobs is discussed below.

Programs and Policies

Since the early 1960s the federal government's efforts to train youth have cost more than $15 billion. One of many groups eligible for assistance under the Manpower Development and Training Act of 1962, youth became the focus in 1964 of the Neighborhood Youth Corps, which provided work experience but little training or support services for economically disadvantaged youth, and the Job Corps, a more intensive and comprehensive effort to attack a range of problems affecting hard-to-employ youth. In 1973 the Comprehensive Employment and Training Act decentralized and decategorized most manpower programs, including the Neighborhood Youth Corps but not the Job Corps. Even by the mid-1970s the success of these efforts to raise the earnings and employment prospects of youth remained unclear. As a result, the Youth Employment and Demonstration Projects Act was passed in 1977, establishing four primary demonstration programs and a number of other experimental activities designed to increase understanding of the training process. As the 1980s begin, only the most preliminary results are available from the 1977 act. Although a consensus has not been reached on such fundamental questions as what kind of training is best suited for various categories of youth and whether the benefits of training programs exceed their costs, some lessons have been learned:[31]

1. Work experience by itself, particularly of a make-work kind, seems to have no lasting impact on a youth's chances in the labor market. Such programs should be justified, if at all, by their current benefits in providing income supplements or for carrying youth through an unstable time of life.

31. For summaries of youth experiences with training programs, see Ernst W. Stromsdorfer, "The Effectiveness of Youth Programs: An Analysis of the Historical Antecedents of Current Youth Initiatives," in Anderson and Sawhill, eds., *Youth Employment and Public Policy*, pp. 4-1 to 4-25; and "An Assessment of Youth Employment Policies for the 1980s."

2. Programs that include skill training (vocational or technical education provided by area vocational centers or other institutions) may have a positive but diminishing effect on the earnings and employment prospects of participants who complete the programs, with greater benefits for women than for men.

3. Vocational education as part of a high school curriculum, on the other hand, does not have a clear positive impact on the experiences of young men in the labor market relative to their counterparts who pursue a general academic program. Vocational graduates do seem to benefit in the short run from the placement services of their programs. Women, however, do improve their job prospects by taking a vocational program, apparently because most of them learn clerical skills that are much in demand.

4. The chances that a youth will complete high school are not increased either by work experience programs that provide youth in school with part-time jobs, or (for men) by vocational curricula. Women in vocational programs are more likely to graduate than their counterparts in the general academic track. Preliminary evidence from the Youth Incentive Entitlement Pilot Projects suggests that requiring school attendance (or its equivalent) as a condition of receiving a job is more successful.

5. Although the Job Corps is one of the most expensive programs in terms of costs per trainee, its benefits appear to exceed its costs, in part because it reduces the potential criminal activity of its trainees.

6. Successful programs are not cheap. They require adequate planning time and resources, skilled supervisors for the training component, and support services—most importantly, assistance in job placement.

Although debate will continue over the effectiveness of various approaches to training youth, other unresolved issues from the 1970s will challenge policymakers in the next decade.

PROGRAM ELIGIBILITY. Policymakers face difficult choices in deciding who should be eligible for special programs to combat youth unemployment: youth in school or those out of school; young teenagers (aged fourteen to sixteen) or only older youth; young people from poor families and poverty areas or those who meet other criteria of need, such as unemployment. The most fundamental choice, however, is between focusing assistance on those with greatest need, who are also the most difficult to help, or on a broader, less disadvantaged population where the programs promise to be more effective. Usually these two criteria imply different target populations. The former approach is appealing on equity grounds—if limited resources prevent everyone in need from being assisted, then those least likely to succeed in the labor market on their own should be helped first. The second approach is largely supported on efficiency grounds because more people can be made employable with a given budget. In addition, some argue that programs focused on the groups with highest risk stereotype their graduates and become self-defeating, denying the neediest trainees contact with more successful participants. Since the reauthorization of the Comprehensive Employment and Training Act in 1978, the tendency in Washington has been to favor the former strategy of focusing employment and training programs on the most disadvantaged. Because the problems in moving from school to work are disproportionately concentrated within a small segment of the youth population and will become even more so in the 1980s, it seems advisable on balance to concentrate youth programs on those with the dimmest prospects of success in the labor market.

EMPLOYABILITY. With the solution yet to be found for turning high-risk youth into productive workers, policymakers must nevertheless choose which types of training and which institutions to support with public funds. The relative merits of work experience versus specific skill training versus general, or basic, education continue to be debated. The last approach is currently most favored, in part because whatever other problems high-risk youth may have, their near-illiteracy is bound to be an obstacle, and in part because the other two approaches are associated with the perceived failure of the programs in the 1960s and 1970s. Although analyses of earlier programs do counsel skepticism of work experience for its own sake and of skill training that is not coordinated with the relevant labor market, it seems unwise to expect instruction in basic literacy and computational skills to be the long-sought solution. Given the persistent uncertainty about which approach works for whom, it seems that basic educational competence should be considered a necessary but not sufficient condition for success in the labor market.

Whatever mix of training is chosen, the next question is which institutions should provide it and, in particular, what role the public school system should play. Schools are the institutions given primary responsibility for shepherding children into adulthood, but ample evidence exists that many of the schools that blacks attend are failing to educate their charges. For example, only 58 percent of seventeen-year-old blacks register as functionally literate compared to 91 percent of whites.[32] Among college-bound high school students, only 10 to 20 percent of the blacks score as well as the average white on the College Board Scholastic Aptitude Tests. These and similar statistics persuade many observers that the public schools—particularly predominantly black central city schools—should not be chosen to provide supplementary training for hard-to-employ youth. Supporters of the schools point to the disadvantaged circumstances from which these youth come as explanations for the poor results and maintain that with adequate resources the public schools are best suited—because of their experience and location—for running those programs. Although there is merit to the claim that the schools face severe obstacles in educating these youth, the argument that they have a comparative advantage in serving them is unconvincing. It seems advisable, instead, to encourage a variety of organizations to offer training because no one type of institution has emerged as most effective. The most important contribution that the public schools could make to the school-to-work transition is greater success in educating their charges the first time through. There is no obvious method for achieving this end. Extending compensatory education support into the junior and senior high schools might help, as might fundamental changes in the schools themselves. It is clear, though, that the chances for success in the labor market for a minority youth will remain inferior to that of a white counterpart as long as the school the black attends fails to provide a basic education.

PRIVATE SECTOR INVOLVEMENT. The central challenge for policymakers seeking to involve the private sector in the transition from school to work is to design programs that will simultaneously advance the goals of the government and the firm. The government wants to induce private firms to participate and to accept hard-to-employ youth, but it does not want to subsidize firms for what they would have done anyway or for displacing other workers. For the programs to be successful, however, they must appeal to the self-

---

32. These figures are from the National Assessment of Educational Literacy, sponsored by the Department of Health, Education, and Welfare, and were cited by Robert I. Lerman, "The Nature of the Youth Employment Problem: A Review Paper," prepared for the Vice President's Task Force on Youth Employment, November 1979, p. 55.

interest as well as the public interest of the firms. This means that a balance must be struck in several areas.

For example, firms want a minimal amount of red tape, but the government prefers regulations sufficient to ensure that its purposes are being served. Firms want the most promising candidates, while the government's concern focuses on the least qualified youth. Firms would like to be compensated for more than their actual expenses for participating in the program, while the government wants the subsidy to be just sufficient to induce participation. The public interest will have to be compromised to some extent to obtain private participation. Whether the value of private sector involvement merits these compromises is a judgment for policymakers, but they need more experience with programs such as the targeted jobs tax credit and the Youth Incentive Entitlement Pilot Projects to make an informed decision.

LINKING SCHOOL AND WORK. The need to bring the classroom closer to the work place for disadvantaged youth is widely recognized. The challenge for the 1980s comes in putting substance into the rhetoric. Many approaches, such as career education and cooperative education, have been tried, but there is no easy solution. One obstacle to which federal policymakers need to pay more attention is that political rivalries between the school board and the prime sponsor (often the mayor's office) on local issues can provide disincentives for cooperating in federal training programs for youth. This consideration and other experiences to date suggest that even within the public sector, exhortation alone will not produce coordination when it conflicts with the self-interest of organizations. Consequently, concrete inducements—either in the form of requirements or incentives—for schools to work with employers must be included in any program where such cooperation is desired.

Legislation for the 1980s

In light of the uncertainties surrounding both the transition from school to work and ways to make it smoother, it is unfortunate that Congress and the administration view the expiration of the Youth Employment and Demonstration Projects Act in 1980 as an opportunity for a major legislative initiative on federal employment and training programs for youth. Although the act was designed as a series of experiments to provide information and successful models for youth programs, any legislation enacted this year will derive little benefit from those projects, because at most two years of operating experience will be available.[33] In such a short period, little insight can be gained on the impact or outcomes of the programs, although some lessons can be learned on administering programs. But years divisible by four have a logic of their own in Washington.

The administration's proposals for the 1980s adopt a two-pronged approach. For young people still in school, the initiative proposes to spend $1 billion a year through the Department of Education to fill gaps in existing programs. It would extend federal support for compensatory education to junior and senior high schools in economically depressed school districts and would increase funding for vocational education in those areas. For youth out of school in areas of high unemployment, the Department of Labor would receive another $1 billion a year to expand and consolidate current employment and training programs, with more emphasis on strengthening their implementation than on revising their content. Both the labor and education components concentrate on the youth most in need of assistance and emphasize planning, incentives for linking training programs to the schools and to the private sector, and standards of performance for the youth and the providers of services. Like their predecessors, these proposals will not work miracles—they will not transform urban schools into model institutions nor guarantee harmony of effort by all concerned with the transition from school to work—but they offer a reasonable response to the challenge of youth unemployment.

Higher Education

Between 1960 and 1970, total enrollments in higher education increased by 136 percent; from 1970 to 1978, enrollments increased by 34 percent; during the 1980s, enrollments are likely to increase very little, and may even fall. Although many economic and social forces will bear on colleges and universities during the next decade, none will have more impact than the changing demography of the U.S. population and its effect on the demand for higher education. The size of the population between eighteen and twenty-four years of

33. Most projects were not truly operational until spring 1978, and any evidence from evaluations that could influence reauthorization would have to be collected before spring 1980.

age will reach a peak of 29.5 million in 1981, and then fall to 23.2 million by 1995, a drop of more than 21 percent. Because students in this age range currently account for 82 percent of total full-time enrollments in higher education, this sharp decline in the dominant applicant pool will send shock waves throughout the system of higher education for years to come. (This impact will vary by region, as some areas experience greater than average loss, while others continue to grow.) Institutions that have experienced an environment of growth for a quarter of a century will have to adjust to a decade or more of limited growth and, in some instances, decline. Most of the important policy issues for the 1980s arise from this central economic fact.

Another important demographic trend is the shifting racial composition of the group aged eighteen to twenty-four. All the decline is in the white population; the number of nonwhites in this category remains relatively constant at about 4.5 million, but increases over time from 14.2 to 19.3 percent of the total.[34] Thus the minority-group population will become increasingly important to the colleges and universities, and efforts can be expected to increase the college-attendance and retention rates of those students during the next decade.

What are the implications of this drop in the traditional college-going age group? First, and foremost, there will be sharply increased competition among institutions for enrollments and for support. Unlike the situation of elementary and secondary schools, where students have limited mobility and generally enroll in the local school, potential college students exercise much greater choice in deciding whether—and where—to enroll. The "market" for higher education is extraordinarily diverse and differentiated: some colleges and universities draw students from throughout the nation; others serve primarily a state or region; and still others, a section of a state or a local community. Many colleges have religious affiliations and mainly serve church members, while others, such as the single-sex or historically black colleges, serve those particular groups within the population. The diversity of U.S. higher education is one of its great strengths, as is the tradition of autonomy and local decisionmaking.

---

34. These data, based on live births in the United States and collected by the National Center for Health Statistics, include persons of Hispanic origin within the white population.

For these reasons, the coming struggle for students and for resources will be hard fought. The swing from a seller's to a buyer's market, however, will pose thorny policy questions in areas such as educational quality, "truth in advertising," consumer protection, and government regulation.

Second, there will be increased interest on most college and university campuses in extending access to "nontraditional" students, primarily adults who enroll on a part-time basis, often in nondegree programs. The community colleges have led the way in developing this market, having embraced service to the entire community as their mission. The principal policy question that this type of education poses is: who should pay for it? Most state and federal student aid programs are designed to foster more equal opportunity, and are thus directed toward full-time, degree-seeking students. Lower priority has been placed on financing education for older, part-time, nondegree credit students. The rationale for their support would require a broader philosophy that stresses the value of formalized lifelong learning. So far, this case has not been persuasive in the political arena.

A third implication is that there will be little hiring of new Ph.D.s for the faculties of colleges and universities during the 1980s. The two main sources of demand for new faculty are enrollment expansion and replacement for turnover and retirements; we have seen that there will be little demand from expansion and, given the existing age distribution of the nation's faculty members, relatively little replacement demand until well into the 1990s. The prospect of a "missing generation" of young scholars has serious implications for the vitality, productivity, and morale of college and university faculties, with diminished quality of both teaching and research a serious concern.

Fourth, just as the 1980s will see a push for direct federal aid for elementary and secondary education, so too will there be a renewed effort by colleges and universities for some form of federal institutional aid. The catalyst for such an effort could be the bankruptcy of one or more reasonably well-known private colleges, with the accompanying fear that without federal aid, many more closings would follow. Efforts will also be directed at state governments to increase their support for private colleges and universities; if successful, these efforts will further blur the distinction between public and private sectors of higher education.

Prospects for the Sectors of Higher Education

The nation's major research universities, no more than 100 in number, should have no problem maintaining their undergraduate enrollments, but will face severe difficulties in financing graduate education and maintaining their strength as research institutions. Financial support for graduate students is down sharply from a decade ago; budgets for library acquisitions have fallen far behind the increased costs of books and periodicals; and much of the scientific equipment in research laboratories has become outmoded or obsolete.[35] Graduate education and research are high-cost activities, heavily dependent upon support from the federal government, and the continued strength of the research universities, more than any other group, will depend upon policies set in the nation's capital.

A more troubled group of institutions will be the former teachers' colleges that began to develop into comprehensive state colleges and universities during the 1960s, but now find themselves stranded in states of semidevelopment with unclear missions. These institutions will not become major research universities within our lifetimes, and are likely to experience much of the enrollment loss in the public sector. Location will be of prime importance in determining which of these institutions thrive and which decline; those in large cities are most fortunate because they can emphasize an urban mission, concentrating on professional graduate programs short of the Ph.D., aimed at older, part-time students who are currently employed.

Private, liberal arts colleges face an equally difficult future, for their heavy dependence on tuition makes them particularly vulnerable to enrollment losses. Inflation and the sluggish performance of the stock market have severely eroded the value of endowments, reducing their contribution to operating budgets. Tuition increases are limited by competition from other colleges, particularly publicly supported institutions that charge considerably less. As many as 200 of these small colleges may close or merge with other institutions during the next decade.[36] The factors that will ultimately make the difference are

35. See *Research Universities and the National Interest: A Report from Fifteen University Presidents* (Ford Foundation, 1977); *Scholarly Communication: The Report of the National Enquiry* (Johns Hopkins University Press, 1979), chap. 4; and Bruce L. R. Smith and Joseph J. Karlesky, *The Universities in the Nation's Research Effort* (Change Magazine Press, 1977).

36. See David W. Breneman and Chester E. Finn, Jr., eds., *Public Policy and Private Higher Education* (Brookings Institution, 1978); and Robert D. Behn, "The

location, reputation, a clear sense of identity and mission, loyal alumni, good trustees, and intelligent management.

Community colleges increased in number and grew more rapidly than any other part of higher education during the past two decades, and the conventional view holds that if there is any sector likely to thrive in coming years, it is the two-year colleges. The National Center for Education Statistics projects their enrollments will grow by 54 percent between 1976 and 1986, based largely on increasing numbers of part-time, adult students. Although this forecast may prove accurate, an equally plausible view is much less sanguine about their prospects, based on the growing tension between the evolving mission of community colleges and their financing. Community colleges are likely to lose some of their full-time, transfer-oriented students to four-year institutions that recruit aggressively. Continued expansion of financial aid based on student need will reinforce this tendency. The number of adult, part-time students may not continue to increase because of saturation of demand, effective competition from other sectors, or because of the unwillingness of local, state, or federal governments to subsidize such education. Community service activities may be forced to remain on a "pay-as-you-go" basis, and taxpayers may resist increased financing for adult, remedial instruction, preferring instead to concentrate resources for that purpose in the secondary schools. The vocational-technical programs seem reasonably secure, but there is a risk that the comprehensive community-college mission may be lost, with the colleges becoming essentially technical institutes. In short, community colleges seem to face the most volatile future, in which the very nature of the institutions may change; there is no reason to believe that they will emerge unscathed from the next decade.

Policy Issues for State Governments

The most critical public policy decisions affecting higher education in the 1980s will be made at the level of state government, as governors, legislators, and statewide governing or coordinating boards shape policies for an era of enrollment decline.[37] State officials will

---

End of the Growth Era in Higher Education" (Duke University, Institute of Policy Sciences and Public Affairs, 1979).

37. This section does not address the important administrative actions that will be necessary on campuses during the next decade. For a discussion of institutional management, see Lewis B. Mayhew, *Surviving the Eighties* (Jossey-Bass, 1979).

have the following types of questions thrust upon them: can a reasonable division of labor among institutions be sustained in the face of pressures on many institutions to search for new markets and activities? Does an enrollment-driven budget formula serve the system well at a time of stable or declining enrollments? What policy should the state adopt toward its private institutions, and what should it do when bankruptcies loom? If state colleges have excess capacity, should recruitment of out-of-state or foreign students be encouraged? Can educational quality be ensured in off-campus programs and in other entrepreneurial ventures that the 1980s will spawn?

There are no simple or obvious answers to these questions, primarily because of the zero-sum nature of many of the choices: one institution's enrollment or financial gain will often be another's loss. For example, if state officials place high priority on maintaining low public tuition, the competitive position of private colleges within the state will suffer in the absence of increased financial aid for students. In states where the principal research university is located away from the centers of population growth, state representatives may have to decide whether to maintain research excellence where it currently exists or to redirect resources for graduate and professional education to emerging urban universities. In cities where two-year and four-year colleges coexist, a shortage of full-time undergraduates may force a choice between shutting down the first two years of the four-year college or closing the transfer programs at the community college. These are the types of decisions that most elected officials would prefer not to make, relying instead on the verdict of the market, but it is unlikely that the existing higher education marketplace will yield a socially desirable outcome in the 1980s. Private colleges in many states will bear a disproportionate share of the losses, but because tuition prices in the various institutions bear little relation to the costs of education, there will be no reason to applaud that outcome. Nor are market forces likely to resolve the issues of program duplication and relocation. Establishing rational prices in higher education as a means to guide resource allocation appears to be impossible politically, leaving increased decisionmaking at the state level as the alternative. Whether the relatively new coordinating agencies in many states will be able to function effectively—and in the public interest—in the politically charged atmosphere of the next decade is, at best, an open question, worthy of investigation in its own right.

There are several actions that state governments can take, however, to reduce unnecessary conflict and to increase the chances that the adjustment to the 1980s will be less haphazard. First, financing formulas for public institutions should be examined to see whether they provide sound incentives for the changed circumstances of the coming decade. The typical state formula is enrollment-driven, and provides either a dollar amount per student or a personnel entitlement (such as one faculty position for every twenty full-time students). These formulas, which are commonly based on average, not marginal, costs of instruction, worked to the benefit of public institutions during the years of enrollment growth, but there are at least two problems with them for the coming decade: they do not accurately reflect the cost structure of colleges and universities, thereby penalizing institutions harshly when enrollment falls; and they provide an incentive for each public campus to strive for continued enrollment growth.

On the latter point, the competition for students promises to be sufficiently intense without fueling it further by linking budgets tightly to enrollments. One way to change that incentive would be to reduce sharply the state payment for any enrollment increase over the average level at an institution during the preceding three years. By paying only the marginal cost of any enrollment gain, the incentive to grow beyond current size would be virtually eliminated. If the larger, more attractive public institutions were not motivated to recruit quite so strenuously, the pressures facing smaller, less selective institutions, both public and private, would be lessened.

For those campuses that do lose enrollments, however, current formulas based on average costs could be devastating. A campus that loses 10 percent of its enrollment cannot promptly or easily reduce its costs by 10 percent. Most college and university costs are relatively fixed in the short run, and some costs, such as those of basic administration or building maintenance, do not vary much with enrollments. Consequently, there is a strong incentive under current formulas not to let enrollments decline because costs cannot be cut proportionately without seriously damaging the institution. The solution to this problem is to break the formula into fixed and variable components or reduce appropriations by marginal, rather than average, costs when enrollments decline.

Second, each state with any sizable number of private colleges should establish an explicit policy toward its private institutions and their students that reflects the value and importance of those institutions to the state. Procedures should be established in advance to govern the state's response to potential closings of private colleges. Guidelines should specify under what conditions (if any) the state would take over an institution and incorporate it into the public system; under what conditions (if any) financial assistance short of a state takeover would be granted; and, if a closing is inevitable, what responses the state would make to assist students to complete their education with minimal loss of time and money. Because it is possible to foresee the extreme financial pressures that many private colleges will experience during the next decade, states would be well advised to establish explicit policies in advance of the inevitable crises, so that the pressures of the moment do not produce ad hoc, ill-conceived, and costly responses.

Third, states must weigh the costs and benefits of increased state-wide planning for the 1980s. Additional planning would reduce institutional autonomy, restrict innovation, and in the view of some, would ultimately weaken higher education. On the other hand, states without master plans run the risk of eroding whatever institutional division of labor currently exists, contributing needlessly to increased competition for resources. This issue will be most pressing in the newer, nontraditional market for adult education, remedial education, community-based education, off-campus education, and the like. In these newer areas, a clear sense of who can best perform has not been established, nor is there a good understanding of who should pay for such programs. If financing becomes assured, however, the struggle among providers will grow more intense, and the merits of a market free-for-all versus an explicit allocation of responsibilities and support must be debated, and policy determined.

Finally, the higher education officials of a state will have to be alert to issues of educational quality, particularly in judging the more entrepreneurial ventures that some colleges and universities may undertake in the 1980s.[38] Thus far higher education has avoided the erosion of public confidence that plagues the elementary and secondary schools; confidence could easily be shattered in today's cynical climate, however, and it is the responsibility of all concerned with

---

38. For several examples, such as low-quality graduate programs offered on military bases, see Kenneth H. Ashworth, *American Higher Education in Decline* (Texas A&M University Press, 1979).

governance, financing, and management of colleges and universities not to let that happen. While not losing sight of the primary responsibility of trustees, administrators, and faculty for determining educational policy, state officials should examine their financial and programmatic policies to be sure that they are not inadvertently encouraging questionable programs or practices.

Policy Issues for the Federal Government

The most significant question regarding federal policy for higher education in the 1980s is whether the federal government should attempt to influence the outcome of the coming struggle for enrollments and resources, or remain officially neutral and above the fray. Although neutrality toward institutions is notoriously difficult to achieve, particularly in the domain of student financial aid, where the interests of public and private colleges often conflict, there is every reason to think that the federal government will—and should—avoid the temptation to try to shape the future of higher education. Given the complexity and diversity of higher education in the fifty states, it is unlikely that even a well-intentioned federal effort would be accepted politically in the states.[39] The fate of individual institutions is better left to state governments and to private organizations and individuals.

There are two groups of institutions, however, that the federal government has been directly concerned with in the past: the major research universities (including medical schools) and the historically black colleges. The universities are the country's principal performers of basic research, financed largely by federal grants and contracts. Because the benefits of basic research accrue to the nation as a whole, federal financing is essential if the nation is not to underinvest in new knowledge. In addition to research support, federal agencies are properly concerned with the supply and utilization of highly trained individuals, with the obsolescence of scientific equipment, with the incentives that encourage (or discourage) the practical application of research findings, and with the age distribution and vitality of the faculties of major research institutions. Although relationships between the federal government and the universities have been severely

---

39. See Breneman and Finn, eds., *Public Policy and Private Higher Education*, pp. 427–33, for discussion of a possible federal effort to influence state policy toward private colleges and the resistance it would meet.

strained in the last decade by cutbacks in support for research and graduate education and by sharply increased government regulation of virtually all aspects of university operation, both parties (and the nation) have too much at stake to countenance continued deterioration in their relationships.

The nation's historically black colleges are principal beneficiaries of institutional support under the "Strengthening Developing Institutions" program.[40] Although grants under this legislation were not meant to be a continuing source of support, in several cases the funds have become an essential part of operating budgets, and their withdrawal would threaten the survival of the colleges. The result is a highly politicized program, plagued by instances of mismanagement at both the campus and the federal levels.[41] There are good reasons for a federal interest in these colleges, but this program is certainly no model for the delivery of institutional aid, serving instead as an object lesson in the perils of direct federal entanglement with institutional support.

Assuming that Washington steers clear of institutional aid in the 1980s, the federal legislative agenda embodied in the Higher Education Act of 1965, as amended, is essentially complete, with few new initiatives likely to mark the next decade. This judgment should not be interpreted, however, as diminishing the need for reform in several of the student aid programs. Congress is currently engaged in reauthorizing these programs, and while the final shape of the Education Amendments of 1980 is not yet definite, a major problem that requires—but may not receive—attention is the burgeoning cost of the guaranteed student loan program. In 1978, in order to stave off enactment of a tuition tax credit, Congress passed the Middle Income Student Assistance Act. This legislation removed the family income limitation governing eligibility for subsidized student loans; any student can now borrow up to $2,500 a year interest-free while enrolled, with interest at 7 percent during the repayment period. Not surprisingly, the response to this offer was prompt and substantial; according to preliminary estimates by the Congressional Budget Office, the number of loans increased by 50 percent between 1978

40. Title III of the Higher Education Act of 1965, as amended.
41. General Accounting Office, *The Federal Program to Strengthen Developing Institutions of Higher Education Lacks Direction,* HRD-78-170, February 1979. See also Lawrence Feinberg, "Order Barred Cuts to Colleges," *Washington Post,* December 13, 1979.

and 1979 (from roughly 1.0 to 1.5 million), and the amount borrowed climbed from $1.94 billion to $2.97 billion. The Congressional Budget Office estimates the cost of this program to the federal government in fiscal 1981 to be $1.37 billion, with over $1.1 billion of that amount being interest subsidies. Also in need of reform is a provision that allows state agencies to reap sizable profits under the program by issuing tax-exempt bonds and lending the proceeds to students. Because the federal government guarantees that all lenders will receive a market rate of interest for student loans, state lending agencies receive the difference between their tax-exempt borrowing rate and this reimbursement rate. Federal outlays under the guaranteed student loan program are uncontrollable because the subsidies are an entitlement, and these rapidly growing costs, coupled with pressures on the budget, threaten the annual appropriations for the student grant programs.

Furthermore, in November 1979 the House of Representatives passed its version of the Education Amendments of 1980, which sharply expands the benefits available to students under these grant programs. The centerpiece of the bill is a much-trumpeted "student aid compromise," agreed upon by all major college and university associations. That an agreement was reached on issues that have been in dispute for years suggests one fact about the compromise—it is expensive. In return for sizable increases in the maximum award under the basic educational opportunity grant program (which the private sector wanted), a provision that limits grant awards to "half-of-cost" will be relaxed (as insisted upon by the public sector).[42] The Congressional Budget Office estimates that these two changes will raise costs in fiscal 1981 by approximately $1.0 billion. The compromise also calls for increases in other programs, such as the supplemental educational opportunity grants program, which are particularly important to the private institutions. Further provisions of the bill expand eligibility for aid by not including equity in a home in the calculation of financial need, and by providing the same opportunities for aid that dependent students now have to independent students with dependents (that is, a parent who attends college would

---

42. The "half-of-cost" provision is clearly inequitable because it penalizes the poorest youth attending low-priced institutions. An increase in the maximum award could also be justified to account for inflation. Thus the compromise can be interpreted as serving reasonable, if costly, social ends.

be able to qualify for aid on terms similar to those of a child). The House bill does nothing to reduce significantly those subsidies in the guaranteed student loan program that are unnecessary and wasteful.

If the Senate accepts the House bill and it is signed into law in 1980, higher education will enter the decade with legislation that allows some form of federally subsidized support for virtually every person enrolled for credit in a college or university, regardless of income. Should that happen, the authorizing legislation will have failed to address the difficult choices among competing groups and purposes that is the essence of setting educational priorities. In the presence of an inevitable budget constraint that will prevent the authorized levels of spending from being met, the power to set educational priorities will shift from the education committees to the appropriations committees. The higher education associations need to consider carefully whether that is the best place to have their differences settled, although there may be no realistic alternative, given the divergent interests within that community.

The outlook for higher education policy in the nation's capital, then, is essentially "business as usual" during the next decade. No striking new initiatives are apparent, nor are existing programs or purposes likely to change much. The support that the federal government provides to students and, indirectly, to institutions will remain vital to the financial well-being of colleges and universities, but the most important decisions about the future of higher education will be made at the state, institutional, and private levels. And that is as it should be.

CHAPTER EIGHT

Intergovernmental Fiscal Relations

GEORGE F. BREAK

WHEN the Founding Fathers established the outlines of the federal system of government, they could hardly have foreseen that it would take the better part of the republic's first century to determine what federalism was to mean in a political sense and possibly more than the second century to define federalism in fiscal terms. Especially since the end of World War II, the federal government's response to the question of what is involved in establishing justice, ensuring domestic tranquillity, and promoting the general welfare has amounted to acceptance of vastly increased responsibility for channeling financial assistance to state and local governments. The large scale of this distributive mission has required great ingenuity in the creation of a lavish array of complicated arrangements for moving money from Washington to practically every political subdivision of the nation. The thirty-five-year crescendo of this money-moving activity has recently shown signs of slackening. This change of pace, though not yet great, could be one of the significant features of budgets in the next few years.

Recent Trends

Federal grants-in-aid to state and local governments, which in 1946 amounted to a mere 0.5 percent of gross national product,

I am indebted to Helen S. Break for assistance in preparing the manuscript and to Florence C. Myer for secretarial support and editorial comments.

247

Table 8-1. Federal and State Intergovernmental Grants as a Percent of Gross National Product, Selected Years, 1946–78

Year	Federal grants	State grants
1946	0.5	1.0
1950	0.8	1.5
1955	0.8	1.5
1960	1.3	1.9
1965	1.6	2.2
1970	2.5	3.0
1975	3.6	3.4
1976	3.6	3.3
1977	3.6	n.a.
1978	3.6	n.a.

Sources: *Survey of Current Business*, various issues; for state grants before 1960, U.S. Advisory Commission on Intergovernmental Relations, *The States and Intergovernmental Aids, The Intergovernmental Grant System: An Assessment and Proposed Policies*, Report A-59 (U.S. Government Printing Office, 1977) p. 9.

n.a. Not available.

reached 3.6 percent by 1975 and then began to level off (table 8-1). State grants-in-aid to local governments followed a parallel course, rising to 3.4 percent before leveling off. Federal grants now appear to be dropping—projections for the 1980 budget show them declining to 3.2 percent of gross national product and for 1982 to 3.0 percent. It seems reasonable to assume that there will be a concomitant lessening of state aid to localities.

To appreciate the magnitude of these deceptively modest-looking percentages it is necessary to realize that in 1947 expenditures in the public sector amounted to only $42.5 billion, or 18.3 percent of gross national product. By 1978 they had risen to $686.0 billion, the federal share (excluding grants-in-aid) amounting to 18 percent of gross national product and the state and local share to 14 percent. These are impressive rates of growth, but it may be significant that the 1978 levels were below those reached in 1975 when federal spending was 20 percent of gross national product and state and local was 15 percent.

Even more can be learned about the changing nature of the federal system by studying the alterations that have taken place in government spending patterns. In 1948 nearly half of federal government expenditures went for purchase of goods and services, with 31 percent allocated to national defense and 17 percent to nondefense uses; a third of the federal budget went for transfer payments to private individuals and business; a mere 6 percent went in grants-in-aid to states and local governments. Thirty years later the proportions were very different: defense expenditures had shrunk to 21.5 percent of the budget and nondefense purchases to 12 percent, while transfer payments had escalated to 40 percent and grants-in-aid to 17 percent. More and more of the federal budget was being passed through to private individuals and households and to state and local governments, while budgets at the lower levels were allocating increasing amounts to purchase of goods and services and less to transfer payments.

The shift in the configuration of government purchases of goods and services is important because this category of expenditure represents government's share of the economy's total productive activity. While only a dyed-in-the-wool conservative could agree with Adam Smith that such expenditures largely go for "maintaining unproductive hands," the striking growth in the amount of total output absorbed by government is significant for the economy. In 1947 government output amounted to 10.9 percent of gross national product, almost equally divided between the federal and the state and local levels. By 1978 government consumption of resources amounted to 20.5 percent of gross national product, with the federal level accounting for only 7.2 percent and the state and local sector 13.3 percent. Clearly, government was a growing force in the economy, and most of that growth was occurring in the state and local arena.

Such enormous changes in spending patterns involve equally great changes in governmental structure. As more and more of Washington's energy has been devoted to channeling money to other parts of the nation, the transfer of funds has itself grown into a major industry. Finding appropriate means for directing and regulating this flow has been an intense preoccupation of government during the past quarter of a century, and experimentation with different methods and approaches nears a new critical point as revenue sharing comes up for renewal in the fall of 1980.

The evolution of federal grants-in-aid, which are the lifeblood of fiscal federalism, has been, like all undertakings in a democracy, a complex mixture of pragmatism, politics, and principle. Before anything can be done, there must be an identification of needs and of goals to be served. These may vary greatly from one section of the country to another, and critical decisions must be made about how to equate different needs and how to weight different goals. This process raises questions about how and where the decisions can best be made —whether in Washington or in the field. With huge quantities of money at stake, the choices are momentous.

Fortunately for the decisionmakers, the historical development of federal grants-in-aid, which now exceed $80 billion a year, began rather slowly. In the nineteenth century there were federal grants (often in land) for the construction of wagon roads, railroads, and canals, and at one affluent period a distribution of surplus revenue.[1] In 1950 the first broad-based grant program, school aid to areas whose populations were swollen by federal undertakings, was enacted. From a level of $2.3 billion in 1950, federal grants began a trend of steady, slowly accelerating growth, reaching $10.9 billion in 1965. The first special revenue-sharing program, comprehensive health grants, came into being in 1966, and general revenue sharing was inaugurated in 1972. Within the past decade the dollar amounts of federal grants have more than tripled. For state and local governments they amounted to more than 26 percent of expenditures by 1978, up from only 10 percent in 1950 and 1955. The 1980 budget, which shows that federal grants fell to 25.6 percent of state and local expenditures in 1979 and estimates a further drop to 25.3 percent in 1980, is the first hint of a decline.

Although federal grant-making may appear to have progressed from specific-purpose funding to broad-gauge functional aid to general sharing of revenue, the fact is that each successive form has been added to the existing types of intergovernmental assistance. The most specific form, categorical grants, accounts for over 75 percent of the aid transferred. Those grants with the fewest strings attached (principally revenue sharing) make up less than 11 percent of the total, and broad-based grants just under 14 percent. Revenue sharing has been and remains the most controversial of the three basic approaches, and its future is the most uncertain.

1. In 1836, during Andrew Jackson's second administration, the federal treasury was so swollen with receipts from the sale of public lands and from customs duties that Congress passed the Surplus Distribution Act, apportioning among the states the surplus above $5 million. This process was interrupted by the panic of 1837, and the payments stopped after about $28 million had been distributed.

Categorical Grants

In political, if not economic, terms categorical grants seem to be the easiest (for Congress at least) to justify. They finance nearly five hundred separate programs. For Washington they have the great advantage of maximizing its control over the use of aid funds. It is true that in fact the federal government may achieve only an opportunity to bargain with state and local governments and that grant agreements are likely to reflect the priorities of all parties.[2] Nevertheless, in its categorical programs Washington can impose more specific constraints and pressures on grantees than it can either with block grants or through revenue sharing.

In their simplest forms, categorical grants lend themselves readily to policy guidelines. The funded program must serve some identifiable national interest and produce some broadly disseminated benefits. A significant portion of the benefits accrues locally, however, so that it is logical to introduce a matching element, with the local jurisdiction paying an agreed portion of the program cost. Such joint ventures are also easy to justify as a means of giving both sides of the partnership a stake in the efficient management and ultimate success of the program. So it is in theory.

In practice, unfortunately, this neat blueprint becomes blurred. The precise extent of the national, or even local, interest in a program may be impossible to determine. The raison d'être for the funding thus may shift from ends to means—from the stake that the nation has in the activity to the achievement of a cooperative intergovernmental arrangement for operating the program (whatever the interest served). Although the benefits may be largely local, federal help then serves to provide expert knowledge and skills or to achieve greater coordination among related activities throughout the country. Such a rationale—using operational rather than functional goals—raises entirely new questions about both political and economic justification. If improving local operational efficiency is in itself a national goal, federal subsidies make sense; if not, they are decidedly questionable.

Because there are so many variables to be considered, categorical grants have taken a number of different forms. In fiscal 1975 nearly

2. Helen Ingram, "Policy Implementation through Bargaining: The Case of Federal Grants-in-Aid," *Public Policy,* vol. 25 (Fall 1977), pp. 499–526.

Table 8-2. Number and Outlay of Federal Categorical Grants, by Type, Fiscal 1975

| | Grants | | Outlay | |
| | | | Amount (billions of | |
Type	Number	Percent	dollars)	Percent
Formula-based grants	146	33.0	25.8	69.0
Allotted formula	97	21.9	8.6	23.0
Project grants subject to formula distribution	35	7.9	2.8	7.4
Open-ended reimbursement	14	3.2	14.4	38.6
Project grants	296	67.0	11.6	31.0
Total	442	100.0	37.4	100.0

Source: Advisory Commission on Intergovernmental Relations, *Categorical Grants: Their Role and Design*, Report A-52 (GPO, 1978), p. 92. Outlays are estimated.

one-fourth of all categorical grant money distributed was allotted by formula (table 8-2). These grants require that there be a clearly defined population of eligible recipients with demonstrable needs, and that there be objective measures of those needs to serve as factors in the allocation formulas. Depending on the needs and the fiscal capacity of the recipient jurisdiction, a matching requirement may be attached. These are extremely variable. In fiscal 1975 nearly 39 percent of federal categorical grant programs had no statutory matching requirements; 12 percent required nonfederal matching of only 5–10 percent of the total grant; and only 13 percent required that donees match 50 percent or more of grant funds. In reality, both needs and fiscal capacity prove extremely difficult to measure objectively, and theoretical clarity tends to give way to practical negotiation. Nevertheless, the matching principle continues to be an important conceptual part of categorical grants, not so much in order to tie funding to benefits as to create a spirit of partnership and provide an incentive for grantees to handle the work efficiently. Where local funding is not available, some programs allow grantees to fulfill their matching obligations by contributions in kind rather than in cash. There is considerable controversy over whether these "soft matches" stimulate the same measure of participation as cash contributions.

A further aim of matching is to stimulate spending by recipient governments on programs considered important by Washington. The many approaches to this goal have included relating grantee contributions inversely to the degree of national interest in the aided program; varying federal contributions inversely with the level of grantee spending, as in aid to families with dependent children, in order to stimulate at least a minimum level of activity everywhere; and gradually raising the level of contributions by the grantee as a program matures and simultaneously phasing out the federal "seed" money. Some grants require a maintenance of effort by grantees, stipulating that they must not diminish spending from their own tax sources during the lifetime of the program. All these efforts to ensure conscientious stewardship and enthusiastic participation by recipient governments are fraught with hazards and may produce perverse effects. Relating grant eligibility to earlier expenditure levels may, for example, penalize energetic and innovative grantees whose maintenance levels were higher than those of more cautious grant recipients. And maintenance-of-effort requirements pose a threat in recessionary periods by creating adverse fiscal pressure unless state and local budgets are protected by other federal programs, such as antirecession fiscal assistance. Inflation is no less of a problem, when the value of the federal matching funds is declining and ever greater financial commitments to the program are required from the grantee.

One additional feature sometimes built into allotted-formula grants is aimed at stimulating very specific kinds of activity in certain program areas. By targeting stated percentages of the grant funds on particular population groups, these grants can induce spending for pinpointed needs and also stimulate greater local spending on whole programs.[3]

The majority of individual grant programs are not suited to the allotted-formula design because they are not aimed at a well-defined group of eligible recipients and cannot be tied to good measures of fiscal need or capacity. A totally different format is used to fund projects related to service areas specified by Washington but designed by interested state and local authorities who apply for financing. Project grants tend to be relatively small in dollar terms, accounting for less than one-third of total federal grant funds. The choices that must be made in selecting among competitors for available funds are based not only on need but on the project's likelihood of success. Unfortunately these two criteria often conflict, with the neediest

3. See, for example, Martin Feldstein, "The Effect of a Differential Add-On Grant: Title I and Local Education Spending," *Journal of Human Resources*, vol. 13 (Fall 1978), pp. 443–58.

jurisdictions able to offer the least promise of success—a problem that puts a considerable strain on administrative judgment. Matching requirements may be attached and grantee spending stimulated by varying matching ratios inversely with the grantee's elasticity of demand for the aided output. Project grants are particularly well suited to undertakings of limited duration involving research, development of new techniques for production and delivery of services, or capital construction.

Whereas project grants satisfy the grantor's desire to channel money into high-priority activities, they impose heavy costs on potential grantees and on government efficiency. They have generated an entire new bureaucratic specialty, known as grantsmanship, that rewards adept players but often penalizes deserving candidates whose projects are not presented salably. The format is, nevertheless, well suited to certain kinds of program objectives. This form of aid is sorely in need, however, of systematic and continuous monitoring to make sure that grants are fulfilling their purposes and that fund procurement is not becoming a goal in itself. Such control could be accomplished by enactment of a "sunset" system for all federal grants that built terminal dates into contracts and that permitted renewals only after review, evaluation, and explicit reauthorization of the contracts.

The largest single share (nearly 40 percent in 1975) of categorical federal grants-in-aid to state and local governments is given in the form of open-ended matching grants, which commit the federal government to pay a fixed percentage of an indefinite total of program costs (table 8-2). The two major programs that receive this money are aid to families with dependent children and medicaid. How well suited these major health and welfare programs are to the matching-grant principle is a matter of heated controversy. Those who hold that the distribution of such aid should be the sole responsibility of the federal government believe that nationwide income support levels, adjusted for regional differences in the cost of living, should be established and fully funded by the federal government. Others take the position that attitudes toward income redistribution vary from region to region, and that therefore states and localities should have considerable latitude in determining support levels. An open-ended matching program offers a substantial degree of local autonomy in this matter, providing a ready means of equating local costs with perceived local benefits. In addition, a federal commitment to match local expenditures may provide a strong incentive for grantees to spend their own funds on the aided programs. If that is so, a shift to full federal financing of nationwide minimum welfare floors, supplemented by full state and local financing of any additional benefits, might well reduce total welfare outlays significantly.[4]

Fiscal federalism has come to mean a good deal more than the sharing of federal money with state and local governments. Increasing federal support has been accompanied by an expanding circle of federal standards that must be observed in the process of spending the funds. Before 1960 most of the requirements associated with federal grants had to do with efficient management of the subsidized programs. Since then a lengthening list of national policy goals has become an integral part of all programs receiving federal support. These general requirements deal with civil rights and nondiscrimination, environmental protection, planning and project coordination, labor and procurement standards, public employee standards, access to government information and decision processes, and the side effects of urban renewal and other grant programs. The wide-ranging federal requirements impose substantial compliance costs on the funded programs—costs that tend to be undervalued or even ignored in congressional evaluations and that in effect reduce federal matching ratios and distort state and local participation in different programs. The proliferation of controls has even led to talk of state and local governments' withdrawal from federally aided programs to give these governments the greater freedom that financing their own activities allows them. Such reactions could lead to increased pressure for federal tax reduction.

The Scylla and Charybdis of federal grant controls are the possibilities that highly specific requirements will ignore the wide diversity in the needs and the incentives of different state and local governments, and yet that very general guidelines will leave room for unintended and counterproductive action by either federal administrators or grant recipients. Complex economic and social problems unfortunately defy simple, clear administrative directives; protracted bargaining thus often serves as a substitute for effective control mechanisms. When, as a consequence, grantees have a high degree of

4. Larry L. Orr, "Income Transfers as a Public Good: An Application to AFDC," *American Economic Review,* vol. 66 (June 1976), pp. 359–71.

discretionary power, they may use grant funds in unintended ways, leading to disputes that can be settled only in the courts.

Another problem inherent in the federal categorical grant realm, either because of its nature or because of the way it has developed, is its fragmentation. Reformers have for years been urging greater coordination, but the impediments to accomplishing this have not yielded readily. Three broad-scale, multifunctional, targeted grant programs, adopted with coordination as one of the explicit objectives, provide valuable evidence about what may be hoped for in that regard. The community action, Appalachian regional development, and model cities programs all attempted to bring together a wide variety of grant-assisted public services in order to focus them on the solution of complex social and economic problems affecting a specific target population or geographical area. These efforts to get a wide range of agencies to coordinate their activities and work in concert toward the solution of multidimensional problems met with little success. For better or for worse, existing agencies have their own goals and their own bureaucratic patterns and procedures, and they tend to remain unconvinced of the desirability or possibility of adapting these to other, peripherally related, purposes. Even general national policy requirements are interpreted differently by the various federal grantor agencies, so that greater coordination here would be difficult to achieve despite the fact that it might reduce both program costs and the frustrations of state and local officials.

Block Grants

If coordination is a hopeless ideal, consolidation has offered a somewhat more viable means of rationalizing at least portions of the apparent chaos of the federal grant system. The first major move toward consolidating categorical grants, in 1966, was the merging of nine related health categories into the partnership for health program. Two years later this concept was pushed another step forward when a whole "block grant" program, aimed at crime prevention and the administration of justice, was created de novo rather than from an amalgamation of existing programs. President Nixon in his 1971 budget message to Congress proposed a major revision of federal aid to state and local governments, one big part of which was to be known as "special revenue sharing." One hundred and twenty-nine categorical grant programs would be consolidated into six block grants in the broad functional areas of education, law enforcement, manpower training, rural community development, transportation, and urban community development. The hope was to reduce administrative and compliance costs, to increase state and local flexibility in using federal aid, to strengthen state and local fiscal positions by removing matching and maintenance-of-effort requirements, and to shift political power from functional specialists to elected generalists. The consolidation was seen as a major move toward decentralizing fiscal operations while still directing expenditures toward broadly outlined national objectives. As usual, the grand design was considerably diminished by political reality.

After much delay the new approach to block grants was initiated in 1973 with the consolidation of seventeen categorical grants into the comprehensive employment and training program. The following year, six urban aid programs were merged into the community development block grant program, and in 1974 social services grants (after a checkered and difficult start) were made into a block grant program by title XX of the Social Security Act.

A kind of cousin program was added to the block grant family by the Public Works Employment Act of 1976, which as an antirecessionary measure authorized a group of grants to finance a wide variety of state and local capital projects. The effectiveness of this kind of spending stimulus has long been questioned by economists, primarily because of the potentially long lags to which it is subject. The expenditures authorized by the 1962 accelerated public works program, for example, were spread out from 1963 through 1971.[5] The timeliness of the employment-creating effects of grant-assisted state and local public works appears to be even more uncertain than that of federal projects.[6] The funds that the 1976 public works program made available seem to have had perverse effects, inducing state and local governments to delay their own discretionary capital spending while awaiting word on their qualification for full federal funding for the same undertakings.[7]

5. Nancy H. Teeters, "The 1972 Budget: Where It Stands and Where It Might Go," *Brookings Papers on Economic Activity, 1:1971*, p. 233.

6. U.S. Congressional Budget Office, *Temporary Measures to Stimulate Employment: An Evaluation of Some Alternatives* (CBO, 1975) and *Short-Run Measures to Stimulate the Economy* (U.S. Government Printing Office, 1977).

7. Edward M. Gramlich, "State and Local Budgets the Day after It Rained: Why Is the Surplus So High?" *Brookings Papers on Economic Activity, 1:1978*, pp. 208–09.

As their rather piecemeal development suggests, the cluster of block grant programs was shaped more by historical accident and political compromise than by clear design. The somewhat heterogeneous characteristics of the member programs are evidence of their diffuse origins. Nevertheless, despite their generic diversity and lack of clear definition as a specific type of fiscal instrument, block grants have provided a useful bridge between the Washington-directed, restricted, and controlled assistance offered through categorical grants and the unrestricted, decentralized approach afforded by revenue sharing, which was formally launched in 1972.

Evaluating the fiscal effects of the hybrid block grant mechanism in shifting spending authority from the federal level to state and local governments is a difficult if not impossible task. Neither have related categorical grants been fully consolidated nor have recipients gained unlimited discretion in applying federal funds to the designated problems, but block grants have contributed to the decentralization process. Two major factors, pulling in opposite directions, obscure their effects.

One of these factors is the fungibility of grant funds. Funds flowing into state and local treasuries are hard to keep neatly identified; expenditures are often sufficiently interrelated to permit many recipients to spend earmarked revenue pretty much as they please. This fact of life makes it hard to draw a clear distinction between the effects of block grants and revenue sharing. Actually, the biggest difference may be in the minds of the grantors—they may find it politically easier to justify appropriations of money presumably directed toward specific problems than those offered on an unrestricted basis according to a fixed distribution formula.

While fungibility means flexibility in the use of federal money by state and local governments, the rapidly proliferating strings that Washington is attaching to the use of its funds pull strongly in the opposite direction. The lengthy list of extraneous requirements not only stipulates who is to be hired for grant projects, and for how much, but imposes many conditions on the decisionmaking process and on the environmental effects of the funded projects. These relatively recent mandates are becoming burdensome and costly enough to cause many state and local officials to question the net gain to their jurisdictions from federal grants. They are particularly troubled by the possibility that either Congress or the courts will make the fungibility of grant funds an issue in the noncompliance suits they are constantly faced with; this could make virtually every program of a recipient government subject to the federal grant regulations.

Although these obfuscating elements make the effects of block grants hard to measure, it seems probable that the economic objectives of the grants have been better served than their political goals. The hopes of strengthening general rather than special-purpose governments and of vesting more decisionmaking authority in elected officials have been as often frustrated as advanced by the multidimensional, overlapping, and occasionally contradictory aims and requirements of the programs. The same is true of the hope of strengthening lines of responsibility between state and local governments.

The economic goals have proved in some ways less elusive. During the first year of the community development block grant program, some 85 percent of the funds was used either for new spending (53 percent) or for program maintenance (32 percent) rather than to replace existing sources of funds or to build up reserves (7 percent). Only 0.5 percent was used to stabilize or reduce taxes.[8]

Another avowed economic aim of block grants was to finance activities, such as slum clearance, directly benefiting low- and moderate-income families. In the first year of the community development program, however, only a little more than half of the money appears actually to have been spent in that way.[9] Such findings led the Department of Housing and Urban Development in 1978 to issue a directive that (unless strong reasons to the contrary could be adduced and an exception explicitly granted) 75 percent of the money received by any locality under the program should be used to provide direct benefits to low- and moderate-income families. While this approach presumably helps to focus expenditures on the desired objective, it raises important questions about the appropriateness of intergovernmental grants as an instrument for alleviating individual poverty. Direct transfer payments or subsidies are much more efficient routes to that goal. Intergovernmental grants are well suited to the financing of urban public goods and collective services, but these, by their very nature, confer their benefits on all the people in a given area. Trying

8. The remainder was unallocated or went for miscellaneous purposes. Richard P. Nathan and others, "Monitoring the Block Grant Program for Community Development," *Political Science Quarterly,* vol. 92 (Summer 1977), pp. 225–26 (Brookings Reprint 326).

9. Ibid., p. 227.

to set rigorous limits on how the benefits are to be distributed risks eliminating projects whose benefits are not precisely allocable or are too widespread. It is entirely possible that the strict requirements eliminate some projects that would actually be of greater advantage to the poor than others that satisfy the regulations.

Intense concern with goals raises another question about programs with multiple objectives. The Comprehensive Employment and Training Act, for example, stipulated three major goals—job creation, provision of useful public services, and targeting assistance on economically disadvantaged and structurally unemployed individuals. Although the program may have proved to be a "workable bargain,"[10] it is far from clear that this approach is the best or most direct way of getting to those rather disparate goals. Here is yet another example of the fundamental conflict between the requirements of economic efficiency and political feasibility, the former calling for (at least) one instrument for each separate goal sought and the latter for many different goals for each instrument used.

How block grant funds are to be allocated is, of course, a major issue. The standard approach ties the formula to the particular purpose of the program—manpower grants to unemployment rates and community development grants to such indicators of urban stress as the incidence of substandard or overcrowded housing. This seemingly simple logic, however, becomes irrelevant if the funds are highly fungible and consequently simply another form of shared revenue. It would make more sense to tailor the allocation formulas in order to complement those used in the revenue-sharing program. The sentiment in favor of keeping, or even tightening, the strings attached to block grants seems so strong, however, that this approach to funding has little promise of becoming popular.

The most frequently used allocation factor in block grants is population. The partnership for health, crime control and safe streets, and social services programs use it exclusively, and community development grants include it along with other measures of urban need. Comprehensive employment and training grants are allocated partly on the basis of unemployment rates and partly on the incidence of low-income families. As with many other aspects of the intergovern-

---

10. Richard P. Nathan and others, *Monitoring the Public Service Employment Program: The Second Round,* A Special Report of the National Commission for Manpower Policy, no. 32 (GPO, 1979), p. 105.

mental grants picture, the measures selected represent a mixed blend of economic, political, and pragmatic considerations. Local area unemployment rates, for example, are one important indicator of economic distress in principle, but in practice the data used are little better than guesses. Improving these measures would achieve greater fiscal equity but would add new expenditure commitments to an already tight federal budget. The great attraction of population as an allocation factor, of course, is its availability on a relatively current and accurate basis. In any case, grant allocation formulas and procedures will continue to be the subject of much pushing and hauling each time they come under congressional surveillance. Because they determine who gets the money, they are at least as important to the political powers as how the money is spent. The fact that both questions apply with approximately equal weight to block grants is perhaps the clearest evidence of that program's intermediate position between categorical grants (focusing on how the money is spent) and revenue sharing (which concentrates on who gets it).

A tightening federal budget makes that intermediate position a vulnerable one. A major issue in intergovernmental policymaking is whether federal controls should be tightened by favoring categorical grants, moderately loosened by greater use of block grants, or minimized by expanding the role of revenue sharing.

Revenue Sharing

Despite the many difficulties encountered in trying to solve with pinpointed, earmarked grants the highly diverse and complex problems of a far-flung, pluralistic society, Washington was not quick to accept the idea of unrestricted allocations of money to state and local governments. This approach began to gain momentum during the 1960s, when it appeared to offer a means of treating two particular economic ailments, fiscal drag and fiscal mismatch. Strange as it seems today, the federal government then faced the problem of an overflowing treasury, brought on by rapid economic growth and a growth-sensitive tax system. This situation worried macroeconomists, who were concerned about the relatively high unemployment rate and feared that a federal revenue surplus would exert a drag on the economy by depressing aggregate demand and so prevent an early return to full employment. They were also bothered by the fact that state and local governments were facing the opposite problem, with their spending requirements far outpacing their revenues. Where the needs were, the money was short, and vice versa. To economists a broad, no-strings distribution of federal monies seemed an ideal way to counter both the fiscal drag and the fiscal mismatch. But the Johnson administration opted for a variety of Great Society programs with strong categorical features. While these did help to eliminate much of the fiscal drag and mismatch, they carried the project-categorical grant concept to such an extreme that the stage was prepared for a new approach. The rapid proliferation of categorical grants was viewed by some critics as a worrisome extension of federal power and influence over the economy and as an excessive vesting of authority in the hands of professional program specialists. Such concerns did much to revive the idea of general revenue sharing, which was finally enacted in 1972.

One striking feature of the State and Local Fiscal Assistance Act, which authorized revenue sharing, was its omission of any explicit statement of purpose. Presumably there were so many different goals in the minds of its diverse supporters that no simple listing would suffice. To some it was an opportunity to lighten the growing burden of state and local taxes by substituting federal taxes—and in the process to increase the progressivity of the total tax system. To others revenue sharing meant more money for new programs or for capital spending. A complication arose over the lack of clarity as to whether the shared revenue was to be an infusion of additional federal money or was to replace existing federal aid funds. This doubt caused considerable consternation among state and local officials, particularly when President Nixon, at a time of budgetary stress in 1973, used his powers of impoundment to stem the flow of categorical grant funds. This cutback, as it turned out, did not make any long-term dent in the general outward expansion of the flow of federal money to state and local governments.

Distribution of Funds

How to distribute the $30.6 billion appropriated for the five-year trial period was the most difficult problem to solve in getting revenue sharing enacted. It was at least as much a political problem as an economic one, and the complicated solution that was worked out was attractive chiefly because of its acceptability to a wide diversity of interest groups. Efficiency considerations would have suggested limiting the recipient local governments to a small number of populous cities and counties (as few as five hundred had two-thirds of the nation's population at that time). Political salability, however, required a much larger group of beneficiaries. The final decision was to make funds available to all general-purpose local governments—then nearly thirty-nine thousand. This massive task could have been handled only in an age of computers.

All funds were initially allocated to the fifty states and the District of Columbia, and local distributions were then determined within each state allocation. Because different allocation formulas were developed in the two houses of Congress, state allotments were computed under both, and each recipient was granted the larger of the two. The Senate formula was based on three equally weighted factors: population; general tax effort measured by the ratio of total state and local tax revenue to state personal income; and relative state income status, entered inversely by using the ratio of U.S. per capita personal income to each state's per capita income. The House formula used the same three factors plus urbanized population and state income tax collections and weighted them differently.

Once the state area amounts were adjusted to fit the total appropriation, one-third of each state allocation was apportioned to the state and the remaining two-thirds to all eligible local governments. Those funds were first broken down by county area on the basis of a formula that gave equal weight to population, inverse per capita income, and tax effort adjusted to exclude school taxes (no area could receive less than 20 percent nor more than 145 percent of the statewide average per capita amount for local distribution, however; any remainders or deficiences were spread proportionately among the other county areas).

Before the county area amounts could be allocated among the general-purpose governments in the area, allocations were made to Indian tribes and Alaskan native villages on the basis of relative population. The remaining funds were then assigned to the county government, municipalities, and townships on the basis of nonschool tax revenue. Within municipalities as a whole and townships as a whole, each jurisdiction's allocation was based on the formula used to determine the countywide allocations, including the 20 percent and 145 percent per capita limits plus a ceiling on shared revenue funds equal to 50 percent of the local government's nonschool tax revenue and intergovernmental grant receipts combined.

These complex allocation rules, arrived at because each factor has plausibility that makes it, in combination with the rest, politically acceptable, were left unchanged in the 1976 legislation extending the program. Among the many questions that have been raised about them, the main ones focus on the equity of the allocation formulas, the effects on intergovernmental fiscal relationships, and the value of the allocation limits.

Fiscal Need and Capacity

The way in which relative fiscal need is determined is the critical factor in any unrestricted grant program. This is a matter not only of identifying existing needs but of assessing the capacities of individual state and local governments to meet these needs on their own. Critics of revenue sharing's use of population and inverse per capita personal income as indicators of fiscal need have stressed the lack of precision of these measures. Among the alternatives they have suggested is the percentage of families within the jurisdiction below official poverty lines. Much as it might show about poverty, such a measure is not really appropriate for revenue sharing, since either direct government transfers to the families or categorical grants for programs directed at poverty groups would do the job more effectively than unrestricted grants would. The purpose of revenue sharing is to provide broadside support for state and local programs, and it should be based on a needs factor correspondingly broad in scope. Several researchers have proposed the development of an index based on the cost to each state or local government of providing some average menu of public services. Assuming that working agreement could be obtained on what a standard menu would be, such an index could gauge relative fiscal need more equitably than the present indicators do.

The measures of fiscal capacity used in the allocation formulas for revenue sharing are no more satisfactory than the measures of fiscal need. Both the House and the Senate approaches make use of per capita personal income and take no account of the differing abilities of state and local governments to export some of their tax burdens to outsiders. If all goods produced in a given area were consumed there, personal income would be a good measure of the ability of that area to impose and bear tax burdens. Interregional trade, however, creates an important distinction between jurisdictions of origin (such as central cities) and of residency (such as suburbs). Both can tax the income flows occurring within their boundaries, and in cases of conflict, priority is usually given to jurisdictions of origin. Because personal income is normally measured on the basis of residence, it cannot provide a complete picture of a jurisdiction's ability to raise tax revenue. Personal income, in other words, may be a comprehensive measure of ability to bear tax burdens, but it is only a partial measure of ability to impose them.

A really adequate measure of an area's taxing potential, then, would take into account both income originating in the area and income received there. The representative tax system index devised by the Advisory Commission on Intergovernmental Relations is based on the revenue potential of a typical state-local tax system. A national average tax rate is computed for each of the twenty-three components of the system.[11] When these tax rates are applied to the corresponding tax bases in each state, the resulting measures of tax capacity indicate a very different allocation pattern for shared revenue than that based on personal income. For 1972 the commission index would have increased the shared revenue distributed to ten states by 5 percent or more and reduced that distributed to twenty-two states by corresponding amounts. The states that would have gained tended to rank high in per capita personal income and degree of urbanization, while those that would have lost were typically mining, farming, or tourist oriented.[12]

Another way of approaching the problem of measuring fiscal capacity is to try to separate a community's actual capacity from other factors—what it needs and what it is willing to spend—that affect its spending decisions. Innovative attempts to separate these behavioral factors from the capacity to spend have sorted out, by statistical analysis, the variables that determine spending tastes and needs. One of the more obvious of the capacity variables is median family income; one of the less obvious possibilities is that different kinds of

11. U.S. Advisory Commission on Intergovernmental Relations, *Measures of State and Local Fiscal Capacity and Tax Effort,* Report M-16 (GPO, 1962), and *Measuring the Fiscal Capacity and Effort of State and Local Areas,* Information Report (GPO, 1971).

12. Richard P. Nathan, Allen D. Manvel, and Susannah E. Calkins, *Monitoring Revenue Sharing* (Brookings Institution, 1975), pp. 136–40.

property (residential, commercial, or industrial) may contribute differently to a community's tax capacity. Identification and careful measurement of such variables could lead to the development of more effective ways of comparing the abilities of different jurisdictions to finance given levels of public services. A major hurdle in getting such measures incorporated into the allocation formulas, however, would be selling them to Congress as credible and politically acceptable.

Tax or Revenue Effort

The distribution formulas for revenue sharing include another factor that is closely related to fiscal capacity—tax effort, which is normally defined as the ratio of tax collections to some measure of a jurisdiction's tax capacity. While plausible, such an indicator of tax efforts makes no real distinction between relatively deserving and undeserving recipients. High tax effort may signify above-average fiscal need or below-average fiscal capacity, but it may also reflect wasteful management, exploitation of passive local taxpayers by powerful special interest groups, or simply strong voter taste for public services. Furthermore, the measures of tax effort used for revenue sharing may assign high values to jurisdictions with an above-average ability to export tax burdens and thereby reward not those who most help themselves (as the formula is meant to do) but those who can pass on their public service costs to others. This bias in the allocation formulas could be corrected by shifting from per capita personal income to a representative tax system as a measure of fiscal capacity. Or tax effort could simply be eliminated as a factor in allocating funds. States with lower per capita income would thereby receive relatively more money, rural states less, and those with the largest concentrations of black and poor people more. On the other hand, dropping this factor from states' distributions to county areas, municipalities, and townships would mean lowering central cities' shared revenues by 20 percent and raising neighboring suburban communities' share by more than 10 percent.[13]

Another problem with the grant-allocation formulas under revenue sharing is the narrowness of the revenue measures used. User charges

13. National Science Foundation, Research Applied to National Needs (NSF-RANN), *General Revenue Sharing: Research Utilization Project*, vol. 3: *Synthesis of Formula Research* (GPO, 1975), p. 71, and Richard P. Nathan and Jacob M. Jaffee, "Effects of the Statutory Formula Alternatives," in vol. 1: *Summaries of Formula Research* (GPO, 1975), p. 10.

and fees are excluded, thereby providing some incentive for local governments to steer away from direct benefits-received financing. Yet judicious use of benefits financing is widely seen as a way of improving both the equity and the efficiency of state and local revenue systems. Including the most commonly employed user charges and fees in revenue-sharing formulas would result in a shift of funds from counties to municipalities, sometimes in significant amounts.[14]

In some ways the complexity of the distribution mechanism is the greatest asset of revenue sharing. This not only widens its political appeal but frustrates attempts by recipient jurisdictions to manipulate the terms to their own advantage and impedes the development of systematic methods of exploiting loopholes.

Antirecession Fiscal Assistance

While revenue sharing is directed at the general support of state and local governments in a high-employment economy, similarly unrestricted aid has been widely discussed as a means of cushioning the budgetary impact of recessions on those governments and helping to stabilize the whole economy in the process. In 1976 Congress enacted the antirecession fiscal assistance program, which offered additional aid to revenue-sharing jurisdictions whose unemployment rate was greater than 4.5 percent. One-third of the money was reserved for states, and the remainder was allocated to local governments in proportion to the product of each jurisdiction's unemployment rate in excess of 4.5 percent and its latest revenue-sharing allocation; all funds had to be spent on maintaining basic public services. The program was intended to be temporary, explicitly offering its funding only as long as the national unemployment rate stayed at or above 6 percent. When it expired in 1978, some observers gave it relatively high ratings for its employment-generating powers; others contended that direct federal expenditures or lower federal taxes would have been more effective. Some critics suggested that because of the wide variations in economic circumstances among state and local governments, some index of budgetary disruption ought to be constructed to make recessionary aid more sensitive to need. As a countercyclical measure, antirecession fiscal assistance may have been greatly hampered by its failure to attach requirements governing accumulation or dispersal of budgetary surpluses. It is quite possible that beneficiaries

14. NSF-RANN, *Synthesis of Formula Research*, pp. 74–75.

could begin to rely on such federal help and thus modify or abandon their countercyclical tendency to accumulate surpluses during good times and draw them down during recessions. On balance, those who have studied the 1976 program give it substantially higher marks as a means of treating secular economic problems than as a countercyclical device. Redesigned, however, the program might help mitigate some of the distortions that recessions create in state and local spending behavior. Such help would be especially valuable to state and local sectors that were no longer growing rapidly and hence were more vulnerable to economic downturns.

State-Local Fiscal Relations

One of the arbitrary features of the legislation that created revenue sharing, the across-the-board allocation of one-third to the state government and two-thirds of each state's allotment to local governments, ignores the wide variation among the states in the sharing of responsibility for financing public services. A more equitable division of revenue-sharing funds within each state, based on relative fiscal responsibility, might be derived from measures of direct general expenditures, own-source revenues, or both. One proposed composite index for distributing funds showed an average state-local division of responsibility in 1972 of 53–47 for the country as a whole, with a range of from 80–20 in Hawaii to 38–62 in New York.[15] Basing the state-local division of revenue-sharing funds on such an index would take explicit account of the nature of intergovernmental fiscal relations in each state.

Statutory Floors and Ceilings

The statutory floors and ceilings imposed on the distribution of funds to local governments are another important source of variation in the effects of revenue sharing. The guarantee, for example, that no jurisdiction will get less than 20 percent of the average per capita amount allocated to local governments in its state means that somewhat vestigial governing units, such as midwestern townships and New England counties, are kept alive when their limited functions, in the opinion of many proponents of governmental reform at least, might better be taken over by larger jurisdictions. Supporters of a

15. G. Ross Stephens, "State Responsibility for Public Services and General Revenue Sharing," in NSF-RANN, *Summaries of Formula Research*, pp. 91–105.

wider degree of public choice, on the other hand, applaud this support of small governing units. Fear that these minimums might lead to a proliferation of small, limited-function jurisdictions has for the most part failed to materialize, but the long-term possibilities are still there. In the first distribution of revenue-sharing funds the 20 percent floor came into play to the advantage of one-third of all townships and one-sixth of all municipalities.[16]

The 145 percent per capita ceiling penalizes some hard-pressed central cities, leaves others unaffected, and holds down benefits to industrial, commercial, and tourist enclaves.[17] It may also inhibit potentially beneficial mergers of municipal and county governments in metropolitan areas. It certainly limits the redistributive impact of revenue sharing, rendering it relatively ineffective as a way of ameliorating the problems of severely distressed central cities.

The ceiling that limits revenue-sharing funds to 50 percent of a jurisdiction's nonschool tax revenue plus receipts from intergovernmental grants has been the strongest of the tax effort incentives. It affected about 10 percent of all general-purpose local governments in 1972 and prompted some to reach for the carrot—fifty cents in new entitlements for every dollar of additional nonschool taxes. The impact of this incentive may have been blunted, however, because of the uncertainty and the slowness with which the complex allocation process operates. Lowering the revenue limit from 50 percent to, say, 20 percent would reduce the incentives and also lower allocations to small units and to less active jurisdictions.

Net Distributional Effects

Assessing the complex effects of revenue sharing has become a whole new industry for economists and political scientists. The Brookings Institution, for instance, maintains a regular service monitoring sixty-five governmental recipients of revenue-sharing funds. From the information gathered, analysts study the changing patterns of expenditure, tabulate the grant recipients' own explanations of what they spend revenue-sharing funds for, and draw up simulations of the effects that different patterns of funds distribution would presumably have. These findings, however, are approximations only; no one, not even the recipient jurisdictions themselves, can really be sure

16. Nathan, Manvel, and Calkins, *Monitoring Revenue Sharing,* p. 160.
17. NSF-RANN, *Synthesis of Formula Research,* pp. 76–77.

what their budgets would be like in the absence of this federal infusion of money.

If there were no revenue sharing, there might be lower federal taxes or higher federal expenditures of other kinds, or perhaps lower federal deficits and borrowing. Local conditions would then vary also —local revenue potential would increase because of lower federal taxes or even because a different pattern of federal expenditures might bring more money into a particular area. Though it is impossible to say who would win or who would lose under changed circumstances, research can indicate what the results would be of holding some variables constant while adjusting others. For example, in 1971–72 a 17 percent reduction in other federal grants would have financed the $5.3 billion shared revenue allocation of that year. Such a substitution of funds would have left twenty-nine states and the District of Columbia (or two-thirds of the nation's people) worse off, and twenty-one states better off. The largest losses would have been $82 and $76 per capita in the District of Columbia and Alaska, respectively, while the biggest gains—$9 and $10 per capita—would have gone to Mississippi and Wisconsin. In general, revenue sharing was more generous than other federal grant programs to low-income rural states, but not consistently so.[18]

Probably the most common assumption is that revenue sharing is financed by higher federal taxes. This real possibility is appealing to many supporters of revenue sharing because it indicates a strengthening of the redistributional effects, from high-income to low-income states and regions, that they see as a major goal of the program. Per capita shared revenue received in 1972 by Mississippi, the poorest state in per capita income, amounted to 153 percent of the national average, while Connecticut, the richest in per capita income, got only 85 percent of the average. In that same year, however, shared revenue was 284 percent of Mississippi's prorated share of total federal receipts and only 57 percent of Connecticut's.[19]

Such broad-scale evaluations are about as far as the net redistributional effects of a tax-financed revenue-sharing program can be figured. For one thing it is not clear which taxes would be lower in the absence of revenue sharing. The chances are that the likeliest candidates would be the corporation and personal income taxes. Allocating

18. Nathan, Manvel, and Calkins, *Monitoring Revenue Sharing,* pp. 73–77.
19. Ibid., p. 72.

the burdens of the corporation tax is particularly difficult, as there is no consensus on its incidence. As for the individual income tax, the geographical pattern of its burdens can fairly readily be traced, but the specific structure of the tax reductions that would be made cannot —and that would make all the difference. Although since 1964 the general trend in tax reductions has been toward increasing the progressiveness of the income tax, a turning point may have been reached in the Revenue Act of 1978. Simply to assume a proportionate reduction in each taxpayer's share of the burden, then, would amount to only a first approximation.

Another major assumption about the fiscal impact of revenue sharing is that the grants reduce other federal expenditures more or less proportionately. Again the measurement problems are serious. While it is easy enough to allocate transfer expenditures geographically, doing the same for the government component of gross national product is a different matter. Either the regional incidence of federal expenditures on goods and services must be traced, or the benefits to people generated by federally financed programs must be allocated to different parts of the country. Only the first approach offers any real possibility of clear answers, yet it involves such intractable tasks as trying to follow all government payments to prime contractors in one area to subcontractors elsewhere.

The net distributional effects of revenue sharing, then, are somewhat of an enigma—too important to be ignored, yet often too imprecise to depend on in formulating policy. Handled skillfully, nonetheless, they can provide useful guidance. A simple allocation of grant funds on the basis of population, for example, would appear to be mildly redistributive, but when combined with and financed by a progressive tax system it would be significantly redistributive. Careless measurements of net distributional effects can be hazardous; they may give rise to unjustifiable, and even counterproductive, interregional disputes if they cause states that are really gainers to regard themselves as losers and act accordingly.

Taxing and Spending Effects

Measurable or not, the net distributional effects of federal revenue sharing are present and active in influencing the reactions of recipient jurisdictions. One important question is whether the funds are used by the recipients to reduce taxes or to expand expenditures. Determining this disposition with reasonable accuracy is the first step in getting at the fundamental question of the program's impact on the size of the public sector. The second step (assuming the program is financed by higher federal taxes) is to compare the state and local tax reductions induced by revenue sharing with that proportion of a federal tax reduction that would remain in the private sector and not be transferred back to the public sector by offsetting increases in state and local taxes. Assuming there is a tendency for money to remain in the sector in which it is first received, a federal tax reduction would mainly stimulate private spending, while federal revenue sharing would mainly stimulate public spending. If so, one important effect of a tax-financed revenue-sharing program would be to enlarge the state and local government sector of the economy.

Pinning down the effects of shared revenue on recipient governments' spending is an elusive and intriguing problem in political-economic sleuthing. Governments that simply merge shared revenue with other monies must be distinguished from those that treat it as a special kind of increment, to be spent differently. The pattern of spending shared revenue for the first group can be predicted from estimates of the usual state and local government marginal propensities to spend on different programs. But for the second group, clues must be carefully followed to determine how the funds have changed the scope and nature of the recipient governments' activities. The question of which governmental units react in which ways and under what circumstances is one of the pivotal issues in revenue sharing.

Among the standard research methods being applied to the question, surveys of government officials, by mailed questionnaire or personal interview, have enjoyed unusually high rates of response. Econometric behavioral models have been applied both to standard fiscal data and to the tabulations of special surveys. The Brookings monitoring program has from the inception of revenue sharing kept a careful watch on the state and local governments in its sample in an effort to determine what these recipients have done differently because of the existence of the program. One finding from this sustained surveillance and other research is that by far the largest share of the money has gone into an expansion of the state and local government sector. Approximately 20 percent seems to have gone either to reduce taxes or to avoid tax increases in the recipient jurisdictions. The findings vary with the type of recipient. Tax reduction has been a significantly stronger effect in localities with more than 100,000 population than in smaller units and has occurred most frequently where fiscal pressure has been either extremely great or virtually absent. Besides population and fiscal pressure, the key determinants seem to be per capita income, regional location, per capita grant revenue, and uncertainty about how long revenue sharing will be continued.[20]

Interest has also focused on the kinds of spending being induced by revenue sharing and especially on whether the funds are being used to support existing programs at current levels or to underwrite innovative and expansionary programs. The Brookings study shows that through mid-1974 state governments were using 47 percent of their retained revenue-sharing income for new capital projects, expanded current operations, and increased pay and benefits and the remaining 53 percent for supportive purposes (program maintenance, restoration of federal aid lost when other grant programs were cut, avoidance of borrowing, and increased fund balances). Local governments, in contrast, used 65 percent of their shared revenue funds for new and expanded programs and the remainder for existing program support.[21]

Local governments have tended to use shared funds to reinforce their public safety, transportation, and recreation programs. They seem to have put relatively little directly into education, which is consistent with the general finding that they have tended to use the funds primarily in areas not already supported by federal and state grants. On the other hand, state governments have tended to direct shared revenue more into education and less into welfare, health, and transportation than their earlier, typical spending patterns would have suggested. These spending trends do not necessarily coincide with the planned uses reported by the governments themselves. The fungibility of virtually all grant funds, especially revenue sharing, makes it as much a problem for researchers to detect where the money does go as it is for congressmen to try to attach strings to grants-in-aid. It is much the same as trying to trace the source of specific drops of

20. Richard P. Nathan and Charles F. Adams, Jr., *Revenue Sharing: The Second Round* (Brookings Institution, 1977), pp. 31–41.

21. Ibid., p. 31. These percentages were calculated by deleting the tax reduction and tax stabilization categories used in the Brookings tabulations. More recent figures indicate that this trend at the local level has declined. Charles F. Adams, Jr., and Dan L. Crippen, *The Fiscal Impact of General Revenue Sharing on Local Governments* (U.S. Department of the Treasury, Office of Revenue Sharing, 1979), p. 11.

water in a bay that is fed by numerous streams, rivers, and springs. Planned-use reports by state and local officials can be honest efforts at reporting or calculated attempts to please or influence the readers, but their accuracy is probably as hard for the writer as for the reader to verify. Most are undoubtedly a complex mixture of fact, guesswork, wishful thinking, and political strategy.

Process and Structural Effects

Those who had hoped that revenue sharing would result in a major shift of program responsibilities from the federal to state and local governments and transfer operational power from bureaucratic specialists to elected generalists, and possibly lead to improved government structure by encouraging consolidation of inefficient and unresponsive governmental units, have yet to see most of their hopes materialize. Similarly, those who hoped for marked broadening of hiring policies and greater participation by the public in budgetmaking have not seen their dreams come true, but there is evidence of some shifting of political influence, with a strengthened role for generalists and broader public participation in decisionmaking. Two prominent issues in the congressional debates over extension of the revenue-sharing program in 1976 were civil rights and public participation. The amendments of that year expanded the nondiscrimination provisions and mandated public hearings on how revenue-sharing funds are to be used. While these requirements were tightened, the already weak programmatic strings were further loosened by the elimination of the original law's categories of priority expenditures and the prohibition against using shared revenue to match other federal grants. Otherwise, few significant changes were made. Congress seemed to be putting more emphasis on process while trying to influence program less. At the same time, however, it shortened the extension period to three and three-quarters years and did not provide for any increment in the annual funding level of $6.85 billion. The subsequent high inflation rates, as a result, greatly eroded the real value of revenue sharing.

The Role of the States

The revenue-sharing program is approaching its October 1, 1980, expiration date in a general fiscal environment very different from that of 1972. The federal government faces escalating costs in its own program operations, continued pressure for new programs, demands for tax relief, and broad public support for a balanced budget. The last goal, like the mechanical rabbit at dog races, seems to become more elusive the harder it is pursued. Although several major cities hover on the brink of insolvency, state governments in general are enjoying remarkably good fiscal health. Partly this is due to broadened, more balanced state revenue systems. More of them make use of both the personal income tax and the general sales tax (37 in 1979 as compared with 19 in 1960), and state and local tax systems are better coordinated and less regressive (making wide use of state-financed property-tax circuit breakers and sales tax credits or exemptions). Whereas in 1965 state governments collected somewhat less total revenue than local governments, they are now raising substantially more. To a large extent the states owe this affluence to the thriving condition of the personal income tax. Aided by inflation and real economic growth, some states have built up large surpluses (half of the total is in California, Alaska, and Texas), but since fiscal surpluses are seldom allowed to accumulate, or even to arise at all, state tax reductions are a better indicator of fiscal ease, and these have been frequent in recent years.

Looking at this situation and comparing it with the relatively tight fiscal position of the federal government and the continued heavy fiscal pressure on local governments, a number of influential members of Congress have urged that state participation in revenue sharing be ended. Such a move would change the whole character of the program as well as the direction in which federal grants-in-aid have been working during the past decade.

A persuasive case can be made for not eliminating the states from revenue sharing. While some state governments are currently in a strong financial position, others are not, and even the well-being of the few could be reversed by an economic downturn.[22] The wide disparity in the fiscal responsibility that states assume for basic public services (such as education) constitutes a strong argument for not arbitrarily eliminating this level of government from the revenue-sharing picture. To make the cities and other local jurisdictions wards of the federal government while ignoring the parental role of the states

---

22. The operating budgets of state and local governments shifted from a surplus of $2.6 billion (seasonally adjusted at annual rates) in the first quarter of 1979 to deficits of $6.3 billion and $1.8 billion in the second and third quarters, respectively.

would profoundly affect the structure of the federal system and serve to diminish its logic. The vast resources of Washington tend to obscure the fact that the federal government is a creature of the states, not vice versa. And the attention focused on local governments may blind some to the fact that they are political subdivisions of the states. Channeling revenue sharing around state governments, thus reinforcing the direct flow of money from Washington to localities, could produce major changes in the way the American republic operates.

For those who find the states highly unresponsive to critical urban needs, of course, a major reorganization of the federal system may seem a price well worth paying. A simple redirection of unrestricted federal grant money, however, is not likely to accomplish much by itself. The urban problem is a complex and ever-changing one, requiring the use of a well-coordinated and carefully directed set of policy instruments. Few would rank revenue sharing high on that list. Its goals are different and must be evaluated within the framework of the entire federal grant system. What does seem clear is that if revenue sharing is worth having at all, the states should play a significant role in its operation. Elimination of states from the picture would be especially ironic at a time when state aid to local governments is expanding steadily—it rose from $13 billion, or 43 percent of local general revenue from own sources, in fiscal 1964 to $61 billion, or 60 percent of local own-source revenue, in 1977—and states are taking an increasing interest in the problems of distressed communities, both urban and rural. Dropping the states from the revenue-sharing program would not only undermine the importance of their intermediary role in the whole grant-in-aid system[23] but could create considerable confusion about the place of the states in the division of intergovernmental responsibilities.

Conclusions

Making decisions about the size and structure of the federal grant system when pressure for defense spending is rising at the national level and movements to limit taxes and expenditures are spreading at the state and local levels is not a task for the fainthearted. For one

23. In 1972 direct federal aid to local governments was $4.6 billion; federal aid to state governments was $26.8 billion, $7.1 billion of which is estimated to have been passed through to local governments.

thing, the efforts to limit taxes and spending send out conflicting messages. On the one hand, the tighter budgetary conditions created for state and local governments increase their desire for outside funds and would add to the distress caused by any sharp cutback in federal aid. On the other hand, federal policymakers may well see the movements favoring limitations as a broad and growing public desire for less government spending, federal grants included. What may be less obvious is that most of these movements are not only recent but assume the existence of revenue sharing and other federal grant programs. If this important source of support were greatly diminished, many jurisdictions (and possibly most) would be left periously swinging in the wind.

Anyone evaluating the intergovernmental grants system as a whole comes inevitably to the conclusion that it is badly fragmented and needs some major overhauling. Each of the three broad types of federal aid serves a purpose, but there is much room for greater efficiency in all of them. Categorical grants are useful instruments for dealing with pinpointed problems, but ways should be found to reduce the paperwork and red tape they involve and get more of the money to the program objectives. The principle of block grants is sound, but greater coherence needs to be brought into their management so that the multifaceted programs they finance work more harmoniously toward their common purposes. Funding terms and expectations should be clarified so as to minimize the paralysis that results from uncertainty. Periodic reviews, either mandated by sunset laws or ordered by the budget office, should be made of all grant programs. The value of each program, the nature and strength of the national interest in it, and the suitability of the grant instrument to the goals sought should be carefully considered. In some cases, grants would remain as the preferred policy instrument but with improved designs; in others, they would be replaced by better means of achieving the same ends. Prominent among the potential improvements in grant design would be more effective matching and maintenance-of-effort requirements, more equitable allocation formulas, and more cost-effective regulatory standards.

Reforming the structure and general workability of federal grants would be an important administrative advance but would leave the fundamental policy questions unanswered. How much reliance should be put on categorical and block grants? What should be the future of revenue sharing? To give coherent answers to these questions, federal policymakers must establish some clear priorities. Depending on these priorities, three alternative policy options seem open.

If the choice is to give clear priority to the accomplishment of specified national objectives, revenue sharing should be allowed to expire as soon as possible. Block grant programs should be more sharply focused on the desired goals through greater use of targeting, project grants, and federal administrative discretionary funds. Federal controls over categorical grants should be tightened. This option would fly in the face of recent history and reduce the flexibility needed in dealing with some of the country's most pressing problems.

If the choice is to put emphasis entirely on state and local priorities, revenue sharing should be renewed for a limited number of years in its present form, at funding levels that would take into account the effects of inflation on state and local budgets. During this third phase of revenue sharing, other possible arrangements for distributing federal funds without any controls or constraints should be carefully analyzed and discussed. In particular, consideration should be given to a national value-added or retail sales tax, with part of the proceeds to be returned to the jurisdictions of origin—either to states as a whole or in allocated shares to states and general-purpose local governments. If revenue sharing, with its inevitable strings and controls, were replaced by this kind of tax sharing, state and local governments would simply receive a portion of the tax revenues collected within their jurisdictions by the federal government. Sharing a national sales tax rather than the federal individual income tax would offer the advantage of producing less unequal revenue shares among states and localities. This arrangement would, of course, not deal with the problem of state and local governments with high fiscal need and low fiscal capacity. That would present no real obstacle, however, since direct transfer payments to low-income families confront the problem more squarely, and their use could be improved and expanded if revenue sharing were replaced by a tax sharing plan. In the event that a value-added tax was not enacted, a tax sharing arrangement could be applied to the federal individual income tax. Returning some percentage of tax collections would obviously favor high-income states, but this bias could be reduced by returning instead a flat percentage of the tax base.

In addition to the continued use of either revenue or tax sharing, a policy package emphasizing state and local priorities should incorporate in the regular assessments of categorical grants the possibility of their consolidation into single block grants. In the absence of good reasons to the contrary, the block grant should be considered preferable to categorical grants. The same priorities would prescribe loosening the strings attached to block grant programs and minimizing federal control and direction of them. Consideration could even be given to folding block grant programs into the tax sharing plan by reducing the federal portion of shared tax revenues. This policy option would provide maximum scope for decentralized management of the federal fiscal system.

A more balanced set of priorities would give equal weight to national and to state and local interests. Implementing such a policy would mean evaluating categorical and block grants on their own merits, with no presumption about the way that conflicts of national with state and local priorities should be resolved. Revenue sharing should be renewed on an indefinite basis. Its structure should be improved, but if this cannot be done before the October deadline, the current program should be renewed and the federal government's commitment to structural reform affirmed. A new design could then be drawn up to deal with these major needs:

1. Annual fund appropriations should be indexed for inflation.

2. The allocation formula, giving one-third of funds to state and two-thirds to local governments, should be changed to take account of differences among states in the division of state and local fiscal responsibilities.

3. The measures of fiscal need and fiscal capacity used in the allocation formulas should be improved—for example, the representative tax system of the Advisory Commission on Intergovernmental Relations could replace per capita personal income in the formula for state allocations and the incidence of low-income households in the formula for allocations to individual municipalities and townships.

4. The statutory ceilings and floors on allocations should be eliminated.

5. A minimum of revenue-sharing funds should be allowed to go to small, inefficient governmental units.

6. The balance between legislative and "public hearing" responsibility in the allocation of revenue-sharing funds should be improved

—where many voices and rules are involved in decisions, it is hard to hold elected representatives responsible; indeed, the special-interest lobbying that has been stimulated by revenue sharing may be a major factor contributing to the movements for tax and expenditure limitation.

Acceptance of a policy of balanced priorities would continue the recent course of intergovernmental fiscal relations, leaving a high degree of federal control in the categorical and block grant area while allowing for a more comfortable fit of revenue sharing to the varying dimensions of state and local needs. It would cause the least disruption and offer the combined advantages of political feasibility and fiscal continuity.

The only part of the intergovernmental grants package that requires immediate decisionmaking by Washington is revenue sharing. Its very existence for the better part of a decade has created changes in national fiscal patterns. If there is one strong message that seems to be emerging from the recent tax rebellions, it is that wasteful bureaucracy is a distinct irritant. Whatever may be said against revenue sharing, its administrative costs are minimal—in sharp contrast to the high costs of administering categorical grants and of working out the bureaucratic coordination of block grants.

Even if the categorical and block grant programs were made more efficient and effective, the logic of unrestricted aid would still give it a strong claim to a place in the system. Part of this logic is the simple argument of economic efficiency—the federal government has a comparative advantage in taxation, while state and local governments can better allocate the proceeds among programs with significant regional or local benefits. This applies regardless of the relative ease or stringency of budgets at any level of government. The wide differences among states and localities with respect to both needs and tastes for services are strong arguments for allowing the kind of flexibility that only unrestricted aid can offer. Revenue-sharing funds may also be viewed as compensation for the unreimbursed costs imposed on state and local governments by federally mandated programs; they offer a means of helping with such costs without adding an entire new department to the paperwork empire.

Revenue sharing has not proved to be the panacea that some expected it to be, but measures of its effectiveness have shown that, in general, it is getting to the places of need. Improvements in the way it is allocated could make that record more impressive.

Federal grants as a whole now supply about one-fourth of the revenue expended by state and local governments and are particularly important to central cities. Withdrawal of revenue sharing would be a serious setback in the effort to meet local needs. Although more categorical aid would undoubtedly be supplied in its stead, the move would be backward from fiscal flexibility and decentralized decision-making to greater dependence on the politics and bureaucracy of grantsmanship. Such a retreat could hardly fit the mood of an aroused and patently rebellious taxpaying public.

CHAPTER NINE

Defense Policy

WILLIAM W. KAUFMANN

PRESIDENT CARTER, on January 28, 1980, sent Congress his five-year defense program and budget. The president requested total obligational authority of $158.7 billion for fiscal year 1981, an increase of $8.1 billion in real terms over fiscal 1980, and projected that total obligational authority would rise to $188.6 billion (in fiscal 1981 prices) by 1985.

If the program is fully implemented, as Secretary of Defense Harold Brown has pledged it will be (insofar as the Carter administration can make such a promise), it will carry the country through September 30, 1985, and result in a 25 percent real increase in total obligational authority for defense. Moreover, since Secretary Brown has also pledged to protect the integrity of the program against the ravages of inflation and extraneous changes made in it by Congress, the total and percentage increases could be even higher.

These added resources will presumably be used for five major purposes. First, the existing force structure will be brought to its authorized strength through the provision of increased modern equipment, training, and war reserve stocks, at a cost of at least another $80 billion (in fiscal 1981 prices). Second, the United States will develop, produce, and begin to deploy in Europe 108 Pershing II ballistic missiles on launchers and 464 ground-launched cruise missiles—both types armed with nuclear weapons—at an estimated real cost of at

I thank Kathleen Elliott Yinug and Kirk W. Kimmell for secretarial assistance.

least $3 billion during the five-year period. Third, naval general purpose forces will be expanded to about 500 active ships at an estimated real cost of about $8 billion. Fourth, air and sea mobility will be increased by new programs for maritime pre-positioning ships (floating depots for matériel and supplies) and wide-bodied aircraft at an estimated incremental cost of around $10 billion (in fiscal 1981 prices). Finally, research and development will grow cumulatively by another $15 billion, in real terms, to ensure that a number of long-range technical options are kept open. In sum, the total new resources required to fund these five programs will amount to about $116 billion (in fiscal 1981 prices). These programs appear to explain why the real growth rate of total obligational authority during the life of the five-year defense program will average around 4.6 percent a year.

Because the Carter program covers half the 1980s, it can be regarded as a defense blueprint for the decade. Nonetheless, it may be too early to ask in detail whether it plans to do too much or too little, allocates resources more or less sensibly, or incorporates too many or too few hedges against possible future developments. There are a number of uncertainties about the Soviet Union and other parts of the world, and more time will be needed to resolve these questions. But it is not too early to spell out certain realities that should serve as guides in assessing the Carter program and determining the course that should be set for the 1980s. Some of those realities relate to the national security decisionmaking process as it now stands and to the methods currently used to analyze problems. Others relate to the international environment and what can be done to deal effectively with it.

Organization

Americans like to believe, and probably do believe, that their national security institutions and procedures are well adapted to the problems raised by the modern technical and international environment. In reality they are not. Traditional divisions of labor among various national security agencies are no longer relevant, and the line between civilian and military prerogatives has become increasingly blurred. Much of this has happened because nuclear weapons appear to make the delegation of authority risky, and because greatly improved satellite and other communications permit central control over even small operations at great distances.

The trend has accordingly been toward increased centralization and more layers of authority in an effort to impose some degree of order and coordination on the many and disparate groups in the national security community. But more often than not, the effort has led to the overburdening of a small number of senior officials with the details of foreign policy, defense planning, arms control, and crisis management.

This overloading has had a number of undesirable effects, among them crisis management as a way of life and reaction to events rather than planning and initiatives; inadequate staffing of positions simply because the principals usually lack the time either to determine what kind of support they need or to absorb the results of the work that is done; the ability to handle only a very small number of issues more or less simultaneously; the tendency of the staffs to coordinate and compromise at the lowest common denominator rather than let issues escalate to their harried principals; the exploitation of this process by the ambitious to make their mark, expand staffs, and attract notice; and leaks as disaffected staffs become alienated from this interminable process or are unable to make their views heard.

In recognition of these effects some efforts have been made—at least in the Department of Defense—to decentralize the process again and to delegate some degree of authority under guidelines devised or agreed to by the principals. For the most part, however, these efforts have not been notably successful.

A case in point is the defense planning guidance, which had its recent origins in the early 1970s, but dates back to the basic national security document of the Truman and Eisenhower eras. The planning guidance purports to set certain boundaries within which defense programs for the coming fiscal year are to be developed. Since these boundaries consist of general statements about policies and priorities, without accompanying resource constraints, the program planners go about their relatively microscopic business as though the guidance did not exist. As a consequence, the secretary of defense finds himself still immersed in detailed programmatic issues that he is forced to resolve on narrow grounds. He has no macroscopic model of what various budgets and forces will produce in the way of deterrence and defense; he lacks a basis against which to compare what has been produced by the planning and programming process; he sees a great many trees, but few forests. Thus, to the extent that the Carter defense program (or practically any other for the past decade) meets national needs, it is as much by accident as by design. Clearly, it is necessary, and possible, to do better than that.

Problems of Assessment

Another reality of the 1980s (as of previous years) is that, short of the test of actual combat, existing methods of assessing needs for deterrence and defense are primitive, and the results are subject to large margins of error. Perhaps the most popular and least reliable methods are those based on simple comparisons of opposing forces. It is bad enough that the procedures for counting these forces are frequently suspect, that different types of weapon systems are frequently lumped together (as though interceptor and attack aircraft were identical), and that counterpart rather than competing systems are compared (so that tanks fight only tanks rather than antitank weapons as well). But even worse, most of these "static" comparisons leave out such important factors as accuracy, reliability, protection, geography, terrain, weather, training, combat readiness, sustainability, and objectives.

It is true, for example, that the Soviet Union has nearly three times as many attack submarines as the United States according to standard counting procedures. But Soviet attack submarines, many of which are still diesel-powered, are divided into four fleets, two of which could hardly threaten the main U.S. lines of communication in the Atlantic and Pacific. And even the more threatening submarines would have to pass through narrow and dangerous waters to reach those lines of communication. To defeat their attacks, the United States could deploy its own submarines (which are quieter than Russian submarines) in advantageous geographic positions and provide them with valuable information about enemy locations and directions; it could also use mines, aircraft, and surface combatants to attack opposing submarines. Any study that compared only the number of Soviet and U.S. attack submarines and then reached conclusions about the outcome of an attack on U.S. sea lines of communication would not simply have a high probability of error; it would not even have provided an adequate data base for any such conclusions.

To make more realistic predictions, simulations of actual combat engagements would have to be attempted. These simulations, or "dynamic" analyses, usually incorporate more of the relevant determinants of performance than the simple static comparisons. Moreover, they force the planner to focus on outcomes rather than selected inputs of data. But some of the simulations must create wars that nobody has ever experienced (as with nuclear exchanges); others must simplify the complexities of actual combat; and all of them must deal with specific cases, none of which may materialize.

It is little wonder in the circumstances that a great deal of military judgment about force requirements is based on rules of thumb derived from previous combat experience and expressed conservatively so as to hedge against uncertainties about the types and numbers of future contingencies that may have to be faced. The Navy thus has felt more or less comfortable in peacetime with fifteen aircraft carriers and around one hundred attack submarines. The Army likes to maintain a total force of roughly twenty-six divisions (active and reserve) at all times. The Air Force considers roughly five fighter squadrons for every Army division adequate in peacetime but emphasizes aircraft designed primarily for air superiority and interdiction (in contrast to the Army, which wants them primarily for close air support and will acquire attack helicopters for that mission to the extent that the Air Force ignores it).

These numbers have evolved from and stood up well in the past and are expected to do equal service in the future, provided always that the weapon systems themselves are kept technologically advanced. Unfortunately, it is impossible to be entirely confident—as opponents change and become more proficient industrially and technologically—that the numbers will prove comparably effective in dealing with the problems that lie ahead.

This methodological difficulty is not trivial. In the past, because the United States rarely constituted the first line of defense, it could depend on the experience of others and, to some degree, on trial and error (as it did in adapting the B-17 bomber and its fighters to the rigors of World War II) to dictate the size and composition of its forces. At present and in the foreseeable future, Americans are much more likely to participate in the initial stages of any conflict; consequently the decisions made in peacetime are bound to be of much greater gravity. Indeed, now that the United States and its opponents have a wide range of lethal mechanisms available—including conventional ordnance, fuel-air explosives, biological and chemical weapons, and a host of nuclear devices—some of which have never been fully tested in combat, planners are more than ever the captives of their hypotheses and calculations. These are increasingly important not only in determining the size and composition of U.S. forces, but also in deciding which components it would be advantageous to stress and even use.

It is therefore imperative to abandon the shopworn debate about civilian whiz kids versus experienced military officers and get on with the task of improving analytical capabilities. They will be needed in the 1980s more than ever before, both for campaign analyses and for detailed weapon systems comparisons.

International Trends

Published reports about campaign analyses, particularly those relating to potential conflicts in the region of the Persian Gulf, indicate that political sensitivity is not one of their strengths. Accepting major international trends and relating the evolution of the U.S. defense posture to them seem to be equally difficult. Nevertheless, some of these developments constitute inescapable realities that must be taken into account in defense planning more than has been done in the past.

U.S. Involvement

For example, like it or not, the United States will be even more dependent on the outside world in the 1980s than in the 1970s. And some of the areas on which it depends most heavily will be subjected to violence or the threat of violence to a greater degree than in the recent past. These realities, in turn, mean that the United States will find itself more rather than less deeply involved in international politics, with all the dangers of confrontation and crisis that invariably accompany those politics.

Why these realities are inescapable is no secret. The growing economic dependence of the United States on the outside world is most spectacularly documented by its imports of oil. By a more rigorous policy of conservation and the substitution of other fuels, it can hope to reduce its dependence on foreign oil. But even the most ambitious peacetime plans will not end that dependence for at least another decade. And oil is of course only one—though the most conspicuous—external need. The whole U.S. economy is increasingly geared to worldwide supply and demand. It used to be said that when the United States sneezed, everyone else caught cold. Now Americans are equally susceptible to the ailments of others.

The problem is not only that the United States needs access to these areas and worldwide markets, but also that it cannot afford to see them controlled or conquered by another great power. It has already participated in two great wars to prevent Germany from dominating Europe (and in World War II, to keep Japan from controlling much of Asia and the western Pacific). It now has an equal interest in preventing the Soviet Union from seizing and exploiting the human and material resources of Western Europe, China, Japan, and the broad area of the Middle East (including the Persian Gulf).

Such a concentration of power, even when allowance is made for all the inefficiencies of the Soviet system, would constitute a standing threat to U.S. well-being, freedom, and territorial integrity. No attempt to retreat into isolation could remove that threat. No elaboration of nuclear defenses could credibly save America from a skilled and determined enemy. The reality is that the United States has become mixed up with the rest of the world and will remain that way.

During the past decade this country has greatly exaggerated its limitations as a world power, finding it convenient to forget that only now, with the 1981 defense budget, is it committing anything like the same amount of real resources to the military establishment as it did before the war in Indochina. As a percentage of a much larger gross national product, that budget of course is substantially lower. The burden is not heavy—a great deal more could be added without serious sacrifice.

Even so, unless the United States is to become an armed camp, with vast legions stationed overseas, or is to try once again to rely on increasingly implausible nuclear threats to forestall every danger, it must preserve its alliances. They serve both as clear indications of what interests are considered essential and as a way of sharing the costs of collective security. These commitments—many of which are on the periphery of the Soviet bloc—remain in force thirty years or so after their ratification. The fact that they have not been abrogated symbolizes the persistence of danger in the international neighborhood and the magnitude of the task that faces the United States and its allies.

Danger is taken for granted, regrettably, in most urban areas of the United States, and resources are lavished on forces to deter and deal with attacks in such neighborhoods. There is little reason to believe that the international need is any less great.

Some of the dangers to U.S. friends will undoubtedly come from internal activities or even external activities that are difficult to suppress by what Americans would consider the acceptable use of military capabilities. Where grievances within a society are so deep that revolution becomes their only outlet, the United States will probably continue to believe that any military intervention by it (or any other outside power, for that matter) should be ruled out except to protect its citizens. If essential U.S. interests are jeopardized by these convulsions, undoubtedly other means for their protection will be used.

But just because so much of this kind of turmoil exists—in Southeast and Southwest Asia, the Middle East, Africa, and Latin America —does not mean that, without effective countermeasures by the United States and its friends, organized warfare has become a thing of the past. Surprise attacks to overwhelm weak, isolated, or disorganized opponents are always preferred by some to the slow and uncertain course of political action, terrorism, subversion, or guerrilla warfare.

Soviet Propensities

The Soviet Union has already demonstrated its preference for the use of force and deception on three separate occasions during the last twenty-four years: in Hungary, in Czechoslovakia, and now, outside its own bloc, in Afghanistan. These incursions, limited though they have been so far, are not the only evidence of the Soviet view that military capabilities are still an important instrument of international politics, at least when the price looks right. There is also the long record of Soviet military buildup, which seems to have accelerated after the fall of Nikita Khrushchev and the ascendancy of Leonid Brezhnev, with his emphasis on "peaceful coexistence."

That record can probably be explained in part by the fears of a despotic regime that is hated at home and has suffered near ruin from external attack. But when those fears turn into paranoia, when the only real security lies in far-flung domination, and when those who are not dominated must perforce be considered enemies and undermined by all available means, the traditional distinction between defense and aggression rapidly loses its meaning.

Clearly such an outlook combined with a military effort that has increased so steadily—regardless of the strategic arms limitation talks (SALT), regardless of détente, regardless of any U.S. restraint in defense budgets or weapon deployments—and now exceeds that of the United States by between 35 percent (if both are priced in the Soviet economy) and about 50 percent (when both are priced in the U.S. economy) does not suggest stability in the decade ahead. Of course, a trend that has been described by the last four secretaries of defense can be ignored. Soviet leaders can be mistaken for likable but somewhat primitive and sensitive types who suffer from an inferiority complex and just want to be treated as equals. A blind eye can even be turned to where they are headed: toward what they refer to as a war-winning nuclear capability; toward the achievement of conventional power much superior to that of their neighbors; toward greater air and sea mobility and the development of the land and naval capabilities necessary for the overseas projection of military power. Alternatively, they can be recognized for what they are. Their pretensions can be taken seriously and at the same time their accomplishments kept in perspective. Americans can avoid panic, stop exaggerating Soviet capabilities, and call a halt to the unnecessary denigration of their own. The Soviet Union in 1980 is not a military giant and the United States is not a military pygmy.

Such a balanced view is admittedly difficult to maintain in light of the frequent "revelations" about the Russians' superiority. There they are, as the public is so frequently reminded, with nearly 1,400 intercontinental ballistic missiles and 950 modern submarine-launched ballistic missiles in 62 more or less up-to-date submarines, while this country deploys only 1,054 ICBMs and 656 SLBMs in 41 modern submarines.

One may say, and even believe, that this is a relationship of rough or essential equivalence. To suggest that a somewhat comparable relationship exists at the tactical level—both nuclear and nonnuclear—is apt to be regarded as sheer folly. It remains the case, nonetheless, that much of what passes for analysis of Soviet theater capabilities confuses size with effectiveness and extrapolates from the carefully studied elite units (such as the Group of Soviet Forces in Germany) to the entire Soviet force structure. Such analysis would have one believe that a society that is singularly inefficient in the civil sector of a command economy has managed to become more efficient in its military sector, even granting that the military sector gets first call on Russian human and material resources. It encourages the view that a government that seeks to import Western technology, including a whole truck-manufacturing plant, is on the verge of achieving technological superiority over the United States in all its weapon systems. Even worse, such analysis demands acceptance on faith of such assertions as the one that endows the Soviet Union with 45,000 tanks and tank production of at best 4,000 tanks a year (admittedly more impressive than U.S. output), yet argues that the Soviet army is undergoing continuous and rapid modernization.

None of this is to say that the Soviet Union should be given anything less than the highest marks for effort. It is persistent; it sees itself in competition with the United States; it is an aggressive competitor; and it is eager, wherever possible, to equal and overtake this country —as it is demonstrating in the nuclear realm. Even though it would be well to discount the more extreme claims of the Russians' competence and strength, their competition must be taken more seriously in the future than in the recent past.

Other States

Similarly the capacity for trouble of North Korea, Vietnam, and Cuba under their present leaders must be recognized. Individually they may no longer seem worthy of much U.S. attention, especially in an age of relativism when no distinction is made between North and South Korea and Castro's Cuba is seen as a model for social reform. But with encouragement from Moscow, and under the mantle of Soviet power or in collaboration with the Kremlin, all three can still challenge U.S. commitments. No one can say what they might do if the United States were to become deeply involved in Europe and the Persian Gulf and had no power left to confront them.

The Role of Military Power

The international arena of the 1980s is clearly not one Americans should enter poorly armed or reluctant to do whatever is necessary to fulfill U.S. commitments. Military power is no panacea; it will not solve all the problems likely to arise in the decade ahead. But it can lend a certain persuasiveness to other efforts by the United States. It can strengthen the confidence of friends and increase the hesitation of foes. As a last resort, it can defeat attacks on U.S. friends and on the United States itself. That the United States should have it in ample measure is hardly an issue in a world where the institutions and rules of law are honored mostly in the breach, and where force is so often the final arbiter of competing claims. What is and will remain at issue is the appropriate composition, size, equipment, deployment, readiness, mobility, and sustainability of U.S. forces.

The United States could, as in the 1950s, place main but not sole reliance on nuclear weapons at the expense of its conventional capabilities. It could attempt, as in the 1960s, to achieve modern, ready, sustainable forces capable of exercising a wide range of nuclear and nonnuclear options and adapted to a number of contingencies that could arise in connection with its commitments. It could rest on its somewhat tarnished laurels, as it did through most of the 1970s, and preserve all the facade and some of the capabilities for a flexible response. It could focus its planning, its forces, and its deployments on the particular theaters it deemed of greatest importance to it. The menu of postures and defense budgets from which to choose is large.

But which one should be chosen for the 1980s? And at what cost and risk? Which one best suits U.S. needs and purse? The answer is obviously sensitive to a variety of factors, including what the United States thinks the Soviet Union will do. It is an answer that must be reviewed each year as the five-year defense program is extended.

Whatever the answer selected, international politics can be expected to continue their rough-and-tumble course in the 1980s. Despite impending changes in the Kremlin's leadership, the Soviet Union can also be expected to pursue an aggressive defense of "socialism," to continue the improvement of its military capabilities, and to exploit Western vulnerability where the opportunities arise and the risks of weakening the West (or gaining leverage with its members) are not considered high. But unless the United States is to make its own capabilities a mirror-image of the Soviet Union's—which would be foolish and wasteful—it must find other grounds on which to base its choice.

Nuclear Capabilities

Nowhere is this task more difficult than in the choice of nuclear capabilities. Even here, however, there are several realities that, if acknowledged, should help in the design of an appropriate posture.

Clearly, where only one side in a conflict possesses nuclear weapons, and their number is significant, the other side is virtually at the mercy of the monopolist. Even where both sides have large numbers of nuclear weapons (that is, thousands), it remains possible—at least on paper—for one side to achieve an exploitable military superiority over the other, although this kind of superiority is much more likely to be achieved at the strategic than at the tactical level. Despite this possibility, any nuclear exchange, strategic or tactical, would be fraught with the danger of escalation to unrestricted bombing and unprecedented civilian and military damage.

These realities have several major implications. One is that even when opposing nuclear forces are quite asymmetrical in several dimensions (including numbers) the side with the notional advantages may not really have a usable capability. Another is that nuclear capabilities, whether for strategic or tactical targeting, are now worth having almost exclusively as a counterweight to those of an opponent and as a deterrent to the opponent's use of them.

The idea that the United States, or for that matter the Soviet Union, is straining at the nuclear leash or is likely to launch nuclear weapons except in almost unimaginable circumstances is simply at variance with these realities. The decision is too hard, as anyone who has come at all close to it in the last twenty years knows only too well. Talk about an early use of nuclear weapons—even when it appears in supposedly serious Pentagon studies—is either the equivalent of cocktail party conversation or sheer bluff.

Concepts of Nuclear War

Nuclear weapons and their effects are different in scale and kind from anything previously experienced. They are not simply another explosive. Their use makes it extremely difficult not to kill large masses of people very quickly. They do not fit well into traditional concepts of how wars can be fought and hence deterred.

At the tactical level attempts have been made by the United States, as well as by the Soviet Union, to force them into the traditional mold.

But all the analyses of this kind of warfare, unless they are quite abstract, suggest that both the battlefield and the rear areas of the belligerents would rapidly be reduced to chaos.

At the strategic level what may be more plausible and feasible types of exchanges have been invented. But even these have an air of artificiality. They usually lack a political beginning or ending. More often than not, the war is stopped after several volleys, residual weapons are counted and compared, and the side with the larger number is declared the victor. Even where, in the hypothetical campaigns that are more seriously conducted, some more exploitable form of leverage begins to emerge, it looks at best precarious and dangerous to exploit for any purpose commensurate with the costs already incurred and the risks ahead.

U.S. and Soviet Objectives

For all these reasons, whether strategic or tactical nuclear deterrence (to the extent that they are separate) is being considered, it seems a wasteful and futile exercise to seek nuclear superiority over a moderately competent and determined adversary. It would be far better to set a more modest and feasible objective: to ensure a stalemate in these two arenas and use U.S. resources for other, more profitable purposes.

This is not to say that the other side will settle for a comparable objective. Nor does it mean that settling for a stalemate, which is what now exists, will prove either easy or cheap. Indeed, despite Brezhnev's willingness to sign SALT II, the Soviet Union has undertaken many of the programs necessary to the acquisition of one form of strategic nuclear superiority. It is already well on the way to developing elements of a highly effective counterforce capability against U.S. fixed, hard ICBMs. It keeps striving, though with little success thus far, to achieve the capability to locate and destroy U.S. SLBMs on station. It continues to modernize its massive air defense system against low-flying bombers and cruise missiles. As permitted under SALT, it still pours resources into the development of antiballistic missiles. And unlike the United States, it maintains a large civil defense organization and is gradually expanding what is considered in this country to be so far a relatively ineffective system of blast and fallout shelters.

Of perhaps greater importance, the Russians have developed an increasingly elaborate and hardened system of command, control, and communications. Although the data are poor, it has to be assumed that this system gives them some flexibility in managing their strategic nuclear capabilities.

The Conditions of Stalemate

Whether the Soviet Union has put all these pieces together in a coherent effort to achieve the capability for war-fighting and damage-limiting campaigns remains uncertain. But given the persistence and magnitude of the programs (which have proceeded independently of SALT), even maintaining a strategic stalemate will be challenging. This is so not only because it pays to be conservative in the design of U.S. forces for this strange contest, but also because even a strategy of deterrence by stalemate requires that the United States continue to maintain and improve the capability for controlled and selective responses that it instituted nearly twenty years ago.

The Triad of strategic offensive forces obviously serves both these purposes. The United States already has the capability, on a second strike, to cover a large number of relatively soft military, political, and economic targets in the Soviet Union. But the U.S. ability to conduct a counterforce duel initiated by the USSR against U.S. ICBMs (however implausible such a limited exchange might be) is weakening. The Minuteman III with the Mark-12A reentry vehicles will have a respectable hard-target kill probability, but it will be vulnerable to a Soviet first strike. Cruise missiles on alert bombers will also be effective in this role, but on the average they will not reach their targets until after eight hours of flight, and then only if they successfully penetrate Soviet air defenses.

These presumably are some of the reasons the Carter administration has decided to go ahead with the full-scale engineering development of the MX ICBM. It is hoped that the MX will be based in a less vulnerable mode than the Minuteman III, and it will certainly provide greater assurance of rapidly destroying ICBM silos than either Minuteman III or cruise missiles. Also, the MX will force the Russians to consider how to cope with the vulnerability of their ICBMs, limiting their ability to transfer further resources to the neutralization of U.S. SLBMs and bombers.

The MX program, combined with the modernization of the other legs of the Triad and improved command, control, and communications, will undoubtedly drive the total obligational authority for U.S.

strategic nuclear forces to over $20 billion (in fiscal 1981 dollars) by fiscal 1985, although this total will still be less than 11 percent of the projected defense budget. Without eventual ratification of SALT II, the percentage might become somewhat higher—or the entire defense budget might have to be expanded—largely because of the insistence that the United States maintain the appearance of essential equivalence with the Soviet Union, whatever that term means. It is also assumed that the USSR, without SALT, would add to its offensive forces rather than improve its strategic capabilities in other ways. Whether additional Soviet ICBMs or SLBMs would have any further effect on the nuclear stalemate is a question that appears not to have been raised, much less answered.

The Price of Stalemate

No matter how these particular issues are resolved, it is essential that the United States and its allies finally acknowledge that the strategic and tactical nuclear forces will only deter the use of nuclear force by others, particularly the Soviet Union. If they do not face this reality, there is no assurance that they will get on with the serious business of coping with the more likely and more imminent dangers.

There continues to be an understandable U.S. reluctance to spell out this reality. The fear is that if U.S. allies are finally forced to face it, they will become more loath than ever to expand their conventional capabilities and may decide either that they have been left entirely exposed to Soviet pressure or that they must acquire new or expanded nuclear capabilities of their own to preclude such an eventuality. The truth, though, is that the pretense of being willing to initiate nuclear warfare should allied conventional defenses break down has not resulted in substantially improved allied conventional forces. Instead, it has led to excessive complacency about the Soviet nonnuclear buildup punctuated by crises of confidence over the strength and credibility of the U.S. nuclear deterrent.

In the past, the United States dealt with these crises, first, by putting forward a proposed multilateral nuclear force, and then by falling back on a North Atlantic Treaty Organization (NATO) nuclear planning group, which at least gave European allies some voice in U.S. nuclear programming decisions. The United States is now engaged in repeating part of that process, this time with the Pershing II ballistic missiles and the ground-launched cruise missiles, both under

U.S. control, as substitutes for the old multilateral nuclear force, which would have consisted of Polaris missiles on ships manned by multinational crews. Indeed, the United States acts as if this were its only recourse (at a total acquisition cost of $5 billion in fiscal 1981 dollars) in view of the Soviet deployment of the mobile SS-20 intermediate-range ballistic missile equipped with multiple independently targetable reentry vehicles (MIRVs), which is now said to be on more than a hundred launchers, and of more than fifty Backfire medium-range bombers.

There is, however, another way to proceed. Washington can, after all, indicate that there is a plausible stance between the extremes of the dangerous pretense that the United States would strike first against these and other Soviet systems and the abandonment of its allies, which it has no intention of doing. The plausible stance is that while a first use of nuclear weapons by the United States can never be completely ruled out, the real U.S. commitment is to respond appropriately with nuclear weapons to their first use against U.S. allies and other friends.

Such a position, combined with the programmed improvements in U.S. strategic and tactical nuclear forces, at least has the merit that it substitutes credibility for a pretense that is being combined with expensive expedients. The decision to initiate the use of nuclear weapons under present conditions is virtually unbearable for any reasonably sane policymaker, whatever his or her nationality. The decision, on the other hand, to respond to a first use of nuclear weapons is not only less of a burden; it can be further eased by the availability of well-designed second-strike forces armed with options. Furthermore, this position provides U.S. allies with the missing incentive to strengthen their conventional defenses. The terrifying nuclear decision would be placed where it belongs: on the shoulders of those who would disturb the peace in the first place. Allies would be no less protected than they are now, but a pernicious illusion would have been destroyed.

Such candor undoubtedly has a price, although the price is not necessarily the one associated with it. It requires that the United States and its allies develop a conventional posture that can stand up to attack without nuclear crutches. But this is a capability the United States has sought to achieve for the last twenty years. Candor also confirms to the Soviet Union the existence of a situation that, in other terms, the United States has already proclaimed: a nuclear stalemate and mutual nuclear deterrence.

It is nonetheless important to be clear about just what that confirmation does not signify, as well as what it does. It does not signify acceptance of the cliché that the world of an acknowledged nuclear stalemate is radically different from the previous world of nominal U.S. nuclear superiority. In that earlier world, despite the current mythmakers, Americans were not much impressed with their superiority; it is difficult to find an occasion on which they exercised it to any effect, even during the Cuban missile crisis. Whether the Russians were impressed by it is simply not known. However, it is known that their behavior was at least as atrocious as it is now. True, they have invaded Afghanistan. But twelve years ago they invaded Czechoslovakia, and Hungary suffered an even worse fate twenty-four years ago. True, they are now providing Angola, Ethiopia, and Yemen with military assistance, military advisers, and Cuban mercenaries. But thirty years ago they encouraged the North Korean attack on South Korea, and thirty-two years ago they blockaded Berlin.

No doubt the Soviet Union has a longer military reach today than it did so soon after World War II, although it is a reach that still extends beyond the Soviet periphery only at the sufferance of the West. Perhaps because of this tolerance and its own military buildup (nonnuclear as well as nuclear), it may misjudge Western resolution in the future. The USSR may prove more tenacious in defending its alleged interests and in exploiting opportunities to weaken the West than it was in Berlin and Cuba, when the nuclear superiority that was nominal to Americans may have seemed operational to the Russians. But that is all the more reason for dropping the pretense that nuclear weapons will somehow extricate the United States from the confrontations and hazards of the future. They will not. Only adequate nonnuclear capabilities will.

Nonnuclear Capabilities

Like Molière's bourgeois gentleman from the country, who discovered, after taking lessons in Paris, that he had been speaking prose for forty years, Americans are discovering yet again that they have been engaging in conventional international politics, with its emphasis on traditional conflict, for nearly the same length of time. This reality needs to be recognized if this country is to fulfill its commitments.

The Soviet Posture

Another reality is that the Soviet conventional posture at present is not nearly so out of proportion to that of the United States and its allies as is popularly supposed. Soviet ground forces consist of about 1.8 million men, roughly double U.S. ground force manpower (counting both Army and Marine Corps personnel) if paid reservists (over 600,000 men) and civilian manpower (360,000 employed by the Army) are not included.

From its personnel, the Soviet Union manages to extract over 170 divisions, whereas the United States has only 19 active-duty and 9 reserve Army and Marine Corps divisions, plus 5 active and 24 reserve brigades that are usually overlooked. However, most Soviet divisions are less than fully manned, many of them are less capable and ready than the U.S. National Guard and Reserve divisions, and there remain questions about how much equipment of what vintage is held by the less ready Soviet divisions.

In peacetime, most of the Soviet divisions appear to lack many of the support forces that would permit them to sustain a military operation for more than a couple of weeks. As was evident in Afghanistan, it takes the Soviet establishment a substantial amount of time—months rather than weeks—to organize a small operation against a weak and relatively disorganized country. The forces, once in occupation, seem to devote as much as 40 percent of their manpower to combat service support—that is, primarily to logistic and maintenance functions.

The Soviet tactical air forces (known as Frontal Aviation) are numerically no larger than comparable U.S. Air Force, Navy, and Marine Corps tactical air forces. Frontal Aviation has been undergoing a substantial modernization with late-model MiG-21s, MiG-23s and -27s, Su-17s, and Su-24s. But while some of these aircraft may be the equivalent of the more advanced F-4s and F-5s, they are not on a par with the newer U.S. aircraft. Beyond that, Soviet pilots are less well trained than their American counterparts, fly fewer hours, and exercise less initiative because of constraints imposed by Soviet ground control.

The Soviet Union has obviously dedicated substantial resources to its naval forces, and now deploys an oceangoing fleet that, at least superficially, rivals that of the United States in surface ships and exceeds it in submarines. Appearances, however, are deceptive. Soviet surface combatants are heavily armed for their size. But they appear to carry only small reserves in missiles and ordnance; their cruising range is limited; and crews' quarters are crowded. Larger ships are under construction—such as the 27,000–30,000-ton cruiser being built near Leningrad—but it will be some years before significant numbers are deployed.

Although the Soviet navy pioneered in arming surface combatants with cruise missiles, it is not clear how accurate these missiles would be when fired at targets over the horizon. They could be aided by spotter aircraft, helicopters, and surfaced submarines and, in principle, could be defended by carrier-based aircraft. In practice, the newer light aircraft carriers such as the *Kiev* and the *Minsk* cannot provide this kind of protection since their deckloads consist of helicopters and vertical takeoff and landing aircraft with limited combat radii and light armament. U.S. land-based and fleet aircraft armed with the Harpoon (later the Tomahawk) cruise missile should be able to do well against them and any other surface combatants that ventured from under the cover of Soviet land-based aircraft. It is worth remembering, furthermore, that Soviet surface combatants are divided among four fleets. Two of them—in the Black Sea and the Baltic—are virtually landlocked, and even the Northern and Pacific Fleets would have to pass through narrow waters and a number of man-made barriers to reach U.S. and allied surface combatants and merchant ships.

Soviet attack submarines armed with torpedoes and cruise missiles are similarly divided and would have similar problems reaching their targets. Soviet nuclear submarines are admittedly faster than most U.S. nuclear submarines, and the new *Alfa*-class titanium-alloy submarine has demonstrated impressive speed and deep-diving characteristics. However, all Soviet submarines carry limited numbers of torpedoes and cruise missiles; they are also noisy. All would have to run the gauntlet of various U.S. early warning systems, mines, antisubmarine aircraft, quiet submarines armed with high-speed torpedoes, and surface combatants equipped with sophisticated detection gear and antisubmarine helicopters (of which there will be around two hundred aboard surface combatants).

Relatively speaking, the Backfire bombers being assigned to Soviet naval aviation are coming to be viewed as a bigger potential threat to U.S. maritime capabilities. On a naval mission the Backfire is expected to have considerable range (especially if flown subsonically at high altitude and refueled), good target-location capabilities, and two air-to-surface missiles, which it can fire at ships from distances of hundreds of kilometers. If concentrated in large numbers against a U.S. carrier battle group or a convoy of merchant ships, Backfires could presumably saturate current defenses with their missiles and score a significant number of hits. Countering this is the U.S. program of cruisers equipped with the AEGIS system, which is designed to detect and track large numbers of objects and manage the defense against them. It is conceivable that in some areas, such as Japan and along the Greenland-Iceland-United Kingdom barrier, land-based aircraft will also have an important role to play against the Backfire.

While the architects of Soviet naval forces thus face a number of difficult problems in making their present fleet effective (other than as an important political and deterrent weapon), the United States must not only expect them to continue building defenses against its ballistic missile submarines and carrier battle groups and to seek the ability to sever its sea lines of communication; it must also anticipate that they will continue to develop the elements of long-range power projection. The Russians have little capability for this kind of activity at present. Only a few of their surface combatants have the range and firepower to sustain an attack on a distant defended area. They still lack reliable and secure overseas bases and the logistics ships to supply a distant fleet of any size. As currently constituted, their forces would be vulnerable to air and submarine attack. However, there is every indication that these forces will grow in size and effectiveness and that they will be supplemented by long-range sealift (based on a growing fleet of roll-on–roll-off ships), airlift substantially improved over the force currently available—which did not perform with éclat in the buildup against Afghanistan—and light naval and airborne infantry.

The Present Situation

If the Soviet Union is so constrained, why does so much pessimism exist about the ability of the United States to cope with its capabilities by conventional means? The reasons are numerous; two are worth stressing. First, the vulnerabilities of U.S. and allied forces are known in great detail, but the USSR is assumed to have overcome all such problems despite much evidence to the contrary. Only when it undertakes an operation such as the unopposed invasion of Afghanistan does the West realize (and then forget) that Soviet forces fall short of perfection as well. Second, planners have an understandable propensity to confuse the future with the present. They see Soviet ground forces becoming more mobile and better equipped with protected firepower, Soviet Frontal Aviation evolving from a collection of interceptors to a force increasingly capable of fighting deep air superiority and interdiction campaigns, and Soviet naval and projection forces beginning to adopt many of the characteristics of comparable U.S. forces; and they anticipate, with the strengthening of Soviet forces in Eastern Europe and the Far East, that the Russians will be able in the future to conduct offensive operations simultaneously in two or more theaters. What they expect the Soviet Union to be able to do some years hence—and what the United States must allow for in its defense programs—they credit the Soviet Union with being able to do now. To those who have little confidence in the ability of democracies to plan ahead, this propensity to confuse the future with the present may even seem justifiable.

Perhaps they are right. But a price accompanies this kind of well-intentioned confusion. Great Britain's Royal Air Force discovered as much after it had overrated the German Luftwaffe in its reports to Neville Chamberlain before his visit to Munich in 1938. Indeed, exaggerated statements—whether about the present or the future—can lead to despair instead of the determination and higher budgets that are sought. Such estimates can cause an unnecessary deflection from what really needs to be done. Worst of all, they can result in the appeasement they are intended to avoid. Accordingly, it is vital to be realistic about the present as well as the future.

What, then, is the current nonnuclear situation? U.S. techniques for assessing it are not strong, but they do indicate that in any given theater—assuming it is the only active one—the position of the United States and its allies has not deteriorated nearly as much as the conventional wisdom implies.

Even in Central Europe, where the Soviet Union is credited with its greatest concentration of conventional strength, the opposing NATO and Warsaw Pact forces do not differ much in capability when reasonable measures are equitably applied to them. The main current problems lie elsewhere. NATO would presumably obtain prompt warning of Pact preparations for an attack, but whether NATO members would respond promptly and efficiently to the warning is much less certain. Although NATO would have the advantages of the defense, at least in the initial stages of such a conflict, it would have to distribute its forces along a front of considerable length, whereas the Pact could concentrate the attack at a point of its own choosing and possibly achieve tactical surprise in the process. The Supreme Allied Commander, Europe, would need a mobile reserve to cope with this eventuality and, with the active forces in its inventory, the United States could provide such a reserve. Whether it could be deployed fast enough to prevent a breakthrough is much more debatable. Based on the time it took the Russians to prepare the Afghanistan invasion, the odds remain good, even now, that there would be sufficient warning to allow the United States to get its forces on line before an attack came. But the odds are not as favorable as they used to be, and they will become less so unless the United States and its allies respond to the ongoing Soviet improvements with continued programs in NATO.

On the Korean peninsula, despite the North Korean ground force buildup of the 1970s, the military situation still favors South Korea. The North Koreans, although they have added manpower, tanks, and artillery to their ground forces, are still short of offensive air power. Moreover, they would have to smash through the heavily fortified lines south of the demilitarized zone separating the two countries or somehow circumvent those lines and disorganize the substantial South Korean defense forces. In doing so, they would have to cope with in-place South Korean and U.S. tactical airpower, the Second U.S. Infantry Division, the rapid U.S. reinforcement of its deployed forces with ground and air units from Japan (Okinawa), and further air and ground reinforcements brought in by air from Hawaii and the continental United States. Without major support from the Soviet Union, the North Koreans could not count on the success of such an attack.

A Soviet attack on Iran is one of the most dangerous contingencies facing the United States, largely because of the distance its forces would have to be moved, the limited airlift at its disposal, and the lack of bases on the way to and in the area. Nonetheless, with time, it would not be beyond the capability of the United States to project a significant amount of military power into the region. Admittedly, the Soviet Union has strengthened its posture there, at least temporarily, by increasing the readiness of the divisions facing Iran and in Afghanistan. It may be better able to foment trouble among such groups as the Baluchistani. Because its troops are now deployed to the east as well as to the north of Iran, its strategic position may have improved, although the terrain in both areas interposes major obstacles to a large and opposed movement of mechanized forces. It is one thing for airborne and motorized rifle units, virtually unopposed, to seize key points in a country such as Afghanistan. It is quite another to attempt a comparable operation in the teeth of air attacks with modern nonnuclear ordnance.

If the invasion of Afghanistan is a good example of Soviet mobilization in the region, several months would probably be needed to set up an operation against Iran. The United States would almost certainly have prompt warning of these preparations. As has been pointed out publicly, it should be able—with its entire current airlift and sealift capability—to position a three-division corps in the region within about sixty days, put two or three carrier battle groups into the Arabian Sea, and deploy as many land-based tactical fighters as the available base structure within striking distance of the Soviet forces could handle. Such a force, which would consist of as many as five hundred combat aircraft and the equivalent of more than six Soviet-style divisions, would have a good chance of preventing the seizure of the principal Iranian oil fields and production facilities. If Iranian resistance proved effective and if other forces from the region joined in the defense, even more ambitious objectives might be worth attempting. In these circumstances, the Soviet Union could have little expectation of achieving much to its long-run advantage. However, it could expect to pay a heavy price in local and Western hostility and in a major U.S. military buildup.

Should any one of these three contingencies arise—in Europe, on the Korean peninsula, or in the region of the Persian Gulf—the U.S. Navy should be fully capable of protecting U.S. sea lines of communication to the theater. Even in the event of a major nonnuclear war in Central Europe, U.S. and allied naval forces would have the capability to defeat the surface combatants, submarines, and aircraft of the Soviet Northern Fleet. However, the process of containment and destruction (or bottling up of these forces) might take as long as three months. During that time, U.S. naval vessels and merchant shipping would probably suffer serious though not crippling losses.

No doubt these assessments of the overall military situation, as it is measured in these three crucial areas, will be regarded as excessively optimistic. Yet to the extent that anything as intrinsically uncertain as the outcome of a conflict can be estimated, there is good reason to doubt the more pessimistic appraisals of the ability of the United States and its allies to defend against each of these attacks. The pessimism, for the most part, is based on exaggerated estimates of current Soviet capabilities and deflated assessments of U.S. and allied capabilities.

Current Problems

None of this should be taken to mean that the present situation, more broadly considered, gives cause for great optimism. There are two reasons for considerable modesty and some anxiety about the adequacy of the U.S. nonnuclear posture even today.

The first is that, while the Soviet Union still may not be capable of conducting more than one offensive operation at a time, it appears to be able to do at least that much without substantially disturbing its forces in Eastern Europe and the Far East. Should it wish to, it could certainly give the impression with these forces—by increasing their readiness and changing their deployments—that it was ready for action in these two theaters. Also, of course, North Korea, Vietnam, or Cuba could choose such a crisis to settle some scores of their own. Without prompt countermeasures on the part of the United States and its allies, there is no telling what they might be tempted to do.

Not only would such a pattern of behavior force the United States to take precautions in a number of places; it might also be forced to put its strategic nuclear forces on high alert. But a worldwide alert—and this is the second reason for concern—would severely strain existing capabilities. The United States now has the combat force structure to deal simultaneously with one major and one minor nonnuclear contingency. It does not have the combat force structure necessary to reinforce Europe to the level planned, to hold forces of any magnitude in the western Pacific and Hawaii, and to deploy a corps with air support to the region of the Persian Gulf. The U.S. defense posture may have the naval forces to protect U.S. lines of communication in the Atlantic and the Pacific, but it probably lacks the capability for covering these sea lanes, holding the eastern Mediterranean, and dispatching several carrier battle groups to the vicinity of the Persian Gulf simultaneously. And combat force structure aside, it is seriously short of the readiness and long-range mobility to complete all three moves in an acceptable period of time. Even two simultaneous deployments of any consequence would overburden existing mobility capabilities, at least in the short run.

The Carter administration is attempting to minimize the near-term risk in several ways. Through an ambitious program of pre-positioning ground force matériel and stocks of combat consumables in Europe, it is improving the U.S. ability to reinforce NATO rapidly both in the Central Region of Europe and on the northern flank without having to subtract much of the outsize and oversize airlift that might be needed for another contingency. At the same time, it is looking into the availability of bases in the vicinity of the Persian Gulf, entering the commercial market for roll-on–roll-off ships that could be used as floating storage depots in the Arabian Sea, expanding facilities at the British island of Diego Garcia in the Indian Ocean, planning an increased number of naval ship days in the Indian Ocean (probably at the expense of deployments in the western Pacific and the Mediterranean), and raising the readiness of key units that, in an emergency outside Europe, would become part of the Rapid Deployment Forces.

Future Problems

To deal with the longer term dangers brought on by the continuing Soviet military buildup and the likelihood of further international turbulence, the plans of the administration are more open ended. It is now more widely appreciated that, barring increased internal problems and an unlikely change for the better in the existing leadership, the Soviet Union's military capabilities will become more ready and agile, its reach will lengthen and strengthen, and its logistics will be able to support larger forces in more places at any one time. Whether or not the Soviet Union has better than a one-contingency capability now, the possibility that it will be acquired during the 1980s cannot be precluded.

In anticipation of this possibility, a number of programs are being extended or begun. The U.S. forces currently deployed in Europe—

which, along with allied forces in Germany, are judged adequate to deter a surprise nonnuclear attack in the Central Region—will presumably remain at present levels. But their equipment, readiness, supplies of modern munitions, and ability to coordinate with allies will be substantially improved. Additional measures will be taken allegedly to permit U.S. tactical air forces in Europe to be tripled within seven days and ground forces there to be increased by 75 percent within two weeks, all without requiring much of the current airlift. A combination of maritime pre-positioning ships (with heavy Marine equipment stored on board) and additional airlift—in the form of civil reserve air-fleet modifications, more flying hours for the C-5A aircraft, large new tanker aircraft (the KC-10), and a new airlift aircraft capable of transporting outsize cargo (such as tanks) —will help the United States to respond simultaneously and promptly to other contingencies. So will increased funding for the material readiness and training of the units designated for the Rapid Deployment Forces. An expanded five-year shipbuilding program, entailing the funding of an average of nineteen new ships each year, will not produce results for some years. Hence it will not appreciably expand the 500-ship active force toward which the Navy is headed, but it will ensure staying at that level as the Navy retires its older ships. Whether a still larger effort is deemed necessary will presumably depend on a further assessment of Soviet intentions in Southwest Asia and the Persian Gulf and on more data about the evolution of Soviet nonnuclear capabilities.

This caution is understandable. As the secretary of defense has pointed out, to confront the newfound national consensus for additional defense appropriations with a major expansion of the armed forces might make that consensus collapse. So might the demand for a significant increase in military personnel, which, unless there was an emergency, could probably be obtained only by large pay increases for the entire defense establishment. Bringing the existing force structure up to its full effectiveness is a substantial task in itself, and probably makes more sense than a rapid expansion. However, it is not too early to clear the decks for what may prove to be necessary but selective additions to the combat force structure.

The chief reason for considering these additions is that the current planning concept for the general purpose forces is beginning to break down under the weight of events and growing Soviet nonnuclear flexibility. This planning concept originally required the Department of Defense to generate the forces to deal simultaneously with two major contingencies and one lesser contingency. This requirement (if its conditions were met) also provided the option of dealing simultaneously with one major contingency and several minor contingencies. In 1969 the original concept was modified in two ways. One of the major contingencies was dropped, leaving the Department of Defense with the requirement to plan for two simultaneous contingencies: one major and one minor. At the same time, it was indicated rather casually that, if the two simultaneous contingencies became unmanageable or if more than two contingencies arose at the same time, the United States would resort to the use of nuclear weapons.

This piece of bravura has since been forgotten or dropped. But planning for the general purpose forces is still based on one major and one minor contingency. In principle, except for mobility, the demands of the concept have been satisfied, primarily by means of 19 active Army and Marine Corps divisions, 26 Air Force tactical air wings, 3 Marine Corps wings, and a two-ocean Navy with 12 attack carriers and perhaps 430 other general purpose ships and submarines. These forces permit the allocation of as many as 16 divisions and 24 fighter wings to a major contingency (with a European contingency as the basis for generating such a force), while supposedly leaving at least 3 divisions and 5 or more air wings (depending on the availability of carriers) for the minor contingency. But whether these forces will be sufficient for future U.S. needs is bound to become increasingly doubtful.

There are two grounds for this growing doubt. The first is that, more than ever, the United States will have to face the prospect of at least three military crises arising simultaneously: in the Persian Gulf; in Northeast Asia, Southeast Asia, or the Caribbean; and in Europe. In other words, the demands on the nonnuclear defense posture could easily run to the forces for one major contingency and two or more lesser contingencies. The second reason is that a crisis in one region —particularly if it involved the Soviet Union or one of its surrogates —would almost certainly set the alarms ringing in other threatened regions. It would be difficult and might seem excessively risky in these circumstances to "borrow" from the major-contingency forces (as was done in Southeast Asia, even after the Army and the Marine Corps had been expanded by over 700,000 men). And even the three divisions for a minor contingency might prove out of reach unless the crisis were in Northeast Asia, where the United States already has three divisions close at hand (in Korea, Japan, and Hawaii).

As the forces of the Soviet Union and its satellites gain in mobility and readiness, these problems will become more acute. The equivalent of nearly six divisions and more than eight fighter wings are already deployed in Europe to help guard against surprise attacks by the Warsaw Pact. The three divisions and four air wings (Air Force and Marine Corps) in Hawaii and the western Pacific have a somewhat similar function in relation to North Korea, although the specific need is less well defined. This leaves ten active-duty divisions and seventeen tactical air wings (Air Force and Marine Corps) in the continental United States, some of which are annually committed to NATO and the defense of Europe. To the extent that forces might have to be deployed elsewhere for comparable purposes, the remaining divisions and tactical air wings could be drawn on, at least in relatively quiet times, although this would constrain the U.S. ability to reinforce Europe in a worldwide crisis.

So far, the Soviet Union has been careful—whether deploying missiles to Cuba or invading Czechoslovakia and Afghanistan—not to exert pressure on other points, such as Berlin, and it may continue to be cautious in the future. But that cannot be counted on. Moderately conservative planning suggests that the United States should consider steps to expand the combat force structure as well as the mobility forces and be prepared to station ground combat as well as tactical air forces in the Persian Gulf region without disrupting its other deployments and reinforcement plans.

These forward-deployed forces would probably be given two immediate missions. In the event of Soviet preparations for a move toward Iran, establishing a firm base for the reception of reinforcements from the continental United States would be desirable. Also desirable would be the ability to conduct air operations against the precarious lines of communication over which the Soviet Union would have to launch and supply an invasion. These two missions might require at least a brigade of ground forces and three tactical air wings in the immediate vicinity of the theater for rapid reaction. As backup, a corps force of three divisions and another three tactical air wings would probably be needed to establish, at a minimum, a well-defended perimeter on the northern shore of the Persian Gulf.

Forward-deployed forces could in principle be positioned on bases in countries such as Oman and Somalia. In practice, it would almost certainly be better to give the forces the independence and flexibility of forward basing at sea. This in turn would probably require, at least for the near future, the concentration of all U.S. amphibious lift in one ocean so as to have the ships necessary to maintain three battalions of Marines near the Persian Gulf at all times. To keep as many as three carriers on station in support of them would necessitate diverting both carriers from the Seventh Fleet in the western Pacific and one carrier from the Sixth Fleet in the Mediterranean. To compensate, additional land-based fighters could be stationed in Japan and Turkey, where they could perform most of the functions currently assigned to the carriers. Also, more carriers could be assigned to home ports overseas, which would permit keeping more of the total force on station at any one time.

It may eventually be decided to add new divisions and air wings to the active-duty forces based in the United States to make up for these additional deployments and to ensure that the corps force could be made available without either eroding the capabilities for a major contingency or drawing on the forces deployed in Northeast Asia. But neither of the two methods available for this purpose looks attractive for the near term. Trying to acquire additional volunteers would probably be prohibitively expensive. Reviving the selective service system and drafting the necessary personnel at current pay scales would almost certainly prove impractical unless there was a national emergency. As one alternative, the United States could insist that its European allies take greater responsibility for their own forward defenses so as to reduce the need to provide so many U.S. reinforcements. As a practical matter, however, only the Federal Republic of Germany would be able to provide the necessary manpower, and its NATO partners might not acquiesce in such a development. No doubt Moscow would have something to say about it as well.

Another alternative would be to make much better use of the National Guard and Reserve ground and air units than at present. The Air Force fighter squadrons are already of high quality and would probably require relatively little additional training to enable them to augment or replace active forces on short notice. Army National Guard divisions are alleged to lack a comparable proficiency. But as the Israeli experience has shown, this is not a necessary condition for reserve ground forces. With better equipment, which they would actually be allowed to keep, with more training in larger units in the field, and with improved leadership, they too could be brought to a sufficiently high state of readiness to substitute quickly for any active units that might be drawn into the Rapid Deployment Forces. Additional costs would be entailed, but no additional active-duty personnel; further inducements might also have to be offered to increase the number of volunteers for the Guard and Reserve ground forces. They would be well worth their cost if they contributed to increased flexibility in U.S. nonnuclear capabilities.

Other precautionary measures should also be considered. The base from which to increase military personnel has fallen into disrepair, and the ability to expand the production of military goods rapidly has weakened, partly because of resource constraints and other priorities, but also because of the view that any major conventional conflict would either be short or quickly escalate to an even shorter nuclear exchange. Because of the uncertainties ahead and the growing doubts about this view, the U.S. lack of basic preparedness now seems an unnecessary risk. Prudence suggests that the United States should be ready to expand its nonnuclear capabilities. The Carter administration is already proposing that the selective service system be restored and, perhaps too hastily, calling for a limited form of pre-draft registration. A number of other measures may be needed as well. If use is to be made of any additional personnel provided by selective service, the military training base and other facilities will have to be expanded. Also, it should be decided which is the most efficient process at present: to increase the production of existing military goods and stockpile them to equip new units if they are formed or to create the kind of standby "shadow" production facilities that served the British so well in 1939 and 1940, when they had to speed up their production of aircraft and other weapons. Developing designs and plans for weapon systems and other military goods that can be mass-produced in short periods of time by relatively unskilled labor should be considered too. Americans have become the medieval craftsmen of the weapons world. So long as the armed forces are limited to around two million people, perhaps it makes sense to provide them with exotic capabilities that spend more time in the repair shop than on the combat line. With massive mobilization, this would no longer do. Some degree of quality would have to be forgone in favor of the quantity that stood America in such good stead in past wars. Finally, as the administration recognizes, mobilization procedures need to be practiced and improved to prepare not only for a major international crisis, but also for the more protracted but still rapid buildup that the 1980s may require.

Conclusion

In 1979, when the most recent debate on U.S. defenses began, it focused on SALT and the state of the strategic nuclear forces. Since that time the appearance and disappearance of the Soviet combat brigade in Cuba, the seizure of American hostages and the turmoil in Iran, the Vietnamese military activities along the borders of Thailand, and the Soviet invasion of Afghanistan have refocused attention on the U.S. nonnuclear posture.

Although this cannot help but be a healthy development, it is still necessary to make sure that U.S. nuclear forces have the numbers, accuracy, reliability, survivability, and flexibility to maintain their essential second-strike role. As far as can be foreseen, continuation of the Trident, cruise-missile, and MX programs should provide the necessary confidence that the Soviet Union will never see any advantage in launching nuclear attacks on the United States and its allies. The stalemate, in short, should hold.

The Soviet Union may be foolish enough to believe either that a tactical nuclear campaign can be conducted for more than a few hours or that it can be "won" without unacceptable damage and rapid escalation. If so, the United States already deploys the forces to deny them any plausible objectives, although a good case can be made for modernizing and improving the survivability of these forces. Whatever is done with the strategic and tactical nuclear forces, however, it is essential that the United States and its allies recognize that they cannot realistically rely on these nuclear capabilities except to deter the use of nuclear weapons by others—an entirely feasible task and a credible stance. They must also acknowledge that great reliance needs to be placed on conventional forces to defend against and hence to deter the more traditional forms of attack.

Accepting this reliance is difficult not because the Soviet Union is overwhelmingly strong in nonnuclear capabilities or because a more sensible nuclear policy will tempt it to exercise this strength any more than in the past. Instead, it is because, as the Soviet position improves and revolutionary ferment spreads, more military threats to U.S. commitments could arise than this country is now equipped to handle.

Current difficulties can be overcome to some degree by completing the modernization programs for the nonnuclear forces and by improving the combat readiness and increasing the long-range mobility of existing forces. But owing to the way in which U.S. forces are deployed and the commitments the United States has made, it may become necessary to go beyond the administration's five-year defense program to be able to deal simultaneously with at least one major contingency and several lesser ones. If the United States is not prepared for such a possibility, it might find in an emergency—as it discovered in late 1979 and early 1980—that it could not readily provide as many deployments as it wanted or sustain them for as long as the situation demanded.

As noted, the Carter administration plans to increase total obligational authority by an average of 4.6 percent a year in real terms over the coming five years. But even if it is decided that any short-term need for additional forces and mobility can be met by bringing selected reserve units to a higher state of readiness, these increases may not prove to be sufficient.

It will no doubt be said that despite the occasional Soviet aberration, such as the attempt to control unruly neighbors in Afghanistan, the problems of the 1980s will not yield to military solutions. In the many instances where strictly local economic, social, and political grievances result in widespread unrest, that claim will prove well founded, at least as far as the application of U.S. military power is concerned. There nonetheless remain many functions that U.S. military power can perform in a world that seems headed toward greater instability. It can help to deter the overt use of external force against the United States and its friends; it can defend those friends and U.S. citizens abroad if deterrence fails; and if U.S. nonnuclear forces are equal to their tasks, they can—along with flexible, second-strike nuclear forces—keep America and its friends a safe distance from the terrors of nuclear warfare. Because of the existence of U.S. military power, and in some instances its presence, local governments can reject external threats with confidence and deal more compassionately with strictly internal problems. Military power may not be (and almost certainly is not) a sufficient condition of international stability in the areas of U.S. commitment. But it is a necessary condition. It affords this country the opportunity and the time to use the other measures on which it prefers to rely—diplomatic, economic, legal, and administrative. Without it, nothing much is likely to work at all.

When international politics are relatively placid, Americans like to pretend that the Russians are somewhat distorted mirror-images of themselves. When the amenities of détente are being followed, they like to relax, neglect their defense, and act as though the world were a safer place than the District of Columbia. When the Soviet Union emerges from its shroud of secrecy and uses its military power with deception and brutality, Americans become outraged and overreact. On these occasions, and for six months thereafter, they remember (perhaps too well) the rise of Hitler and the lack of European and American preparedness, or the charge of the North Koreans across the 38th Parallel and the desperate measures that a virtually disarmed America had to take to stop it. The tendency then is to try to make up for past neglect, which gives the impression that Americans can think and act in military terms only.

The last reality to be acknowledged, however, is that, whether the Soviet leaders differ from Hitler or not, the process the world is engaged in today differs greatly from that of the 1930s. The United States and its allies are neither as weak nor as bemused as they were then. The fear of nuclear warfare hangs over aggressor and victim alike in a way that strategic bombing never did. And the Soviet Union thus far appears more cautious and less demon-ridden than Hitler, more willing to give "the forces of history" a healthy push than to risk everything on a single throw of the dice, especially when the dice are not heavily loaded in its favor.

The United States may need more ready strength (and military skill) to deal with this alien force. But this will not reduce the need for it to continue what will remain a delicate but protracted balancing act. Despite Afghanistan, despite Sakharov, the United States cannot abandon its efforts to reassure the Russians of its respect for their legitimate security interests. Nor can it fail to maintain at the ready (and expand as necessary) the nonnuclear power required to constrain those Soviet fears and ambitions that infringe on long-standing U.S. and allied interests.

The balancing act will not be easy to perform, but the 1980s will demand no less. Great responsibility will continue to go with great power. Now is none too soon to behave accordingly.

CHAPTER TEN

The Middle East

WILLIAM B. QUANDT

THE 1980s will be a decade of unparalleled change, development, and quite probably international conflict in the Middle East. This region, because of its location, its history, and its resources has always attracted the interest of outside powers, and in the 1980s it is certain to be the arena of intense U.S.-Soviet strategic and economic competition. These outside pressures will severely test the capabilities of the states in the region to pursue their preferred courses of national development, and will place an extraordinary premium on statesmanship if superpower confrontation is to be avoided.

The Regional Setting

The strategic environment in the Middle East in the decade of the 1980s will stem in large measure from a series of crucial developments in the last years of the 1970s. Of cardinal importance was the collapse of the imperial regime in Iran in early 1979 and its replacement by a self-styled, militant Islamic republic. This, coupled with the Soviet invasion of Afghanistan in December 1979, raised the danger of instability in the largest oil-producing area of the world. The second development of particular significance was the achievement of the peace treaty between Egypt and Israel, a development that set off shock waves in much of the Arab world and brought particular pres-

I am grateful to Ellen N. Pyda for typing the manuscript.

sures to bear on the conservative monarchical regime in Saudi Arabia. The third development was the return of power to the oil cartel of the Organization of Petroleum Exporting Countries (OPEC), a power demonstrated by the doubling of oil prices in one year, from less than $13 per barrel in December 1978 to an average of over $26 at the end of 1979. The upward escalation of oil prices, and the rapid infusion of billions of dollars into the underdeveloped economies and societies of key Middle Eastern countries, is bound to have unsettling and unpredictable consequences for the region. Among other things, a new hierarchy of super-rich countries coexisting with some of the poorest countries in the world is now a fact of life in the Middle East. How long this can continue, given the fragility of many of the oil-rich regimes, is open to question.

Developments in Iran

Whatever the historical verdict on the Pahlavi regime in Iran, the fall of the shah in February 1979 and the creation of an Islamic republic under Ayatollah Ruhollah Khomeini will be viewed as a watershed in Middle Eastern history. For the region as a whole, the most immediate consequence was a change in the local balance of power. Iran, which was acquiring weapons at an astounding pace and developing the strongest military establishment in the region, was suddenly reduced to near impotence. This has created new uncertainties in the Persian Gulf, where Iran was both feared and respected for its power. Iran was strongly committed under the shah to a Western orientation and used its power on behalf of conservative regimes in the region. The new Islamic republic of Iran, whatever its ideological preferences, no longer has the military might to enforce its will in the surrounding region. And it will take many years to reestablish the position of power that the shah's Iran reached in the late 1970s.

Iran also served the United States as a strategic ally, allowing sensitive intelligence installations to be located on Iranian soil. The new regime adopted a policy of nonalignment, and the United States lost access to strategically important facilities that had contributed to monitoring Soviet strategic weaponry development. This loss has clouded, for the short term, prospects of successfully negotiating and ratifying strategic arms agreements with the Soviet Union.

Further, Iran's new orientation dictated a policy of nonreliance on foreign technicians to help with the management of its primary resource—oil. As a result, Iranian oil production plummeted from about 6 million barrels a day in the late 1970s, to an average of only half that under the Islamic republic in its first year. This removed a significant fraction of oil from the world market, created artificial shortages, and set the stage for massive price increases in 1979. There was little reason to believe that production would return to the high levels maintained by the shah, and many expected that Iran would find it difficult to keep production even at 3 million barrels per day.

Iran's loss of military and economic strength has created a new balance of power in which its immediate neighbor, Iraq, assumes much greater influence in the Persian Gulf. Iraq's position is by no means totally secure because it has internal weaknesses, including a large part of its population that feels unrepresented by the current government. Nonetheless, Iraq enjoyed a degree of political continuity in the 1970s, which allowed for positive internal economic development and the building of a strong military establishment. Oil income is high and appears likely to rise, and Iraq, as a result, is certain to be a dominant influence in the Gulf region in the 1980s. Already it is apparent that countries such as Jordan and Saudi Arabia are paying more attention to Iraqi policy than at any time in the past. Iraq, formerly isolated in inter-Arab councils, has played an active role in shaping a tough-minded Arab consensus in opposition to Egypt and the United States.

For the United States, the fall of the shah has led to considerable rethinking of Middle Eastern priorities and policies. During most of the 1970s the shah was the recipient of extraordinary quantities of American arms. Iran was the primary beneficiary in the Middle East of the so-called Nixon doctrine approach to regional problems. Growing out of the Vietnam conflict, this view maintains that the United States cannot afford to supervise directly all its global interests, and therefore it needs to encourage and strengthen regional allies who could play a stabilizing role on behalf of American interests. The shah was an enthusiastic supporter of this concept and enjoyed giving the impression that Iran was an emerging power of great strategic importance to the United States. The one concrete example of the contribution of Iran's power to regional stability was the dispatch of an Iranian brigade to Oman in 1975 to help suppress the Dhofar insurgency.

The shah's downfall, however, has called into question the underlying logic of the Nixon doctrine. If a country as powerful and as developed as Iran could not play a regional peacekeeping role in partnership with the United States, what other country in the region could? Increasingly, Washington is placing emphasis on the need for an American military capability to defend U.S. interests rather than depend on regional surrogates. In addition, the mood in the United States opposing activities abroad has begun to shift, and a more permissive environment can be expected in the 1980s if some form of U.S. diplomatic or even military intervention in the Middle East seems to be in the national interest.

Both the Soviet Union and the United States seemed to be surprised by the developments in Iran, but unlike the United States, the Soviets were short-term beneficiaries of the new situation. Initially, they supported the Islamic revolution. Subsequently, they labeled the Khomeini regime reactionary, although they strongly encouraged the Islamic Republic in its anti-American policy. Khomeini's inability to consolidate power raised the prospect that the Soviets might increasingly throw their support behind one of the disparate groups on the left, or behind the various regional separatist movements such as those in Azerbaijan, the Kurdish areas, Baluchistan, or even the oil-producing region of Khuzistan. In the event of a prolonged period of anarchy in Iran, during which strong regional separatist movements might develop, the Soviets may become involved on behalf of any of these groups.

The Egyptian-Israeli Peace Treaty

The most threatening dimension of the Arab-Israeli conflict was the Egyptian-Israeli dispute. Of all Israel's Arab neighbors, only Egypt possessed a military capability that could pose a real danger to Israel. It was Egypt, under the leadership of President Gamal Abdel Nasser, which successfully mobilized much of the Arab world behind the crusade against Western colonialism and Zionism. This entailed an opening to the Soviet Union as a supplier of arms and political support. Indeed, it was the Soviet presence in Egypt in 1970 that brought the conflict to one of its most dangerous levels.

The achievement of peace between Egypt and Israel was a landmark in the history of the Middle East. It was welcomed as a contribution to stability, to removing or at least reducing the risk of war, and to opening the way to normal, peaceful relations between Israel and the Arab world. It further held the promise that Egypt would be able to turn its resources and energies to improving its own society and economy, a long overdue task.

But critics of the peace treaty were numerous, especially in the Arab world, but also in Europe. Some thought that the removal of Egypt from the confrontation with Israel would ensure that the remaining issues in dispute—the future of the Palestinians, the Syrian front, and southern Lebanon—would never be seriously addressed. The Saudis in particular were apprehensive that a separate Egyptian-Israeli peace would leave much of the Arab world subject to radical influences and would ultimately prove to be destabilizing.

The treaty is likely to pave the way for normal relations between Egypt and Israel, although the scope for genuine cooperation between these two countries may be limited. President Anwar Sadat seems determined to carry out the provisions of the peace treaty; and in return, Israel will withdraw from all Egyptian territory. This process will take several years to complete, and there is always the chance that it could stall in mid-course, or that a successor regime might be less committed to peace than President Sadat appears to be. Nonetheless, the prospects for a lasting peace between Egypt and Israel are remarkably good.

President Sadat has been the architect of Egypt's shift in foreign policy toward the West and away from the Soviet Union and confrontation with Israel, even at the expense of his relations with his Arab neighbors. The key to Sadat's strategy seems to be his belief that the United States can offer Egypt more than any other power can.

The United States has not only been able to use its influence with Israel to mediate an Egyptian-Israeli peace treaty, but it also represents the source of scientific, technological, economic, and military assistance for Egypt's future. President Sadat appears to be fascinated by the prospects of gaining access to American technology, both for rebuilding Egypt's economy and strengthening its military forces. He knows that the condition for large-scale aid to Egypt from the United States is observance of the peace treaty with Israel. Any breach in the treaty with Israel would immediately call into question American support for Egypt on the scale that Sadat desires. This is a powerful incentive for President Sadat to fulfill the terms of the treaty with Israel in good faith.

Sadat's desire for a close strategic relationship with the United

States also helps to explain his conduct in inter-Arab relations. Although the United States may consider it desirable for Egypt to maintain close relations with Saudi Arabia, this has not necessarily been Sadat's perception. Since spring 1979 he has let few opportunities pass to provoke the Saudis. This has resulted in the suspension of virtually all official assistance from Saudi Arabia to Egypt, and many observers have been perplexed by Sadat's apparent indifference to this development.

While Sadat was not adverse to the aid the Saudis provided, he did not want to accept any strings that might have been attached. In addition, his hopes for large-scale American aid were not fully consistent with a continuation of sizable Saudi financial assistance to Egypt. From this perspective, Egypt, having isolated itself politically in the Arab world, having taken significant risks for peace, and having no other prospects for economic assistance, could count on generous American aid. It almost seemed that Sadat took U.S.-Israeli relations as something of a model. The Israelis were isolated in the region, without other potential donors, and the United States had no real choice but to help Israel in those circumstances.

Sadat has attempted to turn Egypt's isolation into an advantage in his dialogue with the United States, adding a new dimension by arguing that a strong Egypt, with American support, could become a factor for stability in the entire Middle East. Accordingly, Egypt, even more than Israel, could be a strategic asset for the United States. It could extend its influence as far as Sudan, the Horn of Africa, and possibly the Arabian peninsula. Sadat spoke boldly of bringing Egyptian military power to bear against such unpleasant regimes as those in Libya, South Yemen, and elsewhere. He advertised Egypt's willingness to support Oman, Morocco, and the Gulf emirates if they were to come under threat from radical forces. Offers were made to the United States to use Egyptian military facilities at some future time. Occasional arms shipments to Somalia and Morocco served as concrete evidence of Sadat's regional ambitions.

All this was designed to make an impression on American officials, especially on the congressional leaders who would be asked to support increases in aid for Egypt. On the whole, Sadat's strategy was quite successful. In fiscal 1980 Egypt was able to count on nearly $1 billion in economic assistance, and over $2.5 billion worth of credits over a three-year period for the purchase of military equipment. In September 1979 for the first time Egypt received sophisticated combat aircraft from the United States. The F-4 Phantom aircraft was flown in the ceremonies commemorating the outbreak of the October 1973 war. Shortly thereafter, the United States promised in January 1980 to provide Egypt with as many as eighty F-16 fighters.

President Sadat's attempt to present Egypt to the United States as a strategic asset may succeed in generating large amounts of assistance. But there are dangers in relying on Egypt's role as a regional peacekeeper. Egypt's capacity for military action outside its borders is relatively limited. In the 1960s Egypt sent over 50,000 troops to North Yemen, but they were unable to tip the political balance in favor of a friendly regime. It may be equally difficult in the 1980s for Egypt to send effective aid to other Arab countries far afield. Perhaps Sudan will be an exception; Egyptian interests are substantial there, and previous experience suggests that limited military action in support of a regime in Khartoum can be effective.

Serious dangers would lie ahead if Sadat were to launch his American-equipped military into reckless adventures against other countries, particularly those such as Libya that have strong Soviet support. If Egyptian forces were thrown into battle without prospects of rapid success, one might anticipate a mounting degree of frustration within the Egyptian military establishment, a development that could bring political problems to the Sadat regime. Thus, as much as Egypt may wish to present itself to the world as a dominant power in the Middle East and North Africa, the United States has no interest in feeding illusions of a major Egyptian peacekeeping role in the region.

Nonetheless, a friendly regime in Egypt can mean a partner for the United States in developing the capacity to respond to some kinds of contingencies in the region, and on that level U.S.-Egyptian cooperation may develop smoothly. In some circumstances, access to Egyptian airfields, ports, and transit through Egyptian airspace might be of importance for the United States if it were anxious to send support to a country in the Arabian peninsula. In this sense, Egypt may offer valuable strategic assistance to the United States.

If Sadat has set himself an objective of consolidating a close military and economic relationship with the United States, does this necessarily mean that he has no interest in resuming normal ties with

Saudi Arabia? For the moment, there are no signs that Sadat is prepared to pay any price for the resumption of Saudi aid. He seems to believe that if and when rapprochement is desirable, it can be effected essentially on Egyptian terms. Insofar as Saudi Arabia is important to his larger regional designs, Sadat appears to assume that the United States can deal with the Saudis. Nonetheless, one can sense in Egypt an uneasiness about the breach between Egypt and the richest Arab state. Many Egyptians also favor better relations with Saudi Arabia because of its important role in the Islamic world and particularly because of its role as guardian of the holy places of Mecca and Medina. As Islamic sentiment in Egypt is strengthened, so is the desire for improved relations with Saudi Arabia. At some point, this may prompt Sadat to seek reconciliation with the Saudis. He seems confident that there will not be a permanent breach.

While much of Egyptian foreign policy can be explained in terms of the normal pursuit of Egyptian national interest, there is no question that President Sadat has personalized Egyptian foreign policy to a remarkable degree. None of his advisers encouraged him in his historic initiatives for peace, beginning with his trip to Jerusalem in fall 1977. Most of his associates were more concerned with Egypt's relations with the rest of the Arab world than with the benefits to Egypt of the Egyptian-Israeli peace treaty. Few of them have appeared to appreciate Sadat's larger strategic design.

This does not, however, mean that Egyptian foreign policy would move in radically different directions if Sadat were no longer in charge. The commitment to peace with Israel, the shift away from dependence on the Soviet Union, and the desire for closer relations with the West, particularly the United States, have found support in Egypt at all levels. This is largely because of the expectation that peace will bring tangible economic benefits to Egypt.

Precisely this concern with improving the domestic situation in Egypt could lead a successor regime toward renewed cooperation with Saudi Arabia and the Arab states of the Gulf. After all, nearly one million Egyptian workers are employed outside Egypt—primarily in Libya and Saudi Arabia—and their remittances are a major source of hard currency for Egypt. In 1979 nearly $2 billion flowed into Egypt from the earnings of these Egyptian workers abroad. Many Egyptian planners fear that continued strain in Egypt's relations with the rest of the Arab world will lead to an eventual replacement of Egyptian workers by non-Egyptians, thereby cutting off Egypt from that source of income. Many would therefore like to see a restoration of good relations with Saudi Arabia.

From Israel's point of view, it gained a genuine degree of security from the peace relationship with Egypt. Israel's military and security problems are greatly simplified by Egypt's removal from a posture of hostility. This was the main strategic objective of the Israelis in the peace treaty negotiations with Egypt, and the final result of the negotiations came close to meeting the Israeli preference for a separate peace—that is, a peace treaty with Egypt that is not conditional upon further moves toward peace on other fronts.

Israel did, however, commit herself in the course of the Camp David negotiations to peace talks on the future of the West Bank and Gaza. Although these talks are independent of the peace treaty with Egypt, they nonetheless could affect Israel's relations both with Egypt and the United States. According to the Camp David Accords and the subsequent agreement between Egypt and Israel, the negotiations for self-government for the West Bank and Gaza inhabitants should be concluded by May 1980. How to proceed in those negotiations has been the subject of controversy in Israel, and the Begin government has found it difficult to develop credible proposals for granting genuine autonomy to the Palestinians in the West Bank and Gaza. And the Egyptians have not gone much beyond articulating broad principles.

The slow pace of negotiations and the ambiguity concerning Israel's ultimate objective led to the resignation of Foreign Minister Moshe Dayan in October 1979. With his departure, doubts were raised concerning Israel's ability under Begin's government to address the Palestinian question constructively. There were few who believed that the Camp David Accords could be implemented by mid-1980. The weakness of the Begin government added to the difficulties of reaching results in the course of the negotiations.

The lack of progress in the peace negotiations, coupled with a continuation of Israel's policy of establishing settlements in the occupied West Bank and Gaza, are likely to add some strain to U.S.-Israeli relations. Periodic disagreements over the use of American-supplied arms in Lebanon also has had an adverse impact on relations between the Carter administration and Israel. Nonetheless, the basic U.S.-Israeli relationship remains remarkably strong, with high levels of economic and military assistance continuing to flow to Israel.

OPEC's Reassertion of Power

In 1979 there was a dramatic reassertion by OPEC of its power to raise international petroleum prices. Only once before, in 1973, had that organization succeeded in pushing prices dramatically high. From 1974 through 1978 it had done little more than maintain the real dollar value of petroleum in the face of spiraling inflation. But in 1979, in large part because of the panic created by the temporary halting of Iranian production late in 1978, OPEC dictated a 100 percent increase in the price of crude oil. Even this increase left the OPEC price well below the spot market, where prices reached more than $40 a barrel.

Significant price differentials existed among the OPEC countries; Saudi Arabia sold oil for most of the last half of 1979 at about $18 a barrel, while other producers were able to obtain from $23 to $25 a barrel for their highest quality crude. Thus, although individual members of OPEC were able to push prices to high levels, the organization itself was unable to discipline its membership to adhere to a common pricing schedule.

At the December 1979 meeting in Caracas, the differential price pattern continued. The Saudis held to a price of $24 a barrel, as others sought prices of $30 or more for their premium crudes. In the absence of significant production cuts, it was widely believed that these prices would lead to a greater supply of oil than demand by spring 1980. That could bring prices down somewhat, or create an unprecedented problem for OPEC of formally agreeing on prorationing of production to sustain high prices. But before agreement on prorationing could be achieved, a uniform pricing schedule would be needed.

OPEC actions in 1979 further slowed growth in the industrialized countries, forced underdeveloped countries to accumulate even more debts to pay for their oil bills, added to the inflation spiral, and put pressure on the dollar. Within the Middle East, the consequences were also dramatic. Some countries saw their revenues rise significantly, particularly Iraq, Saudi Arabia, the United Arab Emirates, Libya, and Algeria. Iran was able to earn as much revenue from oil production of 3 million barrels a day in 1979 as it had from producing 6 million barrels a day in earlier years.

The lesson was not lost that greater income could be gained with less production, and a number of countries, particularly Kuwait and Libya, announced plans to reduce production. Contrary to many expectations, the Saudis decided to keep production at high levels throughout 1979, resulting in an average of 9.5 million barrels a day for the last half of 1979. This generated sufficient income for Saudi Arabia to restore its balance of payments to a surplus position, following a two-year period in which expenditures exceeded revenues. Whether the Saudis will maintain such high levels of production into the 1980s is an open question. In any case, modest cuts by a number of other oil producers could offset any expansion of Saudi output. In the future, a number of oil-producing nations acting individually or collectively will have the capacity to keep the petroleum market sufficiently tight to ensure continued high prices.

Saudi Arabia has clearly been the dominant power within OPEC on pricing decisions in the past. By increasing their production, the Saudis have been able to moderate prices. In previous periods of potential glut, they have cut back to ensure that prices would not tumble. As the 1980s unfold, however, that nation is likely to be in a less commanding position to dictate its preferences to other OPEC members. Its ability to increase production depends upon large investments in developing and maintaining its oil fields. Little evidence exists that Saudi Arabia has made a determined commitment to expand production much above the current maximum sustainable capacity of 10.5 million barrels a day. The Saudis talk of an ultimate goal of 12 million barrels a day by the early 1980s, but there is no apparent inclination to exceed that level. Without such spare capacity, Saudi Arabia will be unable to meet modest increases in demand or to increase production temporarily to keep prices from escalating to unreasonably high levels; and it will not have the capacity to help meet emergency situations, such as the possibility that Iranian production might once again drop to nearly zero.

The Saudis have also lost some of their flexibility to cut production in order to maintain high prices. Unless the production cuts result in significantly increased prices, they would be taking a net loss in revenue, while some of their regional rivals, particularly Iraq and Iran, might profit at their expense. The Saudis have little desire to forgo current income, particularly with their present high levels of spending.

Despite all the concern with surplus "petrodollars" in the mid-1970s, the Saudis have learned to spend and invest their oil income, even though that income has been accelerating at remarkable rates. It is unlikely that they will curtail current spending and drastically reduce oil production. If this analysis is correct, their realistic choices range from a low of perhaps 8 million barrels a day to a high of more than 10 million barrels a day.

Why does Saudi Arabia deny itself the option of increasing oil production? One explanation is that the Saudis want to conserve their resources far into the future. While this is undoubtedly true, it does not explain why a higher productive capacity is not being developed to meet temporary emergencies, even if Saudi Arabia prefers to produce at lower rates as a long-term average. Another explanation, which is gaining increasing support, is that an installed capacity to produce 12 or 14 million barrels a day of oil will mean that Saudi Arabia may be subjected to intense pressures from the Western countries, particularly the United States, to maintain that level of output. At the same time, the Saudis will also be subject to pressures from their OPEC partners to refrain from using their full capacity because of the dangers that this would create surpluses and soften prices. To reduce such pressures, the Saudis seem to be deliberately narrowing their range of options. Unless the United States can find new incentives for them to invest the billions of dollars necessary to increase productive capacity, Saudi Arabia seems determined to keep its maximum capacity lower than the Western world would like in the 1980s.

Apart from the dilemmas that the new oil prices and demands for increased production pose for Saudi Arabia, other countries in the region are also affected by the continuing escalation of oil prices. A substantial gap is emerging between the "oil rich" and the "oil poor." A look at Iraq and Syria is instructive. The two countries have populations similar in size, Iraq being somewhat larger. Both have relatively good agricultural resources and comparable social and political problems. Both have developed large armed forces, primarily with Soviet assistance. But on most indicators, such as per capita income, education, literacy, and development spending within the country, Iraq is now far ahead of Syria.

If these trends continue, Iraq will become a much more powerful country in the region than Syria, and may seriously challenge others in the region as well. Even smaller countries, such as Libya, are able to use their oil revenues to develop large military forces and to conduct aggressive and often troublesome foreign policies. Those without substantial oil resources, such as Egypt, North Yemen, and Jordan, are finding a large part of their work force migrating to the oil-rich countries to earn higher salaries. This trend has ambiguous consequences. On the one hand, it leads to the repatriation of a large amount of income to Egypt, North Yemen, and Jordan. But it also creates manpower shortages in critical sectors of their economies, such as construction in Egypt, which may exert a constraining effect on longer term development.

From the perspective of the Middle East, oil developments reinforce other trends that are making the Gulf an important arena of potential conflict. The superpowers are showing increasing interest in this region, and the oil producers are anxious about their long-term viability and are seeking ways to ward off inevitable pressures that accompany immense wealth. The political turmoil in Iran has produced grave uncertainty, compounded by the emergence of Iraq as the most powerful regional actor. All these trends suggest that the Persian Gulf in the 1980s will be a region of intense international competition, possible instability, and great danger to the economic health of the world, as well as to the prospects for international stability.

Current Issues

In this strategic setting in the Middle East, several issues will take on new forms in the 1980s. On the cultural and political levels, one can anticipate changes in the nature of inter-Arab relations stemming from the erosion of the ideology of Arab nationalism, and a stronger assertiveness by sectarian and particularly Islamic sentiments. The Arab-Israeli conflict will remain important, but will be dealt with largely through diplomatic means, with emphasis on finding steps toward resolution of the Palestinian dimension of the conflict. On the military front, each superpower can be expected to try to enhance its presence in the region and to strengthen bilateral relations with individual countries by providing substantial quantities of sophisticated arms.

Ideological Trends

From the mid-1950s to the mid-1960s, nationalism was the paramount ideology professed by leaders of most Middle Eastern countries. The struggles for independence were still vivid memories, and the political elites in many countries derived their legitimacy from participation in those struggles. In the Arab world, nationalism was tinged with a commitment to social justice and populism, and some nationalists were also secularist in their basic political philosophy. Egypt's President Nasser and the Baath parties in Syria and Iraq were the main conveyors of the ideology of Arab nationalism, which for a period was a serious influence in most Arab countries. Rivaling this current of thought were always narrower political concepts, such as state nationalism or sectarianism, as well as a broader commitment to the Islamic community as a whole. But in its heyday, nationalism dominated all other ideological currents.

After 1967 Arab nationalism took a beating. Israel had defeated the combined forces of the Arab world in the 1967 war, and the Palestinians, who had depended heavily on the unity of the Arab world to help restore their rights in Palestine, began to argue that reliance on collective Arab action had been a mistake, and that the Palestinians should take matters into their own hands. Thus emerged a stronger sense of distinctive Palestinian nationalism, a noticeable departure from the earlier period.

Elsewhere in the Middle East, nationalism was also a strong current. In Iran, the shah tried to strengthen support for his regime by glorifying the Persian empire. He emphasized the Persian tradition of kingship, which had existed for 2,500 years, in contrast to the more conventional emphasis on Iran's Islamic history. He changed the calendar to one based on pre-Islamic Persian tradition, thereby alienating traditional Muslim elements in the population. But Persian nationalism was the glue that could hold the many diverse ethnic groups together in Iran, whereas Shiite Islam was a broader basis for emphasizing political solidarity but also highlighted differences between the main branches of Islam within Iran.

With the death of Egypt's President Nasser in September 1970, the folk hero of Arab nationalism was gone. His successor, Anwar Sadat,

initially pursued a foreign policy similar to that of Nasser, characterized by rhetoric about Arab nationalism and Arab unity. However, it
was increasingly clear that Sadat's Egypt would place Egyptian interests first, and Arab interests a distant second. Sadat also began to
liberalize Egypt's economic policies and seemed to be less hostile to
organized Islamic groups than Nasser had been. To some degree,
these trends could also be seen in other self-styled Arab progressive
regimes, where the emphasis was heavily on state interests, the need
for mixed economies, and greater sensitivity to traditionally influential groups. The net result was the weakening of the appeal of pan-
Arab nationalism and its replacement by a more diffuse set of political
identifications—some emphasizing the priority of individual state
interests, some building on sectarian differences, and some turning to
Islam as a source of political and moral inspiration.

Western observers tended to attribute far too much importance to
the resurgence of Islam after the fall of the shah of Iran. They neglected to note that religion has always been a powerful force within
Islamic societies, and that no distinction between religion and state
has ever been accepted by Muslims. At frequent intervals in contemporary history Islam has been a dynamic and assertive force for
change, as was the case in the reformist movements of the 1930s and,
more recently, in the events in Iran leading to the fall of the shah.

It would be a mistake to predict that Islamic revolution is the wave
of the future in the Middle East. For the near term, leaders will show
increased deference to Islamic sensibilities, and sectarian rivalries
may be somewhat exacerbated by the greater assertiveness of the
Muslim communities. The experience in Iran, however, is likely to
demonstrate that Islam does not hold all the answers for the management of complex modern societies. It has no simple solutions to the
pervasive problems of economic development, social integration, or
the reduction of disparities in wealth, education, and status.

Efforts to establish a pure Islamic order as the means to solve modern problems, like other attempts to impose rigid orthodoxies on the
mosaic societies of the Middle East, will face grave obstacles. Ultimately, Middle Eastern leaders will be obliged to recognize that no
ideology, whether socialist, capitalist, or Islamic, can resolve the
dilemmas of modernization for their societies. The process of change
will be frustrating, and those who try to reduce its complexities to
simple ideological formulations are bound to see their efforts

thwarted. In time, one can anticipate renewed efforts in Iran and elsewhere to find a balance between deference to Islamic values and the need for modern technologies and organizational skills. But recent events in Iran and elsewhere in the region suggest that the notion of secular, Western-style democratic socialist states has failed to attract the loyalties of the largely Muslim populations.

The Arab-Israeli Peace Negotiations

The Egyptian-Israeli peace treaty of March of 1979 will have a profound impact on any further negotiations between Israel and its other Arab neighbors. The Camp David agreements signed by Egypt and Israel in the fall of 1978 envisaged a two-phase peacemaking process. The first part consisted of the Egyptian-Israeli treaty, which would be implemented in stages. According to the agreements, Israel is to complete the withdrawal from all Egyptian territory by spring 1982, by which time normal relations between Egypt and Israel will be well under way. Ambassadors will be exchanged and full diplomatic relations will be established by spring 1980.

The second part of the peace process is negotiations on the Palestinian question and, in particular, on arrangements for a transitional period of five years for the West Bank and Gaza. During this transition, the Israeli military government will withdraw from the territories and will be replaced by a freely elected Palestinian self-governing authority. An Israeli security presence will remain, with its precise scale and function to be negotiated. While in principle this arrangement could be open-ended and might lead to a number of possible outcomes, the Begin government quickly narrowed its definition of self-government to preclude extensive authority in the hands of the elected Palestinian body. And Begin made clear that, at the end of five years, Israel will assert its claim to sovereignty over these areas.

It thus seems that one outcome of the transition, according to the Israeli government, may be the annexation of the West Bank and Gaza to Israel. This is an outcome that no Palestinian or Jordanian leader finds palatable, and the credibility of the Camp David approach is consequently suspect.

A second flaw, from the viewpoint of many Arabs, is that Israeli settlement activity shows no signs of decreasing during the negotiations leading up to the establishment of the Palestinian self-government. This raises the prospect that a form of creeping annexation may take place by means of settlements in the occupied territories during the transitional period. A decision of the Israeli Supreme Court in October 1979 prohibiting the seizure of private property for settlements unrelated to security gave some pause to the construction of new settlements, but leaves ample scope for continued establishment of settlements in the name of security on public lands.

In brief, while the Camp David process does not appear to be intrinsically flawed, it has failed to gain credibility with those whose participation is required to produce a positive result. There is little prospect that the Palestinians will overtly participate in the negotiating process, nor is Jordan likely to play a role. The best chance of overcoming this deep skepticism lies in the negotiations between Egypt and Israel, with U.S. participation, on the scope of authority for the self-governing body to be elected. If agreement can be reached on providing broad authority to this body, particularly control over a significant amount of land and water resources, and if the Israeli military presence in the occupied areas can be substantially reduced, it may be possible to elicit considerable interest among the West Bank-Gaza population. In that event, elections may be held, and a fairly high level of participation may be anticipated.

But only optimists see much prospect that the Camp David negotiations will lead to such a positive result. In the views of many, an unsatisfactory negotiation yielding only partial agreement is more likely. The target date for the completion of the talks is May 1980, and few believe that it will be possible to reach full agreement by that point. A weak Israeli government will be hard pressed to make difficult decisions in any case, and the American partner to the negotiations will be preoccupied with domestic political concerns. In addition, President Sadat shows little interest in the details of these negotiations. It is difficult to find any reason for optimism.

The departure from the Israeli cabinet of Foreign Minister Dayan in October 1979 raised questions about the viability of the Begin government. Some expected an early collapse of the Begin coalition and its replacement by a new government under the leadership of the Labor Party. More likely, in the view of many Israeli observers, was the continuation of the Begin government into spring 1981, but with decreasing capabilities to act in foreign policy or to deal with the drastic economic situation within the country. Elections will be held on schedule in May 1981, and it is widely assumed that the Labor

Party will return to power at that point. That could open the way to a renewal of the peace negotiations, with greater emphasis on a negotiation with Jordan over the disposition of the West Bank. The Labor Party does not overtly oppose the notion of a transitional period based on the concept of self-government, but it is much more inclined to discuss a territorial arrangement with Jordan than is the Begin government.

As the Israeli government shows less capacity to act in foreign affairs, the Palestine Liberation Organization (PLO) seems to be gaining international recognition. European countries have routinely begun to take pro-Palestinian positions, calling for self-determination for the Palestinians and recognition of the PLO as the representative of the Palestinian people. As part of its diplomatic campaign, the PLO seems intent upon presenting itself as politically respectable, and thus there is less resort to international terrorism, although attacks continue within Israel and in the occupied territories.

The emphasis on diplomacy includes a dialogue between Jordan and the PLO, which has produced some speculation that a common position favoring Jordanian-Palestinian federation as the agreed long-term objective of the two parties might be announced. This is an idea that could receive considerable support internationally and, if backed by such important Arab countries as Saudi Arabia and Syria, could provide the basis for a new approach to negotiations.

Assuming that the Camp David negotiations will fall short of their announced objective, an alternative approach will need to be considered at some point. If by then the PLO and Jordan have developed a common position favoring confederation, and if a new Israeli government comes to power by spring 1981, a new initiative can be envisaged that will focus more clearly on the future of the West Bank and Gaza. Any positive results from the Camp David negotiations concerning the nature of a transitional period could still be useful, because inevitably the need will arise for a staged transition from the present situation to an eventual territorial compromise involving Israel, Jordan, and the Palestinians.

For the United States, the negotiation of further peace accords between Israel and its Arab neighbors is likely to receive less priority in the future than it did during President Carter's first two years in office. In part, this will be because Egypt and Israel have already made peace. In addition, the focus of American policy in the Middle East is shifting toward the Persian Gulf. But it is precisely because of the concern for the Gulf, and particularly for Saudi Arabia, that the United States will not be able to ignore the question of the Palestinians entirely.

Although no Arab country places Palestinian interests at the top of its list of priorities, there is concern in Saudi Arabia and elsewhere in the region that the Palestinians can be a destabilizing and disruptive force if their political aspirations are continually frustrated. The Saudis, in addition, have a deep interest in the future of Jerusalem, and they will find it difficult to acquiesce in total Israeli control of the third most important city for Muslims. Thus the American preoccupation with stability in the Persian Gulf and the Arabian peninsula will reinforce U.S. concern with the Arab-Israeli conflict, and particularly its Palestinian dimension.

At some point, new initiatives will be required that will broaden the scope of the peace process beyond that envisaged at Camp David. In particular, some effort will be required to build support for a settlement policy based more clearly on the terms of reference of U.N. Resolution 242—withdrawal of Israeli armed forces from territories occupied in the 1967 war in return for real peace and security. Most of the international community does not accept the argument put forward by the Begin government that Resolution 242 does not apply to the West Bank and Gaza. Reemphasis of the principles of this resolution will lie at the heart of any new U.S. peace initiative, and by returning the focus to the questions of territory, security, and peace, the United States will have a chance of gaining support from Jordan, Saudi Arabia, and even Syria.

U.S.-Soviet Rivalry

The combination of oil, instability, and weak regimes in the Gulf ensures that outside powers, most importantly the United States and the USSR, will seek to assert influence through direct and indirect means. Although superpower competition in this region is hardly novel, it is likely to take on new military dimensions in the 1980s. In part this is because of the impressive development of Soviet capabilities for projecting power overseas, and in part it will stem from a renewed American sense of the need to wed power with diplomacy in protection of vital energy supplies.

On the periphery of the energy heartland, the Soviets have developed positions of strength that enhance their ability to use or to threaten the use of force. In South Yemen and Ethiopia the Soviet military presence is particularly impressive. The port of Aden is available to Soviet ships, which more than offsets the loss of the base in Somalia in 1978; Soviet communications facilities exist; the Soviets can use local airfields to conduct reconnaissance flights and to refuel transport aircraft. A large number of combat-tested Cuban troops are in Ethiopia, available for redeployment elsewhere if circumstances require it. In addition, the Soviets and the East Germans are reportedly deeply involved in organizing the security and intelligence services of these two Marxist regimes.

The Soviets have also dramatically deepened their military involvement in Afghanistan, including the sending of about 80,000 combat troops. In December 1979 Soviet forces actively led a coup to replace one communist leader with another more to their liking. In the process, Soviet armed forces virtually occupied the country and assumed a role in fighting Muslim insurgents. It may prove difficult to pacify the countryside, but the Soviets seem determined to keep a friendly regime in power. And with a strong foothold in Afghanistan, the Soviets may hope to extend their influence to Pakistan and Iran in the near future.

The Soviet presence may be less securely rooted in Libya, but is nonetheless significant. Large quantities of modern Soviet arms have been delivered there, including over 100 MiG-23 fighter aircraft and over 1,000 tanks. These numbers greatly exceed Libyan capabilities, which suggests that these arms have been pre-positioned for possible use elsewhere in the region. Alternatively, they may be meant to deter an Egyptian attack on Libya and could be quickly joined by Soviet or Cuban advisers if necessary. In either event, Libya contains an impressive arsenal of well-maintained Soviet equipment for which the Soviets receive much-needed hard currency.

In contrast to the military buildup along the periphery of the Arabian peninsula and Persian Gulf, the Soviets have maintained more conventional arms supply relations with Syria and Iraq. These ties provide the Soviets with some access to Syrian and Iraqi facilities, but neither arms recipient has proved to be a particularly reliable regional ally. The two Baathist regimes have remained remarkably independent in their foreign policies and have been particularly sensitive to any signs of Soviet intervention in their domestic affairs through local Communist parties.

Although Soviet naval strength has been growing in recent years, deployments in the Indian Ocean and Arabian Sea are still relatively modest. But both superpowers seem to be moving toward larger and more frequent naval visits to the region and access to permanent bases.

Complementing Soviet naval strength as an instrument of policy in the region is the impressive airlift capability of the USSR. Demonstrating its effectiveness first in the October 1973 Arab-Israeli war, the Soviets delivered large quantities of arms on short notice during the Ethiopian-Somali war in 1977. Aden proved to be a convenient transshipment point during that operation. In December 1979 the Soviets again used their airlift to move troops quickly into Afghanistan.

As an additional element of their military presence, the Soviets continue to be active in arms sales in the Middle East. Soviet aircraft, armor, artillery, and missiles have found their way into the inventories of Algeria, Libya, Ethiopia, South Yemen, North Yemen, Iraq, Syria, and Afghanistan. In each case, the arms are accompanied by advisers and training programs. And although arms do not automatically buy influence, they do establish a form of dependency, earn hard currency for the Soviets, and provide a particularly valuable point of entry into key institutions of the recipient countries. Egypt has shown that it is possible to switch arms suppliers, but the Egyptian example also demonstrates what a difficult and prolonged effort is needed to restructure an army equipped by the Soviets into one with arms supplied by the West.

To meet the growing Soviet military presence in the Middle East, the United States is planning to increase its naval capabilities in the Arabian Sea and to develop a rapid deployment force that could be sent to the area on short notice.

Not long after the fall of the shah's regime, a decision was made in Washington to expand by three to five ships the Middle East Force that operates out of Bahrain. Subsequently, naval units from the Pacific and Mediterranean fleets were sent to the Indian Ocean and Arabian Sea for frequent patrols.

Another step in U.S. military planning was sparked by the Iranian seizure of American citizens in November 1979. The public mood created by that crisis made it politically wise for President Carter to ask for increased defense spending, some of which was earmarked for the rapid deployment force. In addition, initiatives were taken to explore the possibilities of acquiring access to air and naval facilities in the area. Some officials favored full-fledged bases, while others emphasized alternative means of enhancing U.S. power in the region. The island of Masirah off the coast of Oman was one candidate. The airfields in Sinai were also discussed, as well as the port of Berbera in Somalia.

In addition to seeking air and sea bases in the vicinity of the Gulf, the United States has placed emphasis on the sale of arms to selected countries, especially Israel, Saudi Arabia, and Egypt. Only in Israel and Egypt do these arms transfers create a capability to intervene in other countries, and thus to change the regional balance of power. In Saudi Arabia, little more than a modest self-defense and internal security role is envisaged for its armed forces.

A major question in the military equations of the Middle East is the future of Iran. The Islamic Republic at some point will need to reopen an arms-supply relationship with the United States, the Soviet Union, or Europe. The strategic importance of this choice for Iran should not be underestimated. Whatever the source of arms, it will take years before Iran recovers its former military might. In the interim, Iraq may be strongly tempted to use its military superiority to intervene in Iranian affairs, possibly in support of autonomy for the Arabic speaking population of Khuzistan. More dangerous, the Soviet Union may be tempted to interfere directly in Iran if a leftist regime comes to power or if the country splits apart into warring provinces.

U.S. Policy Choices

During the 1980s the United States will have an overriding interest in assuring the continued supply of large quantities of petroleum from the Middle East at prices that do not wreak havoc in the international economy. Policies designed to reach this goal will have to address problems of regional instability, Soviet influence, and declining U.S. credibility. Demand for oil will have to be constrained by effective energy policies. Finally, specific countries, such as Saudi

Arabia, Iraq, and Iran, will be of particular importance in the years ahead, and the United States will need to devise policies to deal with each of them.

Containing Middle Eastern Conflicts

It has been the view in Washington that conflict in the Middle East, while to some extent inevitable, is most often a threat to Western interests. The record of the past suggests that Arab-Israeli hostilities, as well as inter-Arab quarrels, have provided openings for Soviet influence. In addition, internal upheavals have replaced moderate regimes with more extreme ones.

If the past is to provide some guidelines for the future, the United States is likely to recognize that there are limits to what it can do to resolve most disputes in the Middle East. This is particularly true in the cases of inter-Arab controversies and internal conflicts, such as those involving the Kurds. It is less true in the Arab-Israeli conflict, where the United States has demonstrated since 1973 a unique ability to promote a peaceful settlement through negotiations.

Israel's conflict with Syria, Jordan, and the Palestinians may be less tractable than its dispute with Egypt, but the United States is still the only outside power with the ability and incentive to play an effective mediating role. Whether and how to do this will be a serious policy decision for the 1980s.

Some analysts hold that U.S. interests are not vitally affected by the remaining issues in dispute between Israel and its Arab neighbors; that U.S. influence is in any case limited; and that the Israelis and Egyptians should bear the primary responsibility for stability in the eastern Mediterranean region. Such views would be compatible with continued efforts to negotiate Palestinian "autonomy" within the Camp David framework.

An alternative line of argument places more emphasis on an active, catalytic American role in promoting a Palestinian settlement. More is at stake than Israel's security, which is well assured already by the Egypt-Israel treaty. More broadly, the lack of further progress through U.S.-sponsored negotiations could lead to a radicalization of Arab politics, a decline in U.S. prestige, and eventual instability in countries such as Lebanon, Syria, and Jordan, perhaps to be followed in time by upheavals in the Persian Gulf sheikhdoms and even Saudi Arabia. Although this argument may overestimate the radicalizing potential of the Palestinians, it does accurately note that the U.S. role in working for a comprehensive Arab-Israeli peace is linked to U.S. influence in the area and the chances for stability in a number of key countries. On balance, these considerations will probably continue to influence the thinking of U.S. foreign policymakers.

The situation in Lebanon, together with the Arab-Israeli conflict, is likely to remain on Washington's agenda of problems in the Middle East. But the policy objective for the United States in Lebanon is more realistically defined as containing the dangers inherent in the Lebanese situation rather than seeking a comprehensive solution. Experience has led to low expectations. Attempts to strengthen the central government have been mostly unsuccessful. Intermittently, the United States has succeeded in persuading Israel to show restraint in south Lebanon, but no stable arrangement has yet been found. The Syrian military presence in Lebanon is part of the problem, but the country could well be plunged into civil war by its withdrawal. Thus, few good options seem available. From time to time, conflict in Lebanon is likely to erupt and to attract the attention of U.S. policymakers, but little more than periodic efforts can be anticipated to prevent the tensions in Lebanon from spilling over into the surrounding region.

Less predictable than conditions in Lebanon is a possible conflict between Iraq and Iran. Each party has ample reason to be suspicious of the other. Each is heavily armed, although Iraq currently has clear military superiority. Deep conflicts of national interest exist, apart from the ideological incompatibility of a secular Baathist regime in Baghdad and the Islamic Republic next door. Offsetting these reasons for conflict and tension are several mutual vulnerabilities. War between Iraq and Iran could be accompanied by serious damage to the oil fields of both countries. Each side also has the capability to carry out subversive activities against the other. The Kurds can be armed and assisted by each regime against the other. The Iraqis can provide aid to the Arabs of Khuzistan, and Iran can try to mobilize Iraqi Shiites against the Sunnis in Baghdad.

Added uncertainties stem from the ambiguous relations of Baghdad and Tehran with the superpowers. Iraq depends heavily on the Soviets for military equipment, but has nonetheless pursued a relatively independent policy and would not welcome a pro-Soviet regime in Iran. Nor does Iran under Khomeini's leadership seem likely to align itself with either Moscow or Washington. But his successors, especially if drawn from the military, will at some point need to develop a stable military supply arrangement with the United States, the Soviet Union, or Europe. A shift away from the United States could mean a prolonged period of comparative weakness for Tehran.

Iraq and Iran are both significant countries with which the United States has poor political relations. The dynamics of conflict between these two Middle Eastern countries, however, could provide openings for the United States to improve its position significantly. For example, a serious Iraqi military threat to Iran could enable the United States to take a position in favor of Iran's territorial integrity. Conversely, if Iran were to move sharply toward the Soviet Union, the United States might expect to improve its ties with Baghdad. Insofar as the choice in these matters is made in Washington, the thrust of U.S. policy should be to keep Iran united under centrist leadership. In strategic terms, Iran is still of greater importance to the regional balance of power than is Iraq, although the difference may be narrowing. In its preoccupation with Khomeini, the United States must not lose sight of the longer term stakes in Iran.

Another source of conflict in the area of the Gulf and Arabian peninsula that is likely to concern the United States in the 1980s is the regime in South Yemen. Allied to Moscow, under the leadership of the only ruling Communist party in the Arab world, the Aden regime is genuinely revolutionary and aspires to export its revolution to neighboring North Yemen and Oman at a minimum. Militarily, South Yemen has only modest capabilities, but these could be augmented swiftly by Soviet advisers and Cuban troops from nearby Ethiopia. Apart from conventional threats, however, the Aden leadership is experienced in other forms of political and covert warfare. Propaganda, terrorism, and assassination are all part of the South Yemeni repertoire, and the regimes in Oman and North Yemen are probably more vulnerable to these dangers than to an invasion by South Yemeni forces.

The United States is likely to become involved in the protection of North Yemen and Oman against external threats. The Saudis will probably remain the driving force behind U.S. policy toward Yemen. Although this adds some strain to U.S.-Yemeni relations, the United States will probably not risk offending the Saudis by adopting an independent policy toward Yemen. In the case of Oman, the United

States may develop an interest of its own if it succeeds in acquiring bases or facilities there. The quid pro quo would certainly be some form of increased security commitment to the regime of Omani Sultan Qabus bin Said.

Bilateral Relations

Three Middle Eastern states will receive the largest amount of U.S. economic, military, and diplomatic assistance in the 1980s: Israel, Egypt, and Saudi Arabia. The case of Israel has some unique features, largely because of the strong domestic support for that nation in the United States. This, along with the view that Israel is a stable, pro-American state in an area of turmoil, will assure that U.S. aid will continue at high levels. This will not mean total support for all Israeli policies, and periodic strains in relations are possible, but the fundamental strength of the bonds between the United States and Israel is unlikely to weaken in the 1980s.

Israel may, however, have to compete for U.S. support. Under Sadat's leadership, Egypt has succeeded in laying the groundwork for strategically significant ties with Washington. Economic aid has reached unprecedented levels, but even more remarkable is the pace of U.S.-Egyptian military cooperation. As long as Egypt remains at peace with Israel, it can expect to be handsomely rewarded by its new superpower friend. A reversion to a state of belligerency with Israel, however, could quickly undermine much of what Sadat has achieved.

Saudi Arabia will not be an aid recipient, but will be a major trading partner of the United States. Saudi oil will be sold to the United States and its Western allies in vast quantities, earning the Saudis approximately $85 billion in 1980, most of which will be spent on development and arms, given as aid to third world countries, or invested in the West.

But it is not the management of these sums that will concern the United States. It is rather the physical availability of oil, its price, and Saudi decisions on the capacity for future oil production that give U.S.-Saudi relations their importance. In return for Saudi cooperation on oil, the United States is prepared to go to great lengths to ensure Saudi security. This is appreciated by that nation, but to some extent it is also taken for granted. The Saudis look for more, particularly U.S. efforts to resolve the Palestinian issue, as the extra dimension that would justify their decisions to produce more oil than is required by internal needs. Because of these differing perceptions of national interest, the U.S.-Saudi dialogue will be a difficult one to manage throughout the 1980s.

Although each of these bilateral relations is of great importance to the United States, they do not by themselves ensure stability in the Middle East, nor do they provide an adequate shield for U.S. interests. It would be folly for the United States to entrust its interests in the Middle East to any regional power. There may be moments when friends in the region can be helpful, but the United States must be in a position to act on its own if necessary when vital interests are at stake. This is not just a matter of military forces in the region. It also involves maintaining a wide network of political relations. Despite transient differences over policies or with individual leaders, the United States cannot simply write off Syria, Iraq, Iran, and Algeria, nor can it take for granted the friendship of Jordan, the Gulf states, Oman, North Yemen, Tunisia, and Morocco. An effective U.S. policy in the Middle East will require a sensitivity to developments in each of these countries, and a willingness to help friends and to welcome relations with genuinely nonaligned countries.

Vulnerability of Energy Supplies

U.S. Middle Eastern policy in the 1980s will be affected to an unprecedented degree by world energy problems. American dependency and that of U.S. allies may well extend beyond the 1980s, but if the United States hopes to recover a degree of freedom of action in foreign policy by the end of this century, a credible and effective energy policy is essential. How to achieve this is beyond the scope of this chapter, but there are few steps that could be taken in this decade that would be of more help to U.S. policymakers struggling with the Middle East than to relieve the United States and the rest of the world of its growing vulnerability to disruptions of oil supply from that region.

The greed of the oil producers and their genuine desire not to deplete their limited sources of wealth has driven prices to levels at which incentives are overwhelming to consume less oil and to develop more energy resources outside the Middle East. In time, this may reduce the centrality of the Middle East in the world energy picture. But for the 1980s, at least, there is simply no alternative to oil from the Persian Gulf, and policymakers will have to cope with that reality.

Conclusions

The West's appetite for oil shows no sign of decreasing, and sometime during this decade the Soviets may also enter the market as importers of Middle Eastern oil. With Iran's foreign policy orientation uncertain and the Soviets deeply entrenched in neighboring Afghanistan, the prospects for a direct clash of U.S. and Soviet interests in the Persian Gulf region are consequently very high.

How, then, should the United States respond to this challenge? First, the administration should draw on its strengths. Close relations exist with Egypt and Israel. These need to be maintained and used as the pivot for moving toward a broader Arab-Israeli accommodation. This is important in its own right, as well as for the added security it may bring to the fragile regimes of the Arabian peninsula.

Second, the U.S.-Saudi relationship needs constant attention. The United States should not look to the Saudis as a pillar of the U.S. security presence in the region. Pressures on Riyadh to grant bases to the United States or to support openly the Camp David approach to solving the Palestinian issue are misdirected and could weaken the Saudi regime. Instead, U.S. policy should seek to buffer Saudi Arabia from external military threats, making clear American determination to protect Saudi territory from aggression. U.S.-Saudi military relations should also be reviewed to determine whether they are helping the regime to deal with its internal security problems.

Third, the United States does need the capability to project military power into the Persian Gulf region. This may involve improved airlift, a credible naval presence, access to port facilities, close consultations with friendly regimes in the region, some pre-positioning of equipment and logistical support, and perhaps even bases. But policymakers should bear in mind that the availability of military force is not a guarantee of influence. The Soviets, after all, made some of their most impressive political gains in the Middle East from the mid-1950s to 1970, a period of U.S. military superiority at the global level as well as in the region.

Fourth, the United States must convey to the Soviets a clear understanding of American determination to protect vital interests in the Middle East. Moscow's invasion of Afghanistan demonstrates how far the USSR is prepared to go to bolster its influence. The Soviets must pay a price for their aggressive behavior if they are to be expected to exercise restraint in the future.

Fifth, the United States must think beyond its preoccupation with Iran and Khomeini to the broader issue of ensuring that Iran does not have the same fate as Afghanistan. Within Iran, Islamic leaders, military officers, technocrats and intellectuals are potentially responsive to an American policy that helps Iran retain its unity and respects its independence. It should be clear to many Iranians that the United States is much less of a threat to their country than is the Soviet Union. Iran's orientation under a post-Khomeini regime will be a major factor in the new strategic equation of the Middle East. If the United States can devise policies to help ensure that Iran remains outside the Soviet sphere of influence, this will contribute immeasurably to the restoration of American prestige and credibility in the Middle East as a whole.

CHAPTER ELEVEN

The Soviet Challenge

HELMUT SONNENFELDT

THE 1980s began ominously with the Soviet invasion of Afghanistan. This event highlights the fact that in the decade ahead—as in the thirty-five years since World War II—the Soviet Union will be the single major foreign preoccupation for the United States. And the United States, in turn, will be the major external preoccupation for the Soviet Union. Despite dispersal of many elements of power throughout the contemporary world, these two nations will remain the most potent in military terms; conflicts between them will carry the most catastrophic risks if they escalate into war; an enormous share of national resources will be devoted by each to counter the military forces of the other; and the political values shaping the respective internal systems will remain disparate and essentially incompatible. At the same time, the size, scope, and diversity of interests of these superpowers will ensure a variety of contacts and negotiations between them in which they will continue to grope for a measure of safety and predictability in their relations, albeit from premises and for purposes that, for the most part, will continue to be widely at variance.

To say that each superpower will be thus preoccupied with the other is not, of course, to deny that each will have other concerns as well. On the contrary, the 1980s will almost certainly see the United States and the USSR intensely engaged in their respective domestic

I thank Delphenia W. Brandon for secretarial assistance.

problems, notably economic ones. Both will wrestle with a multiplicity of external issues, many of which will not yield to control. Yet the proclivity of each country to measure its strengths and weaknesses, aspirations and fears, progress and frustrations against those of the other is likely to last for years to come, undoubtedly through the decade of the 1980s.

These broad propositions must be further qualified, perhaps more so in the case of the USSR. The Soviet Union, unlike the United States, exists adjacent to another potential superpower whose future role is bound to weigh heavily on Soviet plans and prospects. Soviet leaders cannot avoid confronting the possibility that China and the United States will form a hostile coalition. Among the priorities of Soviet policy will be to seek, by enticement or threat—or, most likely, a combination of both—to prevent such a coalescence. The United States will almost certainly encounter a growing Soviet presence and influence in many parts of the world in which Americans have major interests, including areas physically close to the United States. But the United States is unlikely, if only because of geography, to face quite as daunting a problem as China presents for the Soviet Union.

Trends and Uncertainties

Although it is easy to foresee a continuing intense mutual preoccupation and interaction between the United States and the Soviet Union, the shape and content of U.S.-Soviet relations are difficult to predict. As the new decade begins, the United States has entered a period in which many of the major trends in this relationship are marked by severe uncertainties and complexities. Perhaps this has always been true at any given time since the United States and the USSR became major antagonists in international politics. But it seems to be especially true now.

Thus, even before the Afghanistan crisis led to a suspension of the U.S. Senate's consideration of the strategic arms limitation treaty (SALT II), the future of SALT and other attempts at regulating the pace and scope of U.S. and Soviet military programs by negotiation seems more clouded than ever. The expectations of many that U.S. unilateral defense efforts could be significantly aided by this method have not been met. In the 1980s the maintenance of an adequate military balance in the face of the growth of Soviet military power, and the protection of American interests against inroads by direct or political uses of that power, will continue to rest predominantly with the defense efforts of the United States and its allies. Whether, in due course, negotiated limitations can make a greater contribution to these efforts remains unclear.

Some observers speculate that the economic problems of the Soviet Union, which are reflected most visibly in a declining rate of growth, may induce Soviet leaders to reduce their military activities or to approach negotiations with greater eagerness or less one-sided objectives. History, however, offers little comfort on this score: economic constraints have always been severe for the USSR. Yet in the past, for the most part, only when Soviet leaders perceived adverse trends in the balance of forces, and consequently strengthened their efforts to induce their adversaries to apply the brakes, did negotiations appear to have some promise. A case can be made—though there is disagreement on the issue—that Soviet leaders did not take an interest in arms limitations until they recognized the seriousness of American programs for antimissile defense in the early 1970s.

Prospects for negotiation thus are likely to be affected significantly by the degree to which Soviet leaders see projected American and Western defense policies as potentially vitiating Soviet defense efforts of recent times. Even then, however, the modest and controversial effects of SALT II and of other arms-control projects suggest that the negotiating track is not likely to accomplish much more than to place modest inhibitions on existing programs (while allowing diversion of resources from constrained to unconstrained activities). In the latter part of the 1970s, as arms control became the mainstay of détente, the United States seemed to focus negotiations on areas of possible agreement. At least for the United States, these did not necessarily coincide with actual security needs. Soul-searching about the purposes, directions, and utility of existing arms-control enterprises has become widespread in the West. The continued relevance of approaches stemming from intellectual conceptions developed nearly a quarter of a century ago and the tortuous history of negotiations will likely mean continued questioning of how and whether negotiated arms control can be made a more useful instrument for the pursuit of U.S. security.

The Effects of Growing Power

The latter part of the 1970s also witnessed a more persistent Soviet push than before for presence and influence both near and beyond the immediate periphery of the USSR. The invasion of Afghanistan dramatized the trend. In earlier periods, notably at the time of rapid decolonization and of the retraction of the power of the traditional European imperial nations, Soviet intrusions into foreign areas, both distant and close, had relatively strong ideological motivations. Opportunities to appear on the scene as the handmaiden of liberation and independence abounded. The Soviets sought to present themselves—not without some impact—as the model for, and disinterested supporter of, newly developing societies. But in this phase the Soviet staying power turned out to be uneven. Soviet military reach, while growing, could not yet sustain Soviet positions of influence when they encountered serious challenge. As many new nations moved beyond achievement of independence to the building of viable societies, they became disenchanted with the Soviet role, and the appeal of the Soviet system lost much of its initial luster.

Soviet involvements tended to be more selective in the 1970s. But where they occurred, the military component was pronounced—Angola, Mozambique, the Horn of Africa, South Yemen, Vietnam. The use of Cuban troops, transported and equipped by the Soviets in militarily significant numbers, along with smaller numbers of East German and other "technicians," added a new dimension that, while keeping Soviet visibility low, gave interventions an effectiveness they tended to lack before. Afghanistan became the first country outside the Warsaw Pact where Soviet forces intervened directly to sustain a pro-Soviet regime. By coincidence or design, the strategic locations of many of these ventures both reflected and reinforced the emergence of the Soviet Union as a power with global military reach. Soviet spokesmen had long emphasized Moscow's interests the world over and asserted a general right to be heard wherever disputes or instabilities occurred. In the 1970s they began to define Soviet security stakes in more expansive and concrete terms. Thus, in 1979, the oceanic routes between the eastern and western parts of the vast Soviet territorial expanse came to be mentioned as part of the Soviet security sphere, a claim that assumed greater concreteness as the invasion of Afghanistan moved Soviet forces closer to the Arabian Sea and Persian Gulf.

Were the 1970s another relatively temporary period of increasing Soviet ambition resulting largely from opportunities that were not initially of Soviet (or Cuban) making? Or did they mark a new phase in an imperial drive, still perhaps opportunistic but now sustained by a power no longer as vulnerable to changing political conditions and much harder to dislodge than before? Could Western nations—and for that matter China—still rely on the forces of local nationalism or on Soviet ineptitude to diminish Soviet influence? What risks would the Soviets run to gain positions and to retain those gained if the United States or other nations moved to challenge them? How serious is the threat of the Soviets to the availability of raw materials, including oil, to the United States and others and to the sealanes over which these products have to be conveyed?

These are questions for the 1980s that have no precise answers. Yet there can be little doubt that the 1970s witnessed the manifestations of Soviet ambition and power in more places and with seemingly more persistence than in the past, and that this outward thrust was in part due to the circumstance that there was little risk of countervailing power the Soviets would encounter. Moreover, the emerging Soviet definition of security interests appeared in a period when the definition of American security interests was, if not contracting, at least uncertain.[1] And other major international actors seemed largely unwilling or unable to draw security conclusions for themselves from the extension of Soviet influence even though much of it occurred—and seems destined to occur—in regions where many Western nations, for example, have crucial economic interests.

The Effects of Growing Needs

The evolution of the nonmilitary aspects of the Soviet Union's conduct in international affairs is another cause of uncertainty in the new decade. In the 1970s, more than in earlier years, the Soviets sought to develop what might be called beneficial foreign connections. Put briefly, the emergence of the Soviet Union into the world as a result of its increasing military power has been accompanied by extensive efforts to meet the economic needs of the USSR through foreign ties. The shortfalls of the Soviet economy have created increasing requirements for capital, technology, machinery, manufactures, agricultural products, and other goods from abroad. Ironically,

---

1. President Carter's assertion in January 1980 of a vital U.S. interest in preventing control of the Persian Gulf by an "outside force" was the clearest such assertion in years. Even so, it raised questions about the U.S. capacity to act if the stipulated contingency should arise.

perhaps, the principal suppliers of many of these items are the advanced industrial nations that have formed defense alliances to deter Soviet threats.

In the early 1970s it appeared that the United States might emerge as one of the USSR's major economic partners. The Nixon administration saw in this possibility one means of obtaining leverage in the power contest with the USSR—that is, of providing added incentives for Soviet restraint in international power contests. The U.S. role, as it turned out, developed slowly and unevenly. Various limitations were imposed by congressional actions, such as the Jackson-Vanik amendment to the Trade Act of 1974, which made the expansion of trade and the use of the Export-Import Bank to facilitate the needed financing conditional upon the liberalization of Soviet emigration practices. Other legislative actions like the Stevenson amendment to Export-Import Bank legislation in 1974 placed additional ceilings on extensions of U.S. government credit.

Nevertheless, by the end of the 1970 decade, the Soviets had established a ramified network of trading and financial ties. Their intention evidently is to expand those ties. Western nations generally have welcomed the opportunities for trade and have been increasingly interested in access to Soviet raw materials, notably energy resources. When economic relations with Soviet partners in the Council for Mutual Economic Assistance (COMECON) in Eastern Europe are added to the picture, the overall balance is tipped in favor of the West, with the difference financed by a steadily growing volume of private and government-supported Western credit.

Questions now arise about how this relationship will be characterized in the future. They are compounded by uncertainties about the Soviet petroleum situation in the next decade. Some authoritative estimates project a Soviet-East European shortfall of more than 500,000 barrels a day, accompanied by a loss of Soviet earnings from oil exports and thus additional needs for foreign financing.

More fundamentally, however, questions can be raised about the extent to which Soviet leaders are prepared to continue the course of deviating from the traditional autarchic proclivities of the Soviet system. In Western nations—not excluding the United States, if legislative restrictions are to be reduced—questions will have to be addressed concerning the wisdom and feasibility of promoting increasing economic interaction with the USSR and the COMECON nations and how best to relate this interaction to the security issues posed by Soviet military buildup and outward thrust.

Debates have persisted on the issue of whether broadening and deepening economic relations will over time stabilize political relation, or whether Soviet needs provide the United States with leverage to restrain Soviet international conduct. This matter of "linkage"— whether it can or should be practiced, and if so, how—has been controversial for most of the 1970s.

In the United States, for example, there has always been resistance —manifested again in the Afghanistan crisis—to the idea of connecting grain exports to Soviet political conduct. More broadly, widespread support also exists for the notion that economic relations should remain separate from the fluctuations of political relations because those relations are based on mutual advantage in the traditional sense. The Soviets, not unnaturally, have also resisted overt connections, although they have unabashedly practiced their own brand of linkage between economics and politics at various times— for example, with Yugoslavia and China.

In addition, the Soviets have not refrained from suggesting that they are in a position to show preference in economic dealings for partners who defer to Soviet political and security sensitivities. At the beginning of the 1980s, members of the North Atlantic Treaty Organization (NATO) are beginning a program to modernize the nuclear forces of the alliance. The vigorous Soviet-Warsaw Pact effort to prevent or delay making and implementing decisions in this area has included intimations that there might be adverse economic consequences for the participants. Western nations that contemplate or maintain large-scale economic involvements with the USSR, including reliance on unhampered access to Soviet resources like natural gas, will need to face the question of whether such reliance might at some point constrain their political and security choices. (At this time it is uncertain to what extent a stake in maintaining economic relations is inhibiting Japan and Western Europe in responding to the Soviet move into Afghanistan.)

The Succession of Soviet Leaders

In all such areas of uncertainty and complex policy choice, the future makeup of the Soviet political leadership clearly plays a major role. Observers can only speculate how the inevitable succession will unfold in the USSR over the next several years, how a new set of leaders will handle the combination of strengths and vulnerabilities it inherits, how the conduct of the United States and that of other external powers will affect the succession and the policies of those who assume power, and how the latter, in turn, will affect the United States.

Leadership will also change in the United States. Three presidential elections and five congressional elections will occur in the 1980s. The past twenty years do not provide assurance that all changes in presidents will occur through the elections. In a sense, changes in U.S. leadership may be more baffling than those of the Soviet Union. U.S. election outcomes are far from predictable, and individuals can rise to political prominence more rapidly than in the hierarchical Soviet system. The United States has also witnessed major shifts in presidential style and changes in approaches to issues. Nevertheless, the American system is geared to periodic change; generational change tends to be gradual rather than abrupt; power is relatively diffuse, and changes in personnel in the various parts of the U.S. government do not necessarily vitiate major institutional and policy continuities.

Certain incontestable realities in the Soviet Union mark the 1980s as a time of fluidity in leadership. Despite the vast Soviet party and governmental machinery, it is fair to say that the country is ruled by about twenty-eight men—fourteen full, or voting, and nine nonvoting members of the Politburo and five members of the party Secretariat who are not members of the Politburo. (Only one woman has in recent times penetrated these male bastions.) Of these twenty-eight, one, General Secretary Leonid I. Brezhnev, is also the head of state and another, V. V. Kuznetsov, is his deputy in that capacity. One man, A. N. Kosygin, doubles as prime minister. Five men double as senior colleagues of Kosygin; another, Yu. V. Andropov, heads the ubiquitous police; and yet another, M. S. Solomentsev, is the prime minister of the largest Soviet constituent republic, the Russian Soviet Federated Socialist Republic. Thus the top party leadership is also the top leadership of the Soviet state. This overlap in party and state leadership functions has not always been as complete, but the pattern has prevailed for many years and probably will continue to do so, although possibly with variations in the years ahead.

Of these top leaders, ten are seventy years of age or older, including Brezhnev, who is seventy-two. Indeed, eight of the fourteen full Politburo members are septuagenarians. Another seven are more than sixty-five years of age; four of these are full Politburo members. An additional five men are aged sixty or more, one a full Politburo member. Only one full Politburo member is less than sixty years of age— Leningrad party chief G. V. Romanov, who is fifty-six. In short, age weighs heavily in the top leadership structure. It appears that during the 1980s about 50 percent of the present full Politburo membership will be replaced.

Two successions may actually occur during the 1980s. They may not be neatly separated, but it seems reasonable to assume that by 1990, all or most of the twenty-two men now aged sixty or more are likely to be replaced, disregarding other casualties, both political and physical, along the way. By that time, but probably beginning some years earlier, the top leadership could be taken over by a new generation, people born around 1930. (Only three of the top twenty-eight come from this group today.)

This does not mean that all will be flux at the top for ten years. Whatever the manner of Brezhnev's departure (for example, if he were to accept the status of an elder statesman or a pensioner, it would be the first time since the Bolshevik Revolution; Lenin and Stalin died in office, and Khruschev was removed and disgraced in a palace coup), a single senior leader probably would emerge. It is conceivable that this might be someone like Romanov at the younger end of the age spectrum.

What kinds of leaders will be emerging as the new oligarchy takes shape?

The members of the intermediate group—those aged sixty or more —are probably not much different from their seniors. Both age groups have participated in building the power of the Soviet Union since the Second World War; they have seen it equal or exceed that of the United States in many categories of military strength; they have seen Soviet influence expand, sometimes with setbacks and frustrations, but impressively nonetheless. They have lived through times of open crisis in the Soviet security belt in Eastern Europe and have participated in the workable but almost surely not enduring compromise between Soviet dominance and modest national autonomy in that part of the world. They have experienced the Chinese break with Soviet hegemony; they have shared in the conservative domestic policies and the stagnations of the Brezhnev era (having earlier ridden Khrushchev's roller coaster). And they have helped guide the gradual and cautious involvement of the Soviet Union in international enterprises, such as the effort to curb nuclear weapons proliferation. World War II and Stalinism remain vivid experiences for this generation.

Thus, allowing for differences in personality and style, rule by Soviet leaders aged sixty or more seems likely to resemble that of today's leaders who are more than seventy years old. This is not necessarily good news for the United States. These leaders, along with their elders, have led the Soviet Union to superpower status and staked out unmistakable claims to a place in the sun. They have amassed military power and ordered the invasion of Afghanistan. They have sought negotiations with the United States and other nations to build margins of safety into the pursuit of Soviet interests. What can be said of these leaders, though, is that they are not likely to adopt drastically different approaches and attitudes.

But it is precisely this that cannot be said with any certainty about the fifty-year-olds. Chances are that as long as the older leaders remain, this younger group will not be inclined to attempt major experiments with the economy. Sometime in the 1980s or shortly thereafter, though, the decline in growth will need to be faced. Soviet leaders must confront, among other problems, lagging productivity, a shrinking labor market with changing ethnic composition, generally inadequate development and adaptation of modern technology, persistent overcentralization and bureaucratization, increasing costs of recovering raw materials and impending energy stringencies, and continuing problems of agriculture (particularly while the increasing consumption of meat remains a major tenet of the regime). And these problems should be especially pressing for a younger generation of leaders, which by all accounts has had better schooling and training and knows more about the outside world than its predecessors.

Such concerns, together with the related need to encourage innovation among the army of managers, professionals, and skilled workers, would suggest a heavy focus on internal matters. And this might be further reinforced by a class consciousness that concentrates on material comforts, shorter workweeks, and so on. This attention to internal needs could serve to stimulate, indeed necessitate, more intercourse with other nations, especially if even a younger generation of leaders were still reluctant to change the centralized structure of the country because of the implications for the monopoly of party control.

To some degree at least, foreign inputs of capital, technology, plant, and manufactures will be sought to avoid politically sensitive reforms of the Soviet system. On the other hand, the outside world may not be wholly without influence as future Soviet leaders address their problems. If economic interactions become more complex, if Soviet raw materials alone become less able to finance Western inputs to the Soviet economy, if Western capital resources become less readily available to the Soviets, the Soviet economy might have to become more export-oriented. In other ways, too, Western economic partners and, in time, international financial institutions might levy requirements on the Soviet Union for openness, although the Soviets have hitherto largely and successfully resisted.

Such possibilities are merely alluded to here to suggest that the United States and other industrialized nations are likely to be involved to some extent, even if an eventual new Soviet leadership were to give major emphasis to the domestic problems of a stagnating and unevenly developing Soviet economy. COMECON countries, even more than the USSR, face serious economic issues that are almost certain to lead to deeper and broader relations with other nations. How Soviet leaders will weigh the needs of their own economy and that of their allies against the risks of excessive interaction with the outside world is among the unknowns. How, beyond that, they will see the trade-off between restraint in international conduct and their chances, with foreign help, to cope with their internal problems is another question, albeit one that also poses major issues for the United States and other nations.

Soviet Military Power

If future leaders of the Soviet Union must face major and difficult domestic problems, and if it is arguable that in doing so they may, on the whole, prefer a fairly tranquil international environment, it is nevertheless also certain that Soviet military power will continue to grow in the future.

The uniformed military and the managers and technocrats of the defense industry occupy a strong position in Soviet politics and in the extended elite that dominates Soviet life. It is probable that any new leadership will seek and need the support of these groups to establish and maintain itself in power. Both the Stalin and Khrushchev successions involved bargaining in which aspiring leaders gave this military-industrial complex assurances that an ample share of the national resource pie would continue to be allocated to the military sector. Although both Khrushchev and Brezhnev tangled with the military at various times after attaining top authority, the Soviet political system, as it has evolved over a quarter of a century, is geared to the priority of defense. And the world of the 1980s seems unlikely to change in the Soviet view. Paradoxically, the more that Soviet power grows and spreads, the more the Soviet sense of encirclement seems to increase. It would be a rash prediction to suggest that a new Soviet generation of leaders, which made its first moves up the ladder when the Sino-Soviet split was most virulent, will easily shed these anxieties.

More than forty years after the pains and agonies of the Second World War, will a new set of leaders, remembering the glory of victory and the remarkable Soviet march to superpower status, wield their military instruments with caution? Will they calculate risks conservatively? Will they see potential gains in their country's position whose attainment may warrant substantial risks? Will they use force to obtain assured supplies of energy? Will potentially adverse developments occur—the growth of Chinese power, the rearmament of Japan, a move of post-Tito Yugoslavia toward closer associations with Western Europe, the relative growth of German military strength, some threat against a distant Soviet foothold important to the security of Soviet maritime communications—that will make the use of force to arrest those actions seem a lesser risk to Soviet interests? Or will those leaders be more inclined to use their power to achieve security and other objectives by trying to negotiate from a position of strength?

Again, none of these questions is answerable. All require a calculus of risks versus gains and hence some judgment about the strength and the scope of the interests and the vigor with which they may be defended by the United States and other nations with whom the Soviet Union coinhabits the globe. The outgoing generation of Soviet leaders has at various times demonstrated caution when faced with military risk: it has not exploited situations of relative military advantage in such nations as China and Romania. The 1980s must include the uncertainty of how a new generation of Soviet leaders will use the

USSR's power to promote and protect Soviet interests. The United States and other Western nations must continue the effort to structure relations so that no Soviet leader can expect to practice assertiveness without risk or penalty—or practice restraint without some expectation that it will be reciprocated. Neither element was sufficiently present to deter the Soviet action against Afghanistan.

Managing Conflict: A More Comprehensive Approach

For the United States the overriding issue in the 1980s will remain how to manage relations with the USSR to avoid both war and injury to U.S. interests. Theories abound on Soviet motives and purposes: that the Soviets operate according to some systematic program of expansion, leading eventually to world domination; that the undoubted growth of Soviet influence and presence is essentially the result of opportunistic exploitation of instabilities, particularly in third world regions, which were not originally caused by the Soviets; that the Soviets basically are still responding to what they consider the excessive power of the United States in the world and to the possibility of a hostile Western-Chinese coalition. Most observers and policymakers agree, however, that the Soviets seek their objectives without war because they must be as aware as the United States is that a nuclear conflict would have catastrophic consequences.

The common fear of war has been widely considered a basis for moderating U.S.-Soviet antagonism and broadening the areas of cooperation, especially in managing crises and minimizing the chance of unintended conflict. In practice, however, the desire to avoid open warfare has not been easy to translate into more concrete kinds of joint action. The danger of war does produce a certain caution—most notably at the height of crises in which there is a palpable possibility of direct U.S.-Soviet confrontation, such as the Middle East in 1956, 1967, and 1973; Cuba in 1962; and Berlin in the 1950s and 1960s. But fear of war can be used as a form of pressure to test the resolve and tolerance of the other side. Broadly speaking, unless accompanied by more immediately compelling incentives for restraint, the abstract fear of war has done little to regulate hostility or to institutionalize the process of crisis prevention. It seems unlikely to do so in the future. It cannot, in the end, be dissociated from the actual risks that either side sees in pursuing particular policies and courses of action. This, in turn, is a function of how one side interprets the interests of the other and how one assesses the readiness and ability of the other to protect those interests.

In the early 1970s the leaders of the United States and the USSR signed a number of joint declarations purporting to establish rules of conduct reducing the danger of war and the intensity of rivalry. The U.S. administration at the time did not, however, view these declarations as self-enforcing—that is, that they would be automatically adhered to simply because they stemmed from a shared fear of conflict and were solemnly signed. Subsequent events (for example, Soviet complicity in the outbreak and course of the Yom Kippur war and intervention in Angola) made it clear that agreements to exercise restraint, respect the interests of others, forgo efforts to achieve unilateral advantage, and to consult have little practical significance in the absence of inducement, whether in the form of perceived risks or potential benefits, to abide by them. Even the principle of mutual advantage, which tends to operate with some effectiveness in more specific and concrete aspects of relations (like trade and cultural exchanges), seems to have only a modest applicability in the less precisely definable realm of maneuver for power, position, and influence.

From the U.S. vantage point, the Soviets failed to live up to the 1972 Declaration on Basic Principles of Relations between the United States and the Soviet Union and the 1973 Agreement on the Prevention of Nuclear War when they encouraged, participated, or acquiesced in various conflicts in the Middle East, Southeast Asia, and Africa. The Soviets have also registered complaints against the United States. They have protested generally that the United States does not in practice accept the concept of equal security and resists whenever the Soviet Union asserts interests to which it is entitled. Particularly in the Middle East, the Soviets claimed, after the brief period of joint action in 1973 to bring about a cease-fire and again after the October 1977 joint declaration, the United States froze the Soviets out at the first opportunity.

In short, neither side seems persuaded that restraint is likely to be reciprocated; on the contrary, the presumption is that it is more likely to be exploited. A course of restraint tends to be seen not as adherence to a set of principles but as a signal that the restrained side does not consider its interests sufficiently engaged in an issue or that it does not possess the power to defend those interests. Rules of conduct are then readily overridden by the quest for gain at the expense of the hesitating side.

Against the background of this experience in the 1970s, it is doubtful that any useful purpose would be served by efforts to devise new or revised principles to govern U.S.-Soviet relations in the next decade. The problem is how to put into practice the principles already promulgated.

For the United States this process must include a much clearer definition of U.S. interests than what has been conveyed in recent years. As the painful experience of Vietnam recedes and the impact of Afghanistan emerges, it should be possible for the United States to make its concerns known to the Soviets (and others). The United States is probably beyond the point at which mere declaratory assertions of interests and concern carry sufficient credibility to command respect. A conscious pattern of actions will be required to establish a well-defined sense of U.S. sensitivities and needs. And as long as the Soviets interpret equal security as entitling them both to accumulate international influence and to probe for U.S. vulnerabilities, the United States is forced to use similar tactics toward the USSR. Such an approach may not be a prescription for détente (defined as the process of reducing friction) in the short run, but it would seem to be a prerequisite for more restrained relations in the longer run.

A conscious U.S. policy of asserting and defending interests against Soviet encroachments requires adequate means for power projection and flexible instruments (such as arms sales and transfers) to support others with shared interests and concerns and to collaborate with formal allies. More broadly, however, the United States should seek to establish the principle that the various components of U.S.-Soviet relations cannot be compartmentalized. In particular, it must be made clear to the Soviet leadership in practice that the extent to which the benefits of international cooperation are available to the USSR will depend on moderation in Soviet pursuit of international aspirations— both in the definition of goals and in the manner in which those goals are pursued.

The United States alone cannot control Soviet access to economic and other benefits in the international community. Wider acceptance is needed, especially among U.S. allies, of the interconnection between fostering beneficial relations with the USSR and the overall conduct of the latter in the international arena. In short, a U.S. strategy of encouraging Soviet restraint by a combination of coercive and cooperative policies will be most effective if pursued in collaboration with other nations.

The Soviets would no doubt interpret more consistent U.S. efforts to achieve multilateral consensus as an intention to bring about a hostile coalition beyond that which already exists in the U.S. alliance system. Such a perception would be accurate precisely because the actual achievement of wider ranging coordination would reflect a new common concern among nations that feel threatened by Soviet power and ambition. On the other hand, multilateral cooperation and coordination could also include extensive beneficial interchanges with the USSR in the context of generally restrained relations. This would imply a calculation that it is feasible and desirable to have more orderly relations—provided that all concerned agree that it is more advantageous to have relations of that kind rather than those based solely on maneuver for advantage and geopolitical dominance.

International relations do not flow from theoretical constructs alone. Conceptions have to be translated into policies applicable in particular situations and circumstances. Still, there needs to be a general orientation that has broad understanding and backing in the American political structure, is comprehensible to the Soviets and, to the greatest degree possible, has the support and reflects the stakes and concerns of America's allies and others.

The pragmatic American tendency is to deal with issues "on their merits," which tend to be rather narrowly construed. Moreover, in relations with the USSR, the United States is inclined to see virtue in cooperation and agreement per se. In the realm of arms control, particularly, the United States has identified progress with the prevention of war so much that Americans have pressed ahead with negotiations, notably on SALT, regardless of the political environment. In the sphere of economic relations, many groups consider mutual commercial advantage in most cases to be the chief yardstick by which to measure the scope and content of contact between the United States and the USSR. Or, to take another kind of example, U.S. human rights policies toward the USSR often appear to have been based on the premise that, despite Soviet sensitivities in this field, various U.S. pressures would have no effects on other aspects of relations.

If the United States is to convey an overall sense of direction in its policy approaches, that direction is unlikely to emerge from a multiplicity of separately motivated and conducted policies. If the United States is to make progress in safeguarding its interests while the Soviet Union, through both its power and its needs, increasingly emerges into the world, U.S. pragmatism must show greater coherence and consistency. And greater emphasis must be placed on the continuity of U.S. policies (and on the adaptation of U.S. governmental actions to such continuity).

The tendency to consider relations with the USSR as choices between rather stark alternatives—such as cooperation versus competition—is likely to be misleading. It seems more accurate to describe relations as a complex intermingling of many characteristics. Americans would do themselves a disservice if they believe they can achieve complete clarity in the nature of U.S.-Soviet relations.

To suggest to the Soviets that they have a choice between friendship and antagonism is unrealistic and infers that some finite point may be reached at which the choice will have been made. It is possible that the United States and the USSR will go to war—and to that extent, clarity would have come to U.S.-Soviet relations. Virtually any state of relations other than war may contain more or less hostility at any given point; but even if cooperative agreements and practices accumulated over time—a situation not sustained thus far, even in the more hopeful phases of détente in the early and mid-1970s—competition and hostility would still continue to be present and would have to be managed. Indeed, cooperation may be seen as part of the process of managing hostility.

Regional Conflicts

The 1980s are likely to be characterized by continued instability and conflict in many parts of the world. As in earlier periods, there will be a multiplicity of causes, ranging from pressures for radical domestic change that may spill over the national borders of a particular country, to more traditional types of territorial or irredentist disputes. Other chapters in this book deal in detail with conflicts in these parts of the world, the sources of such conflicts, and U.S. concerns.

Soviet Capacity and Inclination to Intervene

The Soviets have long maintained that conflicts anywhere are a legitimate concern of the USSR and that its sensitivities must be given special weight in regions physically close to the Soviet Union. The Soviets have also claimed special interest in conflicts, regardless of locale, which by their definition constitute "national liberation struggles" against "imperialists" and former colonial powers or their agents. Further, the Soviets have shown support for full-fledged socialist allies such as Cuba and Vietnam; in the case of Warsaw Pact countries, this interest has also been expressed as a right or duty. The Soviets have also signed treaties of friendship and cooperation with a number of third world countries qualifying as socialist by Soviet definition (for example, Afghanistan, Angola, Ethiopia, South Yemen, Mozambique), although they have not been linked to the USSR as closely or for as long as supposedly full-fledged socialist regimes and the Warsaw Pact countries. (In early 1980 it appears that Afghanistan may assume a status analogous to that of a full-fledged socialist regime. The Soviets cited their treaty with Afghanistan as the legal basis for their military intervention.)

The actual Soviet role in world events has varied. In some instances it is confined to propaganda and diplomatic activities; in others, to massive supplies of military equipment; and in still others, to a combination of military supplies, Soviet technicians, and "proxy" forces. Regular Soviet forces have been directly committed to combat only rarely. The most notable case, apart from Eastern Europe, is Afghanistan.

Although Soviet support differs in its precise form, in several cases it has gone to parties that have expressed or displayed hostility to the United States and one or more Western nations. Support frequently has also gone to parties whose opponents receive U.S. support or have U.S. sympathy. But the Soviets have generally retained flexibility in situations where the United States is directly involved; they have preferred to avoid open and direct confrontations.

Vietnam has been a somewhat special case. Hanoi long received Soviet material support while it was fighting first the French and then the United States. More recently, however, a new burst of Soviet support for Vietnam, including both equipment and some operational assistance, was prompted by the latter's conflict with China.

In some instances, Soviet involvement has included not only support of one of the sides in a conflict but also the establishment of military facilities for Soviet purposes not necessarily related to the conflict. (For example, Soviet naval, communications, air and intelligence facilities in or near Vietnam and Ethiopia serve wider Soviet military purposes than support of a client in a local war.)

In general, it may be said that the USSR did not originate the conflict situations in which it became involved in the 1970s. In cases where local or regional conflict resulted from domestic upheaval, the Soviets by and large were not the instigators of the latter. In some situations, however, such as Afghanistan in 1978, the evidence strongly suggested involvement from the outset, though it still remained ambiguous. But once revolutionary domestic upheaval got under way, the Soviets frequently encouraged it and then moved to sustain or establish supportive relations with the rising regime. In Afghanistan in 1979–80, Moscow took further steps to replace an undesired regime and to occupy the country. Geographic proximity made such action more practicable than in remoter places.

These general patterns of Soviet conduct undoubtedly will continue in the next decade, but probably in intensified form. The degree of Soviet initiative and the scope of Soviet intervention will necessarily continue to be influenced by Moscow's judgment of the risks and costs, including the possibility of confrontation with the United States.

The thrust of Soviet intervention in the Near and Middle East must cause special concern for the United States because of the repercussions for Western oil supplies and because of the strategic implications of strong Soviet influence in countries stretching from the Eastern Mediterranean to the rim of the Arabian Sea, Persian Gulf, and Indian Ocean. Soviet military action in Afghanistan has dangers that extend beyond that country's frontiers: to Iran, Pakistan, and elsewhere. Soviet involvement in conflicts in the Horn of Africa likewise affects the United States, particularly, though not exclusively, because of the proximity of that region to the Arabian peninsula.

Other areas of concern include southern Africa where, in addition to involvement in Angola and in the Rhodesian conflict (largely through proxies), the Soviets have built up the presumption that they will support eventual black moves against South Africa; northwest Africa, where Soviet support generally goes to those opposing Morocco over the issue of the former Spanish Sahara; the Caribbean, where the Soviets extend broad support to the Cubans, who in turn have become more active in some of the independent island nations and in Central America; Southeast Asia, due to the Soviet alliance with Vietnam; Korea, where in certain circumstances the Soviets might support a North Korean attempt to unite the divided peninsula.

Any survey of potential Soviet intervention must also include Europe. In the case of NATO members, the Soviets, who are conscious of U.S. treaty commitments and military presence, have generally observed considerable caution when occasions for possible direct intervention have arisen, such as in Portugal in 1974. This caution is likely to continue, but so will Soviet pressures to prevent NATO members from participating in programs to improve the military capabilities of the alliance and on other issues. At the same time, the Soviets will persist in their efforts to induce European alliance members to avoid becoming embroiled in U.S.-Soviet tensions. The Soviets are aware of the special sensitivities among the countries of Western Europe, and as their stake in contacts with the East has grown, they will seek to apply the tactics of "selective détente."

The Soviets have warned against Spain's joining NATO and might encourage domestic agitation there against such a step when and if it becomes topical. The issue is at least as much psychological as military for the Soviets: Spain already maintains formal defense arrangements with the United States and informal ones with other NATO members, but its actual entry into the alliance would constitute a change in the Soviet definition of the European status quo that is incompatible with their concept of equality. How the Soviets could respond—beyond recourse to agitation—is difficult to predict. (The issue is controversial within Spain, and there are differing attitudes among the existing fifteen NATO members. No formal steps will probably be taken toward membership until Spain's application for entry into the European Community has progressed much further.) For the United States, and for the alliance as a whole, yielding to Soviet pressure would be extremely damaging if Spain and the alliance countries decided to proceed with Spain's membership.

Developments in post-Tito Yugoslavia could bring possibilities of direct Soviet intervention. It would obviously be tempting for the Soviets to achieve the reintegration of Yugoslavia into the Eastern bloc. To attempt to do so militarily against Yugoslav resistance would, however, be a major undertaking in which the Soviets could not be certain of prompt success or of the West's abstention from some form of response. If there were confusion as a result of domestic conflicts in Yugoslavia, it might afford the Soviets the most plausible pretexts for intervention. Another cause for Soviet action might be a tendency in Yugoslavia to move closer to the West. By whatever means achieved, a significant shift of Yugoslavia toward alignment with the USSR would constitute a major adverse change for the United States and the West in the political and strategic map of Europe and the Mediterranean region.

This summary of continuing and potential areas of tension or conflict is not intended to be exhaustive. There are causes for instability in most parts of the world, as indeed there have been for several decades. What has come to be different in the 1970s and 1980s is, first, the Soviet capacity and inclination to intervene and, second, U.S. uncertainty about whether its interests are sufficiently at stake in a particular situation to warrant its active involvement.

Change in U.S. Attitudes and Policy

In the post-Vietnam period the presumption grew in the United States that Americans would do well to review U.S. interests in order to avoid a repetition of frustrating interventions where little of consequence is directly at stake. Legislative restrictions, such as the 1973 War Powers Resolution, were designed to induce greater caution in the definition of U.S. interests and to circumscribe the discretion of the president in undertaking military interventions. Through legislation and other means the United States sought to reduce its identification with governments that failed to meet certain human rights standards in dealing with their own peoples. Actions were undertaken to reduce the volume and scope of arms sales and transfers. Additional legislative restrictions were placed on various kinds of U.S. cooperation, including military, with governments that failed to comply with certain U.S. and international measures intended to curb the proliferation of nuclear weapons capabilities.

These and other policy and attitudinal changes in the United States coincided with the reduced emphasis on U.S. military capabilities pertinent to possible uses in overseas crises. As a consequence, the U.S. military presence has been more thinly deployed worldwide than at any time since World War II. During the Nixon administration and since then, it has been anticipated that the decline in U.S. military capabilities and the contraction of direct U.S. commitments could be compensated for by a number of regional powers that, with U.S. backing in case of trouble, would carry the basic burdens of defense against external pressures or internal upheavals. These expectations have proved to be excessive.

Events in Iran, Afghanistan, and elsewhere at the end of the 1970s appear to have stimulated a gradual shift in the attitudes of the U.S. public and the Congress, suggesting that the post-Vietnam mood of retrenchment was changing. Support for increased defense expenditures became more pronounced, and spokesmen for the administration talked about improving and funding long-range intervention capabilities without encountering widespread or intense opposition.

Clearly, not all changes in governments around the world will be of equal concern to the United States. A master U.S. strategy toward change is neither practical nor realistic: it is neither axiomatic that all change can or should be supported by the United States nor that it should be opposed. What must be recognized, however, is that the Soviets have manifested a new impulse and greater capabilities to turn turmoil and regional conflicts to their advantage in structuring the balance of power for the coming years. And the growing recognition of this development has contributed to the shift in American attitudes.

In the 1980s, therefore, the United States must structure policies, adapted to particular circumstances and geographic regions, which counteract Soviet efforts to coopt aspirations, grievances, and instabilities in various parts of the world for Soviet purposes. Such policies would not seek to exclude all kinds of Soviet influence from a particular region or country. (Such a task is almost certainly beyond U.S. capacity, and may not necessarily be in the U.S. interest.) U.S. policies would, in general, seek to produce greater Soviet readiness to work toward viable settlements.

The general point to be made is that the Soviets should not be able to isolate a particular crisis from the totality of their relations with the United States and, for that matter, with other Western nations. The West, in turn, must be prepared to incur costs if a strategy of noncompartmentalized crisis management is to be adopted. More fundamentally, a readiness to forgo benefits must accompany a sustained U.S. policy to establish that any unrestrained pursuit of expansionary goals carries not only risks in the particular geographic area where it occurs but involves costs in a wider context.

It may be argued that the United States cannot unravel the entire fabric of U.S.-Soviet relations whenever a crisis erupts. And it may be contended that it would be more difficult to find compromise arrangements in a crisis, or at least in the U.S.-Soviet component of it, if the United States escalates the confrontation. Both points have a certain force, particularly as long as the only goal in a crisis is to find a compromise or a solution. If the U.S. purpose, however, is to look beyond an individual crisis to the broader pattern of relations and conduct, the risks may be worth taking. Moreover, if the United States can credibly convey its intention to widen a crisis, if necessary, it may help deter the occurrence of that crisis, or at least Soviet involvement in it, in the first place.

It is often contended that the United States, by backing the wrong or losing side, particularly in southern Africa, opened the way for Soviet-Cuban intervention in 1975. By analogy, it can be argued that U.S. identification with Israel opened the way for Soviet influence and presence in many parts of the Arab world.

It may well be that in some instances the United States can preempt Soviet involvement by backing more radical factions in conflicts or endorsing certain policy positions or drastic demands for change. But it is unlikely that the United States can satisfy the often inchoate demands of various groups pressing for change, the redress of various grievances, and the reshaping of the international system.

The notion that less reactionary and more sympathetic and progressive U.S. policies would reduce Soviet opportunities for intervention is a highly questionable one because it underestimates the momentum of Soviet interventionist policies, which constitute the most challenging problem in the conduct of U.S.-Soviet relations in the 1980s.

Arms Control Issues

The decade of the 1970s saw more negotiations begun and agreements concluded than any previous ten-year period since World War II. Some modest restraints on planned programs were established; introduction of some types of weapons, such as chemical and radiological ones, was curbed; and communication between the two sides was intensified on military questions. But it cannot be said that the principal goals usually associated with negotiated arms control efforts were significantly furthered as a result.

Thus it is difficult to demonstrate that the risk of war was measurably reduced, or that the absence of open warfare between the United States and the USSR (and between East and West generally) was due to the accomplishments of arms control endeavors. Nor are the agreements that were reached likely to contribute to a reduction of the casualties and damage that would result if war were to break out. (It could even be argued that Treaty on the Limitation of Anti-Ballistic Missile Systems (1972) would, if deterrence were to fail, contribute to greater casualties and damage than if those missiles had been widely deployed. On the other hand, the absence of deployed antimissile defenses may have made some contribution to deterrence.) And, finally, it cannot be persuasively argued that arms control efforts contributed to a reduction of the economic burdens of defense. Conceivably, the rate of growth of Soviet defense expenditures (estimated at 3 to 4 percent a year in real terms) might have been higher, but this is largely speculative. In the case of the United States, it is doubtful that arms control justified reduced expenditures for defense during the 1970s. Although some argued during the SALT II ratification debates that failure of the agreement would result in larger increases in U.S. defense expenditures than adoption, no one seriously contended that approval of the agreement would obviate increased efforts. The difference between the efforts necessary if SALT II succeeded or failed remains in dispute; so many variables are involved that the debate cannot easily be resolved.

Strategic Forces and European Arms Control

At the end of the 1970s SALT and, to a lesser extent, other arms control projects were the most concrete and active negotiating issues between the United States and the USSR. It is only a slight oversimplification to say that they were almost all that was left of the expectations of the détente period of the earlier years of the decade. Yet at no time—even before Afghanistan—were more serious questions raised in the United States about the utility and benefits of these endeavors. It is true that both supporters and critics of SALT advocated greater reductions and other curbs in future phases of SALT. But there were few specific and practical proposals on how to implement such far-reaching measures, except for those that, in effect, amounted to the dismantling of land-based missile forces. But although the Soviets also advocated cutting back, they were plainly reluctant to reduce forces that over the years had constituted the greatest and most effective—and, toward the United States, the most threatening—portion of their strategic power.

The Soviets, in fact, asserted that their strategic programs in the 1970s had merely been designed to catch up with the United States. Brezhnev repeatedly affirmed that the achievement of superiority was no part of Soviet military efforts, whether in the realm of intercontinental weaponry or regionally. His major public arms control initiative in the autumn of 1979 suggested a readiness to limit the deployment of Soviet SS-20 intermediate-range ballistic missiles aimed at Europe, but only on condition that the West abstained from deploying any modernized or new nuclear systems in Europe capable of reaching Soviet territory. Along similar lines, the Soviets, whose intercontinental ballistic missile forces were expected to have the capacity to destroy a large portion of U.S. fixed strategic forces by the early 1980s, urged cancellation of U.S. programs (such as the MX program) that would improve the survivability of U.S. forces and increase U.S. capabilities to target Soviet fixed intercontinental ballistic missiles. In short, following logically from their claim that Soviet programs were simply achieving a condition of parity, the Soviets objected to all new American (or NATO) programs that in the Western view were needed to maintain or restore parity. Alternatively, the Soviets threatened to develop additional Soviet programs to counter those of the West.

In addition, the Soviets maintained their long-standing view that their geographical position, the U.S. forward-based systems, the nuclear forces of the United Kingdom and France, and the need for defense against China had to be weighed when judging the state of the strategic balance. From the Soviet point of view, these and other factors entitled the USSR to certain compensations in the numbers and types of their strategic and other forces; any advantages thus conferred upon the USSR were part of the balance that represented a state of "equal security"—a concept long held by the Soviets and mentioned in several joint U.S.-Soviet documents, but never defined.

Such perceptual differences between the United States and the USSR do not provide a favorable platform from which to develop mutually acceptable restraints on strategic programs, although efforts to do so will no doubt continue in the coming years, whether or not SALT II has been approved and implemented.

At the level of intercontinental weapons, the Soviets will presumably wait to see whether the U.S. MX program will go forward and, if so, how rapidly. If domestic resistance or impediments were to slow or abort the program, the Soviets might be even less inclined than they already are to consider reducing their reliance on fixed land-based intercontinental ballistic missiles. But they may in any case supplement the latter with mobile forces of their own to offset increasing accuracies of current and planned U.S. forces, including cruise missiles. It remains to be seen how meticulous the Soviets would be in selecting deployment modes that would permit the counting of launchers in order to maintain SALT launcher ceilings. The United States, for its part, should actively reconsider the planned "racetrack" basing mode for the MX and, if necessary, should seek changes in the SALT provisions to allow a less cumbersome kind of deployment.

There might be scope in such circumstances for certain qualitative limitations—for example, on the number of reentry vehicles per launcher, on testing, on the pace at which new systems can be introduced, on esoteric weapons of various kinds. But it seems unlikely that the SALT process over the next several years will have significant limiting effects on programs now being implemented and planned by both sides.

The increasing vulnerabilities of fixed sites might make it of interest for both sides to consider adjustments in the antiballistic missile treaty to permit certain kinds of point defenses. There may be pressures in the United States to proceed in this direction by unilateral action—that is, by invoking the "supreme interests" clause of the treaty (article XV); but this course could trigger use of the clause, and analogous ones in other treaties, and thus would undo modest accomplishments in strategic arms limitations that have been achieved in the past. If the United States were persuaded of the need for point defenses against missile attack, the route of negotiated change in the treaty would be much preferable to unilateral action. Failing success in the former, the latter would have to be considered.

An important issue that might be addressed in part through negotiations is the security of command and control. Thus efforts to constrain development and deployment of antisatellite weapons should be pursued. The United States should not deny itself devices of this kind if Soviet antisatellite programs go forward. In any event, however, the principal means of safeguarding systems that fall within the categories of command, control, communications, and intelligence-gathering must continue to be unilateral. The Soviets, to judge from what is known publicly of their programs, do not seem to share Western theories of stability, which hold that these elements of an opponent's military capabilities should not be brought under threat of attack or incapacitation.

In late 1979 more active negotiations on regional nuclear delivery systems seemed on the horizon during the next few years. The Protocol to SALT II included a temporary prohibition on the deployment of cruise missiles (besides air-launched missiles) with ranges of more than 600 kilometers. In practice, this provision applied only to the United States because the USSR was not preparing to deploy such systems. The United States, however, did not expect to have its pertinent cruise missiles ready for deployment before the expiration date of the Protocol (December 31, 1981). Soviet and U.S. ballistic missiles and aircraft with similar intermediate ranges were not restricted.

The Soviets indicated that they intend to seek an extension of the Protocol limitations on the United States. Indeed, they mounted a major campaign to try to forestall or slow NATO programs to deploy several hundred ground-launched cruise missile launchers and intermediate-range Pershing II ballistic missile launchers in the early and mid-1980s. The NATO countries declared their readiness to consider numerical limitations on these deployments if Soviet SS-20 missile and Backfire bomber deployments were likewise restricted. (As already noted, the Soviets offered to halt SS-20 missile deployment in 1979 if Western programs were canceled altogether. They subsequently asserted that no negotiations on European theater nuclear weapons could occur unless NATO revoked its decisions to produce and deploy such systems. Afghanistan further diminished expectations of early negotiations.)

A problem for the West in any such negotiations arises because the Western programs were needed to balance not only Soviet intermediate-range systems but also the steady buildup of both shorter range Soviet nuclear capabilities and Warsaw Pact conventional forces. Several Western political leaders, for domestic and other reasons, have alluded to the possibility that Western deployments might be made superfluous by successful negotiations. But the public record does not make clear whether such a bargain would involve only the Soviet SS-20 and Backfire or whether there would also have to be curtailments in the other Soviet and Warsaw Pact forces. From the standpoint of the United States, the preservation of the flexible response strategy in Europe would make the deployment of a modern intermediate-range capability desirable, if not essential, even if the SS-20 and Backfire were substantially reduced in the equation. (Both these Soviet systems could theoretically be moved out of range of NATO targets but redeployed back to the western USSR in a relatively short time. Western systems could not be similarly moved. They probably would not even be produced by the United States if they were not to be stationed in Western Europe.)

Negotiations confined to intermediate-range systems could thus run the risk of leaving important Western programs hobbled in exchange for some limitations on the Soviets without, however, affecting other adverse trends in the European military balance. On the other hand, an agreement that preserved the essential size and nature of the Western program could not be expected to affect the worrisome Soviet intermediate-range deployments.

This unpromising prospect might be improved by relating the negotiations to the mutual and balanced force reduction talks. But here again the prognosis is not favorable, even apart from Afghanistan. The Soviets announced in late 1979 that they planned to make some unilateral reductions in their forces in Central Europe (20,000 men and 1,000 tanks). The West, in turn, was to undertake unilateral removal of 1,000 obsolescent nuclear warheads plus an additional number equal to that deployed under its modernization plan. If implemented, these actions would represent the first reciprocated military reductions in the region. The basic military imbalance would not be affected, however. And the Soviets might simply transfer the withdrawn forces to other assertive uses.

The USSR has rejected the Western view that Soviet modernization programs during the past ten or more years have substantially changed the balance in favor of the East. Although both sides have accepted the principle that an agreement should eventually leave each side with the same number of forces, no agreement has been reached on the data for levels of existing Warsaw Pact forces. The

Soviets have not agreed that unequal reductions will be required to reach equal levels. Among other complications, those related to the way in which reductions would be implemented by countries besides the United States and the USSR have been most troublesome. (The Federal Republic of Germany, for example, has always objected to any implication that the Soviets might have a *droit de regard* with respect to the size of the Bundeswehr.)

It is conceivable that these negotiating bottlenecks will loosen up somewhat, if only because the Soviets might want to impede efforts by NATO, over a period of years, to improve its forces. But it is doubtful that Moscow would offer sufficiently far-reaching adjustments in its force posture in Eastern Europe to produce fundamental changes in the defense problems faced by the West. Moreover, the effects of the asymmetry in the geographic positions of the United States and the USSR vis-à-vis Europe cannot be removed altogether even by the most asymmetrical changes in military dispositions. Since World War II the Soviets have never been prepared to do without massive forces on their Western perimeter; there is no indication that this will change in the 1980s. These forces have always served offensive and defensive purposes—an arrow pointed at the West and a deterrent to rapid or anti-Soviet change in the East. If the 1980s are to be a time of leadership succession, the Soviets will probably be even more sensitive than usual to possible turmoil in Eastern Europe.

Despite these rather sober prospects for both the SALT negotiations and those more specifically related to the military balance in Europe, existing negotiating forums may still survive in more or less the same form. For the West, including the United States, continued efforts at negotiated arms control are required because the public expects them. Support for adequate military forces rests to an important degree on the continued efforts of governments to find agreed ways of restraining competition. At the same time, the decade of the 1980s will be a period when special efforts are needed to strengthen the Western military posture if deterrence is to remain credible and Western nations are to have the general sense of security and U.S. commitment needed to resist Soviet political pressures.

Soviet military advances may have the effect in the 1980s of intensifying dilemmas for Western defense that have never been fully resolved. Evidently unwilling, even though theoretically able, to match Soviet and Warsaw Pact conventional forces, the West has long relied on U.S. nuclear weapons (and to a lesser degree on French and British ones) to deter Soviet attack. But reliance on the role of extended deterrence of U.S. intercontinental ballistic missile forces became more problematic when the Soviets began to acquire their own means of threatening the United States. In the 1950s, therefore, the United States undertook nuclear deployments within the European theater. Possible use of these weapons in a war always posed difficulties for the Europeans, and it has never proved feasible to develop a complete set of criteria for their role. This became even more complicated after the Soviets also entered the era of nuclear plenty and based their own military strategy for a European war on early use of theater nuclear weapons, including weapons located inside the USSR. The effect of these developments was to reinforce the weight of Soviet conventional advantages and to stimulate long-standing European worries that U.S. strategic forces were being de-coupled from the defense of Europe. (Such worries were further intensified by the increasing Soviet counterforce capabilities against U.S. strategic forces.)

In light of these trends, many suggestions have been made to revise Western defense concepts. It is doubtful, however, that a more satis-factory alternative to the flexible response concept can be found in the 1980s and agreed upon by the Western allies. NATO will have to devote its energies to adapting the existing concept to the new and emerging conditions created by Soviet buildups, and, above all, to procuring and improving the forces that give the concept military meaning.

Negotiations with the Soviets—whether bilaterally between the United States and the USSR or in wider East-West forums, such as the existing mutual and balanced force reduction talks in Vienna, the follow-up discussions of the Conference on Security and Coopera-tion in Europe, or possible new conferences—do not seem likely to alter significantly the tasks that must be confronted by the West. As already indicated, adjustments in force and armaments levels that might be achieved and implemented through agreement would not seriously address the Western military problems; these do not so much stem from disparate numbers as from the qualitative changes in Soviet forces. (The Soviets also tend to see their defense problems in Europe as stemming from qualitative changes in Western forces. On the other hand, by contending that they are increasing neither the number of their nuclear and other forces nor the yield of their nuclear warheads, the Soviets seek to play down the qualitative improvements in their own forces.)

Some possibilities for negotiation may exist in so-called confidence-building measures. These may have marginal benefits for the Western military position by restricting the size of maneuvers, limiting other kinds of force movements, and refining certain warning indicators to make planning for a surprise attack more difficult. Such restrictions would also entail some costs for the West if they were to inhibit, for example, trans-Atlantic reinforcement for exercises or for use in times of crisis.

The basic message of this discussion, however, is that the next several years are unlikely to be productive ones in negotiated strategic and European arms control. Some weapons programs may be slowed down and some force disposition may be regulated. But unilateral defense programs will be the chief means of coping with the vulnerabilities and imbalances of strategic forces and the problems of deterrence and defense in the European theater.

Conventional Arms Transfers and Regional Limitations

A number of other arms control projects may be carried over into the 1980s, although the Afghanistan crisis makes this less likely in the short run. Two of these—conventional arms transfers and arms limitation in the Indian Ocean area—stem from the hopes expressed some years ago that a mutual U.S.-Soviet interest in reducing the likelihood of regional conflicts could be translated into certain agreed restraints. Negotiations begun in the early stages of the Carter administration later encountered difficulties, which suggested that either less congruence existed between U.S. and Soviet interests in regional crises than assumed or that overlap was insufficient to make agreements readily feasible.

There was concern during the 1970s in many quarters in the United States that U.S. arms transfer policy needed overhauling and stricter control. In 1977 the Carter administration promulgated a set of guidelines to this end, and a number of congressional actions sought to set firmer conditions for the sale or transfer of military equipment. It was recognized that unilateral U.S. restraint might merely result in replacement by other suppliers where the United States was removing or limiting its supply. Efforts were thus initiated to enlist support from other suppliers, including the USSR.

The Soviets have been using the supply of arms and military equipment as an instrument of foreign policy for a quarter of a century. Many of the more dramatic Soviet breakthroughs in establishing bridgeheads or clients in the third world occurred on the strength of military assistance programs, often undertaken on favorable financial terms for the recipient. Although Soviet propaganda has been second to none in condemning the arms trade as inherently dangerous (when conducted by others), Moscow itself has always been clear in its position of subordinating its arms transfer policies to broader foreign policy goals. At times this has meant that the Soviets have refused to meet all demands made on them because they evidently believed that to do so was too risky. In the Middle East, for example, while making massive arms deliveries to Egypt and Syria since the late 1950s, the Soviets nevertheless withheld certain sophisticated weapons—those they judged would be used to start open warfare in circumstances that the Soviets found objectionable. This relative Soviet caution did not necessarily restrain the recipients; but it indicates that the Soviets have sought to maintain political control over their arms transfer policies—sometimes (as in Egypt) at considerable cost. At the same time, the Soviets have generally not attached restrictions on use for arms they have delivered.

Because the Soviets have calibrated their arms policies to their political purposes, the prospect of working out agreed restraints with them are not good. Predictably, the Soviets have sought to turn negotiations on conventional arms transfers into a means of impeding U.S. transfers wherever these stand in the way of Soviet goals. On the other hand, the Soviets have resisted restrictions on their own freedom of action. Abstract notions about mutual restraint in areas of tension have had little appeal to the Soviets precisely because these are the areas in which the Soviets seek to make political gains. As noted, where the Soviets did practice restraint, it was because of the way they calculated the risks to themselves. Thus, in the Middle East, the Soviets have always taken the view that agreed restraints on arms transfers must follow a political settlement of the Arab-Israeli conflict —that is, the Soviets have refused to accept restrictions on their ability to supply clients (or look for new ones), regardless of the state of tension. But they have applied unilateral limitations when they consider it in their interests. During conflicts in southern Africa and East Africa, the Soviets likewise have shown no interest in agreed limitations but have applied them unilaterally as policy needs or risks dictated.

In light of experience to date, negotiations on conventional arms transfers that are not related to efforts to deal politically with regional conflict situations have little promise of producing results. An exception may be found in possible limitations on weapons types. It is unlikely to be a significant exception, however, because such limitations would probably be applied to weapons that neither side was prepared to export. Still, this aspect is worth pursuing because an understanding might reduce the likelihood of irrational responses to presumed or feared transfers of various esoteric weapons. (Nuclear weapons, for example, are already covered under the Treaty on the Nonproliferation of Nuclear Weapons; antiballistic missiles may not be transferred under the 1972 treaty.)

If efforts to limit conventional arms transfers were designed to reduce the dangers of regional conflicts by inhibiting the flow of weapons for use by regional powers, the arms limitation talks regarding the Indian Ocean represented an effort to reduce these dangers by limiting the military activities of external powers, specifically the United States and the USSR. This project has faced a number of difficulties. Although Soviet naval power has grown and is now a major instrument of Soviet power projection, the United States, on the whole, still relies more heavily on maritime mobility than the USSR. This is hardly surprising, given the relative proximity of Soviet territory to large parts of the Eurasian land mass. Inherently, therefore, limitations on naval movements tend to have more inhibiting effects on U.S. access to regions in Eurasia than on Soviet access. (The crises in Iran and Afghanistan in 1979–80 illustrate this point.) In addition, major U.S. reliance on missile-launching submarines for strategic deterrence makes restrictions (such as geographic ones or by type of ship or by ship-days) unequal in their effects on the two sides. It has also proved difficult to reach common definitions of what constitutes a base or some other military facility, the establishment or use of which might be limited by agreement. Apart from contending that the facilities to which they have access—for example, on the Indian Ocean littoral—are not bases, whereas Diego Garcia is, the

Soviets have also taken the position that if they operate in a country by invitation, they should not be subject to limitation.

These and other difficulties encountered in negotiations to limit regional arms underline the basic proposition discussed above—that limitations on military activities can probably not be isolated from broader political understandings concerning a particular region. Indeed, the United States recognized this interconnection when it suspended Indian Ocean negotiations in 1979 because of Soviet activities in certain littoral countries. In most cases, limitations would tend to operate to the disadvantage of the United States; and for these limitations to be significant and equitable in their effects, they would have to occur in the context of broader political settlements.

Unilateral or Informal Restraints

Since 1962 the United States has imposed limitations on Soviet military activities in the Caribbean. No comparable restraints apply for U.S. forces, apart from general assurances by the United States that Cuba will not be attacked. The Caribbean case, which has its origins in the 1962 missile crisis, is unlikely to be replicated elsewhere. It is a function largely of U.S. ability to enforce the restrictions by the presence of superior regional power and to invoke sanctions against the USSR. Even so, the pattern of the 1960s and 1970s suggests continued periodic Soviet efforts in the next decade to test the limits of U.S. tolerance and capabilities by attempting expanded military activities. As long as the Soviet-Cuban association endures, the United States is likely to be confronted by this problem.

The United States, for its part, has practiced some military restraint in areas considered sensitive by the Soviet Union. U.S. military activities in the Baltic Sea, for example, are modest. In the Black Sea, in addition to restrictions imposed by the 1936 Montreux Convention on the passage of warships through the Turkish Straits (which the Soviets, incidentally, have stretched in successfully declaring their aircraft carriers as cruisers), the United States observes unilateral restraints on the frequency of naval visits, the number of ships, and the types and geographic limits of operational activities. The Soviets are not similarly constrained in these areas. Unlike the situation in the Caribbean, however, U.S. restraints are a matter of unilateral judgment and decision rather than of written agreement. These cases do highlight the fact that systematic restraints—unilateral, imposed, or mutually agreed—have occurred only in areas contiguous to the territories of either the United States or the Soviet Union. If either side succeeded in dominating some third area in a way tantamount to contiguity, similar restraints might come into being there. Barring such developments, explicit restraint generally will be far more difficult to establish in regions remote from either the United States or the Soviet Union. (Antarctica is one exception; the demilitarized regime in this unpopulated area was established in 1955 for economic, political, and other reasons that cannot be duplicated elsewhere, except possibly in outer space.)

Nuclear Nonproliferation

The United States and the Soviet Union first engaged in active dialogue on nuclear proliferation in the aftermath of President Eisenhower's Atoms for Peace proposals of 1953. A perceived common interest in confining the nuclear weapons club to the then-existing membership contributed to the inclusion in the 1956 International Atomic Energy Agency charter of provisions to prevent peaceful uses of atomic energy from being diverted to military purposes.

In the 1960s the negotiations leading to the Treaty on the Nonproliferation of Nuclear Weapons, again conducted initially by the United States and the USSR, sought to establish more extensive means to preclude the spread of nuclear weapons capabilities to other countries. Although many governments subscribed to the treaty—as they had supported the safeguards and restrictions applied by the International Atomic Energy Agency—several countries delayed doing so or declined altogether. For some, this reluctance stemmed from a fear that adherence to nonproliferation would hamper programs for the production of nuclear power. In addition, some countries did not wish to preclude themselves indefinitely from acquiring nuclear weapons.

In the 1970s the United States pursued a more activist policy to achieve cooperation with the USSR and other major suppliers of nuclear materials, equipment, and technology; this policy applied restrictions to exports and called for recipients to accept safeguards and inspecting procedures. U.S. legislation required invocation, in effect, of certain penalties against countries that did not comply adequately with various multilateral and bilateral safeguard requirements. Such penalties included reductions in U.S. economic and military assistance. On the more positive side, efforts were undertaken, multi-laterally as well as bilaterally, to provide security assurances to countries that were denied access to potential nuclear weapons capabilities.

The Soviets in general saw their own interests served in confining the number of countries with nuclear weapons to the smallest possible one. From their vantage point, all countries with nuclear weapons were actually or potentially hostile to them. Most states generally considered capable, through their own efforts, of acquiring nuclear weapons and delivering them would also be counted as hostile or un-friendly to the USSR.

India was probably an exception to this general rule. The Soviets did not let India's peaceful explosion of a nuclear device deter them from continuing to pursue friendly relations, although the supply of heavy water to India was apparently curtailed. The slight cooling in Soviet-Indian relations in the late 1970s was brought about by changes in domestic Indian politics rather than by any Soviet initia-tive stemming from Indian nuclear programs. To what extent the Soviets might have been instrumental in dissuading the Indians from conducting an early second explosion is not clear from the public record.

The Soviet Union has supported and participated in international programs to prevent the diversion of peaceful nuclear materials and equipment to military purposes; its export policies, especially within the bloc, have generally been conservative. On the other hand, no Soviet policy appears to be analogous to the U.S. practice of imposing certain quasi-sanctions on nations that do not fully accept various restrictions on their peaceful programs.

As matters have developed, the United States appears to have car-ried the main political burden of attempting to apply restrictions to the nuclear policies of non-Communist countries. At various times this has led to strained relations between the United States and one or more of the suppliers of nuclear equipment (France and the Fed-eral Republic of Germany, for instance) and between the United States and one or more recipients of external assistance or countries suspected of, or actually working on, potential nuclear weapons pro-grams (Brazil, Iran under the shah, Israel, Pakistan, South Africa, South Korea). These have been, for the most part, countries with which the United States is either allied or maintains generally friendly relations, whereas the Soviets maintain more distant relations with them or none at all.

In a number of the countries allied with the United States there has been resentment at various times over what appeared to be U.S.-Soviet collaboration, or at least consensus, at their expense. This has been the case in the past in France and the Federal Republic of Germany. The Germans, in particular, would probably have been less uneasy about adhering to the nonproliferation treaty if it had been essentially an intra-Western agreement rather than one negotiated principally by the United States and the USSR. These concerns have by now been largely dissipated. But with the deepening of the energy crisis, resentments continue to exist concerning any efforts, in the name of nonproliferation, to curtail options for nuclear power and for doing business in the field of nuclear energy.

Another aspect of the nonproliferation issue is the connection that has been made between it and the disarmament efforts of the super-powers. Many nonnuclear weapons states have asserted that as long as the nuclear weapons arsenals of a few states exist and grow, non-proliferation is discriminatory. Some of these states have conditioned their continuing cooperation in establishing a broad nonproliferation regime on progress in arms control, especially with respect to nuclear weapons. Article VI of the nonproliferation treaty placed nuclear weapons states under a general obligation to achieve such progress. Among the reasons frequently cited for proceeding with a comprehensive nuclear test ban—a matter under active negotiation in the Carter administration by the United States, the United Kingdom, and the Soviet Union—is the presumed effect that an agreement in this field would have in persuading nonnuclear weapons states of the serious-ness of nuclear weapons states in curbing their military programs. Although the nonproliferation treaty, various resolutions of the United Nations, and innumerable statements by nonnuclear weapons states have stressed the connection between superpower disarmament and nonproliferation, this relationship is probably rather complex. Countries that rely on U.S. military guarantees for their security must view limitations on U.S. defense programs with some misgivings and may therefore not be wholly persuaded that agreements in this respect are an appropriate precondition to their own renunciation of nuclear weapons.

One rationale for the U.S. antiballistic missile programs of the

1960s and early 1970s was that they would serve to protect the United States from small-scale nuclear attacks by countries besides the USSR. The freezing or dismantling of the small deployed U.S. and Soviet antiballistic missile systems as a result of the 1972 treaty had the effect of improving the countercity capabilities of small nuclear forces. Thus the British, French, and Chinese may have been beneficiaries of this effect because of their ability to threaten various Soviet targets.

Despite environmentalist and other objections to the rapid development of nuclear power in many Western countries, the mounting uncertainties about the availability of adequate petroleum supplies at acceptable prices will almost certainly increase pressures in the 1980s for additional nuclear power plants and associated facilities throughout the world. The probabilities will rise that potential nuclear weapons capabilities will develop, despite extensive measures to prevent this from occurring. In addition, political conditions and uncertainties about external security guarantees will probably continue to generate pressures for weapons development in several countries. Although the Soviets can be expected to maintain a generally cooperative stance on export policies and international safeguard arrangements, other Soviet policies may well continue to contribute to such pressures. In particular, South Africa and Israel probably will be affected. Soviet policies also played a part in Pakistan's aspirations to achieve nuclear weapons status—or, in the absence of conventional weapons support from the United States, to pursue appeasement of the USSR. (Developments in Afghanistan belatedly led the United States in early 1980 to relax restrictions on conventional arms transfers to Pakistan.)

The United States may well find itself under periodic Soviet pressures to undertake coercive actions in order to arrest nuclear weapons programs in countries like South Africa and Israel if evidence of such programs, however ambiguous, becomes available. The United States will need to deal with such Soviet overtures with caution. Despite the common U.S.-Soviet interest in seeing nuclear proliferation precluded, joint coercive action, U.S. action clearly stimulated by the USSR, or unilateral Soviet action would all pose serious problems for the United States. This would be especially true when previous Soviet policies—such as encouragement and support for black African military action against South Africa—contribute to the causes or pretexts for a decision by a threatened country to acquire nuclear arsenals.

The United States will need to draw a careful line between cooperating with the USSR in promoting international safeguards and other control arrangements with respect to peaceful nuclear programs, on the one hand, and de facto alliances of a coercive character, even under the auspices of the United Nations, on the other.

The United States must also recognize that, although efforts to establish nonnuclear weapons zones—including provisions against the use of nuclear weapons against countries in such zones—may be suitable in certain cases, such zones are not universally appropriate. Western Europe would, for example, be unsuitable for such arrangements as long as the defense of the region relies, in part, on possible first use of nuclear weapons by the United States. Korea is another example where, in foreseeable circumstances, the United States cannot deny itself the option of recourse to nuclear weapons in the event of attack.

In general, while the exclusion of nuclear weapons from a particular geographic zone is probably verifiable within reasonable margins of error, prohibitions of the use of such weapons from launching areas external to the zone would be purely declaratory. As such, they would probably not constrain a country that aspires to nuclear weapons as a deterrent, however minimal, against a potential nuclear enemy. Beyond the arrangements for exclusion of nuclear weapons that have already been undertaken in Latin America, therefore, the United States should treat such schemes with caution.

The 1980s may also witness a revival of the idea of a European nuclear weapons capability, although this seems highly unlikely at this time. The nonproliferation treaty was intended to leave this option open, at least according to the interpretation of the Western signatories. The possibility presupposes the creation of a European political entity into which existing European nuclear capabilities would be merged. The Soviets would no doubt strenuously reiterate their old objections to such a scheme, and this alone would probably be a major impediment to its revival. The United States, however, should continue to keep an open mind.

In sum, the 1980s will probably continue to be a period during which considerable overlap will occur in U.S. and Soviet interests in preventing the spread of nuclear weapons. There will continue to be scope for cooperative or parallel policies to this end. Although the Soviets will not deny themselves opportunities for export of nuclear materials, equipment, and technologies (several Western nations, indeed, rely on the availability of Soviet-supplied nuclear fuel), they will probably maintain tight controls on such exports to minimize diversions to military use. As in the past, the Soviets will also be alert to opportunities for complicating U.S. relations with allies or other non-Communist countries. The United States, in pursuing nonproliferation policies on several fronts, will need to bear in mind its priority interest in the cohesion of its alliances.

The 1980s may experience the emergence of one or more new nuclear weapons states, although such predictions, which have been made for years, should be treated with some skepticism. There is no doubt that if this were to occur in regions of high tension, crises there would become even more complex to manage than in the past. This is not the place to describe possible scenarios. The incentives for U.S. and Soviet efforts to ease tensions would no doubt increase with the prospect that a crisis might escalate to the use or threatened use of nuclear weapons by one or more of the parties to it. Whatever the state of bilateral relations, it is unlikely that either the United States or the USSR would want to be drawn into a nuclear conflict against its will.

Thus new forms of U.S.-Soviet communication and consultation, as well as recourse to international or regional organizations, should be considered—preferably before a crisis reduces decision times. This is a delicate problem. Planning for proliferation and how to manage a crisis involving parties with nuclear weapons in third world areas would amount to conceding the failure of nonproliferation policies. The implication of U.S.-Soviet joint domination may complicate rather than alleviate tension. The rather modest and basically moribund U.S.-Soviet Agreement on the Prevention of Nuclear War (1973) created a certain (misplaced) anxiety among NATO allies. But that agreement, with its provisions for consultations in crisis situations, could sometime in the 1980s be a basis for U.S.-Soviet cooperative activities on this range of problems.

Economic Relations

During the 1970s Soviet economic relations with the outside world increased substantially. Decisions promulgated at the twenty-fourth and twenty-fifth congresses of the Communist Party of the Soviet

Union in 1971 and 1976, respectively, indicated clearly that Soviet leaders recognized the need to expand trade with the industrialized world in order to meet needs for capital goods, technology, foodstuffs, and other items that the Soviet economy and the economies of the USSR's East European allies could not adequately fill. Between 1970 and 1977, Soviet trade with the non-Communist world (including developing countries) increased about 111 percent in real terms. In trade with the non-Communist industrialized world, Soviet imports exceeded exports in all but one year between 1970 and 1978. Consequently, the hard-currency debt of the USSR rose from $1.9 billion in 1970 to $16 billion in 1977. The total net hard-currency debt of all the COMECON countries reached about $50 billion by 1977, when Poland's indebtedness of $13 billion was second to that of the USSR.

Soviet leaders since the days of Stalin have sought to stimulate the interest of the American business community in the opportunities of the Eastern market. These overtures have not been without response, especially as other Western countries began to activate official and private commercial dealings with the USSR. In the absence of most-favored-nation status and access to the facilities of the Export-Import Bank, and with various restrictive U.S. laws, business activity between the United States and the USSR has remained modest. The United States tied any consideration of extending most-favored-nation status and Export-Import Bank facilities to the USSR to a settlement of the World War II lend-lease claims issue, a problem that remained deadlocked for years. The Soviets, in turn, showed no disposition to take action on the lend-lease issue without assurances that U.S. trade restrictions would be removed.

As pressures from several quarters mounted in the early 1970s to reduce the impediments to trade, the Nixon administration sought to formulate a broad approach to U.S.-Soviet economic relations. In contrast to views expressed by parts of the business community and others, the premise of the Nixon administration was that economic interaction required more normal political relations and that the prospect of more extensive economic relations could contribute to incentives for more restrained Soviet international behavior. The Nixon administration was prepared to expedite or delay governmental decisions on trade with the USSR in accordance with Soviet conduct on political issues. This form of "linkage," which may be called tactical, was not, however, the essence of the approach developed in the early

1970s. Its most important objective was to attempt to gear the expansion of economic interaction to the overall state of relations—that is, to view economic relations over the long run as an aspect of the evolving total relationship.

Following the first Nixon-Brezhnev summit in 1972, a series of agreements was reached that removed the various formal impediments to economic relations and sought to place these relations on an increasingly normal basis. In 1972 an umbrella trade agreement was designed to facilitate business activities, provide safeguards against various kinds of disruptive trade practices, and arrange for settlement of disputes. A maritime agreement sought to regulate commercial shipping between the two countries, including that associated with the periodically heavy grain trade. These measures, developed shortly after the 1972 summit, were intended to fit into a broad array of agreements and understandings which, along with an adequate military balance and the use of vigorous actions against hostile Soviet moves, would in time lead to more orderly and less crisis-ridden relations.

The Soviets—with Brezhnev personally taking the lead—seemed eager for massive U.S. and Western investments, especially in Soviet raw material projects in Siberia, which were expected to provide the hard-currency earnings to finance Moscow's increasing import needs. Brezhnev evidently perceived that these arrangements would extend far into the future. He probably recognized that such imports would have an impact on Soviet society, decisionmaking, and the economy. (This may have been a matter of internal dispute among Soviet leaders.) He also seemed to understand that the kinds of relations envisaged would require greater civility and restraint in political relations, and would place the USSR in a state of gradually increasing reliance on the outside world. On the other hand, he no doubt expected that the West would acquire its own stake in the benefits of expanding economic relations with the East.

Whether explicitly planned or not, the growth of Soviet influence and political-military reach on the one hand, and the increasing economic interaction between the USSR and other nations on the other, became the processes that characterized the Soviet evolution in the 1970s. The pattern is likely to continue in the next decade.

Despite these general developments and expectations, U.S.-Soviet economic relations have progressed only modestly. The warming trend marked by the 1972 summit and subsequent agreements coincided with a notable increase in Jewish emigration from the USSR. The Soviets moved to arrest the flow by imposing financial penalties and other forms of discrimination on potential emigrants and others. This led the U.S. Congress to attach conditions regarding Soviet emigration practices to confirmation of the 1972 trade agreements. Although the Soviets reduced their financial levies, other forms of harassment continued. Eventually, despite strong misgivings by the Nixon and Ford administrations, Congress adopted the Jackson-Vanik amendment to the Trade Act of 1974. This required the president to obtain certain assurances from the Soviet Union regarding emigration and to certify that the Soviets were in compliance with standards set by Congress. Other legislation, notably the Stevenson amendment to Export-Import Bank legislation in 1974, placed limits on the amounts of credit that could be extended to the USSR. In early 1975 the Soviets rejected these conditions and refused to let the 1972 trade agreement take effect, although certain specific provisions, such as those governing U.S. business representatives in the USSR, were implemented in practice. Consequently, most-favored-nation status and U.S. government credits remain suspended for the Soviet Union.

During the past few years a number of suggestions have been made in the United States for alleviating the impasse. For reasons not entirely clear but probably connected in part with the hope of building support for modifying U.S. legislative restrictions, the Soviets permitted emigration to increase again in 1978 and 1979, after it had been significantly reduced from the peak reached in 1973.

The Soviet Union has steadily built up economic relations with other Western industrial nations and a modest, if fluctuating, level of intercourse with the United States—largely U.S. grain and machinery exports and U.S. raw material imports. But the Soviets remain eager to develop active trade with Americans. The United States, in turn, has been deprived of a certain volume of business; more importantly, however, the possibility of utilizing economic relations in the pursuit of broader and longer-term policy objectives has basically gone untested. The leverage with regard to Soviet human rights practices afforded by a policy of denial, albeit one modified by modest private commerce and credit, remains open to argument.

In addition, efforts by the industrialized democracies to achieve coordination in their economic policies toward the USSR have almost certainly been hampered by the absence of systematically articulated and implemented policies by the United States. The desirability of developing broadly coordinated economic policies toward the USSR and the COMECON countries is a controversial issue among Western nations. The one existing mechanism in this field, the Coordinating Committee (COCOM), which must approve exports having possible military benefits for the Soviets, has functioned with indifferent success. Inevitably, suspicions arise that one country seeks to use the export-control instrument against another for commercial rather than security reasons. Nevertheless, COCOM provides a forum for some degree of coordination.

In the 1980s Western countries—both individually and as a group—can hardly avoid addressing such issues as the establishment of prudent levels and terms of exposure for private and public lending institutions doing business with the USSR and COMECON countries; safeguards against dumping and other market disruptions by the USSR (the European Community faces this problem in the petrochemical industry, for example); and the dependence upon Soviet sources of supply that is acceptable in a particular sector of economic activity.

Perhaps the most serious and complicated issue is that Western petroleum-consuming nations must face the possibility of COMECON becoming a net importer of oil and must plan for the impact of such a development on oil supplies and prices. Presumably, too, because oil is one of the principal sources of Soviet hard-currency income, a shift from a position of net exporter to one of net importer (at least by COMECON as a group) would produce an additional need for financing, especially if Soviet demand for agricultural commodities, machinery, and technology persists.

In the United States, particularly, the complex issue of technology transfers to facilitate recovery of remote and difficult-to-reach petroleum reserves in the USSR will need to be readdressed. Trade-offs have to be weighed between the benefits that the Soviets might derive from such transfers for their defense establishment and the possible postponement of the time when the USSR might make the world's oil supply tighter. The connection made in the United States between this issue and Soviet trials of dissidents distracted attention from fundamental substantive issues and had doubtful positive humanitarian effects.

In early 1980 the United States is moving to curtail technology exports and grain sales to the USSR because of the latter's invasion of Afghanistan. But these and other economic issues are likely to reemerge during the decade of the 1980s. An eventual new Soviet leadership will have to address the complex problems of the Soviet economy as its growth rate slows, and various distortions and short-comings continue to retard progress. Whether a new leadership will be more or less inclined than the Brezhnev leadership to tamper with the fundamental organization and structure of the Soviet economy remains to be seen. What seems almost certain, however, is that the Soviet Union will become more involved with the world's economy in the 1980s. It is unlikely that any single trading partner will be in a position to induce the Soviets to play by the rules of international economic intercourse. The Soviets themselves will naturally be inclined to make their bargains by appealing to the individual commercial interests of particular countries or firms.

For the United States to deal effectively with the USSR on economic issues and to have any significant influence over the character and direction of East-West economic relations, it will have to find ways of removing or reducing the institutional and legal impediments to the conduct of its own economic policies toward the USSR. The executive branch and Congress will need to undertake renewed efforts to this end, recognizing that trade is not a favor that the United States unilaterally grants to the USSR but can aid in the pursuit of wider U.S. interests.

Given the history of the issues and the powerful political interests that have been engaged in it, it will be difficult to disentangle economic policy from human rights considerations such as emigration. But unless the rigid connection that came into being in the 1970s is gradually attenuated and the U.S. government is given the opportunity and the incentive to formulate broad policy guidelines, U.S.-Soviet economic relations will continue to proceed largely on the basis of individual decisions with minimal purposeful direction. And the capacity of the United States to participate in multilateral approaches with other industrial democratic countries—most of which are also members of Western security alliances maintained to ward off dangers emanating from the USSR—will remain severely hampered. (Experience, for example, has shown that efforts by governments to establish broad guidelines for credit policies toward the East have met with only sporadic and limited success.)

Special mention must be made of the grain trade. Despite Soviet claims that the USSR will soon be independent of agricultural imports, that day will not arrive in the 1980s. The reason is not that the Soviets cannot provide a subsistence-level diet for their population, but rather that the political leadership some years ago resolved to provide the population with an improved diet, with the emphasis on high-protein foods. It seems doubtful that even if Brezhnev's successors were more conservative and draconian than he and his colleagues have been, they would repeal this basic political decision of the post-Stalin regimes. On the other hand, a more experimentally inclined leadership may be prepared to attempt reforms of the basic agricultural organization of the USSR and to give more scope to initiative and private production. Additional investment resources may also be made available to increase productivity and to improve quality, marketing, and the other chronic failings of Soviet agriculture. Even so, however, the need for augmenting domestic production with imports will remain for several years. The precise annual volume of demand obviously fluctuates with the size and quality of the harvest.

Until the Afghanistan crisis the United States was reluctant to utilize Soviet reliance on American agricultural exports to affect Soviet political conduct, although suggestions frequently arose that it should do so—usually in circumstances in which other forms of presumed leverage were considered too risky. Moreover, the American farm community and others concerned with such matters as the U.S. balance of payments and the reduction of restraints on trade have generally opposed government intervention in the grain trade. There has also been widespread opposition on moral grounds to the use of food for political purposes. However, in the case of the USSR the effect would not be starvation. (American trade unions, such as the longshoremen, have not always shared such beliefs. They have used boycotts for a variety of reasons—and are currently doing so because of the Afghanistan crisis.)

Since 1975 the United States has, by formal agreement with the USSR, imposed certain controls over Soviet grain purchases. These were designed in part to prevent large and disruptive fluctuations in

Soviet purchases and to provide the U.S. government with some opportunity to limit exports to the USSR if they jeopardized other U.S. export commitments or more urgent needs, or even for political reasons. In practice, U.S. harvests of the products needed by the Soviet Union and the world supply situation have allowed the U.S. Department of Agriculture to authorize the sale to the Soviets of quantities far above the annual levels envisaged in the 1975 agreement. This policy was in effect in 1979 until President Carter imposed a partial embargo following the invasion of Afghanistan.

Depending on the state of relations when the 1975 agreement lapses in October 1980, the United States will, at a minimum, be well advised to renew the conditions established in the 1975 agreement and to maintain it for the indefinite future. This means that, except in the highly unlikely circumstances of a poor U.S. harvest, the United States will be obligated to sell the USSR at least six million tons of various kinds of commodities a year. But the question of how readily the Americans permit the USSR to buy quantities vastly in excess of the normal ceiling of eight million tons annually ought to be reviewed on the basis of the state of the agricultural market and also the general political situation. This, too, is a delicate potential area of cooperation with certain other supplier nations, such as Canada and Australia, which have not in the past been inclined to participate in coordinated policies on levels of supply and on pricing.

Yet, if, as Afghanistan has shown, the 1980s become a period in which the Soviets increasingly flex their muscles in the world's trouble spots—by using military means amassed at the expense of the Soviet consumer and of the greater efficiency of the Soviet civilian economy —it is not unrealistic to suggest that the Soviet leadership should not be able to count on unlimited food imports from the West.

Human Rights

The regimented and repressive nature of the Soviet regime has always complicated American policy toward the USSR. American decisions in the 1940s to become actively engaged in the containment of Soviet expansion were motivated not only by geopolitical or strategic considerations but by a deep concern that the subjugation of a nation and a people by the USSR would result in profound human tragedy. But successive American administrations have conducted business with the USSR and have sought, where possible, to set limits to hostility and to provide options and incentives for restrained relations. The emigration issue and the human hardships associated with it revived public awareness of the nature of the Soviet regime, which, while eschewing the mass brutalities of the Stalin period, persisted in the violation and disregard of human rights. Congress directed the executive branch to exert influence on the Soviet Union and other governments engaged in violations of human and other rights. The Carter administration made the promotion of human rights a central theme of its foreign policy (although other administrations hardly neglected the issue, even though they may have had different methods of pursuing it).

For the Soviets, rigorous U.S. emphasis on human rights was an instrument of political warfare—something the Soviet Union has never been reluctant to use for its own purposes—in an area in which the Soviets are vulnerable. Moscow reluctantly agreed to meet Western demands to include a major section on human rights, contacts, cultural improvement, and related issues in the Final Act of the Conference on Security and Cooperation in Europe, signed at Helsinki in August 1975. The stirrings of dissidence and demands for compliance aroused by that act in both Eastern Europe and the USSR probably reinforced doubts among the aging, conservative Soviet leaders about the advantages of the Helsinki accords as a means of legitimizing the postwar status of Eastern Europe. Reacting to public and official U.S. pressures and acting on its natural repressive instincts, the Soviet regime cracked down on dissidents. Although difficult to demonstrate conclusively, Soviet sensitivity probably also accounted in part for foot-dragging on SALT—a sort of reverse linkage to matters in which Moscow believed the United States had a major interest. U.S. counteractions, in turn, included postponements of various exchanges, some economic retaliation, and public condemnations.

The Carter administration gradually reduced the vehemence of its human rights policies toward the USSR. The Soviets, for their part, increased emigration, which in several instances amounted to expulsion of dissidents or other undesirable persons. The net effect of several years of U.S. activism on human rights practices in the Soviet Union, and on the people living under Soviet rule, cannot yet be assessed.

There is no doubt that most dissidents and many others in the USSR see in American assertiveness a means of bringing pressure to bear on the Soviet regime to relax its grip or at least to make it pay a penalty for its repressions. Even so, however, the U.S. government must weigh factors in addition to the preferences and pleas of those whose human rights are at stake. The United States faces the Soviet Union on a wide array of issues, and it must balance its concern with human hardship and tragedy in the USSR with other interests, including the security of the United States and its allies. Furthermore, the United States must recognize that direct pressure on the Soviet government, while laudable in its motives and purposes, can also serve to demonstrate the inability of the United States to accomplish its goals. Such demonstrations can have adverse repercussions for the credibility of American commitments and, indeed, encourage the Soviets to seek opportunities to emphasize the limits of American influence.

The active U.S. pursuit of human rights goals for a powerful, repressive regime like that of the Soviet Union will be beset with the most profound dilemmas, both in the weighing of the interests the United States must protect and advance and in the choice of particular methods. The Soviets are to some degree responsive to public pressures; but there is also a line, difficult to discern or define with precision, beyond which the regime feels itself so severely challenged that it reacts by tightening the screws and complicating other aspects of relations.

With the hindsight of more than a quarter of a century since Stalin's death, it can be said that the Soviet regime—together with most of those in Eastern Europe—has reduced the crudest and most brutal forms of oppression. How the outside world can contribute to the maintenance and acceleration of this trend cannot be said with assurance. But perhaps the policies that serve to restrain the external uses of Soviet power and to encourage a more disciplined Soviet participation in international affairs can also serve to mitigate the human pain and suffering that continues for those Soviet citizens who cannot seek refuge in other lands.

CHAPTER TWELVE

The China Connection

KENNETH G. LIEBERTHAL

AFTER a decade of courtship, the United States and the People's Republic of China now seem ready to develop their relations in a way that can significantly influence a range of critical issues. Recent events have riveted attention on the strategic implications of potential U.S.-China military cooperation. But shared opposition to Soviet expansionism is inadequate by itself to provide a basis for close Sino-American ties. Indeed, the degree to which China remains committed to a domestic policy of rapid modernization will fundamentally influence the possibilities for U.S.-China relations in the coming decade. And political crosscurrents in both Washington and Taipei could also seriously affect America's ability to participate in China's modernization efforts. The boundaries of Sino-American relations in the 1980s, therefore, remain unclear. The outcome, however, will prove important not only for both countries and for the strategic triangle but also for determining the possibilities for resolving key Asian and global problems in the 1980s.

The Domestic Factor

One of the major uncertainties in fixing the future agenda of U.S.-China relations concerns the capacities of the two political systems to consolidate and develop their relationship. Both the United States

I am grateful to A. Doak Barnett and John D. Steinbruner for their valuable comments and to Lisa M. Diaz for her research assistance.

and China are large continental countries, where domestic political concerns occasionally shape foreign policy decisions. Neither society, moreover, as yet understands the other, except in a superficial way. Thus actions and attitudes reflecting domestic strains and pressures in each country, exacerbated by the difficulties each side already has in fathoming the other's decisionmaking, might substantially alter the U.S.-China agenda in the future.

In the case of China, the outward-looking foreign policy and desire of Beijing (Peking) to participate fully in the international economy indicates that a leadership committed to rapid modernization of the country has prevailed in the succession struggle to date. The goals of speeding industrialization and securing protection against the Soviet threat (goals that are inextricably intertwined for the Chinese) have virtually required good relations with the United States, Japan, and the industrial countries in Western Europe. But China's leaders are old—most are from the generation of Mao Zedong (Mao Tse-tung) —and it is clear that many of their possible successors disagree with both their order of priorities and their methods. How secure, then, is the modernization program in China? How will the agenda of U.S.-China relations be affected if that program falters? And what can the United States do to affect the outcome?

The modernization program has evolved rapidly over the past two years. Most of the targets announced in February 1978 were scaled down during the spring and summer of 1979 to make the program more realistically attuned to China's economic capabilities. Almost all major architects of this program—in both its original and scaled-down versions—are men who are more than seventy years old, and all have had to confront the question of how to maximize the chances that the commitment to rapid modernization will survive their exits from China's political stage. There appears to have been some disagreement within this group of veteran leaders, however, about how best to accomplish this.

Deng Xiaoping (Teng Hsiao-ping) provided the major driving force behind the modernization effort throughout 1978. From the policies he advocated, it appears that Deng based his program more on a political than an economic calculus. Implicitly, Deng believed that no controversial program of economic development could achieve sufficiently impressive results within three to five years to guarantee that the program would be continued. Thus he placed priority on creating a political momentum behind the program that would carry it through and make it impossible for his successors to chart a radically different course. Deng became committed to shaking up the Chinese system through greatly increased exposure to foreign ideas and standards of living, rapid and far-reaching administrative and political changes within China, and a self-critical frankness that shocked certain elements in his domestic political audience. Deng sought through these measures to create a constituency for modernization that would demand that any successor leadership not slacken the pace. Not surprisingly, a strategy designed to jolt the system produced opposition and confusion as well as support and excitement. A series of problems in the winter of 1978–79—economic shortfalls, budget deficits, rising unemployment, the costs of China's Vietnam invasion—forced a modification of Deng's approach.

A renewed commitment to modernization as a goal but within a less grandiose political and economic strategy resulted. Chen Yun and other leaders of Deng's generation offered a scaled-down economic program that anticipated three years of adjustments and reforms before making the push toward rapid modernization. They packaged this program in political orthodoxy, demanding continued fidelity to leadership by the Chinese Communist Party, to the socialist path for China, to the dictatorship of the proletariat, and to the principles of Marx, Lenin, and Mao Zedong as the guiding philosophy of the country. This new approach remains extremely ambitious and far-reaching. It ultimately aims at major reform of both economic and political institutions that are the mainstay of the political system, and there is no question that it is challenging deeply entrenched vested interests. But it is seeking to bring about these enormous changes at a more manageable pace. On balance, the program should survive roughly intact if—and only if—it can produce tangible rewards to a sufficient cross section of key groups to make them rally to its defense.

But the obstacles facing the program are formidable. China already feeds over 20 percent of the world's population on 7 percent of the world's arable land, and its capital-output ratio in agriculture is climbing. The country's complex bureaucracies are staffed by cadres who have been made skeptical of new political initiatives by the ten years of kaleidoscopic changes during the final decade of Mao Zedong's reign (1966–76). And the current older leaders will have to confront "lame duck" considerations that will increasingly sap their ability to whip the bureaucracies into action as their numbers decrease. In addition, uncontrollable economic elements could dramatically affect the chances of success of the program. Bad weather would preclude the needed rate of agricultural growth. Failure to find sizable amounts of high-grade offshore oil would greatly change current calculations of affordable debt. And rapid international inflation would increase the price of importing capital, while a major international depression would hamper China's ability to generate foreign exchange through exports.

Overall, the most likely prognosis is that the current scaled-down program will fall short of its economic goals, but not disastrously so. If this occurs, there is a good chance that the Chinese government will remain committed to rapid modernization of the economy, although it might find itself forced to use more coercion to contain the tremendous pressures in the system. In foreign policy, Chinese leaders probably will remain committed to extensive foreign trade, including countertrade and direct foreign investment in China. The successor leadership probably will also seek wide-ranging security ties with the advanced countries of the West, including the United States. But it will most likely be politically more orthodox at home than it is now, and thus will seek to keep sharp limits on contacts with the international arena outside the scientific and technological realm broadly defined.

Clearly, the actual course of development in the People's Republic of China can differ greatly from that just described. Economic and political problems might coalesce to produce another bout of relatively xenophobic nationalism—not as inward-looking as was the Cultural Revolution of the late 1960s, but still sufficiently different from today's policies to produce more rigid views in Beijing on such key nationalist issues as Taiwan reunification, freedom of emigration, the role of foreign capital in China's economic development, and so forth.

The United States can do little to increase the chances that the modernization program will remain relatively intact. The program could be set back a bit if the United States tried to block China's access to international markets and technology, but currently there is no interest in doing this. At the same time, it is doubtful that U.S. willingness to normalize economic relations fully will generate much additional momentum for the program, inasmuch as America is only China's fourth largest trading partner to date, and this is unlikely to change dramatically in the future—even though China received most-favored-nation status in early 1980.[1] Paradoxically, the rapidly broadening U.S. contacts with China link America to policies and programs that remain highly controversial and increase the vulnerability of the Sino-American relationship to an attack on these programs in China.

Thus the climate on the Chinese side for this relationship in the 1980s will probably be almost as favorable as that at the end of the 1970s, but the situation could change. The significant chance that Chinese domestic politics will become less congenial to further development of Sino-American relations raises the general issue of whether the United States can and should try to hedge its ongoing policies to cope with this possibility—even if deteriorating U.S. relations with the Soviet Union seem to commend more far-reaching integration of U.S. and Chinese policies.

On the U.S. side, politics can also seriously affect the agenda of U.S.-China relations in the 1980s. Congress will have an ongoing involvement in relations with China, and shifts in congressional sentiment can have serious effects. In addition, the election of a U.S. president who did not think it appropriate to pursue improved relations with China as a high-priority policy might set in motion a process that could seriously upset current expectations. Having such a president in office, for example, might encourage Taiwan to risk assuming more of the trappings of an independent country, even though this could provoke a sharp response from Beijing. This sequence could put the United States in a difficult position as it tried to protect both its ties with Taiwan and its relations with Beijing in an increasingly polarized situation. More fundamentally, U.S.-China relations require continual nurturing, and the interest to do so must exist in the White House. Without this nurturing, trouble lies ahead.

In this chapter, unless otherwise noted, I assume that politics in both the People's Republic of China and the United States encourage the further development of relations between the two countries. Even

1. In 1978 U.S. exports to China were $906 million; imports from China were $323 million. This amounted to 11.5 percent of China's imports and 6 percent of its exports. By far the largest single item in this trade was U.S. exports of agricultural products. Studies have suggested that the most-favored-nation status might increase Chinese exports to the United States by more than 25 percent.

with this optimistic assumption, serious issues will complicate the relationship on (overlapping) bilateral, strategic, regional Asian, and global levels in the 1980s.

Bilateral Relations

Bilateral relations have already overcome seemingly intractable problems. The formula for normalization of diplomatic relations with Beijing finessed the Taiwan issue. The political normalization in turn allows the resolution of outstanding economic issues, and most of these should be cleared away by 1981 or 1982. Failure to resolve these issues—which would most likely occur as a result of political crosscurrents in the United States—would seriously disrupt Washington's ties with Beijing.

Economic Issues

More than two decades of hostility—compounded by trade restrictions governing Communist countries (intended originally to constrain Soviet activities)—have left a complex legal tangle that must be undone if U.S. businessmen are to compete effectively with their Japanese and West European counterparts for a broad spectrum of the Chinese market. Much progress has been made toward achieving this task, although some problems remain.

The wide-ranging trade agreement between the United States and the People's Republic of China, which was approved by both houses of Congress in January 1980, is the centerpiece of the new economic relationship. This trade agreement is required (under the terms of the Trade Act of 1974) for China to receive most-favored-nation status and to be eligible for Export-Import Bank loans and tariff treatment governed by the generalized system of preferences. In submitting the trade agreement to Congress, President Carter had to declare that China has met the emigration requirements of the so-called Jackson-Vanik amendment to the Trade Act of 1974. When President Carter did this, he evidently imposed far less strict demands on the Chinese to document their policy of free emigration than are being applied, for example, to Romania. According to current law, this affirmation must be renewed each year.[2] If a future president demanded more

2. Several resolutions have been introduced in Congress that would extend the renewal period (the longest is for five years), but none of these has passed.

stringent documentation from the Chinese or in other ways raised the threshold for meeting the Jackson-Vanik amendment, the entire trade agreement could be undermined. The agreement recognizes this possibility by declaring, in effect (in article X.3), that the agreement becomes null if, at a future date, China fails to meet the free emigration requirements of the Jackson-Vanik amendment.

A second economic issue concerns America's promise to seek legislation permitting the Overseas Private Investment Corporation to provide guarantees for U.S. investment in China. This will require that the Overseas Private Investment Corporation Amendments Act of 1974 be amended to exempt the People's Republic of China from its strictures. Similar amendments have been passed for Yugoslavia and Hungary.

A third issue is the eligibility of China for the so-called generalized system of preferences. Beijing has made an inquiry about eligibility, and Washington could consider this in the future. China would have to clear several hurdles: first, it must be officially designated by the United States as a developing country, which has been done in article II.3 of the trade agreement; second, it would have to join the International Monetary Fund and the General Agreement on Tariffs and Trade. Both of these require agreements on economic reporting requirements and possible other economic commitments that the Chinese may find onerous, but Beijing now seems increasingly willing to provide others with economic data, and these international bodies have shown flexibility in dealing with other Communist countries. Currently, Australia, New Zealand, Japan, and Canada have extended the generalized system of preferences treatment to China, and the European Community may do so during 1980. According to title V of the 1974 Trade Act, the president of the United States must also declare that China is not "dominated or controlled by international communism" in order for China to be eligible for the generalized system of preferences.

The fourth issue is that the U.S. government has taken action to make available American governmental services to China on a compensatory basis, such as having the U.S. Army Corps of Engineers assist in Chinese hydroelectric power development. This required (under section 607a of the Act for International Development of 1961) a declaration that China is a "friendly country." The U.S. State Department made this declaration in 1979.

As the above brief list indicates, some of these issues require further actions—some sensitive or difficult—to reach fruition. Indeed, as noted above, Congress will play a continuing role in maintaining the viability of the legal framework for this trade through, for example, its ability to require an annual declaration of whether China has continued to meet the emigration requirement of the Jackson-Vanik amendment. Any marked return to a more nationalist and orthodox communist approach to broad political issues in China might well cause that country to run afoul of the requirement. Such easily triggered sanctions increase the difficulty and uncertainty of managing the U.S.-China relationship in the future.

Indeed, the recent history of economic negotiations between the two countries highlights both the tremendous momentum that has built up behind this relationship and the potentially significant adverse possibilities. Fundamentally, the Chinese do not have the highly legalistic approach to problems that characterizes U.S. trade practices, and they do not divide power among their branches of government. Good intentions on both sides may, therefore, be frustrated or seriously tested by tensions between the legal and political dimensions of life in China and the United States. The resolution of the nettlesome issue of claims and assets in 1979 illustrates the point.

In late fall 1950 the United States unilaterally froze the assets of Chinese nationals in America. China retaliated several days later by freezing U.S. assets. This amounted to roughly $196 million of American assets in China and approximately $76 million of Chinese assets in the United States. Because U.S. law provides that a claimant can obtain a court order to attach nongovernmental Chinese property in an unresolved claim, failure to resolve this issue would seriously hamper future trade relations between the United States and the People's Republic of China. But the Carter administration could not agree with the Chinese position that each side should cancel its claims and pay off its own claimants because that would have meant that the U.S. Congress would have to agree to American claimants receiving less than forty cents on the dollar—a lower figure than has ever been found acceptable in the past. In addition, legal title to the blocked assets in America is in many cases unclear, and Washington would have to go through years of litigation to obtain these funds before it could distribute them to American claimants. The solution offered by the United States was to have China directly pay the United States $76 million to distribute to the American claimants, placing the entire burden of litigation on Beijing to obtain the formerly blocked assets in America. This solution in fact plunges China into a legal nightmare, and it is likely to be years before it manages to regain the greater part of the funds. Indeed, some of the litigation could even require U.S. judicial decisions on which of the two Chinas owns particular assets in dispute. There is little evidence that the Chinese realized the complexities involved at the time they signed this agreement.

In sum, rapid progress is being made toward clearing away the legal problems so that U.S.-China economic relations can flourish during China's massive effort at modernizing its economy. But political and cultural differences may yet upset these relations, especially insofar as current U.S. law makes China's future actions on issues such as emigration directly relevant to the treatment of China under the foreign trade laws of the United States.

The Taiwan Issue

The Taiwan issue, which the normalization agreement finessed but did not resolve, lurks beneath the surface as a potential spoiler in Sino-American bilateral relations. Two possibilities—neither of which the United States will be able to control—could bring Taiwan to the fore in a highly disruptive way. The first would reflect changes in domestic politics in the People's Republic of China; the second, decisions made in Taipei.

There appears to be a spectrum of opinions in China on how the Chinese should view their ties with the United States—in the context of the strategic triangle or in more strictly bilateral terms. Deng Xiaoping has been the foremost advocate of the strategic triangle perspective; he says that China must develop its relationship with the United States to gain security against an expansionist Soviet Union. For Deng, the Chinese must be willing to tolerate the long-term separation of Taiwan under a compromise that enables the United States and the People's Republic of China to build their strategic relationship in lieu of settlement of (or, conceivably, even progress on) the issue of Taiwan reunification. The implications of this for U.S. policy toward the strategic triangle are discussed below. In a strictly bilateral context, Deng's position permitted the Chinese to make the significant concessions necessary to obtain the normalization agreement negotiated in December 1978.

But other Chinese leaders disagree with Deng's weighing of the strategic versus the bilateral merits of normalization. They place greater priority on reunification with Taiwan. Significantly, in the views of many of these leaders the U.S. Congress passed legislation to provide the legal framework for America's future relations with Taiwan that does not fully conform with the normalization agreement negotiated by President Carter. The legislation, indeed, can be interpreted as violating the first two of the three major compromises that the United States made to win China's approval of normalization —that is, that the United States would cease to recognize the validity of the government on Taiwan, would terminate its security guarantees for the island, and would withdraw its remaining military forces. To date, the Ministry of Foreign Affairs of the People's Republic of China has lodged a strong protest over this legislation, but Deng Xiaoping has pushed for further development of U.S.-China relations nevertheless. This legislation remains a readily available tool for any opponents of Deng's policy to wield if they want to do so.

In fact, the Chinese who oppose the current approach to modernization may use the Taiwan issue as an emotionally charged vehicle for attacking Deng and his policies. These opponents can make a credible case that Deng's modernization program and strategic views demanded normalization of relations with the United States on a basis that leaves the Chinese with reduced options to bring Taiwan back into the fold. Thus, it can be charged, Deng accepted what all Chinese leaders have consistently said was unacceptable—a de facto U.S. policy of two Chinas. Whether more nativist leaders genuinely disagree over the merits of Deng's normalization package or simply consider that issue as a vulnerable one for Deng is irrelevant. In either case, the Taiwan issue could again be placed on the agenda of U.S.-China relations by Beijing. This might occur in the next three years —that is, from the first sales of defensive weapons and military equipment to Taiwan by the United States in 1980 through the next stage in the succession cycle in Beijing.[3]

3. In accordance with the normalization understanding, the United States made no new military sales to Taiwan during 1979. The United States resumed such sales in January 1980, and the Taiwan Relations Act passed by the U.S. Congress (in sections 3a and 3b) mandates continuation of these sales. China has stated officially that renewal of U.S. military sales to Taiwan will, in the words of Hua Guofeng (Hua Kuo-feng) "not conform to the principles of normalization . . . be detrimental to the peaceful liberation of Taiwan and . . . exercise an unfavorable influence on the peace and stability of the Asia-Pacific region." *Peking Review,* vol. 21 (December 22, 1978), p. 10.

Taiwan itself could precipitate a crisis by increasing the trappings of independence—or even declaring itself an independent country—and asking the United States for recognition and protection. Although unlikely, this possibility cannot be ruled out. It will become more attractive if a candidate for U.S. president who is considered pro-Taiwan is elected in the United States. A more aggressive posture in the People's Republic of China toward Taiwan could also encourage Taiwan to declare independence.

If polarization of the situation over Taiwan occurred because of decisions in either Beijing or Taipei (or both), the United States would have to decide to what extent to support Taiwan at direct cost to U.S. relations with Beijing. Necessary measures might include recognizing an independent Taiwan, helping Taiwan break a blockade imposed by the mainland, providing Taiwan with increased military aid, and applying other sanctions against the People's Republic of China. All these measures would do enormous harm to U.S. relations with the People's Republic of China. At the same time, simply permitting Beijing to put pressure on Taiwan without rendering any support to the island could severely damage America's prestige throughout non-Communist Asia.

The greater likelihood is that Taiwan will remain a manageable issue in U.S.-China relations. China is now developing a program that will permit relatively unrestricted development of certain territories on the mainland near Hong Kong and opposite Taiwan; and it seems that Beijing hopes in time to create enclaves sufficiently similar to Hong Kong and Taiwan that the latter will not view absorption into the People's Republic of China as highly threatening. Beijing's policies toward Tibet during 1979, which brought a largely Tibetan leadership into government office at the provincial level, also seemed aimed at establishing a set of precedents that will make reunification seem less fearsome in Taipei. For Taiwan, although the initial shock of normalization has been weathered and the economy appears strong, there are increasing signs of political polarization and possible instability on the island. Short of some enormous threat perceived by Taiwan's leadership, however, it seems unlikely that these leaders will follow the high-risk policy of moving toward independence.

Under these circumstances, the U.S. interpretation of the normalization agreement commits the United States to a far-reaching, unofficial relationship with Taiwan that includes sales of defensive weaponry and maintenance of adequate defense forces in the area to ensure Taiwan's security. The basic issues that will remain on America's agenda toward Taiwan under these circumstances are, first, how best to cultivate a secure and prosperous Taiwan and, second, whether to go further and actively encourage Taiwan's leaders to begin to establish some contacts between Taiwan and the mainland, perhaps beginning with the relatively peripheral areas of post and telegraph communications, tourism, and limited direct trade.

The United States will face pressure from Taiwan, some of it filtered through sympathetic members of the U.S. Congress, to upgrade the U.S.-Taiwan relationship to a more official status and to provide more sophisticated weaponry and equipment to Taipei's armed forces. Beijing will remain highly sensitive to the way Washington addresses these questions.

Strategic Considerations

Strategic concerns involving the Soviet Union that are so much a part of Sino-American relations in 1980 in fact played a prominent role in U.S. thinking about China throughout the 1970s. Indeed, Henry Kissinger placed triangular considerations uppermost in his recapitulation of the decisionmaking behind the U.S.-China rapprochement in the early 1970s.[4] Throughout the past decade, the growing relationship between the United States and the People's Republic of China has served the interests of both countries in their respective relations with Moscow. For the Chinese, this budding relationship has provided an additional measure of security against Soviet aggression, as demonstrated in the secret U.S. assurance during the Indo-Pakistani war in 1971 that the United States would give China military assistance in the event of Soviet military action against the Chinese.[5] For the Americans, the U.S.-China connection has been developed to maximize Soviet incentives for détente, especially as expressed by Soviet willingness to reach strategic arms limitations agreements and to exercise restraint in U.S.-Soviet competition. This desire to use the U.S.-China relationship to promote Soviet-American détente has, in turn, placed some constraints on the ways in which

4. Henry Kissinger, *White House Years* (Little, Brown and Company, 1979), chaps. 6, 8, 14, 19.
5. Ibid., pp. 910–11.

Washington has been willing to develop its ties with Beijing. On the most general level, the United States adopted a policy of evenhandedness in Washington's relations with the two Communist powers.

The underlying rationale of the evenhanded approach was that America would fare best with both countries if it avoided crude manipulation and maintained good relations with each. To demonstrate that the United States was not trying to develop its ties with either Moscow or Beijing at the expense of the other, Washington committed itself in principle to maintaining a rough balance in its activities with both. This principle has always been a difficult one to apply in practice, given the different economic and military situations of the USSR and China, but America has consistently tried to do so. For example, in 1979 President Carter delayed submitting the U.S.-China trade agreement to Congress because he could not obtain sufficient assurances from the Soviet Union on its policy toward free emigration and, without such assurances, he could not warrant giving the USSR the waiver from the Jackson-Vanik amendment that he was granting the Chinese.

That the policy of balance has not been rigid is illustrated by the fact that in October 1979 President Carter finally submitted the U.S.-China trade agreement to Congress without parallel action vis-à-vis the Soviet Union. Indeed, the very difficulty of determining what is evenhanded has always made the policy subject to controversy and has raised an unending stream of questions about specific transfers of technology. In addition, arguments have been made for interpreting evenhandedness in various ways that would benefit the Chinese—for example, regarding as evenhanded any transfer that did not increase the difference between Chinese and Soviet capabilities; applying a "China differential" in recognition of the Soviet Union's greater ability to exploit much of the technology that can be transferred to both countries; and making evenhandedness apply only to items of military significance but dropping it as a principle governing other dimensions of the relationship (such as granting most-favored-nation status and providing Export-Import Bank loans). U.S. policy to date has not actually been strictly balanced. It has leaned in China's direction on certain issues such as the trade agreement and the sale of some computers and geological prospecting equipment. And it has leaned toward the Soviet Union in other areas, such as in closer consultation about development plans for strategic weapons.

Since U.S.-Soviet détente provided the rationale for evenhandedness during the 1970s, should this policy be abandoned now because of the Soviet invasion of Afghanistan and related Soviet activities? If a new cold war is beginning, should Washington engage China's collaboration against Soviet expansionism through the development of a U.S.-China security relationship?

Several major arguments support strong Sino-American security ties in the early 1980s. Such ties, it has been argued, will further ensure that the Chinese leadership—always acutely sensitive to its own security needs—will not seek a middle ground between the United States and the Soviet Union during the years to come. At the same time, U.S.-China security ties would vastly complicate the Soviet Union's military problems, especially insofar as the U.S.-China security connection was part of a larger cooperative set of anti-Soviet relationships that stitched together the countries of the North Atlantic Treaty Organization, Japan, and China. To the extent that the Soviets in the 1980s perceive that they face a credible threat of a war on two fronts should they initiate major military action in either Europe or Asia, they will probably be deterred from following their worst instincts in either of these two theaters. Finally, U.S. and Chinese military capabilities potentially complement each other in Asia. China excels where the United States is weakest—that is, in the ability to sustain large numbers of ground force units in action with modest support requirements. America, moreover, can help China in areas where there are critical deficiencies in its military capabilities—by providing tactical air support and air interdiction of Soviet supply lines, supplying antitank and antiaircraft missiles (the latter with sophisticated electronic equipment), vastly upgrading China's airlift and general transport capabilities, transferring sophisticated communications technology, and so forth. Overall, then, it appears that the rapid development of a strong U.S.-China security relationship might tie down large numbers of Soviet troops permanently on the Chinese border, while at the same time improving the chances that the Chinese will not in the future decide to move toward a more neutral stance in the strategic triangle.

But these potential benefits of a substantial U.S.-China security relationship cannot overcome other serious considerations. While both China and America want to contain Soviet expansionism, Chinese and American interests do not coincide everywhere in Asia. Indeed, military conflict in the Taiwan Strait or on the Korean peninsula might find the United States and China on opposite sides in a hot war. At the same time, given the size of China and its long historic traditions, the United States could not count on gaining meaningful influence over future Chinese military decisions by virtue of U.S.-China military ties. Thus, even with such ties rather well developed, China might opt for some action that runs grave risks of producing wider military conflict (such as another attack on Vietnam—with the attendant risks of provoking Sino-Soviet military conflict), even if the United States strongly opposed such a move. Indeed, the major object of Sino-American military ties would be to produce more prudent and responsible behavior on the part of the Soviet Union. The development of such ties might well, however, have just the opposite effect—alarming the Soviets so that they feel compelled to act quickly and decisively to alter the course of developments in Washington and Beijing. This rationale could produce direct Soviet military action against China while the military relationship between the United States and the People's Republic of China is still in its nascent stages.

Some disagreement has, in fact, long existed in Washington about how best to influence Soviet foreign policy decisionmaking. Does Moscow have its own hard-liners and moderates, and should the United States try to pursue policies that bolster the position of the moderates and undercut that of the hawks? Or are the Soviets inherently aggressive, exercising restraint only when faced with decisive diplomatic and military obstacles?[6] If the former is true, the United States will want to limit any security relationship with China in order to avoid undercutting Moscow's moderates. This need not preclude all U.S.-China security ties, but it does require that prudence, caution, and flexibility become the watchwords of U.S.-China security relations.

All things considered, what is needed is a new conceptualization of

6. The different American perceptions of Soviet foreign policy decisionmaking are clearly outlined in Lawrence T. Caldwell and Alexander Dallin, "U.S. Policy Toward the Soviet Union: Intractable Issues" in Kenneth A. Oye, Donald Rothchild, and Robert J. Lieber, eds., *Eagle Entangled: U.S. Foreign Policy in a Complex World* (Longman, 1979), pp. 215–19. A variant of the view that posits hard-liners and moderates in Moscow holds that the position of the latter would be strengthened by a bold and forthright U.S. policy that clearly demonstrates the dangers inherent in the approach of the Soviet hard-liners. See, for example, Kissinger, *White House Years*, p. 122.

the strategic dimension of the U.S.-China relationship—one that recognizes the highly significant differences in the thrust of the U.S.-Soviet and U.S.-China relations, while not enhancing the probability of Sino-Soviet military conflict. This new vision of the U.S.-China relationship should distinguish between the activities that legitimately cause alarm in Moscow and those that the Soviets would like to stop but that in fact do not threaten Soviet security interests. The former, such as potential U.S. weapons transfers to China, are truly triangular issues, while the latter, such as granting trade credits, should be free from triangular constraints.

Specifically, America should abandon the idea of evenhandedness, or balance, in its relations with the Soviet Union and China in all nonmilitary spheres and should publicly state the rationale for doing so. The Soviet Union and China are in very different economic situations, and the dynamics of their relations with the United States now differ markedly. For example, the United States is trying to expand its trade with China while it is using trade sanctions to punish Moscow for the invasion of Afghanistan. There is no reason why, in principle, Washington should tie its nonmilitary activities with China to those with the Soviet Union.

On security issues, America should act with great caution. The United States should certainly upgrade its ties with China so that they include everything encompassed by the U.S.-Soviet security relationship in the past. This includes both symbolic and substantive issues, and Washington should call attention to the fact that these policies in principle apply equally to both China and the Soviet Union. Symbolically, for example, the United States should offer to have American naval vessels pay calls at Chinese ports. (This has been offered to the Soviet Union in the past.) Substantively, the United States should make a concerted effort to engage the Chinese in detailed discussions on weapons developments and arms control. In 1979 China launched a three-stage rocket, made progress toward the development of solid-fuel propellants, and appeared to be on the verge of acquiring an operational capability in intercontinental ballistic missiles.[7] These developments mean that within several years China might for the first time be capable of attacking U.S. territory with nuclear weapons. Such a change would in any event heighten the importance of active

7. *Daily Report: People's Republic of China* (Washington, D.C.: Foreign Broadcast Information Service) October 2, 1979, p. L-34 and October 3, 1979, p. L-27.

efforts to bring China into negotiations on strategic arms limitation to control—and eventually reduce—the development and deployment of new strategic weapons. U.S. experience with the Soviet Union, moreover, demonstrates that a long lead time is required to acquire a common vocabulary and sufficient mutual appreciation of the issues concerned to permit fruitful negotiations.[8] Efforts to engage China in a strategic dialogue on arms limitations—and related subjects, such as command and control procedures—should thus be relatively high on the U.S.-China agenda.

With the desire to upgrade U.S.-China security ties providing the overall impetus, theater nuclear weapons may provide the concrete bridge needed to bring China into the dialogue on arms control. If U.S.-Soviet negotiations on theater nuclear weapons materialize, Moscow will probably cite its conflict with China to argue for higher ceilings on its theater weapons such as the SS-20 missile. The United States made a policy decision in the late 1970s to consult intensively with its European allies in order to take their interests fully into account in theater weapon negotiations with the Soviets; in the 1980s it will at least have to take into account the interests of a friendly China.

Going beyond evenhandedness in security-related measures is another matter. America must consider any such initiative in light of the complex and volatile situation in Asia and the possibility of future Sino-Soviet conflict. Détente, for example, will no longer constrain Soviet retaliatory action against China (as it did in early 1979) if Beijing decides that it is necessary to "teach Hanoi a lesson" in Southeast Asia. Any efforts that transcend the principle of balance in the military sphere, therefore, should be undertaken without fanfare, and the United States should avoid rigid, potentially costly commitments. Active cooperation in devising U.S. and Chinese policies toward the security of third countries of mutual concern, such as Pakistan and Thailand, is clearly advisable. Other appropriate areas for developing security ties between the United States and China might include initiating or enhancing pertinent intelligence sharing; continuing current discussions on common military problems; perhaps striving to achieve some de facto complementarity in military deployments in Northeast Asia; and allowing selected Chinese purchases of dual-use technology, on a case-by-case basis, which is important for economic

8. Admiral John M. Lee discusses this point in his "An Opening 'Window' For Arms Control," *Foreign Affairs,* vol. 58 (Fall 1979), pp. 121–40.

or scientific progress in China (for example, computer and satellite technology that will enhance China's capability to do geological survey work).

The objectives of retaining some flexibility and avoiding actions that are unnecessarily provocative to the Soviet Union should preclude other possible security measures, such as direct weapons transfers or joint planning against a Soviet attack on China that includes pre-positioning of appropriate U.S. equipment and supplies in China. Direct U.S. military assistance would create commitments that would become difficult and costly to modify in the future. The long lead times required would create the risk that a changing situation either in China or elsewhere in the region would have made those measures undesirable by the time they became operational. Rhetoric that suggests a far-reaching U.S. commitment to protecting China's future security—with its implications for inevitable growth in U.S. security ties—is so highly irritating to Moscow that it will probably prove counterproductive. And sales of nonlethal, strictly military technology are clearly more provocative than are sales of many types of dual-use technology. In sum, although evenhandedness and balance may have become somewhat outmoded principles for U.S. relations with the Soviet Union and China in the 1980s, America's self-interest will demand that subtlety, caution, and flexibility should govern any future development of U.S.-China security ties in the face of aggressive Soviet activity.

The Asian Setting

Within Asia, the non-Communist countries in general have applauded America's rapprochement with China and value the stability and easing of tension it contributes. These countries have anxieties, however, about the staying power of the United States and about Beijing's future policies in the area. China's anti-Sovietism is welcomed by some, but many look with dismay at the possibility that the Sino-Soviet and U.S.-Soviet rivalries will increase tensions and spread military conflict throughout the region. Some perceive in China's economic development plans the prospect of large-scale, mutually beneficial trade, but others fear China's trade expansion. Asia is complex, and few policies will appeal to all.

China's newly declared willingness to engage in various forms of countertrade and to accept foreign direct investment raises fears throughout Asia about Chinese competition based on inexpensive labor. The United States can do little to affect the impact of China's policies on other Asian countries. Washington will, indeed, face pressures from American businesses to resolve any remaining legal problems that inhibit U.S. firms from taking advantage of this new opportunity on a footing equal to that of their competitors.

The one economic issue that is distinctly a U.S. government question and that has an impact on the entire region is the question of textile quotas. China depends on rapid expansion of textile exports to earn badly needed foreign exchange, and Beijing sees the United States as a major potential market. Protectionist sentiment is strong in the American textile industry, however, and this well-organized sector of the U.S. economy will most likely work effectively through Congress to maintain a controlled market for imports from Asia.

For the United States, the problem will be one of accommodating increased textile imports from China without creating severe problems with America's other major suppliers in Asia—Taiwan, Hong Kong, South Korea, and Japan. Clearly, the basic solution will be to give China an increasing share of the future growth of textile imports, without permitting the Chinese to cut into current quotas of the other countries.[9] But the latter countries will probably consider this solution one that denies them the share of the future U.S. market on which they had counted, and thus some friction will inevitably result. This issue will likely remain as a continuing irritant to the U.S.-China relationship during the next decade.

On the military side, the United States must make basic decisions in the early 1980s about its force posture and the relations between American forces in Asia and both those of the Asian countries and those of the North Atlantic Treaty Organization. Since the Korean War, America has employed the "swing" concept de facto in its de-

9. Sino-American negotiations to reach an orderly market arrangement for the five Chinese apparel products that have the greatest domestic impact in the United States adjourned without agreement in May 1979. On May 31, 1979, therefore, the United States unilaterally imposed quotas on these products. Two more were added to this list in October. China strongly objects to the U.S. textile restrictions but will probably agree to reopen negotiations for an orderly market agreement because the level of textile imports allowed under an agreement would be higher than that allowed under the current quotas. The textile issue reflects a more wide-ranging problem—China is hoping for high levels of exports of light manufactures to the United States in items such as footwear and clothespins, where protectionist sentiment in the United States is strong.

fense planning—that is, in case of war in Europe, U.S. forces from the Asian Pacific area would be moved into the European theater as needed. American allies in Europe have been privy to this order of priorities, but reportedly the U.S. government has not discussed it explicitly with its Asian allies. In 1979 this military strategy became known throughout Asia, and it has resurrected questions about America's defense commitments in the region in the context of strengthened Soviet forces in Northeast Asia and both Soviet and Vietnamese military activities elsewhere in Asia.[10] As the decade of the 1980s begins, the United States enjoys good diplomatic relations with both Japan and China (as well as the countries in the Association of Southeast Asian Nations), which provides dramatic evidence of America's political commitment to remain in Asia even after the painful setbacks of the mid-1970s. The United States must decide, however, on the military content of this commitment—an issue of keen interest to China and to other Asian friends.

This general concern raises a number of specific issues relating to China. How much should the United States count on Chinese military forces to operate in more or less close cooperation with American forces in case of large-scale warfare in Northeast Asia—or in Europe? Whatever the answer, what would it imply both for America's posture toward strengthening Chinese forces and for the U.S. deployments in the region? If, for example, the United States should beef up its bomber and fighter capabilities applicable to north China to make up for critical deficiencies in China's defensive capabilities, how compatible would this be with other U.S. military commitments in the area, notably for the defense of Japan and of the Republic of Korea? Should the United States encourage increased Japanese defense spending concentrated on the specific areas (such as antisubmarine warfare) that would fit most neatly into a cooperative relationship among the American, Chinese, and Japanese military forces?[11] To what extent should any such effort be included in direct negotiations and discussion, or, alternatively, should the focus be on the de facto complementarity that can be achieved by appropriate unilateral decisions on all three sides?

Diplomatically, America's improving relationship with China has

10. *New York Times,* October 9, 1979.
11. Michael Pillsbury explores this issue in "A Japanese Card?" *Foreign Policy,* no. 33 (Winter 1978–79), pp. 3–30.

facilitated a continued U.S. presence in Asia, and has enhanced the possibility of resolving some long-standing problems in the region. Creative diplomacy might permit China to nudge North Korea toward reconciliation with South Korea, while the United States similarly encourages the latter to move toward accommodation. China is severely constrained on this issue by Pyongyang's ability to play off its Chinese and Soviet patrons against each other. But diplomatic windows may open up in the future, and the United States must be fully prepared to take advantage of them.

U.S. cooperation with China will also prove necessary if there is to be any chance of achieving a coalition government to rule over a neutral Kampuchea (Cambodia) in the wake of the fighting there. The possibility for such a government will be determined first on the battlefield. If the Vietnamese can consolidate their hold (through the Heng Samrin regime) and eliminate all effective Pol Pot resistance, a coalition government will prove unfeasible. But should the ground fighting prove to be indecisive, the chances for neutralization could improve, and Sino-American cooperation to bring this about would be fundamental to any resolution of the Kampuchean tragedy.

Unquestionably, events during the 1980s will put additional issues on the agenda of potential areas for cooperation between China and the United States in the Asian arena. These may include such possibly explosive issues as resolution of conflicting claims to resources on the continental shelf. To date, both countries have voiced recognition of their "parallel interests" in many areas. The new decade will challenge American leaders to transform these interests into active cooperation to the benefit of both, while preventing unavoidable differences from creating serious frictions or conflicts.

Global Issues

The development of friendly relations between the United States and China brings together key members of the "first" and "third" worlds, respectively. Inevitably, the broader issues of relations between the developed and developing countries are part of the U.S.-China agenda of the coming decade—and cooperation between these two countries could have wider significance as an indication of the degree to which tensions between such different countries can be bridged by joint efforts to resolve common problems. Indeed, the

United States and China can be characterized in size and economic features as, respectively, the greatest potential donor and greatest potential recipient of benefits conferred on third world countries during the next decade.

China has long approached international military and political problems from a third world perspective in rhetoric, but economically it has practiced a policy of self-reliance. At the end of the 1970s, though, Beijing began to act more as a third world country in the economic sphere also. Reportedly, China now wants to participate in the international financial institutions designed to provide assistance to developing countries, such as the World Bank and the International Monetary Fund. The People's Republic of China has recently begun to accept various kinds of assistance from the programs of the United Nations for developing countries, and it will certainly look for greater aid in the future. It is also seeking concessional developmental aid from several countries on a bilateral basis.

Beijing's decision to make claims on the international economic community as a third world country means, concretely, that the size of the claims or demands of the third world could increase by an enormous percentage within a short time. Where funding formulas are linked to the size of the population (such as, for example, in the Asian Development Bank), China's legitimate share could be a significant percentage of all currently available funds, although its prudence in borrowing will probably set limits on what it requests. If China's demands are great, the implications for India, Indonesia, and other large aid recipients could be ominous, and the United States would have to think through its own aid commitments, both on bilateral and multilateral bases, in light of this new reality.

On most global issues, China has been a staunch defendant of third world positions where clear-cut positions are evident. These include, for example, issues relating to the New International Economic Order, where the People's Republic of China has consistently supported the new arrangements proposed by the developing countries (indexing prices of raw materials and manufactured goods, revamping tariff regulations, and so forth). They also include the positions supported by a majority of third world nations during negotiations in the several sessions of the United Nations Conference on the Law of the Sea.

On other global issues, China has charted an independent course to date. It has, for example, refused to participate in international efforts to resolve the world food problem. China is now one of the world's major grain-importing countries, and its rice exports have a significant effect on the Southeast Asian markets. The fact that the Chinese have an interest in the availability of substantial quantities of food at relatively predictable prices on the international market may make it feasible to try to bring Beijing into cooperative efforts in order to establish a worldwide food reserve system. China is potentially one of the world's largest food importers for the 1980s, while the United States will clearly be the world's major food exporter. America should, therefore, try to use its relationship with China to encourage it to take measures—such as providing detailed statistical information about Chinese agricultural conditions—that will lend greater stability to the international food markets.[12] The 1979 agreement by China to contribute about $1 million toward creation of a Common Fund for commodities under the integrated program of the UN Conference on Trade and Development provides some basis for hoping that Beijing will participate in various multinational commodity stabilization plans in the future.

Other global issues, such as international approaches required to clean up the environment, multinational conventions to protect endangered species, and cross-national cooperation to tackle scientific research tasks, could also benefit from China's greater willingness to be active in the international community. As China's economy develops and its own consumption of resources grows, moreover, its participation in managing global resources will become more important. The United States shares interests in almost all the problem areas concerned and should encourage China to seek multilateral solutions to these common problems.

Conclusions

Despite major progress in the U.S.-China relationship during the 1970s, uncertainties about the context of that relationship plague efforts to think through the agenda of issues for the 1980s. The three major unknowns discussed above are changes in Chinese domestic

12. A. Doak Barnett provides a detailed review of China's relations to the international food system in his *China and the World Food System*, Monograph 12 (Washington, D.C.: Overseas Development Council, April 1979).

politics that affect the modernization program and the related turn toward the West, developments in Taiwan as they affect that island's willingness and ability to play its assigned role in the Sino-American relationship, and changes in U.S.-Soviet relations that influence the perceived costs and benefits of building a more extensive U.S.-China security relationship (which would also involve Japan and Western Europe). Other potential problems beyond the scope of this chapter might also have a major impact, albeit indirectly, on Sino-American relations during the next decade. Most prominent among these is the state of the international economic system and the extent to which global economic problems divide the United States, Japan, and China.

Within this uncertain context, the United States should maximize its economic, cultural, scientific, and political interactions with the Chinese during the coming decade. The activities involved might at least slightly improve the chances that Beijing will remain committed to rapid modernization and an outward-looking foreign policy. They will also increase understanding of China in America, thus possibly improving the prospects for long-term cooperation between the two countries. China's emergence on the world scene during the 1970s had a major impact on the politics of the decade, and a rapidly modernizing China will no doubt continue to force changes—some uncomfortable and upsetting—in the international arena during the 1980s. But the Asian region is rapidly growing in importance in international politics, and America has little choice except to continue to develop its relations to the fullest extent with a country that will be so central to the politics of Asia and the world.

America's policies toward China in the national security arena must comport with the evolution of U.S.-Soviet relations and with U.S. commitments to other friends and allies. If there is a pronounced downturn in U.S.-Soviet relations throughout the early 1980s, a policy that takes maximum advantage of the Soviet Union's concern with China to tie down Soviet forces and complicate Soviet defense planning might appear attractive. America must take care, however, not to provoke the Russians into even more belligerent and aggressive behavior and must remain aware that Washington is not certain about how best to influence foreign policy decisionmaking in Moscow. Additionally, creating firm, long-term security commitments to the People's Republic of China will link the United States to a country whose future actions America cannot control and may well oppose, especially because the overlap in interests between the two countries is greater on the strategic level than on other security issues in Asia itself.

Accordingly, at the beginning of the 1980s it is necessary to conceptualize anew U.S.-China ties as they relate to the strategic triangle. Given the forward thrust of the current U.S.-China relations and the growing tensions with the Soviet Union—combined with the different economic circumstances of the USSR and China—there would appear to be little reason to strive for evenhandedness in nonmilitary relations with the two countries. In the highly sensitive security sphere, however, any moves to establish relations with China that transcend the boundaries America has set on its dealings with the Soviet Union should be structured to maximize U.S. flexibility as future events unfold. And American rhetoric about the U.S.-China security relationship should remain appropriately muted.

On balance, U.S. decisionmaking regarding China during the 1970s focused primarily on knitting together bilateral political and economic relations, even if the underlying rationale for that effort was based on broader strategic concerns. In the 1980s the focus is shifting toward regional and global issues within the context of a rapidly changing strategic triangle. This evolution in U.S.-China relations serves in some ways as a benchmark of how much progress has been made over the past ten years—and as a warning of the difficulties that have yet to be resolved in the decade ahead.

CHAPTER THIRTEEN

The Japan Relationship

PHILIP H. TREZISE

IN 1976 the Republican party promised that if the voters chose a Republican president, Japan would "remain the main pillar of our Asian policy." Not to be outdone in architectural figures of speech, the Democrats told readers of the party platform that "friendship and cooperation" with Japan would be "the cornerstone of our Asian interests and policy."

These lofty expressions of sentiment and intent represent a long-standing estimate of Japan's importance to the American national interest. Within a short time after the end of World War II, American politicians and strategists began to realize that Japan, defeated, de-militarized, and occupied though it was, was destined to have a large role in the emerging world of Soviet-American confrontation.[1] That judgment was soon validated when Japan became the indispensable staging base and supply center for the forces of the United Nations engaged in the war in Korea. Thereafter, through cold and hot war in East Asia and during both confrontation and reconciliation with China, the importance of the link with Japan has been a constant in the American strategic view of the Far East. The party platform

I wish to acknowledge the help of Shujiro Urata in preparing this chapter and of Janet E. Smith, who typed the manuscript.

1. Prime Minister Shigeru Yoshida wrote later that he noted the evidence of a basic shift in American occupation policy from reform to reconstruction and economic recovery in the January 1948 speeches of Kenneth C. Royall, U.S. secretary of the army, and Frank McCoy, the U.S. representative on the Far Eastern Commission. *The Yoshida Memoirs: The Story of Japan in Crisis* (Greenwood, 1963), p. 40.

writers in 1976 were reflecting a policy view that has never been subject to serious dissent.

The arguments for it are readily at hand, self-evident almost. Japan has the third, or perhaps the second, largest economy in the world. Japan is a sturdy democracy, unique in East Asia. The relationship with Japan affords the United States military facilities unavailable elsewhere. Considerations of material interest and political philosophy drive us into close association with Japan. On the other hand, an alignment of Japan's industrial capacity and potential with another great power, an upheaval in Japan's political system, a loss of access to bases in Japan—these would have to be seen as blows of the most damaging kind to America's position in Asia and the world.

The Other Alliance

In its fundamentals, therefore, the case for military alliance and political and economic cooperation with Japan matches the case for the North Atlantic Treaty and our other close ties with Western Europe. The Treaty of Mutual Cooperation and Security between the United States and Japan is our principal defense alliance, after the North Atlantic Treaty. As is true of relations with the Western European states, this other alliance extends well beyond its military dimensions. Japan's economy, like that of Western Europe, is linked by mutual interests with our own, in both its strengths and its vulnerabilities. And Japan's adherence to the principles of political freedom in a region otherwise inhospitable to democracy parallels the distinction between the politics of Western and Eastern Europe.

The apparent differences between the Atlantic and the Pacific connections can be overdrawn. The North Atlantic Treaty obliges its parties to come to one another's aid in the event of aggression: "An armed attack against one or more of them in Europe or North America shall be considered an attack against . . . all." In the mutual security treaty with Japan the United States is obliged to defend Japan against attack, but Japan assumes no commitment to respond to an attack on American territory or forces, not even if those forces are in South Korea, the security of which a Japanese prime minister has declared to be "essential" to Japan's own security. The assymetry, however, is largely verbal. The commitment to Western Europe does not rest on a requirement for European help in resisting an attack on the United States. As a practical matter, both treaties are one-sided promises.

Nor is it entirely so that the North Atlantic alliance is less parochial, more geared to the maintenance of global order. Japan, of course, has steadfastly and successfully resisted all suggestions that the scope of its defense commitment be extended beyond the home islands. A strict territorial limitation on the use of the military, or self-defense, forces is embodied in statute and justified by interpretation of the "peace clause" (article 9) of Japan's constitution.

In NATO, similarly, a narrow construction has been placed on the application of the treaty. When crises involving NATO members have arisen outside the treaty region—Suez, Cyprus, Cuba, the Near East, Indochina—the regional definitions written into the charter have been implicitly or explicitly recognized as binding. The reality is that both Japan and the European NATO powers have considered it politically expedient, or necessary, to confine their commitments to the letter of the treaties.

Of course, a more substantial difference is to be found in the relative degrees of military integration in the two alliances. The North Atlantic Treaty Organization has a fairly articulated structure: a military command, a strategy, a political council, and a bureaucracy. If the elements of commonality are notably fewer in tactics, equipment, and logistics than in command and strategic thinking, NATO is nonetheless history's most elaborate example of peacetime coordination among the armed forces of independent states. By comparison, collaboration between American and Japanese military forces has only just begun to expand beyond the most obvious requirements for periodic consultation between treaty partners. Japan's persistently modest allocation of resources to defense, relative to potential, has been matched until very recently by its reluctance, undoubtedly based on an accurate appreciation of domestic political sensitivities, to explore the putative benefits of joint planning, equipment standardization, and greater complementarity of force structures.

But, as is discussed more fully below, this difference now appears to be narrowing. The mutual security treaty has gained in public support or tolerance, giving the Japanese government more room for maneuver. While Japan will continue to be very much the junior in the military partnership, the initial steps are being taken to give the alliance the elements of a coordinated defense system within its primary locus of concern, the islands and nearby waters of Japan.

To push the parallel a bit further, American economic relations with both Japan and the European states have been extensive, expanding, and frequently troubled. The relatively open economies of the United States, the European Community, and Japan are bound together by trade, investment, monetary links, and commonalities such as a dependence on imported oil. This growing but also disconcerting bilateral interdependence has been as marked with Japan as with Europe. Not surprisingly, notions of national interests have often differed—over policies ranging from agriculture to macroeconomic choices. It is not feasible to determine whether strains have appeared more often or with greater intensity in trans-Atlantic or in trans-Pacific economic relations, but certainly the variance cannot be enormous. (See chapter 3 for a fuller treatment of the effect of economic interdependence.)

In sum, the relationship with Japan has indeed become a cornerstone of U.S. foreign policy as it has evolved since World War II. Comparisons show a parallelism between American relations with Japan and our better-advertised relations with Western Europe. Japan is our other principal ally in all relevant respects.

That said, relations with Japan are different and, what may be more important, are commonly seen as different. In a fundamental sense, it could hardly be otherwise. History, culture, language, and race do set Japan apart. Most Americans are of European ancestry; ties of sentiment and family run predominantly across the Atlantic. Japanese-Americans are a tiny minority—three-tenths of one percent of the population—heavily concentrated in California and Hawaii. Even though large numbers of Americans have become acquainted with Japan during the postwar years—the occupation and the continued U.S. military presence brought hundreds of thousands of Americans to live in Japan for extended periods—it probably remains for most a remote and recondite place.

Many observers thus tend to emphasize characteristics considered to be peculiar to the Japanese or to discover unusual capabilities, or vulnerabilities, in Japan's social and economic system. Henry A. Kissinger, in a basically sensitive and sympathetic report in his *White House Years,* is conventionally extravagant on this score: "For Japan's achievements—and occasionally its setbacks—have grown out of a society whose structure, habits, and forms of decision-making are so unique as to insulate Japan from all other cultures." This kind of hyperbole no doubt derives in considerable part from the fact of Japan's extraordinary postwar economic growth and the social and political stability that has accompanied it. The resilience and adaptability of Japanese society and institutions has rightly impressed foreigners, as they have many Japanese as well. It is beyond argument that Japan possesses important strengths and that the country's leadership has helped to direct these strengths to the general advantage. But one wonders whether, had Japan been less successful, its now perceived uniqueness would have been so noticeable.

The belief that Japan is, if not inscrutable, a country to which ordinary norms do not apply has gone along with closely confined Washington-Tokyo relations. Unlike the European industrial democracies, with their postcolonial connections and their strong intraregional links, Japan's relations with countries other than the United States have been relatively distant, and those with the United States, special. They are special in a sense different from the Anglo-American tie of the early postwar period, for the Japan-American association is notable in its almost unvarying bilateralism. This has been most striking, of course, in defense affairs, where Japanese constitutional and political constraints have precluded any widening of the area of mutual security beyond Japan itself. Past efforts to persuade Japan toward any form of regional defense arrangement have been unavailing and the subject itself for long has been, by tacit understanding, outside the range of direct discussion.

In other respects, also, the pattern has been narrowly bilateral, particularly in economic relations. Habits that grew naturally during the occupation and postoccupation years—when the United States played a benevolent avuncular role toward Japan—have persisted. To be sure, Japan is a member (its initial admission having been at the instance of the United States) of all of the relevant multilateral institutions, including the Organization for Economic Cooperation and Development (where it was the first entrant from a region other than Western Europe or North America). The practice, however, has been to see American-Japanese problems as falling outside the useful reach of these institutions. It has been customary, comfortable, and unquestionably less chancy for both parties to look for solutions in a bilateral setting. This is true of, above all, trade relations, where problems appear with greatest frequency. No trade issue between Japan and the United States has been submitted to the processes provided by the General Agreement on Tariffs and Trade, not even during the extended period when Japan could have been judged to be in wholesale violation of its obligations under this agreement. During the multilateral trade negotiations, 1977–79, the negotiation within a negotiation between American Ambassador Robert S. Strauss and Japanese Minister Nobuhiko Ushiba seemed often to overshadow the main event.

It would be straining things to say that the alliance has been endangered or weakened by an exaggerated sense among Americans of Japan's strangeness or by the undiluted bilateralism of relations. The forces keeping Japan and the United States together obviously have been strong enough to overwhelm recurring misunderstandings or even basic divergences of view. Thus, succeeding American administrations have made the mistake of supposing that a Japanese prime minister and his cabinet could readily comply with demands for actions desired by the United States.[2] But the ensuing frustrations, from Secretary of State John Foster Dulles's failure in 1955 to persuade Japan's political leadership to endorse the concept of regional defense to Robert Strauss's inability to have Japan remove import quotas on oranges and beef, were in due course accepted by Washington. And the closed features of U.S.-Japanese relations may have been as desirable as they were otherwise. It would not have been infallibly a gain to have had South Korea or Taiwan under the aegis of the security treaty with Japan or to have had most bilateral economic issues referred to international institutions for mediation or settlement.

All the same, the association with Japan is no more fixed than any other aspect of our foreign relations. At this time, security relations appear to have reached a new high level of mutual understanding and trust—but with a question about the continuing tenability of the present allocation of the burdens of defense. Economic relations with Japan seem certain to become more complex and less suited to management via a Tokyo-Washington telephone and shuttle service. The issues looming ahead are bound to involve the interests of the major

2. Examples from recent administrations include Richard Nixon's adamant insistence on comprehensive controls on textile exports which, to use Kissinger's phrase, proved to be a "fiasco." One of the trade issues raised by Jimmy Carter's administration was the need to change wholesale and retail distribution in Japan so as to foster imports.

industrial nations, and usually those of the developing countries as well. If the need is for better coordination of goals and policies at least among the big three—the United States, Japan, and Western Europe —it is hard to see how this can be achieved except on an effectively multilateral basis.

In the future, as in the past, the problems of maintaining the Japanese cornerstone of our foreign policy for Asia will fall into the categories of security and economic relations. Although these are not independent of one another, for expository purposes they are best considered separately. Security, which presumably is at the heart of the relationship, is discussed first.

Mutual Security

For the better part of two decades the staple of domestic politics in Japan was the mutual security treaty with the United States. In its 1951 form it was accepted reluctantly, as a price for the treaty of peace.[3] Thereafter the principal opposition party, the Socialists, made hostility to the treaty and to the American military presence in Japan cardinal elements of policy. Moreover, the appeal of the Socialist position extended beyond the party membership to intellectuals, students, and even to many conservatives. In 1960 a prime minister was driven out of office by the turmoil surrounding Diet ratification of a revision of the treaty (ironically, the revision met most of the Japanese objections to the original document).

Opposition to the treaty slowly declined during the next decade, as prosperity abounded under the conservative slogan of doubling national income in ten years—and as the number of American military bases was reduced. By 1970, with the return of the island of Okinawa to Japanese control assured, it was possible to renew the treaty—for an indefinite period—without serious controversy.

Since the 1970 renewal, the Japanese have grown steadily more favorable to the treaty and to the presence of American military forces in Japan. The return of Okinawa and the substantial consolidation and reduction of American military bases doubtless helped to change public attitudes. So must have the American reconciliation with the People's Republic of China, for the risk of becoming en-

3. At that time Japan had two conservative parties, one of which was so divided on the issue that its representative to the negotiations was unable to sign, leaving only Prime Minister Yoshida to sign.

tangled in a Sino-American war had been a long-standing cause for Japanese worry about the alliance with the United States. The American withdrawal from Vietnam may have been the capstone on the series of events that made the treaty and its associated features less troubling to the Japanese. The war was unpopular in Japan and its ending welcome. And the debacle gave credence to the idea that all U.S. military commitments in East Asia might be open to question, with consequences not readily to be faced. Both considerations probably enhanced the value of defense cooperation with the United States. In any case, the pace of improvement in defense relations has quickened since the end of the Indochina war.

To review the current status of the military alliance, there is first the mutual security treaty itself. Now an agreement of indefinite duration, not subject to fixed periodic political review, the treaty has two main clauses. Article 5 states that each party, in effect, will resist an armed attack against "either party" *in Japan*. Article 6 grants the United States the use by its armed forces of "facilities and areas" in the interests of Japan's security and "peace and security in the Far East."

Since the United States has utilized the authority provided by article 6, an attack on Japan almost inevitably would involve American forces stationed there. By the same token, the Japanese self-defense forces could scarcely fail to react to an attack on American military bases located in Japan. The treaty provisions, in short, do constitute a mutual and, in practical terms, closely binding commitment to act together in the specific circumstances of armed aggression against Japan.

American forces assigned to Japan have been reduced over the years, from 260,000 in 1952 when the peace treaty came into force to some 46,000 in 1979. Currently, forces are stationed at five principal air bases, at a large naval base in Yokusuka, near Yokohama, and in Okinawa, where two of the three regiments of a Marine division compose the ground force element in Japan. At the core of the American military force is the Seventh Fleet, which bases one of its two carriers and five other ships in Japan. As the forward-deployed portion of American naval power in the Pacific, the Seventh Fleet's mission extends widely over the western Pacific and the Indian Ocean. Its ability to control the seas, however, is of special importance to the security of the islands of Japan.

Japan's self-defense forces consist of twelve ground-force divisions and one composite brigade (a total of 155,000 men), an air force of ten fighter squadrons and assorted other aircraft, and maritime forces that include 59 destroyers and destroyer escorts, 13 submarines, and 200 aircraft.

It seems it would have been important that these modest—but by no stretch negligible—combined forces be designed, organized, and equipped to enhance their efficiency in defending Japan against some commonly understood danger. Instead, Japan's rearmament, which began only in 1954, and the American deployment of forces in Japan proceeded along separate tracks. The reasons are explicable enough. In Japan, suspicions about American "imperialist" policies in Asia were entertained not only by the left opposition but by the Japanese public. The counsel of prudence for politicians was therefore to take an arm's-length posture toward combined planning and genuine collective defense. As for the United States, its forces were and still are considered to have responsibilities for an area of Asia well beyond Japan. Given that the Japanese military force was bound by the narrowest conceivable geographic restrictions,[4] there were apparent limits on possibilities for coordination.

To be sure, consultative arrangements were devised to deal with the manifold problems associated with the existence of a large American military establishment in Japan. Consultations stopped short, however, of steps toward coordination of the military forces. Not until 1975 was an understanding reached on a joint study of the question, in the course of talks between Prime Minister Takeo Miki and President Gerald R. Ford. A subcommittee on defense cooperation was then established and after lengthy deliberation produced in 1978 "Guidelines for Japan-United States Defense Cooperation," which a delegation from the Senate Armed Services Committee called "a development of major proportions."

It is possible that this description of the guidelines will turn out to be overly exuberant. Nonetheless, the guidelines carefully spell out an agreement to move to joint planning, to conduct joint exercises and training, to coordinate procedures, and to act in complementary ways

---

4. In 1966, Prime Minister Eisaku Sato felt it necessary to say that Japanese forces could not be sent to aid in the defense of Okinawa because the island was still under American political control—that is, was not part of the area that Japan was obliged by treaty to defend.

in emergencies. When it is realized that for the first time ever the two military commands will have to agree on the nature and magnitude of the potential threats against which planning must be addressed, it becomes clear that the guidelines do give the alliance the prospect of reaching a mutuality of purpose heretofore absent. At a minimum, they provide a basis for increasingly effective cooperation in the defense of Japan. And in an addendum to the text there is provision for joint study of the "facilitative assistance" that might be extended to U.S. forces in "situations in the Far East outside of Japan which will have an important influence on the security of Japan."

This gingerly approach to the territorial constraints on Japan's self-defense forces is in recognition of the sensitivity of the matter. Japan's constitution has been construed to mean that armed personnel may not be sent abroad "with a mission to exercise armed action" and that "any role in collective security systems requiring Japan to take action against aggression aimed at allied nations" is prohibited. These strictures mirror Japanese political realities and are not likely to be overtly modified other than in the most compelling circumstances. Their interpretation, however, can be more rigorous or less.

Thus in 1969 the F-4 fighter could not be introduced into the air self-defense force until its "offensive" capabilities (bombing systems and in-flight refueling) had been removed because it was feared that the plane's operational radius might make it appear to be an "aggressive" threat. In 1972 it was possible to acquire a support fighter, the FS-T2 (now designated the F-1), with its bombing system intact. Now, the successor to the F-4, the F-15, is being introduced complete with in-flight refueling, which, it is explained, will not be put to use until the late 1980s.

If Japan has a priority regional interest, it is in the neighboring Republic of Korea (South Korea). But even the most ordinary forms of defense collaboration with the Koreans—exchanges of intelligence, say, or communications regarding overlapping air zones—have heretofore been conducted through a third party, the United States, because of sensitivities in both Japan and South Korea. Now a head of Japan's Defense Agency has been able to pay an official visit to South Korea, and the way has been opened to more direct exchanges—still, of course, in matters that do not connote an external military role for Japan. And Japan's maritime forces for the first time have found it possible, without dissimulation, to take part in a com-

bined exercise with ships from the Australian, Canadian, and New
Zealand, as well as the American, navies.

These thin straws are tentative indicators of greater flexibility in
Japanese attitudes, official and popular, toward the regional exigen-
cies of national defense. They go along with a more thoroughgoing
turnabout in views about American military bases in Japan. As recently as 1975, an experienced American observer found that "the
presence of armed foreigners on Japanese soil has become even less
tolerable" than ever to Japanese opinion.[5] Yet subsequent official
statements and actions are of a quite different sort. According to the
Japanese Defense Agency's 1976 White Paper, "the presence of U.S.
forces . . . serves as an important pillar of . . . peace and stability in
Asia." The 1979 issue says flatly that "the stationing of U.S. Forces
in Japan is the core of the Japan-U.S. security arrangements, and is
indispensable to the security of this nation." As much to the point is
the increase in appropriations for the direct and indirect support of
the American bases. Originally confined largely to rentals for land,
expenditures were expanded to finance a variety of projects on behalf
of the American military forces and their dependents. Costs incurred
on behalf of American forces grew from 147 billion yen in Japan's
fiscal 1975 to 206 billion yen (about $1 billion) in fiscal 1979. In
1978 these costs began to include contributions to local labor costs
and in 1979, contributions to the improvement of facilities on the
bases.[6]

It is true, however, that the bulk of these expenditures, helpful as
they may be, come out of the Defense Agency's budget and might
otherwise be devoted to strengthening the self-defense forces. If there
is a single principal source of future difficulty in the military alliance
it probably is the overall level of Japan's defense spending. The 1979
budget is 2 trillion yen (about $9 billion). With military pensions
added (which are included in NATO defense budgets) defense is
about 1.5 percent of gross national product, less than a third the U.S.
ratio and lower than that of any large NATO power. Criticism of the

5. Fred Greene, *Stresses in U.S.-Japanese Relations* (Brookings Institution, 1975),
p. 47.
6. Of the 206 billion yen for 1979, 166 billion is included in the budget, while
40 billion represents imputed rents for national property and buildings provided to
U.S. Forces Japan. The "direct" U.S. budgetary expenditures for American forces in
Japan—pay and allowances plus operational and maintenance costs incurred *in
Japan*—are estimated at $1.4 billion for U.S. fiscal 1979.

"free ride" is a recurring feature of American congressional comments about Japan, particularly in the context of bilateral economic relations. Not surprisingly, Japan is seen as having consistently devoted fewer resources to its own defense than any other country while vigorously expanding its exports and waxing affluent; rightly or not —and arguments can be offered both ways—a connection is made between cheap defense and economic success. And expectations that Japan would depart from this pattern have been regularly dashed.

There is little reason to project any early change in defense spending. A ceiling of 1 percent of gross national product (not including pensions) has been observed in practice since 1962. In 1976 the outgoing Miki cabinet declared that the 1 percent limit should be formally imposed for the "interim." Although the 1976 statement obviously does not bind subsequent governments, it added status to a figure already well-grounded in custom. Defense Agency planning for the first half of the 1980s assumes that the ceiling will remain. This is clearly based on a sound assessment of political possibilities.

The truth is, the constituencies for greatly increased defense spending are weak. The political influence of the defense forces is minimal. Others willing to be counted are rightist groups outside the mainstream of Japanese politics, a few politicians, and a small number of industrialists. Against are all the major political parties, the youth and "peace" organizations, the trade unions, and, so far as can be judged, public opinion generally. Within the official establishment, the powerful Ministry of Finance has always found desirable a built-in limit on the defense budget, which contrasts with the open-ended claims of, say, the rice farmers. In recent years, when the ministry has had to find ways to finance huge fiscal deficits, the implicit guideline for defense spending has been all the more welcome. Other cabinet ministries, with their own budget wishes to be satisfied, are certainly not going to be advocates of more defense spending.

Realism says, therefore, that short of a near cataclysmic change in the security environment, Japan's defense spending over the next several years will grow at a rate no higher than and most likely slightly below the rate of real gross national product. If the 1985 growth objective of 5.7 percent is achieved and 1 percent goes to defense, the 1985 defense appropriation, in constant 1979 yen, will be about 39 percent over the 1979 appropriation, the equivalent of $12 billion to $13 billion.

The ability of the United States to alter this outlook must be recognized to be very small. If any influencing lever is available in the abstract, it is the prospect of a significant withdrawal of American military power from Japan and the western Pacific. To make such a prospect credible, the reductions would have to be put in train, not merely talked about. This is an ultimate and unlikely form of pressure, however.

It needs only to be noted that if Japan were ever to opt for large-scale rearmament and military independence as a consequence of a much-reduced American presence, the power balance in Northeast Asia would alter and not necessarily to America's benefit. China and the USSR alike seem to be satisfied with the Japanese-American security alliance; whether either would be ready to see the Japanese role enhanced while that of the United States shrank is at least open to question. And if Japan's rearmament were to extend to nuclear weapons, the shock waves would go far beyond Asia, since that would signal the practical end of nonproliferation. Japan is not India or Pakistan. It is potentially a major power. Its entrance into the nuclear field would open the way to an unrestrained scramble for nuclear weapons.

If efforts to push Japan toward a significantly larger military program are likely to be unrewarding, the prospects for a more cost-effective defense association are moderately favorable. With agreement reached on the need for joint planning, the practicable rationalization of American and Japanese military roles and missions is finally within sight. There is already a large measure of interoperability of equipment between the two forces. It will be furthered by Japan's current modernization program, which provides for a strengthening of antisubmarine capabilities[7] and for the replacement of an aging fleet of fighter aircraft with F-15s. It is not beyond expectation that the annual increments to Japan's military budget can be devoted in reasonable part to enhancing the complementarity of the two military forces.

Some changes, perhaps desirable, are not achievable. For example, Japan's military spending is skewed in favor of the ground forces, which received 42 percent of the defense budget between 1970 and

7. An important new acquisition is the Lockheed P-3C patrol aircraft. This procurement decision required the government to absorb negative public reaction to its renewing a relationship marred by a hugely publicized bribery scandal in 1976.

1977, in contrast to 22 percent for the navy and 24 percent for the air force. It is arguable that these proportions should be significantly revised because the naval and air forces are more relevant to Japan's defense. But any major change in the relative budget shares among the forces is out of practical political reach. Similarly, a case can be made against Japan's policy of producing most of its own hardware. Costs undoubtedly are usually higher, because of low volume.[8] The Defense Agency's own studies show that producing the P-3C in Japan under license is measurably less cost-effective than importing the finished aircraft. Again, however, the policy—which can be justified, if at all, only because it provides a production base for emergencies—is fixed (initially it had American encouragement) and is no longer open to effective challenge.[9]

During the 1950s and 1960s American administrations generally took a long view of the military side of the association with Japan. This meant, among other things, accepting the judgments of Japanese politicians about political feasibilities. In the 1970s the political foundations of defense cooperation strengthened steadily, and by some standards remarkably. If the United States can continue to live with a modest Japanese defense budget, growing not much faster than our own stepped-up spending, defense relations can be expected to become closer and this element of our global military position more solid. To look for more promises disappointment.

Peaceful Economic Coexistence?

American views of Japan's economic potential and prowess have gone through two more or less distinct phases.

From early in the occupation—once the decision against a punitive peace had been taken—until the middle 1960s the emphasis was primarily on Japan's vulnerabilities and weaknesses. The lack of domestic raw materials and a chronic foreign trade deficit seemed to justify a guarded, if not wholly dismal, assessment of the country's prospects. Given the pessimism about the balance of payments, it was

8. Because exports are strictly controlled, the domestic market provides essentially the only outlet for the arms industry.

9. Comparative advantage in defense procurement, despite the arguments for it, has not prevailed in NATO either. See Keith Hartley and Alan Peacock, "Combined Defense and International Economic Cooperation," *The World Economy,* vol. 1 (June 1978), pp. 327–39.

quite in accord with the general practice of the time that from the beginning external transactions of all kinds were closely controlled. When Japan became a party to the International Monetary Fund and the General Agreement on Tariffs and Trade, waivers of the resulting obligations to remove controls were readily accorded. An American development assistance program was continued in Japan until 1961.

Irritants in economic relations developed when Japan's "low wage" exports began to come into the American market in large volume. These problems were fairly easily controlled, however, by a series of nominally voluntary and unofficial restrictive arrangements including one covering the sizable trade in cotton textiles.[10] Economic relations into the 1960s otherwise can accurately be characterized as placid.

Attitudes changed as Japan's economy and the state of its external accounts changed. The "miracle" growth rates of the 1950s, far from declining, accelerated, led by a rapidly diversifying manufacturing sector. Exports came more and more from industries like steel, electronics, and automobiles, as those of the traditional labor-intensive industries slowed. By the mid-1960s the trade deficit was replaced by a surplus. Where persisting weaknesses had been, there were increasing—and by some measures alarming—strengths.

Views about Japan were affected also by the slow pace of liberalization of foreign trade and investment controls. Quantitative limits on a wide range of nonagricultural imports were retained until the early 1970s. Direct foreign investments similarly continued to be subject to severe restrictions. Japan was openly in violation of its commitments under the International Monetary Fund and the General Agreement on Tariffs and Trade—its waivers having been relinquished in 1963 and 1964—and of its obligations under the Treaty of Friendship, Commerce, and Navigation with the United States. To the perception of Japan as a vigorous competitor was added a conviction that Japanese economic policies were less than fair and equitable.

The Nixon administration's economic "shocks" in 1971 were in part a response to the revised official view of Japan. "By the middle of 1971, adjustments in our vast economic relationship [with Japan]

10. The original industry-to-industry textile arrangement was undermined by the growth of exports from the Republic of China (Taiwan) and Hong Kong, and in 1961–62 it was supplanted by intergovernmental agreements limiting exports.

had become a pressing requirement of U.S. national policy," President Nixon reported to Congress in February 1972, referring to the new economic policy measures of the previous August. To bring a reluctant Japan to accept broadened restrictions on textile exports, the administration used the "obnoxious threat," in Henry Kissinger's words, of the Trading with the Enemy Act.

In 1973 the United States briefly embargoed foreign purchases of soybeans, one of Japan's chief agricultural imports. Then, in the wake of the Arab oil embargo, as Japan experienced the worst inflation and the deepest fall in national output of any of the large industrial powers, there was an interlude of "no problems" in American-Japanese relations. By 1976, however, a period of confrontation was again in sight. Japan's otherwise modest recovery from recession, 1976–78, was marked by a very strong export performance, a return to an external surplus, and an impressive restoration of price stability—the obverse of the American experience. This performance served to harden a belief in Japanese capacities for managing—or manipulating—economic activities in the interest of the external accounts. It was the more urgent, therefore, that inequities be remedied—and that rising pressure from American industry and labor and from Congress be contained. A series of bilateral negotiations, intertwined with the multilateral Tokyo Round trade negotiations, helped to defuse the more extreme notions of suitable policy toward Japan,[11] and perhaps to provide some of the means for limiting and resolving disputes in the future. The fact that Japan's 1979 current external accounts shifted into large deficit, globally if not bilaterally, contributed further to a reduction in tensions.

If the lesson to be drawn from the past is that economic relations will be comparatively free of severe strain only when the Japanese economy is in difficulty—or at least is not running a big external surplus—then the alliance obviously has an important point of weakness. This should not be overstated. American-Japanese relations have remained close in spite of differences over economic issues; it must be supposed that the compulsions to get along will not lose their

11. One proposal, much bruited in Congress in 1978, was to impose a discriminatory surcharge or import quotas on Japanese goods. In rejecting the idea on behalf of the president, Robert S. Strauss still termed it "a legitimate option." *Task Force Report on United States-Japan Trade,* Committee Print, Subcommittee on Trade of the House Committee on Ways and Means, 95 Cong. 2 sess. (GPO, 1979), app. G, p. 81.

force quickly or easily. Nonetheless, political-security relations cannot have been aided by congressional demands that trade with Japan be treated like trade with the Soviet Union—or by the widened belief among Americans that Japan was not observing the rules of the trading game. More important, perhaps, the fears and suspicions engendered or worsened during the recent period do not provide an optimum setting for the heightened cooperation at both macroeconomic and microeconomic levels that is needed in the future.

For, hackneyed term or not, the interdependence of the American and Japanese economies is real. Policy decisions in either of these big, relatively open economies influence events in the other. A slow-growth policy in Japan undergirds an export boom that makes more difficult the pursuit of a U.S. policy focused on reducing unemployment. Choices made in Washington that encourage American imports of oil impinge on Japan's interest in stable prices for this crucial product. The expectation that flexible exchange rates would lead to quick adjustments between the two economies proved illusory; and since flexibility, a widely moving exchange rate has presented unanticipated problems for economic policy on both sides of the Pacific.

At this time, the outlook for the early 1980s is for slow growth in the United States, the European Community, and Japan, for an extremely fragile situation in energy, for major—even frightening—requirements for industrial readjustment, and for serious balance-of-payments difficulties among developing countries. If these are indeed features of the next period, they set a premium on cooperation, especially between the two biggest market economies. Whether that can be achieved is, of course, an open question.

It is useful, in any case, to survey some of the elements in U.S.-Japanese economic relations for indicators of the possibilities and problems ahead.

Unfairness in Trade

If there is a chronic American complaint about Japanese policy and practice, it is that imports have been discouraged and exports promoted by unfair means.[12] The persistence of a large imbalance in

12. "Japan uses tariffs, quotas, and a variety of nontariff barriers to limit imports; Japanese exporters benefit from tax rebates and other government assistance programs designed to stimulate and to subsidize exports; and finally, Japanese exporters dump products in the American market. . . . Given these unfair acts . . . U.S. industries such as television will find it increasingly difficult to compete in their home

bilateral trade in recent years supports this complaint, but its principal source probably is the accumulation of specific grievances over access to Japan or over the successes of Japanese exporters in the United States. In any case, it provides an inauspicious background for the delicate process of putting into effect new international agreements on trade practices.

So far as the customary sorts of official intervention in private trade are concerned, Japan is not exceptional. It has ended its quotas on nonagricultural imports, except for the special case of leather products. Its average tariffs on industrial goods, according to U.S. calculations, will be the lowest of the big three when the Tokyo Round reductions are completed. Import licensing and prior-import deposits were abolished in 1972. Japan has agreed to the new General Agreement on Tariffs and Trade codes governing export subsidies, customs valuation, import licensing, the application of technical standards to imports, and, subject to further negotiations with the United States, purchasing by public authorities. The commitments involved are not matters for unilateral observance or nonobservance. This agreement, including the new codes, provides procedures for settling disputes and sanctions for violations.

Export dumping—usually thought of as price discrimination by private sellers—is similarly liable to sanction, with the support of the General Agreement. And dumping in the United States has not been frequent. From 1972 through 1977 the U.S. Treasury initiated an average of twenty antidumping cases a year, including a dozen brought in 1977 by the steel industry. Findings against Japanese firms averaged six a year, including six of the steel cases (which were disposed of by the special "trigger price" arrangement rather than by assessing dumping duties).

There is the proposition that official or visible features of Japanese trade policy or practice are supplemented by less visible or extralegal habits, customs, and institutions that foster exports and deter imports. To the extent that this rests on observed Japanese attitudes it cannot be dismissed. Japan does have a tradition of protectionism and a

market." See editor's introduction to an article by John J. Nevin in *Harvard Business Review*, vol. 56 (September–October 1978), p. 165. For a congressional view, see *Task Force Report on United States-Japan Trade*, p. 16: "The [trade] adjustment process has been deliberately and systematically retarded by artificially high consumer prices and subsidized export maintenance programs. . . . Japanese officials and industrialists are unwilling to take these hard steps [to remove trade barriers]."

preoccupation with the hazards of being dependent on imports, and these undoubtedly continue to influence private and official choices.

A specific matter in point is "administrative guidance," a procedure under which an agency of government, without legal authority, may propose or request courses of action by private individuals or firms, perhaps but not necessarily using the persuasive force of future favors and penalties. That administrative guidance has been invoked to restrict exports as well as imports has not made it less a source of resentment abroad; indeed, few things can have contributed more to belief in Japan's unfairness in trade than semicovert governmental interventions to regulate imports.

Still, if we put aside such things as Japan's archaic (in part) internal distribution system—and the Japanese language—which may be import-inhibiting but are hardly open to short-run modification by anyone, it is not plain that the means are lacking for coping with trade practices considered unfair. As has been said, the General Agreement on Tariffs and Trade, including the codes negotiated during the Tokyo Round, allows penalties or retaliation for violations and provides procedures for consultation and dispute settlement. Beyond that, since 1977 the United States and Japan have had a bilateral agreement for identifying and dealing with specific difficulties concerning Japanese trade practices and procedures through the joint Trade Facilitation Committee composed of government officials and the Trade Study Group of business and government representatives.

Then there is American legislation, which abounds in provisions aimed at "unfair" trade. In addition to the antidumping statute and the antisubsidy or countervailing duty clause of the basic Tariff Act of 1930, trade legislation provides for retaliatory "responses to certain trade practices of foreign countries" and for actions to counter "unfair practices in [the] import trade." The antitrust laws, which allow private suits for treble damages, also have been invoked against allegedly unfair and anticompetitive acts.

It is unquestionably important, on both economic and political grounds, that a showing be made that practices generally considered unfair are not acceptable in international trade. In the Tokyo Round, the negotiations were principally directed at this point. The codes or conventions coming into effect in 1980 and 1981 are designed to reduce or eliminate the resort to nontariff measures that can arbitrarily or artificially restrain imports or foster exports. If the codes are applied in roughly equitable fashion among the United States, Canada, the European Community, and Japan, a genuine advance will have been made.

The prospects for equitable treatment are uncertain, however. Although the United States will have a procedure that assures open or, in the current jargon, transparent implementation of the codes, the remedies for unfairness in U.S. trade laws can also be used to harass importers and their foreign suppliers.[13] In the "trigger price" mechanism used to govern steel imports, the United States has applied a specialized if not unique definition of dumping: sales at prices found to be less than the average cost of production are subject to dumping duties even if no price discrimination exists. That is, prices that do not cover full costs, as defined by American law, are per se dumping prices. And the Treasury has found it proper to assess countervailing duties against Japanese export-promotion measures that are used by the United States as well.[14]

On the other hand, in Japan and other nations with parliamentary systems, procedures are likely to be less open. The American emphasis on public hearings, a published record, and an appeals and review process provides a measure of protection against arbitrary decisions. If foreign procedures are not similar, American skepticism is almost inevitable, whatever the applicable laws or regulations say.

The codes have been heavily advertised to Congress and to American business and labor as answers to the unfair trade practices of other countries. If the resulting expectations are frustrated, the new system will be quickly discredited. Meanwhile, little has been said in this country about the application of the codes to the United States. But it is also predictable that unless the United States stands ready to have its own practices examined, the codes will be soon undermined.

In the optimum case, the world could be entering an era in which the General Agreement on Tariffs and Trade is revivified and interna-

13. Imports of Japanese color television sets have been the object of legal actions under the antidumping and countervailing duty statutes, under section 337 of the Tariff Act of 1930 (predatory practices alleged), and under the antitrust laws; in addition, there was an escape clause investigation, which was ended by the negotiation of an orderly marketing agreement limiting the volume of imports.

14. The measures were a tax deferral available to small business for export revenues (comparable to but on a much lesser scale than the U.S. law providing for domestic international sales corporations, or DISCs) and aid from Japan's export promotion service (comparable to our commercial officer and trade center programs).

tional trade put more securely than before under a widely accepted rule of law. If so, it could be expected that the unfairness issue in U.S.-Japanese relations will diminish—no doubt slowly, for perceptions will lag behind reality. It is also possible that the new system will quickly be overloaded with complaints and allegations of bad faith, followed by retaliatory measures, and that the international atmosphere will be worsened rather than improved. The first few years of the 1980s will test whether the principal trading nations have the capability or the will to make the new system effective. What happens can make relations with Japan easier and freer of friction, but an opposite outcome is also possible.

Adjustment to Competitive Change

Even with a strong General Agreement that is closely adhered to, major shifts in competitive positions are almost bound to put strains on international trading relations in the 1980s. Steel, chemicals, and automobiles are among the industries where massive adjustments seem to be in prospect as new suppliers enter world markets or as technology or demand patterns change. It is naive to suppose that these adjustments will be left to market forces alone. At the same time, the countries concerned and the world economy will be ill-served if the adjustment process is so heavily "organized" as to perpetuate inefficiency and high costs.

Until now, in fact, the standard answer to large-scale adjustment problems was to devise special import-protective regimes—invariably outside the general trade agreement, because its requirements for balancing liberalization were considered too onerous. Controls on trade in textiles are now far into their second decade; except for a brief period, the steel trade of the United States has been subject to import quotas or minimum price requirements since 1968; when imports of television sets cut deeply into the American market in 1976, quota limitations were negotiated in the form of an orderly marketing agreement; footwear imports are similarly restricted.

Although Japan has been at the center of most of the publicized product-specific trade issues, it is important to recognize that these issues were not strictly bilateral. In every instance, the trade restraint arrangements had to be made multilateral to be effective. This certainly will not change. It is an argument against the unfortunate but usual practice of singling out Japanese exports for the first application of restraints; the lengthy and bitter negotiation over textiles in 1969–71 got off to the worst possible start in just that way. If it is assumed that trading nations will continue to respond to some adjustment problems with protectionist measures, the case is strong for internationalizing these schemes from the beginning. This will require an extension of the general trade agreement. In the Tokyo Round, the negotiators considered at length a supplement to the escape clause (article 19) that would have allowed—and also set limiting conditions on—various voluntary and orderly arrangements to restrict trade on a product-specific basis. The effort unfortunately failed, mainly because of the resistance of developing countries to the European Community's demand for the right to apply the restraints selectively—that is, discriminatorily. Negotiations remain open, however, and the so-called safeguard addition may still be salvaged; with suitable terms, it could remedy a glaring lack in the international body of trade rules and law.

At best, considerable vigilance will be needed to assure that even arrangements approved by the General Agreement do not saddle the world with permanently protected industries, as textiles seem to have become. One offset may be found in flows of foreign direct investment and the expansion of international trade in components. The Japanese television industry has moved a sizable part of its production for the American market to facilities in the United States, in part because of U.S. protectionist pressure; American producers have sources in Mexico, Taiwan, Korea, and elsewhere for parts or even for finished sets. The impending shakeout of the world automobile industry may well be smoothed by cross-flows of direct investments. Ford and General Motors are setting the pace in moving toward truly internationalized production of standard "world" automobiles. Volkswagen is following. The strongest European and Japanese makers will be pressed to do the same. Out of the competitive struggle looming ahead, it is improbable that more than six or eight of the two dozen or so more or less independent final producers can survive the decade as such. It is possible to contemplate a rather quick evolution to an industry of a few large firms competitive with one another in their home markets and producing and competing in third markets (where government intervention may be more constrained than now by considerations of cost).

Such an evolution cannot take place with crippling restrictions on flows of direct investment. Neither Japan nor the United States imposes special restrictions on foreign direct investment, although Japanese validation procedures are time-consuming and expensive, and occasional congressional expressions of alarm about the implications of foreign ownership could worry would-be investors. But direct investments by one country in the other are not very large: American direct investments in Japan at the end of 1978, at $5 billion, were less than 3 percent of American investment abroad (but more than 100 of *Fortune*'s 500 largest American firms were investors); and Japan's $2.7 billion of investments in the United States came to 6.6 percent of total foreign investment in the United States. (These are U.S. data. While Japanese figures differ, the ratio is not altered.) There thus appears to be substantial room for expansion.

It is essential to recognize the political sensitivities that are exposed everywhere by foreign investment, especially when the United States, the home of the multinational firm, is anything but immune. Even so, the American experience in the European Community, or for that matter in Canada, does not suggest that a large multinational corporation presence is unduly disturbing in fact. Now that Japan has overcome its long-standing apprehensions about foreign investment, additional and growing cross-flows of capital, technology, and management can foster income-enhancing economic integration between the two major Pacific-basin economies.

Agricultural Trade and Food Security

The bilateralism that pervades U.S.-Japanese economic relations has special point when trade in agricultural goods is considered. Japan is the largest single national market for American farm exports, and a highly predictable one at that—in recent years buying about 15 percent of U.S. agricultural exports by value. And for Japan, the United States is the overwhelmingly important source for the most crucial agricultural imports—soybeans, feed grains, and wheat.

This is one of the signal features of trans-Pacific interdependence. A big and growing market in Japan makes possible a more efficient use of American agricultural resources. The availability of American soybeans and grain has permitted a remarkable diversification of the Japanese diet at low resource cost. As matters stand, more than a quarter of Japan's primary food energy comes from the United States.

With Japan's rice consumption projected to decline by a fifth in 1977–90,[15] the prospect seems to be for a continued growth of the market for oilseeds and feedstuffs needed to support expanding livestock and poultry industries.

It could be supposed that both countries would expect to gain from allowing agricultural trade to follow its apparently natural expansionist course. Perhaps that will happen. Japan's alternatives, in the end, are few. After the American embargo on soybean exports in 1973 and the grain price explosion in 1972–73, a try was made for greater food self-sufficiency through sharply higher domestic price supports. The meager results—wheat output remained virtually unchanged between 1973 and 1978 despite a more than doubling of the government's purchase price—suggest that the costs of any significant growth in domestic output would be exorbitant. Self-sufficiency in rice has been achieved—overachieved, for the Japanese citizen buys less and less, despite subsidized consumer prices, and the government must struggle with the problem of disposing of a costly, undesired surplus. Diversification of the sources of the two largest imports, soybeans and feed grains, is a very narrow option, for other suppliers lack the capacity to fill a much larger portion of Japan's requirements, at least at competitive prices. Thus if consumers are not to be further constrained in their freedom to choose (wheat, beef, citrus fruits, and other foods are now subject to quantitative import limitations) the trend clearly will be toward an enlarged American role in the provision of Japan's food supplies.

Japan's politicians and officials—and, probably, the public at large—do not find this prospect a comfortable one. The very real benefits of imports may be recognized in the abstract, but matched against them is an underlying concern about food insecurity. As a leading Japanese agricultural economist put it, "The majority of Japanese may be too pessimistic about future food supplies. However, it is understandable that the psychology of a people whose life is based

15. An extrapolation of the experience of 1965–77 (from Japan Ministry of Agriculture, Forestry and Fisheries), together with the U.S. Census Bureau medium projection for population growth, suggests a decline in rice consumption from 9.5 million tons a year to 7.7 million tons.

	1965	1977	1990
Population (millions)	98.3	113.9	125.9
Annual rice consumption (millions of metric tons)	11.0	9.5	7.7

entirely on foreign supplies of staple foods and petroleum would be pessimistic."[16]

Since it cannot possibly be in the interest of the United States for Japan's fears about food to be realized, the case for mutual efforts to strengthen supply assurances seems clear-cut. The commercial export interest is evident, but so ought to be political and defense relations, which cannot be separated from so fundamental a matter. In 1975, the two countries took account of this mutual interest by an exchange of stated intentions—by Japan to purchase and by the United States to sell at least 14 million tons of grains and soybeans in each of the marketing years 1975–76, 1976–77, and 1977–78. This understanding had the merit of assuring Japan that an embargo on grain or soybean exports was unlikely. The obligation to allow exports to Japan up to the 14 million ton figure, while not immutable, would have had substantial weight in a time of short supplies. Unfortunately, the exchange of commitments was allowed to lapse, apparently because the Ministry of Agriculture decided, somewhat myopically, that it would be politically awkward to announce an intention to buy American grain when rice was in embarrassingly large surplus.

A solution to Japan's food security problem, given all the constraints, would be an internationally agreed system of grain reserves. If we put aside doomsday predictions—crop failures so far-reaching that exporters would simply not be willing to sell—the chief basis for Japanese worry is that natural or man-made disasters will cause periodic upheavals in grain markets, which will impinge heavily on an import-dependent nation like Japan because exporters will protect home markets by controls.[17] National grain reserves, created by international agreement and released according to prearranged guidelines, would in principle protect all in such shortfall periods.

Since the Soviet crop failure in 1972, the idea of internationally coordinated grain reserves has been extensively studied and discussed but unsuccessfully negotiated. The failure to reach agreement on even a scaled-down reserve proposal suggests, however, that the

16. Kenzo Hemmi, "Japan's Food Problems," paper prepared for Conference on Food Policy and U.S.-Japanese Relations, Columbia University, East Asian Institute, March 1, 1977, p. 4.

17. The Japanese authorities conceivably might see the spectre of an OPEC-like cartel for grains or oilseeds; but given the competitive markets for these commodities, cartelization is a possibility so remote it does not justify spending on countermeasures.

negotiating problems—which are unquestionably formidable—will not be surmounted until after the next severe shock to grain markets.

In this circumstance, it is sensible for the United States and Japan to go back to second-best, bilateral possibilities. The obvious minimum step of regular agricultural consultations has been taken: Japan should at least be made aware of the considerations going into American farm policy, and U.S. policymakers need to be exposed to the concerns of Japan's agricultural ministry. A renewal of the earlier supply-purchase agreement would further inhibit any temptation to invoke export controls or to impose severe restrictions on American farm output. It could be supplemented by a Japanese decision to hold more sizable reserve stocks of feed grains and perhaps oilseeds. The U.S. Export Administration Act provides for a guarantee against the use of export control authority on agricultural goods stored in the United States by foreigners for later export, so that Japanese stocks could be held in both countries if that proved to be a cost-efficient option.[18]

Initiatives in these matters have to come primarily from Japan, where the authorities have traditionally been reluctant to take forward positions. Now, however, the overwhelming evidence is that the basic crop, rice, is facing a continuing decline in consumer acceptance, which in turn makes inescapable a readjustment, deliberate or otherwise, of the domestic farm economy. The occasion may exist, therefore, for examining seriously a policy of shifting land and resources (including subsidies) from rice to crops that Japan might produce at a comparative advantage—high among them, livestock and dairy products based on imported feedstuffs. That kind of decision might be fostered by assurance that supplies of feedstuffs are available from the United States, which in all foreseeable circumstances will have to be Japan's dominant supplier.[19] No sector of Japanese society is more resistant to economic interdependence than agriculture; and no other sector has comparable political influence.

18. It appears that some state and local taxes may inhibit the holding of grain stocks in Gulf and West Coast ports.

19. The decision could also be aided if Washington took a longer view of its export interest, subordinating for the time being further claims—pressed so strongly, and to some Japanese unreasonably, during the Tokyo Round—for increased access to the market for beef and citrus fruits. Japanese import policy, especially for beef, has kept consumer prices extravagantly high. But further liberalization will require the passage of time, and neither item is comparable in importance or prospect to the big, staple U.S. exports.

But basic forces push agricultural Japan toward the outside world. A patient and forthright American policy toward Japan's legitimate anxieties about food supplies is in accord with the realities of the 1980s and can work to mutual advantage.

Energy: Dependence and Interdependence

Japan's proximate and appalling vulnerability, as seen by all Japanese, is not food, of course, but oil. Worldwide, oil accounts for about 45 percent of primary fuel energy. In Japan, oil—nearly all of it imported—accounts for 73 percent. Another 15 percent of primary energy comes from imported coal and liquified natural gas. Nuclear power, based on imported fuel, contributes less than 2 percent, and wholly domestic sources—coal and hydropower and small amounts of domestic oil and natural gas—10 percent. And practical relief from energy import dependence is an eventuality too remote to be considered.

It is unsurprising, therefore, that after the 1973 oil crisis Japan's concern for supplies of energy fuels became acute. The Tokyo response to the Arab oil embargo is illustrative. Within a month of being labeled (and only by inference) an unfriendly country by the Organization of Arab Petroleum Exporting Countries (OAPEC), Japan announced a shift from neutrality to a pro-Arab position in Middle East policy and dispatched a senior political figure, Deputy Prime Minister Takeo Miki, to the Middle East Arab capitals to explain the change. This break with the foreign policy of its one ally followed on the heels of U.S. Secretary of State Kissinger's plea to hold fast to its earlier position.

In 1977 Japan's energy nerve was again touched, this time by the U.S. proposal for a moratorium on the development of nuclear fuel reprocessing and breeder reactors. The immediate question was the start-up of a pilot plant with an uncertain and modest potential for reprocessing Japan's substantial accumulation of spent fuel. As a symbol of Japan's commitment to reducing its reliance on petroleum, the reprocessing plant took on significance far beyond its actual promise. In the ensuing Japanese campaign to gain an exemption from Washington, a host of lesser officials and, in time, Prime Minister Takeo Fukuda and President Carter were involved before a compromise could be reached.

Japanese efforts to cope with the oil problem have had limited returns. The 1973 crisis found Japan with few ties to the Middle East oil-producing nations and with only small direct investments in crude oil production abroad. A flurry of diplomatic and commercial activity, with promises of loans and private investments, brought relatively little in the way of the hoped-for assurances of "stable" oil supplies.[20] As the international oil companies have had to cut back deliveries of crude oil to noncaptive refineries, Japan has turned to "direct deals" between private importers and producing governments and to government-to-government purchases, the latter sometimes associated with loan or investment commitments. But there has been no way to get truly credible supply guarantees or to escape from rising crude oil prices.

The nuclear alternative is a disappointment as well. In 1972, when nuclear generating capacity was less than 2.5 million kilowatts, it was considered possible to set a 1985 goal of 60 million kilowatts. As of November 1979 Japan had twenty nuclear plants generating about 14 million kilowatts (2 percent of total energy) and the 60 million kilowatt objective had receded into the 1990s. Other energy sources —coal, liquified natural gas, solar, and geothermal—do not promise to alter Japan's position very much. For the next two decades, barring technological miracles, the supply of energy raw materials will continue to be a preoccupying problem.

But if Japan's energy situation has its special features, it is not unique. Apart from the United Kingdom, no leading industrial nation has a genuine alternative to oil from members of the Organization of Petroleum Exporting Countries. All of them must accept the possibility, or rather the probability, that oil exports from some OPEC countries will at times be interrupted, with potentially disruptive economic consequences. None has any reason to expect that its imports will be cheaper or more secure than others, at least not for any extended period.

By the same token, no industrial country has an inherently greater vulnerability to an import cutoff than any other—unless, that is, these countries are unwilling to stand together. An embargo directed against selected consumers can work only if the other consumers allow the suppliers to dictate transshipment policy; importers who do

20. Mexico reportedly has agreed to provide Japan with 100,000 barrels of crude oil per day (2 percent of current imports) for ten years, beginning in 1980, in return for commitments for loans (up to $500 million) for oil-related projects and other development aid.

not cooperate against an embargo will have to reflect on their own situations the next time around. Furthermore, Japan is not necessarily at an economic disadvantage because most of its energy fuel must be imported. Every country must use economic resources to obtain fuels, whether from domestic deposits or from abroad.

In a crucial sense, the end of abundant petroleum has markedly increased the need for close cooperation between the United States, Japan, and Western Europe—to deal both with short energy supplies and with the consequences of the large balance-of-payments surpluses of some oil producers. And, considering the primitive state of international policy coordination generally, the response to the ongoing energy crisis has been encouraging. The International Energy Agency was created promptly after the 1973–74 oil price explosion. Its members have agreed on a plan for "automatic" sharing of oil supplies in an emergency. National stockpile goals have been set, and some progress has been made toward achieving them. The necessity for bringing oil imports under control was recognized at the highest political levels by the establishment of the import ceilings at the Tokyo economic summit meeting in June 1979. Differences over nuclear power technology have been brought under control, if not resolved. These developments reflect a broadening understanding that energy is a common problem, that all stand to gain or lose together from national decisions on energy policies.

The extent of this understanding can be overstated, however. For instance, although the sharp cut in Iranian supplies in early 1979 did not cause the panicky reactions seen in 1973–74, it did lead to an uncoordinated and costly rush to replenish and increase stocks. In spite of everything, it will have taken the United States seven years to give up in 1981 its import-subsidizing and energy-wasteful domestic price controls. In another case, Congress has set itself firmly against accepting the demonstrable savings in transport cost that would be gained from exporting Alaskan crude oil to Japan and importing like amounts from elsewhere. Japan plainly has not been willing readily to forgo opportunities to improve its supply position, even at high cost and at the risk of damage to its image in the United States.[21]

Still, there is no policy alternative to a continuing drive for energy

21. The "unseemly haste" of Japanese trading companies to buy Iranian oil at high spot-market prices after Tehran had embargoed sales to the United States brought an unusual and sharp expression of American official displeasure in December 1979.

cooperation among the big import-dependent countries. Effective conservation in one country or region can be offset by subsidized consumption in another. Import limits have to be set collectively to be credible. A "dialogue" with OPEC, so ardently wished by the Europeans and Japanese, conceivably could lead to more orderly cartel price policies—but only if the importers hold to common positions. The world energy problem has brought home, in what should be the most sobering fashion possible, the reality of interdependence. If the American, Japanese, and European governments cannot act together on energy, then a true economic and political catastrophe becomes all too believable a possibility.

The United States, Japan, and the World Economy

The forces impelling the United States and Japan (and Western Europe) to seek greater concertedness of trade or energy policies also operate at macroeconomic levels. At successive economic summit meetings since 1975, the elected leaders of the main industrial nations have groped for a mix of national economic goals and policies that might enhance the general prospect for achieving more satisfactory economic performance. That the results are mixed does not argue that the effort was misguided. There had been no summits preceding the industrial world's unplanned rush into inflation in 1972–73 and into deflation in 1974. The recollection of those disasters suggests that the search for a deliberated coordination of policies will not be abandoned lightly.

Indeed, the outlook is for more rather than less pressure for a multilateral approach to macroeconomic policy. The relative decline of the American economic role in the world has been leading to a diffusion of power and responsibilities; no new economic superpower is in sight, nor is genuinely supranational economic management, through, say, the International Monetary Fund, a practical alternative. For the 1980s, therefore, the United States, Japan, and, probably, a loose combination of European Community nations will have to try in some systematic way to accommodate to one another's policy choices or risk a damaging economic and monetary conflict.

Japan in some respects is less well-adapted to a multilateral and basically uncertain situation than the other big market economies. The view of Japan as a small, vulnerable country has had a powerful hold on the minds of Japanese officials. Postwar economic management relied heavily on controls to minimize outside impact on macro-economic decisions; the elaborate foreign exchange controls installed during the occupation are only now being dismantled. An essentially parochial point of view continued to govern economic policymaking long after Japan's actions had come to have an evident and important influence on world economic developments.

This can be seen in the persistent tendency since the mid-1960s to generate a large surplus in current transactions with the rest of the world. A country where savings have forged ahead of the investment demand of the private sector, Japan has a natural disposition to an external surplus—which is to say that Japan normally will be a net supplier of real goods and services to the world. In the textbook model, this should give rise to outflows of long-term capital and make the balance-of-payments problem associated with the surplus more manageable. But the Tokyo capital market has been inhibited, in important part by public policies, from developing a capacity to provide long-term investment funds to capital-short regions overseas; and official development-aid policy has been chronically parsimonious. The Japanese business and banking communities often have been venturesome and innovative in their decisionmaking. It is the official policymakers who have been most resistant to change.

Much of the recent acrimony in American-Japanese relations is traceable to the belief in Washington that Japan's surplus was making it more difficult to cope with OPEC's large—and inescapable—surplus. In 1976–78 this belief had substantial foundation. But a current account surplus is clearly not per se abnormal or undesirable for a high-savings, highly productive economy. To the contrary, Japan should properly be seen as potentially a major and efficient contributor to the capital requirements of the world at large. For Japan to play that role, the nation's economic managers need to develop a less insular view of their responsibilities to the world system. From the American side, there is a parallel need to focus on the right problem, which is how the Japanese surplus is used, not whether it should exist.

There are important tests ahead for American and Japanese capacities for achieving fruitful economic relations. One is the probable role of the yen as a reserve currency. The tide is running in that direction; to a limited extent the yen is already held as a reserve by central banks, and as holdings of dollars are diversified, some of the movement will be into yen. The likelihood that Japan will have a current account surplus for some years to come adds to the attractiveness of the yen in this role. And as long-term funds flow out of Japan, it will be natural for Japan's trading partners to hold counterpart deposits in Tokyo. A reluctant Ministry of Finance will have difficulty in successfully opposing these trends.

The implications of a move to multiple reserve currencies—the deutsche mark and eventually the European currency unit are the other obvious candidates—are not small. Unless reserve centers coordinate their economic, especially their monetary, policies, the monetary system could be chronically in danger of large destabilizing swings into and out of the different currencies. To cope with such a circumstance, the United States, Japan, and Europe will need to give up much of the claim to independence in macroeconomic policy. How these differing democratic governments will respond to the challenge will go a long way toward determining the direction of the world economy during the decade.

Concluding Comments

This chapter begins with a bipartisan political metaphor from the presidential campaign of 1976: a close relationship with Japan should be the cornerstone of U.S. policy in Asia.

Nothing happened between 1976 and 1980 to alter the truth of that metaphor. This is so even though public attention inevitably has been directed to the new relationship with another Asian power, China. The China connection, with its large potential risks and benefits, unquestionably has modified the strategic scene in Asia. But Japan remains the assured and stable partner in a region marked otherwise by uncertainty.

In an important sense, rapprochement with China has given new weight to the alliance with Japan. Japan is a more significant force in the delicate balancing act among the United States, China, and the Soviet Union than it was in the earlier era of Sino-American confrontation. China looks to Japan as a principal market and as a major supplier of capital; in their preoccupation with the Soviet threat, the Chinese leaders have readily set aside old animosities and have accepted Japan as a helpful neighbor. To the extent that outside influences bear on events and policies in China, Japan and the United

States will have a shared role. They share as well an interest in a Sino-Soviet relationship that is neither verging on war nor edging back toward collaboration. The pursuit of that interest will be the easier as Washington and Tokyo concert their policies toward China and toward Sino-Soviet relations. Any genuine divergence would be imprudent in the extreme.

In an earlier section it is observed that defense relations with Japan have passed from arm's-length dealings to relative intimacy. Apart from the eventual significance of this development for military efficiency, the political connotations are far-reaching. Joint military planning with the United States means that the two countries must agree on the character of the threat or threats against which forces are to be maintained and perhaps deployed. More than ever, Japan will be overtly committed to a strategy for Asia coincident with that of the United States.

This is not to suggest, however, that the limits on Japan as a military power are now going to greatly widen. In most foreseeable circumstances the political, legal, and budgetary constraints on the size and use of the self-defense forces will be strong and effective. The continuing gap between American and Japanese defense spending—and defense obligations—is bound to be a source of periodic congressional pressure for a change.

Nonetheless, if the past is any guide, the Japanese political system will not be moved quickly or decisively by any persuasive powers realistically available to the next American administration. (Soviet expansionism may do what the United States cannot, of course.) The wise course, then, is to work with, but not to hope to accelerate, indigenous trends; the military alliance promises to grow stronger and more durable because Japan has come to see it more clearly as in its interest; but potential constituencies for it can only be nourished by politicians attuned to Japanese sentiments; that is, Japanese politicians. The United States can make political life difficult for Japanese leaders but can rarely impel them to go beyond what they consider to be practical domestic maneuver.

Relations in the economic sphere promise to be more complicated than in defense because the issues are more diverse, because the state of knowledge is, if anything, less advanced, and because competitive elements cannot be eliminated. It is beyond argument that each country has a material stake in cooperation with the other: in energy, in

food, in responses to structural change, in relations with the developing world, in macroeconomic policies. But it is also the case that the
sometimes-bruising competition between private sectors will spill
over into intergovernmental relations and that conceptions of broad
national interests may differ.

The reconciliation of disparate economic interests, real or perceived, is an endless task for private markets and for public policies.
There is no general formula or any single conclusion. It is worth considering, however, that the path of American-Japanese economic
relations might be smoothed in the 1980s if American policy could
be disencumbered of views about Japan that are overdrawn or simply
wrong.

Having given up the notion of a weak, vulnerable Japanese economy, many Americans have come to the opposite perception of a
nation with extraordinary capacities for achieving its planned goals.
Japanese government and Japanese business supposedly work
in total harmony; weak industries are ruthlessly discarded and resources promptly transferred to carefully chosen growth sectors, all
according to plan; and the state of the country's external accounts is
within the determining power of the central bureaucracy. It is a
thoroughly managed system that somehow has escaped the inefficiencies and crudeness of the overtly planned economies.

This picture is hardly more accurate than the one painted by most
Japanese of an economy "defenseless on all sides," to use Saburo
Okita's phrase. The strengths of Japan's social and political structure
are real enough, but they are not overwhelming. Japanese bureau-
crats make mistakes, politicians insist on wasteful programs, declining industries are propped up with subsidies as in other democracies.
Most important, political leaders in Tokyo cannot deliver major economic changes more easily than their counterparts elsewhere.

If America continues to operate on the supposition that Japan is an
economic monolith with unlimited capacities, then the danger is that
fear rather than sober assessment will govern our policy choices. A
rational position is to put policy toward Japan on the same base as
policy toward the European Community: we need sensibly cooperative relations with both; it is foolish to expect that we will not have
serious differences with both on particular issues; and the only sound
position is not to accord either one differential treatment, favorable
or unfavorable.

This argues for diminished bilateralism. Not all problems in Japanese-American economic relations can be remanded to the multilateral bodies. But many can, and it will be a healthier relationship if we make clear that the rules are not somehow less applicable when Japan is involved. Now that the domain of a central multilateral institution, the General Agreement on Tariffs and Trade, has been widened, the two principal market economies ought to be in the lead in making the rules for international trade more effective. The principle extends beyond trade into economic relations generally. In the difficult decade that is now beginning, both countries should have a compelling interest in strengthening the international economic institutions. The alternative is a balkanization of the world economy and losses to all concerned.

CHAPTER FOURTEEN

The Atlantic Alliance

CHRISTOPHER J. MAKINS

THE RELATIONSHIP between the United States and Western Europe, like a close relationship between two persons, constantly demands the attention of the two partners, yet always eludes succinct definition. There are several reasons why the transatlantic relationship is particularly hard to define. Most important, perhaps, is the fact that it is a function of the policies and attitudes of the Atlantic countries toward a broad range of international and domestic problems, many of which reach well beyond the Atlantic area. The transatlantic relationship is therefore the intangible product of a calculation that consists of many concrete and heterogeneous terms.

Perhaps because of this complexity some commentators have had difficulty in handling the subject. In the early and mid-1970s it was fashionable for Americans to believe that Western Europe was steadily becoming less important to the United States. "North Atlantic relationships," wrote one observer, "are losing their pivotal role in United States foreign policy." "The appearance of new and urgent global issues and the seeming decline . . . of American-Soviet rivalry," wrote another, "have devalued in the United States the centrality of the American-European relationship."[1] On the threshold of the

I thank Charlotte Kaiser and Margo S. Cibener for typing successive versions of this chapter so quickly and efficiently.

1. The first quotation is from Seyom Brown, "A World of Multiple Relationships," in James Chace and Earl C. Ravenal, eds., *Atlantis Lost: U.S.-European Relations after the Cold War* (New York University Press, 1976), p. 103; the second quotation is from Zbigniew Brzezinski, "The European Crossroads," in ibid., p. 93.

459

1980s, and despite the undoubted rise of "global" issues and the increasing importance to the United States of Asian affairs, such statements seem at best oversimplified and at worst misleading. And indeed in the fall of 1979 a senior U.S. official stated that the "central policy issue" for the 1980s is to strengthen international cooperation and that the key to the matter lies in the U.S.-European relationship.[2]

A second reason for the difficulty of defining the transatlantic relationship is that the many levels on which the relationship exists— security, economic, political, psychological—are often incommensurate. The fact that there is some linkage between them, so that disagreements on one level can undermine solidarity on another, is obvious, even though many Western Europeans have at times denied this. But the connections are less mechanical, and more psychological, than the term *linkage* implies.

The third difficulty in analyzing the relationship lies in the need to discriminate between the surface waves of international politics and the underlying tides of interests, between shadow and substance. Excessive attention to the waves can give a false impression of the ebb and flow of the tides. Shadows can obscure as well as highlight. But much journalistic, political, and even academic comment on Atlantic affairs blurs rather than clarifies the distinction.

The Political Psychology of Atlantic Relations

One can discern two broad schools of thought about the transatlantic relationship. The ideas of the first are summarized by the title of a recent book by A. W. DePorte: *Europe Between the Superpowers: The Enduring Balance*.[3] In essence, this view holds that Western Europe's security interests constitute an unchanging force for the preservation of a relationship that suits all the major countries, East and West, better than any alternative. The United States' interest in providing protection to Western Europe, not least because of its superpower rivalry with the Soviet Union, will remain constant for the foreseeable future; so probably will the Soviet Union's European policy—especially with regard to its Eastern European satellites—

2. Statement by Anthony Solomon, under secretary of the treasury, to a seminar on U.S.-European perspectives for the 1980s sponsored by the Friedrich Ebert Foundation of Bonn at Port Chester, New York, reported in the *Washington Post,* October 28, 1979.
3. Yale University Press, 1979.

and its ability to carry that policy out. Lastly, the interest and ability of the United States and the major countries of Western Europe to defend the essence of the postwar international economic arrangements are likely to persist, despite recent U.S. economic problems and the relative decline in the importance of the U.S. economy. In short, believers in an "enduring balance" would argue that, although there will always be transatlantic friction and time lags in perceptions on the two sides of the Atlantic, the underlying community of interest will remain strong enough in the 1980s to create a self-correcting and adaptable alliance. In this view, neither the United States nor the Western European countries will allow a serious threat to the postwar transatlantic system to develop.

By contrast, the second school of thought sees critical tensions within the transatlantic system that, even if they do not lead to a breakdown, will ensure an unstable relationship. No matter what the common security interests of the United States and Western Europe are in the 1980s, according to this view, the changed U.S.-Soviet strategic balance and domestic social and political fragmentation in the United States will prevent the United States from providing Europe with a credible security guarantee. Moreover, the chronic weakness of the dollar and persistent domestic economic problems will make it impossible for the United States to give the sort of economic leadership that it gave in the 1940s and 1950s. Meanwhile the countries of Western Europe, since their postwar recovery, are neither willing to follow the U.S. lead on many issues uncritically nor yet prepared to assume a larger share of the responsibility and cost of maintaining the international economic system and providing for the common defense. Both the United States and Western Europe are thus seen as beset with dangerous inward-looking domestic trends. Finally, a more assertive Soviet policy in Europe and elsewhere and an increasingly combustible situation in Eastern Europe could, in this view, lead to serious differences of policy across the Atlantic, with Western Europe showing a propensity to accommodate Soviet military strength and the United States determined to confront and deter it. For all these reasons, it would be argued, the Atlantic Alliance is unlikely to prove strong and adaptable enough in the 1980s to withstand the growing divergence of attitudes and policies toward defense, East-West negotiation, economic problems, the Middle East, Asia, and so on.

These two opposing views reflect, among other things, different judgments about how Americans and Europeans will strike the balance between the conflicting interests that create on both sides of the Atlantic a rather schizophrenic mentality about the U.S.–West European relationship. On the U.S. side, bureaucratic simplicity, psychological satisfaction, the force of habit, international prestige, and, some would say, the economic advantage of being the dominant state in the Alliance all dispose the United States to seek to prolong that dominance and to look to Western Europe for willing support of U.S. policy rather than for independent initiative. But at the same time there has been a persistent urge in the United States to establish a more equal transatlantic partnership by encouraging Western European integration and to bring about a fairer sharing of the burdens of maintaining the international systems, particularly in the defense sector. One may question both how realistic the idea of creating a European Community in the U.S. image ever was or how great a price, economic or political, the United States would have been prepared to pay for it. But the effort to promote fairer burden-sharing has continued. It has taken many forms, from President Kennedy's "two pillars" and the tangible threat of Senator Mike Mansfield's resolutions of the late 1960s and early 1970s to the more recent U.S. insistence on sharing with Western Europe the onus of nuclear decisionmaking (for example, on the enhanced radiation weapon and the modernization of the Alliance's longer-range theater nuclear forces), as well as to the arguments about the responsibility of the West Germans, in particular, for sustaining growth and exchange rate stability within the Western economic system.[4] The tension between these two aspects of U.S. policy has been obvious: successive U.S. administrations have urged Europe to adopt a more coherent and united role, while tending to disparage its doing so in any way that diverged from U.S. interests.

European attitudes are also somewhat schizophrenic. Western Europe has had a growing desire for a more independent, or at least distinctive, role, even on some security issues. But Europeans have remained constantly aware of the advantages of the United States'

4. For a recent example, see the statement by Anthony Solomon reported in the *Washington Post,* October 28, 1979: "What is not constructive—and can even be poisonous to the relationship [with the United States] and exacerbate specific problems—is for Europe to cloak its substantive disagreements and avoid accepting its own responsibilities by resting on accusations of failure of U.S. will and leadership."

taking responsibility for the maintenance of the system, of the unattractiveness of any alternative security arrangements, and of the consequent need to avoid provoking a change in U.S. willingness to prolong its security guarantee. Although the European urge for greater independence stems partly from a perception of U.S. weakness during the late 1970s, it began to develop earlier, as a direct and natural consequence of Europe's postwar recovery. Most recently, this sense of diminished dependence and continuing economic success, notably in West Germany, has created a habit that would be hard to break. But it is still not accompanied by a willingness to see a major redistribution of political and economic responsibility within the Alliance.

These conflicting attitudes among Europeans and Americans are familiar enough. And they underlie much of the turbulence within the transatlantic system. Like the equally familiar tensions between parents who want to assert their control beyond their children's need for protection and children who seek to shake free of parental influence before they are ready for independence, the tensions within the Alliance cannot be resolved but can only be controlled and survived. In the 1970s even such emotional episodes as the strident European distinctiveness of Georges Pompidou and Edward Heath, the subsequent Atlantic revivalism of the United States in the "Year of Europe," the bitter U.S. response to European unwillingness to support U.S. policy during the 1973 Arab-Israeli War, or the peak of U.S. anxiety about the growth of Eurocommunism were endured with minimal lasting effects. So it may also be with the recent preoccupation in the United States with the alleged decline of U.S. strength of will and international influence. Although on the surface this "decline" seems to have affected Western European attitudes profoundly, it may have surprisingly little permanent effect. The same would probably be true of any transatlantic tension created by the nonratification of the second U.S.-Soviet agreement on strategic arms limitation (SALT II).

Clouds in a Crystal Ball

The key to the difference between the optimistic and the pessimistic schools of thought about the transatlantic relationship lies in the range of possible assumptions about future changes both in the domestic politics of the United States and Western Europe and in the wider international environment. Some discussion of these various assumptions and their likely implications is therefore essential.

With important elections due in the three major countries of the Atlantic world in 1980–81 (West Germany and the United States in late 1980, France in mid-1981), there is a real prospect not only that the sound and fury of the campaigns will create transatlantic problems but that a new transatlantic balance of political forces will emerge that will differ significantly from the present one. Arguably the most crucial variables relate to the United States. Two rather contradictory anxieties bother informed Western Europeans. First, they fear that the decolonization of the "imperial" presidency by an assertive and unmanageable Congress and a prolongation of the recent polarized debate about the U.S. role in the world brought to a head by SALT II and the Iranian and Afghan crises herald a long period of indecisive U.S. political leadership and poor economic performance. These phenomena have already affected Alliance confidence, notably during the Carter administration, and a failure to ratify SALT II would prolong their effects. But being largely systemic problems, they will not be precisely coterminous with the Carter presidency. Whether their persistence would be the catalyst needed for the West Europeans to make up for some of the lack of U.S. leadership or would merely provoke discouragement and disarray in Western Europe is a more open question than many in the United States would allow. Second, Western Europeans fear an excessively strong U.S. reaction against the perception of American "weakness" in the form of more assertive U.S. policies adopted primarily for domestic reasons—whether vis-à-vis the Soviet Union (in SALT or in third world situations) or on other political and economic issues. Such a reaction could lead to a phase of more exaggerated European self-assertiveness and independence in relations with the United States. On the threshold of a U.S. presidential election in which both major parties are riven by internal tensions and the dictates of political maneuver prevail over substantive questions, prediction is more than usually difficult. But the likelihood that U.S. policy in the next two or three years will strike a balance between weakness and strength that will quickly allay both European anxieties cannot be rated high. At best, therefore, a further period of adjustment to a changing American role seems indicated on both sides of the Atlantic.

In Western Europe the problem is rather different. The central question is whether the close relationship between France and the Federal Republic of Germany, which has underpinned the relative stability of Western European politics in recent years, will continue to flourish. The political incentives for both countries to strengthen their relationship are clear. In the Federal Republic, which, although not wholly immune to the social and economic problems of its neighbors, seems likely to remain quite resistant to them for some years, the French connection will probably not be under pressure. A victory by the Christian Democratic Union–Christian Social Union coalition under Franz Josef Strauss in the elections in late 1980 would probably increase on the surface both domestic tension and intra-European friction, because of the more self-confident attitudes of the coalition and its leaders. But it would probably not lead to basic changes in West Germany's domestic or international policies.

In France, too, the most reasonable assumption would be one of continuing political moderation (including the reelection of President Giscard d'Estaing) and economic advance. But Giscard could stumble. And the latent tensions within French society and the temptations of French economic nationalism remain strong. Both could be aggravated by adverse international economic conditions. France's ability to uphold its end of the Franco-German axis cannot therefore be taken for granted. Should it wane, the effect could be quite serious —on France because it would intensify French insecurity vis-à-vis a dominant West Germany, on Germany because it would revive the unwanted specter of the Federal Republic as an island of economic strength in a sea of weak neighbors. Such a development would intensify German dependence on the transatlantic relationship, aggravate the familiar French search for distinctiveness, and thus complicate U.S. relations with both countries.

The fate of Britain and Italy and the future of the European Community as a whole are also important factors. The persistent arguments that will inevitably surround the domestic policies of Britain's Conservative government, the strong possibility that these policies will fail to revive Britain's economic performance significantly, and the likelihood that Britain will not be satisfied by the European Community's response to its demand for more equitable financial and agricultural arrangements within the Community all suggest that Britain is unlikely to play a much more constructive role in European affairs than it has played in the past few years. Indeed, if things go badly, by the mid-1980s Britain could be pursuing a separate, protectionist course under a new anti-European Labour government. But neither outcome need have a fatal effect on the European Community or on the transatlantic relationship. Both France and West Germany have largely accepted the fact that Britain will not play the balancing role in Europe that they had hoped for but no longer need (though the Germans may still welcome a strong British partner in dealings with the United States). In Italy, no great change in the recent pattern of paralytic political weakness and relative economic success seems likely.

Even if one takes an optimistic view, however, one can foresee for the 1980s strenuous domestic conflicts in most European countries over economic policy and distributional questions and anxiety over the impact of growing international competition in industry, a tight oil market, and a difficult demographic outlook (with rapidly growing labor forces until the mid-1980s, in a period of relatively slow economic growth). All these factors are likely to strengthen inward-looking tendencies, though less so in the economically more prosperous countries linked to West Germany than in the less successful European countries.

This temptation to look inward in Europe will be increased by the problems arising from the accession of Greece, Spain, Portugal, and perhaps even Turkey to the European Community, and by the growing internal financial and, with its newly elected parliament, constitutional problems of the Community even at its present size. These problems will almost certainly compel important changes in the Community and in the goals its members hope to achieve through it. The Community will remain indispensable as a means of organizing the common internal European market (a necessity for even limited political cooperation) and of strengthening its members' hands in international negotiation. And for the larger countries the Community will continue to play the invaluable role of enhancing political solidarity with the smaller members and legitimizing effective Franco-German political leadership. But the recent shift in the major European countries toward dealing with problems by intergovernmental cooperation of the classic kind, rather than by strengthening the Community's institutions and powers, is likely to be intensified by the Community's enlargement, possibly to the point of creating, de facto, the two-tier Community or the inner directorate so often proposed.

Therefore, although the Community and the Commission of the European Communities may increasingly be the single European negotiating partner for the United States and others, they will probably become a still less creative force in international policy in their own right.

Some would argue that such an outlook condemns the transatlantic relationship to frustration because the Western Europeans in general and the West Germans in particular will never achieve political or economic satisfaction without the weight that they would wield—and the self-confidence they would gain—through a more integrated Community. In certain circumstances this view might prove to be correct. But it is not necessarily so. The level of intergovernmental cooperation that is developing, especially between France and West Germany, could adequately substitute for true integration. The real question is whether the drag imposed on Western European countries by their internal problems will frustrate even this more limited form of cooperation between them and so disappoint a United States seeking—and increasingly needing—a more active partner in Europe.

Finally, the transatlantic relationship is obviously vitally affected by international developments that are beyond the sole control of the Atlantic countries. Certain economic developments and events in the Soviet Union and Eastern Europe, in the Middle East and Asia, and in the increasingly heterogeneous group of developing countries all fall into this category. All put pressure on the transatlantic relationship, which it may or may not prove strong enough to bear. Many of these broader problems are discussed below in general terms. But their importance as variables that affect the transatlantic relationship needs emphasis at the outset. So does the possibility that unpredictable or unexpected events will transcend the assumptions underlying an analysis of this kind. Like developments within the United States and Western Europe, these broader influences will be crucial in determining whether the transatlantic balance endures in the 1980s or is destroyed.

Whither European Security?

A primary goal of the North Atlantic allies has been to transform the East-West confrontation. But they have never had a clear and agreed conception of how the two elements of their recent policy, defense and negotiation, would combine to achieve this. Periodic attempts to provide such a conception, of which Henry Kissinger's ideas about the entangling web of East-West relations and the creation of vested interests in the Soviet Union in favor of "good" Soviet behavior were perhaps the most striking example, have rarely commanded a broad consensus. Indeed, the Alliance has only occasionally discussed the broad strategy for achieving détente, at least at high levels, and then usually quite unproductively.

Imprecision was probably inevitable on such an important, and uncertain, matter. But its inescapable consequence was that once the initial steps to promote détente had either been taken (the first phases of strategic arms limitation, the Conference on Security and Cooperation in Europe, increased cooperation in trade and other areas) or attempted unsuccessfully (mutual and balanced force reductions in Central Europe, general cooperation in third areas like the Middle East, and so forth), it became apparent how little they had done to moderate the East-West competition and how hard it was to devise further realistic steps that might be more effective. The nonratification of SALT II would only increase the difficulty.

Yet even these initial steps predictably had some effect on the East-West relationship. Had more steps followed, this effect would presumably have been regarded as intended and desirable. But against the background of a persistent East-West stalemate, the increased levels of (and vested interests in) economic and human contacts in Europe can readily be seen as a source of weakness by those, particularly Americans, who anticipate a prolonged revival of the cold war and foresee a need for a high level of Western psychological mobilization during the early 1980s, when Soviet military power relative to that of the United States will be at its height. Whence the concern in the United States about the "finlandization" of Western Europe, the anxiety about the taste that many Western Europeans have acquired for exploring strategies of negotiation to deal with security problems in Europe.

The halting progress toward détente has had its most direct effect on the transatlantic security relationship by consecrating, through SALT, the principle of U.S.-Soviet strategic "parity." The onset of parity has been incessantly discussed since the mid-1950s. But overt acceptance of it as a goal of East-West negotiation meant that the allies could hardly continue to ignore its implications for Alliance strategy and doctrine as they had often done until the mid-1970s, while trusting in U.S. technological advance to blunt somehow the consequences of parity. Once SALT became a fact, Western Europeans could not easily suppress some unpalatable questions. Now that the Soviet Union had a secure strategic second-strike capability against U.S. territory, how could the invocation of the threat and the eventual use of U.S. strategic forces in the defense of Western Europe be assured? And would the Alliance's flexible response strategy remain acceptable in theory and, more important, workable in practice, given allied conventional and theater nuclear defense programs and political realities?

Adjusting to encroaching parity and receding détente has proved controversial on both sides of the Atlantic. Many conservatives in Western Europe share the apprehensions of Americans who are concerned about the growth of Soviet military strength and activism and the lack of public support for stronger defense policies and higher defense spending and who see in East-West negotiations at best a tranquilizing force and at worst an incentive to appeasement. Likewise many American liberals share the view of Europeans, notably social democrats, who are unimpressed by the claim that Soviet military programs and deployments have created an East-West military balance much more threatening to the West than in the past or that Western security (as distinct from Western influence in the world or Western self-esteem) has been harmed by recent events. In this view, the Soviet Union is seen as an essentially defensive power that is beset by many internal weaknesses and that is likely to find equitable negotiated agreements increasingly attractive.

But though these shades of opinion are mirrored on the two sides of the ocean, different psychological influences and political trends often create different balances between the various schools of thought in different countries at any given time. The scope for misunderstanding or disagreement between governments arising from these differences and time lags is considerable. So is the scope for the manipulation of attitudes in one country for political purposes in another. This point is one to which German Chancellor Helmut Schmidt has often alluded—for example in an interview published in *Time* on June 11, 1979. Asked to respond to reports that West Germany was drifting away from the Atlantic Alliance, Schmidt replied: "That notion is being nurtured by people who for domestic reasons either fight my

government in Bonn or fight the Carter Administration in Washington. . . . The malevolent intention of such rumors is obvious."

This perspective is crucial to interpreting the alleged finlandization
of Western Europe. For differences of opinion, which some people
have an interest in regarding as a consequence of declining political
will and psychological mobilization, are in fact often the result of a
legitimate divergence of political assessments between governments,
all of which understand the dangers of naively seeking a broad accommodation with the East. Some of these differences can reasonably
be expected to diminish over time. Parity was unavoidable and has
become irreversible; negotiations should never have been expected to
lead rapidly to détente, let alone entente. Seeking to restore meaningful U.S. strategic superiority or accelerate progress toward détente
may be seductive psychologically or politically, but it is illusory.
The illusion was becoming harder to sustain, either in the United
States or Europe, even before the Iran crisis and the Soviet invasion
of Afghanistan.

The question remains what adaptations to the Alliance's nuclear
and conventional force programs, negotiating policies, and institutional arrangements have been made necessary by recent events.
These three areas must be examined in turn.

Alliance Nuclear Forces

Anxiety about the inherent difficulty of providing "extended" nuclear deterrence from the United States to Western Europe in the era
of strategic parity will no doubt continue to prompt some Europeans
to look for an alternative to the U.S. nuclear guarantee. In the past
such ideas have often been resisted because of a fear, if not a real
risk, of provoking the withdrawal of U.S. nuclear protection. For
the United States, however, some further diminution of its historic
domination of Alliance nuclear policy might be a small price to pay
for an eventual attenuation of European anxieties about security. But
for the West Germans and other nonnuclear European countries, no
small national nuclear force would appear to be a reliable substitute
for U.S. nuclear protection, even though it might provide some longer-
term reassurance. In any case, the French have ruled out for the time
being any contribution from their nuclear forces to deterrence beyond
France's borders. And for the United Kingdom to perform such a
role, a considerable effort of will and resources would be needed.

Despite its veneer of commitment to the Alliance, British nuclear policy has always been rather gaullist in substance, especially under Conservative governments. And with the likely acquisition of five new Trident I–equipped submarines in the 1980s and early 1990s, British nuclear force budgets will be hard put to accommodate cruise missiles or other elements that would probably be necessary to provide credible extended deterrence to other European countries.

The possibility of a greater role for British and French nuclear forces in overall Alliance deterrence in the future should not be discarded. Indeed, the order of magnitude increase in independently targetable reentry vehicles in a British Trident I force as compared with the old Polaris force would compel attention to the British nuclear capability by the 1990s. But the essential requirement for the 1980s will undoubtedly be to retain as credible as possible a U.S. nuclear guarantee of Western Europe. A—perhaps *the*—crucial precondition for this is the restoration of a degree of domestic U.S. consensus on and confidence in American strategic force programs, with or without SALT II and future agreements. Beyond that, however, comes the question of the role of theater nuclear forces.

Theater nuclear forces are the hinges of Alliance strategy. That is, their importance does not (and, for many Europeans fearful about nuclear devastation, must not) lie mainly in the protection they provide in themselves, but rather in the fact that they strengthen the combination of allied conventional forces and U.S. strategic forces on which Western Europe's security rests. Maintaining European confidence in the credibility of Alliance nuclear deterrence will require not only a much clearer conception than now exists in the Alliance of how theater nuclear forces could actually be used to establish a credible linkage to the threat and eventual execution of strategic strikes but also a corresponding force posture. This would entail both working out options for retaliatory use of theater nuclear forces, which would be comparatively easy politically, and more difficult, planning for allied first use of nuclear forces to reestablish deterrence and to try to terminate a conventional conflict. The latter purposes, in particular, would involve redoubled efforts to reach agreement among allied governments (and not just their military experts) on options for the selective use of theater (and possibly also central strategic) nuclear systems, notably against high-value military targets in the Soviet Union, and on associated concepts of political signaling that could both precede and accompany the execution of those options. The main weakness of the Alliance decision in December 1979 to deploy the longer-range Pershing II ballistic missile and the ground-launched cruise missile in Europe was precisely that the decision was not related to any clear and agreed employment concept. Instead, it was heavily influenced by political considerations, notably in the rejection of the greater survivability of sea- or air-based systems in the face of probable Soviet preemptive strikes. Prominent among these considerations were the U.S. desire to provide visible reassurance, in particular to the Germans, and the Western European desire to receive such reassurance, even at the risk of domestic political opposition to ground-based systems. These political gains could easily prove ephemeral given continuing Soviet defense modernization, particularly of shorter-range theater nuclear forces, and political activism. To maintain confidence in Alliance deterrence in the early 1980s, the allies will have little choice but to confront the unresolved doctrinal and operational issues concerning theater nuclear forces of all ranges.

Conventional Forces

In the age of strategic nuclear parity, the role of conventional forces as a source of deterrence and as a means of increasing the commitment needed by the Soviet Union to achieve a given political or military goal in Europe becomes ever more important. No other policy would be as likely to offer durable relief from European anxieties as improving conventional deterrence. Since 1945 Western European countries have, however, been reluctant to show any willingness to fight a prolonged conventional war in Europe, not least because of the cost of providing adequate forces for that purpose and because of the fear that by doing so they would justify a decoupling of U.S. strategic nuclear forces from European defense. But attitudes have changed. During the 1970s many Western Europeans progressively assimilated the idea that a stalwart conventional defense is an essential foundation of deterrence. They accepted the long-term defense program in 1978, the latest and most ambitious of a series of U.S.-inspired conventional force improvement programs, and the associated commitment to increase defense expenditure by 3 percent a year in real terms for five years.

Further conventional force improvements will remain an important focus for allied efforts. Even if the long-term defense program were fully implemented, it would not yield sufficient improvements to alleviate growing European anxieties about being vulnerable to Soviet pressure because of enhanced Soviet nuclear and conventional forces in Eastern Europe. But it would help. Promising new technologies, for example in electronic warfare and target acquisition and development capabilities, will have to be exploited to the full, especially where they might reduce allied reliance on theater nuclear forces, particularly shorter-range systems, for certain operational requirements. Several old obstacles will doubtless reappear: the need for a two-way transatlantic flow of procurement, the inadequacy (and cost) of war reserve stocks, the lack of standardization and, even more important, interoperability of equipment, the inflexibility (and in some cases incompatibility) of allied tactics and force structures, and the allies' consequent failure to use manpower, equipment, and terrain to the best defensive advantage. Progress will doubtless be slow. But efforts to improve conventional forces will be essential and, if successful, probably more valuable in creating confidence within the Alliance than parallel efforts in the nuclear field.

The Role of Negotiation

Some people would question whether any policy of East-West negotiation to complement allied defense policy is desirable, on the grounds that it is unpromising and likely to tranquilize domestic opinion in the West. Certainly the relationship between the two policies, and especially the role of a strong defense posture as an indispensable basis for progress in negotiation, has at times been poorly conceived. But in noncrisis periods the development and pursuit of some negotiating options are preconditions for any broad consensus on security issues not only in Western Europe but also—to a larger extent than many care to recognize—in the United States.[5] Such a policy should be based on the assumptions that progress toward meaningful détente

5. Henry Kissinger provides an interesting and important illustration of this statement. His Brussels speech in September 1979 contained a characteristically forceful formulation that went largely unnoticed because of his remarks on the credibility of the U.S. nuclear guarantee to Europe. Kissinger listed four reasons why the effort to promote détente was important: (1) to convince the U.S. public that the United States was committed to peace so as to sustain the risk of war; (2) to help hold the Alliance together by persuading the allies that the United States was not seeking confrontation for its own sake; (3) to prevent the Western democracies from having to concede the "peace issue" to their opponents; and (4) to enable a confrontation to be sustained if it occurred by demonstrating that it was unavoidable.

will at best be slow but that even modest steps can be beneficial and can create exploitable vested interests in Eastern as well as Western Europe. The aims should be to build a political framework for longer-term security in Europe, something that defense programs alone cannot do (as many Europeans have with some reason felt about the theater nuclear force modernization question), and to give Western European governments a stronger platform from which to defend the high level of defense commitment that is likely to remain essential in the 1980s.

Formulating a set of negotiating policies in the Alliance will be complicated by a basic difference of outlook between Western Europeans and Americans. In Western Europe, and especially in West Germany, the good-neighbor aspects of East-West relations, such as human and cultural contacts, seem more important than they do in the United States, where East-West agreements have usually been judged in concrete security terms and against the background of the global U.S.-Soviet balance of power. This difference has appeared particularly in regard to economic issues, with the United States inclined to take a harder line toward the Soviets in such areas as high technology exports and export credits. Immediate reactions in Western Europe to the Soviet intervention in Afghanistan again pointed up this difference, with many European countries reluctant to allow disapproval to spill over into economic, commercial, and human exchanges. Such reactions only reinforce (not necessarily rightly) suspicions that Europeans are becoming finlandized by Soviet power. Yet there is a quite cogent case for pursuing, without illusion, some good-neighbor measures, such as those at the heart of the Conference on Security and Cooperation in Europe, to preserve a minimum of East-West confidence and communication at a time when concrete steps like force reductions and constraints on defense programs or deployments are unpromising.

It is beyond the scope of this chapter to define the best allied negotiating approaches or to speculate on how long the climate for negotiations will be as bad as it became after the Soviet intervention in Afghanistan. What is important for transatlantic relations is that whatever approaches are adopted should help to strengthen political support for Alliance policies. Some elements of the present allied approach meet this test. The Conference on Security and Cooperation in Europe has been a good example, and it is important that the review conference due in Madrid in late 1980 should further contribute to this purpose. But other aspects of allied negotiating policies are less satisfactory. The negotiations on longer-range theater nuclear forces proposed by the allies in December 1979 are one example. The Alliance proposal is so narrow in scope (focusing on long-range ground-based missiles) that it is largely irrelevant to the overall theater nuclear force threat to Western Europe (of which short-range forces and aircraft are a major part). Such negotiations would run the risk of appearing to be little more than a fig leaf to overcome political opposition to force modernization. Likewise the negotiations on mutual and balanced force reductions, which at the outset were a good example of how negotiations can strengthen allied cohesion, have reached a point at which they could have the opposite effect. The Alliance decision in December 1979 to modify (by scaling down) its negotiating position will help to avert this danger. For the future, an even broader approach that would avoid some of the limitations of the mutual and balanced force reduction negotiations (such as their narrow geographical focus) might be more valuable as an adjunct to allied defense policies.[6]

Institutional Questions and Alliance Cohesion

The health of the Alliance in the 1980s—and the strength of its deterrence of the Soviet Union—will be as dependent as ever on the smooth functioning of its institutions in reconciling divergent perspectives. This was also the lesson of the last long cycle of internal problems in the Alliance, which culminated in the collapse of the multilateral force proposal, the subsequent creation of the Nuclear Defense Affairs Committee and the Nuclear Planning Group in 1967, and the debate over the flexible response strategy. This experience of the 1960s and that of mutual and balanced force reductions and other issues in the 1970s show how an open, multilateral process of discussion within the Alliance can in itself be a source of confidence and cohesion and can also reduce the time lags in perceptions that have so often been a source of friction between the United States and Europe. By contrast, unilateral dealings on issues that affect Alliance interests generally, as repeated experience during the strategic arms limitation

6. For a more extensive discussion of this issue, see Christopher J. Makins, "Negotiating European Security: The Next Steps," *Survival*, vol. 21 (November–December 1979), pp. 256–63.

talks has shown, can easily increase suspicion, weaken Alliance cohesion, and intensify the problem of time lags.

Following the misunderstandings about cruise missile limitations in SALT II, the allies have improved their multilateral consultative procedures in preparation for a possible East-West negotiation that would cover long-range nuclear forces based in Europe. But short-term considerations of political convenience led the Alliance to an initial conclusion in December 1979 that negotiations on theater nuclear forces should take place in SALT III. This presents the real risk of creating frictions in the medium term similar to those that occurred during earlier rounds of SALT.[7] Although a multilateral negotiation would not of course be problem-free, it should at least reduce these intra-Alliance frictions. If long-range theater nuclear forces are to be covered in a SALT III, great effort will be needed to ensure that allied decisionmaking processes minimize the Atlantic problems inherent in a bilateral negotiation on a subject that affects countries not participating in it even more directly than it affects the two participants. This would doubtless require formal procedures that would give the allies an effective right of veto over negotiating positions and tactics adopted by the U.S. negotiators on issues of direct concern to Western Europe.

Confidence within the Alliance must ultimately be broader than that among governments. As Michael Howard has recently been reminding his fellow strategic thinkers, wide public support for national strategy is essential for its credibility.[8] The comparative lack of such support, notably among left-wing circles in Europe, has been a clear weakness in the Alliance. During the past several years, however, support for maintaining a strong defense posture has broadened in most Alliance countries on both sides of the Atlantic. In the United States the wave of senatorial support in the late 1960s and early 1970s for reducing U.S. troop levels in Europe has faded, and both congressional and public support for the U.S. commitment to the defense of Europe seems relatively strong. In Europe the disappointing experience of the mutual and balanced force reduction negotiations has paradoxically raised the level of understanding of conventional defense problems, at least in the political classes of the major coun-

7. For a detailed account of these frictions and the reasons for fearing their recurrence, see Christopher J. Makins, "Bringing in the Allies," *Foreign Policy*, no. 35 (Summer 1979), pp. 91–108.

8. Michael Howard, "Forgotten Dimensions of Strategy," *Foreign Affairs*, vol. 57 (Summer 1979), pp. 975–86.

tries, as the ready acceptance of the long-term defense program even by social democratic governments suggested. Both these trends could be reversed. The U.S. public, faced with a declining dollar and a recession and offended by the apparent lack of allied appreciation of the U.S. world role or support for the United States in crises like those in Iran and Afghanistan, could turn against the provision of defense assistance to Europe and against SALT and other East-West negotiations judged important by Europeans. Such tendencies have already appeared. European publics could likewise turn against devoting an increasing (or unchanging) share of the gross national product to defense, against "excessively" hard-line U.S. policies, and against the effort to develop a more effective allied nuclear strategy. Broader public support for government policies, both of defense programs and East-West negotiations, must be vigorously promoted to protect them from the pressures of economic stringency and political change.

Special difficulties for Alliance cohesion lie in the internal social and political instability of Turkey and other southern European countries. The problems of Turkey (hyperinflation, rampant terrorism, chronic balance-of-payments deficit, and so on) are serious both in themselves and in their effect on allied relations with Greece. In effect, the other allies have little choice but to work together to try both to prevent the Turkish economy from collapse and to protect the Turkish and Greek membership of the Alliance. These will not be easy tasks. However, the signs are not all adverse. Under West German leadership, the allies did succeed in mounting an economic and financial rescue operation for Turkey in 1979, which was coordinated with the International Monetary Fund and the overexposed private banks as well as with governments. Meanwhile Greek entry into the European Community and the prospect of a Turkish application provide leverage in sustaining political confidence, however difficult Turkey would be for the Community to absorb. Finally, because the Turkish army, for years the ultimate source of political power in Turkey, has increasingly come back into prominence since the fall of the Ecevit government in October 1979, a more realistic view of the problems that the Greek-Turkish dispute has created for the Alliance seems to be influencing Turkish policy.

The common feature of the recent problems of Turkey, Portugal, and Spain is that they cannot be solved by international policy. The most that outsiders can do is to encourage tendencies within those societies toward just social policies and greater economic strength, while also trying to retain the confidence of the political elites. To this end the United States and the major Western European countries have both shared interests and important assets. The assets are not only, or even primarily, economic but also, as was plain after the Portugese revolution and Franco's death, political, not least through the attraction of the European Community. The trick will be for the principal allies to exploit these assets effectively and in a concerted rather than discordant fashion. There is no reason why this should prove impossible.

Beyond the North Atlantic

Responsible observers on both sides of the Atlantic have again been musing about extending the area covered by the North Atlantic Treaty. This idea has been a consistent political loser for thirty years. Its recurrence testifies to the vulnerability of both the United States and Western Europe to developments beyond the Atlantic area and to an allied awareness, despite the predictions of the mid-1970s about the declining centrality of the transatlantic relationship, of a need to try to respond in concert.

That the United States and Western Europe should have differing assessments of, or different interests in, developments outside the Atlantic area is neither surprising nor necessarily serious. Such differences occur most frequently over (1) the relative significance of the geopolitical and the regional or local aspects of developments outside the Atlantic region, and (2) the best ways to seek to protect Western interests in such developments. In general, Western Europeans have in recent years tended to interpret events in, say, Angola, Iran, or the Horn of Africa mainly in terms of local and regional problems and to see less significance in the consequences of Soviet involvement. In the United States the geopolitical significance of such events has tended to be emphasized. Western European countries have therefore tended to seek to advance their interests primarily by accepting the inevitability of long-term changes in local situations and by emphasizing political and diplomatic means of adjusting to them.[9] By contrast, the United States has been inclined to look for

9. British support for the Sultan of Oman and French activities in the Central African Republic and Chad have constituted only limited—and largely anachronistic—exceptions to this general rule.

ways of resisting changes to prevent short-term losses to its international position, and, since 1973 at least, Americans have originated most of the discussion about the possible need for military intervention to defend Western interests, notably in the Middle East.

Superpowers are by their nature sensitive to the advances of superpower rivals and able to contemplate the use of sufficient power to resist them. By contrast, the limited size and the geographic positions of the Western European states have made them dependent on their milieu and less likely to ascribe global significance to every ebb and flow of political events and superpower influence in the developing world. These divergences of outlook are unlikely to disappear. But they may diminish. Western Europeans have become increasingly conscious of their dependence on raw material supplies from relatively unstable areas. And the Soviet intervention in Afghanistan served to heighten at least temporarily European awareness of the malign potential of Soviet meddling combined with local instability. But few Europeans are more disposed than in the past to see the use of Western military means as a lasting—or promising—way of advancing their interests, except in special cases (like the invasion of Shaba in Zaire) or in extremis. The significance of the Afghanistan crisis has been to make an extreme situation less unthinkable to Europeans than it was for much of the 1970s.

The crisis in Iran that began in 1978 was indicative. Rightly or wrongly, none of the European countries was as inclined as some people in the United States to see the transition from the shah's regime to the Islamic republic of Ayatollah Khomeini as a serious threat to Western interests that justified efforts to save the shah. The taking of the U.S. embassy hostages in late 1979 disturbed the natural Western European inclination to try to deal with the emerging political forces and compelled European governments to stand out against the fragile Iranian regime in support of the United States. The differing components of the European reaction to this situation—skepticism about the usefulness of economic sanctions or military force in helping to free the hostages, anxiety about jeopardizing oil supplies in the short term, interest in standing up for the United States and for the observance of international law—lent themselves to all manner of interpretations in the United States of European strength of will and purity of motive. In practice, however, the potential for serious transatlantic differences has mostly been contained by the restraint shown on both sides—by the United States in limiting and carefully timing its demands on its allies; by the European countries in providing a reasonable level of support for U.S. policy, even to the point of eventually backing some economic sanctions. A similar pattern has been evident in the responses to the Soviet intervention in Afghanistan. The possibility of a more aggressive U.S. approach in such situations in the future will, however, continue to create anxiety in Europe, just as an overcautious European policy risks provoking hostile reactions in the United States. But recent experience has shown how careful Alliance management can minimize, if not avert, damaging disagreements.

Africa and the Middle East will remain the areas in which these differing outlooks could be most critical for the transatlantic relationship. The disproportionate European interest in African raw material supplies has recently helped to create a community of interest with the United States, which has been more heavily motivated by geopolitical concerns. Despite somewhat divergent views of the Angola situation in 1975–76, this community of interest has sustained joint, though mainly political, action over Namibia, Zimbabwe, and some less intense trouble spots like Zaire. This pattern could well persist for some time. A severe deterioration of conditions in southern Africa, which would be likely to cause considerable disarray in Western Europe, or political changes in the United States that shifted U.S. African policy toward strong support for the whites in southern Africa could, however, disrupt the pattern and cause serious transatlantic discord.

The Middle East is a more complex case. Some transatlantic differences have faded in importance. The Arab-Israeli dispute has been largely neutralized as a source of U.S.-European friction by the virtual abandonment by the Europeans of any pretensions to diplomatic influence in the dispute. Residual irritation will doubtless persist in the United States at what is (not altogether fairly) seen as the Western European desire to appease the Arabs in the hopes of ensuring preferential access to oil supplies.[10] But failing another Arab-Israeli war, this tacit understanding seems sound.

10. U.S.-European differences on the Arab-Israeli problem long predate the acute phase of the oil problem and go back to the 1940s. Moreover, the link between the settlement of the Arab-Israeli dispute and the resolution of oil supply and pricing problems has, even in European eyes, become less strong than it seemed in 1973–74.

The more sensitive issues involve access to Gulf oil supplies and growing Soviet interest in the area. In terms of political relationships (as opposed to energy policy, which is discussed later), the principal dangers are the interruption—or significant reduction—of Gulf oil supplies because of local political turbulence (especially in Iran or Saudi Arabia). It is tempting for Western Europeans to seek to protect themselves against these dangers, and against the risk that misguided U.S. policy might contribute to some future crisis, by developing close bilateral relations and oil supply arrangements. The recent French-supported proposal for a dialogue between the European Community and the Gulf oil producers can obviously be interpreted in this light, even though U.S. apprehensions about proposals of this kind are seen as largely self-serving by many Europeans. They consider that the United States has maintained privileged relations with Saudi Arabia, and did so formerly with Iran, and see no reason for Western Europe to abstain from such relations.

Experience may, however, be diminishing this potential problem. The oil producers have shown little disposition since 1973 to make deals on terms advantageous to particular consumers. And the French, the most prone of the Western European countries to seek preferential treatment,[11] have arguably become more willing to learn this lesson, as was suggested by the European Community's decision at the Strasbourg meeting of the European Council in June 1979 to accept a collective limit on oil imports. The harmful consequences of the chaotic evolution of the spot market for all oil consumers in early 1979, and the glimpse of the likely intense competition for scarce supplies when the United States took action in the spring of 1979 to prevent certain oil products from being diverted from Caribbean refineries to the Rotterdam spot market, doubtless contributed to the greater French readiness to accept collective action. Even so, undivided Western European support for collective action in a future crisis cannot be taken for granted.[12]

Soviet involvement in any instability in the Gulf would present a further complication, all the more so as the Soviet Union will, assum-

11. The British, who were equally susceptible in 1973, are now being largely protected by North Sea oil.
12. If the emergency oil-sharing scheme of the International Energy Agency were called into play and Britain and the United States had to export part of their domestic production, the difficulty of maintaining transatlantic harmony would only be increased.

ing it becomes a net importer of oil, be able to assert a "legitimate" interest in Gulf oil affairs. Various goals of Soviet policy might be involved: a desire to secure the USSR's own oil and gas supplies, a desire to interfere with Western oil supplies, and a desire to ensure political developments in neighboring countries like Afghanistan and Iran that are congenial to Soviet interests (including its position vis-à-vis China). In a critical situation (for instance, the political disintegration of Iran) the risk of divergent assessments and policies among the allies would be real, with the United States probably more inclined than many Western Europeans to discount any legitimate Soviet interests and to see only a Soviet challenge to U.S.—and Western—influence and prestige. In an ideal world, the problem of the Soviet Union's interests in imported oil, like that of its interest in an Arab-Israeli settlement, would be resolved by East-West discussion and, for example, by Soviet participation in emergency oil-sharing schemes. In reality, no such solution seems likely, and the problem of Soviet involvement in future Middle East crises will remain a potential source of transatlantic friction.

These prospects also raise the issue of military force and the much discussed U.S. "rapid deployment force" for use in the Gulf area. In a situation of severe and indefinite oil shortage, Western European governments might well come to see the need for some military action, although many of the scenarios widely discussed in the United States for the use of force have lacked plausibility. Short of such an extreme situation, however, they would almost certainly look to political measures to achieve a resumption of oil supplies, for fear that military action would merely aggravate the situation. Similarly, proposals for intervention to affect the course of domestic instability, in Iran or Saudi Arabia, for example, would also be unlikely to appeal to Western Europeans except in extreme circumstances. The awareness that such contingencies may justify more active policies than in the past—possibly including the use of military assistance and presence to reassure moderate regimes—has grown in Western Europe, not least in the wake of the Afghanistan crisis. But to go from this awareness to an acceptance of the political and financial risks and burdens of planning for, participating in, or directly supporting U.S. or allied military intervention in a crisis is still a long step for many Western Europeans.

The Economic Key to Transatlantic Relations

Despite the importance of political and military issues, in recent years most of the pyrotechnics in the transatlantic relationship have been set off by economic problems concerning, for example, oil and energy policies, monetary policy, macroeconomic management, and trade and industrial policies. All these are problems to which a trilateral framework, to include Japan, is more appropriate than a purely Atlantic one, since they affect all the industrial democracies in similar ways. One of the advances of the 1970s was the increasingly explicit acceptance of this fact, notably by European countries that were, and to some extent remain, fearful of Japan's entry into the industrialized world. The following discussion, however, concentrates mostly on the impact of these broader problems on the relations between the United States and Western Europe.

Since economic issues are those in which domestic political influences impinge most sharply on international behavior, any analysis must take such domestic factors as its point of departure. It was fashionable in the mid-1970s to see Western Europe as set on a steady course toward socialism or corporatism that would make transatlantic dealings ever more difficult.[13] In practice, the search for more effective techniques of economic management in the 1970s has led many European countries somewhat away from classical socialism and interventionism and more toward the "German model." Committed from the start to establishing a liberal market economy, in explicit contrast to the centrally planned economy of the German Democratic Republic, the Federal Republic has opposed protectionist and interventionist ideas within the European Community as well as in its domestic policies. There is little reason, short of an international economic crisis, to expect this orientation to change in the near future.

France's partial shift away from traditional *dirigisme* to greater reliance on market forces and toward encouraging the adaptation of French industry to international competition, which has occurred under President Giscard d'Estaing and Prime Minister Raymond Barre, has been the classic case of the influence of the German model.

13. See George W. Ball, *Diplomacy for a Crowded World: An American Foreign Policy* (Little, Brown, 1976), chap. 9.

Despite the limited scope of those policies and despite some reverses they have suffered, their essential thrust seems likely to be maintained well into the 1980s if Giscard is reelected in 1981. In Britain, too, the Conservative government of Margaret Thatcher, which, barring an unexpected political reversal, should hold office at least until late 1983, is committed to reducing the role of government in the economy and creating the conditions in which British industry can undertake its regeneration with less official intervention. In both France and Britain influential members of the socialist parties have also come to accept the bankruptcy of much of their traditional industrial and economic policy.

In the European Community, too, there has been an apparent reaffirmation of the traditional role of the Community's institutions as defenders of a liberal international economic order. This has been most obvious in the trade field because of the commission's role in the multilateral trade negotiations. But efforts over many years to promote more direct Community intervention in European industry have not made much headway. Only in obviously declining sectors, such as steel and shipbuilding, where long-standing government subsidization was a large part of the problem, has the commission succeeded in getting much common policy adopted. In man-made fibers a crisis cartel virtually came into existence in 1978, although the commission's Competition Directorate successfully prevented its being formally accepted by the Community. And in telecommunications, where for years parts of the commission have been seeking ways to intervene to bring about a truly European industrial base, its most recent proposals have been limited to the creation of a Community-wide market by means of common standards, open government procurement, and the like. Meanwhile, the Community has continued to impose a useful discipline on the protectionist inclinations of member governments' industrial and employment subsidy policies.[14]

But the struggles in Western Europe between economic liberalism and socialism or corporatism, and between protectionism and free competition, have not ended. Domestically, the success of present

14. For a useful summary of the Commission of the European Communities' present approach, from the relatively laissez-faire standpoint of one of its members, see Christopher Tugendhat, "Europe and Industrial Policy," *International Affairs*, vol. 55 (July 1979), pp. 402–08.

British and even French policies, for example, is still quite uncertain. With the likelihood of several years of economic difficulty ahead, the final mix of the economies of Western Europe has yet to be determined.[15] As current debates about the future programs of the social democratic parties in Scandinavia suggest, the balance between public and private sectors will not easily be struck.

Within the Community, too, internal trade disputes, most recently over textiles and lamb, continually recur. Enlargement of the Community will create further problems in various sectors. And, internationally, protectionism in the Community remains a problem. This is especially true with regard to Japan, toward which the Community has historically taken a much less enlightened approach than the United States. But it is also true with regard to the United States, as recent arguments about synthetic fibers and the continuing saga of the Community's common agricultural policy have shown.

Underlying European debates on these subjects are continuing anxieties such as gave rise to the vogue of *le défi américain* in the late 1960s. The American (and now Japanese) challenge is still perceived in Western Europe as all too real. The lively debate, especially in France, about the implications of American and Japanese domination of the advanced information processing industry for European employment levels and culture testifies to this. Apparent justification for some of these anxieties can be found, for example, in the report of the Organization of Economic Cooperation and Development's Interfutures group, whose industrial sector studies suggested a less promising outlook for European industries in key sectors, such as automobiles and electronics, than for those in either the United States or Japan and its Pacific neighbors. The early 1980s, when the European labor force will still be growing rapidly as the baby boom generation enters the market, will be a period of maximum anxiety about possible deindustrialization and its consequences for employment.

Europeans also have reason to worry about American trade and industrial policies. The apparent strength of protectionist sentiment in the United States—in the labor movement, in threatened sectors of industry, and consequently in Congress—is of concern to Europeans,

15. For a stimulating discussion of the evolving balance between the public and private sectors of European economies, see Andrew Shonfield, "The Trend toward a Mixed Economy," in Karl Kaiser and Hans-Peter Schwarz, eds., *America and Western Europe: Problems and Prospects* (Lexington Books, 1977), pp. 114–28.

especially now that the existence of the multilateral trade negotiations can no longer be used as an argument against the introduction of protectionist measures. Although U.S. industrial problems in steel, automobiles, footwear, and other sectors have helped equalize the misery and deepen mutual understanding, they have compounded the difficulty of transatlantic policymaking. The most reasonable assumption, in the absence of a serious contraction of the international economy, would be the continuation of the generally liberal orientation of U.S. trade and industrial policies. But doubts on this score are not confined to one side of the Atlantic, and the memory of the Connally protectionist measures of August 1971 is still alive in Europe.

Arguments over trade and industrial policies are therefore likely to remain prominent both within the Community and between the Community and other countries in the early 1980s. But recent trends in the major European countries suggest a growing recognition of the importance of working toward a more liberal, open system by means of positive rather than negative adjustment policies. Thus, failing an international depression, in the 1980s governments on both sides of the Atlantic are likely to be willing to resolve disagreements on such issues by pragmatic compromises that recognize the need for the adaptation of existing protectionist structures to a more open system. The codes of conduct on such nontariff issues as subsidies and government procurement agreed to in the multilateral trade negotiations —assuming that their introduction and development is relatively smooth—and efforts through the Organization of Economic Cooperation and Development, for example in the steel and shipbuilding committees, should help to achieve such an outcome.

There have been similar changes in macroeconomic and monetary management. The U.S.–West German argument in 1977 about their respective responsibilities for reflating their domestic economies seems in retrospect quite incongruous. The growing consensus in the advanced industrial world that controlling inflation should be the principal goal of economic policy has tended to make West Germany a model to be emulated, not a villain to be denounced. And the increasing recognition (indicated by the emergency dollar support measures of November 1, 1978, and the stringent domestic monetary measures introduced by the U.S. Federal Reserve on October 7, 1979) that the U.S. economy must be as subject as others to international disciplines should make greater cooperation and less name-calling easier in the future.

International Monetary Affairs

Recent years have also seen persistent transatlantic recrimination over the respective responsibilities of the Western Europeans and the Americans for maintaining a workable international monetary system. This characteristic projection of responsibility onto the other partner has reflected an unwillingness to come to terms with the technical and political problems that inhibit reform of the system. There is no doubt that the Germans have been reluctant to see the international role of the deutsche mark grow and take some pressure off the dollar. In practice, however, the role of the mark has been growing steadily in recent years, so that 11 percent of official reserves were held in deutsche marks by 1979. At the same time, the Federal Republic has tried to ensure that the burden on the mark should be shared by other West European currencies, both in the sense that those currencies would be directly and quite rigidly linked to the mark and in the sense that other West Europeans would recognize a common obligation to manage their domestic economies so as to avoid frequent and large exchange rate fluctuations among themselves.

These were in essence the double purposes of the European Monetary System, established in March 1979. Yet the idea of this system was at first greeted with a chorus of American skepticism that appeared to betray not only technical reservations about whether the Europeans could make the system work, but also a psychological reluctance to see any international asset not under U.S. control which might become a serious competitor with the dollar. (The Europeans concerned were of course well aware of the technical problems but intended to work progressively to reduce them during the early, and supposedly flexible, phase of the system.) At the very least, the European initiative would seem to invalidate persistent American criticisms about European unwillingness to facilitate a change in the role of the dollar.

On their side, however, Europeans have often shown little understanding of the practical difficulties of quickly reducing either the dominant role of the dollar as the principal international reserve and transactions currency or the parallel dominance of the dollar banking system. Talk of an eventual role for the European currency unit or the International Monetary Fund's special drawing rights may make sense for the longer term. But in the short term such alternative assets cannot be expected to take much of the burden off the dollar.

Here again there has recently been some convergence of views. The United States took a softer line toward the European monetary experiment and the International Monetary Fund's proposed dollar substitution account during 1979 and, under the pressure of strong European criticism of U.S. insensitivity to the problems that dollar weakness was creating, accepted the need for domestic and international actions to support the dollar (as noted above). Likewise the early experience of the European Monetary System underlined for Western Europeans two facts: that in the present state of divergence of economic performance among the countries in the system, the system's parities will inevitably come under pressure at times of dollar weakness; and that further steps toward making the European currency unit a more promising international asset face many difficulties. Moreover, discussions among the major central banks on greater regulation of the Eurocurrency markets, an essential foil for their domestic monetary policies, have implied a growing willingness on both sides of the Atlantic to explore the complexities of recent international monetary problems more systematically, even if this particular approach may not turn out to be a fruitful one.

If transatlantic understanding has improved, however, the problems of the overextension of the dollar and the dollar banking system remain, especially because of likely developments in the oil market in the early 1980s. A more successful European Monetary System or an effective dollar substitution account or even, perhaps, some new regulation of Eurocurrency markets would not necessarily take enough pressure off the dollar to make the present arrangements more stable in the next few years. International monetary problems will therefore remain a potential source of trouble for the Atlantic countries.

Energy

The economic issue that more than any other will determine the nature of the transatlantic relationship in the 1980s is the issue of energy, and especially of oil. There are essentially three ways in which the advanced industrial countries could seek to deal with this problem. They could, first, intensify their domestic programs to improve energy efficiency and conservation, which they have done and are continuing to do, and seek stronger international disciplines on their domestic policies. Second, they could accelerate the development of alternative sources of energy. Third, they could revive the idea of seeking, separately or collectively, to negotiate with the Organization of Petroleum Exporting Countries (OPEC) about a long-term agreement on the price and supply of oil and on any other matters (such as development aid and perhaps monetary issues) that seemed to be inextricably related to oil pricing and supply either practically or politically.

To take the third possibility first, the outlook for either the proposed dialogue between the European Community and the Gulf oil producers or for a broader dialogue between all the advanced industrial countries and OPEC is unpromising. The second kind of dialogue may have had more promise in 1973–74. But the West spurned it then, partly because many Americans professed to believe that OPEC would not be able to sustain its price rises and partly because many West Europeans thought they could look after their interests better by not being associated with the United States. But even if the West could now agree to try such a negotiation, success would be unlikely, because of divisions within OPEC and an inevitable suspicion on the part of the consumers that the oil producers would break their commitments if changes in the oil market made it advantageous to do so. In any case, the West would have little bargaining leverage beyond the threat of an international monetary and economic disaster if OPEC failed to offer a reasonable oil supply at a reasonable price. What remains, therefore, is the need to preserve as constructive a relationship as possible between individual oil producers, notably Saudi Arabia, and the West. Here, as in other areas, it would be helpful if the United States shared the burden of making Western policy with its European allies in a way that it has not done in the past (when at times it has not been obvious that policy toward Saudi Arabia was systematically coordinated even within the U.S. government). By doing so, the impact of Western policies on the oil producers might be enhanced. And perhaps as important, U.S. and Western European attitudes and policies would be more likely to keep in step, without the time lags in perception that can be damaging in a crisis.

The greater part of the burden of surviving the coming years without serious oil-related problems will therefore fall on conservation and the development of alternative sources of energy. Though both are essentially domestic policy issues, both can also affect the transatlantic relationship. The creation of a still more effective common discipline on conservation than has already been created through the International Energy Agency and high-level meetings like the Tokyo summit in July 1979 can probably only have a marginal benefit. But to achieve even that, the recent cycle of mutual transatlantic recrimination about energy policy must be broken. In fact, both the United States and Western European countries have had some successes in encouraging greater energy efficiency,[16] but both have done less than might have been expected, especially during periods of faster economic growth. Thus the record scarcely justifies the more extreme claims of either side about the success or failure of their own and other countries' conservation policies. What is required is a common understanding among the advanced industrial countries concerning a fair and reasonable distribution of the necessary domestic sacrifices and, on that basis, greater efforts by governments to use the successes of others, modest though they may be, to stimulate greater conservation efforts in their own countries.

As for the development of alternative sources, governments can probably do little more than they have already done to stimulate joint research and development projects and cooperative ventures. The three main areas that need international attention are cooperation to establish how nuclear energy can be safely developed, an international regime for civil nuclear energy, including the eventual use of plutonium, and the environmental problems associated with increased use of coal.

Nuclear safety is an international problem primarily because of the spillover effect of domestic developments, as the instant international interest in the Three Mile Island incident again demonstrated. Yet there is little scope for intergovernmental action among the Atlantic countries, since the main difficulties lie in domestic attitudes and technical problems for which each country will have to find its own answers. Governments and industrialists in all the Atlantic countries, however, need to have more sensitivity to the damaging effects of

16. According to data of the International Energy Agency, energy use per capita in all the major member countries was either stable or declined between 1973 and 1978, despite continued economic growth. And energy use per unit of gross domestic product, a measure by which the United States is less wasteful of energy than several Western European countries and Canada, also declined in the same period.

negligence about nuclear safety in one country on the interests and programs of other countries. In a sense, the whole Western world is now helping to pay off the mortgage on the exuberant and often care-free early development of the U.S. nuclear industry. The advanced industrial countries could ill afford the accumulation of further liabilities of this kind.

On the question of the international regime for nuclear energy, the conclusion of the international nuclear fuel cycle evaluation should enable all concerned to agree that there is no easy technical way around the problems presented by the expansion of the international nuclear industry. Transatlantic differences of opinion on this subject in the mid-1970s stemmed partly from a U.S. failure to understand the needs and concerns of European countries and partly from unreasonable European obtuseness about proliferation risks. European attitudes—for example, toward the export of reprocessing plants—have greatly changed. The main question now is whether the United States, and particularly the U.S. Congress, will agree that the most effective strategy is to develop an essentially political regime of safeguards that will permit the assured supply of the whole range of fuel cycle services for low enriched uranium and plutonium, on terms acceptable to all. Such a regime should if possible be underwritten by an international organization credible to the developing world. This solution may be less desirable than one that postponed indefinitely the negotiation of an international plutonium regime. And it may need to be supplemented by special efforts among a more limited group of countries to deal with difficult political and security problems in particular areas (for example, the Asian subcontinent) where there are great proliferation risks. But it could be almost as effective a brake on proliferation and should reduce future transatlantic arguments.

Finally, the environmental problems associated with increased reliance on coal need to be considered. Evidence has been steadily accumulating to create concern both about the changes in the earth's carbon budget caused by burning fossil fuels and large-scale clearing of tropical forests and about sulfur dioxide emissions from coal-fired plants. Unlike the environmental impact of coal mining, these are truly worldwide problems, but are ill-suited to treatment by classical intergovernmental dialogue and action. Although the scientific basis for action may still be uncertain, the Atlantic countries should be in the vanguard of those trying to arouse concern about these problems.

The Domestic Roots of Foreign Policy

The element common to all the problems of the Atlantic Alliance countries is the delicate interaction between the rigidities of domestic social, political, and economic structures and the dictates of the international system. Domestic resistance to industrial adjustment threatens progress toward a more open liberal trade regime from which all should benefit. The distributional conflicts that have encouraged many governments to tolerate relatively high levels of inflation and adopt permissive domestic monetary policies have aggravated the problems of the international monetary system and made cooperation in macroeconomic management more difficult. There is debate about how great the changes in life-styles of the advanced industrial societies would need to be to achieve a significant reduction in energy (especially oil) consumption and an increase in the use of the most easily available alternative sources of energy. But domestic resistance to any rapid changes has aggravated the tightness of the world oil market and made all the Western economies more vulnerable to minor disruptions in oil supplies. And the unusually elusive risks that Western societies now see in nuclear energy seem to demand that policy in this area be supported by more than the narrow public majority that most governments command in parliament or in national referenda. Finally, the fact that the tolerance of both Western European and U.S. societies for sustaining high levels of defense spending has been in decline for much of the postwar period has intensified the practical and psychological problems within the Alliance in dealing with the Soviet Union.

This link between the principal sources of potential friction in the transatlantic relationship and the domestic politics of the Alliance countries has always existed. But the undisputed international dominance and relatively strong internal consensus of the United States appeared to make U.S. policy largely exempt from domestic constraints on its foreign policy at least until the late 1960s, and made less relevant the domestic problems of Western European countries, which were not called upon to accept such major responsibilities (notably for international economic matters) in the earlier postwar period as they are now. During the 1970s the situation changed both in the United States and in Western Europe in ways that have highlighted the importance of domestic politics and complicated the transatlantic relationship.

It is easy to take a gloomy view of the future impact of domestic policies on international affairs by evoking the prospect of slow and inflationary economic growth, adverse demographic influences on unemployment levels, intensified distributional conflicts, increasing political fragmentation and lack of leadership, and so on. Many people also profess to see signs of a growing divergence of social attitudes and values across the Atlantic, with European societies evolving through a long period of fragmented and conflictual politics toward new forms of participatory democracy and with the United States increasingly absorbed with its own social problems. The close transatlantic ties of the early postwar period would be less relevant to both. But not all the divergent trends will necessarily continue; some more promising signs exist. The strains of the 1970s have been weathered with surprisingly little challenge to the political institutions of the United States and the major European countries;[17] and developments in Spain, Portugal, and Greece have been benign. These facts, plus the apparently greater recognition in several countries of the need for a more systematic fight against inflation and a growing awareness of external security threats, suggest more adaptability in Western societies than many forecast—or feared.

Conclusion

Three important questions remain. How divergent are the interests of the United States and Western Europe? To what extent can any common interests be translated into common or concerted policies without being undermined by interests that are divergent or competitive? And are the institutions through which the transatlantic relationship is managed adequate to the tasks of facilitating concerted action when it is needed and containing divergence of policy when it is inevitable?

In thinking about basic interests it is necessary to distinguish three areas: security questions, broader political problems, and politico-economic issues. Security, in the classic sense, is the area to which the view of the transatlantic relationship as an "enduring balance" is

---

17. To the extent that Eurocommunism should be classified as such a threat, which is debatable, it is at present in retreat.

most obviously applicable. Whatever may have been the problems of confidence and credibility that have arisen since the 1950s, and whatever may be the differing degrees of exposure to the Soviet threat and the differences of perspective between globalists and regionalists, it is hard to escape the conclusion that in the 1980s the structure of the Atlantic Alliance will continue to suit the interests of all its members better than any realistic alternative.

In the broader realm of international politics the underlying community of interests between the United States and Western Europe is also probably greater than often appears on the surface. Whether it be in Africa or the Middle East, there is a common interest in the emergence of more prosperous, politically stable nations that will be willing members of a free and open international system based on a set of agreed rules for trade, investment, and so on.

In the politico-economic realm, however, there are—and have always been—important competitive elements in the transatlantic relationship. The difference in the resource bases, and therefore in the vulnerability, of the United States and Western Europe creates a different set of attitudes and concerns, notably on energy problems. The range and significance of these areas of difference have become greater with the progressive economic and political recovery of Western Europe since World War II. Nevertheless, it is difficult to argue a priori that in other than catastrophic international economic circumstances these different interests are such that they cannot be contained within an agreed set of common rules (for example, on trade questions) and a structure of close consultation and negotiation. By contrast, it is not hard to make the case that without cooperation on economic issues the advanced industrial countries will grow less rich than they would with such cooperation.

Thus the second question—whether common interests can in practice be translated into common policies and not be overwhelmed by the inevitable elements of competition and divergence—becomes crucial. It is here that the long and continuing history of psychological and political problems in the relationship is relevant. The sense of difference between the U.S. superpower, the two European nuclear powers, the powerful, but militarily and psychologically hobbled, Federal Republic, and the smaller European countries cannot easily be eliminated. Changes in European attitudes toward the United States have highlighted some of these differences. Once regarded as the model for European countries, the United States no longer has the same attraction for Europe, even though, at the level of material goods and as a magnet for investment, its influence may be as strong as or stronger than ever. This change, which derives in part from the recovered self-confidence of European societies and in part from a greater awareness of the problems of the United States (from civil rights and drugs to environmental and energy matters), can hardly fail to have some political effects. The same is true of the corresponding feeling in the United States—frustration over continued Western European political disunity despite the twenty years of Community-building. Finally, the passing of the generation that created and managed the transatlantic solidarity of World War II and its aftermath has left a void that many are conscious of but few see how to fill.

All these influences tend to complicate the management of a relationship in which the basic security bargain increasingly depends for its credibility on a continuous and visible identity of political interests and attitudes. There is no magic formula for achieving this identity: it demands constant and vigorous political judgment on all sides. At present both the will and the ability to exercise such judgment seem to be strong by past standards on both sides of the Atlantic. In fact, a review of the Alliance's numerous problems in past decades prompts the conclusion that, despite a good deal of kicking and screaming, both the United States and the Western European countries have adjusted quite well to the requirements of a more balanced relationship. Therefore, although it is easy to draw up a list of possible transatlantic disagreements in the future, notably over Middle East and Asian problems, it would be wrong to conclude that what is possible is likely, much less inevitable. The idea of an enduring balance sustained by an effective self-correcting mechanism is, in the light of recent experience, rather persuasive.

Whether this situation will continue will depend in large measure not only on political and economic developments but also on the smooth functioning of the institutions within which the transatlantic relationship is managed. Much progress has been made in this regard since the early 1970s. Many of the sterile institutional arguments of that period—about multilateralism or bilateralism, the acceptability of exclusive as opposed to inclusive groups, the issue of summits, and so forth—have faded or even disappeared. The seven-power summits that began at Rambouillet have won acceptance, if not universal

Christopher J. Makins

approval. With their associated (and still perhaps too weak) preparatory and follow-up mechanism, the summits have become valuable, if not uniformly productive, shock absorbers in the Atlantic system. The more restricted meeting at Guadeloupe[18] in January 1979 revealed a growing pattern of four-power collaboration on security and political issues that has similar merits. It is important that this type of collaboration develops further, since it could be a crucial means of avoiding future discord on problems like those of the Middle East and the Gulf. Meanwhile the Organization of Economic Cooperation and Development, the North Atlantic Council, and even the International Energy Agency all provide adequate forums for broader multilateral consultation—if they are properly used, as they increasingly have been.[19]

There is thus no pressing need for transatlantic institutional innovation. But routine diplomacy in the Alliance could certainly be made more effective. And Western European governments also need to improve their ability to analyze and formulate policy on complex international issues, especially in the politico-military area, and to rely less on U.S. competence. The attainment of a capability for truly multilateral policymaking, in which the burden of initiative and responsibility is fairly shared, is essential in order to shorten the time lags in perception that have so often bedeviled transatlantic relations.

It is equally important to strengthen and deepen in each of the Atlantic nations the understanding of the political and social forces at work in the other nations. This should lead to easier and less acrimonious policymaking in which loose allegations of failure to accept responsibility in domestic economic or energy policy and of "finlandization" or "confrontation" in security policy have no place. To understand all in the transatlantic relationship may not be to forgive all. But it should help the Atlantic allies to dedramatize their relations without deemphasizing them—in short, to reach a more mature relationship in the 1980s than in any previous decade.

18. The participants were the heads of state or government of France, West Germany, the United Kingdom, and the United States.

19. A classic example of their *not* being used properly came in May 1979, when the United States decided to use its oil entitlements program to redirect certain oil products of Caribbean refineries away from the Rotterdam spot market and back to their traditional markets in the United States. The fact that International Energy Agency meetings only a few days before the decision was announced yielded no disclosure of U.S. intentions and that the subsequent explanations were so poor showed how difficult it is to accustom national bureaucracies to the requirements of the contemporary international scene.

CHAPTER FIFTEEN

North-South Relations

JOHN W. SEWELL *and* JOHN A. MATHIESON

Two salient features marked the evolution of relations between developed and developing countries in the 1970s. First, the importance of the third world to the economic interests of the rest of the world and to the functioning of the international economic system has increased dramatically. Second, a significant division has grown between developed and developing countries on the issue of the structures, rules, and governance of the world economy, with the former countries advocating gradual changes and the latter pressing for immediate reforms. The involvement of developing countries in international transactions will continue to grow in the 1980s, as will the need for improvements in North-South relations.[1]

The next few years appear to be a particularly inauspicious time for increased attention to the main problems at issue between the United States and the developing countries of the third world. The industrial economies of the North are beset by an apparently intractable set of domestic economic problems—slow growth and lagging

We are grateful to Valeriana Kallab for comments and to Paulette E. Nisbeth, Sue Ratliff, Helen Y. Reber, Theresa L. Robinette, and Devinda R. Subasinghe for their assistance in preparing the manuscript.

1. In this chapter we use the term *North* to refer to the world's rich, industrial non-Communist states that are members of the Organization for Economic Cooperation and Development. Theoretically and especially in terms of policy application, the industrial countries of the Eastern bloc should be considered members of the North, but these nations have for the most part declined to participate in North-South negotiations. The term *South* refers to the world's less developed or developing nations that are members of the Group of 77, the coalition that pursues the economic aims of the South.

productivity; structural unemployment; and rates of inflation that are eroding individual economic gains and leading to a pervasive sense of insecurity about the future.

The developing countries, having weathered the stresses of the last decade fairly well, also face a future of increasing uncertainty. They suffer directly from slow growth in the markets of industrial countries, and inflation affects the price of most of their purchases from abroad. Their debt has grown exponentially since 1974 to over $300 billion, while the commitment of the North to raising or even maintaining present levels of development assistance is weakening, even though poverty in the third world remains widespread.

For the United States, the current period seems particularly difficult. The turmoil in Iran and the sudden intervention of the Soviet Union in Afghanistan has raised the specter of a renewed cold war centered on U.S.-Soviet competition in the third world.

The heightened concern about security issues does not, however, diminish the importance of simultaneously addressing world development problems and formulating longer-range policies on American relations with the countries of the third world. In the 1980s U.S. interests in these countries—whether they concern economic relations and development, human rights and basic needs, or nuclear nonproliferation—can no longer be subordinated to issues of military security or relations with the USSR and with America's industrial allies in the Organization of Economic Cooperation and Development.

Importance of North-South Relations

There are several reasons why the United States should give higher priority in the future to relations with the developing world. One is the increasing interdependence between economic performance in the United States (and other industrial countries) and that achieved in the third world. In chapter 3 of this volume the authors point out that the United States has become more dependent on relationships with the rest of the world. Developing countries represent a major component of those relationships because of their markets for and sources of goods and their financial flows and investment opportunities. Indeed, the world economy is not functioning particularly well for either developed or developing countries. Development was once considered a problem confined to the poor countries, and searches for new sources of growth tended to ignore the third world. Now, however, many realize that the economic performance of these countries can slow or stimulate world growth and that the third world can play a greater role in efforts to regenerate long-term international economic momentum.

Second, dealing with today's global economic problems will require the active involvement of the developing countries. The rising number of countries in the third world is significant: in 1959, 92 countries were independent; at the beginning of the 1980s, the number has grown to 164, and all the new entrants are developing countries. This fact alone would complicate the management of any international problem but, in addition, a number of these countries are now economic actors of considerable importance.

Third, the agenda of North-South issues has broadened considerably during the last decade beyond the traditional concerns of aid and trade. As a group, the developing countries are pushing for major changes in the international economic and political systems created after World War II. Their agenda also includes new rules to govern the oceans, air waves, and other commonly shared global domains; the search for an international energy strategy; ways to increase world food production; human political, social, and economic rights; and new policies and institutions to deal with world economic problems.

Finally, neither the industrialized rich nor the developing countries are addressing what still remains the most pressing humanitarian problem: the plight of the world's poorest people. The conditions in the world's more than forty poorest countries pose a crucial moral issue that will require special measures. The World Bank recently estimated that between 470 million and 710 million people will still remain in what is defined as "absolute poverty" two decades hence, depending on the pattern of growth rates. That is, even after a period of global economic growth, these people will lead a life "so limited by malnutrition, illiteracy, disease, high infant mortality, and low life expectancy as to be below any rational definition of human decency."[2]

These problems pose one of the important priorities of the 1980s —the need to address the issues of world development that no longer

2. Robert S. McNamara, Address to the Board of Governors of the World Bank, Belgrade, Yugoslavia, October 2, 1979.

can be resolved within national boundaries and to integrate a comprehensive approach to North-South relations into American foreign policy.

U.S. Security Interests in the Third World

The instability in Iran and the Soviet intervention in Afghanistan have raised concern about Soviet intentions and U.S. military security to levels not seen in a decade. Current discussions center on the need to increase military expenditures, develop the capability of American forces to intervene in the third world when U.S. interests are threatened, and obtain access to bases in order to enhance that capability.

American policymakers are now reassessing how important third world countries are to U.S. security and which policies can most effectively protect those interests. The United States sees itself as a global power and the ultimate guarantor of world peace. Maintenance of a global strategic balance is crucial as a safeguard against nuclear holocaust. From this perspective, the developing countries are important only to the extent that they affect the strategic balance. At the same time, however, thoughtful analysts realize that there are limitations to U.S. military power and that a number of third world countries and regions are of concern to the United States for reasons only tangentially related to the strategic relationship between the United States and the Soviet Union.

Much more analysis and public discussion of the precise nature of the Soviet, Cuban, and Vietnamese "threat" to the developing countries is needed, as well as investigation of the nature of long-run U.S. security interests in the developing countries. Some observers aim at preempting and denying the influence of the USSR in areas where the vital interests of the United States are at stake, particularly in the oil-producing region in the Middle East. Others feel that the United States should maintain its power throughout the world to preserve freedom of communications, particularly on the high seas, and access to supplies and markets. In addition, there is growing apprehension about the instability of the third world and the longer-run dangers for the United States in the event of widespread deterioration in global cooperation. A Rand Corporation report stated in the late 1970s: "The diffusion of military power and the growing reluctance of the industrial democracies to use force in defense of their national interests will increase the propensity of medium and small powers, especially in the Third World, to resort to violence when their interests clash with those of the United States, Japan, and Western Europe."[3]

But the use of military power to achieve American objectives in the third world may no longer be generally applicable. A recent study identified 215 incidents in which U.S. forces were used for political purposes since the end of World War II (185 of which were in the third world) and concluded that the use of military force to achieve political objectives has primarily a short-run effect and is no substitute for long-run diplomacy.[4] This line of reasoning suggests that U.S. interests can be much more efficiently promoted in the longer run by establishing mutually beneficial relationships with the developing countries.

In the 1980s the possibility of confrontation between the United States and the Soviet Union in the third world remains a worrisome feature of the international scene. The danger of an escalated conflict is particularly marked in the Middle East. In southern Africa, tensions will remain high until definitive progress toward majority rule is achieved. This same potential for conflict is present in other parts of the world, depending at times on the actions of both the United States and the Soviet Union; at other times the potential exists in spite of those actions. In the current environment of concern over security issues, however, the United States should not neglect the fact that U.S. interests in the third world include a broad set of economic relationships and moral interests.

Economic Development in the South

Without question, the symptoms of absolute poverty—hunger, disease, illiteracy, and high mortality rates—are still widely prevalent in many third world nations. However, their *aggregate* economic growth record over the past decade has been surprisingly good despite major differences among them and a rather widespread air of gloom about their future prospects. In the 1970s industrial nations grew at an average rate of 3.4 percent a year, while the developing countries

3. Guy J. Pauker, *Military Implications of a Possible World Order Crisis in the 1980s* (Rand Corporation), 1977, p. 73.

4. Barry M. Blechman and Stephen S. Kaplan, *Force Without War: U.S. Armed Forces as a Political Instrument* (Brookings Institution, 1978).

achieved a growth rate of 5.7 percent a year. Even though markets in industrial countries were becoming increasingly closed to certain imports from the third world, the developing countries were successful in raising their exports of manufactured goods at an average annual rate of over 10 percent. Although the level of official development assistance from the industrial countries is only half that called for by the United Nations (0.33 percent of the gross national product of donor countries versus the 0.70 percent objective) and the bill of oil-importing developing countries rose from $7 billion in 1973 to about $44 billion in 1979, the developing countries still managed to finance most of their own development, largely by saving and investing nearly a quarter of their limited national incomes.

The relatively sanguine picture drawn by these aggregate figures masks what is perhaps one of the most important trends in the third world—the growing differentiation of economic performance among developing nations. A handful of countries have achieved rapid advances in economic and social well-being, but more are struggling to maintain economic momentum, and a number of others are witnessing deterioration in already unacceptably low standards of living. This increasing differentiation is, on the one hand, evidence of success; some developing countries have done very well in the past ten years. But it also has greatly complicated North-South relations, given the need to formulate different economic policies for different countries and the desire of the third world to maintain a unified stand on international economic matters.

Any classification of third world nations is open to argument, but it is useful to define four categories: members of the Organization of Petroleum Exporting Countries (OPEC), advanced developing countries, other middle-income developing countries, and low-income developing countries. The first two groups are of direct and immediate concern to the United States economically and in some cases politically; the latter two are for the most part important to longer-term U.S. economic interests and, in the case of the low-income developing countries, to American moral and humanitarian interests.

The members of OPEC have used their rapidly rising oil revenues in a variety of ways to achieve economic and political objectives. OPEC itself includes a highly disparate group of countries, all in the third world, ranging from Indonesia at the low end of the income scale, Venezuela at about the middle, and Kuwait at the top. Some OPEC members have used their oil revenues to invest in projects designed to provide future income when their reserves are depleted, and some have distributed the benefits of oil income as widely as possible throughout their populations. Still others have concentrated on purchases of military equipment and expensive but unneeded infrastructure projects, and have made few attempts to meet the basic needs of their poor majorities.

The advanced developing countries have also taken on major roles in the international economy, both because of their high growth rates (giving them more promising markets for products of industrial countries), and because of their rapidly expanding exports, primarily manufactured goods, to the industrial countries. Although opinions vary on which developing nations can be called advanced, lists usually include the smaller economies of Hong Kong, Singapore, Taiwan, and South Korea, as well as large and resource-rich economies such as Brazil and Mexico. The growth performance of these advanced countries has been spectacular; from 1960 to 1977 the average annual gross national product and per capita growth rate in all cases were higher than those of the United States, even though their populations were increasing twice as fast. More striking is the ability of the advanced developing countries to expand their exports. Between 1967 and 1977 their average annual growth in exports was 24 percent, compared with 14 percent for the United States and about 18 percent for the industrial countries as a whole.

These advanced developing countries by and large have changed from import-substitution to export-promotion policies. Like Japan in the 1960s and early 1970s, they have pursued an outward-looking growth strategy that concentrates on exporting low-cost consumer goods such as apparel, footwear, and consumer electronics to industrial nations. As a result, many American businesses and unions have complained about the cheap goods flooding U.S. domestic markets, dislocating industries and jobs. Opponents of trade with the advanced developing countries seldom mention the consumer gains, anti-inflationary benefits, and efficiency incentives derived from these imports, or the fact that the markets of these countries are among the most rapidly growing ones for U.S. exports of agricultural products, machinery, transportation equipment, and high-technology goods and services.

The other middle-income developing countries—those with per capita income above $300—consist of a host of nations at widely divergent levels of economic development. A few have successfully expanded their exports of manufactures, but most depend on income from exports of minerals and agricultural commodities. Because of the intense competitiveness of the advanced developing countries and reactions to that competitiveness in the markets of industrial countries, the prospects of newcomers pursuing export-led growth strategies successfully are more limited now than they have been in the past. Most middle-income countries have been buffeted by rising import costs and dramatic fluctuations in demand and prices for their commodity exports. The resulting inflation, balance-of-payments deficits, and debt accumulation have made it difficult for many of these countries to implement expansionary economic policies.

The circumstances of the 1.3 billion people living in the poorest nations of South Asia and Sub-Saharan Africa present the bleakest economic prospects for the third world. These countries have witnessed relatively little change in their economic conditions over the past decade. They constitute about 61 percent of the total population of the developing world, but they account for only 16 percent of the total gross domestic product and less than 10 percent of the total exports of the third world. They are in many ways becoming the forgotten majority of development efforts throughout the world. While the middle-income developing countries increased their per capita income by about $400 during the 1970s, the poorest countries recorded an increase of only $40, or about $4 a year. The average per capita income of middle-income countries stood at $1,225 in 1978, compared with only $185 for the poorest nations. The absolute poverty in this latter group of countries is widespread, and there are countless obstacles impeding their attempts to overcome deprivation.

U.S. Economic Interests in the Third World

The activities of third world countries will be of increasing importance to the well-being of the United States and other developed countries in the decade to come. Developing countries not only supply a growing percentage of raw materials and low-cost, anti-inflationary consumer goods, but they are now major markets for the industries and farms of the United States and the other industrial countries.

During the 1974–75 world recession, developing countries maintained relatively high growth rates by borrowing from abroad, and their purchases contributed significantly to aggregate demand in industrial countries. One analyst recently commented: "This source of demand represented a significant contribution by less developed countries to the alleviation of unemployment in developed countries. . . . the development of the world's poorer countries matters to the health of the economies of the industrial countries."[5]

The importance of the developing countries to the North as export markets as well as sources of oil, raw materials, and consumer goods will continue to grow in the future. Indeed, the third world represents the new growth frontier for the world economy. The essential elements of this potential include low capital-labor ratios, low cost and abundance of labor, possible increases in the sophistication and education of the labor force, opportunities for applying technologies used in more affluent countries, a rich natural resource base, and nearly unlimited—but not yet effective—demand for products, investments, and technologies to satisfy the development and welfare needs of the third world countries.

These factors have been present for some time but have been far from fully utilized. Establishing sound economic and social bases for development takes time, as it did for the industrial transformation in the United States and Europe. A number of developing countries have shortened this period considerably, assisted by the capital and advanced technology of the industrial countries of the North. Efforts to augment and utilize the potential of the third world could, if properly implemented, enhance the international economy's efficiency and equity. Although political and economic constraints must be faced at both the domestic and international levels, such efforts are already well under way in several areas of U.S. economic relations with developing countries.

Trade

As mentioned above, the U.S. stake in trade with third world nations is large and growing. That trade improves the quantity and quality of U.S. economic output, largely because the developing

5. William R. Cline, ed., *Policy Alternatives for a New International Economic Order: An Economic Analysis* (Praeger for the Overseas Development Council, 1979), p. 46.

countries offer both rapidly expanding markets for U.S. goods and services and new sources of competition to spur efficiency measures and overcome the "lost dynamism" that some argue is the core of the economic malaise of industrial countries.[6]

While the composition and volume of U.S. trade with individual developing countries varies enormously, trade between the United States and the third world as a whole follows a predictable pattern: the United States exports agricultural products, machinery, transportation equipment, and other relatively sophisticated manufactures to the developing countries, and they in turn sell oil, other primary goods, and labor-intensive consumer goods to the United States. In other words, trade has evolved as one would expect—according to the relative abundance of arable land, capital, and technology in the United States and of natural resources and labor in the developing countries. Both in theory and practice, these major differences in comparative advantage (differentials in factor endowments and costs) raise the potential for significant gains from trade because trade results in the more efficient production of output.

In 1978 developing market economies purchased 38 percent of total U.S. merchandise exports: 26 percent went to non-OPEC developing countries and 12 percent to members of OPEC. The United States now sells more to the non-OPEC developing countries than to the European Community, Eastern Europe, the Soviet Union, and China combined.

Despite the large volume of American exports to developing countries, the United States is experiencing a significant trade deficit vis-à-vis the third world, amounting to about $20 billion in 1978. But the aggregate figure is somewhat deceptive. Of the total $74 billion in U.S. imports from developing countries in 1978, almost half, or $36 billion, was accounted for by oil and petroleum products.

About 40 percent of total U.S. exports of manufactures are sold to developing countries. Estimates that one out of eight jobs in manufacturing are attributed to exports suggest that about one out of every twenty U.S. jobs in manufacturing exists to meet the demand for U.S. exports to the third world.

Although trade in goods does represent the strongest economic link

6. John P. Lewis, *Development Cooperation: Efforts and Policies of the Members of the Development Assistance Committee* (Paris: Organization for Economic Co-operation and Development, 1979), p. 31.

between developing countries and the United States, overemphasis of the merchandise portion of the balance of payments can be misleading. For example, U.S. income from services exports (investment income, fees and royalties, shipping and insurance income, and interest income) improves the U.S. current account balance. The United States ran a total services surplus of more than $25 billion in 1978, of which over $17 billion was accounted for by net services trade with developing countries (including oil-exporting countries). This surplus directly offsets a portion of the trade deficit in the current account balance.

U.S. imports of manufactures from non-OPEC developing countries are increasing rapidly; they rose at an average growth rate of 22 percent a year during the 1965–77 period, compared to an average 16 percent growth rate for U.S. imports of manufactures from industrial countries. The share of manufactures imports from developing countries as a proportion of total U.S. imports of manufactured goods has risen from 15 percent in 1965 to 24 percent in 1977. Although not large relative to the entire economy, this trade is concentrated in "sensitive" commodity categories (textiles, apparel, footwear, consumer electronics), that is, those requiring labor-intensive production and competing with relatively stagnant sectors in the U.S. economy. This type of trade leads directly to the classical case of increased efficiency in the economy as a whole and welfare gains to consumers, but losses of employment opportunities in declining industries.

A recent analysis based on a survey of actual U.S. retail sales found that imports from developing countries were as much as 16.3 percent cheaper than their domestically produced counterparts of comparable quality. Imports from developed areas were only slightly less expensive (0.4 percent) than comparable U.S. goods. Overall, American consumers save more than $2 billion a year as a direct result of purchasing less-expensive imports. This is particularly important for low-income consumers, who save as much as 13 percent by purchasing imported rather than domestic goods.[7]

Public debates in the United States about American policies on imports from the third world highlight sharp differences on this issue between consumers and workers. The gains to the welfare of U.S.

7. William R. Cline, *Imports and Consumer Prices: A Survey Analysis* (Washington, D.C.: American Retail Federation and National Retail Merchants Association, 1979), pp. 3–19.

consumers from these imports are significant, but they are dispersed widely throughout the economy, whereas displacement of employment opportunities is concentrated in a relatively few U.S. industries. The macroeconomic employment effects of these imports are negligible—especially when compared to other job displacement factors such as automation and shifts in demand and when the job creation effects in U.S. export industries are taken into consideration. However, the fact that job losses are highly visible and subject to national policy has led affected businesses and unions to focus attention on them.

In response to these conflicting interests, the U.S. government has adopted a policy of keeping markets relatively open to imports of manufactures from developing countries, but at the same time placing controls on certain imports growing at above-normal rates in affected sectors. Many of these sensitive products have been excluded from the U.S. generalized system of preferences extended to developing countries, and import quotas or their equivalent have been established or tightened on these products. In addition, the United States has taken the lead among industrial countries in urging the advanced developing countries such as Brazil, Mexico, Korea, and Taiwan to open their markets to imports from developed and other developing countries and accept a reduction in preferential treatment.

Food and Commodities

The United States has a direct interest in world trade of food and commodities because it seeks access to supplies of needed materials at reasonable prices and expansion of sales of the commodities it produces, again at remunerative prices. Added to this are broader interests—the assurance that world demand will be largely met (for humanitarian reasons and to avoid the disruptive effects of shortages), the dampening of major fluctuations in commodity prices, and the promotion of investment in raw materials industries.

Notions that third world countries would organize militant cartels on the model of OPEC for other critical raw materials have faded. However, the boom or bust syndrome of excess supply and excess demand continues to plague both producers and consumers. There is an emerging perception in both the North and the South of the need to stabilize commodity markets, but progress in this area has been slow. The lack of progress is somewhat ironic in view of evidence suggesting that the largest measurable economic benefits from commodity price stabilization would be gains for the *industrial* countries, including the United States, because of reduced inflationary pressures.[8]

The U.S. interest in commodity production and trade is complicated by the fact that the United States is both a large producer and a large consumer of raw materials. Not as dependent on imports of commodities as are the European Community or Japan, the United States nevertheless does import significant amounts of commodities from developing countries. In 1976, for example, U.S. net imports from developing market economies accounted for 88 percent of domestic consumption of columbium, 82 percent of tin, 56 percent of aluminum, and 50 percent of manganese. Literally all U.S. imports of commodies such as rubber, coffee, tea, cocoa, hard fibers, and jute are accounted for by imports from the third world. On the other hand, the United States produces large quantities of minerals such as coal, iron, lead, copper, and phosphates, although most of these are consumed domestically rather than exported. And perhaps most significantly, the United States is the world's largest producer of food exports, supplying about 45 percent of total exports of wheat and 64 percent of coarse grains in the 1978–79 period.

U.S. policies are ambiguous with regard to commodity issues. Historically, the United States has participated in commodity agreements on such items as sugar and coffee. When the UN Conference on Trade and Development first advanced its proposal for an Integrated Programme for Commodities in 1974, however, the United States opposed the initiative, citing fears of new cartels and on the grounds of the long-standing U.S. objection to market interventions in general. This position has been modified in recent years. The United States has negotiated individual agreements and is now a member of agreements governing tin, coffee, and sugar (the last, ratified by the Senate, is still pending the enactment of implementing legislation). Late in 1979 the United States signed an agreement on rubber. Originally a strong opponent of a proposed Common Fund to finance commodity agreements, the United States eventually agreed to its creation, but has succeeded in limiting the amount of direct contributions to the fund. On a separate but related matter, the United States participated

8. See Jere R. Behrman, "International Commodity Agreements: An Evaluation of the UNCTAD Integrated Commodity Programme," in Cline, ed., *Policy Alternatives for a New International Economic Order*, pp. 63–148.

in the negotiation of an international wheat agreement, but it collapsed over the questions of stockpile release prices and maintenance
costs. In sum, the United States has taken a selective approach toward
commodity issues in recognition of the diverse requirements for different commodities and has attempted to bargain strongly to satisfy
the current needs of U.S. producers and consumers.

Energy

Energy is the most critical issue affecting economic relations between the United States and the third world. Energy is still an issue
of confrontation, but it could and in fact must become an area of
North-South cooperation if a solution is to be found: energy is a
global problem that requires a global approach. In the near term, a
global strategy should include three elements. First, strong conservation measures are needed to reduce the consumption of oil, particularly in the United States, because per capita energy consumption in
the United States is far above that in other countries: more than one
and a half times the average for industrial countries, twelve times as
much as in middle-income developing countries, and about seventy
times the average consumption in low-income developing countries.
Second, agreement is essential between producing and consuming
countries to provide sufficient supplies of energy at predictable and
reasonable prices, which is not necessarily the same as low or unchanging prices. And third, assistance is needed for non-OPEC
developing countries whose oil-related deficits and debts are rapidly
reaching crisis proportions.

The longer-run strategy for energy should be implemented simultaneously. Such a strategy should include the expansion of production of traditional sources of energy from nontraditional suppliers,
many of which are in the third world, and a much greater emphasis
on investment in and research and development of alternative sources
of energy, both in developed and developing countries. All these
actions require a new kind of North-South cooperation that has been
totally lacking to date. A global energy strategy will be complete
only if the United States and other industrial countries jointly work
with developing countries to produce, save, and replace oil, and
strive to negotiate some new understandings between oil exporters

and importers. (Energy policy is discussed in more detail in chapter 4 of this volume.)

Investment and Lending

At the end of 1978 U.S. direct investment in developing countries amounted to more than $40 billion, almost a quarter of total U.S. direct investment in other nations. Investments in the third world by U.S. firms are generally large and highly visible; they are an integral part of the trading network, providing the United States with significant amounts of raw materials and manufactures from production in developing countries and increased access to third world markets. In addition, they generate significant revenues for U.S. firms; for example, in 1978, 35 percent of total U.S. direct investment income originated in developing countries. From the perspective of the third world, investment inflows supply income, employment opportunities, and access to technology.

American investment in developing countries and its costs and benefits both to the United States and to those countries has been the subject of intense debate over the past decade. Those who contend that foreign investment promotes American interests hold that investments encourage exports and imports and also provide returns to investors, thus giving the United States a "piece of the action" that would otherwise go to the firms of other countries if capital outflows were restricted. As these advocates see it, foreign investment benefits the United States by encouraging efficiency, raising the quantity and quality of employment and production. Opponents of this view argue that foreign investment undermines American interests by exporting capital and technology, thereby "displacing" domestic investment, employment, and growth. Opposition to direct investment in developing countries concentrates on such issues as the exploitation of local labor and natural resources, the despoiling of the environment, and the lack of sufficient contribution to domestic development efforts.

While the pros and cons of direct investment will continue to receive attention, the widespread antagonism to U.S. foreign investment prevalent in the early 1970s has subsided. Both U.S. firms and the governments of developing countries have learned from their experiences, and bargaining for investment terms in many cases takes place on a more equal footing. This process must continue if developing countries are to receive the capital inflows they need, on terms they can accept, and if the firms are to establish a long-term presence with adequate returns.

In addition to direct investments, U.S. private bank lending to developing countries has rapidly increased in recent years. U.S. bank claims on developing countries (excluding offshore banking centers) amounted to $74 billion at mid-year in 1979, or some 35 percent of total U.S. bank claims on foreign borrowers. Interest from these loans constitutes large and growing shares of total bank revenue. Thus the ability of developing countries to repay their debts, primarily through receipts from exports, is of major concern to lenders. The U.S. seizure of Iranian financial assets, and indications that Iran may not honor some of its debt repayment obligations, have created a cloud of uncertainty for the financial sector. Lenders now are concerned about the security of their assets, and borrowers worry about their access to funds.

As in the goods market, the developing countries have also become an integral part of the international financial scene. The ability of third world nations to repay their debt-servicing obligations—individually and collectively—has a direct bearing on bank profitability (in some cases solvency) and on financial stability. This relationship indicates the need for developing countries to expand their earning potential, primarily through exportation. Also, these countries need forms of credit that permit productive investment rather than merely the financing of current obligations.

North-South Bargaining: The "Dialogue"

Problems in relations between developed and developing countries have been the subject of a long series of sometimes constructive, but more often acrimonious discussions and negotiations between the two groups of nations. Since the 1975 Seventh Special Session of the UN General Assembly, which succeeded in initiating a productive phase of these discussions after a particularly confrontational period, the talks have been known collectively as the North-South dialogue. In recent years this dialogue has focused on various aspects of the third world's demands for a New International Economic Order, most forcefully articulated in a declaration and action program that the developing countries pushed through the UN General Assembly at the height of OPEC's 1974 success in unilaterally raising oil prices.

The fundamental rationale for the New International Economic Order—which is a political movement as much as a set of economic objectives—lies in the third world's dissatisfaction with the international distribution of power, wealth, and income among developed and developing countries. These gaps were initially attributed to colonialism, but when political independence did not yield rapid gains in living standards, third world intellectuals and leaders began to scrutinize the international economic system itself for inequities and for what they considered economic colonialism.

The South's demands call for many changes in the rules governing international economic transactions and cover a wide variety of functional areas: commodity price-stabilization mechanisms based on buffer stockpiling and other arrangements; improvement of the generalized system of preferences, in which exports of developing countries are granted duty-free or reduced-duty entry into the markets of industrial countries; increased access to those markets for third world exports; international monetary reform; and cancellation or rescheduling of debt on a case-by-case basis. Other changes are: codes of conduct for the transfer of technology and for the activities of transnational corporations, increased industrial capacity in developing countries, and the implementation of special measures to help the least-developed third world countries and those developing countries most seriously affected by rises in the prices of essential imports. These demands were designed to be sufficiently comprehensive to invite endorsement by all developing countries because individual proposals would obviously benefit some more than others. The diversity of the third world coalition—market and socialist economies, agricultural and newly industrializing economies, oil-exporting and oil-importing countries—guarantees the absence of a strong consensus on any particular item. Therefore, efforts of the South to maintain political unity have required that they demand implementation of the entire set of changes. This tactic, considered necessary by leaders of the South, has been totally rejected by the North, and therefore has become a major source for stalemate in the negotiations.

Emergence of Southern Unity

Although it gained widespread attention only when OPEC exercised control over oil supplies in the mid-1970s, the push for a new economic order has a much longer history. The origins can be traced at least as far back as the mid-1950s. Fearing domination by the superpowers and the possibility that the developing countries might be used as the staging ground for major power conflicts, the newly independent nations sought to avoid direct political and military alliances with either the United States or the Soviet Union. These concerns led to the creation of the Non-Aligned Movement, which grew out of the 1955 Bandung Conference attended by officials from twenty-nine African and Asian developing countries. Initially the Non-Aligned Movement, whose membership has increased to ninety-five, focused its efforts on the political issues of decolonialization, independence, and neutrality rather than on economic concerns. While it has gradually broadened its mandate to include economic issues, its focus remains primarily political. The Non-Aligned Movement created a basis and a model for unity among the developing countries; it was the predecessor of the "Group of 77," the coalition that pursues the economic aims of the South.

The Group of 77 originated in the North-South economic debate at the first UN Conference on Trade and Development in 1964. Consisting originally of seventy-seven developing countries (at the end of that conference), the group now has about one hundred twenty members. This body is for all intents and purposes *the* "South" as identified in North-South discussions. From the outset, the raison d'être of the Group of 77 has been to press the industrial countries to modify international economic regimes in ways that would contribute to more rapid rates of economic growth in the countries of the third world.[9]

The decade following this first conference can be considered a period of institutional and substantive growth for the unity of the South. The Secretariat of the UN Conference on Trade and Development became a focal point for the development and enunciation of the view of international economic relations held by the South. The basic point of this view is that the world's economic practices sys-

9. Roger D. Hansen, *Beyond the North-South Stalemate* (McGraw-Hill, 1979), p. 5.

tematically discriminate against developing countries. The major example cited to support this belief has been the dependence of third world countries on primary commodity exports whose terms of trade vis-à-vis manufactured goods (and petroleum products) have been seen by some as deteriorating over time. Although the validity of the declining terms-of-trade argument was doubtful in earlier years, it can no longer be questioned. The managing director of the International Monetary Fund recently stated: "The large rise in the current account deficit of the non-oil LDCs from 1977 to 1979 can be wholly attributed to two factors: deterioration of the terms of trade and larger interest charges."[10] In addition, fluctuations in the international prices of commodities have brought economic instability to exporting countries. These factors led the third world to call for stabilizing the prices and improving the terms of trade of raw material exports.

Because of the inability of the third world countries to raise their commodity export earnings (with the exceptions of OPEC and a few other developing nations), the commodity issue has remained the central feature of the New International Economic Order movement. Additional economic concerns, however—some related directly or indirectly to commodity problems—have extended the movement to other areas of economic interchange.

By processing commodities locally into intermediate or final products, developing countries hoped to obtain greater amounts of value added. But they were confronted with effective tariff structures and other obstacles (such as freight-rate schedules) that discriminated against imports of processed goods relative to raw materials. The developing countries recognized the need to diversify into exports of manufactured products in which they had a comparative advantage—primarily consumer goods requiring labor-intensive production. While the strategy proved immensely successful for certain advanced developing countries, their success eventually led to more restrictive nontariff barriers, thus limiting growth potential for them and for latecomers.

Continued and rising current-account deficits in developing countries resulted in their accumulation of large private and public debt. Regardless of the actual causes for the debt buildup (higher priced

10. J. de Larosière, Statement delivered to the Board of Governors of the International Monetary Fund, Belgrade, Yugoslavia, October 2, 1979.

imports of basic goods such as food and petroleum products, economic mismanagement, overambitious development plans, and so forth), many developing countries believed that they were victims of a debt trap not of their own making. As a result they demanded debt relief in some form, although key middle-income countries, aware of their need for a high credit rating, have been conspicuously absent from the ranks of those demanding debt relief.

The combination of these economic dilemmas, both domestic and international, and dependence on the markets, foreign investment, and technology of the industrial countries led many in the third world to the conclusion that their economic fate was not in their own hands. The fundamental changes in international economic relations that these nations consider essential to increase their bargaining power include a code of conduct to govern the activities of multinational corporations, a greater decisionmaking role in institutions and policies affecting their economic interests, and access to technology on more favorable terms. They also call for general or selective reduction of dependencies on the North, which implies much greater levels of cooperation among developing countries, or collective self-reliance. Thus the movement for a new international economic order gradually evolved into a set of demands for reform in nearly all areas involving international transactions.

Early achievements in implementing modifications in the international economy were modest but not insignificant. The UN Conference on Trade and Development was to become the primary institutional vehicle for the expression of Group of 77 demands for economic reform; it provided, in a series of conferences, an ongoing forum in which the third world could discuss economic issues. The first of these conferences, held at Geneva (1964), and the second at New Delhi (1968) focused on elaborating the developing countries' comprehensive view of economic relations between the North and the South. The third world pressed for changes in two areas of trade policy—preferential treatment for exports of developing countries in markets of industrial countries and legal acceptance of the principle of nonreciprocity in the trading system. Little substantive progress was achieved at a third conference held in Santiago (1972), partly because of the public attention devoted to the host country (Chile under Salvador Allende), but also because the prevailing international economic and financial disequilibria dominated the concerns of participants from the North.

Setting the Stage for the Dialogue

The year 1973 marked the watershed for North-South relations and the transition of the new international order debate from a latent to an active phase. In September the South voiced its political and economic concerns at the Algiers summit conference of the non-aligned countries, when this group and most of the Group of 77 coalesced in support of the economic agenda established by the UN Conference on Trade and Development:[11]

This convergence of goals, strategies, and work programs between the Non-Aligned Countries and the G-77 was in and of itself bound to increase the organizational and institutional capacity of the South to press its demands for economic (and associated institutional and political) reforms in the plethora of international and regional organizations and specialized agencies to which most developing countries belong and in which they have a major voice. The greater the unity, the stronger the voice.

This consolidation of third world unity, the culmination of a decade or more of expressions of dissatisfaction with economic progress in the developing countries and of frustration with responses of the North to proposals for change, ushered in what has been termed a strategy of "trade unionism."[12] Thus, rather than negotiating desired changes bilaterally, the developing countries should adopt a common platform for collective bargaining with the North. The Algiers conference put forth an economic declaration and an action program for economic cooperation; it called for the establishment of a new international economic order.

The bargaining power of this "union" was apparent a month later when the Arab oil boycott occurred and OPEC subsequently succeeded in unilaterally raising oil prices fourfold. Conditions were ripe for a shock to the North. There was a boom in demand for commodities to support record levels of growth in all nations. The Club of Rome's report, *The Limits to Growth,* had predicted major re-

11. Hansen, *Beyond the North-South Stalemate,* p. 21.
12. For an early elaboration of this concept, see Mahbub ul Haq, *The Third World and the International Economic Order,* Development Paper 22 (Overseas Development Council, 1976), based on five lectures given in November 1975 as the second series of Turkeyen Third World Lectures delivered in Georgetown, Guyana.

source scarcities. The United States was withdrawing its armed forces from Vietnam after a frustrating military engagement that had created international doubts and internal divisiveness about what the United States could and should accomplish overseas.

With the stage thus set for international conferences to consider economic reform, Algeria (then chairing the Non-Aligned Movement) requested and the UN General Assembly summarily arranged a Sixth Special Session in April 1974 to address the problems of raw materials and development. Despite the objections of several industrial countries, the General Assembly adopted, without a formal vote, a Declaration and Action Programme on the Establishment of a New International Economic Order. In December of that year the General Assembly passed a second resolution, the Charter of Economic Rights and Duties of States (against the votes of six developed countries and ten abstentions), under which the third world sought to establish the right of commodity producers to cooperate in achieving more favorable terms of trade and the duty of consuming countries to refrain from retaliation.[13]

Two months later, in February 1975, participants of the Third World Conference in Dakar proposed adding energy negotiations to general North-South economic issues in order to elicit the support of oil-producing countries for the objectives of the New International Economic Order. This strategy was endorsed by OPEC in March. At about the same time, the UN Industrial Development Organization Conference in Lima adopted an objective: to increase the developing countries' share of world industrial output from 7 percent in 1975 to 25 percent in the year 2000.

In May, after having failed repeatedly to engage the OPEC members in discussions on the energy issue, the United States indicated a willingness to discuss other commodities on a case-by-case basis. The more accommodative stance was elaborated at the Seventh Special Session of the UN General Assembly in September, during which U.S. Secretary of State Kissinger proposed a number of specific measures to promote North-South cooperation.

The apparent willingness of the United States to broaden the North-South agenda triggered action both within and outside the

13. Rachel McCulloch, "North-South Economic and Political Relations: How Much Change?" Discussion Paper 645, Harvard Institute of Economic Research (Cambridge, Massachusetts: August 1978), p. 13.

United Nations. In late 1975 the Conference on International Economic Cooperation first met in Paris; twenty-six countries and the European Community participated in a formal North-South dialogue. In May of the following year the fourth UN Conference on Trade and Development was held in Nairobi, at which time the third world again emphasized commodity issues. The Conference on International Economic Cooperation ended after eighteen months of mutually frustrating negotiations: the United States and other industrial countries were interested primarily in discussing energy, whereas representatives from OPEC and other third world countries refused to focus on those issues unless the industrial countries gave greater consideration to their commodity, debt, and other problems. However, participants at the final session did agree in principle on the creation of the Common Fund to finance agreements to stabilize commodity prices and on substantial increases in official development assistance. Conflicts over the financing, uses, and management of the Common Fund have yet to be fully resolved. At a ministerial meeting of the UN Conference of Trade and Development in Geneva in March 1978, agreement was reached in principle on measures for granting debt relief for the poorest countries in the third world, but donor countries retained the right to implement their own programs.

The accommodative phase of the dialogue in the mid-1970s was again transformed into confrontation by early 1979 because of the emergence of real differences between the positions of the North and the South. Negotiations to establish an international wheat agreement collapsed over a dispute about acquisition and release prices. With the exception of Argentina, the developing countries boycotted the April 1979 initialing of the agreement reached in the Tokyo Round of multilateral trade negotiations. The fifth UN Conference on Trade and Development, held in Manila, consisted largely of a rhetorical exercise castigating the protectionism of the North and its general intransigence on other issues concerning the New International Economic Order. Finally, the nonaligned countries held a well-publicized summit conference in Havana in August 1979. Economic issues were relegated to the background against the more dramatic political confrontations of delegation seating and rivalry between moderate and radical states, and the meeting had the effect of polarizing the North and the South. This dimmed the prospects for generating a more cooperative approach to discussions planned for

1980, particularly those associated with the formulation of a new international development strategy for the Third Development Decade of the United Nations and its acceptance at the Special Session of the UN General Assembly on development cooperation, scheduled to take place in August 1980.

Prospects for the Future

Assessments of the chances for progress of the North-South dialogue range from outright skepticism to cautious optimism. Critics note the rigidity on both sides regarding many of the policy issues and feel that little can be accomplished in global negotiating forums. Optimists, on the other hand, point to positive steps already taken in certain areas, such as trade reform, agreements on commodity arrangements, and commitments to some form of debt relief. It will take time to put these new forms of cooperation into operation, and some will prove more successful than others, but experimentation is preferable to no action at all.

A few efforts have been made to reopen the dialogue. First, under some pressure from oil-importing developing countries, members of OPEC have agreed to reconsider the energy issue on the agenda of a new global round of North-South discussions, which is scheduled to begin early in 1981 under the auspices of the United Nations. Second, two separate, independent commissions have recently supplied sets of policy recommendations to improve North-South relations: the U.S. Presidential Commission on World Hunger and the Independent Commission on International Development Issues, better known as the Brandt Commission, chaired by former German Chancellor Willy Brandt.

In a preliminary report issued in December 1979, the Presidential Commission on World Hunger recommended that the United States "make the elimination of hunger the primary focus of its relationships with the developing countries, beginning with the decade of the 1980s."[14] The report also noted that poverty is the fundamental cause of hunger in the world today and that efforts to eliminate hunger must focus on the eradication of poverty in general. The recommendations are commendable and deserve close scrutiny by Congress and the administration, as well as a positive response by developing countries.

14. U.S. Presidential Commission on World Hunger, *Preliminary Report* (U.S. Government Printing Office, December 1979), p. III.6.

The mandate of the Brandt Commission is much broader; its proposals constitute a more comprehensive response to North-South economic problems. Prepared by leaders from both the North and South serving in their capacities as private citizens, the Brandt Commission report sets forth near-term proposals to be implemented on an emergency basis, focusing on global food needs, greater levels of economic assistance to developing countries, an international energy strategy, and the initiation of international institutional reform. The major long-term recommendations include measures to transform the needs of developing countries into effective demand for products from developed countries, measures to bring greater stability to the prices of raw materials, and a reduction in trade barriers. Also included are institutional reforms to develop new types of lending to developing countries, bring Communist countries into international economic institutions, and alter some of the operations and policies of the World Bank and International Monetary Fund.

Recent U.S. Policy

Assessments of the effectiveness of U.S. policy toward the third world vary, reflecting differing perceptions of the nature of the problems and the objectives. Some argue that relations between the United States and the developing countries have undergone considerable improvement in recent years. Presidential adviser Zbigniew Brzezinski summarized this view: "I think it is fair to say that the hostility toward the United States, which was felt so strongly at the U.N. only two years ago, has dramatically declined. Most Third World countries perceive the United States today as more sympathetic and positive in its attitude."[15] More recently, Assistant Treasury Secretary C. Fred Bergsten noted: "Economic and political relations between the industrialized North and the developing South have improved dramatically since the early 1970s."[16] This theme has been reiterated by U.S. commentators who write that the United States has been responsive to the needs of the developing countries and that its only reward has been a series of attacks in international forums. However, the perception of those whose agenda focuses on the need

15. Address to the Foreign Policy Association, December 20, 1978.
16. "North/South Relations: A Candid Appraisal," Remarks before the Center for Inter-American Relations, New York. N.Y., January 29, 1980.

for international economic reforms is that little progress has been made in improving North-South relations and that the United States is one of the most obstructionist nations among the industrial countries. Willy Brandt recently wrote, "I do not believe that the American people could be indifferent to poverty and starvation anywhere in the world, and US organizations have indeed shown that they are concerned and ready to help. Yet the United States, which in the early 1960s was a leader in this field, has substantially reduced its international development efforts. . . . I understand many of the reasons for the dwindling US commitment but I sincerely hope that they do not reflect unchangeable aspects of American political life."[17]

The first assessment—that relations between the United States and developing countries have improved—is based on the following assumptions: that the international economic system is best governed by countries in accordance with their economic power and the level of their economic transactions; that the international system currently is basically sound and does not discriminate against the South, but does require gradual adaptation to deal with new problems; and that the problems of developing countries can be attributed to domestic rather than international factors, so reforms on the international level will have only a slight (and perhaps negative) impact on efforts to overcome poverty. The policy objectives that flow from this assessment are to pursue U.S. economic interests, while making the changes necessary to avoid confrontation with developing countries, and to make some effort on humanitarian grounds to assist third world nations to develop domestically. In the context of these perceptions and objectives, U.S. policies have been formulated and carried out relatively well.

This diagnosis and policy prescription, however, is fundamentally inconsistent with that put forward by many analysts and leaders—not only those in developing countries. They offer an alternative set of assumptions: because international disequilibria affect the economies of developing countries as much as (and in some cases more than) the economies of developed countries, the former countries deserve a greater decisionmaking role in policies that affect them; the international system does discriminate against them, even if inadver-

17. *North-South: A Program for Survival,* Report of the Independent Commission on International Development Issues, Willy Brandt, chairman (MIT Press, 1980), p. 27.

tently; inequities in international wealth and transactions do act as constraints on efforts to overcome third world poverty, even if poverty is primarily an internal matter; and the industrial nations are in a position to offer much more assistance to developing countries than they have to date. The policy recommendations emerging from this analysis consist of basic institutional and procedural reforms aimed at the transfer of some economic wealth, income, and power from developed to developing countries.

Like most public policy issues, the opposing sides in the debate about North-South relations tend to present their cases in black and white terms. In reality, there is some validity to both arguments. Third world nations have a legitimate claim in calling for measures to bring about a more equitable distribution of global wealth and income, but changes on the international level must be accompanied by domestic reforms. The United States should not be singled out as causing the world's economic problems—other Western industrial nations, countries in the Eastern bloc, and the developing countries share the responsibility—but the leadership position of the United States requires that it play the major role in marshaling international efforts to address these economic ills. In this context the U.S. policy record is good in some areas and bad in others.

The current U.S. administration recognized at an early stage the increasing role of the developing countries and the new problems facing the United States in its relations with them. In an address just before his inauguration, in January 1977, President Carter spoke of "the basic right of every human being to be free of poverty and hunger and disease and political repression." In a speech made to the Venezuelan Congress during his visit to that country in March 1978, the president said, "The industrial nations . . . cannot by themselves bring about world economic recovery. . . . Strong growth and expansion in the developing countries are essential. . . . For the rest of this century the greatest potential for growth is in the developing countries." In his 1980 State of the Union Address, President Carter mentioned that one of the three basic developments challenging world peace is "the press of social and religious, and economic and political change in the many nations of the developing world."

Although official pronouncements have been favorable to the concerns of the developing countries, the United States ultimately must be judged by its policies and actions rather than by its rhetoric. In the area of trade the record is mixed. As noted above, progress toward implementing mutually beneficial commodity agreements has been slow. The administration has resisted pressures to erect new barriers to trade, however, and the exports of developing countries to the United States continue to grow at a steady rate.

The Tokyo Round of trade negotiations, for the most part concluded in 1979, provided some benefits to developing countries, but the absence of third world signatures on the agreements signifies their lack of enthusiasm for the results. The major agreements on both tariff and nontariff items were negotiated among the leading developed countries, with only minor attention being paid to the needs of developing countries. Although this was the first serious effort in the history of trade negotiations to involve the developing countries, the negotiations did not address some of the issues of crucial importance to the third world, such as the elimination of existing quantitative restrictions on certain categories of their exports.

The U.S. record on development assistance is poor, despite the Carter administration's initial commitment to provide more aid. Congressional support for economic aid has dwindled and public opinion is ambivalent; the American people are in favor of efforts to assist the poor throughout the world, but question the efficacy and distributional results of existing programs. The United States has allocated few additional funds to its bilateral assistance program, much of which goes to the Middle East. The seemingly large increase in the U.S. multilateral assistance program—from a little more than $1 billion in fiscal 1977 to about $2.5 billion in fiscal 1979—includes partial payment of pledges on which the United States was in arrears and, at congressional insistence, funds in the form of callable capital (committed but not transferred to lending institutions) rather than actual contributions. The most recent report of the Organization for Economic Cooperation and Development shows U.S. official development assistance in 1978 at 0.23 percent of gross national product, far less than the 0.70 percent objective. This places the United States thirteenth among the seventeen donor countries of the Organization for Economic Cooperation and Development, although it represents a modest increase from the record low of 0.22 percent of U.S. gross national product recorded in 1977.

The United States has supported a number of measures to increase the availability of financing to countries facing balance-of-payment problems, particularly through additional facilities in the International Monetary Fund. But the United States has been less responsive toward rescheduling debt or other forms of debt relief, a major demand of the developing countries. The industrial countries have agreed to consider relieving the debt of the poorest countries by easing the terms on past loans that most of these countries have received. A number of donor countries have already granted debt relief to the poorest countries. But the United States has yet to implement its debt relief program because of the lack of necessary legislative action.

To its credit, the United States has focused on certain issues of concern to developing countries, producing some highly positive results. The negotiation and passage of a new Panama Canal treaty signaled the willingness of the United States to deal with third world nations on a more equal footing. American efforts to reach peaceful settlements to conflicts in the Middle East and southern Africa have been commendable. The United States has taken the lead in extending relief to Vietnamese and Cambodian refugees, but in the latter case the momentum for assistance came from private initiatives rather than from the administration or Congress.

The Carter administration's emphasis on human rights has received a mixed reaction from the third world. The priority placed on human rights has drawn some criticism and has complicated the administration of foreign policy, but it has also attracted international attention to individual freedoms. President Carter has correctly defined human rights as including the satisfaction of at least a minimum level of basic needs, such as adequate food, housing, health care, and education. The long-standing congressional position that U.S. assistance go to the poorest groups within a society has reinforced this theme. Both the human rights and the basic needs themes have been attacked by third world leaders as allowing interference in the domestic affairs of developing countries, limiting levels of aid, and diverting attention from their demands for economic reforms. Many feel that the U.S. commitment toward meeting basic needs has not been backed by concrete actions.

Despite the positive elements of U.S. policy, relations between the United States and the third world have reached a low point in recent years. Americans are frustrated because the United States is not recognized for its good will, and developing countries wonder why the United States and other industrial countries are reluctant to do more.

To some degree this conflict is inevitable—as long as the United States remains the leading industrial country and there are large gaps in wealth and income between the rich and poor countries. However, the current feeling of mutual distrust and even antipathy can perhaps be reduced if both North and South will step back from their strategies of confrontation, reassess the needs and capabilities of the pertinent countries, and design realistic policies to improve the workings of the international economy and the development prospects of the third world.

Priorities for the Next Decade

The increasing importance of the third world in the international economy and basic differences over the functioning and management of the economic system suggest a number of general policy directions for the United States and other industrial countries, developing countries, and all countries combined. The North needs to develop an understanding of its interests in the developing world; the developing countries must acknowledge their stake and responsibilities in the international system.

The North must come to realize that it has a substantial economic interest in the present and future prosperity of the South and that there are a number of fruitful areas for mutually beneficial cooperation. Serious attention should be given to efforts assuring that the developing countries become an integral part of the engine of world economic growth. The adoption of coordinated fiscal and monetary policies by the countries of the Organization for Economic Cooperation and Development in order to revive economic growth, control and reduce inflation, and correct current account imbalances are critical economic objectives that will also benefit the developing countries. It will be difficult, however, for the industrial countries to achieve these goals in an unhealthy international economic environment. In short, strong economic performance in the developing countries will support strong economic performance in the industrial countries.

For their part, the developing countries should take into account the legitimate concerns of the industrial countries when formulating their proposals. The refusal of developing countries to discuss the energy supply issue in the context of the North-South dialogue has alienated the North and precluded serious negotiations on other economic matters. The third world also needs to acknowledge that not all their economic proposals are in their interests nor do all necessarily lead to either greater international efficiency or greater equity.

These general policy orientations can be translated into several specific courses of action for the 1980s, which do entail some short-term costs. The United States and other industrial countries should increase their efforts to enhance economic progress in the developing countries, both on humanitarian grounds and for their own long-term self-interests. The United States should play a major role in the initiation of these efforts.

In the area of trade, there needs to be a renewed commitment to liberalization, not only in accepting the new codes established at the Tokyo Round but also in further negotiations to reduce existing quantitative restrictions on imports from developing countries. The United States should press for agreement on an acceptable safeguards code that requires discipline on the part of countries imposing temporary import controls. In fact, given the complexity of negotiations and their usefulness in containing protectionism, preparations should soon be made for a new round of trade talks in the 1980s to focus on North-South trade issues. At the same time, major initiatives are needed in the North to assist workers, industries, and communities affected by changing trade patterns and other dislocating factors. Current policies of adjustment assistance are almost totally inadequate to deal with the shifts in patterns of production needed in the decade ahead to meet the needs of both the United States and developing countries. In their place, a set of comprehensive industrial policies is needed, one that does not isolate trade as the only cause of dislocation and that anticipates structural change.

U.S. export performance will also have to be improved in order to respond to a more competitive international environment. This will require a reassessment of export policies both by private firms and by the U.S. government. The recent reforms in the trade structure of the U.S. government are a beginning, but American business will have to play a major role. Care must be taken to ensure that these reforms do not increase the leverage of groups interested in protection, and that trade policy takes into account the needs of developing countries.

The industrial countries should demonstrate their commitment to increase development assistance by moving as rapidly as possible toward the goal of transferring 0.7 percent of gross national product to developing countries as concessional aid. This does imply a shift in priorities, but not one of great magnitude. In recent years, for example, U.S. federal budget outlays on domestic social programs have been over forty times as large as U.S. foreign economic assistance expenditures. Most of the additional aid should be directed at meeting basic needs in the poorest countries and in the poorest sectors within middle-income developing countries. This will require new types of cooperation with recipient countries and new strategies to make industrialization objectives compatible with efforts to overcome the worst aspects of absolute poverty.

The industrial countries must also increase investment in the key sectors of food, energy, and raw materials in both developed and developing countries to reduce bottlenecks and inflation and assure adequate long-term supplies throughout the world. Private firms doing business in the third world have to pay closer attention to the development needs of those countries. At the same time, developing countries must realize that these firms need some degree of certainty about the conditions and rules under which they operate. In addition, greater levels of investment will be enhanced by more cooperation between the private and public sectors, such as joint financing in which private banks participate in World Bank investment projects.

In the 1980s the developing countries will also have to acknowledge the differentiation among their own countries and to recognize the economic needs and constraints of the industrial world without jeopardizing their own progress. Policymakers in these third world countries need to accept the premise that mutual benefits imply mutual responsibilities, and that a new economic order must also benefit the industrial countries. The economically advanced developing countries must assume a growing share of responsibility for increasing the efficiency and equity of the international economic system by opening up their markets to both rich and poor countries, and eventually by extending assistance and preferences to the poorer developing countries. In addition, these countries should recognize that too rapid a disruption of existing trade patterns will lead to a backlash detrimental to both rich and poor countries. Thus, increasing but nondisruptive access to markets of the developed world should be negotiated. Developing countries also need to expand their domestic markets and lower their barriers to trade among themselves in order to raise their total exports and decrease pressures on econmies of the North. Third world countries also need to implement the difficult domestic economic measures necessary to meet the basic needs of their poorest inhabitants, both for their own sake and to meet the legitimate concerns of those in the North who feel that equity within nations is as important as equity among them.

Finally, developed and developing countries must together seek new methods to arrive at mutually beneficial changes in the existing international economic system. This will require shifts in perceptions and in procedures. Both North and South must begin to show a greater sensitivity to the concerns and needs of the other side and find areas of common interest where progress is possible. Reaching agreements on substantive issues such as trade in energy products, manufactures, commodities, international investment, finance, debt, and rules for governing the exploitation of global resources will require reforms of institutions and of the negotiating process itself. Currently negotiations are hampered because international institutions are either dominated by the rich countries (as in the case of the International Monetary Fund) or by the poor ones (such as the UN Conference on Trade and Development) or, like the UN General Assembly, because they include so many participants that detailed negotiations are cumbersome. Attention must also be given in some cases to changing the rules or membership of existing institutions to increase the participation of the developing countries. Where necessary, new institutions may have to be created to deal with special circumstances. In the new International Fund for Agricultural Development, for instance, voting power is shared equitably between donors and recipients and between developed and developing countries. In sum, the North, and particularly the United States, must overcome the strong aversion to innovations in the rules and institutions regulating economic relationships between developed and developing countries. The South, in turn, must enter into negotiations with a much more realistic appraisal of what can and should be accomplished to make the international economy more efficient and equitable.

Progress toward better North-South relations will not necessarily come smoothly and harmoniously; the choices are not easy, and one should not underestimate the necessary adjustment and costs in the short run. Policymakers should expect a high degree of volatility in the third world. Most developing countries have relatively short histories as independent nations, and so they are still groping for economic and political structures capable of achieving their various objectives. Change involves conflict, and the United States and other industrial countries must be prepared to live with conflict that arises from changes in policies and governments in the third world. The unity of the developing countries will remain strong, however, despite their growing economic and political diversity because they share a common set of interests. The leaders in industrial countries must therefore develop policies that respect that sense of unity while also reflecting third world diversity.

The world economy has changed considerably over the past decade, and adjustments to those changes are required by both industrial and developing countries. Urgently needed is a new program of global cooperation that gives priority to increasing the efficiency and equity of the international economy. Progress toward achieving these goals depends to a large extent on the willingness and ability of the United States to take the lead in North-South relationships in the next decade.

CHAPTER SIXTEEN

The Crisis of Competence in Government

JAMES L. SUNDQUIST

WHEN President Carter came down from Camp David, in July 1979, to talk of a national "malaise" and warn his countrymen that "a crisis of confidence" was "threatening to destroy the social and political fabric of America," he gave his political rivals in both parties an unintended issue. As the campaign got under way in the fall, Ronald Reagan was saying that there was no "failure of the American spirit," only "a failure of our leaders," that the people did not lack confidence in themselves but only in their government. And Senator Kennedy was throwing Carter's words back at him with, "the malaise is not in our people but in our leadership."

The implication, of course, was that confidence could be restored with a change in leadership. But the thesis of this chapter is that the problems of the U.S. government will not be solved by anything so simple as a change in leadership—or a return to office of the incumbent leadership, depending on one's preference. The American governmental system has built-in structural features that have always presented severe difficulties for any president who would provide the sought-after leadership. But deep-seated trends have been, and are, at work that will make effective government even more difficult to attain in the 1980s than it has been in the decade just ended and those that have gone before.

I am grateful to several colleagues for their comments, especially Joel Aberbach and Lawrence Brown, and to Jo Ann Pinero for secretarial assistance.

The Crisis of Confidence

Every poll that has been designed to measure the confidence of the American people in their government has shown a precipitous decline in that confidence since the mid-1960s. No one disputes President Carter on that point. A few figures will illustrate it.

Consider, for instance, the findings of the Center for Political Studies at the University of Michigan, which has asked some questions in identical form and at the same time in each presidential election year. Persons interviewed in its national sample who expressed agreement with five propositions (chosen from a set of answers in a multiple-choice format) can be considered to be alienated from their national government: "you can trust the government in Washington to do what is right . . . only some of the time"; "the government is pretty much run by a few big interests looking out for themselves"; "quite a few of the people running government are a little crooked"; "quite a few of the people running the government don't seem to know what they're doing"; and "people in the government waste a lot of money we pay in taxes." The averages of those who chose these answers were:

	Percent
1964	31
1968	40
1972	47
1976	61

The same general trend appears in answers to the Louis Harris poll question that asks how much confidence the voters have in "the people in charge of running" various institutions, both governmental and private. The percentage of respondents expressing "a great deal of confidence" has been going down for all institutions. Following are the percentages for Congress, the executive branch, and what Harris calls nongovernmental primary institutions (an average of the responses on medicine, higher education, organized religion, the military, major companies, the press, and organized labor) as shown in polls taken at various times during the years indicated:[1]

---

1. Harris survey data, summarized in *Public Opinion*, January–February 1979, p. 24; and ibid., October–November 1979, pp. 30–31.

	Congress	Executive branch	Nongovernmental institutions
1966	42	41	49
1971	19	23	30
1973	29	19	37
1974	18	28	31
1976	9	11	24
1977	16	23	29
1978	10	14	29
1979 (February)	18	17	24

And a corresponding trend marks the Harris index of alienation, which is based on the percentage of the respondents who express agreement with four propositions: "the rich get richer and the poor get poorer"; "what you think doesn't count very much anymore"; "the people running the country don't really care what happens to you"; and "you're left out of things going on around you." Averaging the four percentages, Harris obtains the following proportions of "disenchanted" voters:[2]

	Percent
1966	29
1969	36
1971	40
1972	49
1973	55
1976	59
1977	58

One thing that is clear from the polls is that the steep slide in public confidence began quite suddenly in the mid-1960s. The year 1965 was a high point by any measure. Congress in 1964 and 1965 had put aside all doubt and in a spirit of euphoria had passed the pioneering, hopeful measures that made up Lyndon Johnson's Great Society—the Economic Opportunity Act, civil rights legislation, programs for Appalachia and other depressed areas, medicare, water and air pollution control, federal aid to education, and the rest. President Johnson was riding the crest of popularity; his approval rating ranged about 65 to 70 percent all through 1965, figures averaging well above those of any other postwar president except Kennedy after the same length of time in office. Congress also received then the high-

2. *The Harris Survey,* December 8, 1977.

est approval rating in modern times, according to Harris. Fully 71 percent of the electorate gave it a favorable rating, compared to only 35 percent two years before. So public confidence had been rising. Then, after 1965, it began its slide.

What were the causes? What has made people angry at their government? The polls have not asked that question directly, but they are a rich source of random clues, and anyone who lived through the decade can construct from those clues and from experience and observation a list of events that have contributed to bringing the competence and responsiveness of government and its leadership into question. Most lists, surely, would include these: the Vietnam War, ghetto riots, the rise in crime, Watergate and the Nixon resignation, the Agnew scandal, the highest unemployment since the Great Depression, double-digit inflation, the energy crisis and gasoline lines, and setbacks to the United States in world affairs—in Africa, the Middle East, and elsewhere.

The list could be extended, but in any case a succession of adverse events has produced a generalized feeling about government far more negative than was the case fifteen or twenty years ago—the malaise about which Carter spoke. There is the general impression that government is wasteful. There is the widely shared conclusion that government efforts to solve problems do not usually work, that ambitious initiatives like the Great Society are bound to fail. There is the pervasive feeling that the government is too intrusive, oppressing people and businesses with regulation that brings more burden than benefit. There is the judgment that government does not deliver on its promises, that after all the talk about cleaning up the "welfare mess," closing tax loopholes, streamlining the bureaucracy, and cutting red tape, things always remain the same. There is the suspicion that government looks out mainly for the rich and the "special interests," and the conviction that politicians are not as honest as they should be; corruption and scandal were supposed to have ended with Nixon and Agnew, but the new administration was barely in office when the Bert Lance affair splashed in the headlines and on television news, and the usual quota of Congressmen were caught accepting bribes.

One does not have to share all these negative opinions to reach the essential conclusion: the performance of the government has fallen far short of what the people have expected and have a right to expect. The past fifteen years have seen one long string of mistakes, of commission or omission. Some of the events, the politicians in power at the time may claim, were beyond the control of the U.S. government. But opposing politicians are always around to reject any such attempted alibi and exploit the failure—and the public judgment is not likely to be generous. The people expect the government to control events. After all, candidates for office keep promising that it can do so. They go on insisting that elections make a difference. So each time an election does not, it adds to the disillusionment. And that, in turn, appears to be expressed in the decline in voting participation, which was also precipitate in the 1970s—as Carter noted in his July speech.

The loss in confidence in the early Carter years, in particular, was severe. The polling data suggest that the public mood had experienced some recovery during the brief Ford administration and through the election and inauguration of Jimmy Carter. If the country had not returned to the euphoric heights of 1965, it seemed at least to be pulling out of the doldrums. When Carter was sworn in, the nation faced the future with a fair measure of the optimism and hope that has always marked Inauguration Day. But sometime in 1977, the optimism began to fade, and with it, Carter's standing. By early 1979, the crisis of confidence was again apparent. To turn to the polls once again, the responses to two questions asked repeatedly in recent years measure perhaps as well as any the shifts in the general public perception of how the government is coping with the nation's problems. The first is: "[Are] problems . . . no worse than at other times, [or is] the country . . . in deep and serious trouble?" Among those respondents with an opinion, the percentages choosing each alternative are as follows:[3]

	Problems no worse than at other times	Country in deep and serious trouble
March 1974	32	68
January 1975	29	71
August 1976	58	42
September 1976	51	49
July 1977	59	41
April 1979	33	67

The second question was: "Do you feel things in this country are generally going in the right direction, or do you feel that things have

3. Time-Yankelovich Surveys, reported in *Public Opinion*, June–July 1979, p. 21.

pretty seriously gotten on the wrong track?" The percentages are shown below.[4]

	Right direction	Wrong track	Don't know
October 1973	16	74	10
October 1975	19	71	9
February 1977	41	44	14
February 1979	20	65	15

The downward trend in 1977–79 paralleled the drop in Carter's popularity. The percentage of the voters giving him a favorable rating ranged from 28 to 33 percent in a series of polls between May and August 1979, down from between 60 and 67 percent two years before —one of the steepest declines on record. (That was followed by one of the sharpest surges in a presidential approval rating, after the seizure of the U.S. embassy in Tehran. Whether this reflects a lasting reappraisal of Carter's leadership or simply a support-the-president response to crisis, and whether it is accompanied by any significant revival of confidence in government generally, are not yet clear.)

Late in 1978, President Carter's own pollster, Patrick H. Caddell, asked his respondents how much they thought the government could do to solve certain problems. The percentage that thought the government could do "a lot" was relatively high—46 percent responded that it could bring down inflation to acceptable levels; 38 percent, hold down unemployment to acceptable levels; 52 percent, reduce taxes significantly; 33 percent, reduce crime significantly; 45 percent, improve health care. But the percentages of respondents who considered it "very likely" that the government "will actually be able to do" those things were 10, 9, 11, 8, and 13, respectively. When only 10 percent of the voters believe their government will solve the public problem that weighs most heavily on them—inflation—that is a resounding vote of nonconfidence. And the 10 percent was about equal to the proportion expressing "a great deal of confidence" in President Carter and Congress that was reported a few weeks earlier by Harris.

If all that is the bad news, the good news is that the people have not given up on the American system—not yet, anyway. Pollster Harris asked some questions in September 1978 designed to probe the public's feelings about government itself, as distinct from the people leading it. He identified a series of characteristics that people desire in

4. Roper surveys, reported in *Public Opinion,* June–July 1979, p. 22.

government, and then asked two questions: "Do we have a government that fits these characteristics?" And "Is it possible to have" such a government? The responses given for some of the characteristics are as follows:[5]

	Have	*Don't have*	*Possible*	*Not possible*
Almost wholly free of corruption and payoffs	10	84	48	45
Best people are attracted to serve in public life	18	69	68	22
The good of the country is placed above special interests	26	61	76	16
Public officials really care what happens to people	38	48	81	12

"It is evident," Harris concluded, "that the American people have not given up hope for a better federal government and better people to lead it. In fact, despite the shock waves that have visited the public over the past 15 years . . . there has never been much evidence that most people have gone sour on the system itself and have finally concluded that it is unworkable." So the political gibes that followed President Carter's July speech had an element of truth in them. To a great extent, the crisis of confidence has been a crisis of faith in the people running the government now and their recent predecessors—in Carter's capacity for leadership and in the capacity of Congress as his partner in the government.

A Crisis of Governmental Competence

If the patterns of the last decade and a half continue, the election year of 1980 will see a rise in optimism. Most people will find in one or another candidate someone in whom to place their trust—more tentatively than before, perhaps, but if not with the old confidence at least with hope. The new president—or Carter, if he is reelected—will then have a year or so during which to demonstrate that the government can cope with what the people perceive to be the country's problems. If the new burst of optimism is followed by another letdown, the basic faith in the political system on which the government

5. *The Harris Survey,* November 13, 1978.

rests is bound to be further undermined, with consequences that can only be conjectured.

The fundamental question, then, is whether in the next few years the U.S. government can be made to work—under any leadership. The crisis of confidence turns out to be a crisis of efficacy, or competence, in government. After the shocks the country has suffered, can a series of successes follow?

After what has happened, the day of exaggerated expectations about what government can accomplish may have passed, and fortunately so. Yet, if people are to take the trouble to vote, they must expect *something* from the leaders they choose. What is the public conception of a government that works? At a minimum, I suggest, the people expect this much: first, that a candidate for president have a program to address the central problems that concern the people—not necessarily one with all the answers, but at least a philosophy and an approach that give promise of succeeding; second, that the winning candidate then proceed to accomplish the program—again, not in every detail or all at once, but with enough actual achievement to give the public a sense of progress toward the goals that were projected in the campaign. In short, a mandate to lead the country in an indicated direction is sought and given, and then it is expected to be discharged.

That defines the problem of competence in government. What has always existed in the United States is a gap, sometimes narrow and sometimes wide but always present, between the mandate and its execution. The mandate is granted essentially to one person, the president, but it can be executed only through the collaboration of three separate institutions—the president, the Senate, and the House—elected from different constituencies and free to exercise their powers independently. Two-thirds of the senators did not even run in the election that chose the president, and hence have no share in the mandate. And many of those who were elected with the president—even those of his own party—may have little more in common with him than the date of their election. They were chosen by much smaller electorates, and they presented their individual platforms and received their own distinct and perhaps quite different mandates.

So presidents have always had some trouble getting their programs through Congress. Yet the public has little patience with presidents who blame their troubles on the legislature. The people choose a president to go to Washington and take charge, and if he fails to achieve the objectives he set out, that is his fault, in their view. They may—and usually do—lay the fault on Congress also, but the waywardness of Congress is a constant, taken for granted, and one of the jobs of the president is to "lead" the legislature. If he fails to get his way with it, then his capacity for "leadership" becomes a political issue, as it did in the campaign of 1980. He is expected to stop the incessant bickering, and get things done.

But the degree of harmony among the Senate, the House and the executive necessary for more than routine and incremental legislation —except in situations of manifest crisis—is not the rule in the U.S. government; it is the exception. One can identify only a few brief periods in the entire twentieth century when relations were close enough—or presidential leadership strong enough, which is the other way of describing it—to achieve major innovations in controversial areas of public policy. The most notable of these were the first two years of Woodrow Wilson's administration, when the New Freedom was enacted; the first term of Franklin D. Roosevelt, when the New Deal took form, and the first two years of Lyndon Johnson, when the Great Society was founded. Each of these short but frenziedly active intervals came after a massive presidential landslide, which established the president's credential as a leader (or, in the case of Johnson's first year, after the assassination of a president, which had the effect of unifying the country behind his successor). In each, the legislative agenda was swept clean of long-pending measures; more new programs were initiated, perhaps, than could be sensibly managed. In between these periods, the agenda of unfinished business grew, because few measures could be passed beyond those clearly required by national emergencies or supported for other reasons by an extraordinarily high degree of consensus in the country.

But the prospects for attaining a sufficient degree of unity among president, House, and Senate to enable the government to move forward confidently and energetically to cope with the country's problems are even smaller now than they were in the time of Woodrow Wilson, or Roosevelt, or Johnson. If attaining governmental competence has been always difficult in the past, it will be even more arduous in the future. For in the last decade or two, the political scene has changed profoundly, and the changes all militate against governmental effectiveness.

Four of the trends, all interrelated, affect the government's ability to formulate policy: the disintegration of political parties, the popularization of presidential nominations, the rejection by Congress of presidential leadership, and fragmentation of authority in Congress that prevents its development as an alternative source of policy integration and leadership. A fifth trend is the gradual deterioration of administrative capability. The remainder of the chapter addresses these in turn, and then considers what, if anything, can be done to alleviate the crisis of governmental competence.

Party Disintegration

Political scientists who for generations have pondered the built-in disunity of the U.S. government have generally sought the solution in an institution that the Founding Fathers did not contemplate and that George Washington warned against—the political party. The party, they found, was the "web" or the "bridge" that bound together the separate elements of government. As late as the mid-1960s, the political party was strong enough to serve that purpose, when circumstances were favorable. A Democratic president then could lead the Democratic House and Senate majorities for a time because all felt a party bond and a commitment to a party philosophy and program. But in the past fifteen years, a process of party disintegration, already under way, has accelerated. By now, the web has lost much of its tensile strength, the bridge its carrying capacity.

What held American parties together was not so much their ideologies or their programs (except in periods of realignment, like the 1850s or the 1930s, when for a brief time issues predominated) as two other factors: patronage and the control of nominations for the elective offices that dispensed the patronage. In the past one hundred years, these two bonds have eroded almost to the point, now, of nonexistence. Patronage has been diminished by civil service, by the creation of public agencies to dispense welfare benefits once handled by the parties, and by the development of the ethic—enforced by open and quasi-judicial processes of administration monitored by the media as well as the courts—that partisan favoritism shall be forbidden in the distribution of governmental benefits. And the control of nominations has passed almost completely from the party's leadership to its mass membership—in other words, to the public at large—through the direct primary system. At the national level, that revolution is now complete. Until 1968, party leaders still had some part in choosing presidents; now a state chairperson or national committee member has not much more influence than any other individual voter. Parties are even giving up the business of campaigning; candidates are marketed through television by advertising specialists.

One can hardly regret the passing of old-style political machines, with their corruption, bossism, and cronyism. Few persons nowadays suggest returning to the "smoke-filled room" as the way of selecting presidents. The new ideal is for open, participatory parties, united by program objectives rather than by patronage. Yet only in a few places do such new-style party organizations have cohesion approaching that of the old machines (and even in those places, their durability has yet to be proved). Consequently, within what are loosely referred to as the Republican and Democratic "parties," the trend has been steadily toward an every-candidate-for-himself kind of campaign.

Today candidates for the House and Senate—sometimes even presidential candidates—refer to the party platform rarely and reserve the right not to be bound by it. The platforms of presidential candidates are whatever they say they are during the campaign, but the candidates speak only for themselves, not for those who share the ticket with them. The latter have their own platforms. So when those who together carried the standard of the victorious party take office, they do not necessarily have a common program or even a shared philosophy. And not since Wilson's first two years, when the House and Senate Democrats held caucuses to hammer out the party program and bind the party members to support it, has there been in either party even a mechanism for formulating a party program. During the two later periods of historic legislative achievement, under Roosevelt and Johnson, the party's program was simply announced by the president, and because he had demonstrated overwhelming popular support in a landslide election, Democratic senators and representatives closed ranks behind him. But party cohesion lasted only as long as popular support for the president remained at its crest. When it began to fade, legislators again looked to their own constituencies for their own mandates, and began to go their own ways. Coalitions, such as the old Republican-southern Democratic alliance, formed across party lines and often took effective control of one or both houses of Congress.

The political party has been steadily weakening, then, as a force for unifying the separate policymaking elements of government—president, House and Senate—even when all are controlled by the same party. But with the decline of parties and the concomitant rise in independent voting has come a new phenomenon of extraordinary import for governmental competence—divided party control. As voters pay ever less attention to the party label, picking and choosing among candidates (for the presidency, at least) as individuals in a kind of personality contest, straight-ticket voting disappears. In personality contests, because neither party has any inherent advantage, the winners are distributed between them on a random basis. The result in the case of the president and Congress has been for more than two decades what random selection would be expected, mathematically, to dictate. Half the time the country has had divided government, something rarely known in the days of strong party organization and identification. During the twenty-six years from 1955 through 1980, the Democrats have continually controlled Congress, but during fourteen of those years the Republicans have held the presidency—six years of split control when Dwight Eisenhower was in the White House and all eight years of the Nixon and Ford administrations.

At such times, the normal tendency of the U.S. system toward deadlock becomes irresistible. Harmonious collaboration, barring national crisis, is out of the question. The president and Congress are compelled to quarrel. No presidential proposal can be accepted by the legislature without raising the stature of the president as leader. Similarly, no initiative of Congress can be approved by the president without conceding wisdom to his enemies. The conflict, bickering, tension, and stalemate that characterized the fourteen years of divided government were inevitable.

Given the continued predominance of personality as distinct from party voting, the odds are close to fifty-fifty that in January 1981 the country will enter another four years of divided government and its accompanying incessant conflict. If that happens, confidence in government can only be damaged further. When the president is constantly denouncing Congress as prodigal and irresponsible, and Congress in turn is rejecting his ideas as fatuous and unworthy, will not the people inevitably come to believe both?

But the bonds of party have proved too weak to bridge the gap between the branches even when the president and the congressional majority are of the same party, as they have been in the four years since 1977. President Carter's first term has not been one of the rare historic periods of fruitful collaboration, and the limited legislative output—as in the case of energy—has disappointed almost everyone. The effect on public confidence in government has been direct, and disastrous. To the data on public opinion presented above can be added one more item: A *Washington Post* poll in July 1979 found that two-thirds of the sample believes that President Carter and Congress have not worked well together. Of those, 86 percent said that lack of cooperation was harmful to the country. They absolved neither Congress nor the president, although they considered the legislature somewhat more at fault.

Haphazard Presidential Selection

In all democratic countries, by definition, the people make the final choice among the parties' nominees for national leadership. But only in the United States do the people themselves also make the nominations.

When the state presidential primaries became the mode rather than the exception after 1968, a basic safeguard in the presidential election process was lost. Previously an elite of party leaders performed a screening function. They administered a kind of competence test; they did not always exercise that duty creditably, but they could. More important, however, they could—and did—ensure that no one was nominated who was not acceptable to the preponderance of the party elite as its leader. Even if a candidate swept the limited number of primaries, he could still be rejected, as Senator Estes Kefauver was in 1952. Usually, then, the nominee was an insider in the political system, a person who had established some credentials as a politician or an administrator, or both, of national stature and of demonstrated competence. The party leaders who approved the nomination were then prepared to follow the nominee, and to mobilize the party on his behalf.

Since 1968, all that is changed. There is no screening mechanism. A party's nominee for president now is someone who has been able to devote enough time to shaking hands in the early primary and caucus states and to forming an effective get-out-the-vote organization there, who has raised enough money to put himself on television throughout the primary season, and who has proved to have popular appeal. He may be an outsider to the national political process. He may have no experience in the federal government he seeks to head. He may be a neophyte in dealing with complex issues of foreign relations and the domestic economy. He may be in no sense the natural leader of large and crucial elements of his own party. If elected, he may be a stranger to the people in Congress with whom he has to work, and he may have little sense of how to get along with them. He may have little idea of the kind of talent he needs to help him run the executive branch, and no network of experienced advisers to help him find them. All this was true of Jimmy Carter.

A president may have the capacity to learn fast, as seems to have been the case with Carter—at least in some elements of the job. But that, if true, is pure luck. And in any case, for a country suffering a crisis of governmental competence, it is perilous to devote the first year or two of a new administration to little more than on-the-job training for an inexperienced president and an even more inexperienced entourage, without knowing how much competence will prove to be there when the training period ends.

Without passing judgment on President Carter's personal capacities, about which people differ, this much can be said with certainty: those who find this particular president—or any successor—deficient as a national leader should look with some urgency to the shortcomings of the system that selected him. Jimmy Carter, the outsider, would not have been the nominee in 1976 of an organized political party; he is what can happen when the choice of party leader is taken entirely out of the hands of the party elite and turned over to the people.

In this lottery, some future president—if not chosen in 1980, then in some future year—could conceivably have all of Jimmy Carter's weaknesses without his strengths. The adverse effect on competence in government—and public confidence, and national malaise— would be immeasurable.

Rejection of Presidential Leadership

The theorists who envisaged the majority political party as the institution that would unify a government of separated powers considered the president as the leader of the party, the natural leader of the government. And this view went beyond the theorists. The public at large has come to look upon presidential leadership as an essential feature of twentieth century government in the United States. Looking back over history, it is the strong presidents—Washington, Jefferson, Jackson, Lincoln, the two Roosevelts, Wilson—whom Americans revere. The presidents of the nineteenth century who limited themselves to presiding over the executive branch, while letting Congress direct the nation's policy, are forgotten. And just as the public came to expect presidents to be strong leaders, so did the nation's politicians—including those in Congress.

Indeed, the modern powerful presidency could not have been created except by Congress. The presidency did not grow by seizing power. Rather, statute after statute—many initiated by Congress itself—bestowed new functions on it. The Budget and Accounting Act of 1921, a congressional initiative, required the president to lay out a program for the entire government—which chief executives had not done before. The Employment Act of 1946 required the president to have an explicit program for economic prosperity, growth, and stability—which, until the Great Depression, presidents had not had. The National Security Act of 1947 affirmed the president's primacy in foreign and national security affairs. Beginning with Franklin Roosevelt, Congress expected the president to lay out its legislative agenda, to plan with the Senate and House leaders the strategy and tactics to get the legislation passed, and to help gather the votes. In short, the president was installed as the effective head of the legislative branch. Congress organized itself to respond, to criticize, and to follow, but not to lead.

Because this concept necessarily depended on the willingness of the legislative majorities to accept the presidential leadership, it was bound to run into serious trouble in the years from 1955 through 1960, the first of the two periods of divided government that mark this midcentury. In foreign and military matters, the Democrats who controlled Congress were inclined not to challenge Eisenhower's enormous prestige, but in domestic affairs he had no equivalent respect. On those matters they refused to follow where he led, and he, as might be expected, was even less inclined to follow them. So the government went through six years of stalemate and drift, able to adopt noncontroversial measures or compromise on incremental legislation but to accomplish little more. Later, in the second period of divided government from 1969 through 1976, the model of presidential leadership and congressional followership collapsed entirely.

Had Nixon been another Eisenhower, benign and somewhat passive in his dealings with Congress, the model might have survived. But in Nixon's first term, he became increasingly the aggressive partisan. By the end of that term, he was pushing his powers to the limit, seemingly determined to impose his program on the country in defiance, where necessary, of the legislative branch. In doing so, he aroused the collective anger of Congress and provoked it to fight back.

A series of events converged in the winter of 1972–73 to bring executive-legislative relations to a crisis and arouse a wholly new congressional assertiveness. One issue was fiscal policy: Nixon had humiliated Congress in a struggle over a spending ceiling in the fall; when Congress failed to come up with the budget cuts he demanded, he took power into his own hands and impounded $9 billion (by the narrowest definition of the term), thus unilaterally repealing laws Congress had enacted. Another issue was the war power, a question that had been long festering: while Congress was in recess, Nixon without consultation intensified the bombing of North Vietnam and mined the port of Haiphong. A third was executive privilege: Nixon was asserting unlimited power to withhold any information from Congress, solely at his own discretion.[6] A fourth was reorganization: Nixon put into effect the basic features of a plan for reorganizing the executive departments that Congress had explicitly rejected.

When the Ninety-third Congress assembled in January 1973, its members were in a fighting mood. But it was also a mood of great anxiety. The members sensed that, as Senate Majority Leader Mike Mansfield put it, "the fault lies not in the Executive Branch but in ourselves." The problem, they finally admitted to themselves, ran deeper than just the curbing of the Nixon excesses. Even without these, Congress had lost what its members repeatedly referred to as its coequal status under the Constitution. And it had done so consciously and deliberately, in successive abdications. It had built the presidency, one brick at a time, into the structure that now towered

---

6. "Statement About Executive Privilege, March 12, 1973," *Public Papers of the Presidents: Richard Nixon* (U.S. Government Printing Office, 1973), pp. 184–86; and testimony of Attorney General Richard G. Kleindienst on April 10, 1973, in *Executive Privilege, Secrecy in Government, Freedom of Information,* Hearings before subcommittees of the Senate Committee on Governmental Operations and Committee on the Judiciary, 93 Cong. 1 sess. (GPO, 1973), vol. 1, pp. 18–52, especially pp. 45–46, 51.

over the legislative branch. It had elevated whoever occupied the White House to become the dominant figure in the government.

In the course of a single Congress, the Ninety-third, of 1973 and 1974, the legislature went a long way toward rectifying the previous six decades or so of continuous decline. As the Watergate scandal closed in on Nixon, Congress took advantage of a collapsing presidency to shift the balance. It did all it could by law to recapture the war power—or at least a partnership role in it—through the War Powers Resolution, enacted over Nixon's veto. It regained control of fiscal policy—the power of the purse—through the Congressional Budget and Impoundment Control Act, accepted by Nixon in one of his final acts in office. (Meanwhile, President Nixon voluntarily discarded his reorganization scheme, and the Supreme Court stripped him of his claimed unlimited right of executive privilege—though it did not define what the limits are.) Beyond those specific statutory monuments of the new assertiveness, the congressional mood expressed itself in many diffuse ways. Both houses officially instructed their committees to exert more effort in overseeing the administration of the laws, and for the first time the legislature looked closely at agencies it had earlier let slip out of sight, including the Central Intelligence Agency. A device that had been used somewhat sparingly, the legislative veto of contemplated administrative action, was extended over a new and wide terrain. And Congress entered a phase of freer intervention in matters of foreign policy.

All these actions enabled a Democratic Congress to assert leadership and control over an executive branch that at the time was in Republican hands. But in 1977, the presidency reverted to the Democrats again. What, then, of the new relationships? In practice, there was a pronounced easing of tensions. Mutual recrimination largely ended. Rather than being under compulsion to try to discredit a president of the opposition party, the congressional majorities found themselves under pressure to make their own president look good; party labels had not lost their meaning altogether, and congressional Democrats had to expect to run on the same ticket with Jimmy Carter in 1980. By the same token, the president had to be conciliatory because he knew he would need the support of all those Democrats in their states and districts. Democrats in both branches had a political interest in the record on which they all would run.

Nevertheless, the formal balance of power has remained the same as it was when Gerald Ford was President. All the innovations of the Ninety-third Congress have remained in effect—war powers, budget process, impoundment control, legislative veto, expansion of oversight activities. The aggressive and vastly enlarged congressional staffs that were formed when Congress resolved to reject the leadership of a Republican president and oversee and control executive activities have not been disbanded, and they would find scant joy in working for a passive Congress that followed presidential leadership. Congress shows little tendency toward relinquishing any of its new authority; while moderating the tone, it is not giving up the substance of the new assertiveness.

This would be no problem if Congress had the capacity to set the country's course, as the substitute for presidential leadership. But there are severe limitations on the capability of the legislative branch to develop integrated and coherent policy. If the model of presidential leadership and congressional followership is to be discarded (or suspended), no fully satisfactory alternative model of congressional leadership has yet been designed to take its place. And recent trends within Congress make it even less likely than before that such a model can be devised.

Limitations on Congressional Leadership

Whatever else may be said about it, the executive branch is well organized to prepare a comprehensive and internally consistent governmental program. With its hierarchical structure, it can represent divergent views at the lower levels but blend and reconcile them at higher levels, with a point of decision at the top. Each autumn the entire executive branch goes through an elaborate process of policy integration, out of which emerges "the program of the President." During this process, contradictions among specific programs and policies can be worked out, so that their aggregate effect will serve the broad policy objectives—fiscal, economic, foreign, military, urban, energy, and so on—that the president has set. The program of the president—and it is significant that the noun takes the singular form —is embodied at the beginning of each new year in a series of state papers, the State of the Union Message, the Economic Report of the President, and the budget. These are followed by supplementary special messages spelling out specific legislative proposals.

Congress, in contrast, had no mechanism for policy integration when its era of resurgence began in 1973. Its policy decisions had traditionally been piecemeal, put forward by separate committees and considered separately, at different times, by two independent houses, without benefit of any controlling philosophy or set of policy objectives for either house, much less for the legislative branch as a whole. That had worked reasonably well, most of the time, because Congress had been willing to look to the president to do the integrating. It could then modify and adapt and adjust the elements of the president's program, without destroying its essential unity. But in the era of the new assertiveness, Congress insists upon a freedom to reject the president's program outright. During the period of divided government that ended in 1977, it did just that, and in future such periods it will surely do so again. In that event, the government's policymaking process—barring congressional reorganization—will be left without even a coherent body of policy objectives and proposals acceptable as a basis from which to begin.

The competence of the policymaking processes depends, then, upon the extent to which Congress, in assuming its new responsibilities, creates new machinery to match. But any effective mechanism for establishing broad policy objectives and developing a coordinated and integrated program to support them would require the delegation of considerable new power to the congressional leadership, or to powerful centralized committees of some kind, and centralization of power runs directly counter to the current temper of Congress. Ever since "Czar" Joseph G. Cannon was dethroned as speaker in 1910, the trend in the House has been toward dispersal of power, and the trend gathered new force in the 1970s when committee chairmen were stripped of much of their power and the seniority system that protected them was abolished. The same tendencies have been apparent in the Senate. If one characteristic of Congress of the 1970s has been the new assertiveness, another can be called the new individualism. And they are basically incompatible.

Political individualism is both the consequence and the cause of the decay of parties, which was discussed above. As the old-style machines faded away, either the vacuum was filled by new-style, program-oriented party organizations—widely participatory, undisciplined, individualistic—or it was not filled at all. In either case, from this different political milieu came a new kind of candidate, for

Congress as well as for other offices. Because these new candidates did not arise through disciplined organizations, they are individualists from the beginning of their political careers. As candidates they were self-selected, self-organized, self-propelled, self-reliant, with no habit of being deferential to the established and the powerful, and they will not be so in Congress, either in committee or on the floor. When there were enough of this type of member in Congress, the nature of the place was bound to change.

And everyone agrees it has. In both houses new members are seen as being different from their elders and introducing new modes of conduct. "Sam Rayburn used to be able to glare people down," said House Majority Leader Thomas P. O'Neill, Jr., in 1974. "These new members are brighter, better educated, more talented. . . . You just don't glare these people down." The House, said O'Neill, was "extremely difficult to coordinate." Machine politics "is dead" in the country, he went on, and hence in the House as well.

And that was even before the Watergate class of 1974—the largest body of newcomers since 1948 and surely the most assertive in many years. A survey of House members by the *Washington Post* in 1975 showed that a majority of the members thought the class of 1974 was indeed different from its elders. The new members were described as "wild, uninhibited . . . feeling their oats," "less willing to go along to get along," "in a hurry to make a record," "younger, brighter, more active, involved and vocal," "more questioning of our institutions." The younger members "resist the idea of elders calling the tune," was a news magazine's summary in April 1975. But the elders did not really try—not in the old manner, at any rate. "The 'go along, get along' idea never has been pressed by the leadership," testified Jerome A. Ambro, chairman of the freshmen Democrats' organization in 1976. A member of the leadership, Chief Deputy Whip John Brademas put it this way: "1976 is not 1966 and it's not 1956. I don't think, given the changes in American society, that intelligent and highly motivated young men and women will sit back and wait for a few years before speaking out." "The juniors are no longer on their knees," said Senator Adlai E. Stevenson, in his fifth year in Congress in 1975. "We're not asking, we're demanding. We're organizing and using power."

"No one can lead men and women who refuse to be led," complained journalist David S. Broder in 1975 in diagnosing the ills of a "floundering" Congress. "The House juniors have overthrown the old power centers. Yet they consistently refuse to heed even those they installed in power." The Democratic Study Group that year found the lowest party unity scores in twenty years.

Speaker O'Neill, who took office in the following Congress, is generally credited with being the strongest speaker since Rayburn. Yet the attitude of the membership toward party discipline appears essentially unchanged. "It is . . . an atomized House, increasingly resistant to leadership," wrote another newsman, Dennis Farney, in 1979. The members themselves confirmed the judgment. "It's not enough any more to say to people that the leadership is for something, so they should be for it," remarked Representative Richard A. Gephardt of Missouri, an influential junior Democrat; "people vote for things if they want to vote for them."

With so unruly a followership, the tendency of the leadership in both houses has been to avoid trying to impose its will, or at least to choose its fights carefully to avoid risking defeat and exposing its weakness. "I don't twist arms. I shake hands," was Speaker Carl Albert's way of putting it. "The Senate never wanted a leader," observed Senator Edmund S. Muskie, "and it has seldom had one, at least not one in the sense of somebody who could mobilize a majority." "I don't feel pressure to go along with the party position," said Senator Gary Hart, a first-term Democrat from Colorado, in 1979. But the party position in the Congress is still either the president's program or none at all. Neither in the House nor the Senate, even in the periods of divided government, has the majority leadership presumed to put forward any alternative program of its own; it has not even made policy pronouncements or assembled a staff that in size or backgrounds would enable it to do so.

Nevertheless, Congress has experimented with a device for policy integration more in the pattern of legislative bodies—the committee. In the important field of fiscal policy, new machinery has been created, a budget committee in each house and a Congressional Budget Office to provide analytical support. That machinery has been remarkably successful on the whole, far exceeding the expectations of most observers (if it is judged on its ability to produce a considered and rational congressional fiscal policy, not if it is judged solely—as some critics insist on doing—on whether that fiscal policy conforms to the critics' view of what the policy should be).

The House and Senate budget committees, through a process analogous to that of the executive branch, prepare in the early months of each year their versions of an integrated budget and fiscal policy. Each house acts on the policy developed in its committee, and after the two bodies have reconciled their measures in the usual way through a conference committee, the agreed-upon resolution, adopted in May, serves as a guide to all committees and to both houses thereafter. In the fall, Congress reviews its earlier decisions and, in the light of subsequent actions, sets its final policy. With the new process, the former acknowledgedly irresponsible procedures of Congress have given way to responsible ones. Assuming that the process continues to work as it was intended to (which may be open to some question because, as this chapter is being written, it appears doubtful that the budget committees will be able to enforce the spending ceiling adopted by the two houses for 1979–80), Congress will have developed a wholly new policy leadership capacity of its own.

But the happy precedent of the budget process has not been extended beyond the fiscal field. True, Speaker O'Neill experimented in 1977 with the use of ad hoc committees as integrating devices in two other fields, energy and welfare. They did serve to overcome jurisdictional jealousies and bring forward a legislative product with remarkable dispatch (if only by adopting essentially the administration's program). But this promising device can at best be used only on a limited number of issues in any session. And, lacking the statutory deadlines of the budget process, it does nothing to compel the integration of House and Senate policy. The welfare bill produced by the House ad hoc committee and passed by the House was not even seriously considered in the Senate. And the momentum of the House energy bill was wholly lost in a conference committee deadlock that was not broken until the end of the next session in the following year. Since then, O'Neill has not repeated the experiment.

With no continuing integrative devices except in the field of fiscal policy, Congress cannot prepare a comprehensive program corresponding to that of the president. If the budget process continues to provide a means for bringing the spending and revenue components of all its legislation into harmony with a general fiscal policy, Congress will have solved a considerable part of the problem of program integration, but by no means all of it.

Both Congress and the president have recognized that the many policies that have an impact on urban areas should be brought into consistency with a general urban, or urban growth, policy. The president has contended, and Congress appears to agree in principle (as shown by its ad hoc committees) that the country needs an integrated energy policy. Not all economic policy is encompassed within budget policy; Congress created the Joint Economic Committee to consider all elements of economic policy in relation to one another, but since the committee is strictly advisory, without legislative jurisdiction, it is in no position to produce and implement an integrated economic policy for Congress.

Most crucial of all is the realm of national security. More than three decades ago, Congress established the National Security Council as the instrument for coordination of foreign and military policy in the executive branch, and throughout the postwar period (as well as during the war), the executive branch has been committed to the concept of policy integration in this broad area. Every aspect of foreign relations and every issue relating to the size, composition, and deployment of the armed forces has been subject to constant examination in terms of a central strategic question—how the fundamental competition between the U.S. and Soviet systems would be affected.

Yet Congress, when it set up the National Security Council, organized no comparable machinery on Capitol Hill. This caused no great difficulty until the late 1960s, because in national security affairs presidential leadership was taken for granted. But then came the schism over Vietnam, and the new assertiveness spread to foreign policy. With a deep sense that it had been misled, deceived, and betrayed by presidential leadership, Congress began to make foreign policy decisions. And here the new individualism manifested itself in its most chaotic form. Various committees in the two houses went their separate ways, and the committees themselves were fragmented. Leadership began to come from almost anywhere, inside or outside those committees, unpredictably. On a series of critical issues—aid to Vietnam, the Greek-Turkish clash over Cyprus, intervention in Angola, Jewish emigration from the Soviet Union, the Rhodesian chrome boycott—Congress took it upon itself to reverse the presidential policy. Yet it did so on a piecemeal basis, emotionally, under the pressure of constituency groups at home, sometimes almost whimsically, rejecting presidential strategy without the benefit of any substitute global strategy of its own. General George S. Brown, Chairman of the Joint Chiefs of Staff, remarked that conducting foreign policy in the United States was like being in a chess game where one of the players has a kibitzer who "occasionally reaches in and moves a piece and thereby screws it all up."

People may disagree as to whether the president or Congress, in the individual instances, proposed the right decision. But to debate that point is to miss the fundamental question, which is the method by which decisions are made. Given the present state of congressional disorganization, the choice is to have a national security and foreign policy made by the president or not to have a coherent and consistent policy at all. If one concedes an element of truth to the chess game analogy, and acknowledges that decisions on Cyprus or Angola or Indochina need to be taken with full regard for their bearing upon the central relationship with the Soviet Union, then the new assertiveness of Congress without organizational reform to match can only be cause for deep concern. The new assertiveness compounded by the new individualism becomes the new anarchy.

Deterioration of Administrative Competence

The discussion thus far has concerned the difficulty of making policy through the legislative process. But the crisis of competence extends to administration also. Getting sound and adequate legislation passed—in the field of energy, say—is only part of the problem. The other part is achieving the legislative goals with faithfulness, dispatch, and equity.

That requires administrative skill, at all levels of the executive hierarchy. But it is the top level that is critical, for improvement of administrative skill at the lower levels is one of the responsibilities of top management, which institutes an organization's policies for selecting and upgrading the men and women who make up its staff, and then motivates, directs, and supervises them as they carry out their duties. And at the top levels of the U.S. government, administrative capability has been allowed to decline, over a long period, with a resulting loss of capacity throughout the executive branch.

This is necessarily a subjective judgment because there are no direct measures of administrative capability. But it is a judgment widely shared by the general public. The people clearly see their government as wasteful, inefficient, and "bureaucratic"—a catchall term connoting insensitivity, rigidity, and a devotion to procedure for procedure's sake. Indeed, the title "civil servant," once a term of respect, has been replaced by "bureaucrat," usually uttered as an epithet. An important element in Jimmy Carter's appeal as a candidate in 1976 was his promises to reorganize and simplify the government and eliminate waste. His civil service reform bill was supported with enthusiasm by Congress and the public because he presented it as the way to rid the "bureaucracy" of drones and deadheads. Besides being a campaign issue, administrative capacity is a legislative issue when any measure proposing a new program—national health insurance, for instance—is advanced. "Would you want the *government* to run that?" is always one of the questions asked, and the opposition gains support from the pervasive assumption that, if the government takes on responsibility for anything, it will bungle it.

But even widespread perceptions can be wrong. A conclusion that the government is in fact administratively weak must rest on other grounds. I rest my own judgment on several rather elementary propositions that, I believe, have been proved through the experience over a long period of many organizations—particularly business organizations, which prize managerial capability—and are generally accepted by them. These propositions are:

First, a person selected for a top administrative or managerial post on the basis of demonstrated administrative or managerial capacity is more likely to possess that capacity than one chosen for other qualities.

Second, a person with administrative or managerial experience is not likely to be a fully effective administrator in an organization highly dissimilar to the one in which the experience was gained until after a period of acclimatization.

Third, a person's administrative or managerial competence improves with experience, not only administrative experience in general but experience in a particular organization, until physical and mental vigor begin to decline.

If these propositions are correct, it is easily demonstrated that the U.S. government has been losing administrative capability, because each of the precepts implicit in them has been violated on a growing scale. Except for a few areas of the government that have been the domain of elite organizations—the military, the foreign service, some technical bureaus—management in the U.S. government has been entrusted to a steadily increasing number of political appointees. These are persons who are brought in by each new administration mainly from outside the government, who are chosen primarily for qualities that are distinct from administrative competence—their policy views, the constituencies they represent, the political services they have rendered, and so on—and who, for the most part, do not stay in the government long enough to become skilled governmental managers. Those who do are replaced in any case whenever the White House passes from one party to the other.

The United States is unique in this regard. Other countries severely restrict the number of political appointees placed at the head of executive departments. Those appointees function as policymakers, not as managers; management is the responsibility of a corps of career administrators with long experience, who—though doubtless there are exceptions—have risen to the top on the basis of demonstrated administrative competence. But in the United States the notion that there should be a corps of career governmental administrators who would be politically neutral, serving with equal loyalty whichever party came to power, has never really taken root (again, with the exceptions of the military, foreign service, and technical bureaus). After Andrew Jackson, at least, administrative jobs were seen as patronage, to be distributed as rewards to party organizations. When the civil service system was established, top positions were exempted, and through the years the exempt layer at the top has widened. The process has been called politicization of the civil service; it could also be termed amateurization.

The trend has been particularly marked since 1952. The quality and the capability of the civil service perhaps reached its peak in that year, for the reason that the country had seen twenty years of control by the same party, which happened to be the Democrats. This does not mean that the Democrats are more favorably disposed toward professional civil servants than Republicans, only that partisan control of the executive branch had not changed for two decades, and young persons who entered government service early in the Democratic era had risen through the ranks to high positions. Managerial jobs at the "political level" were filled in many cases by careerists, as the Roosevelt and Truman administrations learned that persons trained in the government's own bureaus not only were equal to outsiders in native talent but also had the added advantage of years of pertinent experience.

The problem was that these civil servants were assumed to be Democratic sympathizers rather than political neutrals in the tradition of a European administrative corps—and, to a large extent, the assumption was correct. They had been enticed into government service, in many cases, by the excitement of the New Deal. All their service had been under Democratic presidents. Their promotions had come from Democrats. So when President Eisenhower took office in 1953, they were suspect. Some left voluntarily, some were asked to leave, and the new administration brought in outsiders with Republican credentials to replace them.

Since then, the process has been repeated regularly, at eight-year intervals, and on a steadily expanding scale. Politicization progressed downward through the administrative levels, and outward from the Washington headquarters to regional and field offices, particularly in agencies administering politically sensitive programs. As it did so, the ceilings on the aspirations of career civil servants were lowered. The more enterprising of the careerists tended to leave; others tended to avoid responsibility and identification with the party in power. Each incoming administration, finding a career force drained of talent and enterprise, naturally looked outside. The result was politicization of more jobs, thus further damaging the career service, which provided the incentive for further politicization, and so on, in a vicious spiral.

No business organization operates that way, or could survive if it did. But management-by-amateurs is now generally accepted as the right way to run the government, taken for granted by politicians and by the general public. Establishing professionalism and continuity in governmental management, on the European model, is not even on the agenda of public issues. But it is difficult to see how the crisis of governmental competence can be overcome without a strong and conscious effort in that direction.

Searching for Remedies

None of the five interrelated trends discussed in the preceding sections is easily reversed. They arise from fundamental forces within the American political culture, and have become more or less established habits of political thought and action. Traumatic historical events can set new forces into motion, which in turn can alter the way people think and act, but between such events existing institutional patterns remain, and solidify. However, the crisis of confidence in government the country is now experiencing may prove to be in itself a traumatic event. Some change has already occurred, and if the government continues its record of failure, advocates of more fundamental institutional change will surely gain a growing audience. Even so, consensus on specific remedial measures will be difficult to attain, even if appropriate measures can be conceived.

The Party System

There is no lack, to return to the first trend, of persons who deplore the decline of political parties. Leaders of the two parties would surely like to head stronger organizations, but they have found no way to bring them into being. People do not identify with parties, join them, support them, and believe in them as an end in itself (except, perhaps, in the few places where anachronistic, patronage-oriented machines survive). Parties are embraced, rather, when people see them as useful means toward achieving some desired public policy. Parties have formed, or re-formed, at times when great issues have seized the country and polarized the voters—as the slavery question did in the 1850s, or populism and free silver in the 1890s, or relief of hunger and unemployment in the 1930s. At such times, new parties spring into being or old parties take on new meaning because they become instruments for the achievement of goals about which the voters deeply care. But such powerful issues come and go, and when they have gone the parties begin to lose relevance. The last period of polarization, when the current alignment of the two-party system was shaped, is by now almost half a century past. To young people in particular, what the parties stand for, what the difference is between them, why they matter, even why they exist, has become obscure. Revival, then, depends on something outside the party system itself—some kind of crisis that will arouse the people, polarize them, and impel them to organize politically to attain their ends. In the meantime, advocates of stronger parties can do little more than remain alert to the incidental effects on party organizations of particular legislative measures, specifically those governing elections. Public financing of campaigns, for example, can help or hurt parties, depending on whether the money is disbursed to the party that nominates the candidate or directly to the nominee.

Presidential Selection

Parties would be strengthened, and some of the risk removed from the presidential selection process as well, if the trend toward proliferation of presidential primaries could be reversed. Conceivably, a retrenchment in the primary system could begin spontaneously in the 1980s in reaction to the exhaustion and the expense of the long ordeal that the presidential campaign has become. Such a swing away from the direct primary occurred early in this century; after the initial burst of enthusiasm for the new device during the Progressive Era, some eight states repealed their laws and others made significant modifications to give the party leadership more control over the choice of convention delegates. But there are few signs now of any such reversal. The voters seem to prefer the primary system. Widespread participation, open decisionmaking, and freedom from "boss control" have become accepted as political ideals. The states that have the primaries like the attention of the media and the business the primaries bring in. The party organizations that would be the natural advocates of a return to less participatory procedures hardly exist to lead any such struggle. And finally, even if some states discarded primaries in favor of choosing delegates through caucuses and conventions, the rules that require the caucuses to be open and to encourage wide participation, and that serve to discourage the selection of uncommitted party leaders as convention delegates, would undoubtedly remain. So the risks inherent in allowing tens of millions of voters, rather than party elites, to choose the presidential nominees are not likely soon to be eliminated.

Presidential Leadership

In contrast to the changes in the party and electoral systems, the breakdown of presidential leadership and the accompanying new assertiveness of Congress are the result not of long-term forces but of a series of events. As the memory of these events fade—if, in other words, presidents continue to behave in the relatively restrained fashion of Gerald Ford and Jimmy Carter and continue to be open and candid with Congress—it is reasonable to expect that the same fundamental forces that brought about the modern strong presidency in the first place will again assert their influence.

That is not to say that the pre-Nixon balance of authority between the branches will be restored—nor should it be. The old norms of presidential dominance and congressional passivity contained dangers that are now clear to everyone, including members of Congress. In any case, the many profound institutional changes made in the past eight years to undergird the legislature's new importance will not be undone; Congress will not repeal the War Powers Resolution or the Congressional Budget and Impoundment Control Act, nor is it likely to disband the vastly enlarged staffs that enable it to exercise tighter control over the executive and play a greater role in the legislative process.

Yet there can be some retreat. Congress seems already to be identifying what can perhaps be called the excesses of the new assertiveness, and to be modifying them. The congressional intervention in operational decisions of foreign policy that marked the Ford administration has diminished in the Carter period. And the tide of legislative veto provisions may have crested; the sheer workload that is imposed on an overburdened Congress by each new veto clause is bound to compel second thoughts about adding any more.

So it is not unreasonable to expect a gradual warming of relations between president and Congress, a restoration of greater trust in presidential leadership, and a resultant reinstatement of the efficiency of the policymaking processes—*provided* that the lottery of presidential selection installs in the White House a candidate with a reasonable measure of the credentials necessary to become accepted as the leader of the congressional majorities. A look at the field of candidates in 1980 suggests that whoever is elected this fall will have a strong probability of acceptance as leader of Congress—if it is controlled by his own party. For the Democrats, President Carter is no longer an outsider and Senator Kennedy has never been one. For the Republicans, any president elected with Republican majorities in Congress would take office as a phenomenally powerful leader because he would take the credit for carrying those majorities into office with him—and, in 1980, that would mean unseating at least nine Democratic senators and fifty-nine representatives. In any of these circumstances, the prospects for progress toward more harmonious and fruitful relations between president and Congress would be good.

There remains, then, just one circumstance that could severely set back the progress. That would be a decision by the voters in 1980 to deny a clean victory to either party—that is, to inflict divided government once again upon the country.

In an article that concluded the volume of *Setting National Priorities* published in 1976, I laid much of the blame for the governmental ineffectiveness of the preceding years on the incessant, bitter conflict between a Republican president and a Democratic Congress.

Before any improvement in governmental performance could be expected, I argued, that error would have to be corrected, one way or the other. Either Congress should be given a Democratic president to lead it, or a Republican president should be given a Congress of his party. Let each voter choose whichever party ticket appeared superior, but vote it straight. The message was not received, of course, and in November, voters split their tickets with as much abandon as ever. Yet by the random consequence of their choosing among candidates on the basis of whatever considerations moved them, divided government was in fact ended. Later, when it became clear that Jimmy Carter was having his own troubles with Congress, I was chided as having overestimated the difference that undivided party control of government, in itself, would make.

Yet some improvement in relationships is undeniable. Presidential proposals have at least been given a hearing in Congress, instead of being rejected out of hand because they came from the leader of the opposition party. Congressional initiatives have been accepted by the president, rather than vetoed automatically. Compromises have been hammered out more readily among fellow partisans than across the party lines that previously separated the branches. As noted above, Congress has shown a marked reluctance to upset Carter's foreign policy, where it showed no such forbearance in reversing that of Ford. The tone of communication has changed; where there was loud recrimination before, there has been in the past four years no more than quiet grumbling. That in itself must have prevented public confidence from dropping further.

The promise of undivided government was limited, however, by other factors, some of which have already been suggested. In 1976, Jimmy Carter was the archetype of the outsider that only in America can be thrust largely unprepared into the top position of governmental leadership. Rarely has a new president been in a weaker position to try to act as the country's legislative leader. But, for the reasons given earlier, if the voters give the country an undivided government in 1980, these circumstances are not likely to be repeated. Those voters who mark a straight ticket for the national offices on their ballots can expect to realize in fuller measure than after 1976 the potential benefits of unified control of the executive and legislative branches.

If, despite all this gratuitous advice, the voters nevertheless choose divided government, Congress will be little better equipped than it was before its post-1973 resurgence to set the country's course. Fragmentation and dispersal of authority within Congress reflect the disintegration of political parties in the legislature as in the country, and the new individualism can be expected to prevail until new and unforeseeable issues arise to bring about the creation of a new party system or the rejuvenation of the old.

Administrative Competence

As for the improvement of administrative capability, any movement toward a remedy would depend upon a higher degree of consensus than now exists as to the nature of the problem. If the analysis offered above were accepted, the way to proceed would be clear enough: the number of politically appointed, amateur managers in the government would be drastically reduced and a professional corps of career administrators would be developed to assume enlarged responsibilities. In essence, the United States would adopt the European model, with a clear distinction between a thin layer of political policymakers at the top and a neutral permanent civil service responsible for implementing the policies. The objective would be to provide each top political appointee—Cabinet member, bureau chief, and so on—with a deputy from the career service who would have the necessary experience and training, the knowledge of how to use the resources of the organization, and the managerial skills to make the policies effective.

But the decision to move in that direction would have to be made by the policymakers themselves, and for every politician in the new administration who would favor an expansion of the role of the career civil service, there will undoubtedly be many who would seek the solution to administrative incompetence by moving in the opposite direction—by supplanting more careerists with transient political appointees.

The Civil Service Reform Act of 1978, however, could conceivably prove to be a turning point in the enhancement of the status and responsibilities of the career civil service, even though it was not presented to Congress and the public as a measure for that purpose. It was put forward, rather, as a means to discipline the government's employees and to bring them, through more flexible systems of rewards and punishments, under tighter control by political executives.

And it did nothing to narrow the layers of political appointees at the top of the government's departments and agencies. Nevertheless, it did establish for a trial period a Senior Executive Service, which conceivably could evolve, if it is accepted and continued, into a professional managerial corps on the European pattern. But to move in that direction would require a conscious, deliberate decision to do so, and that would demand what does not now exist—a wide measure of national agreement.

So the crisis of competence in government is not easily resolved. Many of the trends that have brought about the crisis, and intensified it in recent years, have roots deep in the traditions of American political behavior, if not in the constitutional structure itself. To that extent, incompetence is endemic. Yet there are ameliorative measures that can be taken, and taking some may lead to creative thought that may devise still others. What is necessary, first of all, is that those who decry the shortcomings of governmental performance recognize that the fault does not necessarily lie in the individuals who happen to occupy the White House or sit in Congress, and replacing them with other individuals will not necessarily help. Severe institutional and structural problems must be addressed. Only when acceptance of that proposition is wide enough will a concerted attack upon those problems be possible.

TYPESETTING *Monotype Composition Company, Inc., Baltimore*
PRINTING & BINDING *R. R. Donnelley & Sons Company, Chicago*